S0-BMD-281

FUNDAMENTALISM in American Religion 1880 - 1950

A forty-five-volume facsimile series
reproducing often extremely rare material
documenting the development of one of the
major religious movements of our time

■ *Edited by*
Joel A. Carpenter
Billy Graham Center, Wheaton College
■ *Advisory Editors*
Donald W. Dayton,
Northern Baptist Theological Seminary
George M. Marsden,
Duke University
Mark A. Noll,
Wheaton College
Grant Wacker,
University of North Carolina

A GARLAND SERIES

■ Volume 1

Second Coming of Christ: Premillennial Essays of the Prophetic Conference held in the Church of the Holy Trinity, New York City [1878]
[Includes an introduction to the set]

■ Volume 2

Prophetic Studies of the International Prophetic Conference, Chicago, November, 1886
bound with
Addresses on the Second Coming of the Lord, Delivered at the Prophetic Conference, Allegheny, Pa., December 3-6, 1895

■ Volume 3

Addresses of the International Prophetic Conference, held December 10-15, 1901, in the Clarendon Street Baptist Church, Boston, Mass.
bound with
The Coming and Kingdom of Christ, a Stenographic Report of the Prophetic Bible Conference held at the Moody Bible Institute of Chicago, February 24-27, 1914.

■ Volume 4

Light on Prophecy, A Coordinated, Constructive Teaching, being the Proceedings and Addresses at the Philadelphia Prophetic Conference, May 28-30, 1918
bound with
Christ and Glory, Addresses Delivered at the New York Prophetic Conference, Carnegie Hall, November 25-28, 1918

■ The Prophecy Conference Movement

Volume 2

Edited by
Donald W. Dayton

Garland Publishing, Inc.
New York & London 1988

For a list of titles in this series, see the final pages of volume four.

The facsimile of *Prophetic Studies* has been made from a copy in the Billy Graham Center of Wheaton College, that of *Addresses on the Second Coming of the Lord* is from a copy in the Moody Bible Institute.

Library of Congress Cataloging in Publication Data

The Prophecy conference movement/edited with an introduction by Donald W. Dayton.
p. cm. — (Fundamentalism in American religion, 1880-1950)
Reprint of works originally published 1879-1918.
Contents: v. 1. Second Coming of Christ: premillennial essays of the Prophetic Conference held in the Church of the Holy Trinity, New York City — v. 2. Prophetic Studies of the International Prophetic Conference. Chicago, November, 1886. Addresses on the Second Coming of the Lord, delievered at the Prophetic Conference, Allegheny, Pa., December 3-6, 1895 — v. 3. Addresses of the International Prophetic Conference held December 10-15, 1901, in the Clarendon Street Baptist Church, Boston, Mass. The Coming and Kingdom of Christ: a stenographic report of the Prophetic Bible Conference held at the Moody Bible Institute of Chicago, February 24-27, 1914 — v. 4. Light on prophecy: a coordinated, constructive teaching being the proceedings and addresses at the Philadelphia Conference, May 28-30, 1918. Christ and glory: addresses delivered at the New York Prophetic Conference, Carnegie Hall, November 25-28, 1918/edited by Arno C. Gaebelein.
ISBN 0-8240-5005-3 (alk. paper)
1. Eschatology—Congresses. 2. Millenium—Congresses. 3. Second Advent—Congresses. 4. Bible—Prophecies—Congresses. I. Dayton, Donald W. II. Series.
BT21.P76 1988
236'.9—dc19 88-24301

Design by Valerie Mergentime
Printed on acid-free, 250-year-life paper
Manufactured in the United States of America

CONTENTS

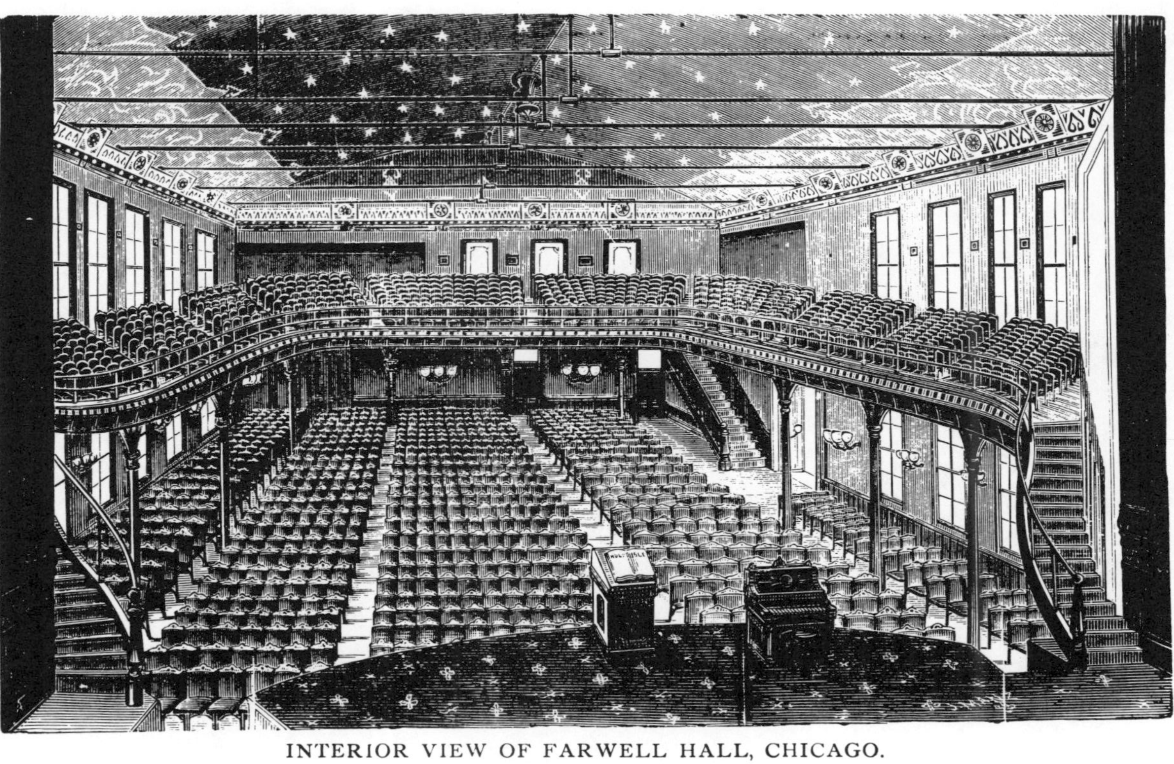

INTERIOR VIEW OF FARWELL HALL, CHICAGO.

PROPHETIC STUDIES

OF THE

International Prophetic Conference,

(CHICAGO, NOVEMBER, 1886.)

CONTAINING CRITICAL AND SCHOLARLY ESSAYS, LETTERS, ETC., UPON

THE NEAR COMING OF THE LORD.
ITS LITERAL AND PERSONAL CHARACTER.
THE DEVELOPMENT OF THE ANTICHRIST.
THE FIRST RESURRECTION.
THE JEWS AND THEIR FUTURE.
PREDICTED JUDGMENTS.
THE MILLENIUM.

AND KINDRED TOPICS AND EVENTS; TOGETHER WITH THEIR PRACTICAL APPLICATION AS AN INCENTIVE TO EVANGELISTIC AND MISSION WORK, AND PERSONAL CONSECRATION.

BY THE FOLLOWING EMINENT BIBLICAL STUDENTS:

W. R. NICHOLSON, D. D., Bishop R. E. C., Philadelphia.
MAURICE BALDWIN, D. D., Bishop of Huron, Ont.
Prof. D. C. MARQUIS, D. D., McCormick Theo. Sem.
Prof. W. G. MOOREHEAD, U. P. Theo. Sem., Xenia.
Prof. E. F. STROETER, Central Wesleyan College, Mo.
Prof. J. T. DUFFIELD, D. D., Princeton, N. J.
Prof. HENRY LUMMIS, Lawrence University.
Prof. JOHN GUSTAV PRINCELL, Chicago.
Rev. NATHANIEL WEST, D. D., Presb., St. Paul, Minn.
Rev. GEORGE BISHOP, D. D., Dutch Ref. Orange, N. J.
Rev. E. P. GOODWIN, D. D., Cong'l, Chicago.
Rev. A. J. FROST, D. D., Baptist, Sacramento, Cal.
Rev. A. J. GORDON, D. D., Baptist, Boston.
Rev. A. T. PIERSON, D. D., Presb., Philadelphia.
Rev. P. S. HENSON, D. D., Baptist. Chicago.
Rev. HENRY M. PARSONS, Presb., Toronto, Ont.
Rev. JAS. S. KENNEDY, D. D., Abingdon, Va.
Prof. F. GODET, D. D., Neufchatel, Switzerland.
Prof. VOLCH, D. D., Univ. of Dorpat, Russia.
Prof. FRANZ DELITZSCH, D. D., Univ. of Leipzig.
Prof. A. KOCH, D. D., Oldenburg, Saxony.
Rev. A. R. FAUSSETT, D. D., Canon of York, Eng.
Rev. ANDREW A. BONAR, D. D., Glasgow, Scotland.
Rev. ARCHIBALD G. BROWN, London, Eng.
Mr. D. L. MOODY, Northfield, Mass.
Rev. F. L. CHAPELL, Baptist, Flemington, N. J.
Rev. W. J. ERDMAN, Cong'l, Boston, Mass.
Rev. ALBERT ERDMAN, Presb., Morristown, N. J.
Rev. J. D. HERR, D. D., Baptist, Milwaukee, Wis.
Rev. J. F. KENDALL, D. D., Presb., Laporte, Ind.
Rev. J. M. ORRICK, Editor "Messiah's Herald," Boston.
Rev. GEO. N. H. PETERS, Evan. Luth., Springfield, O.
Rev. GEO. C. NEEDHAM, Evangelist, Boston.
Mr. WM. E. BLACKSTONE, Methodist, Oak Park, Ill.
Rev. WM. DINWIDDIE, Alexandria, Va.

FLEMING H. REVELL,

CHICAGO: 148 AND 150 MADISON STREET.
NEW YORK: 148 AND 150 NASSAU STREET.

TORONTO, CANADA: S. R. BRIGGS.

PREFACE.

The essays which comprise this book are those which were delivered at the Second American Bible and Prophetic Conference, held in Farwell Hall, Chicago, Nov. 16 to 21, 1886. At the time of presentation they created a profound impression throughout the country; THE INTER OCEAN, with characteristic enterprise, publishing them verbatim from day to day throughout the conference.

In the year 1878, the first general American Bible and Prophetic Conference was held in New York City. The addresses delivered on our Lord's personal and pre-millennial return to this earth were then eagerly heard by the hundreds of ministers, and thousands of intelligent Christian people who were then and there assembled. The New York *Tribune* published an extra of 50,000 copies, giving in full these essays, which, afterwards, were edited carefully by Dr. Nathaniel West, and published by F. H. Revell, Chicago, in one large volume entitled "Pre-Millennial Essays." Such was the influence of the movement that for more than two years following the Conference important and valuable discussions on prophetic themes occupied the pages of not a few of our religious newspapers, journals, and magazines, and a new impetus for Bible study was given to multitudes whose attention had so long been turned away from the great and almost entirely neglected fields of divine prophecy.

The following Resolutions passed by that Conference in its closing session express in brief, the views of the large body of ministers who participated in or were present to sympathize with the proceedings:

1. We affirm our belief in the supreme and absolute authority of the written Word of God on all questions of doctrine and duty.

2. The prophetic words of the Old Testament Scriptures concerning the first coming of our Lord Jesus Christ were literally fulfilled in His birth, life, death, resurrection, and ascension; and so the prophetic words of both the Old and the New Testaments concerning His second coming will be literally fulfilled in His visible bodily return to this earth in like manner as He went up into Heaven; and this glorious Epiphany of the great God, our Savior Jesus Christ, is the blessed hope of the believer and of the Church during this entire dispensation.

3. This second coming of the Lord Jesus is everywhere in the Scriptures represented as imminent, and may occur at any moment; yet the precise day and hour thereof is unknown to man, and only known to God.

4. The Scriptures nowhere teach that the whole world will be converted to God, and that there will be a reign of universal righteousness and peace before the return of the blessed Lord; but that only at and by His coming in power and glory will the prophecies concerning the progress of evil and the development of Antichrist, the times of the Gentiles, and the ingathering of Israel, the resurrection of the dead in Christ, and the transfiguration of His living saints, receive their fulfilment, and the period of millennial blessedness its inauguration.

5. The duty of the church during the absence of the Bridegroom is to watch and pray, to work and wait, to go into all the world and preach the Gospel to every creature, and thus hasten the coming of the day of God; and to His last promise, "Surely I come quickly," to respond, in joyous hope, "Even so; come Lord Jesus."

In addition the following resolution was passed not only unanimously by the conference, but by the vast audience voluntarily rising en masse to its feet—a magnificent spectacle not soon to be forgotten:

"*Resolved*, That the doctrine of our Lord's pre-millenial advent, instead of paralyzing evangelistic and missionary effort, is one of the mightiest incentives to earnestness in preaching the Gospel to every creature, until He comes."

These resolutions were reaffirmed at the Chicago conference, the whole congregation responding with evident enthusiasm and remarkable unanimity.

The Prophetic Conference committee of 1878 in response to many urgent appeals decided to hold the second prophetic meeting at the date above mentioned. The committee issued a call for signatures to which their names, with those added to the original number, were appended as follows:

J. H. Brookes, Editor of "The Truth," St. Louis.
A. J. Gordon, Pastor Clarendon Street Baptist Church, Boston.
Maurice Baldwin, Bishop of Huron, Canada.
W. R. Nicholson, Bishop of Reformed Episcopal Church, Philadelphia.
H. M. Parsons, Pastor Knox Presbyterian Church, Toronto, Canada.
W. G. Moorhead, Professor U. P. College, Xenia, Ohio.
W. W. Clark, Pastor Dutch Reformed Church, S. I., New York.
W. J. Erdman, Pastor Olivet Congregational Church, Boston.
J. D. Herr, Pastor First Baptist Church, Milwaukee, Wis.
J. M. Orrock, Editor "Messiah's Herald," Boston.
Wm. Nast, Editor "Der Christliche Apologete," Cincinnati.
J. F. Kendall, Pastor Presbyterian Church, Laporte, Ind.
E. P. Goodwin, Pastor First Congregational Church, Chicago.
D. W. Whittle, Evangelist, (Chicago Avenue Church), Chicago.
A. J. Frost, Pastor Baptist Church, Sacramento, Cal.
James S. Kennedy, Pastor M. E. Church, Abingdon, Va.
Nathaniel West, Pastor Presbyterian Church, St. Paul, Minn.
S. H. Kellogg, Pastor Presbyterian Church, Toronto, Canada.
L. W. Munhall, Evangelist, (M. E. Church), Germantown, Pa.
Addison Blanchard, (Congregational,) Superintendent A. H. M. S., Kansas.
George C. Needham, Evangelist, (Clarendon Street Baptist Church), Boston.

Committee.

The call with singular promptness was heartily indorsed by hundreds of pastors, theological professors, evangelists, missionaries, and Y. M. C. A. secretaries. Many also of post-millenial faith ratified the call, and were present at every session as interested listeners.

From the large correspondence entailed in the essential preparatory work of the prospective meeting devolved upon us we are persuaded that since the New York Convention in 1878, the doctrine of our Lord's expected advent has gained ground among spiritual believers of all churches, as the revival of no other truth in modern times has done.

The conference gave no opportunity for modern *prophets* to ventilate their calculations or speculations; it was rather an occasion for *students* of *prophecy* to present the weighty matters found in the Written Word concerning "last times" and "last things." The brethren who were appointed to bring to the Conference the results of prayerful and careful Bible study are neither idle star-gazers, eratic time-setters, nor theological adventurers.

We believe their names, their ecclesiastical standing, and their spirituality of heart, to say nothing of their scholarship and their eloquence, will compel respect, disarm prejudice, dissolve doubts, and establish faith in "the testimony of Jesus, which is the spirit of prophecy." They submit their interpretations, convictions, and conclusions to the severest test of candid criticism. The enterprise shown by THE INTER OCEAN is a marvel of modern journalism. The half a dozen essays, of unusual length, delivered daily by the respective speakers appeared verbatim in the next morning's edition of the above named newspaper. This book is made up from stereotype plates made from THE INTER OCEAN reports, but in large part revised, though hurriedly, by the respective authors. If, therefore, typographical errors should be occasionally met with, the reader will kindly take the circumstances into consideration. In order to meet the immediate demand for the book, the publisher, with extraordinary rapidity, has sent it flying through the land in one week after the conference closed its final session.

And as it carries within its pages the sublimest doctrines of salvation, in their original development and glorious consummation, do we heartily bid it God-speed. It is, indeed, our earnest prayer that through its silent agency our Lord Jesus Christ may be abundantly glorified in the hearts and lives of all who look to Him as Prophet, Priest, and King.

GEORGE C. NEEDHAM.

Manchester-by-the-Sea, Mass., Nov. 29, 1886.

REV. GEORGE C. NEEDHAM,
SECRETARY AND ORGANIZER OF THE PROPHETIC CONFERENCE.

CONTENTS.

NOTE.—Possibly a few typographical errors may be found in the following pages, as the book has been issued with a promptitude seldom equaled. It is believed, however, that few such inaccuracies will be found; but for these, and also for the capital sub-heads, the publisher, and not the authors, is responsible.

STUDIES

—OF—

THE PROPHETIC CONFERENCE.

HELD IN CHICAGO NOVEMBER 16 TO 21, 1886.

FIRST DAY.

OPENING EXERCISES.

The Bible and Prophetic Conference, called for the study of Bible prophecy, met for the second session in its history at 10 o'clock on Tuesday morning, Nov. 16, in Farwell Hall. There were present ministers of all denominations from all parts of the United States and Canada. Nearly all the city clergy were present, and hundreds of earnest Christians of every shade of belief from every church, charitable institution, and missionary society in the city. The Rev. George C. Needham, of Manchester-on-the-Sea, Mass., formerly pastor of Moody's Church, Chicago, opened the meeting. Mr. Needham has been the man of all others on whom the success of this great gathering has depended, and it was singularly appropriate that he be chosen to open it.

The first hour was devoted to religious and devotional exercises. The first notes of prayer and praise were the long meter doxology. The Rev. Dr. Davis, city missionary of the Presbyterian Church, led in a fervent prayer. The conference then sang "Crown Him Lord of All." The singing was led by Mr. J. H. Burke, with Mr. William B. Boomer as organist. Mr. Nichols sang an advent hymn, and short addresses and prayer were made by Dr. Parsons, Professor Moorehead, and others.

At the conclusion of the devotional exercises the first paper of the session was read by the Rev. E. P. Goodwin, of Chicago.

THE REV. DR. GOODWIN.

THE RETURN OF THE LORD.

In considering the subject which the committee have assigned to me, "The Return of the Lord, Literal, Personal, Visible," I need hardly say that I have no expectation of presenting anything new or striking upon it. The ground has all been traversed, and the teaching of the word of God thoroughly and nobly set forth by many whose names are as household words to most of the members of this conference. But the truths of the word will bear oft repeating; especially these truths about the last things. And this the more because in the minds of the many of the Lord's people they seem to be of so little significance. It is probably not to much to say that the great majority of believers feel little or no interest in this whole range of inquiries respecting the coming of the Lord and the truths related thereto. Very largely they deem them matters of speculation, subjects only hinted at in the scriptures, and as to which, so far as it concerns practical Christian life, it does not signify which of two or three or more different opinions be held. I have even known quite earnest and faithful Sunday School and Bible class teachers to regret that the International sermons had anything to do with the

PROPHETICAL BOOKS

of the Bible. I sometimes wonderd if the great adversary, hater of all truth as he is, has not a special dislike for the truth of the word concerning the things to come. You remember that when in the third year of Cyrus, Daniel set himself to search out and understand the visions of the Lord, the angel said to him that he set out to bring him an answer to his prayer, and to give him understanding of the visions of God, but was hindered by the Prince of the Kingdom of Persia, i. e., the angel of darkness charged with caring for that kingdom in the interests of Satan, "one and twenty days." And he was only able to overcome by the help of Michael, the archangel (Dan. 10). Now, the things which the angel of the Lord was sent to reveal unto the prophet were the things not merely relating to the return of the chosen people from the Babylonish captivity, but concerning their final restoration to God's favor, the overthrow of anti-Christ, and the glorious resurrection of the just. Such a foreshowing of the release from his tyrannous ruleship, not only of the nation he so long had tortured through their rejection of God, but of the whole race as well, and with that release his own utter and everlasting overthrow, the great adversary did not want made. And so he fought it desperately as the record shows. Not unlike that is his hostility in our day, I sometimes think, to the understanding of these identical truths about last things. Whoever discerns these will of necessity discern the

ONCOMING TRIUMPH

of the Son of God, the sure defeat of the prince of darkness, and will be inevitably and mightily inspired for witnessing and warfare. Hence if believers can be kept blinded as to the nearing end of satan's reign, or unconcerned about it, or better still, can be prejudiced against the idea of such certain and speedy overthrow, there will be so much clear gain to this active foe of God and man.

Be this as it may, there is profit in being put in remembrance of the most familiar truths, and my hope is, if nothing more result, that this representation of the scripture doctrine of the Lord's return will serve to set the blessed hope more clearly before our minds and above all make us sharers in a larger measure in that consuming zeal for Christ and for souls, with which it so grandly inspired and energized the early church.

The question before us, I need hardly say, is purely a question of scripture. Outside of these sacred writings we know and can know nothing whatever on the subject. Speculation, philosophy, the learning, the logic of the schools has no part nor lot in this discussion. Do the Scriptures teach that our Lord is to return literally, and in a personal, human, visible form, and at a given time, or do they teach that He is to come in

SOME OTHER WAY,

impersonally, invisibly, spiritually, and at no particular time? Did He come at the destruction of Jerusalem? Does He come at the believer's death? Is His coming the same thing as the spirits coming into the heart? The whole subject, I repeat, is one to be settled only by scripture testimony. Not what ought these witnesses to say? What would it be rational for them to say? What would harmonize best with science, with advanced thought, with enlarged conceptions of God, and improved conceptions of man? Nothing of this, but simply what, fairly taken, as we read and understand language elsewhere, do these men, speaking as they are moved by the Holy Ghost, say as to the manner of the Lord's return.

Some latter-day theorists upon this subject quite overlook this. They raise objections based upon what they conceive to be certain impossibilities connected with the appearing of the Lord in a personal, visible way, and, therefore, declare the doctrine can not be taught. This is largely the ground of objections urged by Dr. Bushnell, Dr. Lyman Abbott, Dr. Warrens Parousia, and others.

But all such reasonings and speculations have no value whatever in determining what the truth is. As well say the creation of the world out of nothing is irrational and inconceivable, and hence the first chapter of Genesis is a fiction. As well say it is utterly irrational and inconceivable that a human and divine soul could dwell together in one person, and that person could be born both of the Holy Spirit and of the Virgin Mary, and, therefore, deny the twofold nature or the supernatural birth of Jesus Christ; or, again, it is irrational and conceivable that bodies once turned to dust and scattered perhaps to the ends of the earth should be reconstructed and made to reinvest the spirits that once dwelt therein, and, therefore, scout the doctrine of the resurrection. That is precisely the method of reasoning by which some excellent people get rid of the doctrine of an expiatory atonement, and others of the doctrine of miracles, and others still of the imprecatory psalms, and all such stories as the deluge and

DESTRUCTION OF SODOM,

and Jonah and the whale. There is no sort of trouble in having a Bible exactly according to our mind, when we set up this modern principle or canon of authority which so many adopt, that only that is true which in its own pet phrase "finds me," carries the assent of my inner consciousness.

But that is not what settles questions according to this book. This claims to be of God, to voice His thoughts, to reveal his will. And the men who made this book did not write down what they thought or imagined or presumed or reasoned out; not what would accord with other men's thoughts or reasonings or speculations; not what would seem wise or beneficent, but what God thought and chose to say, and what He commanded them—the writers of the book—to say. "Holy men of old spake as they were moved by the Holy Ghost." And our attitude before their testimony is simply that of accepting and obeying what they declare as the truth of God. We have no option whatever and no right of speculation or debate as respects the things revealed. We are as law students before the statutes of the State. The only question for us is, what do these authorities—these books of God's revealed will teach? No matter whether we can understand or explain, or harmonize their teachings with our views of things or not. They give us what God says, and we believe them because of that, and not because of our ability to explain or expound them.

I may not carry the assent of all the members of this conference in this affirmation. I certainly do not carry that of a large number of Christian ministers and teachers with respect to the inspiration and

AUTHORITY OF SCRIPTURE.

But this is where I stand, and is, I humbly conceive, the only ground upon which any authoritive utterance of the word of God can be had. The chief difficulty in all discussions upon Scripture doctrines lies in my judgment in this, that the authority of Scripture is not made supreme. So long as men insist upon squaring belief to the canons of philosophy, or science, and demand that everything shall approve itself before the bar of their reason, so long there can be no certainty in the things of faith. This one will hold this thing and another that as to what the Scripture doctrine is of God's moral government, or sin, or the atonement, or regeneration, or resurrection, or retribution. There can be no unity of faith until the standard of authority is fixed, and it is idle without that to raise any such questions as this programme involves. We might as well engage in seeing who could blow the most brilliant soap-bubbles. But once agree that human speculation, opinion, and reasoning have no more to do in settling what we shall receive and believe as students of this divine word than they had in determining what the people of old should receive and believe when Moses came out from his closetings with Jehovah on the cloud-wrapt mountain top, and declared the message with which he was charged, and then there is an end of controversy. And this, I repeat, is where I stand. I assume the absolute, infallible authority of this book as the word of God. And on that basis, believing that

ON THIS SUBJECT IN HAND,

as upon all others essential to the right understanding of the plan of God in redeeming lost man, the Holy Spirit has given clear and decisive testimony, I propose to ask what saith the Scripture on the question of the manner of the Lord's return.

What the belief of the early church was as to the teaching of Scripture I need not stay to consider. It is sufficient to say, without taking time for the citations that could easily be made, that not a single authority in church history pretends that for 250 years, at least, the early disciples held or so much as knew of any other view than that of the Lord's literal, personal, and visible return. It is agreed on all hands that as to this there is not among apostles, apostolic fathers, or apologists down to Origen a single dissenting voice.

And it may almost be said that, taking the church as a whole, this early belief has never been lost nor modified. The faith-symbols of every branch of the Christian household have most clearly and emphatically put forward this doctrine. What need, then, of arguing for it in such a conference as this? Simply because in this day of so-called advanced thought and of new departures men set to be teachers of the Lord's people in pulpits and editorial chairs, and some who are charged with training those who are to expound this word of God, have abandoned the faith of the fathers. Or rather, I should say, they have, as they claim, improved upon that faith by taking out of it the hyper-literalistic element and so making it accord with the figurative and spiritualistic way of putting truth, which, as they affirm, is a prime characteristic of the Scriptures. Hence such views as those advocated by Dr. Bushnell and the editor of the *Christian Union*, and Warren's "Parousia" and Whiton's book on the resurrection. The pulpit of our day, and not in any one denomination, is leavened with such rationalistic teachings. It may even be doubted whether a majority of our young ministers do not doubt as to any actual fulfillment of the Scripture declarations as to Christ's return. And a great multitude of disciples, if they

DO NOT SHARE SUCH DOUBTS,

are at least in a great maze as to what to believe. It will be ample reward for this undertaking if it shall help any student of theology to stand fast by the old historic faith, and any perplexed child of God to cling steadily to that ancient, blessed hope of one day seeing the Lord face to face and of being from the hour of that beholding forever with him and forever like him.

1. First, then, the language of Scripture gives as much reason for believing in the literal, personal, visible second coming of the Lord as in such a first coming. If it was intended by the Holy Spirit that there should be a distinction made between these comings, that one should be taken literally and the other figuratively, obviously there would have been a difference in the use of the language setting them forth. But there is nothing of the kind. The same personality underlies the testimony in both cases. "Occupy till I come." "If I will that he tarry till I come, what is that to thee?" "Judge nothing till the Lord come." "Ye do shew the Lord's will till He come." "Waiting for the coming of our Lord Jesus Christ." "When Christ, who is our life, shall appear, then shall ye also appear with Him in glory." "And to wait for His Son from heaven whom he raised from the dead, even Jesus, who delivered us from the wrath to come." These are representative passages. And no one, it is perfectly safe to say, reading them without previous bias in favor of preconceived opinions, would ever think of their meaning anything else than the literal return of the Lord. So everywhere in the Word; the most superficial reader of the Scriptures can not fail to have noted how particularly the prophecies set forth the facts concerning the first coming of Christ, the place and circumstances of His birth, His mother, His name, His character, life, sufferings, death, and resurrection. It is almost like having his life history written, or one might say photographed, in advance. But the same kind of particularity precisely characterizes the prophecies of His second coming. Indeed, by so much as the incidents of that coming are grander and more royal than the former one, by so much are they set forth in fuller statement, in more vivid and imposing imagery, and in profounder emphasis. Whatever principle of interpretation we apply to one part of His career, obviously we

MUST APPLY TO THE OTHER.

If we take the first set of prophecies to be literally fulfilled, and this we know to be the fact, we must needs, upon the very ground of such fulfillment, look for a like literalness as to the fulfillment of what remain. It is impossible to divide the testimonies of the Sacred Word concerning our Lord at His resurrection, and say of those preceding that these are to be all taken as they read, the foreshowings of literal facts; but this other half from the resurrection on, though given by the same prophet, and side by side with the other declarations, are to be taken symbolically, figuratively, not as they read. Such a reading of Scripture, as of any other book, is absurd. Take as an illustration the familiar passage in Luke, i., 31—33. The word of the angel to Mary: "And behold thou shalt conceive in thy womb, and bring forth a son, and shall call his name Jesus. He shall be great, and shall be called the Son of the Highest: and there shall given unto Him the throne of His father David, and he shall reign over the house of Jacob forever: and of His kingdom there shall be no end." No one questions that there is taught here a literal birth a literal name for the child, and a literal greatness to be His portion as the Son of the Highest. By what principle, then, can the exegetical knife be run through this prophecy and stab the literalness of the second part, so that there shall be no literal throne of David; no literal reign; no literal house of Jacob; no literal personal, visible manifestation of the Son of the Highest in His glory? But all attempts to dissolve out of these Scriptures the literalness of the Lord's return and His Kingship as related thereto, and to keep in the literalness of His humiliation, His sufferings, are faced with precisely such absurdity.

2. But again, take the words which are especially used in setting forth the Lord's return. There are three of this in the Greek, apocalypsis, epiphanicia, and parousia. The first signifies an unveiling, a disclosure, a manifestation, and would suggest naturally to every Greek scholar when coupled with a person, the idea of some visible, external appearance. II Thes. i., 7 is a good example. "When the Lord Jesus shall be revealed with His mighty angels." Angels, we know, have forms, and when they are "revealed" are literal, visible personalties. And like their revelation or disclosure, will be that of the Lord Jesus. This is the natural meaning and use of the word as applied to persons.

REV. E. P. GOODWIN, D. D.,
PASTOR FIRST CONGREGATIONAL CHURCH, CHICAGO.

THE SECOND WORD, EPIPHANEIA,

is still more emphatic in its witness. It is a word which is never used except of some external, visible and imposing manifestation. It is used five times in connection with our Lord; once as to His first advent, and four times as His second. And in each instance it denotes His personal manifestation. Titus ii., 13, is a good example: "Looking for that blessed hope and the glorious appearing of the Great God and our Savior Jesus Christ;" or, as the revised version gives it: "Looking for the blessed hope and appearing of the glory of our Great God and Savior Jesus Christ." As Professor Kellogg well says: "It would be impossible to find in New Testament Greek any word which should more precisely and and unambiguously denote the visible, bodily appearing of the Lord."

But the word oftenest used is parousia. This occurs in twenty-four passages. In two of these it is rendered "presence," and in the rest "coming." The revisers have left the translation unchanged, but in the margin of the twenty-two passages having the word coming have put the word presence. Seventeen of these passages refer to the coming of the Lord. The root idea of the word, according to the lexicographers, is to be there, as indicating the arrival of one that has been absent. As, when Paul says (I. Cor. xvi., 17): "I am glad of the coming of Stephana, and Fortunatus, and Achaicus;" and II. Cor. vii. 6, "Nevertheless God comforted us by the coming of Titus." Or as when He speaks of himself to the Philippian Christians, i. 26, "That your rejoicing may be more abundant in Christ Jesus for me, by my coming to you again." So when He speaks of His bodily presence (parousia) being weak (II. Cor. x. 10) and exhorts the Philippians to obey, not as in His presence (parousia) only, but much more in his absence (Phil. ii. 12). Precisely of a piece with these are the passages respecting the future coming or presence of Christ. Matt. xxiv. 3, "What shall be the sign of the coming and of the end of the age?" (I. Cor. xv. 23.) "But every man in his own order: Christ the first—fruits. Afterward they that are Christ's at His coming." (I. Thes. ii. 19.) "For what is our hope, or joy, or crown of rejoicing? Are not even ye in the presence of our Lord Jesus Christ at His coming?" These are merely representative texts.

IT IS SIMPLY IMPOSSIBLE

to read out of these passages everything objective, real, visible. Whoever can do that with this word that in every instance denotes a literal, special presence can make his Bible mean anything he chooses, and there is an end to all authority.

3. But let us advance the argument. I affirm, then, that the Lord's return must be literal, personal, visible, because he must needs return as a true and proper man. That He was such when He was upon earth, and as truly such subsequent, as prior to his resurrection, admits of no doubt. It was as the man Christ Jesus that he appeared to Mary Magdalene, and the other women, to Peter, to the disciples on the way to Emmaus; to the eleven when Thomas' doubts were removed; to the 500 in Galilee; to the little company that saw Him ascend from the slopes of Olivet into the clouds of heaven. Up to that vanishing point we know past a peradventure that our Lord was a true and perfect man, and that He took with Him into the heavens a true and literal, though glorified, human body. What I say now is, that of necessity He will return with that same body, a body that can be seen and touched, and personal fellowship as true and real, and loving and blessed be had with Him who wears it, as in the days of his dwelling upon the earth. This is exactly what, if there had sprung up no men wiser than the men who wrote these Scriptures, every one would say was what the angels meant, when after the ascension they said to the wondering disciples, "Why stand ye gazing up into heaven? This same Jesus which is taken up from you into heaven, shall so come in like manner as ye have seen Him go into heaven."—(Acts i., 11.) The point of the angels' message is not so much the fact of the return as the manner of it. This same Jesus is to come as he departed, in the air, in the clouds of heaven. The rationalizers may refine as much as they please upon the phrase, "in like manner," and seek to make it agree with

THE SPREAD OF CHRISTIANITY.

or the destruction of Jerusalem, or the manifestation of the spirit in the heart, but there will still confront them this unquestionable fact, that in the minds of those to whom the angels spoke these words they had an altogether different meaning. They went forth looking for the return of the "same Jesus" whom they had seen depart, and for His coming in the clouds. And the best scholarship of all the ages is agreed that this is what the language signifies. Says Hackett: "The expression, 'in like maner,' is never employed to affirm merely the certainty of one event as compared with another. It signifies 'in what manner'; i. e., visibly, and in the air." So Bengel, De Vette, Meyer, Olshausen, Lange, Alford, Jamison, Faussel, and Brown. To make these angels mean what these spiritualizing interpreters of this passage say they meant, is to make their testimony a cruel mockery to these longing hearts they were sent to comfort. Nay, it is to make the Holy Spirit, whose messengers and mouthpieces they were, put off upon the early church a virtual deception, and suffer them, unchecked, to cherish and rejoice in and treat it as the one peculiarly blessed hope by which their hearts were unspeakably comforted and inspired. God does not comfort and inspire His people in that way. These angels meant exactly what they said. And that "same Jesus," a true, personal, visible man, is to come as He went, in the air, and wtih power, and great glory.

But how do we know, it may be asked, that He has not laid aside His humanity, and so will return in a spiritual way? I answer, in the nature of things He can not lay aside His human nature, but must keep it forever. There is much loose and unscriptural thinking and speculation among Christian people here. Jesus Christ, when He was born of the virgin and entered this world as the incarnate Son of God, took upon Him our nature. He was not a make-believe man, a god disguised in a human form, as some have held from the earliest ages, but a literal and true man. He was as truly man as if He were not God; as truly man as He was truly God. So that as He was God of God, very God of very God, He was man of man, very man of very man. That is, He had a true, rational, human soul and a true flesh-and-blood body. And "it behooved Him" to be made thus; "for as much as the children are partakers of flesh and blood"—i. e.,

THE RACE HE CAME TO SAVE—

"He also Himself likewise took part of the same." He must needs become one with those whom he would rescue, must in the most literal sense be identified with their nature. But having so wedded himself to the seed of Abraham by being born of the virgin, by that fact he made himself thenceforth forever a true and literal man. We talk loosely and lightly about our bodies. We seem to think they are the mere houses in which for a time we dwell; or they are related to us as the casket to the jewel, or the shell to the seed which it encloses. Not so the scriptures. In their view man is a complex being. The body is not the man, nor is the soul the man, nor the soul and the spirit. He is made up of all these factors, and neither of them can be left out, and the true, complete man remain. As in the divine idea of the tabernacle, the shechinah glory and the tent in which it dwelt were to be inseparable, so the divinely bestowed soul and the humanly created body, which constitutes a man, were never to be divorced. The law of God concerns both factors; sin concerns both; redemption concerns both. Their future destiny for weal or woe is, according to scripture, indissolubly linked.

When, therefore, Jesus the Christ was born, He took our nature to keep it. The indispensable condition of His becoming our redeemer was that He should become our kinsman according to the flesh, and that He should remain such forevermore. And rightly speaking, philosophically speaking, as well as scripturally, He could no more lay aside His humanity than we can lay aside ours. In the language of the early time, the time of the great councils that shaped the faith of the church virtually for all the centuries, Christ was on His human side consubstantial with men, and on the divine side consubstantial with God. Hence He was and continues to be both God and man in two distinct natures and one person forever. (Councils of Chalcedon and Constantinople, Hodge Sys. Theol. vol. 3, p. 651, also vol. 2, p. 388.)

And so far

AS THE SCRIPTURES TESTIFY

at all upon this point, they emphasize this permanency of our Lord's human nature. Paul say in Acts xvii. 30, 31: "And the times of men's ignorance God winked at, but now commandeth all men everywhere to repent; because He hath appointed a day in which He will judge the world in righteousness, by that man whom He hath ordained; whereof He hath given assurance unto all men, in that He hath raised Him from the dead." Up to the hour of the judgment, then, we have the express witness of the word that Jesus Christ retains His perfect humanity. Then it is affirmed of Him—Jesus, the Christ—names both of them applied to Him in relation to His human nature—that He is "the same, yesterday, to-day, and forever." (Heb. xiii. 8). And among the last testimonies of this book, speaking of the fellowship with their Lord, which His redeemed and glorified people shall enjoy after the judgment is passed, and the new heavens and new earth are come, and the holy city descended out of heaven to earth, it is said, "And His servants shall serve Him, and they shall see His face, and shall reign (with Him) for ever and ever." Such language by any ordinary rules of interpretation would certainly seem decisive as to the unchangeable and everlasting humanity of our Lord. But whether it demonstrates that or not, it does make it certain that when the Lord returns, He will return the same literal, visible divine man as when He left the world.

4. But there is far stronger ground than the necessity which attaches to the abiding humanity of Christ for affirming such a literal,

personal, visible return. The Scriptures set the seal of a divine certainty upon it, in the doctrine of the resurrection. That the Lord now retains His proper humanity, and has a literal, human body, localized and visible, we know from various scriptures As being such a glorified man he was seen of Stephen at His martyrdom; by Paul on his way to Damascus,. and by John as recorded in the Apocalypse. That perfect humanity furthermore he must keep in order

TO BE OUR INTERCESSOR.

For the vital thing about His filling that office, that which conditions all His success in our behalf, lies in this, that He is a high priest sharing our nature, tempted in all points like as we are, and therefore able, as one touched with the feeling of our infirmities, to present our needs before the Father and to secure for us grace to help in time of need. But the Scripture doctrine of the resurrection emphasizes this fact of Christ's abiding humanity, and of His coming again in visible and glorious demonstration of the fact. Modern theorizings, some with Swedenborg and some with German rationalism to lead the way, have attacked the literalness of the resurrection. A part teach that the resurrection takes place at death; that then we drop the material body, but that our immaterial—or psychical—body, in which the soul dwells, passes into another state of existence. Others say all this language about resurrection is figurative, only an intense form of expression to emphasize the wonderful transformation the soul experiences when it is set free from the bondage of its earthly body. It rises up, breaks forth into a new life, just as the soul does when the touch of God first comes upon it to quicken it when dead in its trespasses and sins. That is called a resurrection, and what occurs at death, or after death is only a more pronounced form of the same experience.

But neither of these views is what the Scriptures teach concerning this great truth. They set forth unequivocally and emphatically the doctrine of a literal resurrection of the body. No language could be more clear and decisive than the language they use. It is the bodies, not the souls, of men that are to rise again. "They that are in the graves shall hear his voice, and shall come forth" (*John* 5, 28-29). "He that raised up Christ from the dead shall also quicken your mortal bodies by His spirit that dwelleth in you" (*Rom.* 8, 11). "Who shall fashion the body of our humiliation, that it may be conformed to the body of his "glory" (*Phil.* 3, 21, Rev. Ver.). Then the mighty argument of the great apostle in that wonderful resurrection chapter, I. Corinthians, xv., of itself ends all debate. The whole pith and force of it turns on the fact that Paul is speaking of the resurrection of the body. The seed that is put into the ground has a body, and that new growth which is developed therefrom has a body, and

EVERY SEED HAS ITS OWN BODY

—i. e., a growth-form peculiar to itself and given to it of God. There are also celestial bodies and bodies terrestrial, and each with its appropriate and divinely appointed glory. So also is the resurrection of the dead. It is sown a natural body; it is raised a spiritual body. "It"—the natural body—"is sown in corruption;" "it"—the spiritual body—"is raised in corruption;" "it"—the natural body—"is sown in dishonor;" "it"—the spiritual body—"is raised in glory;" "it"—the natural body—"is sown in weakness;" "it"—the spiritual body—"is raised in power." The argument hangs absolutely upon the literalness of a bodily resurrection. It is this mortal that puts on immortality, this corruption that puts on incorruption. It is not some awakening of the soul as from a sleep, nor some sudden development of it into a larger activity, nor some mystical dropping of its gross outer enswathement and a passing into a freer and higher state of existence. What these Scriptures teach is that the same body that is put into the ground is the body that is to be raised. Just as truly and literally of our bodies, and more, as it was of the body of the Lord Jesus Christ. He wos the first fruits, and the harvest must needs be identical in kind with the first sheaf. He was the first born from the dead of God's great redeemed family, and the rest of the household of faith must needs be like him. And this they clearly cannot be except by the literal resurrection of the body. No matter as to the question involved, what the difficulties may be, difficulties as to bodies burned and their ashes scattered to the four winds, or as to bodies drowned and devoured by the fishes of the sea, or as to bodies buried, turned to dust, and their elements incorporated into trees, animals, or other human beings. These are God's questions, not ours. With Him nothing is impossible, and the resources of omnipotence are as ample now as when they availed, however unphilosophically, or in contravention of natural law, to create a universe out of nothing, and make the original man out of the dust of the earth. Of one thing we may rest assured, whatever the pledges of this Word, God will make them good in every jot and tittle. Our concern is not with the difficulties of the Word, but with its teachings. And these compel us to hold that these bodies are to be resurrected, and that in the resurrection, although transformed and

INEFFABLY GLORIFIED,

they will be just as identical with what they now are as was the body of our risen Lord with the body laid in the tomb of Joseph. They will be literal, visible, glorious, just as His was, and because His was.

You have anticipated, no doubt, the force of this as related to the subject under discussion. The doctrine of resurrection not only makes our future bodily existence certain, but it conditions that future estate upon the bodily existence and return of our Lord. It is at "His coming" that the righteous dead are to be raised, and with believers then living are to be caught up to meet Him in the air, and, as in the twinkling of an eye, changed into His image. I need not stop to cite the passages so familiar to all upon this point. I. Cor., xv., 23-52; I. Thes. iv., 14-17; Phil. iii., 20-21. But you will notice this: that the resurrection of the bodies of the dead saints and the transformation of the living saints is conditioned not only upon the fact that our Lord actually rose from the dead and that He is actually to return, but that at His coming He shall possess still His body, the identical body with which He left the tomb. For only so can the bodies of our humiliation be conformed unto the body of His glory. Only so can we see Him as He is, and therefore be like Him. Only so can we meet Him in the air, and in our transformed and glorified bodies, the likeness of His own, abide with Him forevermore. It is, therefore, the clear necessity of the Scripture teaching as to the resurrection that our Lord's return should be literal, personal, visible. And this is precisely what we know it must be from other testimonies of the word. For these require that He should come "in the clouds of heaven;" that "men shall see Him," that "they that pierced Him shall look upon Him," and that He shall "come as the Redeemer to Zion," take the "throne of David" and "reign over the house of Jacob forever."—*Matt.* 25:30; *Rev.* 1:7; *Zech.* 12:10; *Is.* 59:20; *Luke* 1:32.

Standing now on the ground of this argument, there is

A SWIFT AND SHARP ANSWER

furnished to all the variant theories as to the Lord's return which do away with this literalness. There is just one trouble with them all. They are, some of them, very learned, very philosophical, very satisfying to men's reason; but they lack one thing—the authority of God's word. These Scriptures are against them one and all. Take the view e.g. that seeks to identify the Lord's return with the destruction of Jerusalem. These Scriptures declare that at that time "Shall all the tribes of the earth mourn," that "Men shall see the Son of Man coming in the clouds of heaven with power and great glory," that then "He shall send His angels with a great sound of a trumpet, and they shall gather His elect from the four winds, from one end of heaven to the other."—Matt. 24:29-33. Not taking into account now the manifest absurdity of making an idolatrous Roman General the representative of our Lord, and his heathen legions the type of holy angels, the facts do not agree with these prophetic testimonies. For all the tribes of the earth did not then mourn, nor was the Son of man seen coming in the clouds of heaven, nor were the elect gathered from the four winds. More than that, the gospel was not preached in all the world, as a witness, the voice of the archangel, was not heard, nor the trump of God, nor were the righteous dead raised, and living believers caught up to meet the Lord in the air; all which events are explicitly declared to be the accompaniments of the coming of the Lord. Only an exegesis which is bound to make Scripture harmonize with its prearranged conclusions can possibly construe these prophetic utterances as aimed at setting forth the destruction of Jerusalem. The same minimizing way of expounding Scripture does away entirely with the final judgment, the new Jerusalem, and the glory of the saints in their final estate.

Take, again, the view which identifies the Lord's coming with the death of believers. This, like the theory just considered, is without Scripture warrant. Its favorite passage, "I go to prepare a place for you, and if I go and prepare a place for you, I will come again and receive you into myself," has no reference to death. Our Lord nowhere taught His disciples that He would come for them at death, and nowhere else in Scripture is the doctrine taught. The teaching of the word is, that when the believer dies, he

DEPARTS TO BE WITH CHRIST.

and his longing is to be absent from the body and present with the Lord. Hence, Stephen, when the mob were stoning him to death, saw the "heavens opened, and the Son of man not come down to earth, but standing at the right hand of God." And a little later he said, "Lord Jesus, receive my spirit," and passed into the presence of his Lord, waiting to give him glad welcome in the skies. It was a company of angels, not the Lord, that came for Lazarus when he died; and perhaps they often come to convey God's children home in triumph when their work is done. But the Lord himself is never represented as coming with them, nor bearing them away. Nor did His disciples so understand Him to teach. They very clearly understood that He did not so come at death. For when He made answer to Peter concerning John—"If I will that he tarry till I come, what is that to thee?" John adds, very significantly, "Then went this saying abroad among the brethren, that that disciple should not die." So far were they from supposing that our Lord meant death by His coming that they imagined Him to mean that the beloved disciple should not die, but should tarry till the Lord returned, or be caught up into heaven. Hence the tradition that prevailed in the early Church that John did not die, but, like Enoch and Elijah, was translated. The true Scripture idea is that death is our great, cruel, relentless foe, and that the mighty adversary of our souls, to the utmost of his power, seeks to invest it with terrors. Its coming has in itself nothing but dread, and never ought to be in a believer's mind made the same thing as the coming of the Lord. He who rides upon the pale horse, and who goes forth to kill with the sword, and with hunger and with death, and with the beasts of the earth, is surely not to be confounded with Him who rides upon the white horse, wearing many crowns called Faithful and True and followed by the armies of heaven! He that has redeemed us

HAS INDEED CONQUERED DEATH,

and pledges us victory likewise. But we must face the grim foe as He did, and feel to the last hour all the pangs His malignity can inflict. We may indeed see our Lord's face beaming on us in the struggle, and catch even His words of cheer. But it will be as with Stephen, with the Blessed One standing not on earth, but at the right hand of God, and waiting to receive us there. We have the best of rights to say over the caskets of God's chosen, "Blessed are the dead that die in the Lord," and "where is thy sting, O death, and where thy victory, O grave." Yet this largely over the final release from long-continued torture, and the faith-discerned issues of the struggle which even the King of Terrors can not shut out from the soul. But a day is coming when this mighty shout of triumph shall burst from ten thousand times ten thousand lips, because when He for whose appearing we watch, and toil, and pray shall come, the sacred dust of all the ages shall catch the trumpet's sound and recognize its Lord and spring to meet Him, clothed in immortal beauty like His own. And then, and not till then, will there roll round the world as the mighty pean of this uprisen host, "Death is swallowed up in victory!"

(c) But one other view—and the favorite view with many—must not be overlooked. That which identifies the Lord's coming with the work of the Spirit in the hearts of believers, and in the hearts of men to convert them to Christ. All quickened spiritual experiences, all conversions, and all revivals are a true coming of the Lord. And this view, it is held, puts honor upon the Holy Spirit, while that of the Lord's personal return does Him dishonor by belittling His competency to save man. As Dr. Lyman Abbott puts it: "Far better for Christian work and Christian character is the universal presence (the Holy Spirit) than the localized one; the invisible Christ than the visible one." "It would be difficult to conceive anything more disastrous to the healthful and moral activity of the Christian church than a return of Christ to the earth to reign in the flesh in Jerusalem."—*Christian Union* Sept. 2, 1886. And similarly Dr. Bushnell. "There is nothing, I must frankly say, that would be so nearly a dead loss of Christ to any disciple who knows Him in the dear companionship of faith, as to have Him come in visible show. Nothing could be more inexpedient, or a profounder affliction, than a locally descended, permanently visible, Savior." (Christ and His Salvation, pp. 334-336.)

THIS IS STRONG LANGUAGE.

If these brethren are right, I am most certainly wrong in this presentation. But to the law and the testimony. Is this theory of the coming of the spirit as identical with the coming of Christ, what the Scriptures teach as to the Lord's return? Far from it. They never confound the gift and indwelling, or work of the spirit with the coming of the Lord. The spirit is another comforter. His office is to glorify Christ by taking the things of Christ and showing them to His disciples. He is the representative of Christ, taking his place in the world, and doing His work. It is true that through Him Jesus Christ is spiritually with and in believers, is their life, has His image formed within them. But all this not as personally present with them in the same sense in which he is personally at the right hand of God, but in the same sense in which God the Father is so present in their hearts. (John, 14: 23 and 17; 21-23). That is to say, Christ is potentially in the hearts of his disciples, thereby His spirit to teach, guide, admonish, comfort, help, purify, empower for service. This is what the spirit was sent into the world for by our Lord after the ascension, while He remained at the right hand of God clothed in his glorified human body, and personally visible there as our High Priest, our Intercessor.

And just here is where those who hold to the theory of the coming of Christ in the spirit seem to halt in their readings of the Word. They recognize the office of Christ as advocate, and the work of the spirit as dwelling in the hearts of believers and accompanying the preaching of the word and making it the power of God to save souls. And they seem to forget that according to the Scriptures all this looks to something further on. They seem never to ask whether there was any ulterior purpose in the Lord's going away beyond the gift of the Spirit. Whereas the testimony abounds, and that of the plainest sort, that He went away in order that He might come again. This is what parable after parable is specifically aimed to teach. This is what He says Himself when He gives the

PROMISE OF THE SPIRIT,

and this, be it noted, is the continual witness of the Spirit when he has taken the Lord's place in the church, and is teaching truth and managing everything according to His own supreme wish and will. It is He that testifies that when the times of restitution of all things shall come, Jesus Christ will come to set up His throne and fill the world with His glory. It is He that testifies of that coming day when the Lord shall descend from Heaven with a shout, and the dead in Christ shall rise, and the living saints shall be caught up to meet him in the air, and to comfort one another in this hope. It is He that exhorts believers to be patient because the coming of the Lord draweth nigh; to live soberly, righteously, and godly in this present world, looking for that blessed hope and the glorious appearing of the Great God and our Savior Jesus Christ. Surely, if this doctrine of the literal personal visible return were one that puts dishonor on the Spirit, this is strange testimony for the Spirit to bear concerning it! To keep it always in the foreground, to emphasize and magnify it as the one especial secret of realizing closest fellowship with Him, highest allegiance to the Lord Jesus, and fullest measures of the peace and joy and power to love others that he himself could impart! If this be dishonoring the Spirit, he has wonderfully made the wrath of man to praise Him. No, brethren, these advocates of comings that leave out the personal visible Lord, misread their Bibles, and they misread the history of the church as well. The witness of the spirit in the word and in the work agree. You can not unthread this doctrine out of this sacred book and have a living word left. As well unthread the nerves out of the body and have a living organism left! And you can not unthread it out of the faith of the church without driving the knife to the heart of thousands of its godliest confessors. Say what men may, one thing stands well attested through all the ages, that wherever this belief in the soul's literal return has gotten possession of men's hearts, it has invariably exalted the

AUTHORITY OF THE WORD OF GOD,

emphasized all the doctrines of grace, lifted high the cross of Christ, exalted the person and work of the Spirit, intensified prayer, enlarged beneficence, separated believers from the world and set them zealously at work for the salvation of men. I say it deliberately. I say it as the profound conviction of my soul, no greater blessing could come to the church of our day than a revival of the ancient faith. It would lead God's people oftener to their closets and keep them longer there. It would make them more reverent, more diligent, and more prayerful students of God's word. It would lead them to long more earnestly for the full indwelling of the Spirit and for the life hid altogether with Christ in God. It would open their purses and pour forth treasures with unstinted hand for every form of gospel work. It would send them forth to personal service in comforting the saints and saving the lost. It would lay upon their hearts the burden of the unevangelized millions of the race, and give them no rest till the gospel should be preached to every kindred and people and tongue under the whole heaven. It would fasten their eyes on the promise of the Lord's return, and by day and by night keep them toiling, praying waiting with ever increasing earnestness and longing till the flash of his glorious coming shall burst athwart the sky. It would hasten mightily that coming and thus the infringing of the kingdom whose glory is to fill the world!

PROFESSOR E. F. STROETER.

CHRIST'S COMING PRE-MILLENNIAL.

The exercises of the afternoon session, beginning at 3 o'clock, were conducted by Mr. Benjamin Douglas, of Chicago. A large audience was present. Local and visiting divines and laymen occupied the platform. The hymn, "We're Saved by the Blood," was sung, and the Rev. Dr. William Dinwiddie, of Alexandria, Va., offered prayer. After the singing of the hymn, "Thou Art Coming, O, My Savior," Professor E. F. Stroeter, of the Wesleyan Institute, Warrenton, Mo., read the following paper on the subject: "The Second Coming of Christ Pre-Millennial."

The time has been in the history of the church when the term "premillennial," in connection with Christ's advent, was unknown and unheard of. Primitive Christianity had no need of it. Why? Simply because in those early days post-millennialism was unknown and unheard of. Professed believers in the personal, visible return of the Son of Man from heaven were not then, as now, divided on this aspect of that glorious event. The general expectation was that at and with the

RETURN OF JESUS

from heaven his Messianic kingdom on the earth would be made manifest in great power and glory.

It has been reserved for a later age to deny this significancy of Christ's second advent, and to draw before the eyes of the hoping church a very different picture. We are told that the church is to all intents and purposes Christ's kingdom on earth; that all demonstration of the kingdom that will ever come to Jew or Gentile on this side of the final judgment, is to come through the church in its present unglorified and corruptable state. By some happy combination of human progress, spiritual power and favorable circumstances, the gospel of the kingdom will gradually accomplish the conversion of the world to Christ, and the subjection to Him of all powers and governments; the removal of most, if not all, the terrible evils under which society groans, the abolition of wars and iniquitous statecraft, in short, a millennium of peace, prosperity, and power for the church. The visible, bodily appearance and presence of the Son of Man is considered in no wise essential to the fulfillment of the millennial prophecies. We are given to understand that it is a disparagement of the Holy Spirit to look for anything beyond the operations of His power in and through the church. We are charged with judaistic and carnal misconceptions of the Christ as

A WORLDLY RULER.

Unbecoming pessimism in the face of the marvellous progress of the church in conquering the world, which is statistically demonstrated—is laid at our door. Yea, we are accused even of cutting the very nerve and motive power of missionary and evangelistic effort by proclaiming the ultimate failure of the gospel to convert the world en masse.

In the face of these and a host of other charges it behooves us to give a reason for the hope that is within us, to examine again and again the Scriptural and reasonable grounds for believing that there will be no millennium before or without the visible presence of the glorified Jesus. In order to do this intelligently let us consider:

1. The essential features of the predicted millennium.

2. The true character of the church under the dispensation of Comforter in the absence of her bridegroom—Christ.

1. The millennium, what will it be? We can not, for lack of time, dwell upon more than the most essential features of the Scripture millennium.

1. Our first proposition is: There will be a fundamental change in the condition of physical nature; the curse being removed, the earth and all that dwell therein will have

A GLORIOUS SABBATH REST.

The curse is a fact. The subjection of the creature to vanity is another fact. But the Word declares it is subjected in hope, and the creature itself shall be delivered from the bondage of corruption into the glorious liberty of the children of God. (Rom. viii., 20-21.) When? As soon as the children attain the redemption; i. e., the resurrection of their bodies (v. 23). This, then, establishes the removal of the curse from nature at the resurrection of the saints, and this is coincident with the return of Christ from heaven. These are what Peter calls the times of reanimation (refreshing—anapsyxis) from the presence of the Lord. (Acts iii., 20.)

When the Messiah first appeared among the chosen people he showed them that the kingdom of God was indeed come nigh, even among them. By what means? By the works of power he did on the mortal bodies of sinful men in the flesh. Moreover he walked on the sea, commanded wind and waves, thus vindicating man's original God-intended power over nature's forces. When he showed the select disciples the kingdom on the mount of transfiguration, the glory of eternal life radiated not through his own mortal frame only, but his very garments, of whatever animal or vegetable fiber they were woven, shone

WITH HEAVENLY SPLENDOR

and whiteness. All nature responded to the touch of the second man—the Lord from Heaven. While this gospel of the kingdom was preached to Israel these signs and wonders continued for a witness to those who knew from the scriptures what was prophecied of the day of the Son of Man.

Are all those millennial prophecies, that in that day the wolf shall dwell with the lamb, and the leopard shall lie down with the kid (*Isa.*, 11, 6), that the earth rejoice and blossom as a rose (Isa. xxxv, 1) that the Lord will lay no famine upon His people any more (Ezek. xxxvi, 29), but that the land shall become like the garden of Eden (Ib. v, 35)—shall all these and many more receive nothing but that fragmentary, mere introductory fulfillment? God forbid. For all things must be fulfilled, which were written in the laws of Moses and in the Prophets and in the Psalms concerning Him (Luke xxiv, 44).

The word of God knows no irreconcilable discrepancy between nature and spirit. Nature is indeed last to be reached by the life-giving spirit, but reached it will be. This much is guaranteed by the resurrection of Jesus from the dead. And the resurrection of His first-born church at His return will mark the beginning of a new era in all cosmic life. New potencies and forces will then be introduced on a large scale into nature and be productive of a yet unknown and to human wisdom unknowable and

INCALCULABLE NATURAL EXISTENCE.

Mere scientific deductions from the laws governing nature at present are of no consequence or trustworthiness. They are not when the question is of nature's past before sin entered, they are not when it regards the body-life of Him who is the first fruits of the resurrection, they can not be for that time when the resurrection powers of the Sinless One and His glorified host shall become dominant over the power of corruption in the earth.

The great mystery of Godliness, "God manifest in the flesh," is not to be reduced or limited to the Christ life manifested by the Spirit in the mortal believer. It is not to be overlooked that the Son of God entered into this earth-life not only to comfort unhappy humanity in life and in death by His model life, but also to redeem that humanity which He took upon Himself, and that same earth from which He took His physical nature like unto us, from the curse and corruption by the power of His life out of death. Is Jesus the God man, God manifest in the flesh, then He is for the earth and for humanity the principle of regeneration (palingenesis), not only morally and spiritually, but also physically, socially, and politically. Indissolubly has the Holy One implanted Himself into our being. So surely as the devil by introducing sin introduced physical evil, so surely will and must the redemption of our spirits from the bondage of sin be followed and made complete by the redemption of our mortal body and of all physical nature after it by

THE BLESSED RESURRECTION.

If, therefore, the millennial prophecies of delivery for the groaning creature are to be fulfilled, then Christ must first come and raise all His saints to that incorruptible life which is from thenceforth to be the dominant force in all creation, and to usher in a new era for all cosmic life.

Our second proposition is: (2) The millennium will be characterized by fundamental changes in matters of government and politics. Cast your eye over the pages of human history! What a harrowing spectacle! What hecatombs of human life and countless treasure sacrificed on the reeking altar of human ambition! What has been achieved. "Present agencies" have been at work among the nations for nearly nineteen centuries. Are the nations of the earth, nay only those of Christendom, happy and at peace? Not even the most enthusiastic post-millennarian optimist, though he does not object to mortal and corruptible rulers and law givers in his millennium, is sufficiently optimistic to accept the present state of governmental affairs in the world as altogether glorious and worthy of perpetuation for a thousand years.

Here the question is: Has the earth ever seen a perfect government? Yes, once—and only once—in all the world's history there was a perfect, holy, incorruptible and infallible

KING AND LAWGIVER

who entered into covenant relations with an earthly people. But the only people that had the Lord Jehovah for their political ruler have rejected Him, His statutes, His servants, yea, His only Son, and are now become the byword of the nations, and their holy city, the city of the Great King (Matt. v., 35) is to this day trodden down by the Gentiles. (Luke xxi., 24.) God, indeed, did undertake the establishment of a perfect government in the earth. Man, His chosen people, caused the attempt to fail. Has God given up the plan forever? No; his gifts and calling, even to Israel, are declared to be, by the apostle to the Gentiles, without repentance. (Rom. xi., 29.) There will be, yea, there must be once a perfect, indestructible, righteous government in the earth, something "new under the sun" Israel must and is preserved to be chief among the nations. (Jer. xxxi., 7.) Out of Zion shall go forth the law and the word of the Lord from Jerusalem. (Isa. ii., 3.)

Mundane history is to find its teleology, and "God in History," his final theodicy in that kingdom of life and peace in the earth, where His will shall be done as it is in Heaven. The as yet unceasing conflict between earthly human injustice and the eternal righteousness must and will find their solution and end. To expect the fulfillment of the Scripture prophecies of a kingdom of peace and righteousness

BY GRADUAL DEVELOPMENT

in the present dispensation by means of existing agencies is simply preposterous, and makes sad havoc with plainly revealed truth.

In the first place Jesus Himself has declared of His first advent, that He was come not to send peace on earth but a sword (Matthew x., 34). To the literal truth of this more than eighteen centuries filled with wars and rumors of war, especially connected with the historical development of Christianity, bear witness.

2. The relations Jesus maintained invariably at His first advent to the hostile world powers have been the exact reverse of those foretold in the millennial Messianic prophecies.

3. The Holy Spirit, the agency pre-eminently relied on for establishing righteous government in the world by our opponents is nowhere in the New Testament declared to be the representative of the Messiah in His royal prerogatives and powers before the world. Not to prevent or make impossible the hostile attitude of the world power, but to give us strength by reason of hope to bear and thus to overcome it, even as Christ did, is the Spirit's glorious mission.

4. The theory that the spirit of Christ is eventually to control the existing governments of this world and to permeate them with Christian principles of necessity requires two things, the logical outcome of which must prove absolutely fatal for the post-millennial theory in the eyes of all spiritually minded Christians. In the first place all the

LAWS AND STATUTES

of the nations must needs be brought at some time or other into conformity with the Spirit of Christ as expressed in the New Testament. Christian principles, to be of any avail for governmental purposes with mortal men, must be embodied in statutes and their enforcement provided for. To be entirely consistent, then, our post-millennial friends will have to labor not only for an acknowledgment in a general way of Almighty God in our Constitution, but also of His Son, Jesus Christ, and Him crucified, and of the Holy Spirit, and, furthermore, to have all our statutes made to agree in spirit at least with that Magna Charta of the kingdom of heaven, the Sermon on the Mount. Considering the fact that several humanitarian, but not one of the essentially Christian, principles have ever been adopted and made statutory by any government on the earth, it will be seen that our friends have considerable work before them. But not the laws only must be made to conform to the Spirit of Christ but also the law givers and the executive officers. The most perfect laws will not execute themselves, and to secure their proper execution in righteousness the executive must needs be actuated by the same spirit that pervades the law. Of necessity then nobody but genuine saints, men full of the Holy Ghost and of power, must and should be secured for all the high places of the earth. It behooves, then, the

TRUE CHURCH OF CHRIST

no longer to be satisfied with her low estate but to mind, at last, this interpretation of her "commission," the high things of this world.

In all candor, where is the consistency any longer in throwing stones at our Roman Catholic neighbors, who are assiduously following out this very principle? The church above and in everything, the church wielding all power and authority under heaven, the church issuing and executing all laws for humanity—the system is true throughout to the post-millennial standard. Only Rome is more honestly logical in not affecting to desire a mere spiritual supremacy and reign. But Protestant post-millenialism paves the way no less effectually for the manifestation of the Anti christ as does Roman Catholic post millennialism.

No, no, not to any body of mortal men, in the flesh, however holy, however wise, however spiritual is committed the establishment and maintenance of righteous judgment and government in the earth. To Him alone, who in the very first chapter of the New Testament is genealogic.lly established the son of David, belongs the government of Israel and the ruling of the nations. (Is. ii., 6-8) He is the only legitimate King of the Jews, according to the covenant God affirmed to His father David with an oath.

Many commentators, indeed, are very ready to simply spiritualize away all that is prophesied to the political Israel and to the geographical Palestine of restitution and rehabilitation under "His servant David" (Ezek. xxxiv. 23, ch. xxxvi. 24, ch. xxxvii.) and to appropriate quietly to the Gentile church all there is predicted of

BLESSING TO ISRAEL.

They instruct us simply to substitute the church whenever we read of Israel or the prophets, a seemingly simple and plausible, but fundamentally wrong, proceeding. The words of the apostle to the Ephesians and Colossians should forever guard us against this presumption. Paul emphatically declares that this mystery (of the position and relation of the Gentile church) "was in other ages not made known unto the sons of men as it is now revealed unto His holy apostles and prophets by the Spirit," but that this from the beginning of the world has been hid in God. (Compare Eph. iii., 5, 6, 9, with Col. i., 26, 27 All this would be idle boasting of the apostle if the matter were as plain and easy as some commentators will have it; just read "church" where it is written "Israel"—that is the whole mystery.

The hope of Israel is twofold. The promised seed has indeed come in the flesh. The church knows this by the Spirit. But neither the world nor Israel have yet acknowledged it. But the kingdom of David, in the land of promise, where is it? Without the equally literal fulfillment of this aspect of Israel's hope—to which Jesus himself and His disciples likewise stand committed—Israel's glory among the nations is lost forever. To transfer David's kingdom to heaven is absurd, for no man nor devil doubts or disputes the reign of the Eternal Word in heaven. The issue is His dominion in the earth. The world will never believe that Israel, despised Israel, did bear and bring forth the Holy One as the promised seed, until to the holiness of Abraham's son be added a revelation of his covenanted power as son of David manifest

TO ALL THE WORLD.

Without a glorious Messianic kingdom, a re-established, perfect, and imperishable theocracy of incorruptible priests and kings in the redeemed land of promise, the name of Israel will continue a reproach forever among the nations.

3. Our third proposition is: The millennium will be a period of great and general salvation. Israel as a nation will accept her once rejected Lord (Matt. xxiii., 39, Rom. xi., 26); all nations will see the salvation of God; the earth will be full of knowledge of God (Isa. xi., 9], and holiness will be the general characteristic of earthly life (Zech. xiv., 20.

On this point our post-millennial opponents are inclined to grant us nearly all we claim, only we must not expect the fulfillment of it by any new agency, such as the appearing of the Son of Man from heaven with His risen and translated saints. The world, we are told, is to be converted and filled with the glory of God through the missionary agency of the unglorified church by the power of the Spirit. Are our opponents altogether consistent when they disclaim any radical, dispensational change to bring on this millennium? Something new must, even on their theory, step in to make men at large more willing to love the truth than they have been hitherto. For never yet, while the spirit of truth has been abroad in the world, and the church has faithfully spread the gospel of glad tidings, has at any time or in any place the truly regenerate body of believers outnumbered,

OR EVEN EQUALED,

the merely nominal, half-believing, or unbelieving hearers. The world has loved and still does love darkness rather than light. Again, something new will have to be introduced for the purpose of better preserving churches in their spirituality and power. Never yet, wherever churches have been planted, have they been able to hold their own against the inroads of worldliness, corruption, or formalism. The pathway of Christianity through the Eastern and Western worlds is marked with churches either mummified in rigid formalism or more or less secularized. It is a very pleasing fancy to imagine our own churches proof against these persistent forces of corruption—but, alas, no more than a fancy! This must be changed, however, and radically, or else the progress of Christianity through the world will be an endless round of flourishing and decaying.

If "present agencies" alone are to enter into the calculation, we would suggest the propriety of counting in this universal and unexceptive tendency to corruption in everything in which unglorified humanity, whatever the demonstration of God's spirit, has any part.

We would also suggest that the agency of the evil one, who has his work in the children of disobedience, be not overlooked. The power of the Holy Spirit to convert and sanctify, however wonderful and mighty, is absolutely limited to those that believe; while the very same power of truth inevitably tends to

HARDENING OF HEART

in those who disobey. There is no power predicated of that spirit to break or crush or remove the resistance of conscious, willful, and persistent disobedience to the truth in Jesus. Men are and must remain at liberty to disobey, to hate and to persecute the truth, under the gospel.

All Bible readers and believers will readily acknowledge the wonderful hindering and restraining influence of the Holy Spirit over the powers of darkness. But nowhere is this declared to gradually become a converting power by which the attitude of the Devil might be eventually changed to at least peaceable submission. The Devil is and must be at liberty, under the gospel, to work out his purposes in his children. This is essential for the trial and test of our faith. As soon expect the sun to dry up the ocean as the power of gospel truth to remove or neutralize the existing power of darkness in the earth. The very intensity of gospel light has caused the darkest combinations of organized wickedness and godlessness to appear in the very heart of Christendom. The most fiendish cruelties and tortures, oppressions and persecutions have been invented and practiced in the bosom and in the name of Christianity. The most grievous and sickening moral leprosy breaks out in Christianized society. The most diabolical

ORGANIZATIONS OF ANARCHISM

and nihilism are known only among so-called Christian nations and civilizations. Whatever good results have been accomplished in the world either by sanitary measures, by the industrial and political elevation of the people, by the development of religious and educational facilities—almost every progress, every attainment of any age has become and still becomes a lever of perdition. The Spirit from beneath takes possession of everything, so that the enormous progress of our age in civilization and general culture does not indeed cause, but accelerate disintegration and decay. This is precisely what the predictions of Christ and His inspired apostles lead us to expect from the course of world development in this present evil age. As it was in the days of Noah and of Lot, so shall it be when the Son of Man is revealed. (Luke xvii.,26-30). The last times of this age shall be—not glorious—but perilous times. (2 Tim. iii.,) Iniquity and anti-Christian opposition will reach their culmination in that Lawless One, the son of perdition, who shall make war with the saints and overcome them, whom all the earth will worship, but whom the Lord shall destroy by the brightness of His coming. [2 Thess. ii.,8]

No, not the mortal, fallible, erring church, whose knowing is in part and whose prophesying is in part (1 Cor., xiii 9), is called to fill the earth with the knowledge of

THE GLORY OF GOD.

Not the mortal, diviced, scattered, broken church, which partly from want of love, partly through unavoidable imperfection, partly through death and the grave has never been able, and never will be able this side of her resurrection to demonstrate to the world the wonderful reality of her oneness in and with Christ her head—shall bring an adoring world to the Redeemer's feet.

But when He shall appear, and all His saints with Him, when the bridegroom has joined his bride, complete and perfect, not having spot or wrinkle, but holy and without blemish (Eph., v., 27), when that which is in part shall be done away (I Cor., 13:10), when there will be but one fold and one shepherd (John, x., 16), then, and not till then, will our great high priest see the desire of his soul: then will they be one in Him and in the father; then will the world believe that the Father had sent the Son. (John xvii:21.)

II. Let us now yet briefly consider the true character of the church in the present dispensation of the Comforter in the absence of her Bridegroom, Christ.

1. The life of the believer is hidden life, life hidden with Christ in God. [Col. iii, 2.] St. John declares of God's children: "The world knoweth them not, because it knew Him not." 1 John, iii:2.) This hidden life of the true disciple is so unspeakably precious that any attempt at laying it open, before those who know it not equals a desecration.

ALL ATTEMPTS

of the church to make her true inward being manifest to the world must result in dismal failure and caricature. Jesus himself could not reveal himself to the world as He did to His disciples. His resurrection life especially was entirely unseen by any but believing eyes. It belonged to His self-humiliation, to know himself to be the Son of God and to be unknown and unacknowledged by the world. Thus, then the more Christlike the Christian is in this world, the more is painful holding still and being impressed his lot. The natural man proceeds to expression and full development of his being. To this the spiritual man may in this life never attain. Self-manifestation is absolutely out of the question. The formative process must continue until the resurrection will bring the glorious possibility of free spiritual creation and of full and adequate expression.

What spirit is this which makes the great churches of to-day restive and fretful under this divinely imposed secretness of her true character? The tendency and avowed purpose is to be known and appreciated as a calculable factor by an admiring world. Numbers, wealth, culture, position and influence of adherents are statistically paraded before the world. Boastful calculations of approaching victory over all opposing evil forces are built upon this array of numerals. Post-millenialism

CAN NOT THRIVE

without fostering this tendency to self-willed demonstration, it takes its very life from these numerical paradings.

2. The life of the church, like that of her Lord, is life come out of death. It means death to the world. The true Christian is crucified unto the world and the world unto him (Gal. vi., 14). Christ has become our life and peace, not by some gradual and peaceful process of assimilation, but by bringing about the rupture, by inexorably pointing out the radical and irreconcilable contrast between the natural world life in us and the spiritual life of the kingdom of God.

Separation from, not alliance with and reliance on, the natural world forces is God's purpose with Abraham's children. The gospel of the kingdom is to be preached, not to improve the present condition of the world, but to save men out from it; not to court its approval and admiration, but to incur the hatred of the world by showing up its death nature and its inborn devilish tendencies.

Let us then be faithful to the church in warning her to come out and be separate from the world, not by holding up before her the delusive and false hope of gradually overcoming the deadly enmity of the world. But rather let us hold up before the church her high calling after she has by faith overcome this present evil world to sit with Him

IN HIS THRONE,

even as He also overcame and is set down with His father in His throne (Rev. iii, 2). 3. The greatest prerogative of the church in the present age is service, suffering, and sacrifice with Him who came into the world not to be ministered unto but to minister (Matt. v, 28), to be made an offering and a sacrifice (Eph. v, 2), and to be made perfect through sufferings (Eph. ii, 10). All our hope of future glory is bound up with our present suffering. (Rom. vii, 17; 2 Tim. ii, 12.) By reason of this hope the Christian life naturally becomes one of of self and world denial and patient sufferance. We resist not the present evil. But now let only half of the millennial expectations be fulfilled in the present dispensation to mortal men and women. What a sorry church that would be without world opposition, without constant opportunities to test the real power and consolation of the word in the face of devilish enmity against her, a church of weaklings, not of men strong in the faith which overcometh the world. Surely that church would have but meagre opportunities to be like the Master in this and in all other respects.

When Peter, prompted by natural love and enthusiasm, suggested to the Lord, "Be it far from thee to suffer and be killed; this shall not be unto thee," the Master sternly reproached him, saying, "Get thee behind me Satan, for thou savorest not the things that be of God, but those that be of men."—Matt. XVI, 23.

WE ARE ASKED

at this present day, in all seriousness, to exchange our hope of future glory after present suffering for one in which the very same suggestion is held out as the prospective and desirable future of the church in this world. Past-millennialism holds out to the reach of mortal believers the yet forbidden fruit of honor, glory, power, and enjoyment in His unglorified state.

This has been the tempter's tactics all along the line. Adam anticipated at the devil's suggestion what God actually meant him to attain. The sin is not now, that the church wants to exchange the condition of servitude and suffering for that of mastery and enjoyment at all, but that she wants to take beforehand, to anticipate. What a powerful struggle in the second Adam not to accept joy, honor glory, and dominion, because He came to His own when He came unto this world. Herein He has shown us the only true exaltation. It is intrinsically carnal and Judaising—a mixture of flesh and spirit, of Christ life, and world death—this millennium for and with an unglorified, corruptible church in the flesh.

No, our first and only object in this world must ever be to become entirely God's through obedience, sanctification, making ourselves of no reputation and denying ourselves all premature power, honor, and beauty.

Thus we know if so be that we suffer with Him, that we shall also

BE GLORIFIED TOGETHER.

(Rom. viii., 17.) For our light affliction, which is but for a moment, worketh for us a far more exceeding and eternal weight of glory, while we look not at the things which are seen but at the things which are not seen, for the things which are seen are temporal, but the things which are not seen are eternal. (2 Cor. iv., 17, 18.) Beloved, it doth not yet appear what we shall be; but we know that, when he shall appear, we shall be like Him; for we shall see Him as He is. (1 John, iii., 2.)

The hymn, "Rejoice, Rejoice, Believers," was sung, and a collection taken, inasmuch, as Mr. Needham explained, as the conference is held under the auspices of no denomination, and must necessarily maintain it from time to time during its session in this way. A short recess was taken and the hymn, "When Jesus comes to reward His servants" sung. By a change of programme, in the absense of the Rev. J. H. Brookes, of St. Louis, the Rev. F. L. Chappell, of Flemington, N. J., was introduced, and he read a paper on "The Holy Spirit in Relation to Our Lord's Return."

THE REV. F. L. CHAPELL.

THE HOLY SPIRIT.

When our Lord ascended He left with His disciples two pre-eminent promises. One was the promise of the Spirit; the other was the promise of His Own return. Both of these promises were very vivid in the minds of the apostles, and for both of the things promised they earnestly looked and prayed. And in their minds both of these things were harmonious, tending to the same end—namely, the establishment of the kingdom of Heaven upon earth. In the Old Testament Scriptures and in the sermons of the apostles these two things blend and coalesce. The outpourings of the spirit run into and join with the notable events of the day of the Lord. Ergo, the prophecy of Joel, quoted by Peter on the day of pentecost, as explanatory of the events of that day. "And it shall be in the last days, saith God, I will pour forth of my spirit upon all flesh; and your sons and your daughters shall prophesy, and your young men shall see visions, and your old men shall dream dreams; yea, and on my servants, and on my handmaidens in those days will I pour forth of my spirit, and they shall prophesy. And I will show wonders in the heaven above and signs in the earth beneath; blood, and fire, and vapor of smoke. The sun shall be turned into darkness and the moon into blood before the day of the Lord come—that

GREAT AND NOTABLE DAY.

And it shall be that whosoever shall call on the name of the Lord shall be saved." Or again, the exhortation of Peter after the healing of the lame man: "Repent ye, therefore, and turn again, that your sins may be blotted out, so that there may be seasons of refreshing from the presence of the Lord; and that He may send the Christ, who hath been appointed for you, even Jesus; whom the heaven must receive until the times of restoration of all things, whereof God spake by the mouth of His holy prophets which have been since the world began."

The outpourings of the Spirit and the return of the Lord are here represented to be in one and the same category. There is no break or change of agency. The work of the Spirit continues, intensifies, and outreaches till all things, external as well as internal, material as well as spiritual, are reached and restored or perfected. The atonement of the Son is the basis on which the spirit works. But the work itself is all done by the spirit. That there was any separation, or rivalry, or change, or antagonism of agency between the Son and the Spirit was not dreamed of in apostolic times. But, very disastrously for the cause of truth, these two agencies, which, in the minds of prophets and apostles, were co-ordinate and harmonious, have become, in the minds of men of modern times, separate and antagonistic. Slowly and stealthily, through the subtlety of the God of this world, during centuries of worldy conformity and ignorance of the Scriptures, men have been led to regard the Spirit as their Savior and the Son as their judge, until practically these two persons of the trinity are esteemed so antagonistic that it is supposed that they can not co-exist on the earth, but that when one appears the other retires. I have seen it stated, in respectable religious literature, as a sort of axiom to be admitted on all hands that "we can not have but one person of the trinity working on the earth at the same time;" that is, while the Spirit works the Lord will not come, and when the Lord comes the Spirit will depart; or, in other words, that when the Lord comes the work of salvation is at an end. This was the doctrine that prevailed during the middle ages, and in consequence the coming of the Lord was regarded as the most dismal, dreadful, direful event imaginable; so that, whoever hoped and looked for salvation,

PRAYED THE LORD MIGHT NOT COME,

since, if He did come, all hope of salvation would forever be at an end. Luther tells us that, when a boy, he was so taught to regard Christ that he trembled and turned pale whenever the name of the Savior was mentioned. We of to-day can hardly understand how utterly destructive and void of all hope was the coming of the Lord during the middle ages. It was under the spell of this dark thought that that renowned and sublime judgment hymn was written:

> Dies, irae, dies illa,
> Solvit saeclum in favilla,
> Teste David cum Sibylla,

which furnished the foundation of nearly all Advent hymns until within the last fifty years, thus popularizing its underlying thought There is, indeed, a mighty and solemn truth presented in this hymn. But it is a one-sided truth, or a half truth, which tells a lie when exclusively presented. That last line of the first stanza should put us on our guard,

"Teste David cum Sybilla."

Whenever Sibylline oracles are mixed with God's truth we should beware. And yet many good people of our own day are still dominated by this thought and feeling, so that, if you ask them to pray for the speedy coming of the Lord, they reply that they can not so pray till their loved ones are saved. And who can be blamed for hesitating to pray "Come quickly," if the answer means the end of salvation for the race of man; such a prayer is at best, like an imprecatory psalm. But in these latter days, as the Bible has been more read and studied, it has appeared plain enough that the coming of the Lord means salvation; as the Scripture explicitly says: "He shall appear the second time without sin unto salvation." It has been seen that the chief hopes of our race cluster around the coming of the Lord, and that nothing generally decisive and victorious can obtain on earth until He does come. So freshly and grandly, however, has this truth dawned upon some minds, that a party has arisen with the feeling that the spirit has somehow failed to save the world, and that the Son must come to do a work for which the Spirit was inadequate. And, as the Scriptures are very explicit in stating that there is coming, at some time, and by some means, a period of general Righteousness—a period usually styled the Millennium—the Christian world is now divided into two parties—post-millennialists and pre-millennialists, the former of which holds that the Spirit will bring the millennium, after which Christ will come; while the latter claim that

CHRIST WILL BRING THE MILLENNIUM

by His own coming; and as some may have asserted by their mistaken zeal, or others may have referred from their own views without the aid of the Spirit. Thus do opposite parties in the church of to-day seem to make the Spirit and the Son rivals or antagonists in the work of salvation. And the post-millennialist seems never to tire in telling the pre-millennialists how he dishonors the Holy Spirit. Yea, more among pre-millennialists who are looking and praying for the coming of the Lord, some are so dominated with the thought of the judical side of His work in that day, that, in their view, the salvation, which He comes to effect is only the perfection of those who have previously believed. They see, indeed, the risen and raptured saints and a glorified earth as their habitation. But that is all. No future salvation for Israel or of the nations dawns on their sight. The day of the Lord's coming is, in their estimation, the day of final doom for the race of Adam, except for the elect, who have previously believed. With them the long suffering of the Lord in not coming is salvation, but His actual coming is destruction, except for those who have previously believed. Most of premillennialists, however, are impressed with the many and glowing promises, which seem to pertain to men in the flesh, under the reign of Messiah; and, therefore, see a remnant brought through the terrors of judgement, and a future era of peace and righteousness for Israel and the nations.

Now, we freely admit that it is a difficult matter to harmonize all that the Scriptures say concerning the mysterious, sublime, and far-reaching events of the day of the Lord. We freely admit that there are texts of scripture bearing on this theme, which seem to man's hasty and narrow view somewhat contradictory. But this is not the first time in the history of Christian doctrine that such has been the case, e. g., the reconciliation of God's sovereignty and man's free agency is far more difficult than the harmonizing of the work of the Son and the Spirit, or of the judicial and the saving aspects of the Lord's coming. Nothing is gained by ignoring one class of scripture and confining the attention to another. Nothing is gained by separating the Spirit and the Son, and assigning salvation to one, and destruction to the other. All the scriptures are consistent when understood. And, while we do not expect to solve all difficulties connected with this theme, we are persuaded that a right understanding of the Spirit's relation to our Lord's return will help in removing some of the obscurities, and assist in enabling the watchmen to see eye to eye.

THE SUBJECT IS GREATLY CLARIFIED,

as are so many difficulties of Scripture, by considering Jesus Christ, the apostle and high priest of our profession. He, in his own blessed person, is the way, the truth, and the life. If we wish for light on the wide career of his cause in the earth we have but to look at his own personal career; and as we look upon Him the potent and significant fact that meets our gaze is, that He was what He was, and is what He is, and will be what He will be by reason of the Holy Spirit. He was "conceived by the Holy Ghost" (Mat. i, 20) in order to become flesh. He was "anointed with the Holy Ghost" (Acts x, 38) in order to follow his earthly ministry. He "cast out devils by the Spirit of God" (Mat. xii, 28) in order to show his method of victory. He "through the eternal spirit offered Himself without spot unto God," (Heb. ix., 14), in order to make His great atonement. He was raised from the dead or "quickened by the Spirit" (1 Pet. iii., 18), in order to be fully manifested as the Son of God. His intercession is also by the spirit, for "the spirit Himself maketh intercession for us" (Rom. viii., 26). And His future coming is to be no exception to the method of His past career. For, as we have already seen, prophets and apostles discern the grandest outpourings of the Spirit as in the same category with the coming of the Lord. He is the high priest of our profession, and surely the reappearing of the high priest from the holy of holies to bless the people was a part of His work, performed in the same manner, and by the same potency as was the sacrifice and the intercession. But if Christ's person and sacrifice and intercession is by the spirit, surely His reappearing is by the same. Yea, His whole atoning work was to secure the spirit. He went to heaven to secure the spirit for earth. And as soon as He arrived there He sent some measure or installment, as Pentecost witnessed, which the apostle recognized as earnests or pledges of what should more fully come on the day of His return. Instead of the spirit being withdrawn at the coming of the Lord, He will then be manifested as never before. It is then that the earth shall be baptized or flooded with the spirit. Then will occur the proper fulfillment of the promise of the baptism of the Holy Ghost and fire, of which Pentecost was but a faint earnest. Then will be the restoration ot all things, material as well as spiritual. Whatever workings of the Spirit there have been through through all the Christian centuries are but little

INSTALLMENTS, OR EARNESTS, OR PLEDGES

of what is coming at the Lord's return. To use an illustration from every-day life: If a man should go to some distant land to gain a fortune for his family, and while absent should send home a few hundred dollars from time to time for their immediate necessities, and should prosper in his enterprise, so that at last he himself with all his fortune should return, would we say that when he arrived home his family would have no more money since now they had his personal presence? No, indeed! But we should, rather, say: Now they will have more than ever, since he has come with all his fortune. Why, then, talk of the withdrawal of the Spirit at the Lord's return? And Why say that earnest looking and praying for the Lord's return dishonors the spirit? If ever the enemy completely reversed the truth, it is upon this point. And yet this idea is so firmly imbedded in many minds that it may be well to consider some of the reasons why it so firmly holds its ground. And one is, doubtless, because Jesus said, when upon earth: "If I go not away the comforter will not come;" from which saying some may have inferred that the presence of Jesus here was a hindrance to the coming of the Spirit, and that, having gone to heaven, and the Spirit come to earth, if He should return to earth the Spirit would depart therefrom. But this does not at all follow. It was expedient and necessary that Jesus should go away to heaven to finish the sacrificial work, and so to obtain the fullness of the Spirit for earth. We make too much of Christ's saying on the cross, "It is finished," if we take it to mean that his whole priestly office was finished. His sufferings were, indeed, finished. But his intercession was only begun. He ever liveth to make intercession. This intercession of Christ in heaven, though mysterious to us, is an integral part of His atonement. It was necessary, therefore, that he should go away to heaven to perform it, else earth would never receive the fulness of the Spirit. But by no sort of means does it follow that when this necessary work is done the Spirit will be withdrawn. Just the opposite follows. The Spirit will then be given as never before. To refer to our homely illustration: The man might say to his sorrowing family, as he was about to depart for the foreign land, "it is expedient for you that I go away:

IF I GO NOT AWAY,

the money will not come." But it does not at all follow that when he returns all their money departs, for he goes to secure the money. Christ goes to heaven to secure the Spirit, and when He returns He brings the fullness of the Spirit. But, second, this idea is fostered by the thought that the return of the Lord has so much to do with judgment and the destruction of enemies. The day of the Lord is popularly called "The Day of Judgment," and, therefore, many see in it no salvation. But just here two things are to be remembered. First, judgment works salvation: and second, the Spirit executes the judgment of the Son. Do you not remember the fate of Ananias and Sapphira, and the result of it? They lied to the Holy Ghost and were smitten by the same. Their judgment could not have been any more summary and effective if the Lord Jesus had appeared there in person. And the result of this judgment was that "great fear came upon all the church, and of the rest durst no man join himself to them, and believers were the more added to the Lord, multitudes both of men and women." The very judgment wrought salvation! On the other hand, the appearance of Jesus to Saul of Tarsus, was, doubtless, something of the same sort as that in which He will appear in the day of His coming. Yet it did not in the least hinder, but rather made possible Saul's conversion and endurement with the Holy Spirit.

Judgment is always a part of mercy. That appearance of Jehovah, which overthrew Pharaoh and his hosts, wrought great salvation for Israel. So that the very first recorded song of salvation is a song of judgment. "Sing unto the Lord, for He hath triumphed gloriously; the horse and his rider hath He drowned in the sea." Did you ever know any very extensive work of salvation that was not, in some way, connected with judgment? Are there not degrees of blindness and infatuation that can only be broken by some such manifestation of the Lord as that which came to Saul? Would anything awaken this careless world to-day like the appearance of the Lord Jesus Himself?

If, then, it be asked, Why do we so urge men to believe before the day of judgment and during the day of grace, lest the door of hope be shut upon them? It may be replied, First: Life is even now

EXCEEDINGLY PRECARIOUS;

death is even now knocking at every sinner's door; and how much more will it be so when the day of judgment begins to dawn! Well might Balaam exclaim, as he saw this day from afar, "Alas! who shall live when God doeth this!" Eight persons were, indeed, brought through the flood to stock the renewed earth, but what were they in comparison to the multitudes that perished? And even these were believers in some sense; not walking with God as did Enoch, indeed, so that they could be caught up alive; but still having some kind of faith and obedience, so as to be brought through the judgment as a remnant or seed. But surely there is not much hope that can be held forth to sinners from such almost infinitesimal chances as these!

But it may be replied, second: There is a blessing accorded to those who believe without sight that is not accorded to those who believe with sight. As Christ said to Thomas, "Because thou hast seen Me thou hast believed; blessed are they that have not seen and yet have believed." It was not, I think, without reason that Paul recorded himself so low in the apostolic band. There is, doubtless, far more difference in the different classes of the saved than we have generally been wont to suppose. The Bride of Christ may be one class, the wise virgins another class, and the foolish virgins still another class. Indeed, there are various weighty questions connected with the Lord's coming, which I do not feel prepared to dogmatise upon. But this much seems certain, that the Holy Spirit is to work more powerfully in connection with the second coming of Christ than ever before. And that, although the Lord is to appear personally on the earth, the work of salvation, including judgment, is to be performed as it always has been, by the Holy Spirit.

A third reason why this idea holds so firmly in some minds may arise from the truth regarding the removal of the hindering cause to the revelation of Antichrist. We are told that "the mystery of lawlessness doth already work, only He that now hindereth will hinder till He be taken out of the way, and then shall that wicked one be revealed." This hindering cause to the revelation of Antichrist is, doubtless, as some of the best interpreters hold, the Holy Spirit as He works in the world calling out the elect. And it is consequently said that He will be

WITHDRAWN FROM THE EARTH

with the raptured saints at the parousia of the Lord. And the further inference may unconsciously be drawn that He returns no more to His gracious work in the world, but that thereafter the Lord alone visits the earth with His judgments. At all events that solemn truth seems somehow to militate against the thought that the work of salvation can continue on the earth. But upon this point two things may be said. First, There is a difference between the general or restraining and the special or elective work of the spirit. He puts His general restraint upon even the unbelieving world while He is calling out the elect. Now, He may see fit to withdraw that general restraint in order that the wicked may show out their true nature, and that Antichrist and his hosts may be ripened for judgment. But even this is for ultimate salvation. He has not withdrawn from His great work in the world, but only from the wicked, that he may the more fully and clearly condemn them. Even this sort of withdrawal is but temporary, for when the wicked have ripened and the man of sin has been revealed, then the epiphany of the Lord occurs, when the manifest working of the Spirit returns with the manifest return of the Lord. The action of the Spirit in this removal is, then, only for a purpose, and temporary, and does not at all interfere with the fact that He is to work more mightily than ever on the earth during the day of the Lord. And thus, in every way in which we view this subject, we find that there is no valid ground for supposing that the Spirit ceases His work in the world at the second appearance of Christ. But rather, on the other hand, we find that the chief, grand displays of His power—the baptisms of the Holy Ghost—are to be experienced during the day of the Lord, or the millenium, if you please so to call that happy period. There is, therefore, absolutely no ground for the post-millennial objection that pre-millennialism dishonors the Holy Spirit. Yea, rather, pre-millennialism assigns a far more extensive office and work to the Holy Spirit than does post-millennialism. It looks not merely for the conversion of the elect and the restraining of the wicked during the present age; but also for the

EXTIRPATION OF EVIL

from the earth, and the reorganization of all things both spiritual and material in the age to come; all of which is done by the Holy Spirit. When the work of our great High Priest is finished and He comes forth again in the light of His waiting people, then the spirit will also exercise the fulness of His office. Therefore with reason does the Spirit as well as the Bride cry in this present age, "Come." And He so cries, not with the idea of resigning his office, but rather that He may exercise it more fully and effectively.

Having now established this general relation of the Holy Spirit to the Lord's return we pause to notice briefly what general action of the Holy Spirit may be expected as the day of the Lord draws near. And here again the career of the personal Christ will be our guide. There were three distinct epochs in the career of Jesus Christ, each produced by a special action of the Holy Spirit. 1. He was begotten or constituted a son of God by the Holy Ghost. But in this capacity He was hidden. His nation knew nothing of Him. He lived in obscurity in Egypt and Nazareth for thirty years. 2. He was anointed with power by the Holy Ghost for His witnessing ministry. And in this capacity He filled the land with His mighty works and wonderful wisdom, thus witnessing to His divine sonship for three years. 3. He was raised from the dead and glorified as to His physical being by the spirit of holiness, and was thus declared or manifested as the son of God. In this capacity He lived on earth for forty days, and then, ascending, continued this His perfect being in the heavens. These three epochs were distinct, although there was before each of them some anticipation or foreshadowing of the next succeeding. Thus we find that His Old Testament theophanies foretokened His incarnation. His visit to the temple, at the age of 12, foretokened His ministry. And His transfiguration on the mount foretokened His risen or glorified state. We notice, moreover, that the enemy made special attempts to thwart Him at each transition or as He entered upon each successive epoch: First, to kill Him as an infant; second, to seduce Him in the wilderness; and third, to overwhelm Him in Gethsemane and the tomb. If, now, we observe the career of the general, visible body of the sons of God in the historic world, we shall find these same three stages. First,

ISRAEL WAS BEGOTTEN

or constituted by the Holy Ghost as God's son. But in this capacity she was hidden. The great world knew nothing of her. She lived in obscurity in Egypt and Palestine. Second, the church was anointed with power by the Holy Ghost to go into all the world and to be a witness to all the nations. And, though she has been far too recreant to this her specific duty in past centuries, she is now awakening to it, and the testimony is being rapidly given to all the world. The third stage is to be the resurrection and rapture, or the glorification or manifestation of the sons of God, together with the liberation of the groaning creation in the day of the Lord.

If now we are approaching the close of the second epoch and the beginning of the third, what special action of the Spirit may we expect in the present time? Manifestly the intensification of the work of the second epoch; and some slight anticipation of the work of the third, together with some earnest and cunning efforts of the enemy to prevent the transition.

And surely these are the very things that we now behold. That the nineteenth century has witnessed a marvelous intensification of missionary zeal is among the tritest of remarks. This is such a generally recognized sign of the times, and will be so fully and ably presented by others that I will not stop to enlarge upon it, but pass to inquire: How about anticipations of the third special work of the Spirit, namely, the glorification or perfection of our physical natures? Perhaps some are ready to say that surely nothing of this kind is occurring. But not too fast. These things are not trumpeted abroad. The transfiguration was witnessed only by three, and even they were charged to tell no one until the event, which it foretokened, had taken place. But certain it is, that the power of the Spirit over material things, and particularly over our own bodies, is one of the thoughts that the Holy Ghost is forcing upon the attention of those who really know the Lord. The quickening of mortal bodies, or "divine healing," as it is more popularly called, is one of the most significant signs of the times to every one who is sufficiently instructed in the mysteries of the kingdom to recognize it as an earnest of the resurrection life. But this aside: certainly any one may notice that the doctrine, at least, of the resurrection of the dead and of the rapture of the living, holds

A MUCH LARGER PLACE

in the thought of the church than it did fifty years ago. Many minds have been revolutionized on this matter, so that the apostolic sayings "We shall not all sleep;" "for this cause many are weak and sickly among you and many sleep;" "we look for the Savior who shall change the body of our humiliation," etc., are coming to hold something of their proper place in the Christian dialect of the day.

But perhaps the true situation is better discerned by observing the tactics of the enemy. Satan is wiser than men and more on the alert to foresee what is coming. And he is now seeking most earnestly and adroitly to forestall with his lying wonders, and so to hinder the work of the Spirit in this regard. Why is it that we hear so much in our day about theosophy and spiritualism and esoteric Buddhism and Christian science, falsely so called? Why is it that spiritualistic cures are wrought, that alleged spirits are materialized, that corporeal bodies are levitated, and that astral bodies are separated, except to forestall and hinder the genuine work of the Holy Spirit in this department? It is but a little while since the reign of law—the impossibility of anything supernatural in physics—was the stronghold of unbelief. Why is the enemy now changing his tactics? It is, I believe, because the Holy Spirit is soon to work His third work for the sons of God. Without entering into any minute portrayal of these various signs and lying wonders of Satan, it is enough to say that their central thought is spiritual evolution as distinguished from the spiritual involution of the Scriptures. To get the soul free from the clogs of matter is the gospel that the devil preaches. To bring the spirit more and more into the realm of matter, until He shall control and glorify it, is the gospel that Christ preaches. One is the gospel of death, the other is the gospel of life—of glorified, organic life. One is in harmony with the present order of decaying nature; the other is the glad evangel of the supernatural immortality, illustrated in the risen, glorified, ascended Christ, who is soon to come again to restore all things. The abolition of death, the glorification of living humanity, and the glorification of even the material earth, is the grand hope set before us in the gospel. The swallowing up of death in victory is the goal to which we hasten.

ULTIMATE CHRISTIAN AMBITION

is not to die and go to heaven, but to live immortal on the earth.

But against this glorious, revealed destiny the enemy has so successfully set himself, holding man's attention to the things that are seen in the present age, that many professed Christians do not know that they are virtually heathen. Error has entwined itself even in our songs of praise; e. g., we sing:

"This robe of flesh I'll drop and rise
To seize the everlasting prize,
And shout, while passing through the air,
Farewell, farewell, sweet hour of prayer."

How directly in antagonism is this to our bodily rising and ascending Lord, or with the cry of the souls under the altar, "How long, O Lord!" Sad it is, indeed, that penal nakedness, through the wages of sin, should be mistaken for the everlasting prize of the gospel! or again, how the heathen Adrian's address to his soul, translated and versified by an English deist, has been incorporated into Christian psalmody:

"Vital spark of heavenly flame!
Quit, oh quit, this mortal frame!
Cease, fond nature, cease thy strife,
And let me languish into life."

Pure heathenism, except that it accomplishes at one bound what the Buddhist requires many transmigrations for.

But, thanks be to God, the Scriptures stand uncontaminated. They not only point out the grand goal, but they give us fair and plain and repeated warnings of the false doctrines and lying wonders that Satan will interpose before the goal is reached. To disentangle the sure word of prophecy from all beguiling admixtures of error is the duty of the hour. The watching prayer of God's people is not to their souls or minds to go from this dying scene of decaying nature; but it is, rather, to the spirit of the living God to come into it, and to restore and perfect it. This third office of the Spirit is fully indicated in the Scriptures, and the events of the day of the Lord will fully verify what is there indicated. And while we wait we cry, "Come, Holy Spirit," "Come, Lord Jesus," fully assured that these cries are wholly in harmony, and that when both are answered the kingdom will have come, and the will of God will be done on earth as it is in heaven. "He which testifieth these things saith: Surely I come quickly—Amen. Even so, come, Lord Jesus."

The Rev. W. J. Erdman, of Boston, pronounced the benediction, and the session adjourned until the evening.

THE REV. DR. LORIMER.

ADDRESS OF WELCOME.

The evening meeting drew out the largest attendance of the sessions of the day. Great general interest was shown in the exercises, which were opened with the singing of the hymns, "When He cometh, when He cometh;" "Our Lord is now rejected;" "Look, ye saints, the sight is glorious," and two others. The hymns were sung with an enthusiastic and inspiring ring. Prayer was offered by the Rev. Dr. Frost, of Sacramento.

The Rev. George C. Lorimer, D. D., of Chicago, delivered a very hearty and cordial address of welcome to the members of the conference, which it is to be regretted was not taken in full. "You are entitled," Dr. Lorimer said, "to a hearty and warm reception at our hands, apart from the important object that brings you together. As the representatives of the divinest thoughts, for there is surely no thought diviner than that we have in God's own word; as the disciples of the sublimest leader, for never man spoke as did the Christ; as the advocates of the purest reforms, for there is no philanthropy like that of the gospel of Jesus, our Redeemer; and, as the believers in

THE PRECIOUS HOPE

of His coming, for hope grander is there not beneath the stars than this, you deserve a place in our hearts and the kindest office of our hospitality. We extend to you a hearty Christian welcome, and may the Lord's gracious benedictions rest upon you while you are in our city.

"I bid you welcome in the name of all the Christians of Chicago, and especially of the pastors of this city."

THE REV. DR. PIERSON.

PREMILLENNIAL MOTIVES TO EVANGELISM.

A hymn was sung and the Rev. Dr. A. T. Pierson, of Philadelphia, interrupted often by approving applause, delivered the following brilliant and scholarly address on the subject: "Our Lord's Second Coming, a Motive to World-wide evangelism."

The tree is known by its fruit, but it is the fruit which is naturally grown on the tree, not that which is artificially tied to its branches. So doctrine is known by practice, but only by the practice which it naturally begets. Truth does not become a lie because it is perverted, otherwise grace would lose its glory when men take advantage of it to continue in sin.

We say this as a word preliminary. The question is, what is truth? That being accurately answered, our next concern is to apply the truth in the best and most helpful way. But if what was meant to be a tonic and stimulant is used as a sedative and narcotic, ours is the guilt and responsibility of the perversion. The same sun that softens and mellows and melts, also hardens, encrusts, bakes. When, therefore, we boldly affirm that our Lord's second coming furnishes the highest motive to world-wide evangelism, we do not thereby affirm that in every believer that grand truth brings forth fruit which, either in quantity or quality, adorns the doctrine; but only that in this truth lies the possibility and potency of all evangelism; that here is the seed which, planted in good soil, taking deep root, having room to grow, unchoked by the thorns, will develop the blade, the ear, the full-grown corn in the ear; will find the perfection of its growth, its

FINAL RIPENESS IN REPRODUCTION

—"seed for the sower as well as bread for the eater." In other words, the blessed hope of our Lord's coming when unhampered and unhindered in its normal action makes every true believer fruitful in the seed of propagation, fits and prompts him to sow the seed and himself become the seed of the Kingdom.

1. Foremost among the peculiarities of Scripture teaching touching our Lord's second coming is its imminence.

Imminence is the combination of two conditions, viz.: certainty and uncertainty. An imminent event is one which is certain to occur at some time, uncertain at what time. Imminent is not synonymous with impending. It is not exact to say that what is imminent is near at hand; it may or may not be. It is therefore unfair to discredit the imminence of our Lord's coming by saying that it is a mistake into which even apostles and early disciples were betrayed: that they thought the Lord would come in their day, and as He did not it was proven a misapprehension into which modern disciples have the less reason to fall, since they have this warning before them. Such argument frames into its structure a fallacy if not a sophistry. Primitive disciples believed that Christ might come in their day; they could not say that He would; the difference may seem slight, but it saves them from the charge of deception or delusion. Your brother is in Europe, and may return at any time, even by the next steamer; you do not say he will, and so you are not mistaken if he does not. Any man in this assembly may die to-day; yet I do not affirm that anyone will, and should all live to see the next day, or the next century dawn, no error has been made in the above statement.

The New Testament uniformly teaches the

IMMINENCE OF OUR LORD'S COMING.

It is an event which in this sense is ever at hand. "Behold, the Judge standeth at the door." His hand may be on the latch. But when he will enter no man knoweth, not even the angels in heaven. When He does, it will be suddenly and without knocking. His last word is "Watch and pray; for ye know not when the time is."

How does this imminence of His coming affect missionary zeal? How can it affect it otherwise than to inspire, quicken, stimulate evangelistic activity?

Our ascending Lord, just before His departure, repeated the solemn words of His last commission: "Go ye into all the world and preach the gospel to every creature." "Beginning at Jerusalem, repentance and remission of sins, to be preached in His name among all nations," and His disciples to be "witnesses" unto Him "to the uttermost parts of the earth." The Son of man going to a far country, committed unto His servants and stewards this great trust, saying, "Occupy till I come." Of the hour of His return He gives no hint that they may be always ready.

What would be the natural consequences? Every faithful servant would hasten to invest his talents in trading, that at His coming He might receive His own with usury. And such was the historic fact. There are two immutable things in the plain records of those early days. First, the church was premillennial in doctrine, and, second, the church was evangelistic in practice. To the student of church history both these facts are indisputable. The church of the first century looked for our Lord's coming as liable to occur at any time; it was so really, vividly imminent that Thessalonian disciples failed to give sufficient

EMPHASIS TO THE ANTICHRIST

and the apostacy that must precede it. Yet never was the church—the whole church—so permeated and penetrated by missionary enthusiasm. Even while the apostles were still at Jerusalem, those humble disciples "scattered abroad and went everywhere preaching the word."

There is a living link joining this blessed hope and this spirit of evangelism. They looked for their Lord and King to return, and they knew not the hour. The King had entrusted them with the grand commission, and the King's business requires haste. There was to be no tarrying save for that enduement from on high, which was their equipment for their work. To the outmost bounds of Judea, Samaria, Galilee, they bore the message; then to Antioch, the eye of the East, Cyprus, Asia Minor, Greece, Rome—then, while Peter went eastward toward Babylon, to the elect dispersion, Paul, burning with seraphic ardor and fervor, swept like a flame across Palestine and Syria, farther and farther into Europe till he touched not only Italy, but, as some think, Spain and Britain. Within the life-time of one generation the gospel message was borne to the outskirts of the Roman Empire, and the heathen priests trembled lest the fanes of their idols should be forsaken of worshipers.

This heroic evangelism of the primitive church was inspired by their love and loyalty to Him who was to them the coming One. They were "looking for and hastening unto the coming of the day of God." Their ascended Lord was only veiled behind the cloud that received Him out of their sight, but still near them, with them alway, even to the end of the age, and that end might be very near. That cloud might at any time

DISCLOSE HIM ONCE MORE

to their expectant, enraptured eyes; and that "same Jesus" who had so suddenly been "taken up from them into heaven," would with equal suddenness "so come in like manner as they had seen him go into heaven." And when He did come He would claim His own, rewarding faithful stewards and judging the unfaithful. The question was thus ever forced upon every disciple, "Are my talents put to use, or put away in a napkin like a buried treasure?" "A dispensation of the gospel is committed to me;" am I dispensing that gospel?

Christ himself warns us of the danger incurred by those who say, 'My Lord delayeth His coming.' To lose sight of its imminence tempts to *self-Indulgence* and to *controversy on minor issues.* Under the blessed impulse of primitive piety, stimulated by this hope, all self-denial was cheerfully endured, and all petty jealousies rebuked. The church, 'all at it and always at it,' worked as though the time was short and the duty urgent. To-day the hope is so obscured that the bulk of professed disciples push our Lord's coming into a very remote future; and the church is leisurely working, if not flippantly playing, at missions, as though there were geologic cycles in which to witness to the world.

2. Again, our Lord's second coming is a motive to world-wide evangelism, because it is inseparably associated with the glorious compensation for all service, suffering, and sacrifice for His sake.

"Behold I come quickly, and my reward is with me to give every man according as his work shall be." It is

NOT OUR DEATH, BUT HIS COMING

that is linked with the wedding feast into which the wise virgins enter with that joy of the Lord of which faithful stewards partake; with that award of prize to those, who so "run as to obtain." It is when He comes that martyrs "faithful unto death" "receive the crown of life;" those who "love His appearing," the "crown of righteousness;" those who as shepherds fed the flock, "the crown of glory;" those who win souls, "the crown of rejoicing," and those who "keep the body under and bring it into subjection," the "crown incorruptible."

What incentive and inspiration to carry the cross at all risks to the very summit of Satan's citadel, and to every point in the parapet, that the humble follower of Jesus is filling up that which is behind of the afflictions of Christ in his flesh for his body's sake, which is the church. He is looking for the coming of the King, when he who has fought a good fight shall exchange the armor of the warrior for the crown of the victor. Death may usher him into Paradise, but the resurrection of the just represents the full glory and complete reward of self-denying service and sacrifice. It is then, and not till then, that they that be "teachers shall shine as the brightness of the firmament, and they that turn many to righteousness as the stars forever and ever."

Paul tells the Philippians of his renunciations and compensations. He counted his gain as loss, and even refuse, to be trodden underfoot; and it was all joy to him because he looked forward, not indeed to death, but to the exanastasis, that out resurrection from among the dead. He could accept the fellowship of Christ's sufferings in view of the fellowship of His glory;

COULD DIE WITH HIM AS A MALEFACTOR

that he might rise with Him as a benefactor; dying while others live, that he may live when others are dead.

It is to be regretted that with even the majority of the disciples this whole revelation of rewards is obscure. In fact, many are in doubt whether rewards can have any place in an economy of grace since "to him that worketh is the reward not reckoned of grace but of debt."

The sermon on the mount teaches us that salvation and reward are not identical, "except your righteousness exceed the righteousness of the Scribes and Pharisees ye shall in no case enter into the kingdom of heaven." The one condition of entrance is a divine righteousness, imputed to us and received by faith alone. But, having entered, there, our place, our relative position there, is determined by the measure of fidelity with which we "do" and "teach" the words of God. Christ taught the woman at the well, that eternal life is the gift of God to be had for the asking; but that chapter also contains an additional revelation touching rewards; "he that reapeth receiveth wages and gathereth fruit unto life eternal." Wages for work differ from a gift bestowed without reference to service rendered. The sinner is saved by grace; the saint is rewarded for work done.

So, in First Corinthians, Paul tells us that a man may be "saved" and yet "suffer loss" of his work being burned, and may both be saved and "have a reward," his work abiding. The Christian worker, dying daily, bearing in his body the marks of the Lord Jesus, lifts up his eyes and sees redemption drawing nigh. He follows his Lord in his humiliation, remembering that "in the regeneration, when the Son of Man shall sit on the throne of His glory,

HE SHALL SIT WITH HIM."

This blessed hope of the Lord's coming with his reward is an hourly inspiration. He watches prayerfully, toils wearily, waits patiently; the Lord is at hand; at any moment "this same Jesus" may "so come in like manner" as He was seen to "go into heaven." Then shall the wrongs of the ages be righted, and the martyrs of Jesus shall receive their long-deferred crown.

The whole tendency of such a hope is to unfix the disciple from the world and the world from him. Those who say, "My Lord delayeth his coming," may be tempted to self-indulgence, hoarded treasure, intoxicating pleasure. But the steward whose Master may at any hour return to call him to account can not bury his talent in houses and lands, costly plate and shining gems, stocks and stores; he feels that he must invest it—it must be currency—current from hand to hand, increasing as it goes. And so wherever he is laboring "the time is short;" the "Judge standeth at the door," and when He knocketh he must be ready to "open to Him immediately;" his work always done and ready for rigid scrutiny.

3. The practical effect of the blessed hope of our Lord's coming is to make disciples unselfish and spiritual; to relax the hold upon worldly things and carnal lusts and make all seem small and insignificant beside the magnitude of eternity. The consistent believer in this truth can neither lay up treasure upon earth nor lay out vast plans for indolence and indulgence. While preparing for a long life of luxurious ease the midnight cry may be heard.

"THE END OF ALL THINGS" MAY BE "AT HAND,"

and he wants no treasures or pleasures, pursuits or possessions which His coming can interrupt, or condemn, or bring to nought. But if, step by step, human enterprise, worldly civilization and ecclesiastical progress could bring on the latter day glory, we should be justified in building as though everything were to last at least a thousand years. But if all these things are to be dissolved, and may be speedily brought to the fiery ordeal; if only the graces of the spirit and the fruits of walking and working with God are to endure, then let us expend our energy upon imperishable things. And there is no proof or fruit which demonstrates that this doctrine is of God more than this undeniable fruit of its real dominance in the soul, making the believer unworldly, uncarnal, unselfish.

Here is another vital link between this hope and missions. No work demands for its earnest doing, more unworldly and unselfish devotion than foreign missions. Much so-called Christian work may be prosecuted in the energy of the flesh; it promises

A RICH AND PROMPT RETURN

in temporal and financial prosperity. A railway magnate may give money in large sums to build schools and churches in new settlements, along the lines, on commercial principles; the church or school is a nucleus for population; population means travel and transportation; and, so, revenue to the railway, increased value to stock, and ultimate enrichment to stockholders.

The fact is significant that during the first centuries the church was premillenial and evangelistic, and since the Lord's coming ceased to be regarded as imminent, and was projected into a remote future, the evangelism of primitive days has never been revived. Few disciples flame with zeal for foreign missions; the bulk of church members regard the work with comparative indifference, and some even contend that "it does not pay."

When we pierce to the core of the difficulty we find it is simple selfishness. Beyond any other form of Christian work, this is carrying the gospel to those so far off, so needy, so distant, and so destitute, that we can expect no returns. They can not recompense us; we must look for our recompense "at the resurrection of the just," and nowhere this side of that. The most frantic appeals for perishing souls along the Congo, beneath the shadows of the Himmalayas, or in the Korean valleys, awaken no response from hearts encrusted with selfishness. Of course foreign missions do not pay, if, by "pay" we mean a compensation to avarice, appetite, or ambition, or any form of temporal interest and self-emolument. To evangelize a great city is applying salve to the festering ulcers upon the body politic; it promotes the safety of our homes, protects life, liberty, property, helps to assure our temporal peace and prosperity, and to

PULL UP ANARCHY BY THE ROOTS.

To evangelize the great West likewise "pays;" the returns will come, though it may take a little longer to reap the harvest. Facilities of travel and harvest do not more surely bring to our doors the granary and treasury of the continent than do the normal growth and healthy development of the remotest members help the whole commonwealth, while a thorn in the farthest extremities inflicts such a pang on the whole body that the whole body stoops and bends, and brings every other member into requisition to pluck it out.

In city missions and home evangelization we may appeal to commercial enterprise and selfish instincts. But when we are pleading for South Sea cannibals, or African Hottentots or the half idiotic Cretins of the Alps, or the despised opium-loving Chinaman, or the stupid Equimaux, or the exclusive Lama worshippers of Thibet, we have no hold on selfish souls. To give money for such a purpose is like putting it "into a bag with holes,"—you will never see it again and may never see adequate results. It is doubtful whether the Lord means that you shall. He puts this work before us as the nearest in spirit and motive to that which brought our Redeemer to this earth. The spirit of missions is essentially unselfish; it is giving to those from whom we can not "hope to receive;" it is bidding to the feast those who "can not bid us again." He who, either in prevailing prayers, consecrated offerings, or personal service, seeks to set up the banner of the cross amid the millions of Brahmins and Buddhists, Confucianists and Mohammedans, Parsees and papists, devil woshipers and fetish-worshipers, must first of all "have the mind of Christ" and

EMPTY HIMSELF OF HIMSELF;

he must consent to "humble himself and be obedient unto death." The carnal must die if the spiritual is to live; the miser dies when the missionary is born; he would "save others, himself he can not save." It is utterly vain to attempt to demonstrate to a selfish disciple that it pays to give his money, his children, himself to carry the gospel to the superstitious ,degraded, half-imbecile pagan. After all the 500 pages of Dr. Thomas Laurie have blazed with their tributes to what missions have done for science, for geography, geology, meteorology, archæology, philology, ethnography; for natural science and social science, medical science, and political economy; for literature and culture, for mechanic arts and fine arts, for history and poetry, for commerce, and common schools, the selfish, carnal disciple can not see that this is the most economical or practical way to spend gold or life blood. To the human view it is comparative if not absolute waste though it may be heroic, for men and women of seraphic natures to go and sacrifice themselves in such a fashion—daring climate, disease, privation, and even human brutes to do their worst. There may be a sweet savor of spikenard amid the deadly rank growths of paganism, but a fair and costly flask of alabaster is broken. Henry Martyn was a mistaken martyr. Wm. Carey would better have stayed in England. Adoniram Judson not only threw himself away in Burma, but withdrew, from civilization to a premature death, three of the grandest women ever nurtured in refined society. Think of Harriet Newell at 21 dying on the Isle of France, and Mrs. Grant in

Persia at 25; of Bishops Patteson and Hannington falling before

THE BLOWS OF BRUTAL ASSASSINS;

of Samuel J. Mills dying on mid-ocean in the service of Africa, and Nott broken like a reed in the first year of acclimation; think of Levi Parsons dying at Alexandria in two years, and Pliny Fisk, that splendid scholar, wasting his five languages in Syria, and following Fisk in two years more; and Stoddard, the young but brilliant astronomer, star-gazing in Persia.

To the average Christian the foreign missionary field is a vast sepulcher of buried hopes and blighted lives. Over six hundred missionary martyrs are buried in the soil of India alone. Hundreds have died on the coast of Africa in the very process of acclimation. In the South Seas scores of saintly souls have yielded their bodies to be roasted in cannibal ovens. "To what purpose is this waste?"

Ah, my brother! vainly shall you seek an answer if selfishness prompts the inquiry. Enough for the true disciple that the Master laid down His life a sacrifice at 33, and prayed for those who crucified Him, and that He, who thus died for sinners, left us "an example of uncompensated love and sacrifice. Enough that He said: "Go ye into all the world and preach the gospel to every creature." We have our marching orders, and if we fail in the unequal contest, let us bear above us the inscription by Simonides over the spartans who feel at Thermopylae, "Go, stranger, and declare to the Lacedaemonians that we died here in obedience to their divine laws."

Now here we find one more link between the hope of our Lord's coming and foreign missions. There is no one thing that compares with that blessed hope in its

REFINING INFLUENCE ON CHARACTER.

Its whole tendency is to make us unselfish, to relax our grasp on carnal pleasures and material treasures, and to fashion us "after the power of an endless life" rather than "the law of a carnal commandment." It makes the time seem short, it dwarfs the world into insignificance and lifts the peaks of the world to come into clearer view, into loftier altitudes, in a nearer horizon.

It makes the present compensation for sacrifice and service of less importance, while it magnifies the approval of our coming Lord. In the seven epistles to the churches which open the apocalypse, our Lord uses His coming as a perpetual admonition and inspiration. The Ephesians could well bear and have patience and not faint; the Smyrnese could endure the ten days of tribulation; the Pergamoans could well hold fast His name and not deny the faith; the Thyatirans might well resist the seductions of Jezebel; the Sardians keep up their watch, and their garments white, the Philadelphians keep the word of His patience, and the Laodiceans turn from luke-warmness to ardent longing—for the Lord's coming was always at hand, when all trials would cease and only eternal things would seem of any importance or value.

Mr. Moody says: "When this truth of the Lord's second coming really takes hold of a man the world loses its grip on him. Gas stocks and water stocks and stocks in banks and railroads are of very much less consequence to him now. His heart is free when he looks for the blessed appearing and kingdom of the Lord." Our brother hits the nail on the head with the blow of his Saxon hammer.

HERE IS THE DEADLY FOE

of the cause of world-wide missions—the world is too wide and selfishness is too narrow. The cares of this world, the deceitfulness of riches, the lust of the flesh, the lust of the eyes, and the pride of life make such unselfish work seem wasteful. Fields planted near by with wheat and corn are more attractive than fields sown far away with gospel seed and yielding slow and uncertain and slim harvests. Fine mansions of marble on the stately avenues of a metropolis are better property to live in or rent to others than the mission churches and schools and hospitals that are always in straits for money to enlarge them or workmen to man them. Self-indulgence promises richer satisfaction in present luxury than self-denial for the tedious process of converting the heathen.

4. Our Lord's coming, when rightly conceived, furnishes a grand motive to a world's evangelization in suggesting a hope which Scripture authorizes and history fulfills. As this is vital to our subject we give it ampler discussion.

Our Lord's coming is marked in Scripture teaching by its dispensational character. It marks a transition; it closes one dispensation and opens another. To understand this dispensational character is of primary importance.

Premillenialism is denounced as discouraging to evangelistic effort, taking out of evangelism all vitality and enthusiasm. It is compelled

TO BEAR THE BRAND OF PESSIMISM.

We propose to show that it inspires instead of strangling hope, but our first appeal must be to the only final authority, the word of God.

What, according to the teachings of our Lord himself, is the purpose of the present dispensation?

Many hold vaguely that it is a world's conversion. According to their view, the gospel is a small mustard seed, set in the soil of society, ever rooting deeper and spreading wider, taking up and assimilating to itself the elements of society and incorporating them with itself, upreaching and outreaching until the earth is filled with the shadow of it and its branches are like the goodly cedars; that like leaven, hidden in three measures of meal—the world, the flesh, and the devil—it is to pervade, penetrate, permeate the whole lump, modifying the evil with which it comes in contact, until it transforms the world into the church, the flesh into the spirit and the devil is leavened out altogether, like the gasses which escape or are expelled from the fermenting dough.

The careful student of Scripture sees another quite different teaching. He finds dispensation succeeds dispensation in human history, all marked by seven features essentially the same. First, an advance in fullness and clearness of revelation; then gradual spiritual declension: then conformity to the world ending with amalgamation with the world; then a gigantic civilization, brilliant but Godless; then parallel development of evil and good; then an apostasy, and finally a catastrophe.

This dispensation began on a higher plane than any that precedes, but bears the same general marks. It opened with the

FULLEST REVELATION OF GOD,

in the written word, the living word, and the coming of the Holy Spirit. It moved step by step downward and backward; primitive piety declined; the church courting and finally wedding the world. The sons of God saw the daughters of men that they were fair, and they took them wives of such as they chose, and of this unnatural wedlock giants were born; but they proved destroyers rather than defenders of the faith. The successive civilization of Egypt, Assyria, Persia, Greece, and Rome trampled virtue in the dust and deified vice with the crown of the gods. Rome made torches of Christian martyrs, and Athens made priestesses of Venus out of unchaste women. Human wisdom built altars "to the unknown god," culture flowered into polytheism and pantheism, and ripened into materialism and atheism. That there has been a growth of good no one will deny, and blessed harvests from the seed of the kingdom, thirty, sixty, even a hundredfold; but there is a parallel development of evil. The tares grow side by side with the wheat, each ripening to the harvest.

It behooves us not to lose our candor even in the heat of controversy. Who can doubt the fact that this high civilization of which we boast is the amalgamation of church and world? The world has become a little churchly, adopting some Christian ideas and sentiments, molding its moralities and philanthropies into a semblance to the gospel pattern; but while the world has grown a little churchly, the church has grown very worldly, hopelessly worldly. The dialect of Canaan is corrupted with the language of Ashdod. Professing disciples do not even profess self-denial. The "strait gate" has given place to

AN EASY AND ATTRACTIVE ENTRANCE,

and the narrow way is broadened into a stately avenue, smoothly paved, and bordered with fragrant flowers. Though there be "no royal road to learning," the church has found a royal road to heaven.

We have spoken of the conformity of the church to the world as hopeless. Satan has for centuries stamped five institutions as especially his own—the card table, the horse race, the dance, the stage, and the wine cup. Professing Christians receive his coals in their bosoms and yet expect not to be burned; they sit till midnight over progressive euchre, enter their steeds on the race course, whirl through the intoxicating mazes of the dance, tipple over the wine glass, and not only go to the theater but introduce it into church entertainments. Our church life is honeycombed and undermined by worldliness. There is little if any practical separation. The bulk of professing Christians if not wholly worldly are worldly holy; at the door of this world's frivolities and gayeties they shuffle off their Christian character as easily as an oriental guest his sandals, and mingle indiscriminately with those who bow at the idol shrines of folly and fashion. There seems to be a process of moral putrefaction, or loss of godly savor, and petrifaction, or loss of godly sensibility, which threatens the very existence of any pure and primitive type of piety. The garment spotted with the flesh communicates the contagion of a worldly leprosy, and those who are warned to keep themselves unspotted from the world are overspread with its uncleanness.

What is the result? Instead of presenting, like Joseph in Egypt or Daniel in Babylon, a perpetual contrast to our surroundings, the only line of separation that remains is the church roll. Instead of being spiritually

ISOLATED AND INSULATED

that we may be charged and filled with the life of God and the power of God, the witness of a separate sanctified life and of the tongue of fire is gone.

What is the real character of our present civilization? We may as well face the facts. It is gigantic in invention, discovery, enterprise, achievement; but it is gigantically worldly; sometimes and somewheres monstrously God-denying and God-defying. This "Christian civilization" has produced giants in these days, men of renown, but they often use their intellect, knowledge, and fame only to break down, as with the iron flail of Talus, all Christian faith. Philosophy now blooms into a refined and poetic pantheism or a gross, blank materialism or a subtle rationalism or an absurd agnosticism. Science constructs its systems of evolution and leaves out a personal God; spontaneous generation becomes the only creator, natural law the only determining power, and natural selection the only Providence. Such men as Strauss and Renan, Hegel and Comte, Goethe and Kant, Mill and Spencer, Darwin and Huxley, Matthew Arnold and Theodore Parker are specimens of men who owe their education, refinement, accomplishment, to the very Christianity they attack. The cubs first nurse the dam and then turn and strike their fangs into her breast. Civilization itself is turned into the stronghold of unbelief; its imaginations and inventions are high towers that exalt themselves against the knowledge of God and the thoughts of our great thinkers have not been brought into captivity to the obedience of Christ.

We have the ripest form of worldly civilization, but the

RIPENESS BORDERS ON ROTTENNESS;

while men boast of the fabric its foundations are falling into decay, and that awful anarchy which is the last result of atheism even now threatens to dissolve society itself. Government is rendered helpless by the destructive forces which science has put into the hands of the ignorant and lawless. The ballot and the bullet alike become weak in competition with dynamite, and war becomes impossible until men are ready for mutual extermination.

There are not wanting those who openly affirm that the millennium is a present fact—this is the millennium! In these days of popular education and rapid locomotion "many run to and fro in the earth and knowledge is increased. In the marvelous triumphs of electricity in telegraph and telephone, the lightning is literally coming from the East and shining unto the West; in the grand achievements of artificial irrigation, agriculture, and horticulture, the wilderness and solitary place are already glad, and the desert rejoices and blossoms as the rose. In the Atlantic cable and kindred transoceanic lines, and the giant steamships that move round the world with such incredible speed, there has come to be no more sea. In the peace societies and courts of arbitration the nations learn war no more.

In the wide dissemination of the Scriptures in nearly three hundred dialects and the dispersion of missionaries in all the lands, the earth is already full of the knowledge of the Lord as the waters cover the sea. In the practical sympathy and unity of all evangelical believers our Lord's prayer is fulfilled,

THAT THEY ALL MAY BE ONE.

In the civilization and enlightenment of the rude and barbarous tribes, the cow and the bear feed; the carnivorous become the graminivorous; the lion eats straw like the ox; the wolfish rapacity and leopard-like ferocity of savage natures is transformed by civilization into lamb-like gentleness. Nay, the prophetic language finds a still more startling fulfillment in the fancy of some, for the English lion and the Russian bear have both become Christian nations, and the little child, youngest born of the great nations, the American Republic, is leading all the rest. Why look for any other millennium when these and other marks of fulfilled prophecy are furnished in current history? Even the symbolic contest of Michael and the dragon may be found in the wars between England and China, whose symbol is the red dragon, and which drew about a third part of the human race after it. And in that war the dragon prevailed not! In a way scarce less frivolous than this have we known modern advocates of an existing millennium to torture prophecy, warping the testimony of the word to fit the crook of their notions.

If the purpose of this last and highest dispensation is to convert the world, developing a millennium by a process of assimilation, this dispensation is so far a failure. That the world has made progress we have already admitted, but it is not progress toward salvation. There have been seven golden ages of history, those of the Ptolemys in Egypt, Pericles in Athens, Augustus in Rome, Leo X. in Italy, Ivan III. in Russia, Louis XIV. in France, Elizabeth in England, but they have all been

AGES OF MORAL PROFLIGACY.

Our golden age is far from unfolding even the promise of a millennium. Beyond any past age science, invention, intelligence and education have reached a lofty level, but human wisdom is a Greek arch, rising high above the earth only to curve back to earth again, instead of a gothic arch, whose highest reach points still upward. The material conditions of the world may advance only to develop materialism, magnifying things seen and temporal and obscuring the unseen and eternal.

I fear we shall be compelled to reconstruct our notions of the millenium and the process by which it is to become a reality. The Word of God does not represent it as a human development, the outcome and outgrowth of civilized or even enlightened society. In the interests both of truth and of evangelism we need to emphasize the fact that the millennium is not a culmination of human progress along an inclined plane of gradual ascent, but the era and epoch of a divine force uplifting, renewing, and transforming human society.

The dream of the image of world power is divinely interpreted by Daniel as a vision of what should be thereafter. There is no hint of assimilation or incorporation of even the best worldly elements into the kingdom of God. Instead of this there is a process of comminution—crushing, crumbling, grinding, pulverizing—that the wind may sweep all away

LIKE CHAFF FROM SUMMER THRESHING

floors. The stone, cut out without human hands, grows without human aid, refusing to incorporate with itself clay and iron, or even silver and gold, rejecting alike the best and worst, most precious and most worthless. That stone is a millstone grinding all alike to powder.

What is the teaching of all this but that the kingdom of God is essentially celestial in its nature and elements? As the wheat does not change the tares so that both are bound in the same sheaves, or the good fish the bad, so that both are put in the same vessels, so the stone does not change the elements of this world, growing by assimilation and accession. This world has ever been only the foe of God, neither worthy nor capable of such transformation and incorporation; its end is to be burned. There will be gold in the city of God, but not coarse opaque metal; it will be transparent like burning crystal or golden sheen of sunlight. The rapid growth of the mustard-seed may mean for the kingdom of God a worldly expansion not wholly of God, attracting to the shadow and shelter of its branches the very birds of the air which catch away the newly sown seed of the kingdom and hinder the harvest. The leaven may represent a false and carnal principle pervading the kingdom as a fermenting element, increasing outward bulk but introducing the forbidden thing.

As Scripture does not teach such a millennium as many look for as the final evolution of human society so the facts do not encourage such expectation. It is patent to the careful observer that so far little progress has been made toward converting the world and those who have cherished such a hope and wrought for such a result, confess that the prospect disheartens. After nearly nineteen centuries of Christian history only

ABOUT ONE-FOURTH OF THE RACE

is even nominally Christian; and three-fourths of these ignorant of the Bible itself and swayed by superstition and priestcraft are but one remove from paganism; the small remaining fraction, nominally Protestant, includes less than thirty million church members. At this rate of progress, it would take a cycle of centuries to convert the world to even a nominal Christianity.

Without being conscious of morbid despondency or pessimism, we cannot but think the present condition of both the world and the church calculated to dishearten of any Christian worker who looks for a millennium upon scientific principles of development, by a process of evolution with natural selection and survival of the fittest Optimists triumphantly array facts and figures to prove the progress of Christianity; but if "facts and figures do not lie" they are sometimes arranged and arrayed in deceptive forms and combinations. The immense "numerical progress of Christianity is like a soap bubble, brilliant but illusive. For example, Seaman's "Progress of Nations" gave the total number of Christians, in 1880, as 317,152,099; and in 1886 this number is swelled to 350,000,000, or one-fourth the population of the globe.

What intelligent man can be misled by such a marshalling of figures: "Of this vast host at least 175,000,000 are under papal sway, and millions of them do not know the Bible from the prayer-book, and are virtually heathens. Eighty millions more are adherents of Greek and oriental churches, having a form of truth and godliness, but denying the power thereof, to both oriental Catholics and oriental Armenians and Nestorians, evangelical Protestant Christendom sends missionaries as to Mahommedans and pagans.

ONE HUNDRED MILLIONS

of "Protestants" remain, but not all are true disciples who are identified with Protestant governments, communities or even churches. Within the ranks even of the Protestant ministry we find included attitudinarians, latitudinarians and platitudinarians, or or ritualists, broad-churchmen and liberalists and retailers of insipid commonplaces; among church members formalists who substitute rites and ceremonies and sacraments for renewing grace, and nominal professors who enter the church at a given age as they would the army, and with no more thought of spiritual qualifications. Nay, as Bishop Foster says, the so-called Protestants are "divided into five hundred sects, and this number of their strength includes also all the thieves, ex-convicts, the debased, besotted, the speckled and streaked in Christendom." We may add, it includes not only scientific sceptics, but materialists, pantheists, and atheists; the blatant blasphemer who goes about lecturing against the Bible, and with his putty-pipe and popgun of cheap satire and borrowed humor, "drawing on his imagination for his facts and on his memory for his wit," must be ranked with the Protestants, because our scientific analysis and classification do not provide a separate species for the man who in pointing out the mistakes of Moses principally reveals his own. And when we come down to the rock basis of solid facts, we find less than thirty millions of church members who can with any fairness be counted as disciples.

It was such insight into the reality of things that constrained such men as Thomas Chalmers to confess that his previous conceptions of the progress of Christianity and the teachings of Scripture had been erroneous, that led him to examine the whole question anew and to write to Mr. Bridges, in 1836, "I am far more confident than I was wont to be

THERE IS TO BE A COMING OF CHRIST,

which is to precede the millennium;" and in 1847 to write to Dr. Horatius Bonar, "I approximate much nearer to your prophetical views than I did in my younger days." Hear again Bishop Foster, speaking on "The Outlook of the World for Humanity," "There are some who too fondly anticipate a millenium. Is our faith supported by existing facts that indicate such a result? I believe that we have drifted so much into enthusiasm that we forget the facts. There is a lack of information on the progress of Christianity. The facts are misstated daily in pulpits all over the country. Ministers hesitate to present the worst side for fear of causing discouragement. They create hopes that are never to be realized. We are not at the dawn of the millenium. Compared with the work to be done the past is nothing. Our children's children for ten generations to come must labor harder than we are doing to accomplish the conversion of the world."

We are told that tares and wheat grow together and ripen side by side till harvest time; and this is what we see to-day. However faithfully we sow the seeds of the Kingdom, Satan's agents outstrip us in sowing tares; disciples are so closely united that only infallible wisdom can discriminate. The parallel development of evil and good will go on until He comes who will separate them for the fire and the garner. Every cast of the gospel net encloses but a few fish out of the world-sea, and even these embrace both the evil and the good, and so

IT WILL BE UNTIL THE END.

Has Christianity—has Protestantism then been a failure, and shall we give up the task as hopeless of evangelizing the world? By no means. Failure is a comparative term. If God meant to accomplish the conversion of the world in this present age, so far there is disastrous failure. But if tares and wheat are to grow side by side, and side by side ripen till the harvest; if the gospel net, cast into the wide world-sea is not to inclose all the sea, but only the select number, and even those inclosed include both bad and good, "sword-fish" and "toad-fish," "man-sharks" and "devil-fish," as well as the delicious cod, the blood-tinged salmon, and the angel-fish, then far from failure, there has been and is exactly what the Lord himself purposed and prophesied as the outcome of thisdispensation.

To see this truth taught in the word and wrought out in the acts of the Holy Ghost and the facts of history from Christ's ascension until now, is to kindle in the despondent breast of a weary workman a new celestial fire of contagious courage and enthusiasm. The handwriting on the wall of this world's palaces of riot and revelry, selfish luxury and profane sensuality may be a sentence of doom, "numbered," "weighed," "wanting," "divided:" but it is the handwriting of God. What if we behold,

Right forever on the scaffold,
Wrong forever on the throne;
Yet that scaffold sways the future,
And behind the dim unknown,
Standeth God amid the shadows,
Keeping watch above His own.

WE ARE NOT DISMAYED

by the double development, the parallel progress of good and evil all along the age. With a holy hopefulness, not as attempting to achieve impossibilities, but as working with God in faith toward a result as sure as His existence, we go to preach the gospel everywhere—to sow the seed of the Word and become ourselves the seed of the kingdom in the whole world field. We see God going before a little Gideon's band, opening doors everywhere and giving access to all nations in His own time and way. We see converts gathered in all lands, but is only an exanastasis, an out-resurrection from among the dead; the great mass still lie in the profound sleep of spiritual death. But it is God's work gathering into the body of His bride the elect witnesses from all nations.

The number grows larger, but it is still the

few that find the strait gate and narrow way. "Iniquity abounds," and "the love of many waxes cold;" but that abounding iniquity in the world and coldness in the church only draw the few holy ones into closer fellowship with each other and closer walk with God. Nay, we are not disheartened in our evangelism by apostasy in the church itself. If the "progressive orthodoxy" of a "new theology" insinuates its subtle serpent coils into theological seminaries; if the "supremacy of the ethical conscience" supplants the supremacy of the cross of Christ in the faith of many a believer; if the speculation on "probation after death" embolden men in sin, harden them in impenitence and cut the nerve and sinew of foreign missions with those who believe and teach it; if millions of believers are by mighty tidal waves of errors swept away from all

MOORINGS OF DOCTRINE AND DUTY,

and the ancient land-mark which the fathers set up are all removed, we are not surprised or disheartened. Prophecy is only finding its Champollion in history; and the obscure hieroglyphus on it monuments have an interpreter. We are persuaded only the more firmly that God rules, and is surely working out His plan. In time to come we expect to see the evil come to its awful ripeness—the full corn in the ear; sin more abundant, flagrant, insolent, triumphant, presumptuous, blasphemous. But this is only the devil coming down, "having great wrath because he knoweth that he hath but a short time." And as surely shall we see Enochs and Elijahs walking closer with God as those who await translation!

Our evangelism is not robbed of its enthusiasm because after nineteen centuries truth and faith, purity and piety are still with the minority. They always were, from Abel's martyrdom till now. In the times of the flood, of Babel, and of Sodom, of Elijah's despondency and Christ's rejection, of the Dark Ages and the new dawn of the Reformation, of the birth of modern missions and the awful maturity of modern worldliness, it has been the comparative few who have entered into the secrets of God. There is not to-day a godly pastor in all Christendom who would think of depending on the bulk of his church membership for prevailing prayer, divine passion for souls, holy self-denial, or even consistent living. We must all learn not to associate power with mere numbers, or to think of God as on the side of the heaviest battalions, to those who would work or war with a will, only while backed by the majority, a candid survey of the facts in the world and in the church will cause a congestive chill that kills all evangelism. But he who is

WORKING UPON A BIBLICAL BASIS

can bear to see the rose-colored cloud of poetic sentiment dissipated and the bald, bare peaks of fact stand out unveiled. He is God's servant. The plan of the campaign, the map of the field of conflict, the weapons of warfare, the strategy of the march he leaves with the general-in-chief. Into the very thickest of the fight, surrounded by the smoke of battle, dimly seeing even his scattered fellow soldiers, it is enough for him that he is obeying marching orders, that the white plume of his leader still moves before him, and the clarion peal echoes all along the lines, "Go ye, disciple all nations!"

This is not a mere question of the interpretation of doubtful Scripture or of historic facts, for undoubtedly both the word of God and the witness of history may be read through colored glasses or distorting lenses. But the interpretation we adopt has a vital relation to the courage and confidence and hopefulness of our evangelism.

What is more discouraging, disheartening than hope not only deferred but defeated. In its actual religious state the world is no nearer a Scriptural millennium than it was hundreds of years ago. Civilization is not Christianization, nor culture piety. None more obstinately resist the direct appeals of the gospel than the worldly religious moralists in our congregation: they are the modern Pharisees, who crucify the Son of God afresh, and the publicans and harlots go into the kingdom of God before them; and the gospel has often cast out the demon of ignorant superstition only to find the house reoccupied with seven demons, all the absurdities of scepticism and rationalism preferred to faith.

The remedy against

DISCOURAGEMENT AND DISPAIR

may be a reconstruction of our hope itself. If we have been looking for a result which the word of God does not warrant, if the Scriptures do not represent the conversion of the world as the end or the aim of the present dispensation some of us have been working on a wrong basis, trying to achieve impossibilities, and of course we are discouraged.

The soldier who mistakes the object of a campaign may see all the movements of the army in a false light. If he thinks the whole force of the foe is to be captured and converted into loyal adherents, the capture of a few leading strongholds is only the next thing to an absolute defeat. But if he learns that orders from headquarters so direct, and that subordinate officers are carrying out the plan of the great commander, seizing and holding in all parts of the enemy's territory the representative fortresses which command the situation, waiting until the general in chief himself arrives on the field with re-enforcements, sounds his imperial clarion along the whole line of battle, and leads on all his hosts to one overwhelming charge. What before seemed next to absolute defeat is now the preparation for final and complete success.

We believe that the word of God will be found on closer study to hold up before us no hopes which are not even now steadily moving on toward full fruition. Nowhere is the purpose of this dispensation represented as the conversion of the world, but always the outgathering from the world of a people for God. As Anthony Grant sententiously said in the Bampton lectures of 1843, "The gospel is not to be in all places at all times, nor in all places at any one time, but in some places at all times and in all places at some time." God purposes that everywhere the banner of the cross shall be lifted as a witness to His grace, and that the church with all its institutions be planted

AS A CONFIRMATORY WITNESS;

that all who are of the truth hearing, shall follow the shepherd's voice and be gathered into the fold. And then shall the end come. A new dispensation inaugurated by the king's personal coming shall gather all the scattered sheep into one flock and achieve triumphs over sin and Satan, to which all previous victories are as ripples to mountain billows or grey dawn to blazing noon.

Our Lord's second coming is a center both of convergence and divergence; all Scripture converges in it, and all final success radiates from it. It is no small matter to have a rational Scriptural hope, for hope is one of the main factors in a joyful, serviceable life; the blow which cuts off expectation is crushing. [The decreptitude of old age is shown by this; "desire shall fail," and then it is that strength also fails, and even the grasshopper becomes a burden.] Whatever quenches aspiration and chills enthusiasm tends to kill hope, and when expectant "desire fails," even the lightest load is an unsupportable "burden."

Many an earnest disciple who has begun working in expectation of a world's conversion has been constrained either to abandon his wrong basis or his fruitless work.

Let the believer once get this scriptural conception as an intelligent conviction rooted within him and he

ORGANIZES VICTORY OUT OF DEFEAT.

Hope that has lost her wings plumes herself for tireless flight. The dirge at the grave of buried expectation changes to the song of rejoicing at the rent tomb from which expectation rises to a new and deathless life. He sees that Satan has no advantage. God's eternal purpose marches on through the centuries and marshals even Satan's forces into line. The whole world with all its oppositions becomes but the scaffolding about the church of God, to be used in its construction, and torn down and burned up when the capstone of God's building is laid.

The Apostle James in inspired words outlined at that first church council the whole plan of the divine architect and builder.—(Acts xv. 15.)

"Simeon hath declared how God at the first did visit the gentiles to take out of them a people for His name. And to this agree the words of the prophets, as it is written: 'After this I will return and will build again the tabernacle of David which is fallen down, and I will build again the ruins thereof, and I will set it it up that the residue of men might seek the Lord, and all the gentiles upon whom My name is called, saith the Lord, who doeth all these things.'" And the apostle significantly adds, as though to assure disheartened disciples that God's plans steadily advance toward completion—"known unto God are all His works from the beginning of the world."

We are not entrusted with a world's conversion, but with its evangelization. The power of man, or of all men combined, cannot convert one soul; that takes Omnipotence, and to combine a million impotences,

WILL NOT MAKE ONE OMNIPOTENCE.

We are responsible, not for conversion, but for contact. "Go ye into all the world and preach the gospel to every creature." There our commission begins and ends. With results we have nothing to do, and are incapable of tracing or guaging them. We are to sow beside all waters, and much seed will be borne by the receding flood to distant fields whose harvests we shall never see or connect with our sowing until hidden secrets are revealed. It is enough for us that God's pledge is given. "My word shall not return to me void; it shall accomplish that which I please and prosper in the thing whereunto I sent it." It is no matter of small moment to get God's point of view and look at this world through His eyes. From that high outlook all needless discouragement vanishes like a cloud, and we breathe the inspiration of a hope that shall never be ashamed, and behold a prospect bathed in the eternal sunlight of his promise. He has told us His pleasure, and the mission whereto He sends forth His word:

first He gathers out from the nations His own elect, then all Israel shall be saved, the times of the Gentiles being fulfilled; and then shall come the true millenium when "the earth shall be full of the knowledge of the Lord as the waters cover the sea."

This promise and prophecy all history is fulfilling. Watch the historic panorama unroll! see each new scene in vivid colors fill out the shadowy outline pencilled by prophecy. Ever since Pentecost gave the tongues of fire God has been visiting nation after nation to take out of them a people for his name. At first the door of faith was opened to the Jew, and the proselytes,

GATHERED FROM ALL NATIONS,

returned like the Eunuch of Ethiopia, to bear witness among the nations where they dwelt. Then the door opened to the Samaritans, Syrians, people of Asia Minor and Greece; then Italy, Gaul, Britain, Germany, and so on till, in our day, God successfully flings wide the portals of India, Burmah, Syria and Turkey, Siam, Japan, China, Africa, Corea and the isles of the sea; yes even the Papal strongholds, France and Italy.

And now Thibet, the shrine and throne of the Grand Lama, the capital of Buddhism, is about to open her two-leaved gates. God is doing just as He said in all these nations, and in some on a grand scale, taking out a whole people for His name. Witness the Hawaiian Isles, now a Christian nation; the half million native converts in India, the scores of self-supporting churches along the Tigris and Euphrates, the Kho-Thah-Byu Memorial Hall, rallying and radiating center for twenty-five thousand Christian Karens; new Japan, with its giant strides unparalleled even by Pentecostal days; the thousand churches of Polynesia, McAll's hundred gospel stations and thousands of converts in atheistic France, Madagascar becoming to Africa what England is to Europe, and China gathering her converts and turning them to evangelists.

Starting from Palestine over eighteen centuries since, and moving westward, the flag of the cross has been successively unfurled in Jerusalem, Antioch, Rome, Alexandria, Constantinople; been borne from shores of Britain to a new world across the sea; then across that new world to the Pacific and the isles of the sea; then across the Pacific to Japan and Corea, and the various lands from the Chinese sea to the Arabian gulf and the Golden Horn; and so completing the circuit of the globe we have once more set up the standard

IN THE PLACE OF THE CROSS

Meanwhile, the girdle of missions is widening into a zone, spreading northward toward the icebergs of Greenland and the snow castles of Siberia, and southward toward the cape of Good Hope and the Land of Fire. We have only to push the lines of missionary effort, until every nation is reached with the good tidings (and hopes shall reap the ripe fruition of Scripture promise). Then, when from gentile nations the last disciples shall have been gathered and incorporated as a member into the body of Christ; when the ecclesia—the called-out ones—shall be complete and the bride hath made herself ready, the Bridegroom shall return to claim his own. The fulness of the gentiles being come in, the blindness of Israel shall be removed; through unveiled eyes, dimmed only with penitential tears, "they shall look on Him whom they pierced" and "wounded in the house of His friends," and "so all Israel shall be saved," and the fallen and ruined tabernacle of David be rebuilt. Then shall the residue of men and all the gentiles see the salvation of God.

The second coming of our Lord is thus vitally related to a world-wide evangelism, for it supplies a motive power in an intelligent and scriptural hope that knows no defeat or disappointment, but rejoices in the visible and perpetual progress of fulfilled prophecy and verified promise. The workman who was the more weary because he looked for results that never were promised and never will be realized, now reading with clearer eyes the purpose of God as enfolded in scripture and unfolded in Providence, lifts up his head; a new joy fills his soul; out of failure courage is born. He sees that he is sent forth

NOT TO CONVERT ALL, BUT TO PREACH

to all the gospel of witness, and from the four winds of heaven to gather out God's elect. Looking for no universal triumph of the gospel until the coming of the King, he is not disappointed.

Our evangelism will be both successful and hopeful, only so far as not misguided by some impracticable scheme having no Scriptural warrant, and aiming at impossible results. Right apprehension of our mission and commission furnish us food and drink. We go forth to work out the decreed, declared plan of God to every land, in His name to call His sheep into the folds, looking for the chief Shepherd to appear and gather all into one flock. No failure can bow us down, for no failure can come. What the promise justifies, results realize. Events evolve what God's eternal plan involved; every crisis was foreseen and provided for. "Known unto God are all His works from the beginning of the world," and He is never taken by surprise. Even the receding wave only prepares for the returning billow that touches higher floodmark.

And so we reach our last argument. Our Lord's coming furnishes a motive to world-wide evalgelism in emphasizing duty rather than success, and our commission rather than apparent results. "Go ye into all the world and preach the gospel to every creature" is a precept, not a promise—our marching orders, not an assurance of large ingatherings. The kingdom of God cometh not with observation, neither shall men say Lo here, Lo, there, as those who point to sudden, startling marvels: great results there have been, and greater there may be, but they are not positively promised until the King by them celebrates

AND SIGNALIZES HIS COMING.

Thus, while pre-millennialism is charged with cutting the nerve and sinew of foreign missions, it supplies their perpetual incentive and inspiration in teaching us that duty is ours; results, God's.

But the faithful evangelist has a promise far richer than any that looks to a wordly standard of success. "Lo! I am with you alway, even unto the end of the world." All through the working and waiting there is a presence, and that presence is power. Results small in man's eyes are great to Him who judges not not by quantity, but by quality. Working with and under the Captain of our salvation, the sense of His presence, the consciousness of His leadership, the assurance of His approval inspire, encourage, enrapture. We may see but a small part of the world field actually sown with the seed of the kingdom, and what is sown may bear but little fruit. The birds of the air may catch away much seed even while we sow; the promptness of its reception may often show how shallow is the soil, in which are no deep conviction, strong affection, rooted resolve; growth that is so rapid and promising may prove lacking in vitality and vigor—a long stalk without ear or kernel—a kind of ecclesiastical uprightness, but no seed of propagation to insure a fruitful evangelism. But some good seed will fall on good soil and yield thirty, sixty, an hundred-fold, showing how God's power abides in the seed and works in the soil. "Instead of the thorn shall come up the fir tree, and instead of the brier the myrtle tree, and this displacement of noxious, offensive, hurthful growths by the fruits of God's own husbandry shall be to the Lord for a name—for an everlasting sign which, though all others fail,

SHALL NOT BE CUT OFF."

6. Thus far our only arguments have been theoretical and philosophical. But we ought not to leave such a theme without at least a word as to the experimental and practical proof found in the actual effect of the hope of the Lord's coming upon saintly souls. The facts are indisputable that from the days of Paul down to those of Christlieb and Moody, Newman Hall and Stanley Smith, the most earnest and ardent evangelists and missionaries have acknowledged this truth as the grand inspiration of their evangelism. The charge that premillennialism "dishonors the Third person of the Trinity and tends to cut the nerve of all missionary and evangelistic enterprises, is based either upon unreasoning prejudice, entire misapprehension of the truth, or total ignorance of the facts.

The mention of such names as Alford and Graham and Craven and Christlieb and Harnack and Delitzsch and Kellogg is enough to show that scholarly exegetes and theologians are represented among the advocates of this view; it is quite enough to name Spurgeon, Newman Hall, Chalmers, Mackay, Bonar, Bishops Ryle and Baldwin and Nicholson; Haslam, Muller, Guinness, Radstock, Varley, Pentecost, Whittle, Needham, Moody, Hammond, Munhall, Brooks Goodwin, Gordon, Moorhead, to show that this hope neither interferes with soundness in the faith, nor with power in preaching, nor with evangelistic zeal.

But we have better work to do

THAN TO DEFEND THE DOCTRINE

by the mention of distinguished names. A truth can not become a lie because it has not won believers among rulers and pharisees, or has no adherents in Cæsar's household. The claims of the truth are quite independent of its following.

A deep conviction, a mighty persuasion sweeps over us like a mighty tidal wave, beneath whose majestic movement all lesser issues are buried. If we discern the signs of the times, the very redness of the evening sky is a hint of the dawn of a new and fairer day. In view of the present crisis of missions, we ought to forget all minor interests and issues and hasten to bear the good tidings to the earth's remotest bounds.

At last, after nearly nineteen centuries the world is open to the gospel. God has flung wide the gates of India, broken down the wall of China, unsealed the ports of Japan; Africa is girdled and crossed, Turkey and Burmah, Korea and Siam invite missionary labor, and France and Italy and Mexico welcome an open Bible and a pure gospel. This has been a divine unlocking of closed doors, with the keys of commerce and common schools, printing press and medical science, arms and diplomacy; nay, even famine and fever and massacre, like "the great armies" of locusts and caterpillars and cankerworms. He has used to force an entrance to Satan's strongholds. What inspiration to zeal and activity when the shining pillar moves before us, and the power and presence of God assure a victory.

IT IS THE STORY OF JERICHO

repeated in modern history. The little missionary band have barely compassed the heathen world, not seven times, but once, bearing the ark and blowing the trumpets, and the walls have fallen flat wherever God's little army stands, the wide world round, every man needs only ascend up straight before him through the breach and take the city. Already the same Omnipotence that has wrought preparation has wrought transformation, and in every field, however unpromising, we have fruits from gospel seed, thirty, sixty, and even a hundred-fold. The harvest is so much more plenteous where the laborers are few that it seems as though Christendom could afford to send half her workmen from home fields to foreign for the sake of reaping larger and even quicker results.

If we do not sow these wide and open fields Satan will. In some quarters the house is empty, swept and garnished, waiting an occupant; peoples disgusted with idols and ignorance, fling away their superstitions and are left without a religion. We must not sleep; our sleepless foe will pre-occupy the house and sow trees in the fallow field. Let the church of Christ but be a pathetic and neglect her opportunity and irreparable damage will ensue. We are sending but one out of fifty-six hundred church members to carry the good tidings abroad, and $1 out of perhaps $1,500 income to support those workmen. The consecration of self and substance in the primitive church leaves ours so far behind that our apathy verges upon apostacy.

This gospel of the kingdom must first be preached in all the world for a witness unto all nations; and then shall the end come. There is a legitimate way of hastening toward, and hastening that end; promptly occupy every open door and amply sow every open field. While we pray Thy kingdom come, we may do much to answer the prayer. The whole creation groaneth and travaileth in pain together, waiting for an apathetic church to do its duty. A thousand

MILLIONS OF HUMAN SOULS

will go down to the grave without light or life, faith or hope, within our generation; one hundred thousand die daily, and thirty millions of evangelical Christians stand idly by and see this wholesale descent into eternal darkness unmoved. Remember there are three hundred Christians who have the message of life to every one of that hundred thousand that each day pass into the great unknown. How far-reaching and potent might be the evangelism of these millions of Protestant believers if organized, economized, and vitalized by the spirit of God and the spirit of missions!

Brethren of this conference, over eighteen hundred and fifty years have passed since the rent tomb, and veil of flesh of Jesus of Nazareth opened a path of life to every believing soul. Through those eighteen hundred and fifty yeays it is estimated that eighteen times the present population of the globe has gone down to the grave from the various mission fields ignorant of the gospel of Christ. Through these eighteen hundred and fifty years, He who is of purer eyes than to behold evil has been hourly confronted by the woe and want and wickedness of heathenism; through all these years God has been preparing his church to enter these now opened doors, and He who was cut off without generation has been waiting to see of the travail of his soul and be satisfied, waiting for his bride to make herself ready and put on her beautiful attire. During the last one hundred years of modern missions, what a series of providential interpositions and gracious manifestations have set the seal of God's sanction upon the missionary work! What colossal obstacles have been removed, what gigantic barriers have subsided, what glorious successes have been granted, the triple marks of divine approval! And do we yet hesitate? Let the shout of this conference arise as the sound of many waters, rallying the Lord's hosts to the onset, that the last fortress of Satan may be stormed and the flag of the cross be everywhere unfurled!

Letters of greeting will be read to-day from Mr. Moody, the Rev. Dr. Bonar, Bishop Ryle, of England, and many others.

SECOND DAY.

OPENING EXERCISES.

LETTERS OF REGRET.

Notwithstanding most unfavorable weather the attendance at the morning meeting of the second day's session of the conference was encouragingly large. The Rev. George C. Needham conducted opening religious exercises, consisting of the singing of several hymns, and prayers by the Rev. Dr. F. W. Baedeker, of Weston Super Mare, England, and the Rev. Jacob Freshman, of the Hebrew Christian Church, of New York. Letters of greeting and blessing were then read from Mr. Moody, the Rev. Dr. Bonar, of Glasgow, Scotland, and the Rev. Dr. Archibald G. Brown, of London, the Baptist preacher. These letters were as follows:

WHEELING, W. Va., Nov. 5.—My Dear Brother: The pressure of work and binding engagements will prevent my attending the conference. I feel for the purpose of the conference the greatest sympathy. May it result in a spiritual quickening in all the churches.

The coming of the Lord is to me a most precious truth and constant inspiration to work.

There can be no better preparation for the Lord than breaking the bread of life to the perishing multitudes.

My prayer is that the conference may result in sending every minister out to evangelistic work this winter. Evangelists can not do one tenth the work called for. Pastors must assist each other. May the Spirit of the Lord for service come upon each one attending the conference. Yours sincerely,

D. L. MOODY.

To Mr. George C. Needham, Secretary.

EAST LONDON TABERNACLE, BURDETT ROAD, October, 1886.—Dear Brother: I am too pressed with home work to be able to write you a paper, however brief, on so important a subject as prophetic teaching. With you I deeply regret that dispensational truth is so ignored. The general idea seems to be that through the influences of Christianity, school boards, etc., the world is going to gradually "level up" into a paradise for Christ. I confess I see nothing of this in the word. If I rightly understand my Bible, this dispensation, like every other, is to end in judgment. Christendom is apostate as well as the world, and is hastening on to her doom. For many years I have found the hope of our Lord's return my brightest joy and my most powerful inspiration for unwearied service. I have no expectation of the world getting better prior to His return, but, on the contrary, expect evil to become yet more pronounced, and this with "a form of godliness," but destitute of power. Conventional religiousness, that knows nothing of the life of Christ in the soul, is too much mistaken for Christianity. I expect that to abound at his appearing. It is, however, a cold, selfish, worldly thing, and will receive judgment at the hands of the Lord. I am looking for Him and waiting, either to be caught up to meet him, or share in the blessing of the first resurrection. With much personal love, yours, in Christ,

ARCHIBALD G. BROWN.

GLASGOW, Oct. 20.—Dear Brother: I have received your notice of the Bible and Prophetic Conference, and read it with deep interest. You ask me to state to you what I have found of benefit and blessing from the cherished hope of the pre-millennial coming of the Lord. In reply let me say that it is nearly fifty years (just before I began my ministry) since I first felt its power; and during all my ministry (now nearly forty-eight years) I can not recollect of any occasion on which I brought to a close the services of a communion Sabbath without reminding my flock of what was implied in "till He comes." As sure as we "sat down" at His table and "watched Him there" in His agonizing suffering unto death, so also we rose from the table looking to the crown and the kingdom.

But more particularly, His "blessed hope" has evidenced itself to be indeed a doctrine according to godliness by such effects as these:

1. It has cast a peculiar light on the pages of the Prophetic Word and on all the Word all through.

2. It has cheered me often when circumstances and times were dark and threatening. I have been able to "lift up my head"

when brethren were letting their "heads hang down."

3. It has proved itself to be an awakening doctrine. There are persons in my congregation who were awakened by listening to the warning: "Behold, I come as a thief."

4. It has also comforted very many saints; and, more than that, it has even led timid and doubting believers to full assurance. For example, a worthy and intelligent member of the church who could not get quit of uncertainty and fear was persuaded to study the subject of the premillennial coming of the Lord. He got deeply interested, and while thus engaged found his eye so continuously resting on Christ Himself that ere ever he was aware he was basking in the light of the law without a fear.

5. This farther let me say, that as for myself, it has stimulated me very greatly to do my utmost through the grace of God to gather in souls at home and abroad, by home mission work and foreign mission work. Though I can not say with old Jerome that "the sound of the last trumpet is ever in my ear," yet I can say that, from time to time, I have been stirred up with new zeal and earnestness in the work of the Lord, from the consideration—"so much the more as ye see the day approaching."

Believe me, my dear brother, your companion in tribulation and patience of Jesus Christ, ANDREW A. BONAR.

THE REV. J. M. ORROCK.

OBJECTIONS TO CHRIST'S PREMILLENNIAL ADVENT CONSIDERED.

While there are many passages in the Holy Scripture which refer to the kingdom of Christ and His saints, there is but one in which the millennium is distinctly named and its coming foretold. But it should be distinctly understood that the repetition of a statement by God does not make it stronger. If it can be shown that He has spoken once, that statement is just as true and may be as fully depended upon as if He had spoken a score of times. The millennial passage is the 20th chapter of Revelation. In looking carefully at it you will find that the millennium is bounded by four notable events, two at the commencement and two at the end. Those at the beginning are bright and blessed, those at the end are dark and dreadful. At the beginning we have "the resurrection, the first," that of the "blessed and holy" and the binding of the devil and his incarceration in the abyss for a thousand years, commonly called the millennium. At the end we have the resurrection of "the rest of the dead," the unblessed and unholy—all who had not part in the first resurrection—and the loosing of the devil "for a little season." Now I want you to distinctly note the two events which come together at the close of the millennium. If you pause for a moment to think of what is involved in the resurrection of the unjust you will agree with me that

IT MUST BE A DREADFUL EVENT.

Think how vast must be the multitude brought from the dead at the close of the millennium, when it includes all the ungodly who have died from the first hour of time down to the last moment. Dr. John Gill, a learned Baptist commentator of the last century, held that the hosts of the ungodly thus brought on the earth again by the second resurrection will constitute the army of Satan, metaphorically denominated in verse 8 "God and Magog." They were his subjects previous to death; they are his subjects in the resurrection. They served him in the flesh and were deceived by him there; they will be gathered unto their master again after they have arisen, see him for the first time face to face, and be again deceived. There is no intimation that any saints will be deceived by him after the first resurrection. He can not reach them during the millennium, for he is imprisoned, nor at the end, for they are encamped and in "the beloved city" (v. 9). He only has access to his own subjects.

As to the state of things in the millennium itself the passage assures us that the subjects of the first resurrection live and reign with Christ, are priests unto God, and will never "be hurt of the second death," which is the doom of all the finally impenitent. This for them is the sabbatismos—"the keeping of a Sabbath"—which Paul affirms "remaineth for the people of God" (Heb. iv. 9). There was no higher dignity of old among men than that of kingship and priesthood; and by these figures we are taught the great dignity to which these "blessed and holy" ones will be raised, as well as their intimate communion and sacred fellowship with their glorious head. If Satan is bound and imprisoned when the millennium begins you will readily see that the condition of things then will be in striking contrast to what we have now. At present the devil is very punctual at religious meetings. Jesus said, when the word of the kingdom is preached "then cometh the devil and taketh away the word out of their hearts, lest they should believe and be saved;" but then his church-going will be ended. Now Christians are exhorted to "be sober and vigilant, for the devil, as a roaring lion, walketh about seeking whom he may devour;" but then his peregrinations will be stopped. All agree that when the millennium comes it will be a golden age; but whether to be enjoyed under the moonlight of Christianity, or under the sunlight of the glorious appearing and personal reign of our Lord Jesus Christ is the question at issue. All premillennialists take the latter view; and the diversity of opinion which exists among them is largely owing to what is read between the lines of the famous millennial text of Revelation. There are passages in the Old Testament which speak of blessings to Israel—whether conditional and forfeited, or otherwise—and these are brought over into the millennial age. Some bring more than others, and just to the extent that is done is the difference. But as to the fact that the millennium lies between two resurrections, and is ushered in by the personal appearing of our Lord Jesus Christ, we are a unit. To the views which are believed by us as a body there are

TWO CLASSES OF OBJECTIONS

made, those that pertain to hermeneutics—especially the interpretation of texts bearing on the resurrection, the judgment, and the state of things during the millennium—and those that are of a somewhat popular character. Of the first class I do not intend to speak. In some of the other addresses reference will doubtless be made to them. I shall dwell especially on the popular objections. And *first*, it is said that premillennialism leads to time-setting, and, by consequence of failure, to discouragement and infidelity. As Dr.

Gardner Spring puts it: "It is calculated to produce mischievous and fanatical impressions upon the minds of men in relation to the period of Christ's second coming."—*The Glory of Christ, vol. I. p.* 145. To this we reply: Time is an essential element of all biblical truths. There are prophetic periods mentioned in the Word which have reference to Christ, His Cross and crown and church. It is our privilege to prayerfully study these passages, but not to suppose that we are thereby to be made prophets. Post-millennialists as well as pre-millennialists have erred in calculations of definite time. The passing of a few years does not affect great historical events which are marked out on the pages of sacred prophecy. To illustrate: Suppose a person stands by the side of a marble monument in the midst of a group of others. He has in his mind a matter in which they are materially interested, and in his effort

TO BRING BEORE THEM HIS IDEAS

he takes a piece of chalk and on the stone before him makes figures and marks of different kinds. The months come and go, the winds blow and the rain falls, the frosts and snows of winter come and pass away. You stand the following summer by the side of that monument, but do you find that it is destroyed? No. The chalk-marks are gone, but the marble shaft rears its head just as it did before. So the passing of 1843 without bringing the Lord was as the chalk-mark; the passing of 1866 without bringing the millennium, as some post-millenarians expected, did not affect great historical facts. The passing of a year does not throw us back in the image of empires (Dan. ii.); into the head of gold—Babylonia; nor into the breast and arms of silver—Medo-Persia; nor into the belly and thighs of brass—Grecia; nor into the legs of iron—imperial Rome; but we still stand, as we have stood for more than thirteen hundred years, in Rome divided, awaiting the action of the mystic stone by which all world-powers will be overthrown and destroyed and the kingdom of our God established. There are some who hold that the Lord may come to-day; perhaps more that He will come soon; but all of us are agreed that when He does come it will be before the millennium. The position we endeavor to occupy is that of waiting, watching, and working in the blessed hope of the second coming of our Lord.

A *second* objection is that pre-millennialism leads to undue excitement and fanaticism. When proof is demanded we are at once referred to

THE GREAT ADVENTIST MOVEMENT

of forty or fifty years ago. Of those times we are told that ascension robes were made and used, and you could read all about them in the newspapers and magazines. Now, I have been connected with this movement since 1843. I saw some excitement then, but I never knew of a case of ascension robes being made or used. I am perhaps as conversant as anybody with the leaders in that movement. I have questioned them closely on the matter, and they tell me they never knew of a single case like the one in question, though they had investigated with great care. It would not be wonderful if such a case had occurred. But the reports of these cases have always come second-handed, and we have no hesitancy in pronouncing them falsehoods. The cry of fanaticism was made by the priests of the church in the days of the Reformation. The early movement of Wesley and Whitefield was attended with great excitement. I do not sympathize with fanaticism, but I believe that people of ardent temperament are apt to get excited over other things than religion. If it must be, I should rather be tied to a man that has fits occasionally than to a dead man. In the words of the late eloquent Dr. John Cumming, of England, a staunch Scotch premillenialist: "Mine be the rolling waves of the ocean rather than the putrifying Dead Sea. Mine be the roaring cataract rather than the stagnant marsh. Mine be all the excitement of living truth rather than the quiescene of pestilential error. 'A living dog is better than a dead lion.'"

A *third* objection is, that premillennialism is burdened with materialism, seventh-day Sabbath keeping, and other errors from which we had better stand aloof. Very likely. But many a good thing has been burdened by a bad one. The college of the apostles was burdened by a Judas, and the early church had dissensions. The reformation of the sixteenth century was almost wrecked on the rock of fanaticism. Premillennialism is not responsible for the vagaries that are charged upon it. This year the Congregational Union of England and Wales elected as its Chairman the Rev. Edward White, who is well known as a believer in "conditional immortality"—as the materialistic doctrine of the extinction of the being of the wicked is called on the other side of the sea—though it is really a misnomer, as all evangelical Christians hold to conditional immortality in the Biblical sense of the term. Others besides premillennialists have materialism among them; yet so persistently have many holding to the Lord's speedy coming pressed their views of the state of the dead and destiny of the wicked as to give the impression that the leaders in the revival of second advent truth in this country were materialists, and so are premillennialists generally; and yet this is an error. I hold in my hand a copy of the oldest prophetic journal in America, now known as *Messiah's Herald*, on the first page of which has stood for many years the announcement: "It is especially devoted to the advocacy of the speedy, personal premillennial advent of Christ, the glorification of the church at that epoch, the dissolution of the heavens and earth by fire, their renewal as the everlasting inheritance of the redeemed, and the establishment of

THE KINGDOM OF GOD,

rejecting, as it has from the commencement of its existence, the doctrine of the unconscious state of the dead and the extinction of the being of the wicked." Evangelical adventists are not materialists; nor are premillennialists in the various evangelical denominations to be thus reckoned.

A *fourth* objection is that premillennialism has the weight of numbers and scholarship against it. This is an old objection to God's truth. They said of Christ, "Whence hath this man letters?" and of some of the apostles that they were "unlearned and ignorant men." It was brought up at the time of the Reformation, and Luther said, "The multitude is always on the side of error." The time was when the objection had more weight than now. Those were the times when the people had to read the Scripture, if at all, in a foreign tongue.

"But Wicliff, by the grace of God,
In hand the Bible took,
And into English language turned
That ever-blessed book."

And since then translation has followed translation, until in the Revised Version we have the latest results of scholarship. Since the days of the "pious and profoundly learned Joseph Mede" (as his biographer calls him), who died in 1638, there have been many scholars who have committed themselves to the doctrine of the pre-millennial coming of our Lord. But we do not deem great erudition necessary to an understanding of either the last things or first things connected with our Redeemer and His work. If a man has good common sense, a fair English education, and is taught of the Spirit in the Word, he will know more of the mind of the Lord than college professors and doctors of divinity who are not humble enough to bow and

TAKE GOD AT HIS WORD

Indeed, in reading some criticisms one is ready to question whether the writers really believe anything; for they seem more like men sinking in sand than standing upon a rock. The objection about scholarship has little weight.

A *Fifth* objection is that premillennialism requires the re-introduction of bloody sacrifices after the second coming or Christ, offered by the restored Israelites. As Dr. John C. Rankin expresses it: "For these favored ones the old sacrificial system and the former modes of worship which neither the fathers nor the apostles were able to bear, will be restored in part at least, if not in whole."

There are many premillennialists, however, who do not hold to the restoration of these bloody sacrifices during the millennium. This is one of the things that is read into the millennial text of Rev. 20. The Rev. George N. H. Peters, A. M., in his "Theocratic Kingdom of our Lord Jesus," argues ably against it, and shows that the principal text supposed to teach it, Ezekiel, chapters 40-48, does not sustain it. "The key to it, "he says, "is not found in chapter xliii., 7-11, where the establishment of the theocratic rule is conditioned by, 'Now let them put away their whoredom, and the carcasses of their kings, and I will dwell in the midst of them forever *if* they be ashamed of all that they have done,' etc. It is expressly asserted that this prediction is given that they may be 'ashamed of their iniquities,' in order that what is promised may be verified. The simple question is this: Did the Jewish nation, after the prophecy was given,

REPENT OF ITS SINFULNESS

and manifest by its shame that it was worthy of such a reconstruction of its government? Let the facts as given in history witness, and we are forced to the conclusion that the reason why no such theocratic restoration * * * was effected was owing simply to the lack of a national repentance commensurate to the bringing it into operation. After carefully regarding the prophecies and reading the reasoning assigned in its behalf, we are forced to the conclusion that it is nowhere taught in the Bible, and that, therefore, no such apparent contradiction as is alleged can be legitimately forced upon our system."

This is the position which I was led to take many years ago, and is in harmony with the general rule of God's dealing with the nations as expressed through Jeremiah (xviii. 7-10): "At what instant I shall speak concerning a nation, and concerning a kingdom, to pluck up and to pull down, and to destroy it: if that nation concerning whom I have pronounced turn from their evil, I will repent of the evil that I thought to do unto them. (Illustrated in the case of Nineveh.) And at what instant I shall speak concerning a nation, and concerning a kingdom, to build and to plant it (as in the case of the Jewish nation), if it do evil in My sight, that it obey not My voice, then I will repent of the good wherewith I said I would benefit them." Under this divine arrangement, and in harmony with the covenant made with Israel at Sinai, many things promised were not realized but have been forfeited.

A *sixth* objection is that premillennialism destroys the missionary spirit. A sufficient reply to this can easily be drawn from historical facts in the history of the church. Turning to I. Thess. i. 9, 10 we read: "Ye turned to God from idols to serve the living and the true God, *and to wait for His Son from heaven*, even Jesus whom He raised from the dead." This was the position of the church in the first century. Justin Martyr, in his "First Apology for the Christians," addressed to Antoninus Pius, the Roman Emperor, says: "You see all sorts of men big with the hopes of His second coming in glory, who was crucified in Judea, after which crucifixion you immediately became masters of their whole country." He calls it "the general expectation of His second coming; a truth your own eyes bear witness to." (Second century.) St. Cyprian, on the Lord's Prayer, speaks of Christ as the one "whom we day by day desire to come, whose advent we crave to be quickly manifested to us." (Third century.) Thus it will be seen that during "the three first and purest ages," as Bishop Newton calls them, when Christians "went everywhere preaching the word," the church was looking, not for the conversion of the whole world, but for her Lord. Her premillennial faith and hope was far from making her inactive; indeed, it had the very opposite effect.

In the dark ages there was but little missionary work done. The witnesses prophesied in sackcloth. In the great reformation of the sixteenth century the reformers, though not strictly speaking premillennialists, were not looking for the world's conversion before the Lord should come. John Knox, of Scotland, cried out: "There is no final rest to the whole body till the head return to judgment. (*Sermon on Isaiah*, 26.) Calvin said: "There is no reason

WHY ANY PERSON SHOULD EXPECT

the conversion of the world; for at length (when it will be too late and will yield them no advantage) they shall look on Him whom they have pierced." (*Institutes, Book* 3, *chapter* 9.) Luther, the great German, said in his comments on John x. 16: "Some in explaining this passage, 'Other sheep I have,' say that before the latter days the whole world shall become Christians. This is a falsehood forged by Satan that he might darken sound doctrine, that we might not rightfully understand it. Beware, therefore, of this delusion." So the work of the reformers in the diffusion of truth was not done under the influence of the present post-millennial hope.

Notwithstanding these facts it may be said that the theory must paralyze the missionary spirit; for if more are to be converted and saved *after* Christ comes than before—if the Jews and large remnants of the gentile nations are to then be speedily brought in—why should we specially concern ourselves about them now? To this we reply: "Be it enacted," is enough for a loyalist; and if the King of kings has said, "Be it enacted: 'Go ye into all the world and preach the gospel to every creature,'" it is enough for His loyal embassadors. Moreover, those who expect the offers of salvation to be extended to Jew and gentile after the Lord comes, hold that *before* He can come His mystical body must be completed, the number of His elect made up, the bride make herself ready; and by hastening forward this elective work, more speedily will be brought in the reign of righteousness. The thought, too, of rewards in that day (Dan. xii. 3), and of the superior dignity of those saved here and now urges them onward in the mission work. There are, however, many premillennialists who do not look for this extension of the offers of mercy after the Lord comes. They consider New Testament teaching to be explicit on this point, for example, Luke xiii. 24-29, Rom. ii. 6-16, II. Cor. v. 20-21, with vi. 1-2, II. Thess. i. 6-10, II. Pet. iii. To them this world is like a sinking ship; it is destined to go down in universal judgment at the end of this age, and all who are saved must be saved *now*. Such can not well do otherwise than work with a will to save souls. If the sun is near setting we feel that we must work the harder before the darkness comes.

A *seventh* objection is that the Scriptures teach the conversion of the world to Christ by the gospel; whereas by premillennialism "the gospel dispensation," as Dr. Rankin says, "is belittled into a practical failure." When asked for these Scriptures there are a few texts which, like "ready change," are forthcoming. Psa. ii. 8, for example: "Ask of me, and I will give thee the heathen for thine inheritance, and the uttermost part of the earth for thy possession." But why not quote the next verse to show what shall be done with them? "Thou shall break them with a rod of iron; thou shalt dash them in pieces like a potter's vessel." Surely ruling with a rod of iron can not mean governing with the scepter of love, nor dashing them in pieces like earthenware denote the careful preservation of them, which must be the case if they are all to be converted and saved by the process. But do we not read in Isa. xlv. 23: "I have sworn by myself, the word has gone out of my mouth in righteousness, and shall not return, that unto me every knee shall bow,

EVERY TONGUE SHALL SWEAR?"

We do; but the New Testament application of the text is neither to prove universal salvation for all time, as some affirm; nor universal salvation for a thousand years, as others, but a judgment to come. Paul says in Rom. xiv. 10-12: "We shall all stand before the judgment seat of Christ; for it is written, as I live, saith the Lord, every knee shall bow to Me, and every tongue shall confess to God. So then every one of us shall give an account of himself to God." The truth taught is, that however much the claims of the Lord Jesus may now be denied the day is coming when all shall be brought to confess, whether willingly or otherwise, that He is King of kings and Lord of lords, though the confession of some then will no more save them than it did the demons at His first advent, when they exclaimed, "We know Thee, who Thou art, the Holy One of God" (Mark i. 23, 24).

But time fails me and I must close. I can only add that my conviction is, the lack of grace in the heart is the more common difficulty in the way of the reception of the doctrine of the speedy, personal, premillennial coming of our Lord Jesus Christ. The apostle affirms that "*the grace of God* which bringeth salvation to all men hath appeared, teaching us," not only "to live soberly, righteously and godly in this present world," but also to be "looking for that blessed hope and the glorious appearing of our great God and Saviour Jesus Christ" (Titus ii. 11-14). In proportion then to our yielding to be taught by divine grace will be our interest in the prayer of the seer of Patmos, "Come, Lord Jesus; come quickly." Do you hesitate to join in it because should He come now He would find the world so unprepared to meet Him and so many must perish? Think again, that if He delays to come how many will die in their sins! and that whenever He does come He will find the world as it was in the days of Noah and of Lot—the multitudes in the broad road (Matt. xxiv. 37-39). Moreover, when we thus pray we petition the Lord to hasten forward the work that must be done before His return—to speedily "take out of the nations a people for His name." And then our world's history will end, as it begun, with Paradise. Earth's Creator will be its Regenerator (Rev. xxi. 1-5). The divine hand will sponge out the stain which sin made six thousand years ago. And when the redeemed "out of every nation, kindred, tongue, and people"—from the ranks of infancy and of riper years—shall find their everlasting home in the deathless land and sorrowless clime of the kingdom of God, it will be seen that, though all men are not saved, nor the whole world converted by the gospel, yet is not God's work in this and past ages "belittled into a practical failure?" The millennium comes, but the Lord of the millennium comes first; and His own coming will effectually answer every objection that has been raised against it.

PROFESSOR HENRY LUMMIS.

CHRIST'S PREDICTIONS.

The Rev. Dr. A. J. Gordon, of Boston, presided at the afternoon session, which was largely attended. After a hymn had been sung and a prayer offered by Dr. Gordon, Professor Henry Lummis, of Appleton, Wis., read the following paper on the subject, "Christ's Predictions and Their Interpretation."

Have we an open Bible? No one doubts that there is entire freedom to study the word.

But is this open Bible, after all, largely a sealed book? Is it so full of mysticism that it needs a mystical seer to reveal its true meaning? Was it written in such ambiguous style that it may be fairly understood, as were many of the ancient oracles, in either of two antagonistic senses?

The Bible needs no seer to unfold its thought. Its utterances are not parallel to those of Delphi or Dodona.

There are unquestionable difficulties in our sacred book. Some cases occur that the light enjoyed in the present life may never satisfactorily enable us to explain. The key has been lost, possibly never to be recovered. It may be that the name of a bird, of a reptile, of a plant, can never be identified with the thing. Perhaps the loss of a prenoun or of a negative of two letters makes a harmony of parallel passages impossible.

But how little of the holy volume is affected by a dropped word by an animal or a plant not identified. It is like the map of some bay or gulf. The trend of the shore is definite, though here and there there may be a minute cape unmarked, an estuary at the mouth of a small stream unnoted.

My theme directs attention to one line of thought. It is asked, sometimes seriously, are not the prophecies difficult to understand? A dogmatic yes is no uncommon answer. "Even the predictions of Jesus are to be understood only after they have been fulfilled" is the explicit affirmation of high authorities.

If this affirmation be true, it is also true that the Bible is largely a sealed book. The New Testament, which contains, as we have held, so clear a bringing to light of life and immortality in the gospel, gives, after all, only light enough to make the darkness visible.

I do not admit the affirmation. I insist that the New Testament statements conform to the laws of language as truly as do those of Xenophon. And the predictions of Jesus are as easy to be understood, even before their fulfilment, as are the utterances of Peter in his sermon on the day of Pentecost, or the words of Paul when he addressed the Athenians on Mars Hill.

The Savior's language in the sermon on the Mount is

NO SIMPLER, NO MORE NATURAL,

no more comprehensible than the language employed in his prohecies.

"Blessed are the meek, for they shall inherit the earth," is as easily understood by the masses as "Lead us not into temptation, but deliver us from evil."

Christ's "I will come again and receive you to myself," addressed to the anxious disciples, is no more mystical than the declaration, "Now ye are clean through the word which I have spoken unto you."

Some one may ask the meaning of mystical as here used. It is not taken as the opposite of literal. Figurative is the proper opposite of literal.

Evidently Christ's prophetic and likewise His didactic utterances, as quoted above, contain some figurative words. "Inherit," in the prophecy, is certainly figurative. So is "clean," in the text, Now ye are clean. Mystical, as employed above, signifies, having a secret or hidden meaning. I give an illustration.

An eminent interpreter in explaining the first chapter of Exodus writes thus: "By Pharaoh's daughter, I suppose the church to be intended, which is gathered from among the gentiles. She pities the infant; that is, the church finds Moses—the law—lying in the pool, cast out and exposed by his own people, in an ark of bulrushes daubed over with pitch, i. e., deformed and obscured by the carnal and absurd glasses of the Jews, who are ignorant of its spiritual sense, and while it (the law) continues with them is as a helpless and destitute infant, but as soon as it enters the doors of the Christian Church it becomes vigorous, and thus Moses—the law—grows up."

It seems astounding that such interpretation ever prevailed in the church.

It has been well said of such exegesis: "A passage may be obliged to say anything or nothing, according to the fancy, the peculiar creed, or the caprice of the interpreter."

Our task is to maintain that none of Christ's predictions can be fairly treated like the above; that on the other hand they are just as easily apprehended by the common sense of the common people as are His teachings in respect to duty.

At the last supper of the Savior with His disciples He said: "All ye will be offended because of me this night." Peter promptly replies: "Although all shall be offended, yet will not I." Jesus says to him: "Verily, I say unto thee, that thou this day, in this night, before the cock crow thrice wilt deny me thrice." But Peter declared: "If I must die with Thee, I will not deny Thee." We have the fulfillment of this prediction recorded.

In the detail of Peters trial and fall many things are mentioned that are not contained in the prediction. That a maid should question him, that she should affirm; "thou wast with Jesus of Nazareth." That another should declare: "This is one of them." That Peter should utter profane words, do not belong to what had been foretold. But the three denials, the crowing of the cock twice, prior to the last denial, its occurence in the night of the very day on which the prophecy was made, these definite things did occur, they occured in the order foretold, the word used in the prediction exactly signifies the thing that takes place in the fulfillment of the prediction. The statement of the Saviour requires the adoption of no mystical sense to harmonize His words with the facts. A child of twelve, with ordinary intelligence would understand the prediction as Christ declared it and understand it just as well as he would the Evangelist's statement which gives the history of the fulfilment.

No special pleading can make a case, here, of prophecy not understood until its fulfilment. And one case like this overthrows the statement so often made that a prediction can not be understood until it has been fulfilled. Peter understood

JUST WHAT HIS MASTER MEANT.

His positive assertion that he would not do what Jesus had said he would shows beyond a rational doubt his clear comprehension of the Lord's declaration. The essential features of prophecy are found in the warning given to the too confident Peter as really as in any prediction of Isaiah or of Malachi. What was thus given in sharp detail, naming the time, the things, the circumstances—not, indeed, all the circumstances, but what was least likely to have been suggested to mere human wisdom; was beyond finite vision and in the realm of the knowledge belonging to God only.

We respectfully ask that some theologian who holds the necessity of fulfillment for the comprehension of prophecy will sustain his claim by as pertinent a case. Eight years ago in an editorial in a prominent religious weekly published in Boston, after referring to the theory of literal interpretation of prophecy held by a school of exegetes, the editor remarked: "This canon of interpretation when once accepted must be honestly obeyed, and this literal interpretation leads to the most extraordinary and ludicrous results."

We invite the editor to point out the ludicrous results from the sharpest application of historico-grammatical interpretation, in the illustration taken from Peter's predicted sin. Any one familiar with the history of prophetic interpretation finds not merely the ludicrous and extraordinary in the theories that ignore literal interpretation, but results that distort language and make it utterly worthless as a medium for communicating thought.

A second case of fulfilled prediction occurs in predictions uttered in regard to Lazarus. Word had come to Jesus from Martha and Mary saying: "Lord, behold, he whom thou lovest is sick. Jesus says: "This sickness is not unto death but for the glory of God, that the Son of God may be glorified thereby. The disciples evidently misunderstand this non-prophetic utterance of the Savior. They apparently infer that Lazarus is not to die from this sickness. For when Jesus a little time afterward says: Our friend Lazarus is fallen asleep; but I am going that I may wake him out of his sleep; they supposing that Christ referred to their common friend resting in sleep, replied: "Lord, if he fall asleep, he will recover." Christ at once corrected their misapprehension. He said plainly: Lazarus is dead. Christ's words to his disciples have now become: "Lazarus is dead and I am going to wake him out of his sleep." This, though containing two figurative words

WAS NO MORE FIGURATIVE

than a score of passages that will occur to any one familiar with the history of the kings of Israel. So David slept with his fathers and was buried in the city of David. This is a paragraph of history. Yet it contains the same kind of figurative word, that is, sleeps in the figurative sense, to signify is dead. If an expression in Christ's conversation had not led the disciples to infer that Lazarus would not die from this illness they would naturally have inferred that sickness had resulted in death, and so would have understood that the awakening was to be an awakening from death's slumber. Is it a lack of perspicacity or of attention that allows the critics who attack the doctrine of literal prediction to assume that literality excludes the occurrence of any word not literal in a prophetic chapter, or in a chapter historic, like Matthew II. No literalist entitled to respectful attention claims a literality of statement beyond that of ordinary history. A metaphor, a synecdoche, a metonomy, a simile may, instead of obscuring a sentence, illuminate it. Does any Sunday-school girl of ten, as she joins in singing—

Asleep in Jesus! blessed sleep,
From which none ever wakes to weep!

imagine that merely ordinary sleep is meant? But the figure is precisely that used by Jesus in speaking to the disciples about Lazarus, when Christ said plainly: "Lazarus is dead," though he does not change the rest of the sentence, "I am going that I may awake him," every one in the company comprehends just what He meant. When the company reached Bethany, and Martha, meeting Jesus, said: Lord, if thou hadst been here my brother had not died. But I know that even now whatsoever Thou wilt ask of God, God will give. Jesus replies: Thy brother shall rise again. Here the prediction was as simple and literal as it could be, but Martha did not interpret the Savior's statement as was natural from her own words: I know that even now whatsoever Thou wilt ask of God, God will give. Perhaps it was to come at the intention of Christ more definitely that she replied: I know that he shall rise again in the resurrection at the last day.

The prediction was so exactly stated that after its fulfillment a simple change of tense would have turned the prophecy into history: thy brother has risen again.

When any one says of a writer: "His articles are full of figures," does any one who understands English conclude that every noun and adjective, and verb, and adverb is figurative?

If not, one who understands English is not authorized to infer that a believer in literal interpretation whether of prophecy or of other writings, holds that every word is to be taken in its literal meaning.

To reach the actual sense is to reach the literal meaning. The figurative word is no bar to the actual sense, if the reader or the interpreter understands the figure. The tyro who should take the words of a simile as if they were metaphorical would confound the meaning by such a course. "Harden not your heart"

HAS TWO FIGURATIVE WORDS,

but the ordinary hearer catches the actual sense, and gets below the figurative words as if the thought were expressed in the most literal terms throughout.

The true literalist makes no protest against metaphor, metonomy, or any recognized figure. He only protests against interpretations which violate the laws of rhetorical figures, and also against that mysterious figure unknown to Quintilian or to Whateley, yet the favorite of the spiritualizer.

When a metaphor, a metonomy, or a simile is recognized, and its meaning is clearly brought out in exegesis, the interpretation gives the thought just as well as if no figurative word had been used; and interpretation that brings out the strict sense of the passage is properly literal interpretation of the passage.

The vice of the spiritualizer is his use of what he is pleased to call a figure, yet a figure to which no rhetorician of ancient or modern times has ventured to stand sponsor. Its lineage is unknown, and it is an evident stranger to him who presses it into his service. Its seeming use is to turn the ordinary statements of the Scriptures into allegory, not to explain allegory. I remember a bright sermon preached in the city of Wilmington, Del., on one occasion, from the text: "Gather up the fragments, that nothing be lost." The theme educed was "Economy." and one head, "Economize the Minutes." The thought was a good one, but to assume that Jesus intended it to teach such a lesson has no warrant in genuine hermeneutics. We have not the slightest hint that Peter or any of the other apostles employed it to teach political or domestic or personal economy.

Is it not a remarkable fact that so many of Christ's predictions outside of a certain line are accepted in their natural meaning as natural as "thou shalt love thy neighbor as thyself?" and yet that many of those thus receiving them when some passage is presented at variance with a favorite theory of theirs fall back on the relief of the obscurity of prophecy. We invite this class of friends to account for their admission that the following list that might be greatly enlarged from Christ's own words are to be taken in as literal a sense as the non-prophetic parts of the sermon on the Mount:

Whosoever shall speak a word against the son of man, it shall be forgiven him; but unto him that blasphemeth against the Holy Ghost it shall not be forgiven him. Luke xii., 10.

Except your righteousness shall exceed that of the scribes and Pharisees ye shall in no case enter into the kingdom of heaven.

When thou prayest enter into thy closet, and when thou hast shut thy door, pray to thy Father who is in secret, and thy Father who seeth in secret

SHALL REWARD THEE OPENLY.

Thou Capernaum which art exalted unto heaven shall be brought down to Hades * * * it shall be more tolerable for the land of Sodom in the day of judgment than for thee. (Matth. xi. 22.)

The men of Nineveh shall rise up in the judgment with this generation and shall condemn it. (Matth. xii. 41.)

For there is nothing covered that shall not be revealed, nor hid that shall not be known. (Matth. x. 26.)

Whosoever shall confess me before man, him shall the son of man also confess before the angels of God. (Luke xii. 6.)

These shall go away into eternal punishment and the righteous into life eternal. (Matth. xxv. 46.)

If there be a true principle like this: Prophecy is obscure and ambiguous until it is fulfilled, why may not those who would fain be free from accepting some of these passages in their strict significance have that right as those who affirm the principle chiefly in reference to those texts that treat of the Lord's return, or of the resurrection of the body, or of the degeneracy of mankind just prior to the second advent?

If it be sound orthodoxy to doubt, not simply the speedy coming of the Lord Jesus Christ, but that He will ever come personally, why under the same exegetical law may we not doubt, I do not say the eternal punishment of the wicked, but their future punishment? The punishment of the wicked in this solemn verse of Matthew (xxv. 46) has not been fulfilled. Is its meaning ambiguous, is it obscure?

It is certainly evident that the canon,

"Unfulfilled prophecy is obscure,
Fulfilled prophecy is clear"

is unsound.

The battle over the 24th Chap. of Matth.,

as applicable throughout its prophetic portions to the destruction of Jerusalem, completely refutes the canon.

If all the predictions in that chapter were fulfilled by the Roman armies in the overthrow

OF THAT DOOMED CITY,

there ought to be no dispute. But even among those who insist upon the clearness of prophecy fulfilled there is no such harmony of what verses 30 and 31 mean in Matth. 24, as of what verse 2 in the same chapter means.

Even with the minute detail of Josephus, an eye-witness of the siege and of the capture of the famous city, no adjustment of the prediction contained in verses 30 and 31 can be made to the facts given by the historian. Let no one say: You must clear up all the difficulties of prophecy. When the difficulties of interpretation found in the simple teachings of Christ are all cleared up, then the demand may be fairly made. "This is My body" is not a prediction, but its real meaning divides Christendom to-day. "Thou art Peter, and upon this rock I will build My church." The sentence I will build my church is a prediction. The Catholic and Protestant would agree as to its meaning. The other part not prophetic is the part that has been a battle ground for centuries.

The most eminent exegetes in the Christian church to-day recognize the directness, the simplicity, the naturalness of the language in which Christ couches his predictions. The monstrous character of the style of interpretation called spiritualizing is also recognized by the most eminent authorities. A distinguished man in my own denomination recently said to a brother clergyman, "I do not believe that Christ will ever be present on earth any more than He is now."

He explained the Parousia as a spiritual coming of Jesus, as others have explained the first resurrection to be a spiritual resurrection. This kind of interpretation is utterly without a recognized principle. No two independent interpreters without some common leader like Origin or Swedenborg could reach any common result. The fancy that one saves the credit of Scripture by any such methods is as mistaken as it is dangerous. It has led to the conclusion: "Anything can be proved by Scripture." By a like use of mathematics two may be shown to be ten, and the largest sum that can be named equal to the smallest.

Exegesis has become a science. But it can only use what is known. Added knowledge often clears up an exegetical difficulty. But the realm of prophecy is no more the realm of mystery than is history, or government, or biography. And Christ's predictions, whether with or without figurative words, are as simple and as comprehensible as are his words of instruction to his disciples.

THE REV. DR. GEORGE S. BISHOP.

TIMES OF THE GENTILES.

The second paper of the afternoon was read by the Rev. Dr. George S. Bishop, of the First Reformed Dutch Church, of Orange, N. J. Its reading was preceded by the singing of a hymn and by a prayer by the Rev. Dr. P. S. Henson, of Chicago. Secretary Needham announced that no more collections would be taken, since the balance of the money required for conference expenses would be privately raised among various gentlemen interested in the conference. Dr. Bishop spoke as follows on the subject, "Times of the Gentiles," his pungent discourse exciting deep interest and frequent applause:

"The times of the gentiles" is a comprehensive expression, and can only be understood when taken in contrast—vis-a-vis—with the counter-expression, the times of the Jews.

"The times of the gentiles"—"Times," says Olivier, "rather than time, because of the relations of successive alien nations to one permanent Israel"—represent that course of ages which begins with God's rejection of His ancient covenant people, and the transfer of earthly kingly dominion from David's throne and house to Nebuchadnezzar; thenceforth they include the whole interregnum, or period of gentile supremacy—i. e., from Nebuchadnezzar to the re-transfer and reversion of royalty to the last living prince and lineal successor of the House of David—i. e., to Christ at the coming of Christ.

The times of the gentiles include the church dispensation, but the phrase does not include the thought of the church, which, looked upon as heavenly, is outside of the scene altogether, and, incognito, waits for her rapture.

Focalize the Scriptures, and they teach that all the lines of God's eternal purposes as to the future blessing of the world meet their fulfillment—not mystically in Christianity and figuratively through the church, but literally after the church has been caught away into heaven—in the restoration of the Jews, God's chosen earthly people to their original and promised land—and in the reign and glory of Messiah as the second Adam. Meanwhile the times of the gentiles are being fulfilled—they march in decadence—

THEY RIPEN TO ANTICHRIST.

In those times of the gentiles it has pleased God that we should have our life, and life-work. We wish, therefore, to understand them. We wish to take in our surroundings, to have before us the projection and the framing of the ages, and to know the ruin that is impending, that we may not be deceived, nor flattered, nor cajoled by any false appearances; but resolutely stand against the tide and flow of vast ungodliness, and in the midst of it, save principle, and from it rescue souls.

An outline of this decadence, this development, the real evolution—they called it "evolution" at Harvard University the other day; and so it is, but only down, not up—the real evolution of our human nature is presented in the book of Daniel, supplemented by St. John's Revelation, the one book being the flower and consummation of the Old Testament as the other is of the New.

For, as revelation in the Old Testament begins with theophanies, or direct appearances of God, followed by prophecy or a subjective communication, and ending in Apocalypse, the objective, where the veil is swept away and the subject himself rises like Daniel into the scenes and realities of the heavenly world, so is it in the New Testament, where we have first the manifestation of God in the flesh in the gospel; then New Testament prophecy in the Acts and Epistles, and, finally, the ravished Seer of Patmos companioned by angels, outside of all earthly horizons.

Daniel, at the close of the Old Testament, is the resume of all preceding prophecy. In him the coming star of Jacob and rising Sceptre of Israel, seen in Balaam's vision, and which should "smite the corners of Moab and destroy all the children of Sheth—which should triumph over Asshur, the Orient and over Kittim, the Occident —whose glories enlarge over all the expanses of after prediction down to the mystic horses in the myrtle bottom, and to the four carpenters and horns of Zechariah, in him all this in final panorama, telescopic for its reach, microscopic, for exact minuteness of detail, pours forth as streams which swell to Amazon, and Amazon which swells to an Atlantic, the ocean-like fullness and depth of the manifold wisdom of God.

Nay, more; Daniel, the chief and colossal Seer of the old dispensation, "the prophet," as our Savior calls him. Jew, though he was, outside of Zion, outside of the limits of Palestine, unfettered by the lines of any race distinction—broad as humanity itself, goes back to Eden and to the Dawning Evangel." "In the Antichrist of Daniel," says Auberlen, "we have the last and complete realization

OF THE PRINCIPLE OF SIN

introduced into the world by the fall, just as the 'Son of Man' in Daniel corresponds to the 'seed of the woman' of Genesis iii. The "beasts" of Daniel are to Daniel's "Son of Man" what the seed of the serpent is to the seed of the woman. The last beast which heads up in Antichrist and which comes up from the sea (Revelations xiii.) has the dragon—the old aboriginal serpent—behind him, just as behind the Son of Man, who comes down from heaven, is God."

And of this prophecy the Revelation is the supplement, giving to us the woman as well as the beasts, and showing us the place of the true church caught up, as also the work of the false church, the harlot.

Such are our sources of light on the phrase, "The times of the Gentiles," the Scriptures, and especially the prophetical Scriptures; and especially again, the Apocalyptical Scriptures, the writings of Daniel and of St. John.

Turning to these, then, let us consider:

I. The outline or sketch of the times of the Gentiles.

II. Their character.

III. The Power that puts an end to them—the handless stone.

IV. The bearing of all this upon us modern men, especially on young men of whom Daniel is peculiarly a type.

I. Then, the outline or sketch of the times of the Gentiles. This is given us twice—

1. In the successive parts and members of a statue-like world-man.

2. In the succession of four beasts which represent those parts or periods again, but from another point of view, the first is man, the race, as seen by Nebuchadnezzar, i. e. within nature's horizons. The second is the race seen by Daniel, and, from the heavenly view-point, by God.

Let us begin then

WITH THE GREAT IMAGE.

There have been four, and only four, universal world empires—Babylon, Persia, Greece, Rome. The world-man and the beasts, set forth those four.

The head of the image represents Babylon. (Dan. II. 38.) "Thou art this head of gold. The arms and breast of silver represent the double kingdom of the Medes and Persians. (Dan. v. 28.) "Peres, thy kingdom is divided and is given to the Medes and Persians." The belly and thighs of brass represent the "brazen clad" Greeks. (Dan. viii. 20.) "The ram which thou sawest having two horns are the kings of Media and Persia, and the rough goat which "smote the ram" and "broke his horns" and "stamped upon him," is the king of Grecia." The legs of iron, with feet and toes of iron and of miry clay, are the great Roman Empire, split into the East and West and prolonged in the ten kingdoms of our modern Europe (Luke ii., 1). "There went out a decree from Cæsar Augustus that all the world should be taxed;" that decree is not repealed to this day.

The world of the present is Roman. Its social fabric is Roman. Rex, regal; princeps, prince; dux, duke; martius, marquis; comes, count; vice comes, viscount; eques, esquire —this whole social fabric is Roman. The laws of the world are all Roman. Their character is that of iron mixed with miry clay; of will, now arbitrary, and now shifting; Justinian in the state; tradition, in the church; the opposite of pure theocracy; the rule of Scripture and Christ.

Iron is the character of Rome. The crown of Charlemagne was iron. The crown of Charles V. was iron. Napoleon was crowned with iron. The crown of Germany is iron. The crown of Italy, worn by Humbert and handed down from the year 590, is iron.

IRON REPRESENTS

hardness, severity. It is more perishable, more easily corroded, rusted, than brass or silver or gold; but in the form of steel it is harder than any, and cuts through every other metal. Such has been Rome—inexorable, pushing everywhere a reign of arbitrary law—now iron and now shifting, as the *Emeute*, the *Chartist*—Communism, gets the upper hand.

This outline of the times of the Gentiles, my brethren, is that of the Bible. These things are the discoveries and plain assertions, not of man, but of the Bible. Reject them, and we see no loop-hole of escape but to give up the Bible. And, right here, we must urge that we have no philosophy. The question with us is one of accepting or giving the lie to plain, unequivocal statements of Scripture. It is the question whether infallible Scripture is to be laid alongside and explained by infallible Scripture, and whether we still shall hold to the Scripture in spite of all counter assertions of man.

But the interpretation thus far has been conceded by unbelievers and by believers alike. "The four empires," says the infidel historian Gibbon, "are delineated with as great a clearness in the prophecies of Daniel as in the histories of Justin and of Diodorus."

The same sketch of the kingdoms comes to light again in the successive symbolism of the beasts.

Here we have God's view of the on-rolling a ges as opposed to that of man. To Nebuchadnezzar, who sees things only in their outer semblance; all has the gleam of gold, the sheen of silver, the brilliancy of brass, the irresistibility of iron.

THE FLASH OF THE GREAT WORLD—

man through the monarch's dream is simply the expression of that universal vanity writ high as on the portals of the palace of Versailles: "A Toutes les Gloires Francaises"—to all the glories of a fallen nature.

The beast, on the contrary, represents God's view of the same subject. The image is Nebuchadnezzar and his successors walking on the roof of the palace—the beast is that same image below, a lunatic herding with oxen.

"Man being in honor abideth not; he is like the beasts that perish." This is true of fallen nature in the individual, as Adam, as Nebuchadnezzar, and in the aggregate.

The image is without dependence on God. It looks down; it runs down. Its trend is not up.

The glory of man is dependence on God. That is the concept of creature. True manhood consists in the knowledge of God, in communion with God, in sharing the imperial and condescending honors of a gracious covenant. The true man, then, the real Son of Man, both in His person and His members, comes down, is born from above, and walks below, in fallen scenes, linked up to God.

Other than this, man, set up anywhere, in any position, for any purpose, is only a beast. Left to himself, he will dash the crown from his head and dim the fine gold into clay, and twist the lion-like in him down to a serpent. Man is capable of but one possibility and but one potency, and that self-ruin. If any man be damned, his own will damns him; if any man be saved—Oh, miracle of grace!—God's will it is that saves him. All history and all experience and all theology are here at one.

A BEAST HAS STRENGTH

and also intelligence, but no higher nature. His eyes are downward, his appetites are earthly, his instincts are selfish. The slave of his senses, he is without any right recognition of self or of God.

The beast, then, is the flesh. Both words point out man fallen from his first estate—led captive by his lusts and having all his home and all his interests in a material world.

The beasts of Daniel, the winged lion seen to-day on Babylonian tablets; the bear of Caucasus, the rapacious appetite of Persia; the spotted, four-headed leopard representing the rapidity of march, and the mottled heterogeneous elements of Alexander's great army—breaking up as it did in four heads—under Cassander, Lysimachus, Seleucus, and Ptolemy. And, finally, the nameless, terrible beast that sat upon the seven hills—Rome, the creation, counterpart, and incarnation of the dragon—in its final form, the little Horn, or Antichrist, purely satanic, all these represent again the four kingdoms—the rule and ruin of our weltering and lost humanity—the times of the Gentiles in contrast to and so oppressive to the Jews—the times of chastisement—so ominous in forecasts of the great tribulation—so vividly repictured in Hosea xiii., 8, 9: "Therefore will I be to them as a lion—I will meet them as a bear that is bereaved of her whelps; as a leopard by the way will I observe them: the wild beast, the terrible creature, shall tear them. O, Israel, thou hast destroyed thyself, but in me is thy help!"

This outline or sketch of the times of the gentiles thus drawn out before us let us

II. Study their character.

It is decadence—

PROGRESSIVE DETERIORATION.

The tableaux themselves—the image and the beasts suggest this. The Scripture confirms and declares it.

The metallic values of the image are found to decline. Silver is worth less than gold, brass than silver, iron than brass, and clay than iron.

The ponderousness or the weight of the image declines. The specific gravity of gold is 19.5; of silver, 10.47; of brass, 8; of cast iron, 5; of clay, 1.930. So top-heavy, so unstable is this image, running down from from 19 to 1, that the slightest touch upon the toes must bring it over in fragments.

So, too, with the beasts. They begin with the lion, the king of the animal tribes, and with him winged as celestial, and they run down to a monster emerging from mud—half hippopotamus, ending in serpent.

The Scriptures declare that the world, the natural around us moves on a descending scale, grows worse and worse.

Two awful facts, starting volcano like, up from the surface of Scripture prove this; one of them judgment to come; the other, Antichrist.

Judgment to come! If the world is hastening to judgment, if judgment be the next thing to expect, then the world is not growing better and better, but worse.

Another thing, Antichrist. The Roman empire, like one vaster maelstrom, sweeps into its swirl the evils and the virus of the former empires, and the "little horn" as opposed to the "Horn of salvation," gathers up into itself the virus of this; and so the beast that "was," "is not," i. e., now lies lost to actual regards beneath the fragments of the European empires, and "yet shall be," finds its last expression, resurrection, reorganic culmination in the man of sin and the son of perdition.

IN HIM APOSTACY CULMINATES.

"It is Pharaoh," says Henri Bettex crying "Who is the Lord?" It is Nebuchadnezzar, commanding the people to prostrate themselves before an idol. It is Darius forbidding any man to pray or make a request to any god but himself. It is Alexander assuming the honors of Jupiter Ammon. It is the divine Augustus, to the genius of whom each Roman legion must, on pain of death, offer the sacrifice.

It is all these, my brethren, and all the Cæsars and Napoleons rolled in one—a grand Satanic and self-deifying ecclesiastico-political leader, heading up, in open war with God, the damnable revolt of nature.

Is Popery this newer Rome—this coming man? In fact, no. Inchoatively, I for one am constrained to say—yes. There is a false system on earth—a church mixed with the world and apostate. Where is it? When we were in the White Mountains we found a little rattlesnake not more than six inches long. The flash of his eyes, the dartings of his lambent tongue, his lightning-like contortions all showed what he was, where he came from, what he was going to become. Now I do not say a little rattlesnake is as bad as an old one, full grown, but it is easy to surmise what any snake left alone will become, and you don't cotton to a snake, especially a rattlesnake—and this one's rattles ring down all the ages—simply because he is small.

The moment we admit these things, my brethren; the moment we concede a drift that heads toward Antichrist, that moment we deny the world's improvement.

Outwardly things may seem to improve.

FOOLISH MEN AND EVEN MINISTERS,

foolish in this, however they may laugh at our wisdom in other departments, may talk of progressive perfection. They may point to the telephone and the Chicago limited express and tell us that one is quicker than thought and the other quicker, almost, than motion. We see all this, we take it all in as much as the natural man does or can, but we oppose to it all, in spite of appearances—Antichrist; Judgment.

The world is growing worse and worse. All the while Tubal Cain was hammering out his new machinery, and Iubal was building his big organs, the world was growing worse and worse, and preparing for the deluge, and so is it now.

Nature grows worse and worse. The natural man grows worse and worse. He may flesh up, wear better clothes, make a more handsome figure, climb to a superior place, be flattered, be courted, but all the while he is deteriorating, growing worse and worse inside, more the prey of the devil, like a worm-eaten apple, more brilliant and riper than its companions, because of decay at the core.

Deterioration is the rule of the times of the gentiles. Deterioration in what?

Not in all respects; not in the outward; not that Greece with the blaze of her brazen pretension, her genius which reflects as in the broken mirror of her bright Egean the light of the Orient, her tragedies whose deep intensity is toned from Hebrew prophets, her mystic legends which retrace their homes and inspiration to the Asian shores—not that Greece makes no advance on Babylon and Persia—not that the image does not grow broader

AND THE ANIMALS MORE RAMPANT

as they move down; but

One thing: There is delusion in form. Not only is the head higher up than breast, than thighs, and than feet, but—The first rule is a unit; the second comprizes two kingdoms—Media, Persia; the third, four—Macedonia, Thrace, Syria, Egypt; the fourth kingdom, ten, and so less and less constitutional unity—more and more of what is divisive as ages roll on.

And with this the steady decay of the notion of stewardship—of delegated power received from God and exercised for God.

God made Adam in Eden the head of creation. "How came such a thing as a kingdom on earth?" says the Chartist. The answer is there.

In Adam all kingdoms—mineral, vegetable, animal—were headed up, just as in Nebuchadnezzar the iron, brass, and silver were headed up.

Kingdom rule—constitutional rule—is God's rule. "If I were not a Christian," says Bismarck, "I would be a communist," but now I believe in government established upon everlasting justice, in the hands of men ordained by God, accountable to God.

Kingdom rule is steward-like rule, founded on law and on justice behind it.

And whatsoever force there is in any government to-day is kingdom force. I mean that government is built on law, and law on penalty, and penalty, at last, on hell.

Law without penalty is mere advice. You tell me to do something, but unless you have the right to punish me if I refuse, and do threaten to punish, what you say is advice—is not law, I may do as I please and remain without harm or regret.

PENALTY MAKES LAW,

and the certainty of penalty, the force of law. There comes to light the radical necessity of hell. Put hell beneath God's law and you put stern penalty, evadeless, beneath every law. Shake everlasting hell and you shake the deepest foundations of justice; conviction and nerve to inforce any penalty, anywhere; and you thus leave both law and government prostrate.

Kingdom rule is therefore the force, whatever force there be, of every government on earth. Call it a republic, call it what you like—the loftier the notion of stewardship; the more sublime the conviction of ordination from God, the more theocratic it is the nobler and purer the power.

God made Adam, his steward, the head of creation. That kingdom rule failed. Bestowed again upon Noah, he failed. Devolved upon David, his dynasty failed. Transferred to Nebuchadnezzar, it runs from the gold of autocracy, down to the heavings of the socialistic clay.

The first notion of God—the innate idea—is linked with a sense of dependence and of responsibleness. Those two—dependence, responsibleness—are the factors of stewardship. Adam as head of the lower creation felt his dependence on God for his place, and his responsibility for its holding.

But from Adam down to Antichrist one finds the gradual descent and diminution of that light of stewardship and denser darkness.

"God hath spoken once," says David—"Twice have I heard this that power belongeth unto God. Nebuchadnezzar knew this. He was made to feel and confess it. The modern blasphemous doctrine of popular sovereignty had not been broached in his day.

You see Nebuchadnezzar down on his knees before God. You read his magnificent declaration of the divine autocracy. You see the King of Nineveh and his court and his subjects and slaves and his

CATTLE COVERED WITH SACK-CLOTH,

bowed in the dust before God. You read the decrees of Darius and Ahasuerus and Cyrus concerning the temple and the worship of the true Jehovah and you find yourself back in a light upon man's felt dependence, his confessed responsibility to God as far above the popular expressions of our day as gold is above earthenware and mud.

I do not stop now to show, as a matter of fact, how government ran down from the autocracy of Nebuchadnezzar—through the parliament of Persia and the oligarchies of Greece—to that mingling of the communistic "clay and clamor" which created imperators and dethroned them, and at last upheaved them all in the vast hordes of those barbaric tribes which like a restless sea flowed over and submerged old Rome.

The descent through the ages is from God's will to man's will. This is not affected by civilization. A civilized man is no nearer to God than a savage. An American citizen boldly blaspheming under the light of the gospel is no advance upon the devout Abimelech of the days of Isaac and Job. The mere fact that he lives in a house with modern improvements and reads his paper by an electric light helps nothing.

God says that nature and the natural man grow worse and worse. That as the ages roll on they are becoming more reckless and willful.

God says that which is born of the flesh is still flesh. Pass it from nature to culture, it is still unregenerate, natural, lost.

More than this—"All history," says Delitzsch in speaking of the of the old world culture which was born among the sons of Cain—

"ALL HISTORY HAS SHOWN

that the refinements of civilization are always in direct relation with forgetfulness of God." And Nitzsch says in his "System of Doctrine," "that all progress resulting from the natural faculties and powers of man augments corruption and accelerates the real ruin of race."

In earlier days—in Nebuchadezzar' days—men, our race at large believed Jehovah—received communications from Jehovah. Their eyes were upward—they studied the stars.

Now, men, our race, at large are infidel—deny inspiration, and study slime instead of stars.

A man is what he thinks. If he thinks mud he will be mud. That is why, under the reign of Huxley Darwin and the purient biologic school; reverence is dying away; the sacredness of womanhood dying away; dignities, titles, self-respect dying away, and London becomes like to Sodom and Paris like to Gormorrah.

This ruin we confront. Its tides are rolling on. The presence of the church, soon to be caught away, holds it in check for a moment, but this removed—the coming of the Antichrist—the lawless one is certain. His avant couriers are with us now. Self-will, the vice of human nature, ripened to one revolt will flower in one who comes in his own name, and doing his own will shall deify material force and show Himself as God; and all inventions and improvements binding more and more to the material serve to help on that day.

Humanity shall stand self-deified and self-exalted, as upon the plain of Dura—wondered after and adored by all the world, and then will come the stone.

III. That is the third point, the destruction of Antichrist and end of the times of the gentiles by the

SMITING OF THE MYSTIC STONE.

This stone, hewn from the mountain rock and without hands is Christ, but Christ not in his first but second coming.

This appears, first, from the action of the stone. Christ crucified and His gospel are grace, but this stone is judgment.

Again, the gospel converts slowly, but this stone does the work at once.

Again, this stone smites Antichrist, but Antichrist has not yet come.

Again, the reign established will be glorious, but now it is said, "Ye shall have tribulation."

Again, when this stone falls the Jews will be restored, the visible kingdom will be retransferred and forever; the people of the saints, of the Most High shall receive it, but that was not done at the first coming of Christ.

Once more, the stone itself would seem to indicate the meaning.

A stone is made up of many particles, but has cohesion in the Divine. No one can tell, discover, or lay bare the secret of that cohesion.

There is that, therefore, in the stone which is in no one of these metals, nor in the clay. A metal has cohesion, but it kills the individual fragment. There is only one mass and one will. Clay, i. e., earth, is made up of many gritty independent particles, but falls apart. Take a lump of earth; how it crumbles; no fusion, and no possibility of fusion.

But now take a stone; here are substances; take quartz or granite, or a common pudding stone; fragments, particles as distinct as possible, seen to be so, but fused as in granite or quartz, into one. Hammers can never break those substances apart. Individual they are, yet a unit; an absolute unity. That is Christ and His church; Christ, the Divine and the human together—distinct as finite and as infinite, and yet so close that no edge of the metaphysical chisel can sever between them.

AND SO THE CHURCH—

10,000 separate wills united in the Divine—those wills could never have met in the metal—could never have yielded themselves to melt away into the metal—but fire—the volcanic fire of regeneration; the irresistible pressure of grace has done this miracle—this wonder of wonders—the chief wonder in nature—which is above nature and which in prophecy has been caught up, and now returns, comes down and falls with Christ in judgment.

"And He hath upon His vesture and on His thigh a name written, King of Kings, and Lord of Lords." "And the armies which were in heaven followed Him upon white horses, clothed in fine linen, white and clean." "And the kingdom and the dominion and the greatness of the seven kingdoms under the whole heaven shall be given to the people of the saints of the Most High." "Whosoever shall fall on this stone shall be broken! fused! melted! heart-broken;" but on whomsoever it shall fall in that day, it will grind him to powder.

IV. I come now to the fourth and final point. The bearing of all this upon us modern men, especially upon young men, of whom Daniel is peculiarly a type.

The first bearing of it all is to show the value of prophecy.

The most heavenly man in the Old Testament is Daniel; the most heavenly in the New Testament is St. John. "How did they become so? By their living in prophecy. You see how Daniel began. First Nebuchadnezzar has dreams, and Daniel only remotely interprets—the thing is outside of him. Then Daniel himself has a dream. Then he has a fixed vision, his eyes being open in daylight, what St Paul had—the trance.

FINALLY HE PASSES THE BOUNDS

of the senses and outruns the need of all visions and symbols. Practically he is in heaven, for in the last three chapters, and especially the last, he is found conversing with the angels, just as much at home with them as with his relatives of flesh and blood.

Don't be afraid, my bretheren, of the dream—the vision—the future. If the Bible is a complete revelation from God, it must shed a light on the future. The Bible in one place is compared to a lantern. You don't carry a lantern on a dark night in order to see the path behind, but that which lies before you. Any man with a straight track before him, who knows just where he is going and what to expect, will do better than one who confessedly walks in confusion and darkness.

Prophecy is of value to give us an object—a drift. Man must live in the future. What shall he live for? "The great trouble with the mass of so-called Christians," says Trotter, "lies just here. A man is arrested by conviction in his wordliness and sin. At once he is anxious; gives himself to prayer and reading of the Scriptures and to every means he can think of in order to get peace By and by he is brought to see and to believe the gospel, viz., that what he is vainly seeking and striving to do for himself, Christ has done for him at once and forever by

SHEDDING HIS BLOOD

on the tree. The effect of this we all know. Anxieties and fears are at an end. The soul has joy and peace in believing—is happy, is free. Then what? Ah, what? How sickening and how sad to finish the picture. Little by little the soul bought with blood—redeemed from all iniquity, goes back to worldliness and selfishness and fashion, ease and gain. What is the trouble? What, but that people learn what they are saved from, without going on to learn what they are saved for—without an object before them."

Now prophecy places an object before us. The Thessalonians were turned from dead idols to serve the living God and wait the coming of His Son from heaven. They had their eyes upon their absent Savior to come any moment. That made them earnest, and it made them unearthly. It made them earnest. A person whom I dearly love said to me only the other night: "Doctor, is it not true that every earnest, successful evangelist—man on fire I mean—from Spurgeon down is a millenarian?" Certainly, I said, it is true. Moody, Bonar, all the Swiss men who are on fire, all the Germans, all the English, all Millenarians.

Prophecy makes men earnest and makes them unearthly. The worldly laugh at visionary men, but let them take care. All revelations from God at first

ARE LIKE VISIONS,

not quite distinct, clothed in halo, men like trees walking. Abraham saw the sacrifice first in a vision, then he saw a lamp that passed between the pieces. He saw more distinctly, and he saw Christ.

Not a man who has done anything for God upon the resurrecting palimpsests of all your records, but he was what men style a dreamer, a visionary, a fanatic. Abraham saw visions; so Moses, so Joshua, so Samuel, so David. Lot saw no visions. Korah, Dathan, and Abiram saw none, the ten false spies saw none, Eli saw none, Saul saw none, except to his own condemnation.

Where would the world be if none were uplifted out of the level and mire of a nominal godliness? Where, were there no Luthers—men seeing Christ and devils quite as vividly as other men see flesh and blood? Where would the world be with out such men as Rutherford, Bunyan, Whitfield, Charles Wesley, Jonathan Edwards? They said of Edwards: "He is a dreamer. He don't live on earth. He walks in the woods half in heaven!" Yes, those are the men who have saved the world and will save it. Young man, if you've got no romance of

God in your soul, you are not a young man. You may be but 20, but you are a fossil, without any

FIBER OR SAP.

Oh! if you have born in you only one idea, but one inspiration which strikes away into the future—which breaks the meshes of red-tape, which gets out of the grind, grind, grind of circumlocution, the fussy parade of how not to do it. If you are astir with one notion, honest and downright, and looking ahead and meaning some business, then cling to it, work it—work it till it works itself out. That's prophecy—Daniel.

2. The second bearing of all this, that we have seen, is to show the influence upon the world of one prophetic man. Take Daniel; History will tell us how Confucuis came to Babylon; how Zoroaster borrowed from Daniel; how all the purer teachings of the Vedas sin, atonement—came from Daniel's light, to this day; I have not time to stop on this; the only thing known by the people who live in the midst of the ruins of Babylon is the story of Daniel. The only tradition they have is the den of the lions, the place of which they point out. Daniel reformed the religion of the Magi from Asia Minor to Japan. To Daniel came Thales, Solon, Pythagoras. All the light that there was from Solon to Christ is chiefly due to one man. No wonder, then, that when Constantine built his great city, Constantinople, upon the Bosphorus, upon Sunday, May 10, A. D. 330, 1,000 years after

THE PROPHET HAD DIED,

there was dedicated with most solemn pomp and to the God of the Martyrs an immense statue of brass in the great square of the city—a statue of Daniel, "because he believed in his God."

"Despise not prophesyings," says the apostle. The knowledge of them is power.

But how to get hold of it. How? There is only one way—separation, suffering, prayer.

Separation—You can't keep in with what is called society, and have this knowledge. Look at Daniel. Altogether outside. Society's drift is the world. Prophecy's drift is to God.

Again: Suffering—Something more than intellect and study are necessary for the understanding of prophecy. A worldly heart, a heart undisciplined can never understand it. Nebuchadnezzar saw the image better than Daniel did. He saw it first. He saw it twice over and forgot it both times. It made no impression on him. But it did upon Daniel. He never forgot it, and why? Because he was a sufferer weaned from the world. The poor eunuch, the self-denied man of pulse and water, the man of the den of the lions; the sympathizer and companion of the men who trod the fiery furnace, took it all in. His heart was prepared.

Separation, suffering, prayer Nothing without prayer. Nothing! No sight of the cross, no triumphant assurance, no power, no joy, no vision, no inward and felt and ripening glory. Lord teach us to pray!

THE REV. W. J. ERDMAN.

THE FULLNESS OF THE GENTILES.

The addresses of the evening meeting were made by the Rev. W. J. Erdman, pastor of Olivet Congregational Church, Boston, and the Rev. Dr. A. J. Gordon, pastor of the Clarendon Street Baptist Church, Boston. The Rev. Henry M. Parsons, of Toronto, Canada, presided. The attendance was large. After singing and prayer by the Rev. Dr. Pierson, of Philadelphia, and the Rev. Mr. Parsons, the Rev. W. J. Erdman, an old and most accurate Biblical scholar, read a paper on the subject, "Fullness of the Gentiles."

The question of this paper is touching the import of the phrase, "the fullness of the gentiles," in Romans ii. 25-27, and the special object of its brief discussion is to show that it is not identical with "the conversion of the world" before the return of our Lord Jesus Christ.

THE SCRIPTURE

is as follows: "For I would not, brethren, that ye should be ignorant of this mystery that blindness (hardness) in part is happened to Israel until the fullness of the Gentiles be come in, and so all Israel shall be saved, as it is written. There shall come out of Sion the Deliverer, and shall turn away ungodliness from Jacob. For this is my covenant with them when I shall take away their sins."

These words introduce the great conclusion of that section of the epistle in which are set forth the grounds of the mysterious dealings of God with Israel and the gentiles in this present time.

Paul, the apostle of the gentiles, after confessing his great sorrow and incessant pain of heart for his kinsmen according to the flesh, because of the apparent failure of the word of God in his unbelieving but beloved nation, proceeds to prove that not all of Israel are Israel, that even now there is, as in former dark days of unbelief, a remnant according to the election of grace, and that in due time Israel, though now as a people smitten with judicious hardness of heart shall again be restored to the favor and blessing of God. This due time, however, it is declared will not be "until the fullness of the gentiles be come in."

The announcement of "this mystery" was also intended to prevent the self-complacent conceit of believers from among the Gentiles that, because of the fall of Israel there was for them, as a nation no future of

SPECIAL BLESSING

and pre-eminence. This warning against gentile high mindedness is still most pertinent and necessary; for, many Christians to-day expect no other future for the Jew than such an unscriptural one as the gentile forecasts for himself, and seeks to accomplish before the coming of the Lord.

1. The word "fullness" is used in various senses. It signifies "that with which anything is filled, its contents;" also "that which is filled, the receptacle," "the state of fullness;" and also "the act of filling." Modifications of the primary meaning are "abundance," "full measure," "complement," "supplement," also "full end" and performance. Corresponding to these different meanings of the word, exegetes and commentators have given inharmonious interpretations of the Scriptures containing it. To some it denotes "the elect among the gentiles as the supply of a deficiency so completing the Israelitish people of God;" Olshausen, Philippi; "the recruitment from the gentiles," Michaelis. In this sense they are regarded as filling up the gap made by the fall of unbelieving Israelites.

Others see in the word "a multitude of gentiles," Hodge; "a great multitude," Stuart; "a large concourse," Calvin; "a great mass," Barnes, Cowles; "a vast harvest among the heathen," Wesley; "a great multitude of nations," Adam Clark; "a most abundant supply," Bengel; "the greater number," "the bulk," Tholuck, Wetstein, and other Germans.

The more definite meaning, "the full number," "the totality," is given to it

BY SUCH NAMES

as Cremer, Meyer, Robinson, Brown, Reiche, Godet, Alford, Koch, Luthardt, Lange. and others, but they differ in its application on certain points to nations as nations. Meyer claims the expression must "be taken numerically, the plena copia of the gentiles (of whom, in the first instance, only a fraction has come and is coming in) their full number," and speaks of the "collective number of converted persons" and "the totality of the gentiles" and of that of Israel. Others under this head speak of every nation under heaven, the proper subjects of the preaching of the gospel —Matt. xxiv. 14, Alford; "the totality of the gentile nations passing successively into the church through the preaching of the gospel," Godet; "the totality of the gentiles, not including every individual, but the nations as a whole," Schaff; "not an indefinite mass of gentiles, nor yet all the gentiles down to the last man, but an organically dynamic totality of the heathen world," Lange; "the whole body of the gentiles professing Christianity," John Locke; "the full number of nations made nominally Christian;" "the world of peoples;" "the whole gentile world" as externally Christianized. Koch, Luthardt.

While another class consider "the fullness" as "the elect of the gentiles;" "the full number of the gentiles as foreknown or comprehended in the purpose of God," Theophylact, Augustine, Oecumenius, Chalmers, Gill, Sutton, Haldane, Plumer, Hebart, Theurer, Krummacher; "the full complement of the gentile elect," Lord.

2. The question then arises whether the fullness of the gentiles stands for their full number as nations

OR AS PERSONS;

for the totality of nations evangelized or the complete body of converted gentiles gathered out of all nations and as distinct from the remnant of believing Jews existing during the same time. That such fullness signifies merely an indefinite great multitude or abundance seems not to agree with this part of the epistle. It is hardly in keeping with the tone of rebuke and warning in which Paul addressed these gentile believers, to inform them that blindness in part had happened to Israel until great multitudes of gentiles have come in. That there will be a great multitude of them saved during this dispensation is not in dispute or doubt.

3. There are also some illustrious names, among them Calvin, who, in favor of the interpretation that "all Israel" signifies the so called "spiritual Israel," consisting of all converted Jews and Gentiles of all subsequent ages, would give to the word "until" the sense of "while;" blindness in part is happened to Israel while the fullness of the gentiles is coming in; but insuperable objections lie against such an interpretation.

The word "Israel" is made to stand for two different peoples, for natural Jews and for converted gentiles, in the same verse and in opposition to the whole context and positive statement, "God hath not cast away His people which he fore knew" (ix. 1, 2), and that people is the very people who are

STILL BELOVED

for the sake of their fathers Abraham, Isaac, and Jacob.

In every other place in the New Testament where the word "until" is used to render not one, but two Greek words in connection with the verb in a certain mood and past tense it is impossible to make it mean "while." "Ye do shew the Lord's death till he come." I. Cor. xi., 26. "Hold fast till I come." Rev. ii., 26. Also Acts vii., 18; I Cor. xv., 25; Gal. iii., 19; iv., 19.

It may be added the commentators on Romans are now virtually unanimous in taking Israel in this Scripture to mean the natural, national Israel.

3. Another intrepretation of this prophetic Scripture, of which Mede, Rieger, Gerlach, and others are representatives, locates this gentile fullness not in this present period of Israel's blindness, but in the age of Israel's salvation and glory. This theory does not deem the present ingathering out of all nations as at all to be compared with the world-wide salvation and life from the dead which attends the restoration of Israel to the favor of God. The text of this discussion would then be made to read "until the the fullness of the gentiles "may come in," or "shall come in;" that is, the hardness will continue until the millennial conversion of all nations. The same grammatical objection brought against Calvin's view in relation to time can be laid against this interpretation; the verb as used in this passage and in similar Scripture should, in the almost unanimous opinion of modern exegetes, be translated "shall have come in," or, as in both the authorized

AND REVISED VERSIONS,

"until the fullness be come in." It denotes completed action; the fullness comes in before the hardness ceases.

4. Still another and more alternative view of this question is taken by those who interpret the passage of the totality of nations evangelized or Christianized before Israel is saved. The words "be come in," or "shall have come in," are understood in a general or absolute sense, or as expressing entrance into "the professing church," or "into Christendom," or "into the kingdom of God," or "into a condition of external Christianization."

However it may be with some of these terms, it is not at all Pauline to look upon one portion of the world as externally Christianized and into which the remaining portions successively enter. Even when in his later epistles the deplorable fact of a nominal Christianity is recognized, it is still viewed as belonging to a corporate form and spoken of as "a great house."—II. Tim. ii. 30. But this is an altogether different conception from the modern notion of Christendom, which comprehends within its vast and easily moveable bounds not only what is indeed Christian but all that is ungodly, anti-Christian, atheistic, a changing world whose oldest churches continually need reconversion themselves and whose most civilized nations longingly turn toward that ideal of civilization which belonged to an age when the world by wisdom knew not God.

Even if the word "elect" may not be applied in the strictest sense to this fullness, it can, according to apostolic usage, correspond to the collective bodies or churches to which Paul addressed his epistles, God alone knowing who in such bodies were truly His own.

In this way the seven churches of Asia are addressed, and from such a standpoint the gentile churches at Rome and elsewhere could be warned

AGAINST A HIGH-MINDEDNESS

that might result in a breaking off of the branches once grafted, contrary to nature, in the good olive tree of Israel. It was a corporate testimony they were to bear; it was a corporate unbelief they were to fear; but this was a testimony or unbelief not of evangelized nations, but of bodies out of all nations.

5. It should also be added that this fullness has been deemed by some as the equivalent of the analogous prediction, "and Jerusalem shall be trodden down of the gentiles until the times of the gentiles be fulfilled."—Luke xxi. 24. But the fullness in Romans is found in a text and context touching the theme of the salvation of Jew and gentile, while in Luke the prophecy is concerning the duration in gentile hands of the political and imperial power that originally and forever was granted to David's seed, and which no interregnum however long can annul, but it is in harmony with the prophetic Scriptures that the closing season of the times of the gentiles, and the completion of their fullness, the removal of the hardness of Israel and their salvation both from sins and from enemies, and the return of the Lord, King of Israel and King of nations, shall synchronize in the end of this age.

In support of the proposition that the fullness relates to persons

INSTEAD OF NATIONS,

the following reasons may be given: When Paul changes from the illustration of the olive tree to the formal announcement of the "mystery," not only does a definiteness of affirmation appear both in it, and in the great conclusion which follows, but he expressly speaks of a real faith, and obtaining of mercy by these gentiles viewed collectively as a body of believers in distinction from an existing remnant of believing Jews, and also in distinction from the Israel that should hereafter believe (ii, 28-32), and such living faith and enjoyment of great mercy can not be spoken of nations as an integral mass. It was a positive righteousness that was obtained, a real conciliation that was effected. To quote Meyer, who, however, believes the totality of gentile conversions and "the conversion of the Jews in their totality" to be yet far off, it is "contrary to the language and the context to interpret what is said of individuals as applying to the nations." (On xi. 32.) And another says "the full number ordained of God is, however, not merely externally Christianized, but enters through inward faith into the kingdom of God." (Theurer.)

2. It was affirmed in the council at Jerusalem that God is visiting the gentiles "to take out of them a people for his name." (Acts xv. 14.) With this great purpose Paul opens the epistle to the Romans, saying: "We received grace and apostleship unto obedience of faith among all the nations of His name's sake; among whom ye are also called to be Jesus Christ's." (I. 5-6.) To this he alludes when he says: "Jesus Christ was a minister of the circumcision for the truth of God to confirm the promises made unto the fathers; and (but) that the gentiles might glorify God for his mercy (xv. 8-9); the promises were confirmed by His first coming; they will be fulfilled by His second coming. In the meantime Israel is hardened and the gentiles enjoy a season of special grace. This divine purpose Paul has in mind when, beholding the embodied result of his gospel among the nations, he, with priestly consciousness, calls it a meat offering; saying the grace that is given to me of God that I should be the minister of Jesus Christ to the gentiles, ministering

THE GOSPEL OF GOD,

that the offering up of the gentiles might be acceptable, being sanctified by the Holy Ghost (xv. 15-16). With this, too, he closes this epistle of world-wide significance when, gathering into one grand ascription of praise its great purpose and the kindred theme and mystery of the epistles to the Ephesians and Colossians, that gentiles once "aliens from the commonwealth of Israel and strangers from the covenants of promise" "should be fellow-heirs, and of the same body and partakers of his promise in Christ." Paul in adoration exclaims:

Now to Him that is of power to stablish you,

According to my gospel and the preaching of Jesus Christ,

According to the revelation of the mystery

Which was kept secret since the world began,

But now is made manifest and by the Scriptures of the prophets,

According to the commandment of the everlasting God.

Made known to all nations for the obedience of faith.

To God only wise be glory thro' Jesus Christ forever.

Rom. xvi. 25-26, Eph. i. 9, iii. 3-5, Col. 26, ii. 2.

To this same purpose, ever true, Paul in his last letter, never disconnecting from his preaching of the gospel to all nations the resultant fact of a called out and separated people of God, rejoices that in his defense before Cæsar the Lord stood by and strengthened him, that through him (especially through him) the preaching might be fully known and all the gentiles might hear. (II. Tim., iv. 17.) In eager haste to accomplish the fullness, he declares. "Therefore I endure all things for the elect's sake, that they may also obtain the salvation which is in Christ Jesus with eternal glory" (ii. 10).

It is hard for us gentiles to realize that when Paul declared himself to be the apostle of the gentiles it was in a significant contrast with Peter, the

APOSTLE OF THE CIRCUMCISION,

and that each was engaged in filling up his own elect number, even though both belong to one mystical body in glory. Therefore Paul could talk of "my apostleship," "my gospel," "my preaching;" and Peter, also the apostle of the circumcision, address his letter to the elect sojourners of the dispersion as if a body by themselves. In it he implies a distinct filling up of a gentile number in his passing allusion to "their brotherhood in the world," who were accomplishing like sufferings with themselves, and in his previous exhortation most pertinent to Jewish believers, "Honor all men. Love the brotherhood. Fear God. Honor the King,"—1 Peter ii. 17, v. 9. To love his Jewish brethren, a Jew did only too well, but to exhort Jewish believers to love their gentile brotherhood was at times most necessary. In the Acts of the Apostles Paul, in fulfillment of the same once-hidden purpose of special grace to the nations, is seen traversing lands and seas, and, as avowed in Romans, aiming to reach even the shores of Spain; and the Book of Acts is the permanent symbol and mirror of evangelistic activity among all nations, but surely in it is no hint or specimen of one people converted unto God. Israel's blindness of eyes and deafness of ears and hardness of heart are seen depicted even on its latest page, to show that Isaiah's prophecy will continue its fulfilment so long as a gentile of this special parenthetic fulness ordained unto eternal life remains to be gathered in (xiii, 44-52).

Likewise in passing it may be said the hints and avowals of present grace to gentiles and temporary blindness of Israel and future conversion of the nations are found in discourse and parable throughout the four gospels.

ISRAEL'S TEMPORARY BLINDNESS

in connection with the present world-wide sowing of the word of God is there; the net is cast into the sea of nations, but the fullness of the net is not the fullness of the sea; the rejection of the Messiah by the hardened Pharisees is followed by the eager quest of Greeks who would see Jesus; the destruction of Jerusalem scatters apostle and preacher, the servants far and wide along the highways and hedges and ditches of the gentile world that the wedding may be filled with guests; but throughout it is the fullness of persons and not of collective nations.

4. If now, however, attention should be called to the seemingly distant way in which Paul says, "blindness in part is happened to Israel, until the fulness of Israel be come in," as if he were speaking of the nations rather than of persons. Let the fact be recalled that there was in the apostolic age what may be called a church—consciousness intense, vivid, a realization of the corporate fellowship of Christians thro' a common union with the risen, ascended, glorified Christ, to which the church of to-day is almost a stranger. Because of this Paul, deeply as he loved his nation, must still speak of them as an Israel from whom grace had severed him, and though the apostle of the Gentiles for whose salvation he was becoming all things to all, yet so long they were unbelieving or unevangelized he must speak of them as far off and strangers, and not yet of the same body. So wide, indeed, is now the chasm between him and them. So high the realm of the new life and churchly brotherhood in Christ above both Jew and Greek, that now, as a stranger to his unbelieving kinsmen and a brother by grace to once hated aliens, he can speak of God making known "the riches of his glory upon vessels of mercy which He afore prepared unto glory, even us, whom he also called

NOT FROM THE JEWS

only, but also from the gentiles." (Rev. Vers. Rom. ix 23-24.) That "us" is a word betokening a life hid with Christ in God where all distinctions of earth and time are known no more. It is on this ground a Christian to-day can, like Paul and the believers of the apostolic age, rejecting the word "heathen" as translating "nations," still adopt the divine classification of the world as consisting of "the Jews, the gentiles (the nations) and the Church of God." (I. Cor. x 32.) and not in the pride of a denizen of an apostate of Christendom send the gospel to "the heathen," but in the humble yet sublime consciousness of oneness with Christ in glory send the gospel to the nations, who are to-day for lack of that gospel just what our heathen fathers were a few centuries ago in their gloomy groves of idolatrous hills.

5. Another reason in favor of such fulness as of persons called out, lies in the evident relation the whole argument of Paul sustains to the divine dealings as being of "this present time." Paul recognizes a mysterious break in the continuity of Israel's relation to the promises of God; he mourns over it; he beholds the gentiles coming to the front; he magnifies his office as the apostle of the gentiles by showing his kinsmen what gentiles have gained and Israel has lost, that so by provoking them to emulation he may save some of them; he would preach the gospel to all nations to complete the body of Christ and hasten the day of Israel's salvation, according to the unchanged and unchangeable purpose of God. It was now, "in this present time," the gentiles in large numbers were entering into the possession of the riches of grace, while the Jews were filling up their sins at all times; it was now the time of the ingrafting of the wild olive branches while the natural branches were broken off; it was a present filling, not

A FAR-OFF FULNESS

not yet begun, that was the cause of gentile high-mindedness and self-complacence. It was and is an unexpected present time; and these very three chapters of Romans seem almost as parenthetic in the epistle as the blindness of Israel and the fulness of the gentiles are parenthetic in human history between the first and second coming of Christ.

Nagelsbach, commenting on Isaiah xl. 1-22, even says: "But after the destruction of the earthly Jerusalem, and during the time of the gentiles, when the holy place is trodden down (Rev. x. 2) there is no other Jerusalem on earth than the Church of the Lord, a poor and only provisional form of His kingdom which, for the period between the first and second act of the judgment of the world (Matt. xxiv, 29), i. e., between the destruction of Jerusalem and the second coming of the Lord to effect the first resurrection (Rev. xx. 4. sqq.), has for its task in conflict with opposing forces the calling, gathering, and enlightening of the elect from all nations." P. 654.

In the light of these truths necessarily inseparable from the consciousness and confession of the brethren to whom Paul wrote, it would appear that the gentile readers of this epistle must have understood that they themselves were part of the fulness whose completion may have been deemed to be not far off, (10: 18) but which we know is not yet finished though we can rejoice that the preaching of the gospel has at last reached

THE FINAL PERIOD

in which it need no longer be successive from nation to nation but simultaneous to all nations, its "sound in all the earth, its words unto the ends of the world."

V. However this fullness may be viewed, whether of nations entering the fellowship of the older nations of Christendom or of persons entering into the community of the people of God, whether a present or a future in gathering of gentiles, one general testimony is borne by the great names of the church to the truth that not before the Jews are converted will all nations of the world be converted, that however great the results of missionary activity may yet be in behalf of the fullness of the nations, this fullness can not be compared with the millennial Messianic blessings and riches of salvation, yet to come through Israel and the power and glory of Israel's Redeemer and King.

This is the testimony even of those who may not associate, or are not positively known to associate, the personal return of the Messiah with the conversion of the chosen people. The conclusion of the commentator and exegete is often in strange contradiction to the enthusiastic predictions of the preacher and orator of the same post-millennial school, who do now believe the conversion of the world hinges so entirely upon the conversion of Israel; but it is undeniable that an unbiased exegesis acknowledges the fullness of Israel to be the means and the time of the conversion of all nations to the Lord.

Godet comments: "It will not be till the national conversion of Israel takes place that the work of God shall

REACH ITS PERFECTION

among the gentiles themselves." John Owen, in his work on Hebrews, affirms, "Israel shall be a guide and blessing to the residue of the gentiles who shall seek after the Lord and may be entrusted with great empire and rule in the world."

John Wesley, in his note on Rom. xi. 12, concerning "the fullness of Israel," "There will be a still larger harvest among the gentiles when all Israel is come in." "So many prophecies refer to this grand event that it is surprising any Christian can doubt it. And there are great confirmations by the wonderful preservation of the Jews as a distinct people to this day. When it is accomplished - it will be so strong a demonstration both of Old Testament and New Testament revelation, as will doubtless convince many thousand deists in countries nominally Christian, of whom there will, of course, be increasing multitudes among merely nominal Christians. And this will be a means of swiftly propagating the gospel among Mahomedans and pagans, who would probably have received it long ago had they conversed only with real Christians."

Meyer, though a strenuous advocate of the coming of our Lord and the Messianic Kingdom, yet differing in some important points from others of the same general belief, says: "The conversion of Israel is the last step in the universal extension of Christianity upon earth;" and yet he adds this does not mean "until no people of the gentile world is any longer found outside the church, for this is decidedly at variance with verse 12. Now if the fall of them be the riches of the world and the diminishing of them the riches of the gentiles, how much more their fullness?" and with

THE WHOLE CONTEXT

down to its evident concluding, verse 32, "For God hath concluded them all in unbelief that He might have mercy on all." And this last verse he interprets as spoken of individuals and not of nations.

J. A. L. Hebart in his "Second Coming" says: "By the fullness of the gentiles is not meant the conversion of all the heathen nor the confessionship of the gospel by all nations, but only a definite number of gentiles converted to God. Israel's reception will be a greater blessing to the world than Israel's unbelief and fall. We shall see later on how the nations as such en masse close in on Israel's national conversion." * * * "When the fullness of the gentiles has come in then shall the offspring of Abraham, Isaac, and Jacob, 'all Israel,' as one man be converted really to Christ, and this 'all Israel' is the 'remnant' of which Isaiah prophesied." Isaiah, x. 22-23. Romans ix. 27.

5. In conclusion, if the fullness is of evangelized nations, it does not mean the conversion of the world, for the nations already evangelized are not converted; if it is the fullness of converted individuals, it does not mean the conversion of the world according to the modern, vague notion, for such conversion is foretold to be not until the fullness of Israel takes place.

It can not be the conversion of the world, for Israel is discriminated from the gentiles or the nations in this Scripture and in all Scripture: "Lo, the people shall dwell alone and shall not be reckoned among the nations." (Numb. xxiii. 9), and yet Israel is the divinely appointed heart and core of the race (Deut. xxxii. 8).

Salvation is out of the Jews (John iv. 22). It can not be the conversion of the world for nearly nineteen centuries have not produced one nation

WHOLLY CONVERTED

to Christ much less a world, but their darkness has been illumined and their corruption stayed by the elect of God, Jew and gentile, as the light of the world and the salt of the earth. The very expression "the gospel to be preached for a witness" has itself a hint and flavor of opposition and rejection. It cannot be the conversion of the world, for this very period of the calling out of the church is to close with a consummate apostasy and a tumultuous assembling of angry nations against the coming Kingdom of our Lord and of his Christ. Rev. vi. 14-18. Ps. ii. 110.

It can not be the conversion of the world, for if it is, if the fullness of the gentiles is identical with the millennial salvation of all peoples, and kindreds, and tongues, then the divine distinction between Jew and gentile in this argument of the epistle to the Romans has lost its point and its need since the apostolic day, then Paul's sorrow for his kinsmen according to the flesh was not assuaged by the inspiring promise of their future rerestoration to a predestined pre-eminence over all nations; then God has cast off His people and intends to merge them in the mass of the converted gentiles as if the present elect church took the place of the Messianic Kingdom, then there will be no distinct and separate future holy lump or future ingrafting of holy branches; then there is no mystery at all concerning the present hardness of Israel or need of the warning against gentile highmindedness; then there is no return of the Redeemer, the mighty one of Jacob, to dwell in the midst of his people, Israel forever, but having come to Israel but once, the Man of Sorrows, the pleading lament of Jeremiah would continue forever, 'O, the hope of Israel, the Savior thereof in time of trouble, why shouldest thou be as a stranger in the land, and as a wayfaring man that turneth aside to tarry for a night?" xiv., 8-9. But these things are not so; the everlasting covenant remains as unbroken as the divine covenant with day and night and the ordinances of heaven and earth Jer. xxxiii., 19-26; "the gifts and calling of God are without repentance," Rom. 11-29; and still must we exclaim in adoring wonder, "O, the depth of the riches both of the wisdom and knowledge of God, how unsearchable are His judgments and His ways past finding out. For who hath known the mind of the Lord? or who hath been His counsellor? or who hath first given to Him and it shall be recompensed unto him again? For of Him and through Him and to Him are all things; to Him be the glory forever. Amen." (Rom. xi. 33-36.)

THE REV. DR. A. J. GORDON

SPIRITUALISM, RITUALISM, THEOSOPHY.

After a hymn, and a vote of the conference on motion of the Rev. Dr. Pierson, requesting the committee to supply a programme for Saturday morning exercises, the Rev. Dr. A. J. Gordon, of Boston, a widely known theological writer, read a paper, commanding the closest attention, on "Latter-day Delusions." It was as follows:

"The consideration of this subject will occupy me quites exclusively with a shadowy and somber aspect of the present age. But I must avow at the outset my belief that this is by no means the only or principal aspect. It is the fault of post-millennarians that, looking for the millennium instead of looking for the coming of Christ, they magnify present successes and anticipate the speedy conversion of the whole world, when the Scriptures authorize us simply to look for the preaching of the gospel among all nations for a witness and the gathering out of an elect people for the Lord. It is the fault of many premilenarians, on the contrary, that, looking for the coming of Antichrist instead of looking for the coming of Christ, they exaggerate the

PRESENT TRIUMPHS OF EVIL,

magnifging every shade into a sorrow, and every shadow into a sign of the son of perdition, and so predict the speedy triumph of the Man of Sin. "Watchman, what of the night? And the watchman said, 'The morning cometh, and also the night.'" Also the night, because the morning cometh. For the sunlight always casts a shadow, and the brighter the light the deeper the shadow. Does not the Scripture declare that "Evil men and seducers shall wax worse and worse deceiving and being deceived?" Yes; and the same Scripture saith that "The path of the just is a shining light that shineth more and more unto the perfect day." The one fact is true because the other is true. For Satan mocks the Lord Jesus at every step by matching his work with some counterpart of evil. And if we watch the present progress of evil from worse to worse let us not forget to look at the obverse side of the picture and rejoice, as we may, that the good is growing better and better. To use a household illustration, what progress has there been made in lighting our homes within a single century: from the rude tallow candle of our forefathers, through the sperm-oil wick and the rock-oil lamp and the jet of burning gas, till we have reached the electric light—so surpassingly brilliant that I can not see it without beholding a startling emblem of "that light into which no man can approach." But look at the shadows which this electric light throws upon the pavement at night! Was there ever such blackness of darkness—such a dense and almost tangible

CONCENTRATION OF NIGHT?

Now, I make bold to say that the Church of Jesus Christ to whom he said: "Ye are the light of the world," never since the apostolic age has shed a purer and more widely diffused light upon the world than she is doing to-day. One glance at the work of present-day evangelism will justify the statement: The six thousand missionaries who are preaching the gospel to every nation under heaven; the Bible translated into three hundred and two different languages and scattered broadcast among the nations; the world-wide study of the Scriptures by the millions of adults and youth in our Sunday schools; the earnest evangelism touching court and drawing-room on the one side, and lane and alley on the other; the marked revival of supernatural works of healing and help among God's people. Here is the light, and without vainglory we may rejoice in its beams. But the shadow is correspondingly black. The ship that carries the missionary carries rum and opium, whereby so-called Christian nations are destroying a hundred souls among the heathen where the church saves one. The printing-press which scatters the Bible is flooding the world with infidel and obscene literature, and the Prince of Darkness is on hand to caricature any miracle of mercy with some dazzling miracle of perdition.

Now let us ask, What Satanic delusion especially and peculiarly characterizes the present age? My reply is not with some: Infidelity foreshadowing an approaching atheistical Antichrist. Infidelity is characteristic of our age, no doubt, but not more so than of some other ages. Indeed if we may credit

THE BEST AUTHORITIES

the unbelief of the last half of the eighteenth century was far more wide-spread and paralyzing in Christian countries than that of the last half of the nineteenth century. And so, with Kelly in the preface to his "Exposition of the Apocalypse," I hold that the conception of an avowedly infidel Anti Christ does not meet the requirements of Scripture. The fact is that open infidelity is not especially in Satan's line. His way is to masquerade in the symbols and sacraments of the church, to manipulate the machinery of miracles, and by supernatural signs and wonders to accredit the doctrine of demons." After figuring for ages as an "angel of light" it would be an entirely new departure in his administration for him to propose for himself an open coronation as the prince of darkness. His way has ever been to dishonor Christ by a feigned allegiance and betray him by a deceitful kiss.

Now I open the scriptures for the signs of the approaching end of the age and of the coming of Christ, and what on this darker side do I find? Not atheism so much as demonism and delusion.

In the first epistle to Timothy and the fourth chapter it is written: "The Spirit speaketh expressly that in the latter times some shall apostatize from the faith, giving heed to seducing spirits and doctrines of demons; speaking lies in hypocrisy; having their conscience seared with a hot iron; forbidding to marry, and commanding to abstain from meats," etc. Then I turn for

A SINGLE GLANCE

at the Apocalypse, and the same thing confronts me there. In the sixteenth chapter, after the successive outpouring of the vials and just before the seventh there is a sudden startling note of warning—"Behold, I come as a thief. Blessed is he that watcheth and keepeth his garments." But what is the event mentioned just previously to this note of warning? It is this: "The spirits of demons working miracles which go forth into the kings of the earth and of the whole world to gather them to the battle of the great day of God Almighty." Seducing spirits, doctrines of demons, Satanic miracles—these are the manifestations which Scripture predicts of the latter day, and these are the most appalling characteristics of our own times. The sources from which the unclean spirits proceed are declared in the Apocalypse to be three—"out of the mouth of the dragon and out of the mouth of the beast and out of the mouth of the false prophet." I will not dogmatize concerning the systemsthus indicated. I will simply point out the fact that the present influx of superstition is in these three forms and from these three principal sources:

1. Spiritualism proceeding from the p't.
2. Ritualism proceeding from the papacy.
3. Theosophy proceeding from paganism.

Spiritualism without doubt is ancient sorcery, reappearing under a different name, but with totally unchanged characteristics. And when I tell you that in the city of Boston, where Cotton Mather, that eminent withstander of witchcraft, once lived and labored, there is now a magnificent temple for the worship of Spiritualism, which, being interpreted, means for the

PRACTICE OF DEMONOLOGY

and witchcraft; when I remind you that this dark system claims from ten to twenty millions of devotees, who have been discipled within the less than fifty years of its modern manifestation, and when I repeat its proud boast that it has gone forth unto the kings of the earth and has royal apostles in many of the thrones and palaces of the Old World, you will see that it is no mere insignificant superstition, utterly unworthy of notice. The theory that spiritualism is a system of sheer imposition; is not the one now held by the most candid Christian investigators; nor is it the one most accordant with fact and Scripture. The Bible explicitly forbids intercourse with spirits of the other world, and it would not forbid what is impossible. "There shall not be found among you any one that useth divination, or an observer of times or an enchanter or a witch, or a charmer, or a consultor of familiar spirits, or a wizard, or a necromancer. For all that do these things are an abomination unto the Lord" (Ex. vii. 2). And not only are these things an abomination, but a crime punishable with death. "A man or a woman that hath a familiar spirit, or that is a wizard, shall surely be put to death," (Ex. xxii. 18) saith the Lord. Our rational age congratulates itself on having outgrown the belief in such puerile superstitions. But incredulity is often the next door neighbor to stupidity; and he who boasts himself too wise to believe in the existence of evil spirits, may be the easiest prey to their seductions. God and the devil, the kingdom of light and the kingdom of darkness, are both realities; and in proportion to our belief and realization of the supernal will be our apprehension and dread of the infernal. And not only is the reality of fallen spirits

DISTINCTLY TAUGHT IN SCRIPTURE,

but their power to produce startling miracles. In Thessalonians we are told that "the working of Satan" is "with all power and signs and lying wonders," and in the apocalypse we have the prediction of "the spirits of demons working miracles." The man who supposes that satan would undermine the belief in the supernatural is utterly ignorant of his devices. He has a creed to inculcate and a code of infernal morality to propagate, and he would employ miracles to authenticate his doctrines. Let us remember indeed that in the emergence of modern spiritualism satan actually comes on the stage as a defender of the faith. "This generation has fallen into doubt concerning the immortality of the soul," say his ministers, the mediums or sooth sayers; "and we propose to demonstrate this doctrine to you by calling up your dead and letting them speak to you." Thousands of once professing Christians who are now in the coils of this delusion were first seduced by the plea of larger knowledge and firmer faith concerning the unseen. The ear having been thus gained for the communications of the departed, the instruction has gone on—no rude denials at first but the most soothing platitudes and the most subtle counterfeits, till little by little the whole system of evangelical faith has been supplemented by that soul-destroying creed, "the doctrine of demons." I say "of demons," for I have no question that what are supposed to be departed friends speaking from beyond the veil are in reality fallen spirits, foul, malignant, and seducing, sent to beguile men into the allegiance and worship of Satan. And here as elsewhere the evil one follows most closely the divine method — first teaching through rapping, planchette, and mediumistic writing, and then miracles

OF PHYSICAL HEALING

and materialization to accredit these teachings; "speaking lies in hypocrisy" and confirming the word spoken by satanic signs and wonders following.

And I must tax your credulity still further by declaring my belief in the substantial correctness of Pember's theory, which is held by Alford and many other commentators, that fallen angels have power actually to assume fleshy bodies; and that in the period just preceding the flood these apostate spirits cohabited in the flesh with the daughters of men begetting a forbidden and accursed seed which God destroyed by the deluge. To say nothing of the fact that that mysterious apocryphal record, the Book of Enoch, tells this story with the minutest detail and that the early fathers of the church heed it as a veritable tradition. We believe that a candid exegesis of the Old Testament strongly supports it, while we find that the Epistle of Jude, according to the revised version, explicitly declares that the sin of the fallen angels was identical with the sin of the Sodomites—the "going after strange flesh;" the lust of the disobedient angels, it would seem, culminating in forbidden intercourse with the daughters of men, as the sensuality of the Sodomites culminated in a daring attempt at fleshy defilement with the angels in the house of Lot

REV. A. J. GORDON, D. D.,
PASTOR CLARENDON ST. BAPTIST CHURCH, BOSTON.

And from this statement of Scripture turn to the latest claim of spiritualism: that in materialization the spirits of the departed now actually reappear, habited in flesh and blood, and hold communion with their friends; then listen to the concessions of some of the ablest Christian investigators of this system, who are constrained to admit that they have seen such forms conjured up at seances, that they have handled them with their hands, and, after the most diligent caution against fraud and deception, have been compelled to concede the apparent reality of the phenomena. What a frightful suggestion we do not say demonstration, is there here, of the triumph of seducing spirits in their last irruption upon a fallen race! What a startlingly literal fulfillment our Lord's prediction may we yet have! "As it was in

THE DAYS OF NOAH

—and as it was in the days of Lot—even thus shall it be in the day when the son of man is revealed;" the subtle tuition in free-love and uncleanness which spiritualism has been carrying on, ending at last in a deified sodomy; and its industrious inculcation of the doctrine of demons, ending in the worship of Beelzbub, the prince of demons! Have I hinted at a culmination which is utterly inconceivable? I remind you that the short plummet of present day naturalism may not be able to sound such depths of satan. But lengthen your sounding line by a diligent study of that much neglected subject, the demonology of Scripture, and you may see enough to cause you to start back affrighted, with the exclamation: "Oh the depths!" An eminent writer on prophesy reminds us that the close of every preceding dispensation has been marked by an outbreak of demoniacal manifestation. If the precedent is to hold concerning this dispensation, then in modern spiritualism we have a startling sign of the approaching end of the age.

Ritualism ought not to be mentioned in the same volume with spiritualism, considering that it is an ecclesiastical eccentricity into which men of unquestionable piety and consecration have fallen, while spiritualism is utterly godless. But at the risk of a seeming breach of Christian charity I must classify it where its origin and history place it among the strong delusions which have come in to corrupt the church and despoil it of the simplicity that is in Christ. Most gladly do I bear tribute to

THE HUMBLE SELF-DENIAL

which many of the ritualistic priests are practising, and to the much sound theology which they are setting forth from their pulpits. Nevertheless, I must remind you how often, in the history of the church, the highest saintship has been found in intimate conjunction with the lowest superstition.

John Henry Newman, in a work which he put forth as a justification for his departure to Rome, makes this striking concession. In speaking of holy water and some other elements of the Roman Catholic ritual he declares that originally they were "the very instruments and appendages of demon worship," though "sanctified by adoption into the church." Literally true is this statement, and as comprehensive as true, for it covers almost every element and particular of the ritualistic service.

Going into a church where this system is in vogue you see the congregation turning reverently toward the east at certain stages of the service. It seems innocent enough to assume this position, though you know no reason for it. But you open your Bibles to the eighth chapter of Ezekiel, and there hear God denouncing the abominations which Israel is committing by mingling the worship of Babylon with the service of God. Among these abominations was the spectacle in the "inner court of the Lord's house" of "about five and twenty men with their backs toward the temple of the Lord and their faces toward the east; and they worshipped the sun toward the east." Such is unquestionably the origin of the eastward posture—a relic and remnant of primitive sun-worship.

IN THE SAME CHAPTER

of Ezekiel there is a reference to the ceremony of "weeping for Tammuz." Tammuz being another name for the pagan god Osiris. If in the ritualistic church you see some making the sign of the cross, remember that this was originally a pagan and not a Christian ceremony. For though X, the initial letter of Christ, very early became a Christian symbol the T shaped cross was originally simply the mystic Tau—the initial letter of Tammuz, and this sign was used in Babylonish worship and emblazoned on Babylonish vestments fifteen hundred years before the crucifixion of Christ. [For ample proof of this statement see Hislop's "Two Babylons," pages 322-334.] If the ritualism is sufficiently advanced to make use of the wafer in the communion turn again to the description of Jewish apostacy contained in Jeremiah xlv. 19, where the Israelites confess, "We burned incense to the queen of heaven and poured out drink offerings unto her, and we did make our cakes to worship her." Here the pedigree of the wafer is suggested, and if one will examine the literature of the subject we challenge him to resist the conclusion that it has come down directly from this Babylonish cake. This cake was round, for the reason that it was an image or effigy of the sun, and was worshiped as such, and when it became installed as part and parcel of Christian worship the shape was strenuously insisted on, and is to this day. John Knox, in referring to this fact, says with his usual vigor of speech: "If in making the roundness the ring be broken, then must another of his fellow cakes receive the honor to be made a god and the crazed or cracked miserable cake that was once in hope to be made a god must be given to a baby

TO PLAY WITHAL."

So, too, in regard to that which is universally characteristic of ritualism, the lighted candles about the altar. In the Apocryphal book of Baruch there is a minute and extended description of the Babylonish worship, with all its dark and abominable accessories. Of the gods which they set up in their temples it is said that "their eyes be full of dust through the feet of them that come in." And then it is added that the worshipers "light for them candles, yea more than for themselves, whereof they can not see one." In the pagan worship at Rome, which was confessedly borrowed largely from Assyria and Egypt, we have accounts of processionals in which surpliced priests marched with wax candles in their hands, carrying the images of the gods," and we find a Christian writer in the fourth century, ridiculing the heathen custom of "lighting of candles to gods as if he lived in the dark," which he certainly would not have done had the practice formed any part of Christian worship.

And time would fail me to tell of the confessional, so closely reproducing that imposed on the initiates in the ancient mysteries, and of holy water whose origin has already been pointed out, and of ceremonies and vestments nameless and incomprehensible.

Granting for the sake of charity that altars and incense were borrowed from Jewish worship, which things indeed were done away in Christ, it still remains true that the great bulk of the ritualistic ceremonies were originally part and portion of primitive idol worship. I am ready to challenge anybody who will make a candid investigation of the subject to disprove it. But what if it be said with Newman that these things are "sanctified by adoption into

THE CHRISTIAN CHURCH?"

Our answer would be, alas, how has the Christian church been unsanctified by their adoption! For of what are they the accessories? What have they brought in with them as they have crept stealthily back into the sanctuaries that were once purged of them? These two central errors—baptismal regeneration and transubstantiation—falsehoods of Satan which have done more to deceive souls, and accomplish their present and eternal undoing, than is possible for the strongest language to set forth. Concerning the first—baptismal regeneration—what shall we say? Is it not enough to make one who has any pity for the souls of men weep aloud, to think of the baptized multitudes still "in the gall of bitterness and in the bond of iniquity," who are being betrayed unto eternal death through this sacramental lie?

Concerning the doctrine of transubstantiation, let me quote the words of a godly English rector, whose soul is stirred within him as he is compelled to see what he calls "the center and sum of the mystery of lawlessness" gaining recognition in his own church. He says: "The crowning error in the process of Satanic inspiration is this, that the priesthood possesses a divine power to locate the Lord Jesus Christ on an earthly altar, and to lift Him up under the veils of bread and wine for the adoration of the people." It is in this blasphemous fraud that the Apostle Paul's prophecy finds its accurate fulfillment Of the apostacy forerunning the second coming of Christ; he says that the deluded followers of the lawless one shold believe the lie. Of all the impostures that the father of lies ever palmed upon a credulous world this doctrine, which, both logically and theologically, repeats millions of times the humiliation of

THE BLESSED REDEEMER,

necessarily transcends all." It is worthy by pre-eminence to be called the lie.

Admitting now that ritualism is of pagan origin what is the conclusion to which we are brought? To this: that by its revival in the church there is a repetition of that sin which God so constantly denounces in the Scriptures as an abomination—the mingling of the worship of demons with the worship of God. Here we go expressly by the book. In Denteronmy (xxxii. 17) when the Israelites are charged with provoking the Lord to jealousy by strange Gods, the ground of offense is declared to be that "they sacrificed unto devils, not to God." In the Septuagint version of Psalm xcvi. 5, it reads: "For all the gods of the nations are demons." And in 1 Cor. x., 20, it is written: "The things which the gentiles sacrifice they sacrifice unto demons and not to God; and I would notthat ye should have fellowship with demons." Dr. Tregelles, commenting on this last passage, says: "Did the ancient heathen think they were adoring evil spirits—demons

—when they sacrificed to their gods and demi-gods—when they honored Jupiter and Hurcules? And yet the Scripture thus teaches us that the worship did actually go to demons; it was thus directed by Satan. And this put the idolatrous nations under the distinct tutelage of demons, whose power showed itself among them in many ways. We should form I believe a very inadequate estimate of Romish idolatry if we were to overlook the solemn fact that it is demon worship commingling itself with that of the living and true God, so that Romish nations stand under demoniacal tutelage, just as did the gentiles of old." And this conclusion accords as closely with the teachings of history as with the teaching of Scripture. How can we account for the course of the Roman apostacy for the last twelve hundred years—that career of blood and blasphemy unmatched by anything in human history, except

UNDER THE SUPPOSITION

that behind the scene it is Satan who is the real pope and his subordinate demons who are the real cardinals—that just as through the mystery of godliness the Holy Spirit became incarnated in the body of Christ to guide and enlighten it, so through the "mystery of iniquity" the evil spirit became incarnated in the great apostacy to inspire it with "all deceivableness of unrighteousness." Is then ritualism an innocent ecclesiastical pastime—a harmless freak of religious æstheticism? So it seems to many, even of those who have no affiliation with it. But look at it just as it is. Trace the history of the ceremonies piece by piece back to their original source, till you find that true of almost every one of them which Newman admits of a part of them, that they were "the very instruments and appendages of demon worship," and then imagine the exultation among these demons as they see Christian priests, clothed in their paraphernalia, marching in their idolatrous processions and preaching their delusive doctrines. And how must their joy be enhanced by the anticipation of the yet greater triumphs still to come in the culmination of idolity and man-worship. Those who are looking for a future infidel anti-Christ have imagined how easily some master genius inspired with infernal energy and magnetism might evoke a world-wide allegiance to himself, and out of the restless elements of socialism and atheism and paganism get himself worshiped as a god.

But I ask you to look not at what may be possible, but at what has actually been accomplished along the line which we are considering, and this, too, not merely in the first centuries of the papacy but in our

OWN DAY AND GENERATION.

It is hardly more than fifty years since the tractarian movement began in Oxford. From among the company of its originators we may select two, Newman and Manning, as noble and sincere souls, so far as we can judge, as any age of the church has produced. But they came under the fascination of ritualism; and it threw its spell little by little over their minds. Watch their course from the beginning to the present day. Observe the mental struggles, the ill-concealed reluctances, as fold after fold of mediæval delusion closes about them. Almost can we hear cries of pain here and there as the process of branding the conscience with a hot iron goes on. But at last the work is complete; they have reached old age, and with it the dotage of superstition. And where do we find them now? Prostrate on their faces before a deified man; all the ascriptions which could be claimed by a god on earth they yield without reluctance to the Pope. Infallibility in his decrees, indefectibility in his conduct they now ascribe to him who sits upon the throne at Rome. Cardinal Manning, speaking for the line of popes says: "In the person of Pius IX. Jesus reigns on earth, and He must reign till He hath put all enemies uner His feet." Words, which as I read them, constrain me to ask of this sovereign pontiff: "Art thou the Antichrist that was come or do we look for another."

Cardinal Newman voicing the sentiment of the church, which he calls "a never failing fount of humanity, equity, forbearance, and compassion," uses

WITH SPECIAL EMPHASIS,

these words: "We find in all parts of Europe scaffolds prepared to punish crimes against religion. Scenes which sadden the soul were everywhere witnessed. Rome is the one exception to the rule. The Popes, armed with a tribunal of intolerance, have scarce spilt a drop of blood: Protestants and philosophers have shed it in orrents"—so "drunk with the blood of martyrs" that she does not even know that se has been drinking!

Here is the goal which the advance-courriers of ritualism have reached in half a century; is it unlikely that the thousands of clergymen and laymen who have within a few years entered upon the same path will fail to arrive at the same destination?

To sum up this part of our subject, then, I believe that ritualism is a desperate but marvelously insidious attempt of the great enemy to regain for the Man of Sin what was wrested from him by the reformation. It is a scheme so fascinating that already many of the very elect have been deceived by it, and are being led back to Rome as sheep to the slaughter. To such I would commend again the solemn words of Tregelles: "A recurrence to Romish connection a re-commingly in any way with the maintenance of Romish idolatry would place a Protestant nation again under the sway of those demons to whom idolatrous worship really ascends, whether the name under which they are adored be that of Jupiter or Simon Peter, the apostle of Christ."

All this is hard to say, for one who prefers the charity which covers a multitude of faults to the criticism which lays them bare. And in dwelling on this subject we are not insensible to the perversions of another kind which have crept into our non-liturgical bodies. For, so far as we know, the liturgical churches, have not fallen into the

COOKING STOVE APOSTASY

which is turning so many of our church basements into places of feasting; nor have they been ensnared with the entertainment heresy which sets up all sorts of shows and exhibitions for amusing the unchurched masses into an interest in the gospel. We deplore these things, and here and now lift up our warning against them as another device of the enemy for corrupting and enervating the church of God.

(At the utterance of this sentiment, or its equivalent in an improvised form, Dr. Gordon's colleagues on the platform, Dr. Pierson leading, and the audience as a whole arose to say "Amen.")

But while considering ourselves lest we also be tempted we must none the less warn our neighbors against the fatal infatuation of ritualism. We take up the Trinity Church catechism of Dr. Dix and find it streaked through and through with the tinge of the scarlet woman—baptismal regeneration, eucharistic sacrifice, apostolic succession, prayer for the dead, intercession of departed souls, when we find its eminent author so enamored of the papacy that he draws away from all Protestant bodies and embraces her, declaring that the three chief branches of the holy Catholic Church are the Church of Rome, the Greek Church, and the Anglican Church, and that the body thus formed is the

TRUE CHURCH CATHOLIC,

"because she endures throughout all ages, teaches all nations, and maintains all truth." When we find Protestant ecclesiastics so smitten with what the reformers used to call "the trinkets of Antichrist," as to allow themselves little by little to be reinvested with the cast-off clothing of Babylon, so that a recent writer describes the Bishop of Lincoln as "adorned with mitre and cloth of gold, his orpheys so lavishly decorated with amethysts, pearls, topazes and chrysolites set in silver as fairly to dazzle the beholder;" when we see all these we are moved to repeat with solemn earnestness the warning of Bradford, the Smithfield martyr, "O, England, beware of Antichrist; take heed that he doth not fool thee."

Theosophy, is the latest religion of transcendentalists. In it, the attenuated unbelief of our times is seeking to find relief from the ennui of denial. How to describe that which takes for itself the name of "Occultism;" how to give an idea of doctrines which claim to be hidden from all but the initiated we do not know. It is enough to say that substantially it is Buddhism seeking conquests in Christian lands; "the light of Asia," offering itself to those who have turned away from "the light of Christ." It has its circles in many of our great cities, where its occult philosophy is diligently studied; though its following is small compared with that of spiritualism, it being the religion of the literary elite, as the other is of the common people. If we question it in regard to its doctrines, it tells us that they are the same as those of "the sacred mysteries of antiquity." It inculcates a very attenuated philosophy of evolution; it teaches the pre-existence and the transmigration of souls, and instructs its disciples how by a rigid asciticism they may cultivate what is called

"THE INTUITIONAL MEMORY"

by which they can enter into profound recollection of what they knew in far distant ages. In a couplet which it is fond of repeating it declares that

Descending spirits have conversed with man
And told him secrets of the world unknown.

And these words give the most reasonable hint of its origin. For its creed is "the doctrines of demons from beginning to end." No personal devil that which is mystically called the devil being but the negative and opposite of God.' No atonement except man's "unification" with himself; no forgiveness of sin, souls being required to wear away their guilt by self-expiation; miracles, mysteries, ultimate deification—these are specimen articles of its delusive greed. It's whole character and contents so far as we can comprehend them are yet another phase of satanic delusion. Now if we compare these three sytems, counting ritualism as incipient Popery, we find them agreeing remarkably to fill up the outlines of the predicted apostacy. The "forbidding to marry" realised in the celebacy of Romanism; the enforced continence of theosophy and the anti-marriage doctrine of spiritualism; the "commanding to abstain from meat" appearing in the superstitious fasts of ritualism, and the rigid abstinence from flesh enjoined on the initialtes of esoteric Buddhism; the doctrines of demons manifested in the magic and idolatry which ritualism substitutes for the chaste and simple doctrines of ordinance of Christ, and which in many particulars hold a common ancestry with those of theosophy and spiritualism, and the fartastic miracle-working which characterize them all. All three of these delusions give a practical denial of Christ's second advent—that doctrine at which demons

FEAR AND TREMBLE—

spiritualism and theosophy declaring that in that in them the promised Epiphany of Christ is taking place; while ritualism by its doctrine of transubstantiation makes the communion declare the "real presence of Christ" in flesh and blood, when the Lord ordained it to declare his real absence "till he come"—I mean, of course, bodily absence.

What now is the prophetic significance of all that we have said? This it seems to me, that according to the predictions of Scripture we are witnessing an irruption of evil spirits who are again working powerfully along their favorite lines—ritualism, superstition, and philosophy.

We hear much said about infidelity and communism "heading up" in a personal Antichrist. Believing as I do, that Antichrist came long ago, and that he was crowned a few years since in St. Peter's at Rome as the deified man—infallible and supreme. I see in the present aspect of affairs his final bodying forth, rather than his ultimate heading up. As in the case of Christ, so in the case of "the man of sin," the head is revealed first, and the body gathered throughout all generations grows up in all things into Him who is the head." For the career of Antichrist is the exact parody and evil counterpart of that of Christ. If you say "the Antichrist must be

AN INDIVIDUAL

as certainly as Christ is," I remind that the word Christ does not always stand for a single individual in description, for in I. Cor., xii., the apostle describes the body of believers, gathered to the Lord through all time with its divers gifts and administrations, and this corporate whole with its many members, but "all baptised by one spirit into one body" he names Ho Christos—the Christ. So that evil system with its various offices and administrations yet baptised into unity by "the Spirit which now worketh in the children of disobedience" is the Antichrist. The one is the head of the ecclesia, and the other is the head of the apostasia; but the head and the body are so identical that they bear the same personal name.

"But he is called 'the man of sin,'" you say, "and therefore must be an individual. Not of necessity. For the line of believers extending through all ages is declared by the apostles to be taken out from Jews and gentiles to "make of twain one new man."

I can not believe that "the mystery of iniquity," which Paul declared to be already working in his day, has been toiling on for nearly two thousand years in order to bring forth a single short-lived man, and he so omnipotently wicked that the Papal Antichrist, with the blood of fifty millions of martyrs on his skirts, is too insignificant a sinner to be mentioned in comparison. And now, I hear the objections coming thick and fast. "But is he not an open infidel since he is said 'to deny the Father and the Son?'" Search your concordances for the meaning of the word "deny," and observe how constantly it signifies the denial of apostasy and false profession. But is he not

THE INCARNATION OF SATAN

since he is called "the son of perdition?" Yes; Judas was named "the son of perdition;" and "Satan entered into Judas Iscariot;" but so far from atheistically denying Christ he openly professed Him, saying, "Hail, Master," and then betraying Him with a kiss. But is he not a godless blasphemer, since he is declared to have "a mouth speaking great things and blasphemies?" The counterfeit of Christ again, for Christ was twice falsely accused of blasphemy, because he made Himself equal with God, and because he presumed to forgive sins. The Pope is justly accused of blasphemy on both these grounds, for he profanely calls himself God, and assumes to forgive sins. Said Alexander VI.: "Cæsar was a man; Alexander is a God." But must he not be a Jew established in Jerusalem, since it is said that "He sitteth in the temple of God, showing Himself that He is God?" No. This particular phrase "temple of God," is never in a single instance in the New Testament applied to the temple at Jerusalem, but always to the church, the body of Christ, to its head or to its members in heaven or on earth. But could the Holy Ghost call that "the temple of God" which has become apostate? Just as possibly as Christ could call the apostate Laodiceans whom he spues out of His mouth

"THE CHURCH IN LAODICCA."

"But does not this view commit one to the year-day interpretat'on, since the career of Antichrist is three years and a hal: and the papal system extends through centuries? Yes, for the one instance of prophetic time which has by unanimous consent been fulfilled, the seventy weeks of Daniel is demonstrated to have been upon this scale. Since the period was actually 490 years—a day for a year—and this may be taken as a clue to the prophetic time of Revelation. But if the Holy Spirit meant years in the Apocalypse why did he not say years? you reply. Why, when he meant churches and ministers, and kingdoms and kings and epochs, did he say candle-sticks, and stars, and beasts, and horns, and trumpets? Yet, having used these miniature symbols of greater things, how fitting that the accompanying time should also be in miniature! To use literal dates would distort the im gary—as though you should put a life-sized eye in a small-sized photograph.

I have said that Antichrist is the evil counterpart of Christ. When Satan offered Christ all the kingdoms of the world if he would fall down and worship him He refused, accepting present rejection and crucifixion, and waiting the Father's time for the kingdoms of the world to become the kingdom of our Lord and of his Christ. The papal Antichrist accepted the kingdoms of this world when the temptation was presented him, and proceeded to announce himself the "king of kings" and that the kingdom had come, and that in himself was fulfilled the scripture, "He shall have dominion from sea to sea, and from river to river, ucto the ends of the earth."

The bride of Christ—the church—was left in the world to share her Lord's rejection and cross, enduring present suffering and widowhood, and waiting for the return of the bridegroom. But the harlot bride of Antichrist accepts and earthly throne and a present glory, boastfully saying, "I sit a queen and am no widow and shall see no sorrows." Do we not see that it was this usurpation of the headship of the church by the man of sin; this premature grasping of the kingdom and the setting up of a mock millennium under rules of a pseudo-Christ, that destroys the millennial hope of the church and has

INFECTED GENERATION

after generation, with the delusion of a present reign and a present kingdom, while Christ is yet absent in person from his flock? But this enemy of God and His Saints must soon come to an end. In Daniel and in Thessalonians this end is predicted in two stages: gradual, and then sudden and complete. "They shall take away his dominion to consume and destroy unto the end," says Daniel. "Whom the Lord shall consume with the breath of His mouth and shall destroy with the brightness of His coming," says Paul in Thessalonians. The consuming process has been going on mightily in our generation by the breath of the Lord's mouth in the world-wide diffusion of the inspired Scriptures. "And now the devil is come down with great wrath because he knoweth that he hath but a short time." He is putting forth the energy of despair. He is sending his legions to work along various lines, which all center, visibly, or invisibly, in one head. On the line of sacerdotalism he is seeking to thwart the work of the Reformation by again insinuating popish worship into our churches; on the line of superstition he is aiming to bewitch the godless and curious multitudes through the energy of unclean spirits; on the line of culture he is moving to foist upon the literary elite a diluted paganism as an extra fine religion. But these things cheer us rather than sadden us, for all the shadows point to the dawn. The church's salvation means Antichrist's destruction, and the same Scripture which speaks to us so powerfully to-day in the light of passing evils, "Yet a little while and he that shall come will come and will not tarry," says also, "And the God of peace shall bruise Satan under your feet shortly. The grace of our Lord Jesus Christ be with you, Amen." All this which I have set forth I have declared with unutterable sorrow. All this I can think of only with weeping, crying

"O, BRIDE OF CHRIST.

how are they increased who would rob thee of thy chastity." All this I now review with a fervent prayer that if I have spoken aught against any of the Lord's anointed He will forgive me, while for myself I cry daily unto Him "Deliver me from the evil one."

Men and Brethren: We are here for a candid and courteous discussion of certain great prophetic questions. Among these none is more important as affecting our present testimony than the one upon which I have just now touched.

I need not remind you that one of the first tasks which the ritualistic leaders fifty years ago felt called upon to undertake was that of getting rid of the Protestant interpretation of Antichrist as the Pope of Rome. How desperately they wrought at this task will be apparent to those who read Newman's essay on "The Man of Sin," and observed especially his earnest wrestling with the ominous saying of Gregory the Great, that "Whosoever adopts or desires the title of universal bishop is the forerunner of Antichrist."

If I must take sides between parties on this question my sympathies will be with Latimer and Cranmer and Bradford, whose vision was clarified by the fires of martyrdom, to recognize their persecutor and call him by name, rather than with Manning and Newman, whose eyes are holden by the charm of medievalism.

But our appeal is not to man, but to the sure word of prophecy. The profoundest discussion of this question which has appeared in fifty years in my opinion is contained in the two recent volumes of Mr. Grattan Guinness. There history is shown to answer to prophecy like deep calling unto deep; there the mysterious chronology written ages ago by God is verified point by point by

THE TERMINAL PERIODS

which are running out under our own eyes. Such correspondencies can not be accidental; such clear pointings to the man of sin as a story of his predicted age as 1,260 years gives can not be fortuitous. One of the ablest prophetic scholars of the Futerest school in this country declares that he knows not how the conclusions of these volumes can be gainsaid.

I humbly concur in that opinion. Nay, I speak rather of The Book than of any human books and avow my conviction that the papal "Man of Sin" was accurately photographed on the camera of prophecy thousands of years ago; that no detective searching for him to-day would need any other description of him than that which is found on the pages of the Bible. Taking these photographs of Daniel and John and Paul, and searching the world upside down for their originals, I am confident that this same detective would stop at the Vatican, and after gazing for a few moments at the Pontiff, who sits there gnawing the bone of infallibility, which he acquired in 1870, and clutching for that other bone of temporal sovereignty which he lost the very same year, he would lay his hand on him and say: "You are wanted in the court of the Most High to answer to the indictment of certain souls beneath the altar 'who were slain for the word of God and for the testimony which they bore," and who are crying, 'How long, O Lord, holy and true, dost Thou not judge and avenge our blood on them that dwell upon the earth?'"

My brethren, let us search the Scriptures anew and let us be sure that they do not require it of us before we silence our testimony against the Man of Rome as Antichrist.

THIRD DAY.

THE REV. DR. J. S. KENNEDY.

PRACTICAL INFLUENCE AND POWER.

Snowy, blustering weather was no obstacle to the atttendance of the faithful many at the third day's session of the Bible and Prophetic Conference. In the opening devotional exercises there was congregational singing and prayer by the Rev. Dr. Goodwin, of Chicago. Before proceeding with the exercises the Rev. George C. Needham, Secretary, made the following statement:

"It is hardly necessary to state to this audience that there has been no arrangement or understanding between the speakers at this conference, coming as they have from many States, to avoid repetition in their addresses. In fact repetition is essential and can not possibly be avoided. Post-millenarians have a variety of views on the subject of our Lord's coming. Pre-millenarians the world over are one in their hope. They may differ on the interpretation of Scriptures bearing on events connected with the subject, but the committee had no hesitation in inviting these good brethren of all evangelical churches and from many States to present with the ability given them this subject of our Lord's

PRE-MILLENNIAL ADVENT."

The Rev. Dr. J. S. Kennedy, of the Abingdon, Va., M. E. Church, South, then read a paper on the subject, "Practical Influence and Power of Christ's Second Coming." It was as follows:

Dear Brethren in Christ: "Grace to you and peace be multiplied. Blessed be the God and Father of our Lord Jesus Christ, who according to His great mercy begat us again unto a living hope by the resurrection of Jesus Christ from the dead unto an inheritance incorruptible and undefiled, and that fadeth not away, reserved in heaven for you, who by the power of God are guarded through faith unto a salvation ready to be revealed in the last time.

"Wherein ye greatly rejoice, though now for a little while, if need be, ye have been put to grief in manifold temptations, that the proof of your faith, being more precious than gold that perisheth though it is proved by fire, might be found unto praise and glory and honor at the revelation of Jesus Christ" (I. Pet. i. 2-7).

The Christ of prophecy—"the same yesterday, to-day, and forever"—is not only the Christ of history, but the living sovereign head of the church, "which is His body, the fullness of Him that filleth all in all" Eph. i. (23.)

THIS CHRIST OF PROPHECY—

"being the image of God, the invisible—the first-born of all creation" (Col. i. 15); yea, being "the effulgence of God's glory, and the very image or impress of His substance" (Hebr. i. 3); as the eternal Logos or word of God, "became flesh," the living incarnation of all the treasures of divine grace and truth, in order that he might be fitted to become the "Captain and Prince of our Salvation," and the medium through whom God the Father "might reconcile all things to Himself, in the earth and in the heavens" (Col. i. 20), and "that in the dispensation of the fulness of times He might gather together in one all things in Christ, both which are in heaven and on earth" (Eph. i. 9-10).

Having wrought out the great problem of man's redemption by procuring for him initial salvation "by grace through faith," He then became the "first-born from the dead," the first arising from death to everlasting life, "that in all (possible respects) He might have the pre-eminence," or first place in rank, as well in His Soteriological as in His Cosmical glory.

And now in His exaltation to the right hand of the Majesty on high he abides "in the form of God," being "the brightness of His glory and the express image of His person," and "has been appointed heir of all things" (Heb. i. 2-3). And "to us" Paul declares "there is but one * * Lord Jesus Christ by whom are all things, and we by Him (I. Cor. viii. 6); to whom John in the Apocalypse applies the ineffable name of Jehovah, "The Was and the Is and the Coming One" (Rev. iv. 8).

It is, we think, universally conceded by those competent to judge that in every age the faith and hope of the church of our Lord Jesus Christ have been

DIRECTED TO AND CENTERED IN

the second personal coming of our now exalted and glorified Savior, as the event in which the Lord's redeeming work shall culminate in the resurrection and glorification of His saints, in the full establishment of His messianic kingdom, in the regeneration of this sin-cursed and sorrow-smitten planet, and in the regenesis of the Cosmos in its complete deliverance from all physical and moral evil by His personal reign. This assumes His coming not only to be personal and literal, but also pre-millennial, antedating in time and fact the millennial era. His coming in person must precede His reigning in person on the earth. That is self-evident.

Before proceeding, therefore, to unfold and discuss its practical bearings upon the church of to-day, and the inspiring and transforming power of this "living hope" of the Master's second personal coming, let us consider for a moment some of the reasons for embracing a doctrine of such amazing import, if true, and which by its logical and essential contents, whether we will or not, must sweep away the foundations and traditions of the commonly received post-millennial theory of "the last days." This theory, as all know, puts the millennium before Christ's coming, and conjoins in an inexplicable manner the sublimities of our immortal destiny with the irreconcilable and contradictory diabolism which, if the Scriptures are to be believed, shall immediately precede the second advent. And the more so, if, as we believe, we are standing to-day

FACE TO FACE

with the great predicted crisis of the world's history toward which the sublime march of events is steadily pressing with quickened pace, and converging with infallible certainty. In the very last discourse to His sorrowing disciples before His departure, Christ said, "I go to prepare a place for you. And if I go and prepare a place for you, I will come again, and receive you unto Myself; that where I am, there ye may be also" (John xiv. 2-3). "When the Son of Man shall come in His glory, and all the angels with Him, then (not before) shall He sit on the throne of His glory," and commence his separating judgments upon the wheat and tares (Matt. xiii. 39-43, xxv. 31).

In Acts i. 9-11, it is written that when "Jesus was taken up, and a cloud received Him out of sight," angels said to the astonished Galileans, "Why stand ye looking into heaven? This same Jesus which was received up from you into heaven, shall come in like manner as ye beheld Him going into heaven." Again: "The Lord Himself in His divine-human personality shall descend from heaven with a shout, with the voice of the archangel, and with the trump of God; and the dead in Christ shall rise first." (I. Thess. iv. 16). "And to you who are troubled rest with us, when the Lord Jesus Christ shall be revealed from heaven with the angels of His power." (II. Thess. i. 7). So in Zech. xiv. 5, "The Lord my God shall come, and all the saints with Thee." "Behold, the Lord cometh with ten thousand of his saints," says Jude (14 vr.), to inaugurate the judgments of the millennial day. Daniel, vii.:9-10, also gives us a sublime prophetic description of the same event. And St. John, in his

APOCOLYPTIC VISION

of the "last times," depicts in graphic simplicity the fact, the manner, and the publicity of His coming. "Behold, He cometh with clouds; and every eye shall see Him, and they also which pierced Him: and the kindreds of the earth shall wail because of Him. Even so. Amen!" (Rev. i. 7).

There is not and can not be any dispute, therefore, as to the question and fact of His coming again at some time. Our blessed Redeemer has not gone to heaven to stay there. He has gone there for the benefit of His militant church, to enlarge the scope and multiply the blessings of His high-priestly mediation, "by appearing in the presence of God for us," "an high priest forever after the order of Melchisedec." (Heb. vi. 20).

He will and must return again in majesty and glory, not mediately by His spirit or providences, but directly in His own proper person, to consummate the work of His redeeming love in and for His people. Nor can there be any doubt as to a millennium or era in which truth and righteousness shall universally reign among all nations; "when all kings shall fall down before Him, and all nations shall serve Him" (Ps. lxxii. 11); "when the heathen shall be given Him for His inheritance, and the uttermost parts of the earth for His possession" (Ps. xi. 8); "when the wilderness and solitary place shall be glad for them, and the desert shall rejoice and blossom as the rose" (Isa. xxxv. 1-2); and "when the earth shall be filled with the knowledge of the glory of the Lord, as the waters cover the sea." (Heb. xi., 14).

The literal and personal second coming of the Lord, if we mistake not, is accepted by all

EVANGELICAL CHRISTIANS

as an indisputable doctrine of the Scriptures. It is not a mere dogma or idle speculation.

The differences in the theological views of His coming grow out of this question: How does the event of Christ's second coming, considered as an isolated fact, stand related to the scheme of completed Messianic salvation as revealed in the Scriptures? What is its true and essential place in the system of revealed truth, touching the "last times?"

We believe with all our heart that God's word places or puts this grand and momentous event at the end of the times of the gentiles, called "the time of the end" in Dan. xii., 9; and of which the present Christian dispensation is that part of "the times of the gentiles," called the "gospel of the kingdom," or the kingdom of God "in mystery," during which the gospel is to be preached to all nations "as a witness" of the truth, in order "to take out of (or from among) the gentiles a people for Christ's name (Acts xv. 14), preparatory to their admission into "the kingdom of God" in manifestation (Rom. xi. 25; and viii. 19).

We believe, further, that the second coming of Christ, as an isolated fact, must occur before the millenium, because the fundamental and essential condition causally of the rise and establishment of the Messianic kingdom in open manifestation. If these two propositions are scriptural and true, then the Messianic salvation in its completeness can only be effected by the parousia. But we learn from Col. I, 5 that the fullness of the Messianic salvation, the objective contents of the Christian's hope, "is laid up for him in the heavens;" and that

THE BLESSED RESURRECTION-LIFE,

"hid with Christ in God," will only set in with the parousia in the "future age," at the end of this age. Hear Paul: "When Christ, who is our life (resurrection—life), shall be manifested, then shall ye also with Him be manifested in glory" (Col. iii. 4). "For our citizenship," says he, "is in heaven; whence also we wait for a Savior, the Lord Jesus Christ; who shall fashion anew the body of our humiliation, that it may be conformed to the body of His glory" (Phil. iii. 20-21). This will take place at the parousia.

Moreover, Messianic sovereignty consists in Christ's universal dominion over the world and in the glorious fellowship of His believing saints with Him. "All authority hath been given unto Me in heaven and on earth" (Matt. xxviii. 18). "Wherefore God hath also highly exalted Him, and given Him a name which is above every name" (Phil. ii. 9-11). Again the Master says, "Ye which have followed Me in the regeneration—palingenesis—when the Son of man shall sit on the throne of His glory, ye shall also sit upon twelve thrones, judging the twelve tribes of Israel (Matt., xix, 28; Rom., viii, 12-18). See this, too, follows the parousia.

Pre-millennialism, whose inspiring and uplifting hopes we are to consider, requires, by the very nature of its sublime and awe-inspiring connections, that the true Basileia of Christ belong to the future eon, to be erected after He comes; and that the "ye shall be manifested in glory" simply means the glory of the Messianic kingdom in which believers, ready and "waiting for their adoption," shall in their glorified bodies be manifested visibly at the revelation of Jesus Christ, their divine and risen Head. Till the parousia this glory is "hidden

WITH CHRIST IN GOD."

If these cardinal tenets of Pre-millennialism be true, then we are also obliged to admit that the last sacred historical development in Christendom and in Gentile heathendom, antedating the parousia, instead of producing a millennium by the universal spread of a pure Christianity in the earth, will, on the contrary, embrace and present moral, social, and political phenomena of the most alarming and extraordinary character. Such as fatal and wide-spread ignorance of divine things. (See Isaiah, lx, 2; Hosea, xiv, 9; Rom., xi. 8-10; Rev., ix, 20-21.) General apostasy in the church from "the faith once delivered to the saints"—especially touching the Lord's imminent appearing. (2 Pet. iii. 1-4; Luke xviii. 8). The prevalence of religious formalism, adulterous friendships with the world, the abounding of iniquity, the waning of faith and love, awful and general revolutions and commotions among all the nations, resulting in tyranny, anarchy, destructive wars, famines, and pestilences without a parallel in the history of the race. (See Matt. xxiv. 12; Jas. v. 1-6; 1 Tim. iv. 1-3; Jere. xxv. 15-29; Luke xxi. 7-11; Ezek. xxi. 24-27; 2 Pet. ii. 12-15; Rev. vi. 1-17, etc.)

Christ the Lord must come, therefore, first to receive His church, the Bride, and then to establish His kingdom in judgment and righteousness.

Not until the predicted "fullness of the gentiles be come in," can we hope for the restoration of the Jews and their establishment as a nation in their own promised land, and their subsequent salvation. The mighty deliverer, who is to effect

THE SALVATION OF ALL ISRAEL,

(Rom. xi. 25-26), must come and first destroy Antichrist and bind Satan. In short, the two grand scenes which are eminently to characterize Christ's second personal coming, are the rapture of the church by her risen head; and the return of the Lord with His glorified church.

The scene of the rapture of the church is tersely and comprehensively presented to our faith and hope in 1 Thess. iv, 13-18, in these deeply impressive words: "But we would not have you ignorant, brethren, concerning them that fall asleep; that ye sorrow not, even as the rest, which have no hope. For if we believe that Jesus died and rose again, even so them also that are fallen asleep in Jesus will God bring with Him. For this we say unto you by the word of the Lord, that we that are alive, that are left unto the coming—parousia—of the Lord, shall in no wise precede them that are fallen asleep. For the Lord Himself shall descend from heaven, with a shout, with the voice of the Archangel, and with the trump of God: and the dead in Christ shall rise first: then we that are alive, that are left, shall together with them be caught up in the clouds, to meet the Lord in the air; and so shall we ever be with the Lord. Therefore comfort one another with these words."

The scene of the return of the Lord with His church, the glorified Bride, to judge the world in righteousness, and to inaugurate His glorious reign on earth, is most graphically described in the nineteenth chapter of Revelation. After portraying in sublime beauty the celebration of the marriage of the Lamb and His bride, "the Church of the first-born," St. John

WAS TOLD TO WRITE:

"Blessed are they which are bidden to the marriage supper of the Lamb." And now comes the vision of the Lord's return in majesty and great power:

"And I saw the heaven open, and behold, a white horse; and He that sat thereon, called Faithful and True; and in righteousness He doth judge and make war. And His eyes are a flame of fire, and upon His head are many diadems; and He hath a name written which no one knoweth but He Himself. And He is arrayed in a garment sprinkled with blood: and His name is called the Word of God. And the armies which are in heaven followed Him upon white horses, clothed in fine linen, white and pure. And out of His mouth proceeded a sharp sword, that with it He should smite the nations: and He shall rule them with a rod of iron: and He treadeth the winepress of the fierceness of the wrath of Almighty God. And He hath on His garment and on His thigh a name written, King of Kings, and Lord of Lords." (Rev. xix. 11-16.) With this brief and imperfect survey of the general field of premillennialism, we can not fail to discover many and cogent reasons why we are and ought to be profoundly interested in the Lord's second coming; and why in truth we are bound to place that coming before the millennial era, and the extraordinary events connected therewith.

It may be safely postulated, therefore, that there can be no millennium without the Jews. "For salvation is from the Jews" (John iv. 22). No millennium without a resurrection. No millennium anticipating the widespread and awful antichristian apostasy of "the very last days of this dispensation" (II. Thess. II. 8).

NO MILLENNIUM

antedating the establishment of the Messianic kingdom of God on the earth (Dan. vii. 13-14; Rev. xi. 5).

No millennium so long as the whole irrational animal creation remains "subject to vanity and the bondage of corruption" (Rom. vii. 20-21).

No millennium till the Christ of God and of the Bible, and of the church and of the nations, shall Himself return to this sin-cursed and sorrow-smitten planet, and here on the very theater of the fall and Calvary complete and consummate the work of His redeeming love by delivering the cosmos—the natural and moral creation—from the curse of sin, and by perfecting and finishing forever the reconciliation of the alienated universe with His Father, God; which divine work is and must continue in course of development until the parousia.

What, then, shall we say of the the practical influence and power of Christ's pre-millennial coming? If so many and so great things depend on the second appearing, personal presence, and glorious open revelation of our adorable Redeemer from heaven at the close of "the times of the gientiles," what ends or uses in Christian life and experience does it subserve? If this sublime doctrine is really the corner-stone in the base, and the key-stone in the glorious arch of our millennial hopes, how ought it to affect our faith and doctrinal beliefs?

Faith is for every Christian the means, the divine organon, by which he receives and appropriates all the blessings of life and salvation which we have in Christ, now and forever to come. This faith, therefore, must have in it the elements of an intelligent apprehension of

THE DOCTRINES OF SALVATION,

and of self-active perseverance. We must abide by it. (Col. i. 23). It must not only survey and scrutinize the past with an intelligent and penetrating eye, but it must clearly and definitely apprehend the present, and as with the spirit of prophetic discernment project itself upon the mighty future, and sweep its sublime horizon of oncoming events from the lofty eminences of true spiritual vision—aye, of prophetic inspiration itself.

Does the patient waiting, the earnest looking for the blessed hope and glorious appearing of the Great God, even our Savior Jesus Christ (Titus ii. 13), exert any directing and transforming influence and power over the Christian mind and heart? If so, what? Does it tend to magnify or minify the Christian's faith, hope, and love—those essential and basal elements of the Christ-life in us? Elements which are to survive the fiery and sifting judgments of the millennial day upon and against antichristian Christendom—yea, even the universal conflagration of St. Peter (II. Peter iii. 10), "in the day of the Lord," and to shine on undimmed amid the increasing and intensified splendors of the final new heavens and new earth.

Who will say that subjects of such infinite moment and such appalling magnitude, occupying so large a portion of God's own holy Scriptures, the Bible, and involving immortal destinies, can be matter of indifference to the church at any time! They are pregnant with spiritual instruction

FOR EVERY AGE.

How much more so for us who have so many cogent and satifactory reasons for believing that we are standing to-day on the very threshold of "the time of the end" of the gentile dispensation. If God's word be true; if a just and intelligent apprehension and anticipation of the most extraordinary and awakening coming events, "casting their shadows"—mighty and dark—before the vision of the watching and waiting Christian; and if a lively and animating hope of sharing in the approaching glory of Christ's openly manifested and established kingdom; do not furnish quickening motives and controling reasons for watchfulness, prayer, self-denial, consecration, earnest study of the divine word, and thorough preparation for the Lord's coming, then we know of nothing in the whole scheme of the Christian religion that is practically useful for personal edification.

Let us take illustrations from God's word. For there is, perhaps, not a doctrine of Christianity upon which the light of this great truth does not shine, and render more luminous and instructive by its own radiance. There is no duty in the whole catalogue of Christian requirements which is not invested with higher and holier significance in the light of this great truth. There is no hope which is the subject of Christian promise that is so uplifting and comforting, so rich in

PRESENT PEACE AND BLESSING,

so inspiring in times of trial and affliction, and so all-absorbing and abiding and illimitable in its glorious contents as this "blessed hope." St. Peter, in his discourse from Solomon's porch, urged the second coming of Christ as a prime motive for repentance. "Repent ye, therefore, and turn again, that your sins may be blotted out, that so there may come seasons of refreshing from the presence of the Lord; and that He may send the Christ, who hath been appointed for you, even Jesus: whom the heaven must receive until the times of the restoration of all things, whereof God spake by the mouth of His holy prophets, which have been since the world began." (Acts iii. 19-21. Rev. iii. 3).

It is also used as a motive to incite us to a mortification of earthly lusts. "When Christ, who is our life, shall appear, then shall ye also appear in glory with Him. Mortify, therefore, your members which are upon the earth: fornication, uncleanness, passion, evil desire, covetousness," etc. (Col. iii. 4-6). "For the grace of God that bringeth salvation hath appeared to all men, teaching us that denying ungodliness and wordly lusts, we should live soberly and righteously and godly in this present age; looking for the blessed hope and glorious appearing of the great God and our Saviour Jesus Christ" (Titus, ii. 11-13).

So, too, it is used to incite to general obedience and holy living. "We know that when He shall appear, we shall be like Him, for we shall see Him as He is. And every man that hath this hope in Him, purifieth himself even as He (Christ) is pure" (John, iii. 2-3).

AND "ABIDE IN HIM;

that when He shall appear, we may have confidence, and not be ashamed before Him at His coming." (John ii. 28). "For the Son of Man shall come in the glory of His Father with His angels; and then He shall reward every man according to His works" (Matt. xvi. 27. Rev. xxii. 12).

It is employed as an incentive to heavenly mindedness and holy conversation. "For our conversation (citizenship) is in heaven from whence also we look (wait) for a Savior, the Lord Jesus Christ; who shall fashion anew the body of our humiliation, that it may be conformed to the body of His glory, according to the working whereby He is able to subject all things unto Himself." (Phil. iii. 20-21). Seeing, then, that all these things are to be dissolved, what manner of persons ought ye to be in all holy living and godliness, looking for and earnestly desiring the coming of the day of God" (II. Peter iii. 11-12).

This hope propels us to works of mercy. "When the Son of man shall come in His glory, and all the angels with Him * * * then shall the King say unto them on His right hand, Come ye blessed of my Father, inherit the kingdom prepared for you.

* * * Inasmuch as ye did it unto one of these, My brethren, even these least, ye have done it unto Me" (Matt. xxv. 31-40).

Also to moderation and patience. "Let your moderation be known unto all men. The Lord is at hand" (Jas. v. 7 and 8). "For ye have need of patience, that, after ye have done the will of God, ye might receive the promise. For yet a very little while, he that cometh shall come, and shall not tarry" (Heb. x. 35-37).

It also excites to pastoral diligence and purity. "Feed the flock of God which is among you, exercising the oversight, not of constraint, but willing, * * * ; neither as lording it over the charge

ALOTTED TO YOU,

but making yourselves examples to the flock. And when the Chief Shepherd shall be manifested, ye shall receive the crown of glory that fadeth not away" (I. Peter v. 2-4). "For what is our hope, or joy, or crown of rejoicing? Are not even ye, before our Lord Jesus at His coming parousia?" (I. Thess II. 19 and 20).

It stimulates to greater watchfulness and prayer.

"Let your loins be girded about, and your lamps burning; and be yourselves like unto men looking for their Lord, when He shall return from the marriage feast. * * * Blessed are those servants, whom the Lord, when he cometh, shall find watching" (Luke xii. 35-37). "Take ye heed, watch and pray; for ye know not when the time is," etc. (Mark xiii. 33-37). "Behold, I come as a thief. Blessed is he that watcheth, and keepeth his garments (Rev. xvi. 15; Matt. xxiv. 43 and 44; I. Thess. v. 2-4).

It intensifies brotherly love. "The Lord make you to increase and abound in love one toward another, and toward all men * * *; to the end he may establish your hearts unblamable in holiness before our God and Father, at the coming of our Lord Jesus Christ with all His saints—parousia" (I. Thess. iii. 12 and 13: Phil. i. 9; I. Cor. i. 7).

It is of the nature of this "blessed hope" to kindle in our hearts earnest love of the Lord's second coming itself. We have a beautiful illustration of it in St. Paul. He says: "I have fought the good fight. I have finished the course, I have kept the faith: henceforth there is laid up for me the crown of righteousness, which the Lord, the righteous Judge, shall give me at that day: and not only to me, but also to all them that have loved His appearing" Epiphany (II. Tim. iv. 7 and 8). "Blessed is the man that

ENDURETH TEMPTATION:

for when he has been approved he shall receive the crown of life, which the Lord promised to them that love Him (James i. 12).

This hope invests our faith here with a higher practical value. It enriches it manifoldly during our earthly pilgrimage by opening wide its wings for higher and grander flights above the din and strife and trials of this fallen world. Hence Paul congratulates the church at Corinth "for the grace of God which was given them in Christ Jesus; that in every thing they were enriched in Him; * * * so that they came behind in no gift; wating for the revelation—apocalypse—of our Lord Jesus Christ, who shall also confirm you unto the end, that ye be unreprovable in the day of our Lord Jesus Christ." (I. Cor. i. 4-8).

The parousia, therefore, is the principal event in the future for which the believer patiently waits; because the event of destiny. For whilst performing our ordinary Christian duties so as "to walk worthily of the Lord unto all pleasing, bearing fruit in every good work; * * * and giving thanks unto the Father, who made us meet to be partakers of the inheritance of the saints in light" (Col. i. 10-12); we nevertheless in thus "serving the living and true God wait for His Son from Heaven." (I. Thes. i. 9 and 10).

Let us consider some other fruits of this patient waiting for "the blessed hope." They are eminently practical, and as potential as practical. What does the Christian more need in this world of sin and sorrow, of affliction and trial, of mourning and tears, than sanctification, and uplifting, and

INSPIRING COMFORT?

Whatever elevates and sanctifies the affections and thoughts, and intelligently engrosses them with an ever increasing interests and delight, is obliged to bring comfort and peace. If our hearts be filled with the assured hope of being with Jesus in His glory as His recognized and glorified bride, will we not seek by all possible means to be found of Him at His sudden coming without spot, and blameless, and in peace? And is not the thought of the near approach of the parousia, the personal presence of the Blessed Redeemer, eminently calculated to sanctify and comfort His people by raising their hearts above the world with its engrossing occupations and corrupting lusts? No wonder Paul closes one of his inspired descriptions of the opening scenes of the parousia thus: "Wherefore comfort one another with these words." (I. Thes. v. 18).

Our struggle with sin and the devil, our conflicts with the powers of darkness, our bodily ills and infirmities, our disappointments in life, the loss of friends and loved ones, the abounding of iniquity, and the prevalence of theoretical and practical infidelity, are often very discouraging to the humble and devout Christian. But if he be able to receive in his heart the sweet and blessed assurance that his Lord and Redeemer will soon come in person, and bring an end to all these troubles by the manifestation of His glory, and by ushering in the day of "the glorious liberty of the children of God" (Rom. viii. 21-26), how comforting, how elevating,

HOW SANCTIFYING

is such a hope! We are not surprised that it is denominated by St. Paul, "the blessed hope." Let us glorify God, therefore, by "rejoicing in (this) hope, being patient in tribulation, and continuing steadfastly in prayer," (Rom. xii. 12), that we may "hold fast that which we have till He come" (Rev. ii. 25).

Will my Lord return? Will He come soon? Will He come suddenly, "as the lightning cometh forth from the East, and is seen even unto the West?" (Matt. xxiv. 27). Will He come as my Savior or my Judge? Am I ready for His coming? Am I praying and patiently waiting for it? Has His coming such an absorbing and vital interest for me as to lead me to watch earnestly for it, to pray for its hastening, to look for it continually, to love it and anticipate it with cheerful and fond desire, and to keep myself in constant readiness for it by always "having on the wedding garment," and "oil in my vessel?" (Mat. xxii. 11, Matt. xxv. 1-13, Luke xii. 35, 36, 40).

My brethren, in conclusion I can only congratulate you as you stand upon the very threshhold of the consummation of the covenant of grace with respect to the militant church, and in the very atmosphere and light and quickening power of the dawning "day of the Lord," when the coming Son of man, "our elder brother," shall fully inaugurate the millennial glory of His kingdom on earth, delivering her, blessed be God, from her long and wretched bondage of corruption into the "glorious liberty of

THE CHILDREN OF GOD."

(Rom. viii. 21). And when all God's high and holy purposes concerning Judah and Israel restored and rehabilitated in the land of promise, as also concerning the nations of gentile heathendom and of Christendom, shall have been fully accomplished during the thousand years of Christ's personal reign in righteousness and kingly power; and after that He shall have put down and abolished "all (Anti-christian) rule and all authority and power," "with His enemies under His feet," and Death, the last of them, destroyed; "then shall He deliver up the kingdom to God, even the Father," and the millennial glory of His messianic kingdom, now our "blessed hope," shall then be succeeded by, and culminate in, the unspeakable blessedness of paradise restored and in the eternal glory of "the church of the first born" amid the splendors of "the new heavens and new earth"—the final palingenesia of the redeemed and glorified universe (II. Peter iii. 8-13. Rev. xxi. 1-8).

"He which testifieth these things saith, yea: I come quickly. Amen. Even so come, Lord Jesus." (Rev. xxii. 20). And in the near prospect of the apocalyptic glory surely we may ever more sing:

> Jesus, lover of my soul,
> Let me to Thy bosom fly;
> While the billows near me roll,
> While the tempest still is high:
> Hide me, O my Savior, hide,
> Till the storm of life be past,
> Safe into the haven guide,
> Oh, receive my soul at last."

"The grace of the Lord Jesus be with all the saints." Amen!

THE REV. HENRY M. PARSONS.

JUDGMENTS AND REWARDS.

The Rev. Henry M. Parsons, of Toronto, Canada, read the second paper of the warning, his subject being, "Judgments and Rewards." After congregational and quartet singing, and prayer by Bishop Nicholson, of Philadelphia, the Rev. Mr. Parsons read as follows:

The term judgment is often used in Holy Scripture to express the judicial dealings of God with men, as part of His government. As earthly governments always have the judicial department, so when the day of the Lord is spoken of as a thousand years, and the saints are said to judge the world, the whole term and the exercise of the functions of government are often included in the expression, judgment. The statement of the subject given to me limits the term to those occasions when rewards and penalties are declared. In this view we have three important and final judgment scenes, revealed in the Scriptures, and involving eternal gain or loss for those who are the subjects of them.

These three have also peculiarities defining and distinguishing each.

The first one is a judgment of saints only as to their deeds done in this life, for recompense or rejection, according to the motive inspiring them.

IT IS THE JUDGMENT OF WORKS.

It is described in II. Cor. v. 10:

"For we must all appear before the judgment seat of Christ, that every one may receive the things done in His body according to that he hath done, whether it be good or bad."

We learn from the first verse of this epistle

that it is addressed to saints only, and the manifestation at the seat of judgment is pressed upon all believers as the most urgent stimulus to fidelity and diligence in service for the glory of God. That this refers to deeds only, as to their motive character, is plain from Rom. viii. 1: "There is therefore now no condemnation to them that are in Christ Jesus." And if no sentence be upon them no judgment can be executed. This is plainly seen in the experience of the apostle, which is shared by all believers—that he had been crucified with Christ and in the eye of the law, was no longer alive. But in Christ believers are a "new creation" and "have passed from death unto life." The "life they now live in the flesh is by "faith of the Son of God" is Christ living in them the hope of glory. This shows that their state is everlasting life, the moment they believe, and that according to the word of their risen Lord, "They shall not come into judgment." (John v. 24). The time of this judgment for reward is indicated by our Lord in Luke xiv., 14. "Thou shalt be recompensed at the resurrection of the just." And this resurrection is at the coming of Christ for the saints, according to I Cor. xv. 23, and Thes. iv. 16-17. In the order of the resurrection given in the first passage, none but Christ's people rise when He comes, and according to the last they rise before the living, are changed into similar bodies, and with them meet the Lord in the air. From that moment they are "forever with the Lord." This manifestation of their works is for the purpose of receiving—"something from the hand of the judge—according to the character of the work, under the standard of judgment then to be applied. This accords with the idea of the judgment seat, in the Greek, a raised dais, from which the judge gave the crowns to the victors in the public games. And that these promised rewards then bestowed is seen from the vision of the church in the heavenly places given in the Apocalypse. (Rev. iv. v. vi.). This gives us the locality of the judgment seat. The epistles of the N. T. contain many allusions to this place of reward,

In I Cor ix-27 the apostle urges the control and subjection of all bodily

LUSTS IN THE CHRISTIAN RACE,

"lest that by any means, when I have preached to others, I myself should be a castaway."

The literal meaning of the Greek term is, "unable to stand the test," and the reference is to the test of his deeds at the judgment seat. Again, the same apostle, reviewing his life work, exclaims: "Henceforth there is laid up for me a crown of righteousness, which the Lord, the righteous Judge, will give me at that day; and not to me only, but unto all them also that love His appearing" (Tim. ii. 4-8). This clearly discloses the nature and object of this judgment. It is an inspection of deeds, with a judgment of their proportionate reward, or rejection. And these rewards or losses bear upon the position of believers in the coming kingdom of glory. Agreeing with this we find the glory and honor of saints portrayed in the preparation for the marriage supper of the Lamb in heaven, and the advent of the Lord on earth with His bride. And "to her was granted that she should be arrayed in fine linen clean and white; for the fine linen is the righteousness of the saints. This was her adornment for the marriage. (Chap. xix. 7), "for the marriage of the lamb is come, and His wife hath made herself ready." In their robes of office, the saints who have been glorified and invested with royal honors, come forth with their victorious leader and Lord, to introduce the next scene of judgment on the earth as predicted in Dan. vii. 22. "Judgment is given to the saints of the most high" (Rev. xix. 14), "and the armies which were in heaven followed Him upon white horses, clothed in fine linen, white and clean." Thus the result of the judgment is proclaimed. The future judges and rulers of the earth co-heirs with the Son of man, then enter upon the new field of service assigned to them.

That

THERE ARE DEGREES OF ADVANCEMENT

and glory among the redeemed is evident from our Lord's parable of the talents and of the pounds.

From this testing of works at the judgment seat will result loss as well as gain and reward.

Christ is recognized as the only foundation for life and for character, for power and for works. Upon Him and in Him the builders work. A test will be applied to all this recorded work. This test will be searching and sure. The motive power, "for the glory of God," in the state and actions of this present life, or otherwise, will be clearly distinguished and discerned in that day of sifting and testing (1 Cor. iii. 13, 15). "Every man's work shall be made manifest, for the day shall declare it, because it shall be revealed by fire, and the fire shall try every man's work of what sort it is. If any man's work abide which he hath built thereupon, he shall receive a reward. If any man's work shall be burned he shall suffer loss, but he himself shall be saved, yet so as by fire." Though the specific reference of this passage is to a distinct class of workmen, the principle applied is evidently the same as governs the decisions at the judgment seat. The last statement in the quotation, the salvation of the believer, without any works for reward, proves that this judgment is not of character in the persons judged, but of their works, and the test applied, "the glory of God" as the inspiring motive—shows there is no place for selfish exaltation; and that the personal righteousness manifest in their works flows only from the righteousness of Christ, by whom they are made just and perfect before God, antecedent to any and all works. It is in view of the manifest

MAJESTY AND GLORY OF GOD

at his heavenly tribunal that the apostle finds the strongest impulse to that consecration and persistent service, which secure the triple crown, of life, of righteousness, and of glory. In this related connection of the individual righteousness of the believer springing from the personal righteousness of His Redeemer is found the only ground on which sinners stand at the judgment seat. In Revelations, iv. 10, the holy throng represented by the four-and-twenty elders not only "worship Him that liveth forever and ever," but, in proof of perfect loyalty and absolute submission to Him in all their glory, they "cast their crowns" (*stephanous*, crowns of victors, symbols of all rewards of grace) "before the throne saying: 'Thou art worthy, O Lord! to receive glory and honor and power; for Thou hast created all things, and for Thy pleasure they are and were created." Thus all the works of all believers shall come into judgment. That scrutiny will discover to what extent they proceed from Him who dwells in the temple, the "hope of glory." The spirit of God in this connection urges us to cease from all uncharitable and unprofitable judgments of each other as co-workers here with one common Master. (Rom. xiv. 10), "For we shall all stand before the judgment seat of Christ," and (Rom. xiv. 12), "Every one of us shall give account of himself to God;" (II. Cor. v. 11). "Knowing therefore the terror of the Lord, we persuade men." The great apostle found in this fact the strongest incentive to self-judgment. The searching discriminations found in all his writings and teachings were adapted to make men tremble in view of coming judgment and sift their motives, lest in the day of reckoning they would be found unable to endure the test. No less needful is it in this day of laxity and departure that the servants of God apply unflinchingly the test-motive of the judgment seat of Christ.

II. The judgment of living nations

IS THE SECOND GREAT SCENE

of judgment, to which the Scriptures call our attention. This is recorded in Matthew xxv., 33: "When the son of man shall come in His glory and all the holy angels with Him, then shall He sit upon the throne of His glory, and before Him shall be gathered all nations, and He shall separate them one from another, as a shepherd divideth his sheep from the goats, and He shall set the sheep on His right hand but the goats on the left."

The subjects which have already been treated in this conference have so clearly defined the several relations of our Lord to Israel, to the church, and to the world that we need not dwell on the fact that the judgment scene already considered will be the introduction of the innumerable company of kings and priests, gathered from all nations in this dispensation, to the co-partnership of the throne of glory on this earth. This wonderful company will contribute the special accumulation of glory predicted of our Lord in Isaaih liii. 11, in return for all the travail of His soul. They were a covenant possession given to Him before the foundation of the world. (See Eph. i. 4, I. Peter i. 20, John xvii. 24.) They were purchased by His blood (Eph. i. 14). Their inheritance is co-heirship with Him, and they are in possession of it at the time of this judgment (I. Cor. iii. 21-23). All the circumstances of the judgment of the nations differ widely from those of the judgment seat just considered, and equally from those of the great white throne revealed at the close of the Apocalypse.

Those of the judged nations whom at His coming He shall set at His right hand are called to inherit a kingdom prepared for them "from" (not before) the foundation of the world. The expression *pro kataboles kosmou*—"before the foundation of the world"—found in John xvii. 24, Eph. i. 4, I. Peter i. 20, will

DOUBTLESS BE CONSIDERED

by intelligent students of the Bible to refer to the covenant of Horeb under which God is gathering His elect church to-day to fill the place forfeited by the defection of Israel. The different expression of the passage now in hand (*apo kataboles kosmou*), "from the foundation of the world," will suggest "the relations of the nations to the earth, as intimated in Psalms cxv. 16, and Daniel vii. 27. Another difference is seen in the terms of admission to the kingdom. The different parts of this prophecy, as seen in Matthew xxv., indicate this. For admission to the "kingdom of priests" we have the "wedding garment" (Matt. xxiv. 11-12), "the oil in their vessels, with their lamps" (Matt. xxv. 3-4), "faithful use of talents in service"

(Matt. xxv. 20-30). For admission to an inheritance in the kingdom of this earth at the judgment of the nations, the blessed of the Father receive their blessing on the ground of their works of mercy (Matt. xxv. 34-30), and the cursed are under the curse because they did not do these works. The ways of providence with the nations of the earth, are different from His dealings with Israel the elect nation, and also distinct from His dealings with the Church, the election from among the nations.

As Son of man, our Lord opens this judgment of living nations. This also determines the nature and the object of the decisions. The terms employed, "sheep" and "goats," imply an organized state of Christianity. The fact too, that this scrutiny is an assignment of the respective parties to their own place, in reward and in retribution, suggests that it must be after the "residue" of men, and "all the gentiles" have been

THE RECIPIENTS OF MERCY

through Christ as indicated in Acts, 15-16. In this case the scope of this judgment may include the millenial age which is still future and occurs after the satanic insurrection is quelled and the "devil and his angels" have been consigned to "everlasting fire." Another element in the retribution here declared should be noticed, "these shall go away into everlasting punishment." This certainly describes a state of existence, but the stress of the sentence to be executed, lies in the word "punishment." It contains the element of conscious suffering and torment as endured by those upon whom it is inflicted. This language is chosen by the infinite Son of God to express the divine thought and intent of this judgment sentence. The element of eternity in this retribution and reward leads us to consider it a final settlement with the nations, upon the ground of the gospel preached to them, during the period of Satan's restraint and brief release. The term "nations" is used, and can be used only of living persons. Hence this term separates this judgment from the one revealed in Rev. 20 12, when only those who are raised from the dead are named. The state of those rewarded is also eternal, and the welcome given them into the earthly and eternal kingdom may identify them with the nations spoken of in Rev. 21-24 as basking in the light of the New Jerusalem. "The nations shall walk in the light of it and the kings of the earth do bring their glory into it" (revision). As the Jews are to be the missionaries to the nations in the opening of the next age, and have preeminence among them as God's earthly people, it would seem congruous with the language of this prophecy, and with the substance of this judgment, that it should occur at the close of the millenial age. On this point, however, we will not speculate. The chronological data of the prophecies, the intervals between great and mighty changes are not in scripture so clearly marked as to the date of occurrence or length of continuance as to justify any positive assertions. Whether this judgment take place at the opening or the close of the next dispensation in the economy of the ages, its terms are exact and definite, its issues so tremendous and final that no one can fail to see the vindication of the holy character, and the impartial justice of the Son of man in His glory. The reward announces the glorious deliverence of this earth from the bondage of its oppressor, fulfilling the ancient promise, "The meek shall inherit the earth." "Come ye blessed of my father, inherit the kingdom prepared for you from the foundation of the world." Upon this inheritence the blessed will enter at once, and enjoy "life eternal." The retribution promised is equally decisive and definite. "Depart from me ye cursed,

INTO EVERLASTING FIRE,

prepared for the devil and his angels." This sentence is further described as "everlasting punishment." If words have any fixed meaning by which we may know the thoughts of God, this is a final settlement with those who are here judged and sentenced.

No intimation can here be found from the Judge of all the earth, that either the character of those consigned to this eternal state will ever change, or that the guilty can ever exhaust this sentence. If language can convey the truth of God's heart concerning anything He is pleased to reveal, nothing can be clearer than the terms here employed respecting eternal reward and eternal retribution. They are the words of the Judge himself. Absolutely they have the same import. The very same word is applied to both, therefore the terms of this judicial inquest must be held as absolute, authoritative, and final, by everyone receiving the Bible as the inspired word of God.

III. The last judgment is described in Rev. xx. 11-15: "And I saw a great white throne, and Him that sat on it, from whose face the earth and the heaven fled away; and there was found no place for them. And I saw the dead, small and great, stand before God, and the books were opened, and another book was opened, which is the book of life; and the dead were judged out of these things which were written in the books, according to their works.

"And the sea gave up the dead which were in it, and death and hell delivered up the dead which were in them, and they were judged, every man according to their works.

"And death and hell were cast into the lake of fire.

THIS IS THE SECOND DEATH.

"And whosoever was not found written in the book of life was cast into the lake of fire."

Several incidents in this scene deserve our attention, as separating this judgment from those we have just considered. 1. The earth and heaven are here said to flee from the face of the Judge, the locality, therefore, appears to be some point in space apart from our globe. This would not be incongruous. As we have seen the place of the judgment seat for the righteous only, was not on the earth. 2. All subjects of this judgment are raised from the dead for this purpose. They comprise all who have died in all ages of the race without God, without hope, and who have not been sentenced in the judgment of the living nations.

3. It is a judgment of character as enemies of God, as evidenced by their works. For this purpose the books of remembrance are opened to discern personal character from their deeds; "The dead were judged out of those things, which were written in the books, according to their works." This is very different from the purpose of inspecting deeds at the judgment seat. For then the object is to discern works for reward. They are to "receive according to that (they) have done." Here the object is to show the character, already formed, to be confirmed by their own deeds, and receive sentence accordingly. Nor can this inquest be confused with the glory-throne judgment, for there all the parties are living, and severally named "sheep" and "goats."

4. A special carefulness is manifest in this scrutiny, the most solemn and awful ever witnessed in the universe. The book of life, containing the names of all given in covenant before the foundation of the world, and, therefore, called the Lamb's Book of Life, is searched for the name of every one condemned by his works, to see if by any possibility that account can be found

COVERED WITH REDEEMING BLOOD.

Such painstaking accuracy can never be questioned throughout eternity. Never will there be found a mistake in the books of God. The sentence marks this as a distinct and final judgment. There is no arraignment and no pleading. It is, in fact, an execution of sentence before declared but now made public in presence of the whole universe. The terms imply the inclusion of all the wicked dead of every age. The sea, death, hades deliver up their dead, thus defining the fact of the body, though mortal and corrupt, having in it the seed of the resurrection body, and the spirit, though separate for a time, reunited to the body of shame and death. Death and hades are personified as enemies of Christ, and therefore allied with Satan, whom he has conquered and destroyed.

There is a most important sense in which this is a final and general judgment. It is a revelation of the eternal truth and justice of God in His dealing with sinners. The confessions of the guilty by their speechlessness when confronted with all their misdeeds—not one forgotten—will be the most eloquent though silent vindication of the purity and holiness, and eternal justice of God.

In a sense, all dispensational judgments are prefatory and preparatory to this.

Peter in his second epistle contrasts the deluge with this final day, and as we know that in the destruction by water every soul perished, so the purgation of the earth by fire may be going on at the very time of this assize (II. Peter iii. 6-7). "The world that then was being overflowed with water perished; but the heavens and the earth which are now, by the same word are kept in store, reserved unto fire against the day of judgment and perdition of ungodly men."

In like manner the judgment of the Red Sea and Sodom are set forth by Jude as examples, "suffering the

VENGEANCE OF ETERNAL FIRE."

This dread assize will signally vindicate the equity of all judicial dealings with the wicked, both men and angels. For the same writer declares that the fallen angels "are reserved in everlasting chains, under darkness, unto judgment of the great day." The place into which the persistent and incorrigible enemies of God are cast is called the "lake of fire." "This is the second death." When we consider the use of this term "death" in the word of God we find it applied to man while alive in his body and active in his mind.

In his native state he is "dead in trespasses and sins," utterly separated from the knowledge and the life of God. Separated from the present state he still has a character either in harmony with God or in opposition to Him. The first death separates each responsible sinner—either "to be absent from the body and present with the Lord," or to be "absent from the body and present in his own place." In both cases permanence for eternity is settled. If this be not the assumption—the assertion, and the conclusion of the word of God—then language has ceased to have definite meaning—and plain statements of facts are utterly delusive and misleading. All entreaties and denunciations are

FOUNDED UPON THIS CERTAINTY.

All promises and threatening run in this eternal groove. "As the tree falleth so it shall lie." (Rev. xx. 6.) "Blessed and holy is he that hath part in the first resurrection; on such the second death hath no power." (Rev. xx. 13, 14, 15.) "And they were judged, every man, according to their works." "And whosoever was not found written in the book of life was cast into the lake of fire." "This is the second death."

Another thought pressed upon us by these eternal verities of Revelation is that every judgment contains distinct recognition of personal character and responsibility in those who are judged as continuing forever.

The assumption made by some teachers of the Word, that there is ground for hope in the future, called the "Eternal Hope," either through restoration after ages of suffering, retribution, or of recovery under some future probation, is seen in the light of this judgment to be groundless, and therefore most perilous when insinuated or boldly interpolated within the lines of these judgment sentences. It is simply the old device of Satan. From the beginning he has both questioned and disputed the benevolence and the justice of God, in dealing with rebels against His government and sinners against His laws, until He has boldly said, "ye shall not surely die."

THE CONCLUSION OF SIN,

whether it be rejection of light or violation of law, is death (Rom. ii. 12-16). "For as many as have sinned without law shall also perish without law, and as many as have sinned in the law, shall be judged by the law in the day when God shall judge the secrets of men by Jesus Christ, according to the gospel."

And when we follow the sinner into that state where no mention is made in any revelation we have from God, of any second opportunity or privilege of hearing the message of mercy; when we know from the experience of the present life that no change of circumstances or external condition can cause a change of heart; when we know that continuance in sinning produces greater hardness of heart in whatever part of the universe it is practiced, and increasing guiltiness in the sight of God; when every word of the Bible shows that as long as unfitness for the presence of God continues, separation by reason of sin must not only continue but also increase; when we see the goodness of God in the grace of Christ, visiting all men of every age, so that they are without excuse in their sinful ignorance and rebellion, it would seem to be the madness of impiety itself, to tell men they had not had a fair chance of salvation, and more than that, to declare a future hope of salvation and mercy through Christ when this life is ended, would seem to be blasphemous contradiction of that "grace of God," that bringing salvation "hath appeared to all men." For nowhere in the words of grace is even "to-morrow" allowed the sinner for repentance. "To-day" if ye will hear his voice harden not your heart." This very day of judgment upon which our thoughts are fixed is made an argument for the instant repentance of all men. No one is exempted from the obligation. "But now (God) commandeth all men everywhere to repent because he hath appointed a day in the which He will judge the world in righteousness by that man whom He hath ordained; whereof He hath given assurance unto all men, in that He hath raised him from the dead." (Acts xvii, 30-31.)

The regular Farwell Hall noon-day prayer-meeting, attended by many conference members, was conducted by the Rev. Dr. William Dinwiddie, of Alexandria, Va.

PROFESSOR D. C. MARQUIS, D. D

ESCHATOLOGY, AS TAUGHT BY CHRIST.

Colonel George R. Clark, of Chicago, presided at the afternoon meeting. After the singing prayer was offered by the Rev. F. Osler, of Providence, R. I., and Professor D. C. Marquis, D. D., of the McCormick Theological Seminary, of Chicago, read the follow-paper on the subject, "Eschatology, as Taught by Our Lord:"

[Note—In the literal reproduction of Greek words in English text throughout this paper, the Greek letter "omega" is represented by the English "oo;" and the Greek "eta" by the English "ee."—ED.]

The eschatological discourses of Jesus, as recorded in the twenty-fourth and twenty-fifth chapters of the gospel by Matthew, and in the twenty-first chapter by Luke, have long been a source of perplexity and difficulty to the interpreters of Scripture.

The difficulty appears to be twofold:

1. To bring the two records of Matthew and Luke in harmony with each other.

2. To so interpret the record of Matthew as that it shall be in harmony with itself.

The common interpretation supposes that Matt. xxiv. and Luke xxi. are two reports of one and the same discourse, delivered to the same audience at the same time. There is, indeed, a marked similiarity between the two, amounting to almost complete identity in certain paragraphs. E. g., Luke xx. 18-11, is almost identical with Math. xxiv. 4-7.

Again, Luke, xxi. 29-33, is nearly identical with Math., xxiv. 32-35. But here the identity ends, and features of marked contrast appear.

1. Luke, xxi. 12, goes back and predicts a history that shall precede the events which have just been foretold—*but before all these*, whereas Matt. xxiv. 8, goes forward and predicts a history that shall follow the events thus predicted—*but all these are a beginning of sorrows*.

2. Luke's record makes no mention of the "end of the age," except to affirm (vs 9) that it does not immediately follow the earlier

COMMOTIONS OF THE WORLD.

He does speak (vs. 28) of a redemption of the church which is to be consummated in the beginning of a final tribulation. He also records (vs. 36) an exhortation to watchfulness and prayer on the part of the church that they may be counted worthy to escape this period of trial, and to stand before the Son of man.

Matthew, however (xxiv. 14) speaks of the *telos* as about to follow "then" *tote* upon the universal proclamation of the gospel of the kingdom. He also describes (xxiv. 29-31) the wreck of nature and the glorious appearing of the Son of Man, as about to follow "immediately" *eutheoos* upon a period of trial just described.

3. Luke xxi. 24 pictures the destruction of Jerusalem and its subjection to gentile sway as continuing until the times of the gentiles are fulfilled. Math. xxiv. 15-29 pictures an awful woe upon Judea and a shortened period of unparalleled severity to be followed immediately by the end.

4. Luke xxi. 20 gives the sign for the faithful to escape from Jerusalem to be the beginning of a military siege, Matt. xxiv. 15, gives the sign of departure from Judea to be the abomination of desolation standing in the holy place.

To harmonize these incongruities on the common idea that these are two reports of the same discourse delivered to the same audience at the same time is to my own mind simply impossible. One of the best proofs of its impossibility is the unsatisfactory result of all attempts to work out a consistent interpretation on that line. No commentator whom I have consulted, has succeeded to his own satisfaction, much less to the satisfaction of his readers.

Reconciliation seems equally impossible, too, if we suppose that the passages wherein these incongruities occur refer to the same event, or to the same period of human history, e. g., When Luke's record makes the woe of Jerusalem to be followed by its subjection to gentile domination until the times of the gentiles are fulfilled, that is one thing. But when Matthew's record makes

THE WOE OF JUDEA

and its unequalled tribulation to be followed immediately by the wreck of nature and the coming of the Son of man, that is another and quite a different thing. It is impossible upon any fair principle of interpretation to refer these two woes to the same period of the world's history.

The commentators who have proceeded upon the supposition that the woe of Judea described in Matthew is identical with the woe of Jerusalem described in Luke, and that both were fulfilled in A. D. 70, have ventured upon various solutions of the difficult problem. E. g. one (Morison in loc) finds a transition from the woe of Judea, to the scenes of the last times, in the *tote* of vs 23. He makes *tote* equivalent to *epeita*, and translates it "afterward." Thus, by making *tote* cover the whole of the period between A. D. 70 and the last times he prepares the way for *eutheoos* of verse 29. But this is certainly an unwarrantable use of *tote*. In all the many places where the word is used in the New Testament it expresses either simultaneousness or immediate succession; never indefinite succession. Another (Owen) makes the entire passage, even down to the close of verse 31, to be but a figurative description of the scenes attending the capture of Jerusalem by the Romans, although the glorious appearing of the Son of man is minutely described (verses 29, 30, 31). Still others give to the predictions a double reference (1) to Jerusalem as then existing and (2) to the scenes of the last days, but the attempt to distinguish the one from the other, or to find the double reference extending throughout the prophecy, only makes confusion worse confounded.

I see no reason why the two records (Math. xxiv., Luke xxi.) may not be understood as containing two separate discourses, the one overlapping and partially repeating the other. The discourse recorded by Luke may have been spoken either by the temple wall or on the way to Olivet.

IT WAS IN ANSWER

to the question of the disciples, When shall these things be, and what sign when these things are about to take place?—"these things" referring to the predicted destruction of the temple.

It begins with a description of the trials of the church in its earlier days—trials arising from the pretensions of false Christs and from popular commotions—with an exhortation not to be deceived by these for they are not the heralds of the immediate end of the age (Luke xxi. 8-9).

Instead of these earlier trials, indicating the immediate end, he declares (vv. 10-11) that the world's history shall be a story of wars, famines, earthquakes, pestilences, and at the last, terrors and great signs from heaven. In this brief paragraph (vv. 10-11) we find a succinct history of the world during the present age. For what is history, but a story of wars—nation against nation and kingdom against kingdom—earthquakes, pestilences, famines. The world's commotions, calamities, woes have always been and are to-day the world's great epochs.

Having thus thrust the world's whole history into a nut shell he turns back (vs. 12) and describes more minutely the experience of the church in connection with the nearer woes that are about to fall upon Jerusalem. "Before all these things"—i. e., before the historic scenes just described—certain things will take place. Then follows (vv. 12-19) an account of the persecutions that should befall the disciples in their first antagonisms with unbelieving hate—a prediction which was accurately fulfilled in the history of the early church. He tells them also of the destruction that would come upon Jerusalem, and foretells the sign that would warn the disciples to make good their escape from the doomed city. "When ye see Jerusalem encircled by armies," etc. This prediction was literally fulfilled in the escape of the Christians to Pella at the time of the siege by the Roman forces under Titus. The (vv. 22-24) he describes the awful destruction that would come upon the city and the scattering of the people among all nations, and the subjection of the holy city to gentile domination "until the times of the gentiles are fulfilled."

In that brief sentence "until the times of the Gentiles are fulfilled" is covered

A VAST PERIOD OF HUMAN HISTORY.

It carries us forward by a single step to the closing scenes at the end of the age. He has reached now the very point indicated at the close of verse 11—from which he had turned back—with the words *pro de toutoon apantoon*—to bring up the history more minutely.

Now, when "the times of the gentiles are fulfilled" shall begin (vs 25) the opening scenes of a great tribulation, which is to proceed to the wreck of nature, and to end in the glorious appearing of the son of man (vs 27). But (*de*, the Greek conjunctive, strongly adversative) the beginning of these awful scenes ought to be a time of rejoicing to the believing and waiting church. When these things are beginning to be, then wake, lift your heads, for your redemption is near. This promise, with its accompanying exhortation, points clearly and unmistakably to the separation of the believing church from the world as described in I. Thess. iv. 16-18. This separation of the saints from the world, we are told, shall take place at the beginning of the tribulation. While they are thus separate, in actual enjoyment of their completed redemption, the trial of the world shall go on, as it is here described (vv. 25-26). There shall be signs in the sun, moon, and stars, on the earth distress of nations with perplexity, the sea and the waves thereof roaring and men's hearts failing them for fear because of those things that are coming upon the inhabited earth. And all this commotion and confusion shall end in the final and glorious coming of the Lord; when Jude's quotation from Enoch shall be fulfilled: "When the Lord comes amid His holy myriads" to execute judgment. The beginning of the tribulation marks the time when the Lord will separate His people as foretold (I. Thess. iv. 16-18). Therefore, he says: When these things are beginning to be, lift your heads, for your redemption is near. The end of the tribulation marks the time when He will come with His holy myriads to execute judgment as foretold in Jude xiv. 15.

A natural question just here would be, is there any sign by which we may know with certainty the beginning of the tribulation? As if anticipating this question Jesus proceeds (vs 29) to answer it. The sign is the same in kind as that by which we tell of the coming of summer.

WHEN WE SEE THE BUDDING LEAVES

we may expect the summer, though if we had no experience to guide us we could predict nothing as to the time. Just so when we see these troubles, *ginomenia* in existence we may know that it heralds the near approach of the completed redemption, though, as we have no experience to guide us, we can predicate nothing as to the time. But we may be sure of this, that when the times of the gentiles are fulfilled, and the trials of the last days are begun, the redemption of the waiting church is so near as to fall within the limits of a single generation—*ee genea autee*—this generation. The pronoun is demonstrative, not intensive. This is decided, not by the accent (for that is no part of the inspiration), but by its position. It must describe the generation then existing at the time contemplated in the view-point of the speaker. If it referred to a generation distant from the speaker's view-point, *ekeinee* would be the pronoun employed. The only question, then, is what is the view-point of the speaker? That is determined by verse 31. He is addressing you who see these things *ginomena*, becoming. The divine prophet is standing in prophetic vision amid the scenes above described. He speaks to you, or you, or you, whoever may witness the beginning of these commotions, just as Paul said, "We who are alive," etc. To such he says: "The wished-for consummation will arrive before this generation shall pass away." The general truth taught is, the period intervening between the beginning of the tribulation of the last times, and the "consummation of the age" is very brief. The same generation that sees the sign will also behold the consummation.

The lesson to the church, in view of these disclosures, is not to let that day come upon you unawares. Uncertain as it must ever be as to when the final tribulation will begin, or as to which of earth's constantly recurring woes is the beginning of the final trial—the exhortation must be always timely to watch and pray that we may be accounted worthy to escape those things which shall come to pass. So watch against the excesses and cares of this world, as that, when the church's redemption is consummated, in the raising of the dead and the changing of the living, ye may be counted worthy of a place among the separated ones who shall escape the dire tribulation that has just begun, and be counted worthy to stand with Him in secure separation from those awful calamities which the world must undergo immediately preceding the final judgment.

This ends the discourse as recorded by Luke. Before

PASSING TO MATTHEW'S RECORD

it may be well to call to mind three well-known and generally accepted truths:

1. Luke's gospel was written for the gentile.

Therefore, if among the traditions of the apostolic church, or if among the written *logia* of Jesus, there was found a discourse which portrayed the future of the church during the times of the gentiles, we might expect that the Holy Spirit would direct Luke to incorporate that discourse in his gospel.

2. The gospel by Matthew was written for the Jew.

Therefore, if among the preserved *logia* of Jesus a discourse was found which gave prominence to the future of God's ancient people, as regards their relation to the kingdom of Christ, we might expect the Holy Spirit to direct Matthew to incorporate that discourse in his gospel.

3. The Holy Scriptures, both in the Old Testament and in the New, predict a future dealing of God with His ancient people of some marked and marvellous character.

The prophets are full of it. Paul, in the eleventh of Romans, reaffirms it. The Apocalypse foretells it. The past history and present status of the Hebrew people in the world is a standing witness that some wonderful future is in store for the Hebrew nation.

Bearing with us these three truths, we turn now to the record of Matthew.

This discourse was delivered on the Mount of Olives, in response to the question of certain disciples (Mark gives their names, Peter, James, John, Andrew—distinctive representatives of Judaistic ideas concerning the kingdom) who came to Him privately and asked when shall these things be, and "what the sign of thy *parousia*, and of the consummation of the age." The question contains two points which could not have been suggested by anything which appears in Matthew's record. The "*parousia*" and the "consummation of the age" could only have been suggested to them by their previous hearing of the discourse recorded by Luke.

In answering this question Jesus begins with a repetition, almost word for word, of the opening sentences of the previous discourse. (Matt. xxiv., 4-7.) It is a brief description (vv. 4-6) of the near trials of the early church, with an assurance that these are not the end. Then follows (vs. 7) an

EPITOME OF THE WORLD'S HISTORY,

Nation against nation, kingdom against kingdom, famines, pestilences, earthquakes. Just as in the previous discourse, he condenses the world history into a terse statement of the events which constitute the epochs of that history. So far the two discourses are identical.

But instead of going back as before, and portraying the experience of the church from apostolic days down to the end of the age, he goes forward, beyond the times of the gentiles, and sketches the history of the Jewish people during the tribulation of the last times. "All these—all the experiences of the church during the world history just narrated—are a beginning of birth pangs." All that has preceded, during the times of the gentiles, are as nothing compared with the sharper pains and sorer tribulations that are to come.

The prophecy from this point onward must presuppose, at least, a partial fulfilment of those ancient predictions concerning Israel which the prophets so often repeat, when there shall be a gathering of Israel in their own land, and this "gathering of Israel," Paul intimates (Rom. xi., 26), will be accompanied with a National profession of the faith of Christ.

In that condition this prediction of Jesus contemplates Israel, and foretells something of the trials that will then befal his covenant people.

1. The Nations of the earth will then be roused against them with a peculiar and deadly enmity, because of their profession of the name of Christ.

2. There shall be defections and betrayals among themselves.

3. False prophets shall arise and shall deceive many.

4. The intensified hostility without, together with the falsehood and treachery within will have a discouraging effect upon the professedly faithful.

5. But whoever abides faithful through the trial—without defection or apostasy—shall be saved (vs. 13).

6. And by their very faithfulness they will testify this, the gospel of the kingdom.

THE THING TO BE HERALDED

is the good news that the glorious Messianic kingdom, which the prophets long ago foretold and for which the fathers waited, is at hand. The same gospel that John the Baptist preached—the same that I preached (says Jesus), but which Israel has now rejected, and by that rejection the manifestation of the kingdom is postponed until the fullness of the gentiles is brought in—that gospel shall then be heralded in the whole inhabited world in the certainty of the kingdom's near approach—a witness to all the nations—and then (*tote*) the end will come.

The sure sign of the approaching end will be "the abomination of desolation, foretold by Daniel, the prophet, standing in the holy place." This is demanded by the connective particle *oun*. "When, therefore, ye may see." The *oun* connects this paragraph directly and indissolubly with the *telos*, which precedes. It points to the abomination of desolation as the unmistakable sign of the predicted end. Here, again, the interpreters who strive to locate this passage in A. D. 70, are widely at variance among themselves. Ebrard and Wiesler make *oun* to refer back to the first part of the disciples' question, which had reference to the destruction of the temple. But that part of their question did not ask for a sign. It only asked, "When shall these things be?" The sign is asked for in the second part of the question, and it was to be a sign of the "*parousia*," and of the "consummation of the age." So that, if we grant to the particle a connection so distant, it is still a connection of the sign with the end. Seeing this difficulty, Dorner regards *oun* as "introducing an application of the eschatological principles enunciated in all the preceding verses," though what those "principles" are and what the "application" is, he does not clearly inform us. Morison understands *oun* to point to an inference from all that precedes, "Therefore, flee to the mountains." These are but specimens of the many and varied attempts to dispose of the particle so as to locate the paragraph in A. D. 70. Yet the unbiased student of the Greek New Testament must regard every one of these suggestions as somewhat forced and unnatural. I do not think it either uncharitable or untrue to say that the poor little *oun* would never have been tossed about through

A RANGE OF THIRTEEN VERSES,

like Noah's dove, seeking in vain for a resting place, had it not been necessary to maintain a theory. The plain, simple, logical connection is with the *telos* which immediately precedes. The "abomination of desolation is the unmistakable sign of the end."

The "abomination of desolation" can not, therefore, be descriptive of anything that occurred when Jerusalem was destroyed by the Romans. It must refer to what will take place in the restored Israel after the times of the gentiles. In the midst of hostility without and treachery and apostasy within the faithful are warned that a sign shall be given when the nation must be deserted. That sign is "the abomination of desolation," foretold by Daniel the Prophet standing in the holy place.

Precisely who or what this is it would be unprofitable to conjecture. May it not, by fair interpretation, be identified with that man of lawlessness whom Paul describes as the final development of the world's wickedness (II. Thessalonians, ii.) and whose *parousia* is the certain precursor of the *parousia* of the Son of Man? He is to set Himself in the temple of God and proclaim that He is God.

When He shall be seen standing in the holy place then let the faithful separate themselves absolutely from all association or affiliation with their nation. Let them "stand not upon the order of their going but go at once" (verses 17-18). For then the tribulation will deepen until it will reach a point of dire distress such as never has been nor may be (verses 19-21). It is suffering so intense and terrible that no flesh could endure it if it were to continue long. But for the sake of the elect—(that remnant of Israel whom God hath chosen, whom John describes as the "hundred and forty-four thousand sealed ones (Rev. vii. 4-8)—the period of trial is mercifully shortened (vs. 22).

"Then," (*Tote.* As it is known to the believing ones that this intensity of trial is a predicted sign of the near approach of the Messiah King, it may be expected that the pressure of the trial will bring out pretended Messiahs.) if any one say, "Behold here, or there is the Christ, believe it not." (v. 23).

FALSE CHRISTS WILL BE ABUNDANT.

Some of them will be accompanied by supernatural powers and by wonderful tokens of a supernatural mission, so numerous and marvelous that even the very elect might be deceived, if such a thing were possible.

The ultimate developments of supernaturalism, the germs of which may be seen in spiritism, and mind cure, and faith cure, will then be rife and rampant.

But no matter where they may concentrate their influence and attempt to rally their followers, heed them not. If they send forth their proclamations from the desert, go not out to join them. If it be whispered that Messiah is come and is waiting his opportunity in secret, believe it not. For the *parousia* of judgment will be so open and universally visible that no one can be mistaken about it when it comes. It will be like the flash of lightning, visible from horizon to horizon, illumining all the earth. Just as the eagles light where the carrion putrifies, so judgment will fall where corruption is foul; and as corruption covers the earth, so the coming of the Son of Man to judgment will be everywhere visible (vv. 23-28).

But (*de* strongly adversative) although the judgment *parousia* when it comes will be so manifest as to leave no excuse for deception by any of the pretended Messiahs; it will be accompanied by signs peculiarly its own.

"Immediately"—*eutheoos.* This is a word with which the commentators have hopelessly wrestled. Morison says: "It has been a very rack of torture to such expositors as have lost their way." And he proceeds to verify his statement by losing his own way. Aug. Meyer says: "It may be observed generally that a whole host of strange and fanciful interpretations have been given here in consequence of its having been assumed that Jesus could not possibly have intended to say that His second advent was to follow immediately upon the destruction of Jerusalem," meaning, of course, the destruction of A. D. 70. If this statement means anything it must mean that Meyer would avoid a fanciful interpretation by assuming that Jesus could and did utter a false prediction. Others (Wetstein, E. J. Meyer, Owen,) make the entire paragraph (vv 29-31) to be but a poetic or figurative description of the destruction of Jerusalem by the Romans. But the visible coming of the Son of Man—the mourning of all the tribes of earth—

THE GATHERING OF THE ELECT

by the ministry of angels from earth and heaven—these things present a very bog of difficulties in which that line of interpretation becomes hopelessly mired. Others (Schott, Hammond) try to make *eutheoos* mean "suddenly," as if it were *tacheoos*, but that is simply playing with words for a purpose. Nowhere else in the New Testament does *eutheoos* mean anything else than immediate succession. Others (Morison) find a transition from the Roman conquest of Jerusalem to the last times in the word *tote* of v. 23, translating "afterward" as though it were *epeita.* But that is maintaining the integrity of *eutheoos* by falsifying *tote*, robbing Peter to pay Paul. Even if this were allowable it would not help the matter, because the tribulation referred to in v. 29 was described in vv. 21 and 22 before ever *tote* appeared in the text at all, and *tote* is only spoken for the purpose of injecting a warning against the pretended Messiahs of those days. The plain common-sense meaning of both *eutheoos* and *tote* can be retained, however, and the difficulties of the passage disappear, if we but accept the truth that "the tribulation of those days" is the tribulation of the last times, and that the abomination of desolation is a development of the last times.

Immediately after those trying days the whole framework of nature will be convulsed in the throes of dissolution (v. 29). The relations of the planets of the solar system will be violently disturbed. The very laws that bind material bodies to their orbits, and that hold them in relation with each other will be loosed. The powers of the heavens will be shaken. Then will appear the sign of the Son of Man in the heavens (v. 30). The flashing of His glory, the blazing effulgence of that ineffable brightness which radiates from His glorified person will flash over the heavens and illumine all the sky. Then all the tribes of the earth will mourn. The unbelieving world is roused at last to greet the shining of the glory of the Lord, as it blazes out amid the convulsive throes of nature, with one universal wail of woe and despair. They shall see the Son of Man coming upon the clouds of heaven, with power and much glory. Behold He cometh with clouds, and every eye shall see Him, and such as pierced Him, and all the tribes of the earth shall wail on account of Him (Rev., i, 7).

Then (v 31) the angels,

THOSE SWIFT MESSENGERS

of the providence of Christ, will gather His elect together from the four quarters of the earth, and from the utmost limits of the heavens. The elect of God, those saved through the tribulation and those saved from it, who hailed their redemption as complete in its beginning; the one gathered from the four quarters of the earth; the other, from limit to limit of the heavens where they have been with Christ during the heat of the trial standing before the Son of Man (Luke xxi. 36). All of them together shall be gathered to the side of the King. This is the *parousia* of judgment.

Before proceeding to describe the judgment scene itself he turns aside at this point to repeat what he had previously said in the discourse recorded by Luke, and, from what follows, it would seem that the immediate reference here, as well as there, is to the *parousia* of grace. Its sign is as the sprouting of the tree to the summer (verse 32). Its only sign is the beginning of the tribulation. From the time when the tribulation begins, until the gracious *parousia* that shall separate the believing church from the unbelieving world will be a period so brief as to fall within the limits of a single generation (v. 34). (See page 86). But concerning that day and hour no man knoweth, i. e., the time of the completion of the redemption of His believing ones, which is to come so soon after the beginning of the tribulation. It must always be uncertain which of earth's constantly recurring trials is the beginning of the final one. Therefore no man can know, and it is useless for anybody to predict the time. The angels do not know it. It is a secret locked in the bosom of the divine Omniscience, and the event alone will declare it. But the world will not be expecting it when it comes. It will be just as it was in the days of Noah. Then the people kept on living their accustomed life, eating, drinking, marrying and giving in marriage until the flood overtook them. So will be the *parousia* of the Son of Man, when His saints will be separated and His judgments will begin. Just when men are pursuing their accustomed life, planting, building,

BUYING, SELLING, TALKING POLITICS,

and building railroads the *parousia* will be present and the day of the Lord will begin. (vv. 37, 39.)

Then to illustrate still more forcibly, if possible, the absolute unexpectedness of the event, He pictures two men at work in the field. They are farmers, pursuing their usual occupation. One of them is of the number of the Lord's redeemed and regenerate children. The other is a child of the world. Instantly, in the twinkling of an eye (I. Cor. xv. 52) one is changed to the body of the resurrection and caught up to meet the Lord in the air. The other is left to share the world's tribulation and judgment.

Two women are at work with a hand-mill. If he had said baking bread, or working sewing-machines, or stitching embroidery, it would have the same meaning. It means anything in the line of every day occupation. One is a follower of Jesus The other is a woman of the world. Instantly, just in the midst of their conversation and work, one is changed into the the bodily likeness of Christ and taken with the risen saints to be with the Lord, the other is left to share the tribulation and judgment that are coming upon the world. (vv. 40-41.)

As this is the feature of the *parousia* that most concerns the church, and as the time of it is absolutely unknown and imminent, it behooves the church to watch, and to be always in an attitude of watchfulness. *Dia touto* (vs. 44). Be ye also ready, for just at the time when we think He is not coming, then is the very time when He will come. Our position is that of a steward whom an absent master has left in charge of a property. If we take courage in negligence by His delay and think to indulge our selfishness with impunity, the accounting will be unexpected and the penalty swift and terrible. We have proved our falsehood and unworthiness, and the space for repentance has gone by. (vv. 45-51.)

Then (ch. xxv., 1-13), by the story of the ten virgins, He illustrates the reception He will have from the church at the time of the *parousia* of grace. In ch. xxv., 14-30, by the parable of the talents, He illustrates the principle on which awards will be distributed at the *parousia* of judgment. Then (xxv., 31) He returns to the description of the judgment scene itself, which had been interrupted at ch. xxiv., 32. That is indeed the end. The only thing to follow is the everlasting punishment and the life eternal (vv. 31-46.)

There are four indispensable conditions of correct exegesis which must be constantly observed: 1. The meaning of words. 2. Grammatical construction. 3. Logical connection. 4. Analogical interpretation. I submit whether the interpretation herein outlined does not entirely satisfy the first three of these conditions.

1. The meaning of words is not strained.
2. Grammatical construction is not violated; 3. The logical connection is natural and consistent throughout.

Is the fourth condition also satisfied? That must depend upon whether the Scriptures teach a dual *parousia* (of grace and of judgment) and a dual dispensation (of gentile and Jew) as constituting the age.

It may be said that this attempt at exegesis lacks authority, as being outside of the current lines of interpretation. But if it has (as I believe) the authority of the divine word, that is sanction enough, for there is none higher.

THE REV. DR. ALBERT ERDMAN.

CONTENDING FOR THE FAITH.

In the absence of the Rev. Dr. J. R. Graves, of Memphis, who had been assigned to speak upon the subject, "Palestine Restored and Repeopled," the Rev. Dr. Albert Erdman, of Morristown, N. J., read the second paper of the afternoon on the subject, "Contending Earnestly for the Faith—the Apostolic Faith and the Apostolic Christian."

"Beloved," wrote St. Jude, "while I was giving all diligence to write unto you of our common salvation I was constrained to write unto you (at once), exhorting you to contend earnestly for the faith which was once (once for all) delivered to the saints" (v. 3).

This brief letter of Jude of only twenty-five verses is one of the latest, if not the latest, of the pastoral epistles. Though the date can not be

DEFINITELY FIXED,

it was written probably after the destruction of Jerusalem, and when most of the apostles had finished their work. It contains no less than eleven references to St. Peter's second epistle, and, like that apostle of our Lord, warns saints against the self-seeking licentiousness and apostacy which together with a mocking skepticism will characterize the last days, and which were already sadly prevalent before the close of the first century of the Christian era.

The writer, Jude, calls himself simply a servant or "bondsman of Jesus Christ, and brother of James," a beautiful modesty, for, in fact, he was the Lord's own brother, a son of Joseph and Mary. Mere blood connection is transcended by the grander relationship of faith in the Lord Christ and devotion to His service.

No intimation is given as to what particular people or church he was writing. The epistle has therefore a universal bearing, and belongs alike to us and the church of to-day. We gladly so receive it, even though it speaks so graphically of gross ungodliness and sin, for it also bears the singular and most precious address, "To them that are called, beloved in God the father, and kept for Jesus Christ."

It seems St. Jude had it in mind to write an epistle on the general subject of what he calls "our common salvation," but owing to the rapid and alarming growth of certain kinds of error, he felt constrained to defer the larger project for a more immediate and urgent necessity. I take it we all believe his sudden change of purpose was the divine constraint of the Holy Spirit. And yet how we would have prized a calm, studied

FINAL STATEMENT,

a summing up of the doctrines of grace and salvation, held in common in Jude's day.

But the Holy Spirit did not deem it necessary. He did deem it necessary that the saints should be exhorted to stand fast an[d] to contend earnestly for the faith which ha[d] been delivered to them.

There are those in our day who fancy it would be well if we could have a further deliverance on doctrine, what men ought to believe; if a system of moral and spiritual truth could be given more adapted to our times and circumstances, than it is thought the Scriptures offer. The notion is not at all uncommon, that the whole system of scriptural truth needs reconstruction, or, at least, restatement; and not a few are trying their hand at it. We are told that certain doctrines contained in the Bible, and which were well enough adapted to, and did service in the days of the primitive church, are no longer needed, or, at least, require modifying to modern ideas.

I well remember the shock of surprise, some three years ago, with which I read in one of the prominent so-called religious papers of New York City, that (I give the substance of the article) the doctrine of our Lord's premillennial advent, which the writer admitted was undoubtedly held by the early church, did well enough in times of persecution, and sustained the faith of God's people when the church was yet weak and struggling against mighty foes; but now, when the church has become strong and is on its world conquering way, such a doctrine is no longer of any use, being unadapted to a

TRIUMPHANT CHURCH,

and therefore whatever in the Scriptures seems to inculcate this doctrine must be interpreted in the light of modern history! With such a principle of interpretation the devil could drive a coach and four through any biblical doctrine whatsoever. It's as foolish as King Jehoiakim's pen-knife and fire-pot with Jeremiah's roll of prophecy signed and sealed with a "Thus saith Jehovah."

Now, it was against just such a faith-destroying, God-dishonoring error that St. Jude was sent to protest and warn. He quotes the very words of Peter, "But ye, beloved, remember ye the words which have been spoken before by the apostles of our Lord Jesus Christ, how that they said unto you: In the last time there shall be mockers walking after their own ungodly lusts," and so he exhorts them, "But ye, beloved, building up yourselves on your most holy faith, praying in the Holy Spirit, keep yourselves in the love of God, looking for the mercy of our Lord Jesus Christ unto eternal life." (vs. 17-21.)

He was not permitted, nor was it necessary, to write out an exposition of the doctrines of "Our Common Salvation;" he simply reminds them that "The faith," i. e., the sum of what Christians are to believe, had been "once for all" delivered to the saints, and they must stand up for it like faithful witnesses and true soldiers of Jesus Christ. They had received their orders; they had only to obey. They had got their colors, and they must defend them.

The key to this whole epistle, and the basis of the thought we are seeking to enforce, lies in the

SEEMINGLY INSIGNIFICANT WORD

"once" (hapax), or as it is more truly rendered in the R. V., "once-for-all." It is only a little Greek particle, but yet, as used here and elsewhere, of profoundest meaning. Its use is an illustration of how carefully the Holy Spirit guarded the very words, when "holy men spake as they were moved by Him." Instead of saying that the faith spoken of was at some time past given to the saints, as the ordinary reader of the common version might and probably does infer, the word emphasizes the fact that no other faith will ever be given. It is the only gift of the kind. It has been once-for-all delivered to the saints. No addition is to be made to it, or alteration in it. It is the foundation upon which the believer is built up, and "the foundation of God standeth sure." It is the "pillar and ground of the truth." It is all summed up in Him who is the Christ, the eternal Son of the Living God.

St. Paul, writing to the Galatians, said: "Though we or an angel from heaven should preach unto you any doctrine other than that which we preached unto you, let him be accursed." And he significantly adds: "The gospel preached by me is not after man, for neither did I receive it from man, nor was I taught it, but it came to me through revelation of Jesus Christ." (Gal. i. 8-12).

Although Jude had no time or was not permitted to write of "our common salvation," it is exceedingly significant that in this brief letter he refers to every fundamental doctrine, which in our day is assaulted, disputed, or denied.

In verse 4 he speaks of those, and warns against them who "turn the grace of God into lasciviousness," i. e., because salvation is free and the grace of God

EXCEEDING LARGE,

some take license from this to run into all excesses and fleshly indulgences. They also disregard the church and church ordinances, being, as Jude says, "such as separate themselves, sensual, having not the spirit" (v. 19). Again warning against such, Jude asserts the headship and lordship of Christ, for they deny, he says, "our only Master and Lord, Jesus Christ." And this necessarily implies the doctrine of the vicarious sacrifice of our Lord, for He is made "head over all things to the church" (Eph. i. 22), which He redeemed with His own most precious blood.

The epistle also indorses the Scriptures as the word of God, for it refers to scriptural facts and revelations and reminds us of "the words which have been spoken before by the apostles of our Lord Jesus Christ" (verses 7, 14, 17). Jude also teaches the doctrine of the Trinity, since with special emphasis he speaks of "God, the Father" of our "only Master and Lord Jesus Christ," and of "praying in the Holy Spirit" (verses 1, 20, 21).

The doctrine of a personal devil and of fallen angels is recognized as a part of the primitive faith, for the epistle speaks of Michael, the archangel, disputing with "Diabolus," "the devil," and of "Angels who kept not their first estate," who are kept "in everlasting bonds under darkness unto the judgment of the great day." (vs. 6 and 9.)

And so also the epistle teaches the doctrine of future retribution and eternal punishment, as the passage just quoted implies, with the one immediately following, in which the destruction of Sodom and Gomorrah is set forth as an

EXAMPLE OF "SUFFERING

the vengeance of eternal fire;" and again (verse 13), where mention is made of those who are like "wandering stars, for whom hath been reserved the blackness of darkness forever." (vs. 7-13).

In the "faith once for all delivered to the saints" is also included the doctrine of a bodily resurrection, as the judgments just spoken of necessarily imply, and as is further proved by the reference to "the body of Moses" (v. 9), as well as in the closing benediction, invoking God's power, who "is able to keep us from falling and to present us faultless before the presence of His glory with exceeding joy" (v. 24), which is singularly like Paul's benediction upon the Thessalonian Christians; "and the God of Peace Himself sanctify you wholly, and may your spirit, soul and body be preserved entire, without blame, at the coming (parousia) of our Lord Jesus Christ." (I. Thess. v. 23). And last, but not least, St. Jude dwells with loving emphasis on the ancient apostolic doctrine of our Lord's second coming. After quoting the words of "Enoch, the seventh from Adam," who prophesied the Lord's second advent in judgment upon the ungodly, he reminds the saints of the "words spoken before by the apostles of our Lord Jesus Christ, how they that they said, there should be mockers in the last time, who should walk after their own ungodly lusts," and who, according to Peter, from whom he quotes, will say, "Where is the promise of his coming!" (vs. 14-18 cp. II. Pet. iii. 3-4). And finally he exhorts them to be

BUILDING THEMSELVES UP

on their most holy faith, praying in the Holy Spirit, looking for the mercy of our Lord Jesus Christ (which, as the context shows, is to be fully manifested at His coming) unto eternal life" (vs. 20-21).

Now, let it not be said that these are mere inferences. It is unquestionable that all these doctrines and kindred ones were held and taught by the apostles of Christ, and it is equally demonstrable from Jude's words, his quotations, and references. that he had in mind these vital doctrines of "the faith once for all delivered to the saints," and which would all of them have received a fuller exposition in an epistle had the Holy Spirit deemed it necessary. Neither let it be inferred that Christianity—the gospel—is a mere set of doctrines, that the apostolic faith was a series of abstract notions about God and man, Christ and the church, time and eternity, heaven and hell, and that because once for all given we are "cabinued, cribbed, confined" to a mere creed, castiron, unchanging, and unchangeable. There is unquestionably a growth and development of doctrines—a philosophy of progress in theology, as in any other science. But that is one thing; it is quite another thing to say that the growth and development are in the truths revealed on which the doctrines are founded. There is no change in the facts, but in the fuller apprehension and appropriation of them by

THE BELIEVING SOUL

and the church, in a deeper sense of need and profounder conviction of the truths involved. A true science of theology no more manufactures its facts than does the science of geology. So far as either does this, it is a fraud and a lie.

We say then, the faith delivered to the saints—the "common salvation"—is founded on facts.

Christianity has this peculiarity above all other religions whatsoever, that it presents for our acceptance certain grand realities, certain great historic facts, which through their consequences to the believer, and the uses and application made of them, cease to be mere external facts, but become the warp and woof of a beautiful system of doctrine and life, of faith and feeling, of character and service. The gospel says Bernard is a life rather than a science. It represents a person, rather than a creed."

These facts are five principally: 1. Jesus the Christ is the eternal Son of God incarnate in human form, very God and very man. 2. Jesus the Christ died on the cross on Calvary for our sins, thus paying the price of our redemption. 3. Jesus the Christ rose again from the dead, for the justification of every believer. 4. Jesus the Christ ascended on high to send down the Holy Spirit, to gather out of every nation a people for His name, and to appear in the presence of God for us, making intercession for His people, being in all things their Head and Lord. 5. Jesus the Christ will come again in visible majesty to gather His own unto Himself in resurrection power, to bring Israel back to their own land, and to

FILL THE WHOLE EARTH

with His power, "like the days of heaven upon earth."

These are the facts—the sublime realities—of the Christian faith. And accordingly the church, the people whom Christ redeemed and sanctifies for His own peculiar possession, the bride of His heart and the glory of His ineffable name, as to origin is heavenly, in character is heavenly, in destiny is heavenly. Man did not originate the church or the faith which she holds. It is not the outgrowth or development of this world; its spirit is not the spirit of this world, and the hope of the church is not earthly power or glory, but is set on the grace which is to be realized at the revelation of Jesus Christ our Lord. Four of these great facts of the Christian faith are matters of history, but what joy fills the soul and what inspiration the life that holds them! The fifth and last is yet to come; but already we hear the roll of His chariot wheels upon the mountains; already the sheen of the insufferable glory illumines the eye of faith, and our hearts thrill with inexpressible longing. "Even so, come quickly, Lord Jesus."

Such, though but faintly expressed, is the faith which once for all was delivered to the saints. This is the charge committed to the custody and defence of the men of God. For it we are exhorted "earnestly to contend". It was of this the great apostle to the gentile wrote, when a prisoner in Rome, an old man, wounded and scarred, but a free man in Christ Jesus. Like the grand hero that he was, he exclaimed triumphantly, "I have fought the good fight, I have

FINISHED THE COURSE,

I have kept the faith, henceforth there is laid up for me the crown of righteousness which the Lord, the righteous Judge, shall give me at that day, and not to me only, but also to all them that have loved His appearing."

Brethren and friends, what sort of men did this faith produce? What sort of person was the primitive Christian? In considering this question, briefly, we shall still further understand what that faith really is. The text answers the question—he was one who, accepting the faith, believed it with all his soul, and therefore was ready to contend for it, to defend it, and testify of it, to die for it.

What was the pattern of the life of the apostolic Christians? If you will take the book of the Acts of the Apostles, or the letters of Paul and Peter and John, or better still, that wonderful prayer of our Lord in the seventeenth of John's gospel, the true "Lord's Prayer," in which Jesus forecasts the condition and character of His followers as they ought to be through all succeeding years, you will find three grand elements of character, which at the same time manifested themselves in a multitude of manly graces and God-like excellencies, viz: They were "in the world, but not of it;" they were constantly looking for and watching unto the coming of the Lord Jesus; and they were filled with a great missionary fire and zeal. So Jesus prayed for them and us. (John xvii. 14-20-24).

1. As to the first mark, unworldliness. We have such passages, words of St. Paul. "Here we have

NO CONTINUING CITY,

but seek one to come." Our citizenship is in the heavens, from whence also we look for the Savior, the Lord Jesus, who shall change the body of our humiliation that it may be conformed to his body of glory." To the worldly wise and proud Corinthian Christians he wrote, that they use "moderation in all things, for the time is short and the fashion of this world passeth away." To Timothy he writes: "No man that warreth entangleth himself with the affairs of this life." While John, writing to young men, says: "Ye are strong and the word of God abideth in you, and ye have overcome the evil one;" and says to all: "Love not the world, neither the things that are in the world."

The very metaphors employed in Scripture to designate and describe the Christian show what sort of a man he is to be. He is "a pilgrim," "a stranger," and "sojourner;" a sailor on the deep, greeting from afar the headlands of the hills of glory; he is a runner in the race, with eye on the goal; a wrestler on the sands of the arena, stripped and eager, his breath between his teeth, his body under him; he is a watchman, awake while others sleep, sober while others are drunken and careless; he is a burning torch held aloft to warn and guide the unwary; he is a soldier on the march, in the enemy's country, the color-bearer in the fight, the tallest man in the regiment, and

THE MOST CONSPICUOUS.

and he must "keep" the standard with his life; he is a martyr, witnessing a good confession, and like as not the crown he gets will be burnished in the fire that shrivels up his flesh and leaves only a few ashes to be swept away by the winds that fanned the painful flames.

2. Equally prominent was that other characteristic of the New Testament Christian. He was constantly expecting and looking for the coming of his Lord, the return of the King in His beauty. It was the natural effect as well as a helpful cause of the unworldly spirit. Being wholly given up to Christ, centering all in Him, remembering the testimony of those who had seen Him go up into Heaven from the hill-slope of Olivet, with His last great commission ringing in their hearts, like bells on the wide sea, they could not but gaze often upward, and amid toils and sufferings manifold listen for the sound of his coming again. It was the hope in their hearts, it inspired their lives, it transfigured the cross and shame and death itself. Every conceivable motive in the whole round of an exalted, splendid Christian manhood was taken from and associated with this one hope of the early Christian. We can understand now why and how they made so much of prayer, why like a fountain night and day it rose to heaven; we can understand their hymns of praise addressed to Christ Jesus Lord. We can understand, too, how short and clear and thrilling was their battle cry, given them by the Master himself, "Watch ye therefore, and what I say unto you, I say unto all, Watch!" For this they took the

"SPOILING OF THEIR GOODS

joyfully." If a man is on his way to meet the King, to receive a palace and riches untold, nay, rather if the King is on his way to meet him, to bring him into untold radiancy and glory, he won't be troubled much who takes his rags!

3. What has already been said will easily explain why the church of the apostolic days and immediately after accomplished so much for Christ and the nations as missionaries and evangelists and teachers, witness-bearers

all. Feeling that the time was short, and the Master's great commission must be fulfilled, so that He might be glorified, they went everywhere preaching Jesus and the resurrection, Jesus and the coming glory. No wonder that in a brief lifetime they had sounded His precious name to the farthest limits of the known world. Alas! how the Church has fallen from her high estate and illustrious calling. For though grand work has been and is done for Christ and His cause, yet how little does the Church take to heart the millions of unevangelized? How little does she seem to understand God's purpose. When God would draw out all the fathomless love of a woman's heart He lays a helpless babe on her bosom; to draw out all the passionate, burning love of the Church He lays on her heart the great crying, needy, perishing world of souls! It's not only the cause of the unconverted nations which we plead, but also the cause of divine power and truth which is hindered from descending to the tabernacle with mortals by low thoughts and worldly occupations. Hear how Edward Irving pleads, as he calls it, for the

PERPETUITY OF THE MISSIONARY

form of manhood." "Up, up with the statue of this character; it is high as heaven; its head is above the clouds which hide the face of heaven from earth-born men. The missionary is the hollow of that trump which resoundeth the voice of God. Let us reverence him, he is above us all. I wonder how any one can be so impious toward God, so cruel toward men, as to wish to obliterate one feature of his celestial character."

Such, my hearers, was the character of the early Christian, at least, such is the model presented in the word of God. Take your Bibles and see for yourselves if such be not the case. And now I ask, do you know of any intimation in the book—in the book I say—that all this was to be changed, and that, as is sometimes said and unconsciously held by multitudes, with the change of times and circumstances, a different style of Christian is needed! What other pattern of a Christian is there? What other model than that which the Bible sets forth? Has the truth of God changed? Has His purpose of grace and redemption changed? Have human sin and guilt and sorrow changed?

Nay, brethren, the conditions of holiness, the requirements of a godly Christian example do not change with time or circumstance. Christian life is not an isolated thing. Gospel Christianity has this great and blessed secret, that it is one and the same continually through all the ages.

THE SCRIPTURES,

which are God's thoughts in God's words, are not a collection of mere historical records and traditions, however authentic, but a grand unity of history, and doctrine, and prophecy—one living whole, having but one purpose, the eternal purpose of God in Christ Jesus. That which prophets, priests, kings spake of and waited for, that which angels desire to look into, that which we believe and hope for, that which creation groans and waits for, that which God has promised, and Christ bought with his heart's blood, is all one and the self same thing "that in the dispensation of the fulness of times, God might gather together in one, all things in Christ, both which are in heaven and which are on earth" (Eph. i. 10).

Men, brethren, it's a grand thing to be a Christian. This is life—"life indeed"—to touch interests that run the length of the eternities.

So soon as one is born again—from above—is filled with the spirit, he becomes in every sense a new creation; he steps into the line of all the ages of God's elect; he becomes himself a necessary factor in the eternal purpose of Jehovah. This is our honor, this our calling. "The faith once for all committed to the saints" is in our hands. Let us hold it, live it, "earnestly contend" for it.

Let Dr. Guthrie's favorite lines be ours:

> I live for those that love me,
> For those that know me true.
> For the heaven that smiles above me
> And waits my coming too.
>
> For the cause that needs assistance,
> For the wrongs that need resistance,
> For the future in the distance,
> For the good that I can do.

CANON A. R. FAUSSET, D. D.

A MESSAGE FROM ENGLAND.

The evening paper was read by Professor W. G. Morehead, of the United Presbyterian Seminary at Xenia, Ohio. The usual devotional exercises preceded the reading of the paper, William E. Blackstone making the prayer. Secretary Needham read communications from several people expressing the writers' deep interest in the conference. These gentlemen were the Rev. Dr. A. R. Faussett, the commentator, Canon of York, England; Mr. G. A. Pember, author of "Earth's Earliest Ages;" Mr. James E. Mathieson, of the Mildmay Conference, London; the Rev. Dr. C. K. Turbine, of Jersey City; the Rev. James C. Quinn, of Emerson, Manitoba, and the Rev. Dr. George F. Pentecost, of Brooklyn.

Canon Faussett wrote as follows:

TO THE MEMBERS MET IN THE PROPHETICAL CONVENTION AT CHICAGO, NOVEMBER, 1886.

BELOVED BRETHREN IN THE LORD.—Grace, mercy, and peace be to you from Him who was, who is, and who is to come. Absent from you in body, I feel as present with you in spirit. We are indeed, however, locally separated for a time, united in the one faith of Jesus Christ, the one love,

THE ONE BLESSED HOPE.

I do not even despair of meeting you sometime hereafter in the flesh, if God permit and the opportunity be afforded me, in your highly-favored land. Among the special signs of our times, not the least remarkable is the growing manifestation of the communion of saints. It is just when men's words are "stout against Jehovah," and the world's challenge is "Where is the God of Judgment?" that "then they that fear Jehovah speak often one to another, and a book of remembrance is written before Him for them that think upon His name," and presently follows "Behold, the day cometh." (Matt., ii., 17; iii., 13-16: iv., 1.)

The "gathering together" (episunagoge) for mutual edification now is the earnest of "the coming of our Lord Jesus Christ and our gathering together unto Him" (episunagoge found only in II. Thes. ii. 1 and Hebr. x. 25). The growing inquiry as to the blessed hope and the consequent increase of the knowledge of beliefs respecting it are evidently fulfilling Daniel's prophecy as to "the time of the end"—"many shall run to and fro, and the knowledge (so the Hebrew) shall be increased."

How shall the inquiry be conducted so as to elicit real fruit to the glory of God and the edification of His children? If I venture to suggest an answer it is with a deep consciousness of my own imperfection of vision in

THE DEEP THINGS OF GOD.

First, then, let us search the word of prophecy in the spirit of prayer for heavenly illumination by God the Holy Ghost, and not suffer our imaginations or preconceived theories to turn us aside from the straight path. Let us not take one step in advance, save as we are led on by the written word and the Holy Spirit. Loving tolerance of the opinions of others and a readiness to weigh their arguments from Scripture in a fair balance, and the maintenance of our own views in an humble and undogmatic spirit will best tend to the decision of controverted points and the building up of one another in our most holy faith.

In examining Scripture, my own plan has been, first, to investigate the literal and grammatical sense of each passage, then the context, then the circumstance of time and place, and the immediate aim of the sacred writer; then the ultimate and far-reaching meaning designed by the Holy Ghost, remembering that "the testimony of Jesus is the spirit of prophecy;" finally, the spiritual application to the present elect Church, and each member of it. Augustine well says: "The literal sense of Scripture is the basis of the Scripture, else the latter would be a building resting on air." Another canon to be observed is the promises so full and so glorious to Israel throughout the Old Testament and in the Gospels, Acts, and especially Romans, xi, are to be interpreted in their plain, literal sense. It is clearly erroneous to interpret the curses pronounced against Israel, if disobedient, in

THEIR LITERAL SENSE,

and then to spiritualize the blessings foretold to Israel in the last days, and to appropriate them to the present election church; in fact, to keep the good all to ourselves and to give them the evil.

The order of events is defined for us in Isaiah lxi. 1-9, the passage which formed our Lord's text in the sermon at Nazareth: 1. He declares His own credentials and present mission, "The Spirit of the Lord God is upon Me, because He hath annointed Me to preach good tidings, to proclaim the acceptable year of the Lord" Here He stopped in the middle of a sentence, at the words which mark the limit of our parenthetical dispensation of the spiritual elect church. The next event will be His personal coming to complete the sentence by ushering in "the day of vengeance of our God" upon apostate Christendom, as is also foretold in II. Thess. i. 8: "In flaming fire taking vengeance on they that obey not the gospel of our Lord Jesus Christ." Next, He comes "to comfort them that mourn in Zion, to give them beauty for ashes;" as is also foretold in Zech. xii. 10: "I will pour upon the inhabitants of Jerusalem the spirit of

GRACE AND SUPPLICATION,

and they shall look upon Me whom they have pierced and they shall mourn." "In that day there shall be a fountain opened to the inhabitants of Jerusalem for sin and uncleanness. Behold, the day of the Lord cometh; then shall the Lord go forth and fight against those nations that shall have attacked Jerusalem, and His feet shall stand upon the Mount of Olives, and the Lord my God shall come and all His saints with Thee." Thus shall be ushered in the millennial kingdom, wherein "the Jews shall be named the priests of Jehovah" to the gentile nations, and "they shall call Jerusalem the throne of Jehovah, and all the nations shall be gathered unto it" (Jer. iii. 17).

If, as post-millennarians think, a thousand years must elapse before our Lord's coming, the hope of His coming must practically cease to be what Holy Scripture represents it—the incentive to every Christian grace. The early Christian fathers, Clement, Ignatius, Justin Martyr, and Irendus, looked for the Lord's speedy return as the necessary precursor of the millennial kingdom. Not until the professing church lost her first love, and became the harlot resting on the world-power, did she cease to be the bride going forth to meet the bridegroom, and sought to reign already on earth without waiting for His advent.

So far from the world becoming more and more Christ-like as the age advances, its culture, science, fashions, and spirit, are becoming more earthy, and less like the blessed state foretold as about to

CHARACTERIZE THE MILLENIUM.

This may be a stumbling block to the post-millennarian's faith, but it is a strong confirmation of the premillennarian's expectation. For the fact exactly answers to the prophecy. The Lord foretold, "This gospel shall be preached for a witness unto all nations, and then shall the end come." Not that all were to be converted, and the nations christianized before His coming, but "God has visited the gentiles to take out of them a people unto His name" (Acts xv. 14). All scripture points to apostasy as about to prevail till the Lord shall come to sweep it away by the brightness of His appearing. (II. Thes I x II). The days before the flood are, according to our Lord, the analogue to "the last days." It was when the barrier between the church and the world was broken down by the intermarriage of the sons of God with the daughters of men, the salt lost its savour and was trodden under foot of men, and universal corruption set in. Is not intense worldliness the distinguishing feature of our age? There is a consequent tendency to relapse to heathenism, cultured and refined, it is true, but still heathenism. If you compare the black catalogue of Pagan Sins in Romans i. with that of the "last days" in II. Tim. iii., you would find five of the latter

IDENTICAL IN THE GREEK

with the former, and five more virtually the same in both. "Disobedience" to parents is prominent in each, and in combination with "naughtiness and boastfulness" engenders that lawlessness, foretold in Dan. vii. viii. xi. and Mstth. xxiv. 12, and II. Thes. ii., and already potent on every side.

Spiritualism so-called, which is really necromancy and demon-consultation, is the darkest feature of our times. St. Paul in II. Tim. iii. foretells, that as the magician, Jannese, and Jambres withstood Moses, so the reprobates concerning the faiths withstood the truth. Already the beast God-opposed world is stripping Babylon, the harlot-church, of its possessions, in fulfilment of Rev. xvii.: When God shall have thus fully executed judgment on her, then the three froglike spirits of demons, working spiritualistic miracles, "shall gather the kings of the earth to the war of that great day of the Almighty God (Rev. xvi. 13-14). Then shall the last Antichrist, denying the Father and the Son, be revealed in full malignity.

But his reign is very brief. From the first he is "the son of perdition," doomed to immediate destruction. The darkest hours shall usher in the bright and morning star.

Let us then gird up the loins of our mind, be sober, and hope to the end for the grace to be brought at the revelation of Jesus Christ.

The remarkable outpourings of the holy spirit in connection with evangelistic efforts on every side are hastening the completion of the elect church, and when thereby the "fullness of the gentiles" shall have come in, the Lord will come for His saints, and subsequently come with His saints to reign over Jerusalem and nations "in the regeneration."

Having this hope in Him, dear brethren, lift up your heads, for your redemption draweth nigh.

Praying that your conference may be blessed to yourselves, and through you to the church and world, I am your faithful and respectful brother in the common faith and hope.

ANDREW ROBERT FAUSSET, D. D.,
Canon of York.

PROFESSOR W. G. MOREHEAD.

THE ANTICHRIST.

Prayer was offered by the Rev. Dr. West, of St. Paul, and Professor W. G. Morehead, of Xenia, Ohio, then addressed the conference as follows upon the subject, "The Antichrist;"

That the Scriptures predict the appearing of a powerful foe of the people and cause of God can not be doubted. Enemies, great in number and in might, there have been and there are; for it seems to be the fortune of truth ever to encounter the most determined opposition. But that an evil power should arise who should be pre-eminently the antagonist of the Lord Jesus Christ, whose awful acts of wickedness and heights of blasphemy should surpass all others, every believing reader of the Bible well knows.

The voices of the prophets and apostles unite in announcing the advent of this adversary. Daniel speaks of it in language which betokens the deep interest the spirit of prophecy takes in the subject: "After this I saw in the night visions, and, behold!

a fourth beast, dreadful and terrible, and strong exceedingly; and it had great iron teeth: it devoured and brake in pieces, and stamped the residue with the feet of it; and it was diverse from all the beasts that were before it; and it had ten horns. I considered the horns, and, behold, there came up among them another little horn, before which there were three of the first horns plucked up by the roots; and behold, in this horn were eyes like the eyes of a man, and a mouth speaking great things. I beheld till the thrones were placed, and one that was Ancient of Days did sit; his raiment was white as snow, and the hair of his head like pure wool; his throne was fiery flames, and the wheels thereof burning fire. A fiery stream issued and came forth from before him; thousand thousands ministered unto him, and ten thousand times ten thousand stood before him; the judgment was set, and the books were opened. I beheld then, because of the voice of the great words which the horn spake; I beheld even till the beast was slain, and his body destroyed, and he was given to be burned with fire" (Dan. vii. 7-11).

In terms as graphic and portentous as those of Daniel, the Apostle Paul describes a like adversary: "Let no man deceive you by any means; for that day shall not come, except there come the falling away first, and the man of sin be revealed,

THE SON OF PERDITION,

he who opposeth and exalted himself against all that is called God or that is worshiped so that he sitteth in the temple of God, setting himself forth as God. Remember ye not that, when I was yet with you, I told you these things? And now ye know that which restraineth, to the end that He may be revealed in His own season. For the mystery of lawlessness doth already work; only there is one that restraineth now, until He be taken out of the way. And then shall be revealed the lawless one, whom the Lord Jesus shall slay with the breath of his mouth, and bring to nought by the manifestation of His coming; even He, whose coming is according the working of Satan with all power and signs and lying wonders, and with all deceit of unrighteousness in them that are perishing." (II. Thess. ii. 3-10).

A still more circumstantial account of a like adversary is found in the book of Revelation, an account which gathers into itself all that has been communicated on the dark theme in the word of God. (Rev. xiii., xvii., xix.)

What is thus minutely pictured in the inspired utterances of Daniel, Paul, and John is foreshadowed by other prophets and apostles. There are preintimations of this great evil power running parallel with the predictions and promises concerning the seed of the woman and the Messiah of the chosen people. In every murderous oppressor and son of Belial that came or was to come upon the field of history in opposition to the children of God inspired men saw the precursors of the final enemy who shall afflict and waste Jehovah's heritage. This is a characteristic feature of prophecy; is woven into its organic structure. As the prophets saw in Moses and Joshua, in David and Solomon, the fore-intimations and types of that great and final Savior and Conqueror to come, the Lord Jesus Christ, and in the theocracy of Israel the shadow of the perfected Kingdom of God, so in pre-eminently bad men, in Cain and Nimrod, in Pharaoh and Balaam, and Antiochus Epiphanes, and in the persecuting kingdoms of Egypt, Assyria, and Babylon, they saw the image of the final enemy, the picture of the last persecuting world-power. The shadow was projected before. "Prophecy,"

DELITZSCH SAYS,

"is apotelesmatic." It fixes its gaze on the end; it dips its brush in the colors which pertain to the end. All good tends toward and finds its climax in Him who alone is the absolute good. All evil likewise tends toward a centralization and culmination in some colossus of sin and crime. And it would seem that the Spirit of God in His delineations of the course and progress of evil ever keeps looking forward to its consummation in the last and most frightful form which human apostacy assumes, viz.: the Antichrist. This is our theme—a forbidding one assuredly, but one upon which the word of God has spoken in the fullest and most emphatic manner.

It is scarcely needful to remark that upon the general subject there has been a very whirl of theory, conjecture, argument, and exposition. We have here the three great schools of interpreters represented, the preterist, the presentist, and the futurist; for the question of the Antichrist correlates itself with the other questions which arise in the field of prophecy—with the church, Israel, the coming of the Lord, and the establishment of the promised kingdom. By some, Antichrist is identified with a person or a system that long since appeared in the world and passed away. By others, he is now upon the stage of action awaiting the doom his sins and crimes so justly merit. By others still, Antichrist is regarded as yet to come; that while he has had and now has his forerunners who prepare for him his way, himself is still to appear. It would require a volume of considerable size merely to report the literature on the general topic

In such a maze and labyrinth of conflicting opinion it behooves the student of the prophetic word to move with guarded steps and earnest circumspection. His first and main effort should be to grasp the mighty outlines of the prophecies touching this adversary, with no attempt to master the details.

HE SHOULD FIX A STEADY GAZE

upon the mountain ranges and lofty peaks, leaving the while unscanned the intervening valleys and profound abysses. His mainly should be the survey of the continent, its boundaries, and conformation, with no effort to trace every stream and lake and watershed of the interior. The first instrument he should employ is the telescope, not the microscope. Adhering to the method of investigation thus indicated, let us (1) determine the import of the word.

The term Antichrist is a scriptural one; four times it occurs in the New Testament, (I. John ii. 18-22; iv. 3; II. John vii). In a general epistle, written to no particular church, but to a wide circle of churches, the apostles make this remarkable statement: "Little children, it is the last time; and as we have heard that Antichrist shall come, even now are there many Antichrists; whereby we know that it is the last time." It is obvious from this language that the Christians of John's day were acquainted with the coming of the Antichrist. They had "heard" about it. It formed part of the common instruction of believers. It was distinct and prominent in the writings of the prophets, and it was among the teachings of Christ, and those sent to preach and teach in His name. Thus Paul in writing to the Thessalonians of the man of sin reminds them of his instruction on the subject during his brief visit to them: "Remember ye not that while I was yet with you I told these things?" The apostles were not dumb as to the last times. Eschatology formed no small part of the message they proclaimed. With the blessed gospel of the grace of God which they preached they intermingled solemn warnings of a future apostacy and the

APPEARING OF THE ADVERSARY

who shall meet his doom at the hands of the Son of God Himself. They, therefore, who earnestly give themselves to such studies for their own instruction and for that of their fellows have for their encouragement and comfort apostolic precedent and authority.

In the word Antichrist there is a measure of ambiguity, for the preposition "anti," when compounded with a substantive, in the Greek language, may signify either "instead of" or "against." There are those who see in the word no more than a counterfeit Christ. Thus, Mr. Greswell, whose learning and impartiality none will dispute, conceives of it: "Antichrist signifies neither more nor less than another Christ; a pro-Christ; a vice-Christ; an alter Christus; a pretender to the name of Christ, who in every circumstance of personal distinction that can contribute to determine the individuality of the real Christ, appears to be, and sets himself up as the counterpart of the true." Thus likewise a living writer, whose books are largely read, expresses himself: "The name itself means, not as is sometimes asserted, an avowed antagonist of Christ, but one professing to be a vice-Christ, a rival Christ, one who would assume the character, occupy the place, and fulfill the functions of Christ."

"Antichrist," however, designates more than a pretender to the Messianic office. There is another term in Greek, which means a false Christ, viz: *Pseudo-christos*—a word our Lord employs in Matt. xxiv., 24. Huther's definition of "anti" compounded is exact; it "denotes a subject, whether person or thing, opposing a subject of the same kind." Thus, *antistrategos* is not only a vice general, but one who opposes another general; *anti philosophos* is a philosopher who opposes other philosophers; just as anti-pope with us is not only a rival pope, but the enemy of another pope. In the term Antichrist there is the idea both of

COUNTERFEITING AND ANTAGONIZING

Christ. In this sense it embodies an important truth. That hostility is really formidable in which the adversary preserves the semblance of the characteristic excellence which he opposes.

But whatever meaning the etymology of the word may yield, the fact is not to be ignored that the Antichrist is described in Scripture as the determined enemy of the Savior. It is in accordance with the design of John in his epistles to represent him as the counterfeit of the Lord; for he there deals rather with the spirit and principle of the adversary than with his character and personality. But in the apocalypse the same inspired writer exhibits the beast as pre-eminently the foe of Christ, as one whose sole aim, purpose, and hope it is to extinguish the name and annihilate the person of Christ. So, too, Paul describes him naming him the *antikeimenos*, the opposer, the antagonist of God. A two-fold idea, therefore, inheres in the name which the word of God gives to the adversary; he counterfeits Christ—a blasphemer; he fights against Christ—a hostile power.

II. Identity of the prophecies of Daniel, Paul, and John, that relate to the Antichrist. Reference is had to Dan. vii. 2, Thess. ii., and Rev. xiii. Among evangelical expositors the consensus is almost universal that one and the same evil power is predicted by all. The tremendous portrait is one, although each account has features and lineaments peculiar to itself. By bringing them together the unity of the description and the magnitude of the subject are apparent. The grounds for the identification of these prophecies are moral and historical, ample, and conclusive. The symbols employed by Daniel and John are identical. In both it is a beast.

A RAPACIOUS WILD BEAST

that appears in the field of prophetic vision. Daniel sees four beasts emerging from the sea in succession; but it is on the fourth in the series that interest and attention concentrate; the fourth that for savage ferocity surpasses the others. John's beast combines in itself the characteristic features of all that Daniel saw. It had the form of a leopard, the feet of a bear, and the mouth of a lion. In both the beast arises from the sea, and is a horrible nondescript, a fierce monster with ten horns.

There is no mistaking the significance of the symbol. It is a pictorial representation of the political sovereignty of the world. So the prophets themselves interpret; the "beast" is a "king" and a "kingdom." He has horns, and horns are the symbols of power. He has diadems on his horns, and diadems are the badges of regal dominion. Clearly it is the God-oppressing power of the world that is meant. Nor should the symbol of a beast to represent imperial sovereignty be thought arbitrary or grotesque. The world powers themselves have furnished the example. The dragon, the lion, the bear, and the eagle are emblems emblazoned on the escutcheons and stamped upon the coins of the nations of to-day.

1. The moral features of the adversary in the three prophecies are identical. By all he is invested with transcendent powers. The little horn of Dan. vii., which masters the great beast and becomes his governing and guiding mind, "has eyes like the eyes of a man." Predominant intellect, dazzling intelligence, power to know men and to sway them, distinguish him.. An so we are told

"HE UNDERSTANDETH DARK SENTENCES;"

"he shall practice and prosper;" "and through his policy also he shall cause craft to prosper in his hand," (Dan. viii. 23-25). The beast of the Apocalypse is quite similar. By his prime minister, the false prophet, "he doeth great wonders, so that he maketh fire come down from heaven on the earth in the sight of men, and deceiveth them that dwell on the earth," (Rev. xiii. 13, 14).

The man of sin of II. Thess. ii. comes "with all power and signs and lying wonders, and with all deceit of unrighteousness" (9-10). He is supremely blasphemous. "The king" of Daniel has "a mouth speaking great things"—"speaking great words against the Most High." He stands up against the Prince of princes, magnifies himself even to the Prince of the host; he exalts himself above every god, nor regards the God of his fathers (Dan. vii. 8-25; viii. 11-25; xi. 36-37). To the beast of the Apoc. there is given "a mouth speaking great things and blasphemies; and he opened his mouth in blasphemy against God, to blaspheme His name and His tabernacle and them that dwell in heaven" (Rev. xiii. 5-6). The man of sin "exalteth himself above all that is called God or that is worshiped; so that he sitteth in the temple of God, setting himself forth as God (II. Thess. ii. 4).

He is intolerant, persecuting. "The king" in Daniel wears out the saints of the Most High, casts down some of the hosts of heaven and tramples on them; destroys the mighty and the holy people (vii. 25; viii. 10-24). The man of sin is the lawless one who, impatient of restraint, sets aside all authority, human and divine, and opposes himself to all that is called God or that is worshiped (ii. 4-8). To the beast of the Apocalypse is given power over all kindreds, and tongues, and nations; power to

MAKE WAR WITH THE SAINTS

and to overcome them; and power to kill every one who refuses to worship him and to receive his mark (Rev. xiii. 7-15).

2. The time-notes in the three prophecies are identical. The adversary appears in connection with apostacy. In Daniel the king of fierce countenance makes his appearance when the transgressors are come to the full (viii. 23). In II. Thessalonians the coming of the man of sin occurs when the falling away is at the flood, the hindrance being removed. In the Apocalypse the beast presents himself when men have renounced allegiance to God and pay homage to the monster. Daniel's beast dominates for "a time, times, and the dividing of time," 1,260 days. John's beast continues forty and two months, 1,260 days. Daniel's vision has its fulfillment "at the time of the end." Paul's prediction synchronizes with "the day of the Lord," the time of the end. John dates his prophecy by the "hour," the "day," the "judgment" of Almighty God—the time of the end.

3. The doom of the adversary in the three prophecies is identical. In Daniel the beast is slain by one like unto the Son of Man who

comes in the clouds of heaven. In Thessalonians the man of sin is brought to nought by the outshining splendor of the coming of the Lord Jesus. In the Apocalypse the beast is taken by the glorious Conqueror who comes from heaven, whose name is the word of God. In Daniel the beast is given to the burning flame; in Thessalonians the man of sin is consumed by the breath of the Lord's mouth. In the Apocaypsel the beast and the false prophet are cast alive into the lake of fire! From all these marks of identity we conclude that "the willful king" of Daniel, the lawless one of Paul, and

THE BEAST OF JOHN

are not three, but one, the three-fold picture of the one great enemy of God and all good—the Antichrist.

III. Have the prophecies relating to the Antichrist been fulfilled? Has there appeared upon the field of history any person or any system verifying the description? Two schools of interpreters make answer in the affirmative—the Preterist and the Presentist. The Preterist theory is based on the plausible assumption that the apostles expected the accomplishment of the predictions in their own lifetime, or at most in the generation immediately succeeding them; in consequence, either they were in error, or we must find the fulfilment in some person or event lying near the apostles themselves. And so the Roman Emperor Nero is pitched upon as the Antichrist, and the fall of Jerusalem as the advent of the Lord Jesus Christ. And this in the face of the inspired declaration of the Apostle Paul who solemnly tells the saints of Thessalonica who thought the day of Christ was already come, that that day can not set in unless the apostacy first come and the check of hindrance which holds back the parousia of the man of sin be removed! But let that pass.

There are insuperable difficulties in the way of our accepting the Neronian theory. Nero died by his own hand at the villa of his freedman Phaon, four miles outside the walls of Rome. Daniel, Paul, and John with one voice testify that the Antichrist is destroyed by the coming of the Lord. How does Nero's suicide fulfill the reiterated promise and prediction of the Holy Ghost? "A more notable instance of inadequate interpretation can not be imagined."

Daniel tells us that on the destruction of his fourth beast and its little horn (the Antichrist), "the kingdom and the dominion and the greatness of the kingdom under the whole heaven

SHALL BE GIVEN TO THE PEOPLE

of the saints of the Most High, whose kingdom is an everlasting kingdom, and all dominions shall serve and obey him." John tells us that when the beast and the false prophet are cast into the lake of fire, and Satan is bound, the thousand years of blessedness ensue (Dan. vii. 27. Rev. xix. 20, xx. 1-6). This is the concurrent testimony of all the prophets, of Joel, Isaiah, Zechariah, and of the Savior Himself. The order, the temporal sequence, observed in all, is this: The enemy and his desolating armies; the time of unprecedented trouble and sorrow, the great tribulation; and then the judgment of the Lord which sweeps the earth clear of His foes, and peace and blessedness succeed. What followed the death of Nero and the destruction of Jerusalem? The millennium? Centuries of persecution, the rise of the papacy, the proscription of the gospel, the chaining up of the Bible, the corruption of Christianity, the inquisition and the Dragonades, and war and strife and ignorance and crime have marked the rolling years. If Nero was the Antichrist, and the destruction of Jerusalem the Advent, and ever since the everlasting kingdom has been in the hands of the saints, and has had undisputed and universal sway, then all we have to say is that the magnificence of the promise and the prophecy is lost in the poverty of its fulfillment, "and Scripture is wiped out as a definite testimony to anything."

Finally, there is an extraordinary anachronism in this Neronian theory. If we are to believe the testimony of antiquity, Nero had been dead and Jerusalem destroyed more than twenty-five years before the book of Revelation was written. Irenaeus, appointed Bishop of Lyons A. D. 177, thus speaks: "For no long time ago was it (the Revelation) seen, but almost

IN OUR OWN GENERATION,

at the end of the reign of Domitian." This statement fixes the date of the book at A. D. 95 or 96; for Domitian was assassinated in the last year named. Nero died A. D. 68; Jerusalem was destroyed A. D. 70. Let it be remembered that Irenaeus lived near the apostolic age, for he could not have been born later than A. D. 130; that he was the disciple and friend of the saintly Polycarp who had been the contemporary of the Apostle John himself; that he was the friend and successor of Pothinus, whose ninety years of age takes us back to the generation which saw the last of the apostles; that his testimony is corroborated by Tertullian, Clement of Alexandria, Victorinus, Eusebius, and Jerome, and its validity and force will be recognized. Not until this testimony is set aside by competent authority, far other than that of the notoriously inaccurate Epiphanius, can sensible men hold that Nero was the Antichrist, or that the fall of Jerusalem was the predicted coming of the son of man.

The prevailing Protestant interpretation is that the beast, the lawless one, is popery, gathered up into the person of the Pope; or that papal hierarchy, the head of which is the papal chair. This was the opinion of the reformers almost without exception. It was held by some even in prereformation times. And there is no little verisimilitude in the view. The marks of correspondence between the prophecies and the papacy are extraordinary, almost conclusive. In its marvelous origin and history; in its near relation to the old Roman Empire as its heir and successor; in its wide departure from the truth; in its idolatry, persecuting spirit, daring assumptions, and blasphemous pretensions, Romanism, it must be confessed,

STRIKINGLY RESEMBLES THE ANCICHRIST.

But wonderful as the parallelism between the two is, and traceable to almost any length, nevertheless the papacy does not fill up and complete, as yet, the titanic portrait of the great adversary which the spirit of God has drawn for us in the word of truth. Let us note very briefly some of the differences and discrepancies between them.

1. The Antichrist is thoroughly atheistic. Atheism is his characteristic feature. John says: "This is Antichrist, even he that denieth the Father and the Son" (I. John ii. 22). "And the king * * * shall magnify himself above every god; neither shall he regard the God of his fathers, nor any god; for he shall magnify himself above all" (Dan. xi. 36-37). The man of sin "opposeth and exalteth himself above all that is called God or that is worshiped, so that he sitteth in the temple of God, setting himself forth as God" (II. Thess. ii. 4). Bad as popery is, this it has never yet done. As a system it plants itself as a mediator between heaven and earth; the priest stands between the sinner and God, auricular confession between him and the footstool of mercy, penance between him and godly sorrow, the mass between him and the righteousness of Christ, indulgence between him and a self-denying and earnest life, tradition between him and holy Scripture, and purgatory between him and the heavenly world. And yet the Pope holds the three ecumenical creeds; acknowledges both the Father and the Son, and owns himself to be a worshiper and servant of God. He blesses the people, not in his own name, but in the name of the Father, Son, and Spirit. So far from being the antagonist of God avowedly, as is the Antichrist, he

CLAIMS OF BE AN HUMBLE VASSAL

of the Divine Master, and professes to identify himself with His cause in the world. No Pope ever yet has really deified himself and ventured to supersede God in His own temple. Blasphemous titles may be given him; he has not assumed them. The adoration paid him at his installation, when he is carried into St. Peter's and seated on the high alter by the Cardinals, is a species of idolatry by a mere man; but it professes to be only the adoration of Christ's presence and power in him. The enormous authority he wields he claims not as his own, but God's, vested in him as the vicar of Christ on earth. In his loftiest and most daring assumptions, he shows himself only as God's viceroy. No Pope has ever yet thrust God aside formally, in his impious atheism, and openly put himself in His place. We know not what the Papal system may yet arrive at; but this it has never done. The Antichrist is something else and something worse than this. He stands in opposition to every god, true or false, and in self-elevation above every god, true or false. He will acknowledge no god; will allow no other to acknowledge any god but himself. True, Daniel says "a god whom his fathers knew not he will increase with glory." This strange "god" whom "the king" will thus honor I am inclined to think is his own image, to which the False Prophet gives breath so that it both speaks and causes as many as refuse to worship it and the Beast to be put to death (Rev. xiii. 15). The Beast is the only god, and his image by spoken word and unimpeachable sign attests it. All these betokens a frightful atheism—open, malignant and haughty antagonism to God, and every object of divine worship, something immeasurably worse than even Popery.

2. The Antichrist is uniformly in the Scriptures associated with the civil power, imperial sovereignty, of which he is

THE BLASPHEMOUS HEAD,

and which he controls and uses for his own diabolical ends. He is represented as seizing the political dominion of world, and heading up and wheeling it into line in hostile array against God and His Christ. The papacy has never wielded such power. Its temporal sovereignty has always been a petty rule; and now it is stripped of this semblance of civil authority, and the Pope sits in the Vatican a self-styled prisoner. To the end Antichrist stands at the head of a revolted world.

3. The Antichrist asserts a supremacy unchallenged and all but universal. In the Apocalypse it is once and again declared that all the world shall wonder after the

Beast, that all who dwell on the earth shall worship the Beast, all whose names are not in the Book of Life. One half of Christendom is outside the pale of Rome and in antagonism to the claims of the papacy. Or, will any one venture to say that all who belong to the Greek and Protestant communions are enrolled in the Book of Life? Either we must reduce the colossal proportions of the inspired picture or abandon the theory that the papacy is the Antichrist.

4. Two frightful alternatives will confront men when the Antichrist is present: One is, either men must worship the Beast or die (Rev. xiii. 15). The other, either they must worship God, utterly repudiating the diabolism of the beast, or be tormented with fire and brimstone forever and ever. Rev. xiv. 9-11.) Death in this world, or damnation in the next; that will be the dread choice of men when the beast is here! Will any one venture to say that this has its fulfillment in Romanism, in the past or as it now exists?

5. All evangelical interpreters hold that Babylon the Great is Romanism,

THE APOSTATE CHURCH;

and yet hateful as Babylon is, she contains to the close some genuine believers. Just before the tremendous judgment breaks down upon the unclean thing a voice from heaven cries, "Come forth out of her my people!" But among the worshipers of the beast there is not a single saint. His adherents and followers are doomed, every one of them. Babylon and the beast are two different things.

6. The beast is distinguished from the harlot in Rev. xvii. Two significant symbols are presented to us; a lewd woman seated upon a scarlet-colored beast. The beast is identified with that of chap. xiii. and Dan. vii., for he has the same number of heads and horns, the same extraordinary history. But what is the woman? Who can doubt but that she represents the false apostate church? The revealing angel describes her as the mystic Babylon, the mother of harlots. Everywhere in Scripture an impure woman is the symbol of a system which, professing to belong to God, apostatizes from Him and becomes idolatrous; (Isa. i., 21; Jer. iii., 1, 6-7; Ezek. xvi.; Hos. ii. 5; iii. 1, 6, 8), etc. Babylon is a shameless and seductive influence throned upon the seven hills, and seated also on the beast. She compels him to support her, she guides and uses him for the accomplishment of her purposes. But it is her last, her fatal ride which the prophet beholds, a ride to destruction and death; "and the ten horns which thou sawest and the beast, these shall hate the harlot, and shall make her desolate and naked, and shall eat her flesh and burn her with fire." Lex talionis! The harlot had intrigued and coquetted with the world-power, had intoxicated and maddened it with the wine of her fornication; then she had mounted the huge beast and under whip and spur had ridden to her

PLACE OF BAD PRE-EMINENCE.

God will put it into the hearts of the beast and his ten confederate kings to hate and spoil her, to tear her bedizened rags from her loathsome body, her polluted flesh from her putrid bones! It is a righteous retribution that overtakes Babylon. If the harlot be Romanism, then the beast is not. If the harlot and the beast be the Papacy, then the Papacy is its own executioner! Reductio ad absurdum! Nay, after Babylon is destroyed, there remains the vast coalition of Antichristian powers, with the beast at its head that proudly marches to the battle of the great day of God Almighty, and is forever overthrown by the personal return of the Son of God Himself.

Two great forms of iniquity constitute the burden of prophetic warning. Ecclesiastical corruption and apostasy form the one; the open revolt of the civil power against God is the other. The first culminates in Babylon, the blood-drunken harlot. The second finds its horrible apotheosis in the beast, the Antichrist. The first is already here, although greater depths of wickedness will yet be reached, no doubt. The second is not yet come; he is still the coming prince—he is coming! Believing that the inspired account of the great Adversary has not received its proper fulfillment in any person or system that has appeared in the field of history, we proceed to inquire as to the origin and character of the Antichrist.

1. The Antichrist is a person, an individual man, the man of prophecy. Every quality, attribute, mark, and sign which can indicate personality are ascribed to him with a precision and definiteness of language that refuses to be explained away. According to Daniel, he is the "king" who overthrows three other kings,

OBTAINS THE SUPREMACY

over the "fourth kingdom," does according to his will, suppresses every object of worship, exalts and magnifies himself over all, speaks great words against the Most High, persecutes the saints, and thinks to change the times and the law. Whatever in human speech betokens personality and personal action is employed by the prophet to designate a man, a single individual. According to Paul, he is the man of sin, the son of perdition—names which at once fasten on him the idea of a person. "The man of sin"—he whose inner element and outer characteristic is sin and nothing but sin; who has his being, plans, and activity in sin and in nothing else; who, as the living embodiment of it, is known and recognized as the Man of Sin. "The son of perdition"—he on whom perdition falls as his due and his heritage; he whom John describes as ascending out of the abyss, and who goeth into perdition. "The terse personal language of Paul fore-pictures one man, one human being, as really as the phrase 'son of perdition' described from the Lord's lips the fate of Judas the traitor." (Eadie.)

The person so described is a man—anthropos—a single man, and not a series or succession of men; not the personification of evil influences, or the head of any human organization. This man, made of sin, is the personal antagonist of Christ, is the counter-Christ. Both are individual persons, both come to view, both are "revealed," both have a parousia. The One has life and glory as His destiny, the other ruin and perdition. This man of sin stands in contrast with the "apostacy," and yet is its final outcome. The apostacy gathers itself at length into a monstrous concentration of wickedness and lawlessness which

RECEIVES THE OMINOUS TITLE

of the man of sin. Thus Irenaeus conceives of him: "Summing up in himself a diabolical apostacy."

Thus Justin Martyr views him, calling him "The Man of the Apostacy." Thus likewise witnesses the remarkable document, "The Teaching of the Twelve Apostles": "For in the last days the false prophets and the corruptors shall be multiplied, and the sheep shall be turned into wolves, and love shall be turned into hate; for when lawlessness increases they shall hate one another, and shall persecute and shall deliver up, and then shall appear the world-deceiver as son of God, and he shall do signs and wonders, and the earth shall be given into his hands, and he shall commit iniquities which have never yet been done since the beginning. Then all created men shall come into the fire of trial, and many shall stumble and perish." The closeness of this statement to 2 Thess. ii. is almost verbal. There is first the falling away, then the eruption of lawlessness, and then the presence of the world-deceiver who appears as son of God. The apostacy, as a fact or a system, is not to be confused with the man of sin, for it precedes him and is the condition of his appearance. The Apocalypse is even more explicit. In chapter xix. the beast is distinguished from the kings who are confederated with him and from their armies. He is distinguished from the false prophet, who acts as his great lieutenant. The beast and the false prophet are distinguished in their fate from their armies, for they are cast alive into the lake of fire while their armies are slain with the sword. As Koch writes: "The beast is as little an abstraction as the false prophet is. Both are persons. This is clear from Rev. xx. 10, where it is said that after the thousand years the devil,

WHO IS A PERSON

and not an abstraction, goes to where the beast and false prophet are—two other persons who served him so well, but to their own loss! It is said, moreover, that they are tempted day and night, which no abstraction could be. So sure as Satan is a person, so sure the beast, the Anti, is." The fathers of the church were agreed in considering the Antichrist as a single human being, and not a system of polity or malign influence. It made no difference whether they were advocates or opponents of chiliasm, it was their unanimous persuasion that he will be one man, and his part in the last times will be the part of a literal agent. The terse simplicity and unambiguous unity of the Biblical description of him certainly tend to such a conclusion. On their face these three great prophecies of Daniel, Paul, and John announce the advent of one enemy, draw the portrait of one single adversary, whose character, energy, and perdition stand unmatched in the history of our race.

2. The Antichrist is the supreme head of the world-power in its final and diabolical form. This is evident from the composition of John's great symbol. Daniel's beasts were successive empires—the Babylonian, Medo-Persian, Græco-Macedonian, and the Roman. But the lion, the bear, the leopard, and

THE NAMELESS TEN-HORNED MONSTER,

each distinct in Daniel, are all united in one in Rev. xiii. It is upon this God-opposing power that the judgment of heaven falls. The beast is cast into perdition, and all this world's kings, armies, and administrations end forever. Precisely the same fate marks the huge image of Dan. ii., for while the blow falls on the feet and toes of the statue, the whole image with all its component parts—the iron, clay, brass, silver, and gold—share in the overwhelming destruction. It is the world-sovereignty as it presents itself in the last times, and the beast is its embodiment and consummation.

Moreover, John saw that one of the seven heads of the beast was smitten unto death, but that his death-wound was healed. The same feature in the beast's history appears in Rev. xvii. 8, where we are informed that the beast "was, and is not, and shall come;" or as the Sinai Codex reads, "shall be present again." No doubt it is the Roman empire that is thus characterised, but the empire in its last form. It has, according to the revealing angel, a most extraordinary history, one which is divided into three stages. "It was." In John's day it existed in the plentitude of its resistless power, and the world lay helpless at its feet. With beak of brass and talons of steel the great eagle of Rome had grappled and overcome the human race, and the earth trembled when from his seven-hilled eyrie he flapped his wings of thunder. "It was."

There came a second stage, that of non-existence. Beneath the deadly sword-strokes of the barbarians imperial Rome sank and died. "It is not." From that time onward until now a universal dominion centering in one grand emperor there has not been. Ambitious soldiers have once and again attempted to found one homogeneous, world-wide kingdom in the earth, but without avail. Charlemagne tried it, the first Napoleon likewise, but in vain. Still "it is not." A third stage arrives; and the world-empire, the

SOVEREIGN COLOSSUS,

re-appears. "It shall be present again." "The deadly wound was healed." And at its head stands the peerless man, the Satan-inspired man, the man in military genius, executive capacity, intellectual brilliancy, and savage ferocity surpassing Alexander of Macedon, Julius Cæsar of old Rome, Antiochus of Syria, and Bonaparte of France. It is the man of sin, the Antichrist, from whom the stupendous confederacy takes its name and its laws, to whose will it bows, whose sway it gladly owns—the beast! It is the time of the end; for the beast ascends out of the abyss only to go into perdition. It was a saying in the olden times that Rome would endure to the end of world. The age terminates indeed when the beast is here, and when the mighty conqueror comes from heaven and hurls him into the lake of fire.

3. The origin of the Antichrist is mysterious, apparently supernatural. Twice in the Apoc. it is solemnly declared that he comes out of the "bottomless pit" (xi. 7; xvii. 8). In chapter xiii, 2 it is as solemnly asserted that Satan gives him "his power, and his throne, and great authority." In II. Thess. ii. he is represented as having a parousia, like our Lord, and his parousia is according to the working of Satan with all power and signs and lying wonders. Many of the fathers believed he will be a Satanic incarnation. Hyppolitus calls him "a son of the devil a vessel of Satan." Irenæus speaks of him as "taking on himself all the power and all the delusion of the devil." Origen describes him as "the child of the devil and the counterpart of Christ." Lactantius thinks he will be "a king begotten by an evil spirit." Theodoret believes the devil will be

"INCARNATE IN THE ANTICHRIST,"

and Theophylact, that he will be a "man who will carry Satan about with him." Augustine says that he will be born as other men, "but that the devil will descend on his mother and fill her totally, surround her totally, hold her totally, and possess her totally, within and without, and the thing that shall be borne of her shall be altogether sinful, altogether damned." Some thought he will be Antiochus Epiphanes redivivus. Many held, and not a few among the moderns concur in the view, that he will be Nero, who shall return to earth from the nether-world. Assuredly there is something ominous in these terms—"he cometh up out of the abyss," "whose parousia is after the working of Satan"—something altogether aside from the ordinary way of men's appearing in the world. Nevertheless we cannot believe they import the return to earth of one who has long been dead, nor yet a demoniacal incarnation. They mean, or seem to mean, that, to accomplish his fell purpose, Satan will transfer to the Antichrist his power and throne, and fill him from crown to heel with his own dreadful and apalling energy. As he entered into the heart of Judas, the son of perdition, so he will take possession of the man of sin, inspiring him with power, intensifying his malignity, dowering him with superhuman craft and pride, till he deifies himself!

Nor is it necessary to believe that Antichrist will from the beginning of his career display his devilish temper, or let out any of the God-defying spirit that is in him. The Scripture intimates the exact contrary. He is represented as being a consumate flatterer, a brilliant diplomatist, a superb strategist, a sublime hypocrite. He will mask his ulterior designs under specious pretences; will pose as a humanitarian, the friend of man, the deliverer of the oppressed, the bringer-in of the Golden Age. Nothing less than this will satisfy the descriptions of him as "the deceiver" and the "liar;" as the one who shall intoxicate men with a "strong delusion," who shall fling over the world

A FATAL FASCINATION,

and utterly daze all with his majestic "powers and signs and lying wonders;" who shall deceive, if it were possible, the very elect. His name implies this: He is the pro-Christ, the rival-Christ. He assumes and presumes to be God, shows himself as God; and he takes this blasphemous place and name through the strange witchery of his stupendous powers. We see the same course taken by his proto-types and precursors by Antiochus the Syrian King; by Nero the persecutor; by the first Napoleon who masked his iron despotism under specious pretences, proclaiming himself a Catholic to the Pope, a Musselman to the Moslems, and the Man of Destiny to Europe. But a crisis arrives; the mask is flung aside, and the Antichrist stands revealed as the consummate antagonist and supplanter of everything divine. The occasion which effects this change in his career is, I believe, the subject of Rev. xii. The objections which lie against any interpretation of this most difficult portion of the Apocalypse are confessedly great, perhaps unanswerable; nevertheless, I would venture an opinion upon it.

Rev. xi. and xii., I believe, are both proleptic. While they precede the description of the beast the action predicted in them falls in the time of the beast, and in that stage of his career when he is doing his worst on earth. In chapter xi. we encounter the beast for the first time in the book; and he is found making war with the two witnesses. These two witnesses, whoever they may be, are associated with Israel and Jerusalem, as verse eight clearly shows, and as Dan. vii. and xi. manifestly prove. Their testimony is essentially Jewish, their mission and ministry like that of Moses and Elijah. But

THE BEAST OVERCOMES THEM,

and they are slain. Babylon the harlot, the apostate church is already destroyed; and now the two witnesses, whose presence was a rebuke and whose word was a torment to men, are out of the way, and the world rejoices and makes merry. It is at this point, I suppose, that the Antichrist ventures upon his "divine treason," and his awful blasphemy culminates in his claiming for himself the place and worship of Almighty God—now that he "exalts himself," usurps God's honor, and seats himself in "the temple of God, showing himself that he is God." But an event of world-wide import transpires to mar and blast his hellish triumph. Because of what takes place as represented in chapter 12 the Great Dragon (Satan) is cast down to earth, and in his desperate rage and fury turns to give his power and his throne to the beast. Everything for the beast, now that the transcendent event announced in the chapter has become a historical fact. What is this event? The conversion of Israel! This, upon which so much else turns which destroys the ground of Satan's accusation, which converts the Antichrist from a crafty dissimulator into a headlong persecutor, which brings on the great tribulation, and at length the Advent; this, I believe, is the supreme idea of Rev. xii. I believe the sun-clothed woman about to bring forth is the symbol of Israel's conversion in the time of the end. The words of other prophets confirm and explain the symbol. Micah predicts the first coming of the Redeemer, announcing that He is to be born at Bethlehem-Ephrata; then he foretells

ISRAEL'S REJECTION

and restoration in these words: "Therefore will he give them up, until the time that she which travaileth hath brought forth; then the residue of his brethren shall return with (marg. R. V.) the children of Israel" (v. 2-3). Isaiah, speaking of the same blessed event says: "Before she travailed she brought forth; before her pain came she was delivered of a man-child. Shall a nation be born in one day? For as soon as Zion travailed she brought forth her children" (lxvi. 7-8). It is the picture of Israel's turning to God, the time when Israel shall be saved. And when this glorious event transpires the basis of Satan's accusation is forever destroyed. This national conversion precipitates the crisis, for Israel's unbelief is the vantage ground for the accuser. The moment it becomes a reality the glad shout rings through heaven: "Now is come the salvation and the power and the kingdom of our God and the authority of His Christ, for the accuser of our brethren is cast down" (Rev. xii. 10). Against Israel converted the Antichrist turns his whole rage. Prior to this, it seems, he had been going on with craft and guile, deluding the world with his lying miracles, and exhibiting but little of his real spirit. Now his wrath bursts forth against God, against the woman and her seed, against everything that is called God or that is worshiped. War is proclaimed; the bugles of Antichrist summon his armies to the conflict, and the earth trembles beneath the tread of marching squadrons. The very atmosphere seems populous with forces marching and countermarching for the decisive battle; and the invisible worlds of being pulsate and grow tremulous in sympathy with the contending armies.

THE GREAT TRIBULATION,

of which the prophetic word has so much to say, begins its awful course. It is the time of Jacob's trouble; the time of trouble such as our planet has never witnessed before, never will again; the time when if God did not graciously shorten the days for the elect's sake no flesh could be saved. It is then the enormity of sin and crime, of wickedness and blasphemy, unparalleled in the annals of the world, will be consummated. And when myriads of martyrs have laid down their lives for the witness of Jesus, and hope seems clean gone, and black despair has settled down on the weltering world, and the horrible triad—the dragon, the beast, and the false prophet—have the poor race under their hellish feet, and God seems to have forgotten the earth; then, flashing down from the opening skies, the Blessed Deliverer comes, the Lord Jesus Christ; and Antichrist with his "armor-bearer," is cast alive into the lake of fire! And the kingdom, the glorious kingdom, for which we now long and pant and yearn, is established forever!

4. When shall Antichrist appear? Not until a something that now "restraineth" be removed. Already in Paul's day the mystery of lawlessness was working. Already the germs of a wide defection were planted—germs of continuous and unsuspected growth, whose huge development should be the revelation of the man of sin. The fatal process marked by the apostle is this: The mystery of lawlessness working forward into apostacy, and apostacy culminating at length in the Antichrist. But an unseen power lays its hand upon the process. There is a time appointed for his manifestation, a time neither to be antedated nor postponed. The restraining power, whatever it is, is in God's hand, and not until His set time is come can the malignant

UPBURSTING OF GODLESSNESS

break upon the world. For the apostle assures us that the check holds "until he who restraineth now be taken out of the way." That "until" is fraught with weighty consequences, is filled with unspeakable destinies. The generation, the century, the year wrapped up in this "until" is hidden from mortal eye. The Thessalonian saints knew what it is; we have not the same knowledge, and this fact should repress dogmatic assertion.

To the query, What is the restraining power, two answers are returned. One is, that it is the Holy Spirit in the church, an opinion which has a Scriptural basis, but which does not fall within the limits of the present discussion. The other is, that it is the fabric of human policy, the moral and civil order of society, divinely constituted authority, in short, in the state. This view does not antagonize the other just mentioned; it is, in fact, its correlative and counterpart. The name given to the Antichrist seems to justify this opinion. He is the "Lawless One" in whom all law is discarded, all moral order is dethroned. "When the unseen yet withholding influence of the civil power with its moral and divine order of things is powerless to restrain increasing lawlessness, then the end is near, is come" (Luthardt). Upon the ruins of shattered states and kingdoms the vast empire of Antichrist is built. The revolutionary condition of society out of which the Antichrist and his dominion arise is clearly indicated by Daniel, vii. 2, who says that the four winds of heaven brake forth upon the great sea, and the beasts arose. Out of the same unstable and agitated element the beast of the Apocalypse issues forth. The sea, torn by the winds, is the graphic image of nations and peoples in

COMMOTION AND REVOLUTION.

And this disrupted state of human society plainly hints at the withdrawal of the check, the overthrow of the dam which holds back the antichristian flood. History affords at least one illustrious example of the malignant process through which the world will travel to the man of sin—the French revolution. There was first the preparatory stage, in which widespread attacks were made on religious faith and existing political institutions; the revolution followed which overthrew church and state, society and religion, royalty, nobility, clergy, laws, customs, everything, and then out of this social chaos came Napoleon and his empire, with the subordinate and confederate kingdoms of Westphalia, Naples, and Rome. We have but to imagine this revolutionary condition spread over the whole "prophetic earth" to have an exact picture of the times when the hindrance is taken away, and Antichrist's road is ready, and the great Kaiser comes!

Is this to be the final outcome of the boasted progress and civilization of our modern era? The science, discoveries, "culture;" the energy, activity, and splendid achievements of the age, are they all to terminate in worldwide godlessness and the man of sin? Pessimism, this view is called, and pessimists, they who advocate it. One whose love for men is deathless, whose power is matchless, has said: "As it was in the days of Noah, so shall it be in the days of the son of man." How was it in the days of Noah? The whole world in revolt against God, and true piety reduced to a family of eight souls. Impossible to be realized in our enlightened times, is it said? We have but to remember that less than one hundred years ago, in the most highly cultivated and intellectual country of Europe, in France, society was so wrecked and chaotic, and

ATHEISM WAS EXALTED

to such a height of proud impiety, that the

world witnessed the audacious spectacle of a prostitute enthroned on the high altar of Notre Dame, saluted and worshiped under the title of the "Goddess of Reason." We have but to remember that at this very time there resides in the city of Rome a man whom one-half of Christendom itself honors and adores as the vicar of Christ, the vicegerent of God, infallible, and sole possessor of the keys of the kingdom of heaven—a man who is borne along "in solemn procession on the shoulders of consecrated priests, whilst sacred incense fumes before him, and blest peacocks' feathers full of eyes wave beside his moving throne, and every mortal near uncovers, kneels, and silently adores." We have but to remember that even now there exists a positivist calendar in which each day is appointed for the "cultus" of some man distinguished in art, literature, or philosophy.

There are principles now at work in our modern society which, if left unchecked, will soon make the advent of the Antichrist not only possible, but certain. The lawless drift is already on us, precursor of worse to come.

Who does not perceive that the forces are already loose in the world that tend to the disintegration of the whole social fabric? Who does not perceive that the ax is already aimed at the chief hoops which bind together the staves of the civil polity? Socialism, nihilism, anarchy, naturalism, materialism, humanitarianism, spiritualism—restlessness and discontent everywhere—is it any wonder that already men's hearts are failing them for fear, and for looking for the things about to come upon the earth? We have only to suppose the portentous movements of the time grow and gather head until the hindrance is gone, the barrier thrown down, and then? Yes, what then? Then cometh the Antichrist, the devastator of the world!

The Lord help us to watch and be sober!

Notes—1. That the Fathers regarded the Antichrist as a single person, and as associated with Satan in some mysterious way, is susceptible of demonstration. Besides those named in the preceding essay, the following may be mentioned: Tertullian, Cyprian, Victorinus, Cyril of Jerusalem, Jerome, Chrisostum, Hilary of Poictiers, Ambrose, Ephrem Syrus, Andreas of Caesarea, John Damascene, Abbot Joachim. The same opinion is encountered in the following writings: Epistle of Barnabas, Apostolic Constitutions, second of the Clementine Homilies, De Consummatione Mundi, Disputation of Archelaus and Manes, Recognitions of Clement. The "Noble Lesson" of the Waldenses, of the twelfth century, contains the like belief of a future personal Antichrist.

2. What is meant by the Man of Sin sitting in the "temple" o God? In Josephus, Philo, the Septuagint, and the New Testament, a distinction is made between *hieron* and *naos*. The former (*hieron*) is the name commonly given to the cluster of buildings on Mt. Moriah. The latter (*naos*) designates the temple proper, the sanctuary where the Divine Presence dwelt. Into this most sacred part of God's dwelling place does this proud oppressor thrust himself as if he were its divine occupant.

But what is meant by this *naos*, this "temple of God?" The term may be used figuratively for the church (1 Cor. iii., 16, 17; vi., 19; Eph. ii., 21, 22). In these ethical passages, describing spiritual privilege, blessing, and destiny the body of Christ, the invisible church in dwelt by the Spirit of God, is undoubtedly the subject. But how the Antichrist who is a man and not an abstraction, can in any proper sense be said to take his seat in this temple does not appear. Wherever the word *naos* is applied to a material structure in the New Testament the reference uniformly is either to the Temple at Jerusalem, or to some heathen shrine, like the temple of Diana—never in a single instance to a place of Christian worship, such as St. Peter's at Rome (Matt. xxiii., 16-17; Luke i., 9; Acts xix. 24, etc.) The Scripture usage of the word would lead us to the conclusion that either it is the Jewish Temple to be restored in the future and rededicated to God, or some pre-eminently sacred place like it, in which the Antichrist is to take his seat. The connection of the Adversary with Israel in the last times, as Daniel and John appear to indicate, seems to favor this view. Time alone will tell.

3. Is the Antichrist to be a Jew? So many think, basing their opinion on Gen. xlix, 17; Jer. vii. 16; Dan. xi. 47, 37, etc. These passages, however, are by no means decisive, and may be satisfactorily explained as relating to another subject altogether.

The argument that the Antichrist must be a Jew in order to be received by the Jews has little weight. History records one instance at least when they hailed a great Gentile soldier as their deliverer, and sang his praises in the loftiest strains. In 1806 "Napoleon made overtures to the Jews, and took them to some extent under his protection. He invited them to hold their Sanhedrim in Paris, and in March, 1807, seventy-one doctors and leading men of the nation assembled in that city and formed themselves into a national council, the like to which had not been held for more than seventeen hundred years—not indeed since the destruction of Jerusalem by Titus" (Pember, "The Great Prophecies," p. 131. Drumont in his recent book on the Jews in France alludes to the same fact).

As Napoleon had vast designs touching the founding of an Eastern empire, the part which the Jews were to take in his schemes, and Jerusalem and Palestine likewise, may appear from the following: "Bonaparte made an appeal to the Asiatic and African Jews to rally to his banner, and promised to give them the Holy Land, and restore Jerusalem in its ancient splendor." Groetz History of the Jews, Vol. XI., p. 236.

The *Moniteur*, published in Constantinople in 1799, says: "Bonaparte has caused a proclamation to be published, in which he invites all the Jews of Asia and of Africa to assemble themselves under his flag, in order to re-establish the ancient city of Jerusalem. But it is not only to give the Jews their Jerusalem that Bonaparte has conquered Syria. He has larger designs. He aims to conquer Constantinople!" Mon. 1799, p. 187. The time was not yet come, and so Napoleon failed. One is coming, however, who will not fail; under whom Israel will come into the tribulation, and be saved at length by the personal appearing of the Lord Jesus.

FOURTH DAY.

THE REV. DR. J. F. KENDALL.

THE JUDGMENT.

The conference, in the fourth day of its session, had its usual good attendance. The morning meeting was opened by the regular devotional exercises, the Rev. J. Flint, of Helena, M. T., offering the prayer. The first paper was read by the Rev. Dr. John F. Kendall, of LaPorte, Ind., on the subject, "The Judgment." It was as follows:

Questions concerning what theologians term the "final," or the "general judgment," often arise in, and often greatly perplex the mind of the ordinary believer. It is the purpose of this study to answer these questions, and thereby give comfort to many a perplexed spirit.

1. Immediately after death, the soul is placed at the bar of God and judged. "Individuals are treated according to their desert, and this is done immediately after death." (Dr. Dick, Theology, p, 339.) "The soul, at death, goes immediately to its place of

ETERNAL HAPPINESS OR MISERY,

according to its moral character." (Ms. Lects. of Dr. L. P. Hickok.) Hence,

2. The sentence of God assigns the righteous to heaven, and they enter at once on an everlasting inheritance.

3. The same sentence assigns the wicked to everlasting fire.

4. At the resurrection, both the righteous and the wicked are brought from their respective abodes, when they are judged a second time, and are returned to the place whence they were brought, to remain forever. "The judgment passed upon each individual at the termination of his life will be solemnly ratified at the end of the world." (Dr. Dick.) It thus appears, and this is the accepted orthodox view, that the final judgment is merely confirmatory of that which has passed at death, and not that there has been another chance. This is no scheme of an "Eternal Hope."

A general judgment "seems necessary to the display of the justice of God, to such a manifestation of it, as will vindicate His government from all the charges which impiety has brought against it." (Dr. Dick, p. 339.)

1. "Such a judgment will be a more glorious display of God's majesty and dominion."

2. "The end of judgment will be more fully answered by a public and general than only by a particular and private judgment."

3. "It is very agreeable to reason that the irregularities which are so open and manifest

IN THE WORLD

should, when the world comes to an end, be publicly rectified by the supreme governor." (Edward's works, vol. 4, pp. 205, 206.)

"There will be such a revelation of the character of every man, to all around him, or to all who know him, as shall render the justice of the sentence, of condemnation or acquittal, apparent. (Hodge, Theology, vol. 3, p. 849).

"At the judgment of the last day, the destiny of the righteous and of the wicked shall be unalterably determined." (Idem, p. 850).

"The grand end of the judgment is therefore to stop every mouth, satisfy every conscience, and make every knee bow to God's authority, either willingly in love, or necessarily in absolute conviction." (Dr. Hickok).

The sum and substance of all reasons for a general judgment, is, in some way, a vindication of God. "God would show Himself holy and righteous in all His functions of sovereignty." (Dr. Hickok).

The marked absence of Scripture quotations or even reference, is worthy of note, in all these reasons for a general judgment.

That it may appear how unsatisfactory to their own minds, are their supposed vindications of the divine dealings, I add one or two quotations from themselves.

(Dr. Hodge, vol. 3, p. 849): "Every man will see himself as he appears in the sight of God. His memory will probably prove an indelible register of all his sinful acts, thoughts and feelings. His conscience will be so enlightened as to recognize the

JUSTICE OF THE SENTENCE

which the righteous Judge shall pronounce upon him." These things being so, we may ask, what possible need of vindication can there be?

Dr. Dick: "Among the multitude of the condemned, however severe may be their punishment, and however impatiently they may bear it, there will not be one who will dare to accuse his Judge of injustice. In the mind of every man a consciousness of guilt will be deeply fixed; he will be compelled to blame himself alone and to justify the sentence which has rendered him forever miserable." "The declaration of the Judge concerning those on His right hand that they are righteous, and concerning those on His left hand that they are wicked, will be sufficient to convince all in the immense assembly that the sentence pronounced upon each individual is just."

Thus, while these writers maintain the necessity of a general judgment for the vindication of the Divine character, they themselves proceed to show that no such vindication is necessary.

Dick: "The proceedings will take place in the sight of angels and men." "Countless millions will be assembled to hear their final doom. All nations shall be gathered before the Son of man."

Edwards: "In the great and general judgment, all men shall together appear before the judgment seat, to be judged." "The whole world, both angels and men, being present to behold."

Hodge: "The persons to be judged are men and angels." "This judgment therefore is absolutely universal: it includes both small and great, and all

THE GENERATIONS OF MEN."

Hickok: "All fallen angels are to be publicly judged." "Also, all the human family."

On the disclosures of the judgment opinions seriously differ. Thus Edwards: "The works of both righteous and wicked will be rehearsed." "The evil works of the wicked shall then be brought forth to light." But then he adds: "The good works of the saints will also be brought forth as evidences of their sincerity, and of their interest in the righteousness of Christ. As to their evil works, they will not be brought forth against them on that day; for the guilt of them will not lie upon them, they being clothed with the righteousness of Jesus Christ."

On the other hand, Hickok, as we think, well insists that "the sins of Christians will be brought to light in the judgment," for various reasons; and, as if answering this thought of Edwards, on the ground that "The grace of Christ in their final sanctification can not be fully exhibited without it."

If there is to be such a general judgment, as is generally supposed, then there would seem to be no good reason to doubt that all the deeds, both good and evil, of all who have lived, both good and evil, must then be disclosed. The physical phenomena of a general judgment are a source of no little trouble. Dr. Hodge avoids it, by utterly ignoring questions which will force themselves upon the reader of Scripture. Dr. Dick's troubles appear in the following quotations: "The place where the judgment will be held is this world; and, as it is said, that the saints shall be

CAUGHT UP IN THE CLOUDS

to meet the Lord in the air, it should seem that the wicked should be left standing upon the earth." "The saints being caught up into the clouds by the ministry of angels to meet the Lord in the air, and the wicked being left on the earth, the judgment will proceed."

And Dr. Edwards: "They shall all be brought to appear before Christ, the godly being placed on the right hand, the wicked on the left." "Besides the one standing on the right hand and the other on the left, there seems to be this difference between them, that when the dead in Christ shall be raised they will all be caught up in the air, where Christ shall be, and shall be there at His right hand during the judgment, nevermore to set their feet on this earth. Whereas the wicked shall be left standing on the earth, there to abide the judgment." According to this representation the righteous have been judged before the judgment begins, for they have been assigned to the right hand, where they remain "during the judgment." while only the wicked really "abide the judgment." Now, according to the Scripture, upon which these writers depend to prove their general judgment, viz.: Mat. xxv., 31-46, the assemblage of the universe is to be a promiscuous assemblage, whom after they "shall be gathered," the Son of man "shall separate one from another." Whereas, they both agree that the separation takes place in the process of gathering. But that certainly it does not. The result, according to their view, is a most singular

PHYSICAL PHENOMENON,

viz.: the saints "on His right hand in the air," the lost "on the left standing upon the earth." It is no quibble which makes these suggestions. They deserve to be considered.

One other declaration of Dr. Hodge deserves a moment's notice. "At the judgment of the last day," he says, "the destiny of the righteous and of the wicked shall be unalterably determined." By "destiny," he must mean "ultimate fate." Webster defines "determined," as, "ended, concluded, decided, limited, fixed, settled, resolved, directed." Which does Dr. Hodge mean? In truth, his proposition can in no wise be maintained. All orthodox theologians agree, that for the believer, "to die" is "to depart and be with Christ," and for the unbeliever, it is to "go away into everlasting punishment;" but the "destiny" may be fixed long before that, and so far as we have experience or knowledge, is never fixed "at the judgment." "He that believeth on the Son hath everlasting life," but "he that believeth not is condemned already." (John iii. 36-18.) The "destiny" of every soul is "unalterably determined," on the moment of his final acceptance or rejection of Jesus Christ as a Savior.

What is the meaning of the term judgment? Webster answers: "Theologically." "The final punishment of the wicked; the last sentence." It should arrest our thought, that, in Webster's mind, only the "wicked" have place in judgment.

Cremer's answer (in Theological Lex, under krisis): "Specially in judicial procedure and primarily without particular regard to the

CHARACTER OF THE DECISION."

"Then, of a definite accusation or prosecution, guilt, of some sort of being presupposed, by the judicial procedure. This precise use of the term as equal to judicial process, judgment directed against the guilty, and leading on to condemnation is comparatively rare in profane Greek, whereas it is almost the only one in the New Testament." And he cites (Matt. v. 21-22): "Whosoever shall kill, or is 'angry with his brother without a cause, shall be in danger of the judgment,' and (Mark iii. 29) the blasphemer against the Holy Ghost, 'is in danger of eternal judgment.'" Further: "It is characteristic of judicial process, especially of the divine judgment to which krisis mostly relates that it is directed against the guilty." I John iv. 17, "Hemera, kriseos. Mark v. 15; xi. 22-24; xii. 36 (and others), krisis denotes the final judgment of the world, which is to bring destruction upon the guilty." "In Rev. xiv. 7; xvi. 7; xix. 2, the word likewise denotes the judgment, the act of judging, which discerns and condemns the guilty." And again, under krima, "the decision of a judge, judgment (Rev. xx, 4), the judgment concerning them is given in what follows. * * * Elsewhere in the New Testament throughout, as in later Greek, the word always denotes a judgment unfavorable to those concerned, a punitive judgment, involving punishment, as a matter of course," and he cites (2 Peter ii. 3), "whose judgment now of a long time lingereth not," with Rom. iii. 8, "whose judgment is just," and Rom. v. 16, "for the judgment was by one to condemnation." "For the cognizance of the judge," continues Cremer, "to say nothing of his judgment, implies

A COMING SHORT."

This is a very vital point in our discussion. If the New Testament usage of the term judgment implies guilt, and has but one natural sequence, condemnation, then we effect at once a very large exclusion from the numbers of those for whom a final judgment is intended; no righteous can be there, and such a thing as a general judgment must be forever unknown. It is easy to show by citation of numerous passages that Cremer is right, both as the term is used in reference to man and God.

1. The use of "judge" when applied to man.

"Doth our law judge any man before it hear him?" (John vii. 51.) Pilate said: "Take Him yourselves and judge Him according to your law. The Jews said unto him, it is not lawful for us to put any man to death (John xviii. 31)," as if that were the only possible sentence (see Acts xiii. 27-46; xxiii. 3-6; xxiv. 6-21). Festus said to Paul: "Let them go up to Jerusalem, and there be judged. * * * Then said Paul, I stand at Cæsar's judgment seat where I ought to be judged; to the Jews I have done no wrong." (Acts xxv. 9, 10; xxvi. 6. See Rom. xiv. 3, 4, 10, 13, 22; James iv. 11, 12.) "The men of Nineveh, the Queen of the South, shall rise up in the judgment with this generation and shall condemn it." (Matt. xii. 41, 42.) It is a remarkable fact that in all these cases (few only are cited) "judge" is use in the sense of condemn, and in some instances strikingly so.

2. The use of "judge" when applied to God.

Luke xix. 22: "Out of thine own mouth will I judge thee,

THOU WICKED SERVANT."

Acts vii. 7: "The nation to whom they shall be in bondage will I judge, saith God."

Rom. ii. 12, 16: "As many as have sinned in the law shall be judged by the law * * * in the day when God shall judge the secrets of men by Jesus Christ."

(II. Thess. ii. 12). "That they all might be judged who * * * had pleasure in unrighteousness."

(Hebrews ix. 27-28). "As it is appointed unto men once to die, but after this, judgment, so Christ was once offered to bear the sins of many; and unto them that look for Him shall He appear * * * unto salvation." Manifestly "judgment" and "salvation" stand over against each other. The world was under judgment, and this meant condemnation, for in judgment they were "judged every man according to his works." Justice is inexorable, and since all have sinned, no one who comes into judgment can escape. Hence the divine mercy interposed, and "as" judgment was the original doom, "so," that is "to meet this very exigency of their case," to arrest judgment and offer salvation, "Christ was offered."

"Those that look for Him" are of course, believers, who though "by nature children of wrath," have been "quickened together with Christ," "raised up together and made to sit together in heavenly places in Christ Jesus" (Eph. ii. 5, 6), and that certainly is far above fear of death and judgment. For such there remaineth

NO "FEARFUL LOOKING

for of judgment and fiery indignation which shall devour the adversaries" (Heb. x: 7.) Not to quote a burdensome number of passages the reader will find the term "judge" used in the sense of condemnation in John iii: 17, 18; v. 22, 24, 27, 29, 30; xii. 31, 47, 48; xvi. 8, 11 (see Greek and R. V.); also, numerously in the Apocalypse, Rev. vi. 9, 10; xi. 18; xvi. 5, 7; xviii. 8, 10, 20; xix. 2, 11; xx. 12, 13; James ii. 13. "For judgment is without mercy to him that showeth no mercy; mercy glorieth against judgment." Very striking are the passages, (Pet. ii, 4-9). "God spared not the angels that sinned, but cast them down to hell, and delivered them into chains of darkness to be reserved unto judgment," and "the Lord knoweth how * * * to reserve the unjust unto the day of judgment to be punished," and (iii, 7), "the heavens and the earth which are now, by the same word are kept in store, reserved unto fire against the day of judgment and perdition of ungodly men." See also Jude 6 and 15.

To sum up under the term krisis or judgment, it occurs forty-eight times in the New Testament. In forty-one instances it is translated "judgment," three times "damnation." In more than thirty places it may refer to what we term the last judgment. And in every one of these cases it does not appear that any but the guilty are involved in the judgment, and in nearly every instance, it is evident that the righteous are positively excluded. In those instances in which other than the last judgment is spoken of, the judgment is still only that of the ungodly, and in no case can it be shown that the godly are

BROUGHT INTO JUDGMENT.

And if we look at the close-related word krima, which is also translated "judgment" and "damnation," it is evident in every instance, in which it can be applied to the last judgment, that only the ungodly are included, and judgment is to condemnation. These facts are very striking, and throw a flood of light upon the question of the judgment, which is such a terror to so many of the Lord's people.

But then the question arises, what is to be said of those texts, which, upon their face, seem to teach that there is to be a general judgment, at which all shall be gathered, such as, Acts xvii. 31, "He hath appointed a day in which He will judge the world;" Matt. xxv. 32, "Before Him shall be gathered all nations;" and especially 2 Cor. v. 10, "We must all appear before the judgment seat of Christ." This first: When we find the true interpretation, these Scriptures with the others, there will be no contradiction.

What, then, are all the facts concerning the believer? For 2 Cor. v. 10 refers to him. It is said then, "We must all appear before the judgment seat of Christ. The Greek for judgment seat is bema, and occurs twelve times in the New Testament. It is derived from baivo, "to go, walk, tread, step." The first definition, both in the classical and

NEW TESTAMENT LEXICON,

is "a step." In this sense it is used but once, viz., in Acts vii. 5, "gave him none inheritance in it, not even 'a bema of a foot' "—a step of a foot, a foot breadth, or A. V., "not so much as to set his foot on."

The secondary meaning is an elevated place ascended by steps. (a) A tribune, to speak or read from. In this sense (Acts xii. 21), Herod "sat upon his throne, and made an oration unto them." (b.) The tribunal of a magistrate or ruler.

In this sense it is used of Pilate (Matt. xxvii. 19), "when he was set down on the judgment seat;" (John xix. 13), Pilate "sat down on the judgment seat;" of Gallio (Acts xviii. 12), "the Jews made insurrection against Paul, and brought him to the judgment seat;" (v. 16), "he drave them from the judgment seat;" v. 17, they beat Sosthenes "before the judgment seat;" of Festus (Acts xxv. 6), "the next day, sitting on the judgment seat, commanded Paul to be brought;" v. 10, "I stand at Cæsar's judgment seat;" v. 17, "I sat on the judgment seat." The other two instances of its use are in the connection, "we shall all stand" (Rom. xiv. 10); "we must all appear before the judgment seat of Christ" (2 Cor. v. 10).

In ten of these twelve cases the Greek word is rendered in the A. V., "judgment seat," and the R. V. agrees in every instance. In one case the word, both in the A. V. and R. V., is rendered "throne," while even here the R. V. gives the marginal reading, "judgment seat." In every instance Alford agrees with the A. V.

IT IS WORTHY OF NOTE,

in this connection, that in not one instance in which persons are represented as brought before the judgment seat is any one of them found guilty, or condemned, by the one who occupies the bema. This, of itself, might suggest the more consistent rendering of Rotherham, in nine of the twelve instances, "tribunal," while also, it should raise the question against himself, why he did not so render in the two cases which refer to Pilate.

Now, it is affirmed of the believer that he must appear before the bema of Jesus Christ. For what purpose? Paul has answered: "That every one may receive the things done in his body, according to that he hath done, whether it be good or bad." (2 Cor., v., 1.) All this said concerning those who "know (v., 1) that if our earthly house of this tabernacle were dissolved, we have a building of God * * eternal in the heavens," i. e., believers and believers only. What does it signify? Precisely what is set forth in 1 Cor., iii., 12-15. "Every man's work sha'l be tried." "If any man's work abide * * * he shall receive a reward." This is said only of the believing man, for only such a one is a "laborer together with God," v. 9, and of the one thus tested, it is affirmed that though his "work shall be burned," "he himself shall be saved," v. 15. All works of the believer are to be tried, that it be made manifest, whether or not "they are wrought in God," (John iii. 21). For this trial all are gathered before the bema,

THE UNGODLY

are not there, but there are all believers. Some will receive great "reward" for efficient service and many good works, some a less reward, others less still, and some none at all, their works being done only in the energy of the flesh, being counted utterly worthless and cast into the fire; yet, by reason of a true, though it may be feeble faith, they do not miss salvation. And thus it is that "every man's work shall be made manifest," and its true value be determined. But of "judgment," of which we have seen that it leads on to condemnation, into any such scene the believer shall not come. This is the very word of our Divine Lord: "He that * * believeth * * hath everlasting life, and shall not come into judgment," where the word is the very same which Paul uses when he says after death, "judgment."

It is not difficult to show by irresistible Scripture proof, that no believer shall ever stand in other judgment than this. Because,

1. The general idea of the judgment supposes that the sins of the believer are to be brought there and judged. But this is certainly a mistake. For though "all we like sheep have gone astray," "the Lord hath laid on Him (Jesus) the iniquity of us all," (Isaiah liii. 6), and He "bore our sins in His own body on the tree," (1 Peter ii 24). When Christ thus bore our sins He "condemned sin in the flesh" (Rom. viii., 3); He "put away sin by the sacrifice of Himself" (Heb. ix., 26.) The believer's sins have therefore been judged and condemned already."

"Thy sin was judged in His flesh." For "He died unto sin once" (Rom. vi., 10.) "He was wounded for our transgressions, He was bruised for our iniquities" (Isaiah liii., 5.) Hence, so far as his sins are concerned, the believer looks back to his judgment, and not forward.

2. The oneness of Christ and the believer testifies to the same fact. Every believer can truly say, "I was crucified with Christ" (Gal. ii., 20.) I was "buried with Him by the baptism unto death" (Rom. vi., 4,) hence what Christ's death expressed it expressed for me. "If one died for all, then all died" (2 Cor. v., 14.) Under the old dispensation the sins of the Jews were dealt with on the day of atonement. God dealt with the sin and sins of all time on Calvary. The awful judgment of God against sin there awoke, was there expressed, and there it smote; and so far as His people are concerned that was its final expression forever. The judgment is passed, the sentence executed.

3. Expose the believer to be judged according to his deeds, and you insure his condemnation. "Enter not into judgment with thy servant," prays the Psalmist (Ps. cxliii. 2), "for in Thy sight shall no man living be justified." No one with whom God enters into judgment can be saved. For justice is inexorable. And not only have all sinned, they continue to sin, and therefore, if sins were brought into judgment, one's doom would be inevitable. "No one will be safe who is to have his

ETERNAL DESTINY

determined by his own deeds." Albert Barnes, Com. on Rev. xx. 12.

There remains a further consideration of most serious and solemn moment, viz:

4. To bring the believer into judgment would make the judge the accused. The judge is Christ. "The Father judgeth no man, but hath committed all judgment unto the Son," and "hath given Him authority to execute judgment also," (John v. 22, 27). "It is He which was ordained of God to be the judge of quick and dead" (Acts x. 42). But Christ, the judge, has stood for us. To bring the believer into judgment, therefore, would be to question the worth of what Christ has done, to bring an accusation against Him. It would bring Him down from the place of judgment, strip from Him the ermine of the judge, and place Him be-

fore the bar as a culprit. He died for us, for our sins. Did He make sufficient propitiation? Did His work meet the demand? If so, if His offering was adequate to the purpose, then the believer is justified, and how can one be brought into judgment of whom the divine testimony already is, "there is, therefore, now no condemnation" (Rom. viii. 1): he is "justified from all things" (Acts xiii. 39).

And further, what greater insult could be offered to Jesus, than to bring into judgment, one for whom He has stood? To judge such would be but to judge Himself. "Who shall lay anything to the charge

OF GOD'S ELECT?

Shall God that justifieth? Who is He that condemneth? Is is Christ that died?" (Rom. viii., 33, 34.)

The judgment must therefore deal with Him before it can reach them.

Consider, too, the incongruity of Christ's judging His own bride. Many of them will have been saints in heaven for thousands of years, and how can such ever be put on trial? No, all believers will be gathered at the judgment seat of Christ for one sole purpose, to receive the reward for their works, each "according as his work shall be" (Rev. xxii. 12). And a reward is not a gift. The believer has received the latter, "the gift of God is eternal life through Jesus Christ" (Rom. vi. 23). The former awaits him at the bema. And it should be noted for the comfort of every believer, that the bema is not set to determine or even consider the question of salvation. That is forever settled, when, as one "believeth," so he "hath everlasting life" (John iii. 36). But it is set to determine the value of Christian service, and the reward therefor. The judgment seat of Christ is not for the judgment of the person, but of his works. There is to be determined the value of a "cup of cold water," given in the name of Christ. "For God is not unrighteous to forget your work and

LABOR OF LOVE,

which ye have showed toward His name, in that ye have ministered to the saints and do minister." (Heb. vi. 10). "Whatsoever good thing any man doeth, he shall receive a reward." (Eph. vi. 8). Oh, pity to him, who, though "he himself shall be saved," shall yet "suffer loss" (1 Cor. iii. 15), at the judgment seat of Christ, for such loss will be eternal. It is a solemn thought that what we lose here, in the matter of Christian service and good works, eternity can never make good. The voice of him who is barely "saved, yet so as by fire," will never sound so loud, his harp will never be strung so rapturously, nor his palm be waved so victoriously in heaven, as will fall to the blessed lot of him who has "abundant entrance."

Oh, joy to him on whose labor, when "the fire shall try every man's work of what sort it is" (1 Cor. iii. 13), there shall be no "smell of fire," but all his work, either "gold, silver, or precious stones," shall abide the test, and whose "reward" shall be great. It is surely worth an effort to stand well at the judgment seat of Christ.

The considerations above urged are opposed to the common idea of a general judgment. What then, shall we say to Mat. xxv. 31-33? "When the Son of Man shall come in His glory * * * before Him shall be gathered all nations, and He shall separate them from one another * * * and He shall set the sheep on His right hand, but the goats on the left."

THIS PASSAGE

is constantly quoted and relied on in proof of a general judgment, and is supposed to be parallel with Rev. xx. 11-15: "And I saw a great white throne and Him that sat on it * * * and I saw the dead, small and great, stand before God * * * and the dead were judged out of those things which were written in the books * * * and the sea gave up the dead which were in it, and death and hades delivered up the dead which were in them," etc., etc. The sound of the two italicized phrases in the last two quotations, will easily mislead one who is careless respecting details; when a careful consideration of them will show that these passages can not be parallel, and must therefore refer to entirely different events. The following facts stand in proof of the last statement:

1. The passage from Matthew contains not one word to indicate a resurrection; that from Revelation plainly declares a resurrection, v. 13.

2. In Matthew the dealing is with "nations." What nations? The answer is in Mat. xxiv.: 14, "This Gospel of the kingdom shall be preached in all the world, for a witness unto all the nations. Then, "When the Son of man shall come * * * before him shall be gathered all the nations" before specified. They come as nations. In Revelation the dealing is with individuals: "They were judged every man according to their works," (verse 13) Coupled with this there follows a third fact, viz:

3. Matthew evidently speaks of nations living when "the Son of man" appears, as in (Zech xiv, 2). Revelation specially designates the nations of the "dead."

4. In Matthew we find among the gathered

"nations" two distinct classes, viz.: "the sheep" and "the goats;" and apart from them, a third class, viz: the "brethren," (verses 40-45). The two former classes are separated, on one sole ground, viz.: their treatment of the third class, the brethren. It were absurd to suppose that the sheep were rewarded for what they had done to themselves, or the goats punished for what they had

DONE TO THE SHEEP,

in the face of the distinct affirmation that the one class is rewarded and the other punished for their treatment of a class entirely distinct from either of themselves. Evidently, then, to constitute them either praiseworthy or blameworthy, they must have known them as as the brethren of Christ.

In Revelation we find but one class, no separation, but all "judged out of those things which were written in the books" (v. 12) (not "the book") consigned to the lake of fire, and among them are many who never heard of Christ, and to whom the language in Matthew could not apply.

Now, certainly, it is most remarkable and unaccountable that if the church or believers are to have a place in this stupendous scene, not one word is said concerning them, and the doom of the lost alone appears as the result of the grand assize.

Our study of these passages reveals, therefore, the following facts, viz: that there is to be a judgment of the living nations, and a judgment of the "great white throne," and these are distinct and separate in time and place.

Where, then, will be the church while these judgments proceed? "With the Lord." Their case is set forth in I. Thess. iv, 16, 17. "The Lord himself shall descend from heaven with a shout * * * and the dead in Christ shall rise first; then we

WHICH ARE ALIVE

and remain shall be caught up * * * to meet the Lord in the air, and so shall we ever be with the Lord." This is the first signal of Christ's second coming. Hence these great events, which have so often been regarded with nothing less than terror, by the Lord's dear people, will not concern them in the least, save as spectators, of what their Lord and Master does.

One other inquiry, partly curious, will prepare the way for the general conclusion.

When will the "judgment seat of Christ" be set? We may not dogmatize, as we have scarcely more than hints upon which to base a conclusion. This much is sure, when the Lord comes with a shout the dead saints will be raised, the living saints will "all be changed in a moment" (1 Cor. xv. 51-52), the corruptible will put on incorruption, the mortal, immortality. This, of course, marks the resurrection, "sown in dishonor, raised in glory," "sown in weakness, raised in power," "sown a natural body, raised a spiritual body," (1 Cor. xv. 43-44). Now, in the Revelation xxii. 12-we find Jesus saying, "Behold, I come quickly, and My reward is with Me, to give every man according as his work shall be." See 1 Cor. iii. 13-14. And in Luke xiv. 13-14, He says, "When thou makest a feast, call the poor, * * * the blind, and thou shalt be blessed, * * * for thou shalt be recompensed at the resurrection of the just." These passages may indicate that the time of the church's "reward" is quickly to

SUCCEED THEIR RESURRECTION.

Bunyan: "Now when the saints that sleep shall be raised, thus incorruptible, powerful, glorious, and spiritual, and also those that then shall be found alive made like them; then forthwith, before the unjust are raised, the saints shall appear before the judgment seat of our Lord Jesus Christ, there to give an account to their Lord, the judge of all the things they have done, and to receive a reward for their good according to their labor."

It is evident from all that has been said that the only judgment of the believer is that which attaches to his works, wherefor he receives greater or less reward, or, may be, none.

The final doom of the wicked is also according to his works. (Rom. ii. 6; Gal. vi. 7; 2 Pet. ii. 12-13; Rev. ii. 23; xi. 18; xx. 12). There is, however, a world-wide distinction in the two classes of works. "Then said they unto Him, what shall we do that we might work the works of God? Jesus answered and said unto them, this is the work of God, that ye believe on Him whom He hath sent," (John vi. 28-29). Eject this special "work of God" from the lives of the ungodly, the "work of faith and labor of love," (1 Thess. i. 3), and there is left but a harvest of whirlwind from the sowing of the wind.

To set down our general conclusion in a word, the Scriptures teach that

THERE ARE FOUR JUDGMENTS.

1. A judgment already passed of the sins of the Lord's people. These have been judged, condemned, and the sentence upon them executed in the person of our substitute on Calvary; therefore, the believer "shall not come into judgment" (John v. 24).

2. A coming tribunal of Christ, before which all believers must stand, for the testing of all their work and service. If any are present, other than saints, they can be only the angels of God.

3. A coming tribunal of Christ, when He sits upon "the throne of His glory" (Matt. xxv. 31). Before Him, shall be gathered at that tribunal, "all the nations," then living for his final adjudication, concerning their treatment of Him in the person of His "brethren." Though they come as "nations," sentence will be pronounced upon them as individuals, according as the desert of each may appear.

4. A coming judgment of the "Great White Throne." This is the only proper judgment, in the sense of the Scripture, viz: guilt being present and leading on to condemnation. There are present at this scene only "the rest of the dead" (Rev. xx. 5).

PREVIOUSLY TO THIS,

the saints have been gathered in "the out-resurrection, that from among the dead" (Phil. iii. 11), to be "forever with the Lord;" and now the remaining dead are raised for judgment. This is the "day of judgment and perdition of ungodly men" (2 Pet. iii. 7), unto which the "unjust" have been reserved "to be punished" (2 Pet. ii. 9). Then shall the "Son of man," to whom all judgment is committed, "execute judgment upon all * * * that are ungodly" (Jude, 15). Then, too, "when the Lord Jesus shall be revealed from heaven, with His mighty angels in flaming fire taking vengeance on them that know not God, and that obey not the gospel of His Son, who shall be punished with everlasting destruction from the presence of the Lord, and from the glory of His power," "shall He come to be glorified in His saints, and to be admired in all them that believe * * * in that day" (II. Thess. i. 7-10). The saints will be there, but neither as culprits nor accused. "Then shall the righteous shine forth as the sun, in the kingdom of their Father" (Matt. xiii. 43), and this will be the "day of judgment" of many Scriptures. Amen.

THE REV. DR. DINWIDDIE.

THE PRIESTHOOD OF CHRIST.

In the absence of the Rev. Dr. J. D. Herr, of Milwaukee, who was to have spoken on the "Importance of Prophetic Study," the Rev. Dr. William Dinwiddie, of Alexandria, Va., after prayer by the Rev. Dr. Burton, of Union City. Mich., and a solo by Professor E. C. Avis, of Tennessee, the singing evangelist, addressed the conference on the subject, "The Priesthood of Christ." The substance, in a somewhat condensed form, of Dr. Dinwiddie's address is as follows:

The Scripture which capitally sets forth the priesthood of Christ is the epistle to the Hebrews. Let us reverently follow the guidance of the Holy Spirit in His teachings to us on this great subject.

There are two great aspects under which it is presented to us, one as relates to God in Hebrew ii. 10; "For it became Him, for whom are all things and by whom are all things, in bringing many sons to glory, to make the captain of their salvation perfect through sufferings." The other view of it is what becomes us (Heb. vii. 26-27): "For such an high priest became us, who is holy, harmless, undefiled, separate from sinners, and made higher than the heavens. Who needeth not daily as those high priests (viz: under the law) to offer up sacrifice, first for His own sins, and then for the people's; for this He did once when He offered up Himself."

The marvel is that what became God in this matter is the sufferings of Christ, His being humbled even unto the dust of death; and what became us is His being holy, harmless, undefiled, separate from sinners, and made higher than the heavens. To this we shall recur.

The Spirit first dwells on his divine glory in chapter I. He is presented to us as the Son of God, the appointed heir of all things, the brightness of God's glory, and the express image of his substance, upholds all things by the word of His power, who by Himself made purification for our sins, who is seated at the right hand of the majesty on high,

BETTER THAN THE ANGELS,

who are commanded when He is brought into the world to worship Him. They are servants only; He is the Son. He is addressed also in these sublime words: "Thy throne, O God, is forever and ever, a scepter of righteousness is the scepter of thy kingdom." Lastly, the dread name Jehovah is given Him in this passage: "Thou, Lord, in the beginning hast laid the foundation of the earth; and the heavens are the works of Thine hands; they shall perish, but Thou remainest; and they all shall wax old as doth a garment, and as a vesture shalt Thou fold them up, and they shall be changed, but Thou art the same, and thy years shall not fail."

What higher testimony could be borne to the divine glory of the Son?

And now, even since His humiliation, He holds His superiority over the angels, to none of whom did God ever say at any time, "Sit on my right hand, until I make thine enemies thy footstool." They are only servants to the heirs of salvation, although we not long ago used to teach our children to say "I want to be an angel." What ignorance of Christian position!

We are next brought, in chapter II to behold His glory as the Son of man, to whom God hath put in subjection "the world to come," that is, this habitable earth, as it shall be when everything in it is ordered according to God, when the world-kingdom of our Lord shall have come and He

AND SHALL REIGN FOR EVER AND EVER.

Made lower than the angels for the suffering of death, He is crowned with glory and honor, that He by the grace of God should taste death for every man, as it is in the authorized version, but rather, for everything, or all things, for the universe. The efficacy of Christ's death is not limited to the earth. The purification of the heavenly things is accomplished by it as Heb. ix. 23 asserts. "It was, therefore, necessary that the patterns of things in the heavens should be purified with these (viz.: the Levitical offerings), but the heavenly things themselves with better sacrifices than these." His death, so far reaching in its consequences, is rewarded by His having all things put in subjection under His feet.

The work given Him to do is the bringing of many sons unto glory; not from the angels, for He takes not hold of them, but of men. And in order to bring sinful men to glory in fellowship with Him it became God, His honor and character demanded that the Captain of their salvation be made perfect through sufferings. The Son of man must be lifted up. It was not possible that the cup His Father gave Him to drink should pass from Him. And His death glorified God. As He, to whom the future is as the past, said a little before His death, "I have glorified thee on the earth, I have finished the work Thou gavest Me to do." Then in His own omniscient mind He was enduring the cross, despising its shame, for the joy set before Him, the joy of bringing us, many sons with Himself to glory. He stands in the midst of

THOSE SAVED BY HIM;

He that sanctifieth, and they who are sanctified are all of one; He is not ashamed to call them His brethern; it is His first word to us since He rose from the dead. "Go to my brethren," He is made like unto them that He might be a mericful and faithful high priest in things pertaining to God to make expiation for the sins of His people. He suffered being tempted that He might be able to succor them that are tempted. And what a mighty succor must He bring us, such a Savior sent to us from such a God!

HIS SUPERIORITY TO MOSES.

The Spirit as He presses the claims of the Lord on the Hebrews goes on to show His superiority to Moses. Moses was faithful in all his house as a servant, but Christ as a Son over His own house. Again, He is the true Joshua, and under His captaincy we are on our way to the rest that remaineth for the people of God. The Sabbath is not now God's rest. "My Father is working hitherto, and I work," said Jesus, in the midst of a race of sinners and of the whole creation groaning under the burdens and misery of sin. Joshua did not bring God's people into His rest, for David long after Joshua spoke of it as still future. And still it remaineth. But we are on our way to it under the leadership of Jesus, who will make manifest and bring into full display that new creation of which He, the second Adam, is the Head, in which old things are passed away and all things are become new and all of God, and of which, if any man be in Christ he forms a part. This is our destination, this is God's rest. Are we walking worthy of such a calling as that of

SHARING HIS GLORY?

On which of us does it seem possible, in the most elevated moments of our life does it seem possible, that Jesus could look and say that we are glorious in His sight. It is yet matter of faith, not of sight. The Sons of God are not yet manifested, nor will be until He who is our life shall appear and we shall appear with Him in glory. And how does He fit us for that glory? He sanctifies and cleanses us with the washing of water by the word that He may present us to Himself glorious, not having spot or wrinkle or any such thing, but that we should be holy and without blemish.

What a place in God's plans is given to His word. By it believers are born again, not of corruptible seed, but of incorruptible; by feeding on its sincere milk, being born again, they grow unto salvation; by His word Jesus cleansed His disciples when with them, through it He prays the Father to sanctify them. And see how the Spirit speaks of it here, "For the word of God is quick and powerful, and sharper than any two-edged sword, piercing even to the dividing asunder of the soul and the spirit, the joints and the marrow, and is a discerner of the thoughts and intents of the heart. Neither is there any creature that is not manifest in His sight, but all things are naked and opened unto the eyes of Him with whom we have to do." The word of God, when we honestly apply it, is the very eyes of

GOD LOOKING INTO THE INMOST SOUL.

Putting ourselves under its light we know that in us, that is, in our flesh, dwelleth no good thing; looking around us, we know that all that is in the world, "the lust of the flesh, the lust of the eyes, and the pride of life," is not of the Father, and we see the god of this world going about as a roaring lion seeking whom he may devour, and find our conflict to be not against flesh and blood, but against principalities, against powers, against the rulers of the darkness of this world, against wicked spirits in the heavenly places. To the treacherous sin that dwelleth in us, how fearful and seductive the opposition of the world! How appalling the power and malignity of Satan and the evil spirits in league with him! In such a conflict how pitifully weak and helpless are we!

But a gracious God and loving Father and a sympathizing Savior know thoroughly and have fully provided for all our needs. Under the guidance of the Spirit we see our great High Priest who has passed through the heavens, Jesus, the Son of God. We know He is touched with the feeling of all our weakness, and we come boldly to the throne of grace that we may obtain mercy and find grace to help in time of need.

But with such glories attaching to Him as Son of God and Son of man, as we have been seeking to contemplate under the guidance of the Spirit and in the divine word, yet Christ

GLORIFIED NOT HIMSELF

to be become a high priest, but God so glorified Him, who said unto Him, "Thou art My son: to-day have I begotten Thee." This is the personal glory. And He also saith in another place: "Thou art a priest forever after the order of Melchizedek." This is the official glory. For this priesthood He was perfected through those sufferings in which He learned obedience, and became the author of not temporary deliverance, but of eternal salvation to all that obey Him, and has now entered within the veil as a forerunner for us, for within the veil, in the holiest, is our present and our endless home.

The priesthood of Aaron and the sons of Levi was but a foreshadowing of the priesthood of Christ, and every way inferior. The tribe of Levi in Abraham paid tithes to Melchizedek, and Abraham being blessed of Melchizedek was inferior to Him. Aaron's priesthood was after the law of a carnal commandment; Christ's is after the power of an endless life. The law made nothing perfect. Hence the disannulling of the commandment because of the weakness and unprofitableness and the bringing in of a better hope by which we through Christ draw nigh to God.

There is no succession in the Melchizedek priesthood of Christ. The sum of the Spirit's history of Melchizedek is "He liveth." No account of his birth, his death, his genealogy. There is no change recorded in his priesthood. And so Christ, whose priesthood is after the order of Melchizedek, is able to save to the uttermost them that come to God by Him, seeing He ever liveth

TO MAKE INTERCESSION FOR THEM.

We have had the Spirit's teaching as to what became God in the priesthood of Christ. Now he gives us what becomes us, a high priest who is holy, harmless, undefiled, separate from sinners, and made higher than the heavens, who needeth not daily as those (the Levitical) high priests to offer up sacrifice, first for his own sins and then for the people's; for this he did once, when he offered up himself. For the law maketh men high priests which have infirmity, but the word of the oath which was save the law, maketh the Son, who is consecrated (perfected) forevermore.

It is a wonderful revelation that such a high priest became us! The glory that is to follow the sufferings of Christ is so high, so pure, the glory of which we share with Him, for He says to the Father, "The glory which Thou gavest me, I have given them!" So great is the love wherewith God loved us even when we were dead in sins that it is His purpose in the ages to come to show the exceeding riches of His grace in His kindness toward us through Jesus Christ. To maintain us in such a glory, it becomes us to have an eternal priest, who through the eternal Spirit offered Himself without spot to God once, who has brought in everlasting righteousness, who is the Author of eternal salvation to all that obey Him.

Results to Us—1. Access to God. This the Israelite under the law never had.

IT WAS BARRED BY THE VEIL

by which the Holy Ghost signified that the way into the holiest of all, that is the way of access to God, was not yet made manifest, while the first tabernacle was yet standing. At Christ's death the veil of the temple was rent in twain from top to bottom. The way of access to God is now perfectly open and free, and the only place of Christian worship is thine holiest. Yet many who profess to worship stand afar off in the outer court, will hardly look upon the brazen altar, seldom if ever come to the golden altar to make the sweet incense of thanksgiving and praise ascend to God, and hardly dare think of coming freely into the holiest. Look at the hymnology of Christendom! Even when they profess to come to the throne of grace to obtain mercy and find grace to help in time of need, it is to Jesus they come instead of to the God of all grace who sits upon that throne.

2. But our consciences also are purged. It would be intolerable to be brought into the holiest if any stain of sin rested on the conscience. Did the blood of bulls and of

goats, and the ashes of the heifer sanctify to the purifying of the flesh so that the Israelite with these offerings and sprinklings could stand in peace in God's place of worship and make his offerings with joy? He did, so long as he believed that God, who made these provisions, spoke truth in them. How much more then,

PLEADS THE SPIRIT,

shall the blood of Christ, who, through the Eternal Spirit, offered Himself without spot to God, purge your conscience from dead works to serve the living God? There can not be a spot on my conscience as long as I believe that God, who made this provision to purge it, speaks the truth in this word about it. Christ has entered into heaven itself, now to appear in the presence for us, having offered himself once. And this connects immediately, in the mind of the spirit, with His return. Unto them that look for Him shall He come the second time without sin unto salvation. And so whenever we remember His death in the communion, the spirit again connects it with His return by the precious words: "Till He come."

3. But this condition of access and perfect cleansing is in perpetuity. By the one offering of Himself He hath perfected forever, in perpetuity, without any interruption, them that are sanctified. We are accepted in the beloved, His own lips assure us that the Father loves us as He loves Him. As He is, so are we in this world. His priesthood makes us priests. The only place of true Christian worship is in the holiest, the only character of such worship is priestly. All believers of any and every degree are priests. They can only offer true Christian worship as priests, all of them, and all equally priests. To set up a class or cast of men as having in any degree nearer

OR FREER ACCESS TO GOD

than all other believers have is to deny the very foundations of Christianity. It is to leave the full revelation of God's grace to His children and go back to the A B C's of elementary instruction, to the twilight of Judaism instead of the sunlight of Christian place and privilege.

There is no simpler test of a false religion of more easy application than this: Does any religion put any set or class of men between God and other men? Then it is not of God. How sad to apply this test to Christendom now. Look at the Greek Church, look at Romanism, look at all the phases of ritualism in the Protestant world. They are all practical denials of the whole truth of Christ's priesthood and one perfect offering of Himself, of the divine purgation of conscience effected for all believers by His blood, and of our eternal redemption. And in contending earnestly for the faith once delivered to the saints, as our Brother Erdman so earnestly exhorted us yesterday, at what point along the line do we need more earnestly and urgently to press the contest than in maintaining the true Christian priesthood of all believers equally?

Christ's Priesthood and Advocacy—The perfect word distinguishes between the priesthood of Christ and His advocacy, and we lose much if we confound them. They are both branches of His great and perfect work in bringing us to His glory. Let us look at them in His word: 1 John I-II, 2 gives us the advocacy of Christ. Those

PRECIOUS TWELVE LITTLE VERSES

contain for us God's recipe to keep us from sin.

"My little children, these things I write unto you in order that you may not sin." It would keep us from sin if we kept these things before us in their full light and power. What things? That which was from the beginning, which John had every opportunity to make himself a competent witness about, he had heard, he had seen with his eyes, he had looked upon, his hands had handled of the word of life—that eternal life which was with the Father and was perfectly exhibited to us in Christ—and this he testified to us that we may have fellowship with him and be as dear to Christ as "the disciple whom he loved," rest our very heads on his bosom; nay, more, have fellowship with the Father Himself and His Son Jesus Christ, share whatever the Father and Christ have with fullness of joy. What a contrast to the doubt, the grief, the weakness, the misery of so many of God's children. Whose fault is it? Not God's, for He has had these things written that our joy may be full. Ah! but He is light, and in Him is no darkness at all. If we say we have fellowship with Him, and walk in darkness, we lie and do not the truth. If we say we have no sin

WE DECEIVE OURSELVES,

and the truth is not in us. And if we say we have not sinned we make God a liar, and His word is not in us. But glorious provision for us. If we confess our sins He is faithful and just to forgive us our sins and to cleanse us from all unrighteousness. Let us see all the provision for us in practical application. Jesus, our advocate when we sin, applies it to us and uses it for us. Look at Peter believing himself to be incapable of denying the Lord, though clearly told of it by the Lord Himself. See him through fear of man denying the Lord and calling God Himself to witness to the lie.

And see Jesus, before he denies Him, and while He can not believe it possible, praying for him that his faith should not fail. And when the infuriated crowd with causeless hatred instigated of Satan are surrounding Christ and clamoring for His blood, see Him with the divine calmness of His unchanging love having leisure to look at guilty Peter slunk away into some corner, in his conscious guilt, and by the look bringing His own word in its searching power to break Peter down in confession of bitter weeping, and later on in deepest, thrice repeated, searching of his inmost soul to see and judge the roots of the sin in him, and then the Lord graciously cleanses, restores, and sets him to feed His sheep and His lambs. Sad to say,

WE ALL NEED THIS ADVOCACY.

But is this what we look to God on the throne of His grace for, when we come boldly to that throne for mercy and grace to help in time of need? No. They who come thus are those who are working and suffering for Christ in conflict with the world, the flesh, and the devil. They are looking at God on the throne, and at His right hand our high priest who by Himself made purification for our sins before he took his seat there. God and Christ are for us, no sin is on our conscience, but we see our pitiful weakness and need in presence of our and God's enemies. Were our eyes fully enlightened by the word there is not a moment of our life in this pilgrimage when we should not feel our entire dependence on God for help and strength. And He never fails to give it. For He pities us. His mercy endureth forever. And in His rich grace He is able and willing to do exceedingly abundantly for us above all that we ask or even think. Christ's advocacy takes the poor crippled, bruised, maimed, disarmed, and broken spirited soldier of th cross who has deserted and dishonored his captain, and can only parade about his pains, his weaknesses, and his worthlessness. He heals him, invigorates him, cleanses him, restores him, renews the courage of his heart, and sends him again to battle, clad in the complete armor of God, while Christ's priesthood in this limited aspect of it puts into our hands and at our disposal the whole treasury of God's riches of strength and armor to contend against His and our enemies.

OUTSIDE THE CAMP.

There is a solemn call to the Hebrews in the last chapter to leave the camp and to go forth unto Jesus bearing His reproach. If the Spirit so called out of effete Judaism, how much more out of apostate Christendom. Let any man live godly in Christ Jesus and he shall suffer persecution. Le: any man bear a full testimony for all the truth as it is in Jesus; let him "hold fast His word and not deny His name" and he will soon find in this day that if he does not go forth outside the camp of Christendom to Christ bearing His reproach, he will be thrust out. Like the man whom the Lord healed, and who gave his testimony simply that Christ must be from God. They put him forth, but only to have the Lord meet him outside and make to him richer communications of His truth and love. What rich reward the Lord stands ready to give to all who faithfully witness for Him! And he will set before us an open door of testimony and service that no man will be able to shut. Gathered in this conference to seek to recover to God's church truth lost and buried under the rubbish of tradition and superstition and formalism, we assuredly find we have to go outside the camp, but may richest blessing result, as I doubt not it will, not only to ourselves, but to all God's children to the very ends of the earth; and may even those who, in their own ignorance and to their own loss, ignore or oppose the precious truth of the Lord's coming, have their hearts opened in His long suffering goodness to the truth in all its sweetness and comfort and power! - The

KING OF RIGHTEOUSNESS AND PEACE.

Our High Priest is also a king. King of nations! King of kings and lord of lords! The world kingdom of our Lord and of His Christ shall come. Surely I come quickly. While we look appalled on the future of the unbelieving world, fast rushing on to the apostasy, and the awful reign of the man of sin, so powerfully presented to us in papers read before the conference, if we hold fast to His truth and do not deny His name, He will keep us from that hour of dread and unparalleled tribulation which shall come upon all them that dwell on the earth, and count as worthy to stand before the Son of man.

PROFESSOR F. GODET.

FROM A SWISS DIVINE.

At the opening of the afternoon meeting, the Rev. J. Halsted Carroll, D. D., of Stillwater, Minn., presiding, and prayer being said by Bishop Nicholson, in the usual devotional exercises, the following letter from Professor F. Godet, of Neufchatel, Switzerland, was read by the moderator, the Rev. Dr. Carroll:

THE REV. N. WEST, D. D.—Very honored and dear brother: I have preferred to give you an exposition, brief as the subject admits, and from which you may readily draw the answer to the questions you have proposed, rather than brokenly to reply to them. I could have extended the labor greatly, but I have chosen to condense it as much as possible. Each line might indeed be the text for an entire page. I send you the result to which my study of the Scriptures has led me. God has kindled a flame in my heart and yours, but the fire of the Holy Spirit does not consume the heart, neither is it hindered from transmission to the hearts of my brethren. I thank you for the confidence you have reposed in me, so far as I deserve it, and ask a place

IN YOUR AFFECTION,

and intercession, in Christ. May God bless your reunion at Chicago, and be a living power in your midst. Faithfully yours,

F. GODET.

"THE CLOSING SCÈNES IN THE EXISTENCE ON EARTH, ACCORDING TO THE PROPHECIES: When Moses was granted the favor of a vision of God, he was not allowed, nor was he able, to behold His face. "I will put thee in the cleft of the rock, and cover thee with my hand, and my back thou shalt see, as I pass by, but my face thou canst not see." So, by means of the prophecies we may indeed observe, in advance the grand scenes that will close the terrestial existence of man, while yet we are unable to form to ourselves an exact and perfectly clear idea of them, until after their accomplishment. What I have said is no reason for discarding, as useless, the study of this great subject. Still less is it my purpose to defend the spiritualist who reduces the prophetic pictures to facts already accomplished, or daily occurring, or interprets the prophecies in a merely ethical manner. It is very evident that Jesus has not thus intended it; for He has plainly said, "Heaven and and earth shall pass away but my words shall not pass away." Neither did the Apostles of Jesus so interpret them; and the Apostles of Jesus are not false prophets.

Let us examine in the light of New Testament teachings:

I. The state of things that will precede the coming of Christ.

II. That coming itself.

III. The state of things that will follow the coming.

I. The first advent of Christ in the flesh did not entirely accomplish the Messianic prophecies of the Old Testament. The fulfilled portion is a pledge of the second coming of the Lord that will realize the same in the most literal manner. The Lord Himself

ANNOUNCED HIS PERSONAL RETURN

when uttering, in presence of the Sanhedrin, these words, "Verily, I say unto you, that hereafter, ye shall see the Son of man seated at the right hand of power, and coming upon the clouds of heaven." The history of the church, in its totality, is that second coming of the Son of man His glorious reappearing will be His arrival. In what condition will Jesus find the world at his arrival?

1. As to Christianity in general, this is what the Lord himself has told us in (Luke xviii. 8), "When the Son of Man cometh, think ye that He will find the faith on the earth?" Also (Luke xvii. 26-30)., 'As it was in the days of Noah, so shall it be also in the days of the Son of man," etc. A carnal security will have taken possession of mankind, entirely ruled by terrestrial thoughts. The majority of men will have lost the sense of divine things. St. Paul says the same thing in other terms (I. Thess. v. 3), "When they shall say peace and safety, then sudden destruction shall come upon them as travail upon a woman with child;" besides, this menace addressed by him to gentile Christianity (Rom. xii. 22) "Behold, therefore, the goodness and severity of God; on them which fell, severity, but toward the goodness, if thou continue in His goodness, otherwise thou also shalt be cut off." What the feelings of the faithful minority will be, at that time, the Lord has expressed in these terms (Luke xvii. 22), "The days will come when ye shall desire to see one of the days of the Son of man, and ye shall not see it."

2. As to the condition

OF THE JEWISH PEOPLE

at that epoch, it is described in terms which seem, to me, very clear. In the Book of Revelation, chapter xi., it is said: "Measure not the court which is without the temple, for it is given to the gentiles; but, measure the temple, the altar, and them that worship therein." The rest of the chapter shows what will be the condition of Israel at the end of this age. The larger part of this people will be carried away by gentile infidelity. A select body of worshipers will, doubtless, remain separate and faithful to the God of Abraham. In the second letter to the Thessalonians a revolt is foretold, called an "apostasy," or "falling away." By this expression, the apostle intends to speak of something known and expected, which can only be the great defection predicted by Daniel, and which, according to the description of the prophet, is to take place in Israel. The people so long faithful to the revelation of God committed to them, will, even after their dispersion by the Romans, finally shake off this yoke and, adhering to the materialism that rules even in the bosom of Christianity, will place themselves at the head of open warfare against everything that is divine. Then the prediction of Psalm II. will be fulfilled. "Why do the nations assemble themselves, and the people imagine a vain thing? Let us break," say they, "their bands asunder, and cast away their curse from us." It is of God and his anointed they speak thus.

Thus, from the bosom of this general rebellion will arise that one in whose person

THE "MAN OF SIN"

will be concentrated, as St. Paul shows us in his second letter to the Thessalonians, chapter second; the "Antichrist" of St. John in his first letter, and in the Apocalypse. This one will be the most complete personification of evil in humanity. He will present himself as the incarnation of the infinite principle which animates the universe, and will make himself worshipped as such. His personal will takes the place of all other law, divine or human. St. Paul tells us in II. Thessalonians, that at the moment when he was writing, there was even then a power that hindered the revelation of this diabolical being, whose spirit of revolt was already active. It appears to me that this power can only be that of the Roman Empire, and consequently the Antichrist can only be the false Jewish Messiah, the authitesis of Jesus, the true Messiah. This false Messiah, ever ready to appear, was suppressed continually by the Roman arms. The fall of the Roman Empire is therefore the precondition of his final appearance on the theater of history; and, if he has not yet appeared, it is because the social state founded upon the Roman institutions is still uppermost, and opposes a barrier to the revolutionary torrent from which this Antichrist will issue. The reign of this wicked one is described in the Apocalypse, chapter 13. According to chapter 11 of this book, his residence will be in Jerusalem, and this will be the realization of

THE CARNAL MESSIANISM,

which has always formed the basis of Jewish thought. The satanic rule will be suddenly overthrown, as soon as it reaches the summit of its power (this is doubtless the import of number 3½), by the glorious appearing of the Lord.

II. The seventeenth chapter of Luke represents this event as making itself known suddenly, and at once, and in a manner rapid as the lightning, over the whole earth. This will be the blow of red-hot iron that will make the flesh of sickened humansty quiver, in order to awaken again the powers of life. St. Paul, in Thessalenians, second chapter, shows us the antichristian power crushed by the breath of the Lord, at His appearance, and in the Apocolypse, Chapter 19, we see Messiah himself, as a conqueror, at the head of celestial armies, dispersing the troops of infidel humanity united against Him. The army that comes with the Lord, in this moment of triumph, is not composed solely of elect angels. It comprises also, on the one side, the risen saints, who descend again with Christ, glorified from the height of heaven; and, on the other, Christians still living, at that moment, who will then be transfigured and lifted to meet the Lord in the air, in order to reappear with Him. This is what St. Paul teaches in I. Thess. iv. 15-16. So also we read of the faithful raised in I. Cor. xv. 23, and of the living transfigured in vss. 51-52. Then, doubtless, the physical phenomena, described in Luke xxi. 25-26, "the signs in the sun, moon, and stars," and "the shaking of the powers of heaven;"

THE RENEWING OF NATURE,

which Paul describes in Romans viii. 20-23, or as Jesus calls it, the "palingenesis," or "regeneration" (see Matth. xviiii. 28)—all, the times of resurrection, redemption, and restitution begun.

III. The state of things that will follow the coming. This will be, in fine, the realization of the thought of God when He first placed man upon the earth, a thought whose accomplishment man himself has thus far hindered; upon the earth renewed, a sanctified humanity, displaying, to the honor of God, all the admirable faculties with which He has endowed it, and employing, in this purpose, all the powers of nature. This will be the reign of Christ in the bosom of humanity brought back to God by His glorious appearing. The long sigh, "Thy kingdom come!" will then be stilled. The number of 1,000 years is the indication of a period which nothing exterior comes to limit (Apoc. xx. 4). That will be the complete era of Christian civilization. This period will be, on the one hand, a time of judgment, as it seems to me from Apoc. xx. 4, and 1 Cor. xv. 24-26. "Then comes the end when He shall deliver up ("shall have delivered up" is a false reading) the kingdom to God, even the Father, when He shall have put down all rule, and all authority, and power. * * * The last enemy that shall be destroyed is death." Between the time of the return of Christ and the end when

HE SHALL SURRENDER THE KINGDOM

to the Father, there will be a time of judgment, during which He will put down all the forces hostile to God, and finally, the last, that of death, in taking from it all its previous spoils, and depriving it of its power to make any more. That point of time is the universal resurrection which will close the reign of "the one thousand years," and will precede the submission of the Son to the Father. Then, the destiny of our present earth will be actually achieved. From God a new abode will descend, "the tabernacle of God with men" (Apoc. xxi. 3), and, as St. Paul says, "God will be all in all" (I. Cor. xv. 28), manifesting Himself in each faithful one, as directly as He is manifested in Christ Himself. "Heirs of God," says Paul, "and co-heritors with Christ." Every element of gloom having been cut away by the judgments, there remains in this state of things only the divine light, resplendent with an infinite diversity in these innumerable prisms.

The role of the Jewish people: It only remains to me to say a word in reference to the role of the Jewish people in these last scenes. We left them, at the moment of the general apostacy, making for themselves a ruler in the person of the Antichrist. But we saw, also (Rev. xi. 1), that a remnant of faithful worshipers survive, even at that very time, as always, in the bosom of this people. At Jerusalem, the capital of Israel, externally restored, and where the

ANTICHRIST HAS HIS THRONE,

two powerful witnesses arise. They succumb, bodily, but their death is the occasion of the conversion of that portion of the people dwelling then in the Holy City (Apoc. xi. 13). This conversion is followed, doubtless, by the conversion of other Israelites still scattered in gentile countries, whether before or after the coming of Christ. Paul declares it positively in Rom. xi. 25-26, and he dates from this event an entirely new age in in the religious life of gentile Christianity. The nations who were hitherto only externally converted, from being spiritually dead will become alive. This will be as "life out from the dead" (Rom. xi., 15). We see from this that converted Israel, during the rein of the 1,000 years, will be the center of spiritual life in the whole world.

From these grand events, the time of whose accomplishment God has reserved for Himself, it does not follow that we ought now to cross our arms in idleness and let hings take their course. St. Paul expects himself to magnify his ministry among the gentiles in order to provoke to jealousy the Jews, his own flesh, "if by any means he might save some" (Rom. xi., 13-14). Every living Christian has charge of souls. Let us act like St. Paul. Let us seek to save as many of them as possible! Up! with loins girded and lamps trimmed and burning! If the Lord does not knock at the door of the world during our life, He will knock at ours at our own death. Let us be ready quickly to open unto Him. F. GODET.

Neuchatel, Oct. 24.

THE REV. DR. NATHANIEL WEST.

PROPHECY AND ISRAEL.

The Rev. Dr. Nathaniel West, of the First Presbyterian Church, of St. Paul, Minn., then delivered the following address on "Prophecy and Irael:"

I speak to you of "Prophecy and Israel." We can not interpret aright the fortunes of Israel, the gentiles, and the church of God, apart from a clear understanding of the nature, structure, and development, not only of prophecy, but also of history, as unveiled in the sacred page. A predetermined plan lies at the foundation of the whole evolution of the kingdom of God, in which Israel appears an abiding factor. The fortunes of the chosen people decide the fortunes of the world. History itself is Messianic. Events do not come to pass because predicted, but are predicted because ordained to come to pass. Great historic crises are the occasions of prophecy, from the fall of man down to the final consummation of the kingdom of God. Therefore is prophecy not the result of any private interpretation of the mind of God, but an

INSPIRATION FROM THE HOLY GHOST,

just because history is not man's invention. (2 Pet. i. 20, Acts xv. 18, Eccl. iii. 14-15). The fortunes of Israel are, have been, and will be precisely what God intends, and has revealed, nor can human hermeneutics break the Scripture or divert God's purpose from its course. First, middle, and last, "salvation is from the Jews," eminent at each great epoch-making node of evolution in the kingdom of God, and this, not by any merely natural law, but by the free grace and compassion of God. They alone of all nations are charged with this mission to the world. At the end of the Mosaic age Israel formed the historic basis of the New Testament "church." At the end of this present age Israel shall form the historic basis of the New Testament "kingdom" in its outward visible glory. Israel stands in prophecy, as in history, the elect agent of salvation, in a national sense, as truly as does Messiah in a personal sense, each a "Son of God," and is identified so closely with Messiah Himself, both in suffering and glory, as the "Servant of Jehovah," that it is sometimes hard to tell which of the two is meant. The pre-existence of Levi, in the loins of Abraham, was not more real than the pre-existence of Christ in the loins of Israel, whose crowning glory Paul declares to be this, that "of them, as concerning the flesh, Christ came, who is over all, God blessed forever," (Rom ix. 5), a consideration he urges with great effect, when solving what we are pleased to call today,

"THE JEWISH PROBLEM."

Israel and Messiah, though historically separated now, are indissolvably united, as mediators and bringers of salvation to the world; the one nationally, the other personally, alike in their humiliation and glory. Not Greece or Rome but Israel, not Alexander or Cæsar but Christ, are to bless mankind. Israel's history was the mirror in which Messiah learned to see his own face and discern His own relation to the world. And, just because of this ordained connection in the one redeeming work, "that generation shall not pass away," an expression on which, until modern criticism narrowed its double meaning, the whole Christian church, as Dorner remarks, "rested, for eighteen centuries, her belief in the persistent continuity of that 'race' (Matt. xxiv. 34) down to the second coming of Christ."

THE EVOLUTION OF THE KINGDOM.

It is no objection to this, that Israel has already been in the field, bringing salvation to the gentiles, at the first coming of Christ. Another more glorious calling of the nations still lies in the future, in which Israel shall shine again, as the national leader and light of the world. On this one fact depends the future realization of unfulfilled prophecy. According to the world-embracing plan of God, the kingdom of God is evolved from the purpose of God, and, by this purpose, the times and the seasons, the ages and ends, are fore-appointed, run on, and expire. The "kingdom" is more than the "church," as Professor Cunningham has lucidly shown. It is a vastly larger idea.

EVERMORE, ONE GREAT MOVEMENT

in history emerges from another, the kingdom one in its essence all the way, but many in its forms; in substance eternal, in stages of development limited and temporal; or, as Kitto most aptly expresses it, "essentially one, circumstantially many;" ever widening in its circle, ever rising in its progress; ebbing now, and flowing now, like the ocean tides; advancing and retreating like the waves that break upon the shore, yet destined to its highest water-mark; each succeeding form grander, purer than the one preceding; and yet corrupted by failure on man's part, with renewal by progress on God's part; one dispensation giving way to another; each stadium a mirror of the other, yet in various degree, and all a pledge of one most glorious accomplishment; the whole pushed outward from within, yet growing by accretion; stepping onward and upward, through judgments and mercies; ruled by laws and shaped by catastrophes; persistent amid dissolutions and reconstructions; each throb of the mighty motion answering, from age to age, to the pulse-beat of the one eternal purpose of God, and climbing to its crown of absolute perfection and glory everlasting. A divine causality pervades all. Israel, already in the front in centuries gone by, shall yet be in the front again. The "first" made "last" by unbelief, shall yet become the "last" made "first" by faith. The pouting elder son who, in the parable, now stands sulky in the field, shall yet come in

AND "DANCE" WITH JOY

in the coming kingdom of God, while wondering nations will admire and learn his step and waltz with gladness and adore

The unveiling of this divine plan, in prophecy, is governed by a law, in deference to which the "seer" often sees the near and far horizons of the future melting into one, and Israel, the central figure, bringing salvation to the world. Events and scenes, ordained to occur far apart, seem to lie close together like mountains in the distant landscape, or side by side like double stars upon the sky, though parted by deeps of infinite blue. The prophetic expression is so framed as to cover a whole series of historic sequences or separate fulfilments. It compasses the whole future painted in one glowing scene, the realization of whose events require in history a progressive order and a temporal succession. "Time and space" both disappear beneath the great description. Only by a later revelation of the same events more sharply defined and combined with others previously unnamed, and by what all history has already registered, can this law be detected. Only thus can we properly adjust the seasons and the times, the ages and the ends, and place the future in its true relations. Only thus can we distinguish the absolute from the relative end, the near

FROM THE FAR HORIZON,

the first from the second coming of Messiah, measure the true radius of vision, and catch the scope and harmony of prophecy and history. Much of what appears due at the first coming will be found to belong to the second, and much of what seems due at the second will be seen to belong to an epoch, or age, later on. In the words of one who has a right to speak on this subject, "The later books of the Bible must be the key of the earlier, the presupposition being the unity of revelation. What is indeterminate and general in the Old Testament must be adjusted by the New. The future in prophecy is often presented in a complex way, and looking to the last end, without specification of the individual events or intervals between. The "here and beyond" are viewed on one plane, in a divine light, even as we see the stars in the sky, their remoteness from each other undiscernable. In the Old Testament the work of God is contemplated as a whole, without marking off the final judgment from the special intervening judgments, the absolute end from the previous relative ends. The fulfilment of prophecy, "per partes," has its ground, not only in its complex and apotelesmatic character, but also herein, that it often treats of one subject by a general or collective name, under which, however, a series of individual events, separate in time and space, are comprehended. The subject is a genus, while the predicate contains the species which must be distributed. Thus, the "seed of Abraham" means Israel collectively

AND CHRIST INDIVIDUALLY."

(Delitzsch).

This law throws a great light upon the true understanding of the prophetic word.

Partial fulfillments, predictions accomplished in part, require for ther unfulfilled residuum a larger answering event than has yet occurred, while a true interpretation waits on history to satisfy its wants. Pentecost did not exhaust the prophecy of Joel; nor Maccabean times the prophecy of Daniel; nor Jerusalem's destruction the prediction of our Lord. Israel's history did not fill full the grandeur destined for it, nor did the coming of the Redeemer to Zion 1800 years ago exhaust the content of Isaiah's oracle. Thus has prophecy what Lord Bacon chose to call a "germinant accomplishment;" or, as Bishop Hurd would say an "overflow;" or, more beautifully still, as Delitzsch says, "Prophecy has wings given her of God, by which she flies over from one event to another still more distant in the same expression." We speak of a "leap," a "spring," a "double prophecy," of "intervals" and "gaps." What we mean is that prophecy has a precursive fulfillment in history, and that events, seen in perspective, at the end of the nearer age, are types of similar but far more glorious ones, occurring at the end of the age next following, or even farther on.

"ALL PROPHECY IS COMPLEX

and apotelesmatic" (*Delitzsch*). It looks always to the ultimate end, and covers all intermediate fulfillments; a law unmodified even by prophetic chronology. In the light of this law (first fully explained by Velthusen), as well as by express delineations, we learn that "Israel" does not mean the New Testament Church, nor "Canaan" Christendom. In the light of this law, as by other means, we learn that the whole stretch of New Testament times is but the evolution of Old Testament eschatology, or what should "come to pass in the afterness of the days," each end unfolding itself into a new age, preconditioned by an advent of the Son of God, and Israel in the front. In the light of this law, as by other means, we discern the characteristic difference between our present "times of the gentiles" and the future "times of Israel" in the kingdom when the "seasons of reviving" and the "times of re-erection" shall "come from the presence of the Lord" revealed to Israel once more; millennial times, when, after judgment upon our present age, national and universal Christianity as such, shall come to all the world with the national recognition of Messiah by the Jewish race. Such is the divine plan, luminous as sunlight in the bright, prophetic word, clear as crystal in the thought of Christ, and brilliant in the splendors of the last Apocalypse. Never can the New Testament "*Basileia*" come, in all its earthly glory, apart from Israel's national conversion, and never can that great event occur apart from Christ's appearing (Acts iii. 19-21, Rom. xi. 26, Rev. xii. 40, xv, 3-4, xix. 11-21).

OPPOSITE SYSTEM OF INTERPRETATION.

I am reminded that two different systems of interpretation contend for the mastery here. The "spiritualizing" or "figurative" conception of Old Testament prophecy concerning Israel, starts with the idea that Israel, as such, has been nationally cast away forever, and that the Gentile Church, or New Testament Church, has "taken Isreal's place in the kingdom of God." According to this, all the prophecies concerning Isreal have found their fulfilment in Christianity. A future for Isreal, as a nation converted to Christ, is a fanatical dream. Their only future is that of individual union to, and absorption by the church, in some one or other of its existing denominational forms. Opposed to this, is the "realistic" explanation. It owes its name to the fact that it takes the

PREDICTIONS AND PROMISES,

concerning Israel, in a literal sense, and not as mere metaphors, or abstract spiritual truths clothed in the perishable literary envelope of oriental imagery or Jewish drapery. It does, indeed, apply the prophecies to the church of the New Testament, yet only so far as Israel and the church have anything spiritually in common, while what belongs to Israel, in its solidarity or nationality as a separate and chosen people, preserved for a glorious destiny, it allows to stand unevaporated in the alembic of a one-sided exegesis. It asserts the historical sense of prophecy, in reference to Israel's future as well as Israel's past, and the mother-right of a grammatico-historical exegesis to dominate dogmatics. I adopt this latter mode of interpretation with all my heart.

For 300 years—here and there an exception—the ruling faith of the early church held to a glorious visible kingdom of God on earth, with Jerusalem as its central seat, the other side of this present age, and this side the final regenesis of all things; a kingdom introduced by the second coming of the Son of man, as all the prophets, Christ, and His apostles, had foretold. Had it held fast to this apostolic faith

IT HAD NOT LOST THE KEY

to the understanding of the Old Testament predictions concerning Israel, nor the key to the true interpretation of our Lord's Olivet discourse, nor of John's Apocalypse, Israel in relation to the Church, and the gentiles is that key. It is not possible, it is not conceivable, that either our Lord or the Holy Ghost, in their final unveiling of the future of the kingdom of God on earth could either forget or omit to repeat what is so clearly foretold in all preceding prophecy, concerning the still unfulfilled destiny of the chosen people. A prevailing change of interpretation, however, marks the fourth century, an exposition of prophecy gigantically fatal to the truth, the spreading leaven of which had already begun to corrupt the church. Not merely to a carnal conception of the coming kingdom, a gross judaizing on the part of some ignorant men, blind to the spiritual nature of the kingdom, was this revolution of sentiment due. Far beyond that, it was debtor to a sublimated heathenizing exegesis in the Gentile church itself.

Five adverse influences contributed to effectuate this result; (1) the temporal supremacy of Christianity in the Roman Empire, through a union of church and state, consequent upon the accession of Constantine

TO THE IMPERIAL PURPLE,

and whereby the predictions concerning Israel's future were appropriated and applied to the church of the fourth century, then free from the martyr flame; (2) the false interpretation of the Apocalypse, whereby the end of that book was made its beginning, the sun-clothed daughter of Zion regarded as the Christian Church of the present time (Rev. xii. 1-6), and Israel's conversion when Michael stands up for Israel's deliverance, turned into the victory of Constantine at Saxa Rubra and the Milvian Bridge (Rev. xii. 7-11, Dan. xii. 1-3); (3) the influence of Alexandrian philosophical speculation upon the exosition of the Scriptures; (4) the increasing pride of Roman hierarchical pretension, and (5) the contempt of the Jew known to be under the curse, swept from his home, and hated by mankind. Blighted by such influences, the former orthodox martyr-faith became heretical and the present heretical faith of the State Church became orthodox. And boasting gentile Rome defended it, with almost unbroken continuity, down to the time of the great Reformation.

The magic by which Israel was ousted from his place in the coming glory of the kingdom was twofold, viz: (1) by changing the

SUBJECT OF THE PROPHECY,

and (2) by changing the content of the prophecy. In place of "Israel" the "church" was substituted, through a spiritualizing obliteration of the line between what is common to both, and peculiar to each. Instead of a literal interpretation of the "blessings" promised to Israel, a figurative one was devised. The "curses," however, by a sad inconseqence, were allowed to remain literal, while the blessings promised to the same subject, Israel, were passed kindly over to the church! It is with a sacred indignation that gifted scholar, Da Costa, asks, "Who has given us the right, while contemplating the literal judgments on the Hebrews, suddenly to alter the principle of interpretation, where the curse is changed into a blessing? Who has given us the right, by arbitrary exegesis, to apply the promises to the Christian church of the gentiles, when the judgments evidently could not have been intended for them?" Nor is there a truer word than what that devout and princely critic, Michael Baumgarten, has spoken, when he says, "The devices by which the promises concerning the Kingdom and the people are explained away as referring only to a merely spiritual kingdom of saints, were entirely unknown to the apostles." Thus was Israel spoiled and robbed, in the name of hermeneutics, under the delusion of a fourth century millennium, with an unbaptized heathen on the throne! Yea, more, with a half-Arian "Eusebius,

ENTERTAINING THE IMPERIAL TABLE

with discussions whether the dining-hall of the emperor, the second Solomon, might not, after all, be the New Jerusalem of John's Apocalypse!" (Harnack.) It is Alexandria and Origen, Rome, and Constantine, post-Niceue fathers, mediæval doctors, a State church, and a boasting gentile Christendom of later times, Jacob has to thank for the cloud that blotted his hope from the creed of the "church." Nor was it possible that God's chosen people could ever come to their right, in the faith of the church, save by a reversal of the false view and a return to the true interpretation of Old Testament prophecy; an event first occurring under the labor of a

Spener, Crusius, Bengel. and their school, in the age next following the grand but partial dogmatics that sprang from the reformation. By the forces then set at work, we, of to-day, are animated and sustained.

THE JEWISH PROBLEM.

To warn against this foreseen perversion of the oracles concerning Israel, Paul wrote the ninth, tenth, and eleventh chapters of his epistles to the Romans. They are a philosophy of history, and theodicy too, a vindication of the depths of God's unsearchable judgments in the national rejection of Israel, the calling of the gentiles, the future recall of Israel to faith in Christ, and the transcendant effect of that event upon the world, at the Lord's appearing, and under the power of a second Pentecost. He treads in the steps of all the prophets. The doctrinal part of that epistle had closed with the eighth chapter. The problem now to be solved was this: Why, if the promises were made to Abraham and his seed, has the twelve-tribed Israel historically failed of salvation and the gospel gone to the gentiles? Is God's covenant a failure, as to the land, the people, and the kingdom? Paul regards Israel's defection as complete, and Jerusalem's doom as impending. He assumes, as already accomplished, the judgment on the nation, and the sad dispersion the Savior had foretold. For him, Israel,

NOW, HAS NO PART,

nationally, in the kingdom of God, but is outcast and crucified among the nations, yea buried in the grave. The burning question is whether the present relation of Israel to the kingdom of God is to be perpetual?

Is the covenant of promise made with Abraham a conditional one, like the covenant of the law superadded under Moses, or is it absolutely and forever unconditional, and of sovereign grace, and free compassion—a covenant that even Israel's national apostasy can not invalidate? Are the Jews the children of Moses, or the seed of Abraham? In their "casting away," is it individually, or nationally, God deals with them? And is it only for a time, or always? Have they stumbled forever?

The subblime answer to this, is the celebrated "Three Chapters." And how grand the solution of the great "mystery!" Paul tellsthe gentile Roman Church; he speaks to "Rome," and says: (1) That, because the promises were made to faith, and the righteousness of faith, and not to legal works, therefore believing Israel is the true Israel and inheritor of God's grace, and unbelieving Israel, to whom Christ crucified

WAS A STUMBLING STONE,

has been nationally cast away. The mystery of Israel's rejection is explained by Israel's unbelief. (2) That this hurling off of Israel from their city, temple, land, and all their privileges as God's chosen people; this taking the kingdom from them in its spiritual power, and giving it to a nation bringing forth the fruits thereof, is only temporary. Israel, though punished for apostasy, is not cast off forever from God's covenant. Even in their unbelief they are yet "His people," and in their misery still "beloved for the fathers' sakes. God's covenant with Abraham is all of grace, and therefore unconditional. The superadded Sinaitic legislation was designed to show the impotence of legal works and drive to Christ. True, indeed, Israel, as a nation, brought the Savior to the cross and killed the Prince of life, whom God raised up. An "election" found the great salvation, but "the rest (the nation) were blinded." Still, notwithstanding this, Israel's national rejection is only temporary, and the ordinances of heaven shall sooner fail than Israel cease to be a nation before God (Jer. xxxi. 35-40). Its historic mission as the bringer of

SALVATION TO ALL NATIONS

in their national capacity, is not annulled but only in abeyance. It yet shall be resumed. Israel, as such, can never be amalgamated or lose his right of primogeniture in the kingdom of God. The temporary abcission of the native branches from their "own olive tree" is measured by the limit of the "Times of the Gentiles," when Jerusalem shall cease to be trodden under foot of the gentiles, as is now the case. Then, "all Israel," Israel in their solidarity, acting nationally as one man, shall be saved. (3) That to be "ignorant of this mystery" and its relation to the coming kingdom of God on earth, will breed "conceit" in the church, a conceit begotten of false wisdom, pride, and gentile boasting, such a conceit as will interpret God's word to mean precisely what it does not, viz., that the church, as now existing, has actually "taken the place of Israel," and forever; so that, hereafter, Israel has no other future than Ishmael or Ham, and Jerusalem none other than Paris or Berlin, Rome or Athens, Chicago or New York, in the kingdom of God, nor as much. The odor of this conceit was already in the air when Paul wrote to seven-hilled Rome his celebrated "Three Chapters." Its beginnings already floated in

THOSE CLASSIC GENTILE CITIES

of the Roman world, where the church had been planted; omen of that spreading darkness of understanding whereby, soon, all Christendom would appropriate to itself the prophecies concerning Israel's distinctive future, and tell the world that these are now accomplished in the Christian Church. It is the very apostle who pleads and proves triumphantly that gentile believers are Abraham's spiritual seed, just as Jewish believers are the same spiritual seed, who also lifts his burning protest against the wrong conclusions men will draw from that great truth. (4) He assures Rome and, through her all Christendom, that the time will come when history will strike the hour for Israel's recovery, and that the effect of Israel's reception into the kingdom of God will be to the nations their national salvation; yea, more, that the time of this event will be just what Christ (Luke xiii. 35) and Peter (Acts iii. 19-21) said it should be, the time of Messiah's second coming; the time when "the Redeemer shall come to Zion and shall turn away ungodliness from Jacob" (Rom. xi. 26, Isa. lix. 20)—a set of decisive texts evaded by a hundred exegetes who can not square them with a post-millennial advent speculation. He assumes

THE LITERAL REALITY

of the prophetic word concerning Israel, and sums it up in one free quotation. He nails his argument, then rivets it, by appeal to the unconditional free covenant of God with Abraham, expounded by Isaiah, Jeremiah, and the other prophets, and all it secures for Abraham's believing seed according to the flesh, and protests that nothing, not even Israel's own apostasy, shall be able to annul that pact, or any way frustrate that promise of compassion and immeasurable grace. "For the gifts and calling of God" to that people, "are not to be repented of." (Rom. xi. 29). The gift of the "land," yea, the gift of the "world," the calling to a mission, and a mediatorship, to the nations, and a princely and a priestly throne. These are absolutely irretractable. Here, he rests his argument. God's covenant is an impenitent covenant. God's purpose is an impenitent purpose. (5) He appeals to Rome, an omen wonderful in view of her oncoming boast of supremacy as the "Mother Church," her self-exaltation, pride, idolatry, and Pharisaic formalism, and, through her, to all gentile Christendom as a unit, "Boast not against the branches!" Think not that you

HAVE TAKEN ISRAEL'S PLACE!

"Blindness in part" may happen to you too! "Be not wise in your own conceit!" Take no comfort from the thought that "the branches were broken off that you might be graffed in!" That judgment came to them "because of unbelief, and thou standest by faith." Beware! "Be not high-minded, but fear. For, if God spared not the natural branches, take heed that He also spare not thee!" You may become a "Babylon the Great!" "Contrary to nature," your oleaster twigs were inserted in an olive not your own. Much more then, "conformably to nature," God may graff the native twigs again into their "own olive." Down to the dust with your lofty head! Your proud statistics, and your mighty empire do not show you clean from deep corruption.

Your carnal caricature of the kingdom of God before the time, Israel still a beggar at your gate, may be crushed beneath a stroke of judgment heavy as the doom that fell upon Jerusalem. With all your ethnic expansion nineteen centuries shall flee away, and not a nation on earth acknowledge Christ as king! A thousand millions, then, will not have heard His name! And, in your bosom, lawlessness and unbelief will lift their horrid fronts, and fit you for the winepress of God's wrath! For the same crimes for which Jerusalem was struck you may be stricken too when the mountain-stone shall

SMITE YOUR CHRISTIAN "TOES."

If, at Messiah's first coming, the Holy City was "trodden down of the gentiles," and Rome arose the central seat of gentile Christendom, it may happen that, when He comes again, Rome shall go down, and Jerusalem "arise and shine," a "crown of glory in the hand of the Lord, and a royal diadem in the hand of her God!" (See Rev., chap. 17 and 18, Isa., chap. 60-62.) So does the great "apostle of the gentiles, and speaking to the gentiles, forewarn them of their coming doom, and build his argument—an argument that glows and burns in the pages of John's Apocalypse.

Grand Result of Israel's Conversion—And what the effect upon the world of Israel's national recall to the blessings of the covenant? It is no less than "Life out from the dead!" "If the fall of them be the riches of the world, and the diminishing of them the riches of the gentiles, how much more will their fullness bring a richer and a greater blessing?" There is a climax here. The argument is "a minore ad majus." Israel "diminished" to twelve apostles and 120 disciples has brought

RECONCILIATION TO THE WORLD,

given us Christendom, and peopled heaven with unnumbered souls. What, then, will Israel, recruited or "filled" to the "fulness" of "*all Israel*," converted to Christ, not bring? Other nations have only a church-historical mission. Israel alone is the bringer of salvation to the world. What this greater blessing is we are at no loss to see. It is not merely the "summum gaudium" of the church crowned with charismatic gifts. It is "life out from the dead!" It is the beginning of the world's glorification; life, in its fullest, widest, deepest, broadest sense. It is no less than a resurrection from the dead. A remarkable parallel—wonderful to the last degree, is Paul's argument. He draws a parallel between the two great stages of individual salvation, and the two great stages of the world's salvation. The analogy is most striking between Christ's work and Israel's mission. The law of development is identical in both cases, the phenomena are analagons, the stages answering, one to the other, as face to face in water. In the case of individual salvation, Paul argues Rom. v. 10, that "if when we were enemies, we were reconciled to God by the death of His Son, much more, being reconciled, we shall be saved by His life," i. e., by His resurrection. On the ground of that fact, Christ said of the reconciled believer,

"I WILL RAISE HIM UP

at the last day." John vi. 54. The death of Christ brings reconciliation to men, and the resurrection of Christ brings life and redemption from the power of death in the judgment day. In (Rom. xi. 15), when speaking of the salvation of the world, through Israel, Paul argues, "If the casting away of Israel be the reconciling of the world, what shall the receiving," or opposite of that, "be, but life from the dead?" i. e., "life proceeding out from the dead," as in the case of the resurrection of Christ. Just as Christ's resurrection brought new life to men, so Israel's resurrection shall bring new life to the nations, or the world. It is simply the further development of the same great thought in Peter's Pentecostal discourse, concerning the "times of requickening from the presence of the Lord," (Acts iii. 19-21). Delitzsch, Hofmann, Luthardt, Volck, Meyer, Koch, and Christiani, have all triumphantly expounded it. Who does not see the correspondence of the national to the individual stages of salvation? Of Israel's mission nationally to Christ's personally? If, when the nations were enemies to God. Reconciliation by the gospel came to them through Israel's death, or casting away, much more, being reconciled, they shall be saved by Israel's life, in the hour of national judgment, at the end of this age. It is the climax of the apostle's argument, the whole eloquence of his deep insight into the ways of God. The necessity for Israel's resignation is grouned, not only in God's covenant with that people, but in the condition of Christendom at the end of this age, even after the gospel has gone to the nations. The blessing that then will come to the world

WILL BE MORE AND GREATER

than the "reconciliation" through death. It will be "life" through the resurrection, "life proceeding out of the dead;" the coming of the "first resurrection," and the visible kingdom of glory on earth, yet not without a preceding "tribulation" unparalelled since the world begun. (Dan. xii. 1-3.) The discussion Rom. v. 10 relates to individuals; that in Rom. vi. 10 to nations, and predicts the era of universal and national Christianity as such. The two great stages of salvation are, first, reconciliation through death, and last, life through resurrection, both individually and nationally, each marked by the Lord's appearing; in the first case, in humiliation; and, in the last case, in glory, each marked, in the first case, by Israel's humiliation and death, and, in the last, by Israel's resurrection and life. It is a wonderful argument. As Christ's death and resurrection determine the fortunes of His people, so Israel's death and resurrection decide the fate of the world.

"Life out from the dead!" It is the beginning of the world's glorification at Christ's second coming. Not, indeed, in the sense of annihilating the material theater on which the development of the kingdom of God has hitherto moved; not in the sense of an absolutely "new heaven and earth," which occurs later on,

AS THE CROWNING EVOLUTION,

but as the commencement of that outbursting power of "Life" which, carreering through a millennial age, ends at last in the final regenesis of all things. It is "life from the dead" in a spiritual sense, life in a national sense, life in a literal resurrection sense, life for the sleeping saints of God of both dispensations, and restored Israel in the front of all. Such honor does God put on His own covenant. Then, "at that time," when the "voice" shall thunder over Israel's valley of dry bones, the "voice" of the Son of God, and the "Spirit" shall "come from the four winds and breathe on the slain," Israel shall rise (Ezek. xxxvii. 7-9)! Then, "at that time," when "Michael stands up," Daniel's "people shall be delivered, as many as are within the Book," and, beside these, "many shall awake from among the sleepers of the earth dust" and be assigned to glory everlasting (Dan. xii. 1-3). Then, "at that time," this thrilling word shall be fulfilled, "Thy dead ones shall live; my dead body (Israel) shall arise. Awake! Sing! ye dwellers in the dust! for thy dew is as the dew of herbs, and the earth shall cast forth the dead!" (Isa. xxvi. 19). Then, at that time, "the face of the covering cast over all peoples, and the veil that is spread over all nations,"—the mortuary pall of unbelief

AND SPIRITUAL DEATH,—

"shall be taken away from off all the earth," —not in a "second death,"—but "in victory." (Isa. xxv. 7; Hos. xiii. 14; 1 Cor. xv. 54-55). "Israel shall bud and blossom and fill the face of the world with fruit." (Isa. xxvii. 6). Jerusalem, the "beloved city," (Rev. xx. 9), shall arise and shine under a new "sunrise," (Isa. lx. 1), and become a glory to the nations, and "the glory of the gentiles shall be unto her as a flowing stream." (Isa. lxvi. 12, lx. 10-22). A second deluge shall occur, —a deluge of salvation, "for the earth shall be filled with the knowledge of the glory of the Lord, as the waters cover the great deep." (Hab. ii. 14; Isa. xi. 9, and lxvi. 19). Then, the era of national Christianity, as such, shall have come, when the colossus of gentile politics and power has fallen, and Israel's King is enthroned as the "only potentate," "King of Kings," as "King of Nations," amid wonders of judgment and mercy unknown before; that blessed time when "the root of Jesse shall stand for an ensign of the peoples, and to Him the nations shall seek and glory shall be His resting place" (Isa. xi. 10), "the place of His throne," "the place of the soles of His feet" (Ezek. xliv. 7); when "reigning in Mount Zion and in Jerusalem, glory shall be in presence of His ancient ones" (Isa. xxiv. 23), "the Lord reigning over them in Mount Zion, from thenceforth, even forever!" (Micah iv. 7. Then, in that day of

EFFULGENT MANIFESTATION:

Arabia's desert ranger
To Christ shall bow the knee,
And Ethiopia's stranger
His Glory come and see.

With anthems of devotion
Ships from the isles shall meet,
And pour the wealth of ocean
In tribute at His feet.

Kings shall fall down before Him
And gold and incense bring.
All nations shall adore Him,
His praise all people sing.

For He shall have dominion
O'er river, sea, and shore,
Far as the eagle's pinion
Or dove's light wing can soar.

"Blessed be the Lord God, the God of Israel, who only doeth wondrous things! And blessed be His glorious name forever! And let the whole earth be filled with His glory! Amen and amen! May Joseph soon reveal himself to 'his brethren!'"

THE JUBILEE ON EARTH.

Thus have I endeavored to allow the Scriptures to interpret themselves, and thrown back the Pauline argument into the bosom of the prophecies whence it sprang. And, doing so, what we find is this, that the whole choir of prophets and apostles, led by Christ Himself, sing in unanimous chorus the coming of the kingdom in its earthly splendor only with the coming of the King Himself the second time, and with Israel's rehabilitation. What wonders will not that great event reveal! Great scholars have dwelt upon it with delight. "The confessors of Jehovah," says Delitzsch, "shall be waked from their graves, and form with the faithful living a glorious church. Here is the predicted first resurrection." So Weber, lifelong student of Israel's faith and hope, says: "The Jewish Christian Church shall again revive. From the dispersion shall the living and from their graves shall the dead be brought back to enjoy together in the Holy Land the promised glory of the Messianic age." And Dr. Fuller, with whom that accomplished exegete, Professor Volck, of Dorpat, agrees, adds, in his able comment on Dan. xii. 1-3: "Not merely those who survive the great tribulation shall be delivered, but also many from

THE SLEEPERS IN THE DUST

shall be awakened in order to enjoy the redemption." So have Davidson, Bleek, Hitzig, Drechsler, Kiesselbach, Dæchsel, Weber, Nagelsbach, Hofmann, Van Oosterzee, and others spoken; men of the most divergent theological views. And that illustrious scholar—the only man ever pensioned by the British Government for his scholarship—Dr. S. P. Tregelles, says, in his book on Daniel: "It is at the coming of the Lord Jesus that Israel is delivered. It is then, also, that the first resurrection takes place. And here belongs that promise, 'Israel shall bud and blossom and fill the face of the world with fruit' " (Isa. xxvii. 27-6).

I have said that the New Testament Kingdom of God, on earth, can not come in the shape foretold, until after Israel's conversion, and the coming of the Redeemer to Zion, and that this was the confidence of the early church. Is there anything in the Scriptures, outside the Pauline argument, to confirm this view? Not to enter upon the superabundant wealth of Old Testament prophecy, the New Testament itself presents no other conception of the future. The faith of those who waited for the "consolation of Israel," as Isaiah had predicted, grasped, not only an inward spiritual salvation, but also an outward temporal deliverance, in connection with the coming glory of Israel, and the safe possession of their promised land, under their Messiah's reign. To Joseph, the angel of the Lord announced, that the Virgin's

CHILD SHOULD BE CALLED "JESUS,

for he shall save his people from their sins." (Matt. i. 21). To Mary it was said "The Lord God shall give to Him the throne of His father David, and He shall reign over the house of Jacob, forever, and of His Kingdom there shall be no end." (Luke i. 32-33). And Mary herself sings, in her sublime "magnificat." "My soul doth magnify the Lord, and my spirit hath rejoiced in God my Savior. * * * He hath holpen His servant Israel, in remembrance of His mercy; as he spake to our fathers, to Abraham and His seed forever," (i. 54-55). Zachriah, in his "benedictus," celebrates not only present help for Israel, through "a horn of salvation raised up in the house of David," but a grander coming time of redemption from all external foes, even "that we, being delivered from our enemies, and from the hand of them that hate us, might serve Him, without fear, in holiness and righteousness, all the days of our life," (i. 67-75). Does this look like a carnal conception of the kingdom? It is the farthest possible from it. Does it throw the kingdom, promised by the prophets, into super-earthly sphere? There is nothing clearer than that the Messianic hope looked to this earth itself as the sphere of the Messianic royalty, in days to come, and Israel as the central people. When old Simeon took the infant in his arms, his swan-like song extols the child, not only as "a light to lighten the gentiles," but beyond that,

"THE GLORY OF HIS PEOPLE ISRAEL"

(ii., 32). Not once in Luke, not once in all the Gospels, not once in Acts, not once in all the epistles, nor once in the Apocalypse, does "Israel" mean the gentile church. Not once in sixty times throughout the whole New Testament, does it mean aught else than Abraham's seed, believing or unbelieving. If we gentiles who believe are called the true seed of Abraham and the true circumcision, it is only in the sense in which a David and Isaiah, a Simeon and Anna, were the same—a spiritual sense. But this does not obliterate the great antithesis, nor vacate the oath and covenant of God to the literal Abraham and his literal seed. A foreign grafted branch does not annihilate the tree.

In the parable of the nobleman who "went into a far country" to be invested with his royalty and then return to reign, destroying all his enemies, our Lord set right the false impression his triumphant march from Jericho had made upon the people, who "thought that the kingdom of God should immediately appear." He tells them it will not appear until the nobleman's "return." Plainer words we could not ask (Luke xix. 13). Israel's kingdom, the Kingdom of God, the kingdom of the heavens, can not come in its outward glorious form, until the present sojourn of Christ in heaven is ended (Acts iii. 19-21; Rom. xi. 26-27; Dan. vii. 13-14; Matt. xxvi. 24). And, as that promised glory on the earth is the millennial age, Christ's coming must precede that blessedness. It was expected to attend His first appearing. He tells them that it can only follow on his second coming. Again, in language

PLAIN ENOUGH FOR WANDERERS,

He assures the twelve Apostles that not before but only during the "Regeneration"—by which He means the "Times of Restitution" (Acts iii. 21), and at His own return from heaven—will Israel's kingdom come, and they themselves sit on their thrones. "Verily, I say to you, that, in the Palingenesis, when the Son of man shall sit on the throne of His glory, ye who have followed Me (now) shall also sit upon twelve thrones, judging the twelve tribes of Israel." Yea, more. "And every one"—Jew or gentile, who so follows me—"shall receive a hundred fold, with persecutions, now, in this present time, and in the coming age, shall inherit everlasting life." (Matt. xix. 28-29, Mark x. 30, Luke xviii. 29). And when the mother of James and John, ambitious for her sons' pre-eminence, petitioned Him, "Command that these, my two sons, may sit, one at Thy right hand, and one at Thy left, in Thy kingdom," our Lord arrests her motherly but ill-informed anxiety by saying: 1. That the kingdom can not come, save only after suffering, and they who share such honors must be first baptized with blood. 2. That the disposition of such dignities is reserved for God, the Father, not for Him; and 3. That unlike the gentile polity, he who would be the first must be a servant like the Lord Himself, and least of all. (Matt. xx. 20-29) His words are no repulsion of her hope as to the coming kingdom itself, but a check to her ambition, and instruction for her ignorance of what must intervene. Not only so in the strife among them, which of them

SHOULD BE ACCOUNTED GREATEST."

He not only chides again their present wish, but turns their vision to the future full of hope, and says: "Ye are they which have continues with me, in my temptations. And I appoint unto you a kingdom, as my Father hath appointed unto me; that ye may eat, and drink, at my table, in my kingdom, and sit on thrones, judging the twelve tribes of Israel" (Luke xxi. 30). And, it is John, himself, who, years afterward, when wrapt in holy vision of the "Palingenesis," says, "I saw thrones, and they sat upon them, and the right of judging was given to them; * * * and they lived and reigned with Christ a thousand years" (Rev. xx. 4). Not in heaven, but on the earth (Rev. v. 10). A kingdom coming only after "heaven opened," the King Himself descending (Rev. xix. 11)

Just before His death our Lord predicted Israel's present blindness, and their ultimate conversion. "Behold, your house, (no longer my Father's house') (John ii. 16), is left unto you desolate; verily, I say unto you, ye shall see me no more, until the time come when ye shall say, blessed is He that cometh in the name of the Lord" (Matt. xxiii. 39. Luke xiii. 35). A ray of hope gleams through the awful darkness of the curse. Plainly, three periods are mentioned here: (1) That of their then present beholding of Jesus with bodily sight, a beholding soon, alas, to fade away! (2) A DAY OF FUTURE BEHOLDING and believing welcome to their long-rejected King. 3. An interval of non-beholding, of blindness spiritual, and full of sadness for the Nation. As surely as they saw Him and rejected Him at first, so surely shall they see Him once again, in penitence and faith, and hail Him with hosannas. Not less clearly did He predict the present dispersion of the Jews, their future redemption, and the restoration of Jerusalem. "They shall fall by the edge of the sword, and shall be led away captive into all nations; and Jerusalem shall be trodden down of the gentiles, until the times of the gentiles be fulfilled. * * * And then shall they see the Son of man coming, in a cloud, with power and great glory. And when these things begin to come to pass, lift up your heads for your redemption draweth nigh" (Luke xxi. 24-28). Down to the coming of the Son of man, the Jews shall be dispersed, and unconverted, as a people—a state of things impossible in a millennial age. So long as the metallic image the Chaldean monarch saw shall stand, an image of the gentile politics and power on Israel's neck, and gentile feet upon their ruined city; so long as Israel's last oppressor rages undestroyed, the final Antichrist; so long the promised kingdom can not come. The "redemption" of the "converts from transgression" contemporates with the final rescue of the Holy City from the tread of gentile hoofs. Israel shall be regathered to their land. Jerusalem shall be redeemed. A Jewish-Christian church and nation shall be born. The kingdom then will come.

AND, AFTER HIS RESURRECTION,

six weeks having been devoted to special lessons in the things pertaining to the kingdom, was the Jewish hope of Israel's restoration quenched? So far from this, the disciples ask Him, saying, "Lord, wilt Thou, at this time, restore the kingdom to Israel?" To Pilate's question, "Art Thou a king?" He had answered yes, but said His kingdom was of heavenly origin. In three different languages his title, "King of the Jews," was written on His cross. And now that, by His resurrection, He has shown His majesty, they ask "Wilt thou, now, restore the kingdom!" The kingdom David spoke about, and Isaiah, Daniel, and Ezekiel have foretold? Wilt thou, now? Had He answered "Yes," He would have deceived their faith. Had he answered "No," He would have denied their hope. He does neither. They ask not shall the kingdom be restored? The prophets and Himself had settled that. But is it now, "at this time," to be re-erected? Are the times of the restoring and reviving now? He restrains their curiosity, and points them to the work that first must intervene in gentile lands, the preaching of the gospel, "beginning at Jerusalem" (Acts 1, 6-8 Luke 24-47). What inference could be more clear than this, that, when this gentile mission is accomplished—not the world's conversion—but the witness of the gospel to all nations, then the end of this age shall come, and the times of Israel in the kingdom be inaugurated? (Matt. 24-14. Rom. 11-25).

And when the

ADVENT OF THE HOLY GHOST

was a living fact already, and not a thing still future, Peter, in that Pentecostal time lifts up his voice, and calls on Israel, as a unit, as a nation, to repent, alleging as the prophets all declare, that Israel's repentance brings Messiah back again, and restores the kingdom. He appeals to them by every designation, personal and national, covenant and theocratic, (1) to change their minds and wheel about, in reference to their slain Messiah, and be forgiven, in order that their risen king may be returned from heaven, and (2), that Messiah's sojourn there is temporary, lasting only as long as Israel's impenitence, and punishment endure. (3) That the promised "seasons of reviving" and the "times of re-erection," forespoken by the prophets, shall attend His second coming, as the prophets all declare. Like two great clocks that strike the same hour, one a moment just before the other, so these two marvellous events shall synchronize, Israel's repentance, and Messiah's reappearing in His glory. (Acts iii., 19-21. Rom. ii., 26). Between the departure of their King and the outpouring of the holy spirit; only ten short days intervene. Shall the interval between the next great Pentecost and His coming back, be a longer or a shorter time.

THE SPIRITUAL KINGDOM CAME

at once, with Israel's "remnant" then, converted from on high. Will not the outward glorious Kingdom come when Israel's remnant is a "nation," turned to Christ? The "Apocalypse of Jesus Christ" to John is in perfect harmony with all that we have said. A word is all that can be given to this most wondrous book. It is a "Book of the End-Time," its fundamental note being found in chapter i., verse 7, "Behold! He cometh with the clouds; and every eye shall see Him; and they also which pierced Him, and all the kindreds of the earth shall wail because of Him. Even so, Amen!" Its last note is the same. "Even so, come Lord Jesus!" (Rev. xx. 20). It is a book which follows the universal law of prophecy, and is not only thus "applicable", to the time when it was written, and to the general course of history, but is to be "interpeted" of the scenes and events that attend the second coming of the Lord—a book for all ages, past, present, and to come. The sealing vision (chapter vii.) refers to Israel of the End-Time, preserved from harm amid the storms of trumpet judgments soon to break. Chapter xi., the "crux interpretum," is a vision of Jerusalem in the end-time during the great tribulation under the last Antichrist. The 144,000 are the "our brethren" of chapter xii., the same as the "my brethren" of Matt. xxv. 40, and the "your brethren" of Isa. lxvi. 5, and are seen

ON THE EARTHLY MOUNT ZION,

with the Lamb, in chapter xiv. 1-5, after the trumpet-storms are over. They are the same company as the sun-clothed woman, or Daughter of Zion, in chapter xii. 1-6, the Jewish-Christian church of the end-time, and the same company as the cithara-players on the glassy sea in chapter xv. 1-4, celebrating there their final victory and blending it, in memory, with their first deliverance, singing "the song of Moses, the servant of God, and of the Lamb" (Deut. xxxii. 36-43. Isa. xxvi. 1-21, Rom. xi. 26-27). In chapter xix. the "beast," the last Antichrist is destroyed, Israel's last oppressor. In chapter xx. 1-6 Satan is bound, the blood-witness of Jesus share in the "first resurrection," and the kingdom of "the 1,000 years," the millennial age, begins. It is enough! All Old and New Testament prophecy is organized into unity in this book. What we read elsewhere we read here, only in symbolic dress—the gathering of the nations for the final struggle; the gathering in Palestine: Jerusalem and Zion, being the central point of Israel's last suffering and glory; the desert shelter during the tribulation; the appearing of the Lord Himself for Israel's deliverance and His judgment on His enemies; the close connection between Israel's conversion and the conversion of the nations; the deliverance on Mount Zion;

THE FIRST RESURRECTION;

the holiness of Israel in the last days; the erection of the glorious kingdom of Christ, on earth, with the "beloved city" as its middle point; and the great interval, the millennial age, consequent upon the appearing of the King from the "opened heaven," this interval followed by the judgment of fire upon Gog, the last resurrection, and the new heaven and earth. So does all prophecy, old and new, combine to one result, viz., the assertion of the preservation of Israel as a separate people in the midst, of the nations, so that, converted to the Lord, and re-established in their land, they may accomplish their divine mission to the world, when gentile times are ended, and take their place in the glorious kingdom of God on earth. Jerusalem, recovered from the dust, shall, by reason of the revealed presence of the "Glory," the personal "Epiphany" of Christ, become the sustaining center of the millennial "kingdom under the whole heaven"—her name "Jehovah-Shammah!"—"the Lord is There!" The heaven for height, the abyss for depth, the earth for breadth, and the mind of God for greatness, nor is there a higher, deeper, broader, greater delusion anywhere in the world than this, that the millennial age precedes the second advent, or that the Gentile church has taken Israel's place in the kingdom of God on earth! The popular idea that the world will be converted before Christ comes is a fiction. It has no warrant in the word of God,

NOR IN THE CREEDS

of Christendom, whatever it may find in post-millenial speeches, resolutions, commentaries, and dogmatics. Luther, Calvin, and Knox, all repudiated it, the first calling it "a falsehood forged by Satan to blind men to the truth;" the second saying "there is no reason to expect it:" the third adding, "it will never be done till the righteous King Himself shall appear." And so does all prophecy, old and new, support Paul's grand argument, that Israel's mightiest mission is yet future, and the world's conversion its most glorious result, at the second coming of the Lord.

The Spiritualizing Interpretation.—Justice to God's word, and those who share in such anticipations, requires me, to refer once more to that spiritualizing interpretation to which I have already alluded. Is it likely that such a mode of exposition, so prevailing and full of years, has brought to light absolutely nothing only error? Assuredly not. Extremes must be avoided. We may not hold a realism that restores the "beggarly elements" of a Jewish pupilage, a carnal cult that perished in the death of Christ. The prophetic coloring, in which the worship of the future is described, must be modified by the better coloring the cross supplies, while still we must remember that the "vanishing away" does not destroy the covenanted right of Israel

OR DIVORCE THE "PEOPLE"

from the "land." To conclude, from the restoration of the Jews to the re-establishment of bloody sacrifices is as bad a logic as to conclude from the abolition of the sacrifices to the non-restoration of the Jews. Prophecy is not a ceremonial institution. Israel is more than typical, even a standing factor and the sustaining center in the evolution of the kingdom at its budding nodes. It will not do, therefore, to press realism so far as that while doing justice to Israel's hope, the "Church," shall thereby suffer and become the loser or be robbed of her true nature, mission, and relation to the world. No. It is certainly true that alongside the fact of Israel's hope there remains the equal fact of Israel's temporary rejection, and that, pending this interval of punishment and expectation, the vineyard of the kindom, in its spiritual power, has passed to the gentiles. We dare not deny this. The nations have received the message of "reconciliation" in large measure through Israel's national decease, and are now the broad field where the kingdom is domiciled in mystery, but still without a central local seat. God, in mercy, has "visited the gentiles," individually, "to take out of them a people for His name." Acts 15:14. It is no less true that "through our mercy" Israel is to "obtain mercy." (Rom. xi. 14 30 32.)

WE ARE DEBTORS TO THAT PEOPLE

in the deepest sense, and our imperative duty, to give them the gospel, is designed to hasten the coming of the Lord. It is decreed of God that Israel's conversion, through the missionary activity of the church (Rom. xi. 30-31), and some new Elias (Rev. xi. 5) shall occur immediately in connection with the coming of Christ from heaven (Acts iii. 19-21), the Redeemer's coming to Zion (Rom. xi. 26), the fulness of the gentiles (Rom. xi. 25), the destruction of Antichrist (II. Thess. ii. 8; Rev. xix. 11-15), a mighty outpouring of the Spirit of God (Zech. xii. 10-14), and the resurrection of the just (I. Cor. xv. 23; Dan. xii. 1-3; Rev. xx. 5-6; Isa. xxvi. 19-21); events all so closely connected that for us they are practically contemporaneous, crowded into one transcendent epoch of mercy and judgment, the open door to a new and better age; and to us an epoch not distant, if, as great scholars are thinking, the downfall of the Turkish empire will close the "Times of the Gentiles," and be the occasion of Israel's repossession of their lost inheritance.

Our duty is clear; even to give the gospel to the whole world, Jew and gentile, with unremitting zeal, and "provoke Israel to jealousy" (Rom. xi. 25, 11). Grafted into Israel's "root," we share the "fatness" of the root and the glory of the fruit. Israel's spiritual gods have become ours. Nor is there anything more precious, in all their blessings, than the possession by us of the "lively oracles" committed to their care and

THE "SPIRIT OF ALL GRACE"

so richly promised to them. Nothing can compare with the salvation that is in Jesus Christ—salvation from sin, the law, death, the grave, and hell, to the Jew first, and also to the Greek, unto all and upon all them that believe, for there is no difference. Spiritualism has its rights as well as realism, the inward essence as well as the outward form, and the first pre-eminent in every case. No conflict should be between them. Realism should not be conceived of, as if the Old Testament predictions did not, at the same time, forecast the abolition of the "middle wall" and the formation of the "church," the one spiritual body of which Christ is the head. True, indeed, it was a "mystery" veiled in all the prophets, but yet it still is there, and uncovered, now, in all its preciousness (Rom. xvi. 25; Eph. i. 10; ii. 12; iii. 4-9. Col. i. 26). What we are required to do, if just to God's word, is clearly to discriminate between "Israel after the flesh" and "Israel after the Spirit," the "Jew outwardly" and the "Jew inwardly," both the natural seed of Abraham—the one believing, the other not—and those gentile believers who are Abraham's spiritual seed, by virtue of their possession of his faith—in short, between "the Israel of God," who are one class, and the gentile "uncircumcision," who believe, and are another class, and contrasted with "the Israel of God," in the expression, "the many as walk according to this rule," in Gal. vi. 16.

WHAT IS COMMON

to believing Jews and gentiles, we must not forget. What is peculiar to Israel, as a nation, we must equally remember. Observing this distinction—of the first importance—spiritualism claims, and must receive, our heartiest support. It is the essence of the blessed gospel, the very life of our souls.

But, now, when the prophecy does not simply predict the inward salvation that renews, and sanctifies, and saves the soul, and fills it with the hope of heaven, but describes decided facts foretold of Israel's mediatorship and mission to the nations: and, when, under New Testament light, it discriminates between "Israel," as such, the "church," and "gentiles," or the "nations," it will not do to take from Israel the rights devised to them in perpetuity and secured by unconditional covenant and restrict them to the "church" or abolish Israel's nationality. (Jer. xxxi. 36.) The covenant on which they stand is not the Sinaitic legislation, but the covenant with Abraham. (Gal. iii. 17.) The gospel is a part of that covenant, and powerless to annul one single promise, temporal or spiritual, of its own indenture. The Jews are

NOT CHILDREN OF MOSES,

but of Abraham, and "Jesus Christ was a minister of the circumcision for the truth of God to confirm"—not some, but all—"the promises made to the fathers." (Rom. xv. 8.) Luke i. 72-75: And this includes Israel's mission to the "gentiles," before, now, and hereafter. (Rom. xv. 9-12. Isa. xi. 10-16; lx. 1-22; lxvi. 5-13). Israel's primogeniture, calling, gifts, and throne. (Jer. iii. 16, Matth. xix. 28.)

This makes plain sailing for a homiletic application of prophecy on the one hand, and a true grammatico-historical interpretation on the other. Preach spiritual and glorious sermons if you will, and may with truth, from Ezekiel's valley of dry bones, or Zechariah's day of penitential sorrow for the Jew, or Isaiah's new sunrise over Jerusalem, or David's set time to favor Zion. Make the Old Testament language a divine terminology in which to shadow forth spiritual truth, now applicable to the church, but do not claim that this is its "interpretation," or that Israel's distinctive future as a nation is abolished because the Christian church exists. This will never do.

When, in that sublime overture of the Messiah, by Isaiah, the prophet bursts

INTO A STREAM OF CONSOLATION,

saying, "Comfort ye, comfort ye, my people, saith your God; speak ye comfortingly to Jerusalem" (Isa. xl. 1), and closes the oratorio with the words, "As one whom his mother comforteth, so will I comfort you, and ye shall be comforted in Jerusalem" (Isa. lxvi. 13), and all this in a vision "concerning Judah and Jerusalem" (Isa. i. 1). What he means is that, through God's compassion, the mourning captives shall leave the place where they hang their harps on the willows, and return to the very city whence they were cast out. "Spiritualize" it, if you will. "Apply," if you choose, to yourself, what is common to you and to Israel, God's comforting words in times of affliction. "Apply" it to the "church," if you desire. But do not seek "renovare dolorem" by telling us that God did not mean to deliver the fainting exiles out of the literal Babylon, and restore the outcasts, literally, to the literal Jerusalem, whence they were literally ejected! And when ordained to a richer fulfillment in years to come, and backed by another special prediction and promise that, in the days of the Messiah, the Lord shall "set His hand again, the second time, to recover the remnant of His people, and assemble the outcasts of Israel, and gather the dispersed of Judah from the four corners of the earth," etc., (Isa. xi. 11-16), "apply" it—if, indeed, you so can amuse yourself—to God's deliverance of His elect, who are gentiles, in all parts of the earth, and

CALL THE ROUND WORLD "BABYLON,"

if you desire, but in the name of all that is good, outside an insane asylum, do not tell us that the "second time" means the return from Babylonian exile itself, and that the original march to Canaan was the "first time," the exodus from Egypt a "gathering" and "return" of "outcasts" to a land they never had seen, and from which they were never expelled! Call Canaan the "church," if you will, and Jerusalem the "church," and Zion the "church," and Israel the "church," and Jacob the "church," or, if you prefer it, "Christendom," but again, in the name of all that is sane, leave us our senses, and allow us to believe that God, the almighty, unwearied, unfainting, and everlasting God has linguistic power enough left to say just what he means, and in terms, too, that a child can understand! I insist on the words of Delitzsch, "Application is not interpretation. Anwendung ist nicht Auslegung!"

How far soteriology and eschatology are to be distinguighed, and how far Israel's place in history is stipulated for in the plan of God we are bound to know. The spiritualizing gentile may as little dissolve God's kingdom into mere "inwardness,"

AS THE CARNALIZING JEW

may petrify it into mere "outwardness." It has an earthly and material, as well as heavenly and spiritual, side. It has a body as well as a soul, and will have a fixed and central seat, as well as lasting name. Herein we agree with that deep word of Œtinger, "Corporeity is the end of the ways of God." The world's transfiguration must come, nor may we disturb the modalities of either the catastrophe or the evolution by our interpretation, but leave them just as God Himself has pre-determined them. The time is passed for us to teach, as did Origen and his school, that "the divine promises pertain to nothing earthly," and that "spiritual blessings alone are of any importance." Christianity does not abolish nationality any more than it abolishes husband and wife, or the distinctions of sex, save in the spiritual "image" of God, and in "the children of the resurrection." Throughout the whole Scripture the antithesis between "Israel" and the "nations" is unclouded and unconfounded. It makes the Apocalypse of John just what it is, a beacon's blaze, and, apart from this distinction, it is dark and undecipherable as a sphinx. The work of Lemisch, uttered long ago, that "the Apocalypse is a hieroglyph whose Champollion has not yet appeared," is true no longer. "Israel" is that interpreter! What elsewhere is uttered to the ear in terms of unadorned and naked prophecy, is here offered to the eye in gorgeous images of terror and of glory. It is Israel to the front in the final development of the kingdom of God!

THE FINAL STRUGGLE—VICTORY!

No obscurity need overhang the necessity for Israel's historic mission in the future. It is God's appointment, and that is enough for us. The foretold condition at Christendom at the end of our age will justify it. We glean a light already from the prophecies, and our Savior's words in reference to the closing of the gentile times, as also from Paul's words in reference to the "Fullness of the gentiles." A certain time has been measured off for the proclamation of the gospel as a testimony to the nations, after which judgment comes. The gentiles will not be cast out of their possession, but there shall be a "falling away" from the truth of Christ, under the careering "spirit of the age," and a "man of sin," an "Antichrist," be revealed, in whom the whole God-opposed energy of these closing times shall be concentrated. Our Lord Himself, His apostles, and the prophets have all told us this. In language too plain to be misunderstood we are apprized that when these two concurrent and contradictory facts appear in history, viz: the wide extension of missions and increasing lawlessness and unbelief in Christendom, the "end" of this age is near. And

WARS, CALAMITIES, AND EARTHQUAKES

will attend the evil days (Matt. xxiv. 7-14). Out of this "falling away" troublous times shall come. The true church will then have no quiet resting-place among the nations, and the Lord will stoop to her deliverance and lift her to Himself. But the kingdom of God on earth is not abolished by the judgment. Israel, perforce, must be summoned as a last reserve, and, purged by confl ct, be carried into victory. The church will share in this. It is the way of God, both sovereign and unsearchable, the wisdom of His undirected and uncounselled mind (Rom. xi. 34, Isa. xl. 12-17), and they who are "expecting Jehovah" shall not be disappointed (Isa. xl. 31). In that eventful hour, when the last "adversary" of Israel "invades the land like a flood, the Spirit of the Lord shall lift up a standard against him, and the Redeemer shall come to Zion, clothed with the garments of vengeance, and clad with zeal as a cloak" (Isa. lix. 16-21, Rev. xix. 11-16). Then, "smiting through kings, in the day of his wrath" (Psalm cx. 5), "the judgment shall sit," (Dan. vii. 26), and

THE COLOSSUS OF GENTILE POWER

go down and "become as the chaff of the summer threshing floor," (Dan. 2, 36), and the sovereignty be transferred to Israel's King and His saints. "The kingdom, and dominion, and the greatness of the kingdom, under the whole heaven, shall be given to the people of the saints of the Most High, whose kingdom is an everlasting kingdom, and all dominions shall serve and obey Him." (Dan. 7, 27, Rev. 15, 4).

"And the seventh Angel sounded! And there were great voices in heaven, saying, The kingdoms of this world are become the kingdom of our Lord and His Christ, and He shall reign forever and ever!" (Rev. ii. 15). The Lord hasten it, in His time!

IMPORTANT EXEGETICAL PAPERS.

THE VOICE OF EUROPEAN PROFESSORS.

The following important letters from old-world professors, in addition to that of Professor Godet's, were laid before the conference by Dr. West, who had with much pains secured and prepared them in translated form for this occasion (see note p. 215):

BARDEWISCH, OLDENBURG, Oct. 3.—The Rev. N. West, D. D., St. Paul, Minn. My esteemed brother in Christ: I thank you very much for your valuable letter, in which you allude so kindly to my book on the "Millennial Kingdom." It is a great encouragement to me to learn that my labor has been of any benefit to you and assisted your progress in the perception of the truth contained in the prophetic word. With this letter I venture to send you two productions of mine, neither of which have as yet gone to America. From these you will learn what answer I would give to several of the important questions you ask. With all my heart I wish you the Lord's blessing for the approaching conference in Chicago. May it serve to disseminate a better understanding of prophecy in your far circles of Christian life and civilization. Though absent from you in body, I shall be with you in spirit, beholding your joy and sharing in the same, while offering with you, and for you, my prayer. My answers to the four questions you have submitted you are at liberty to communicate to the conference, if deemed desirable. These answers are:

1. In view of the predictions found in the Scriptures,

IT IS AN ERROR TO SUPPOSE

that the world, in consequence of any increasing progress in the propagation of the Christian faith, will thereby be transformed into the promised kingdom of God on earth. On the contrary, at the very time when the gospel is preached as a testimony in the world, a "falling away" from the Christian faith will prevail, as even already we see it in the principal countries of Christendom, and this will continue as the gospel advances until, in the closing scenes of our age, out of this apostasy, the Antichrist, the "man of sin," predicted in II. Thessal. ii. 1-12, is revealed, whom the Lord Himself consumes with His judicial breath, and destroys with the brightness of His presence. Then, upon the ruins of the Antichristian kingdom, the kingdom of righteousness and peace, will arise.

2. As to the outlook in Europe and the East. In Europe, the two great enemies of the gospel are constantly gaining in power, viz., (1) a superstitious extra-belief (aberglaube) on the one side, as in popery, and (2) a positive and demonic unbelief (unglaube), or infidelity, on the other, whose extreme is represented by socialism. Nevertheless it remains true, as our Lord predicted, that, side by side

WITH THE TARES AND WEEDS,

the wheat ripens also. In the Orient, the steadily delapsing progress of the Turkish Empire, seems to indicate the nearness of a great convulsion. The important question that is now forced upon us is whether, if this empire—of which Palestine is a province—should perish, the "times of the gentiles" within which "Jerusalem is trodden down of the gentiles," according to our Lord's word, shall reach their consummation; and whether, when Turkish tenure is gone, this city will again be taken possession of by the Jewish people. See Luke xxi. 24; xiii. 35. This would be a grand prognostic of the nearness of our Lord's advent and of the coming kingdom of glory on earth.

3. Not by means of the coming of the Lord, nor as a consequence thereof will the Jewish people who shall have returned to their fatherland, be converted, but closely before that coming, and not alone by our mercy, but by a new Elias (Mal. iv. 5, Mark ix. 12). Thereafter this people will have to experience the enmity of the Antichrist they make for themselves, and who will set up the horror of desolation in the holy place. Protected against him, in a refuge where God shall lead them, as once before,

GOD'S SEALED AND CHOSEN ONES

shall be sheltered during the storms and judgments of the last great tribulation, with all the faithful everywhere, and be led, at last, by their returning Lord into the kingdom of His peace.

4. The coming of the Lord is the one great hope of the faithful. This coming can be accelerated by the promotion of missions, for only then the Lord returns, when the gospel of the kingdom has been preached (in all the world as a testimony to all nations Matt. xxiv. 14, Rev. x. 7-11, xiv. 6). The hope of our Lord's return is, moreover, a great incentive to holiness, for whoever entertains and cherishes such a hope will "purify himself, even as Christ is pure," that he may be counted worthy to escape whatever comes to pass" in those awful future scenes, "and to stand before the Son of man" (Luke xxi. 36).

Again, dear brother, wishing you much blessing for the coming conference and its deliberations, I abide yours, in the unity of faith. A. KOCH.

REV. N. WEST, D. D.—My Esteemed Brother in Christ: Your welcome letter has reached me. After having accomplished my day's work I make use of the evening hour of leisure to reply to the same, and take up the questions which so deeply touch the Christian hope, and to which I have turned my attention for many years, and to which I yet devote my thoughts with much partiality. I still believe that the answers to these questions, which I have already given in my book, "Chiliasmus," to be correct and correspondent with the holy word of God in his Scriptures of the Old and New Testaments.

Answering your inquiries in succession I deem it pre-eminently: 1. A necessary part of the hope of the New Testament Church that the Lord will again reveal Himself, and in personal visible glory, to establish His Kingdom on earth. While the life of the children of God is at present "hid with Christ in God" it is, nevertheless, destined one day to be apocalypsed outwardly in glory with Christ at the "manifestation of the Sons of God," and that on the earth.

2. This kingdom of glory is inconceivable before the coming of the Lord. The Old and New Testament alike teach us this. In the Old Testament the time of the kingdom of

glory on earth is pre-conditioned by the revelation of Jehovah

AS JUDGE OVER THE WORLD,

or gentile power, and as the Redeemer of His people from its might. This time is called the "Day of the Lord, "Yom Yehovah." What, however, in the Old Testament is called the "Day of the Lord," or revelation of Jehovah at the close of the present æon, this, in the New Testament is called the revelation, or "Apocalypse of Jesus Christ," in which, as the "Maleach Habberith," or "Angel of the Covenant," the Lord Himself, who has once come to His people, will come again in another fulness of time." (Does not this account for a great part of the angelology of the Apocalypse, where the Lord Himself is personated by an angel, as, for instance, in the case of the rainbow-crowned and solar-faced angel (Rev. x. 1), the sealing angel (Rev. vii. 2), the cloud-seated and golden-crowned angel (Rev. xiv. 14. Compare Matt. xxiv. 30-31, N. W.).

3. The advent of the Lord will occur, not before, but in connection with the "national conversion" of Israel. For this conversion it is our imperative duty to pray. Impossible that we can pray, with intelligent fullness of petition, "Thy kingdom come! Thy will be done on earth, as in heaven!" without thinking of Israel who must yet learn to cry "Blessed be He that cometh in the name of the Lord!" And this is Israel's preparation for the appearing of their long-rejected King. Only, I would not like to speak of

"NATIONAL RESTORATION," FIRST,

inasmuch as merely human hopes and expectations could easily be brought into this connection, but I would rather express myself thus, viz.: that Israel, one day will, penitently and believingly, look upon Him they have pierced, in order to take their national place in the kingdom of God on earth as a converted people.

4. Since the ascension of the Lord we stand in the "Last Days" waiting for His coming again, according to the words of the angels. For this return, also, the church is bound to pray; yet not forget that the Father has reserved to Himself the determination of the "times and the seasons," yea, of the very "hour." We are bound, also, to observe the "signs of the times," which are to instruct us how near we are to that moment when we shall "lift our heads, for our redemption draweth nigh." And, finally, we must keep ourselves from losing interest in the work which the present time devolves upon the Church, and avoid all sentimental expectations of the future.

5. The opinion that the millennium has already gone by I regard as entirely adverse to the sacred Scripture, and I think I have easily proven it, in my work on Chiliasm. We may, in truth, apply what the prophets have said in regard to Israel's future, to the Christian church of the present time, for all believers are, indeed,

"THE PEOPLE OF GOD."

But, on the other hand, we must never forget that the fulfillment of the Old Testament promises, as this lies before us, now, in the Christian church, is only spiritual and preliminary to a greater fulfillment yet future, embracing Israel's inheritance. That perfect fulfillment for this world's history will come only with the coming of Christ. To acquire a complete picture of the future, promised in prophecy, we must combine the first and second comings of Jesus. The millennial age, which commences with the yet future "Apocalypse of Jesus Christ," closes with the last judgment of the world, and with the creation of a "new heaven and a new earth," into which the redeemed will pass over, and find their eternal home.

Accept so much, my dear brother, in response to your welcome communication. I shall rejoice if, in any way, to you, or your dear brethren, these few words shall be of any service. May the Holy Spirit guide your deliberations! Let us remain united in the prayer, "Come, Lord Jesus!" and, meanwhile, work, yea labor, for Him with all our might as long as He lets us live. With a brotherly greeting, yours, ever, in Christ,

VOLCK, Professor.

University of Dorpat. Russia. Oct. 14. 1886.

FROM DR. FRANZ DELITZSCH.

My Dear Brother in Christ: * * * We are agreed in this, that the temporal history of the world closes with a time of complete victory and glory for the church. The prophets can not be understood apart from this supposition. It is true, as you intimate, that the prophetic word of the Old Testament does not separate the "Here" from the "Beyond," "Time" from "Eternity," and that to acquire a Christian hope a spiritual transformation is needed. But, on the other hand, there are predictions of the "Last Things," for example, of the return of Israel to their fatherland, as also of their rehabilitation, and of the future blessedness and peace of that land, whose spiritual interpretation would be a distortion (Verdrehung) of their original meaning, a flat negation of what is said. If we admit that the gospel will finally subdue the hearts of men, and that even the Jewish stony heart will melt, then we admit, thereby, that history will run out into a relative victory of the good over the evil. I say relative, for the ultimate separation only comes as the consequence of the final judgment of the world.

The New Testament Apocalpse represents the "Eschata" in their future successive temporal order and relations. It is, in this respect, the key to the

ENTIRE PROPHETIC WORD:

for example, in the beautiful prediction (Isa. xxiv.-xxvii.) "libellus apocalypticus," which lifts itself up even to the destruction of death through victory. The triumph and the glory of that time form the millennial age. I believe in the literal reality of this apocalyptic picture without pressing slavishly the letter. (See 1 Cor. xiii. 12.) I am, therefore, a Chiliast, but the "Damnamus" in the seventeenth article of the Augustana does not hit me!

According to Apoc. xix. 11, etc., the parousia of our Lord precedes the millennium (xx. 1-6). He comes and destroys the Antichrist (Apoc. xix. 19-20; xiii. 1-6-7; 2 Thess. ii. 8; Isa. xi. 4). Then Satan is bound and a Sabbath-time, a "Sabbatismos" (Heb. iv. 9), begins which is the prelude to a blest eternity. But even this blessed time of peace is interrupted and declines. Once again the power of the wicked one rages against the kingdom of Christ on earth, and now, finally, all temporal history closes with the judgment of fire upon Gog, and with the general resurrection. At this point the Apocalypse says nothing of the parousia of the Lord, but we know that the final advent of the Lord, as judge of the world, connects itself with what we read in Apoc. xx. 9-15.

You refer me to Apoc. xx. 4-6.

IT MUST BE CONFESSED

that upon a comparison of this passage with the words in Isa. xxiv. 23, "The Lord of hosts shall reign in Mount Zion and in Jerusalem, and in presence of His ancient ones shall be glory;" and also with Isa. xi. 10, "It shall come to pass, in that day, that the root of Jesse, which standeth firm for an ensign of the peoples, even unto him shall the nations seek, and glory shall be his resting place"—it is presupposed that the Lord will descend from heaven and show Himself in "glory," and that he will wield His sceptre over the earth, as declared in Psal. cx. 2-3, (and where else than in the holy city?) and, according to the Apocalypse, be surrounded by the risen martyrs of the Antichristian time of persecution, whom He has counted worthy of a part in the "first resurrection," (Rev. xx. 5, Isa. xxvi. 19), and who sit with Him as His assessors; while, on the other hand, the "rest of the dead ones live not again until the thousand years are finished." (Apoc. xx. 5; compare Isa. xxvi. 14).

It does, indeed, seem so. But is it conceivable that the glorified Lord will permanently dwell upon the old unglorified earth? Is it conceivable that the Risen One will continuously associate Himself with men who still have "flesh and blood," which "can not inherit

THE KINGDOM OF GOD?"

Bengel could not conceive of that, and as little could Jacob Bohm, the Teutonicus Philosophus, whose tendency was realist and whose mind was also given to mystery. I have always preferred the exegesis of Bengel, according to which (Apoc. xx. 4) "they lived and reigned with Christ a thousand years," indicates a reigning of ascended risen saints who rule, with Christ, from heaven. The view that our Savior will set His throne in the Jerusalem of the old unglorified earth, and rule from there, seems to me a crass Chiliasm. And, although I am a friend of Israel, yet Christ, exalted to the right hand of God, is to me so much a supernatural son of man that I believe in no reproduction of the Old Testament earthly national theocracy.

Perhaps, dear brother, you may receive but little or no advantage from these lines, sketched by one who is already overburdened. Yet, if you will continue to ask of me I am ready to answer, although it may be not entirely as you might desire. For, we know in part, and prophesy in part, but when that which is perfect is come, that which is in part shall be done away. "For now we see in a mirror, darkly; but then, face to face. Now, I know in part, but then shall I know even as also I have been known," (I. Cor. xiii. 9-10-12. Faithfully Yours. FRANZ DELITZSCH.

University of Leipzig, Germany, Oct. 10, 1886.

The following notes were appended to Professor Delitzsch's letter:

[NOTE A.—The seventeenth article of the Augustana—i. e., of the Augsburg Confession—is, "Damnamus et alios, qui nunc spargunt Judaicas opiniones, viz., quod, ante resurrectionem mortuorum, pii regnum mundi occupaturi sint, ubique oppressis impiis," i. e., "We condemn others, also, who are now spreading abroad Jewish notions, to wit, that, prior to the resurrection of the dead, the righteous shall possess the kingdom, the wicked being everywhere put under foot." Of course, this "Damnamus" does "not hit" the gifted author at Leipzig, nor any premillennarian, anywhere, Lutheran or Reformed. The "Damnamus" is a clear blow at post-millennialism of every kind, be it coarse or fine, be it Jewish or Whitbyan. Melanchthon, in "Variatio," tells us it was levelled at the Anabaptists and Munster men, who believed that, by revolutionary means, the kingdom should be set up in this present age, i. e., "before the resurrection." It strikes also the later "Fifth Monarchy men," in Cromwell's time. It "hits" every theory that makes

THE PROMISED KINGDOM

of glory, on earth, come "before" the coming of Christ, at which time the "resurrection from the dead" occurs. Says Dr. Koch: "Even the finer form of false Chiliasm, according to which church action is gradually and peacefully to sanctify and transform the world into the glorious kingdom of God 'before' the second coming of Christ is condemned, not only by the Augustana, but by the Apocalypse and the whole word of God. According to the Apocalypse and our Lord's Olivet discourse, wickedness and lawlessness do not decline in the course of history, but rather ascend to their fearful Antichristian height, while on the other hand the church is tried and purified." Lange as pointedly says: "The Augustana negatives the assumption of a millennium before the parousia." Richter adds: "There is not a syllable in it against a true, but only against a false Chiliasm." Steffann, in his book, "Das Ende," avers: "Not those who reject a millennial kingdom, but we who teach it as coming after the resurrection, stand upon the Augsburg confession." "What that article condemns," says Rinck, "was a demonic caricature of the hope of the oldest of the church fathers." "With deep insight," says Ebrard, "the reformers saw through the fundamental falsehood of the false Chiliasm, which held a millennium could come

BEFORE THE RESURRECTION."

A careful study of the reformed symbols and of the Westminster standards of faith in the light of history, will show that all these creeds struck at the false Chiliasm only to protect the true.—N. W.]

Note B—The view of Dr. Delitysch is that of Auberlen, viz. that the Risen Bride is retired into the seclusion of heaven, and from there rules, with Christ, over the earth during the millennial age. It was Bengel's, indeed, but based by him upon the doctrine of a double millennium, or two millennia, which, by reason of the absence of the article in Apoc. xx. 2, he thought he saw in John's description: (1) the first millennium being that of the imprisonment of Satan, reaching from the overthrow of Antichrist to the destruction of Gog; (2) the second millennium being that of the reign of the risen martyrs in heaven, reaching from the unchaining of Satan to the general resurrection. But, for this double millennium Delitzsch assures us properly there is "no Scripture proof." (Eibi—propih—Theologie p 137). The venerable and beloved author of the above, letter will agree with us, moreover that, so far as conceivability is concerned, the difficulty of conceiving "how" a thing can be, though a hindrance to understanding and a barrier to faith in some respects, is no bar to the fact itself, for mystery meets us everywhere. (John iii. 4, 9. iv. 9. vi. 42-52; I Cor. xv. 35). "How can these things be?" "How are the dead raised, and with what body do they come?" Theurer has most aptly said, "It is not always true that what is most conceivable is most probable. The fulfillment alone will bring us the surprising solution."

EBRAID FINDS NO DIFFICULTY

here, but holds that "just as, after his resurrection, the risen Lord remained forty days on the earth, the Glorified one among the unglorified, so shall the church, triumphant, rule over the earth throughout the long period designated by the mystic number, the thousand years." He supports this by reference to the visit of Moses and Elias on the mount, and the many who rose at the first coming of Christ and went into the Holy City and appeared to many." (Luke ix. 28-31. Matt. xxvii. 52-53). And Richter has said, "The risen saints are not to be secluded in heaven and hid in God, but openly apocalypsed at the manifestation of the sons of God, in their glory, when earth begins to put on her pristine beauty for then heaven is on earth, and earth has become heaven. As certainly as Christ, the Risen one, was among the not glorified during forty days, so certainly shall the many who are risen with Him be, like Him, among those not raised. Jerusalem shall again be the central seat and city of the kingdom of Christ during the thousand years, as so often promised in the Old Testament. The Apocalypse presupposes the prophecies of the Old Testament concerning the glory of Israel and Jerusalem in the last time."

There is another view, as to the habitat of the bride, in her glory, viz: that during the one thousand years Christ and His glorified church will dwell in the high pavillion-cloud, the Shekinah-glory in the heavens shining over Jerusalem below, as Isaiah is thought to intimate (Isa. iv. 3-6); Christ and His bride descending to earth, first of all, at the close of this period, on the new heaven and earth, described by John (Rev. xxi. 1-2). This view has a number of advocates.

THE THIRD VIEW IS

that the habitat of the bride, or risen saints, is on the old earth, but glorified or transfigured in part, as was the Mount of Transfiguration, by means of the glory of Christ. And yet more, there will be a physical transfiguration of Jerusalem and the Holy Land, both becoming as Eden. Jerusalem will be enlarged, broadened, and adorned, as Isaiah and Ezekiel depict it, and Justin and Irenæus both held. Luthardt informs us that this view has the suffrages of the preponderating number of special investigators. Kliefoth and Keil would identify the millenium and the new heaven and earth, but this involves us in self-contradictions, and contradictions of Scripture as great as does the view of Augustine, or of Hengstenberg, or the Preterists, or Whitby, who regard the millenium as past, or present now, or yet to come before the resurrection. Against all such preadvent millennialism, that of Whitley, Brown, Glagow, and others, the "Damnamus" of the Augustana is leveled as are, impliedly, all the reformed symbols.

With the protest of Dr. Delitzsch against a reproduction of the Jewish Old Testament, earthly and national theocracy, we all most cordially sympathize. But the difficulty felt by Dr. Delitzsch seems to rest upon the assumption of the unglorified condition of the whole earth during the 1,000 years. It is true that the "new heaven and earth" (Rev. xxi. 1) come

ONLY AFTER THE JUDGMENT

by fire on Gog, which itself follows the millennium. But it is equally true that Isaiah perspectively covers the whole millennial age, and the New Jerusalem state, by this one designation, "new heavens and earth," (lxv. 17). It is the manner of the prophets to first strike the ultimate end, in a general expression covering the nearer end, and then, coming back to a point this side of it, travel up to that end, and vice versa (Isa. xl. 1-11, xl. 1-16). We see this especially in the Apocalypse. And it is no less true that Paul and Peter both assure us that a cosmical regeneration begins at the second coming of Christ (Rom. viii. 21; II. Pet. iii. 13. If we take the "conflagration" as the analogue of the "deluge," as Peter, building on Isaiah does (II. Peter iii. 4-7), all is clear. This would remove the difficulty felt by Bengel, and others of his school, and to which Dr. Delitzsch alludes, as to the habitat of the bride. Dusterdiech, referring to this, says: "Correctly do the Chiliasts interpret Apoc. xx., 1-6, when they reject the fond and favorite 'recapitulation theory' and allow the 1,000 years' kingdom to remain in the place where it is found in the apocalyptic picture of the whole end, as Justin and Irenæus did. Both these fathers take the 1,000 years in their literal sense. And more correctly do they interpret than Auberlen who, from the assumption that the not yet glorified earth can not be the abode of the glorified church, concludes that believers who come forth with Christ from their invisibility in heaven shall be

CLOTHED WITH GLORIFIED BODIES

and then return with Christ to heaven, from there to rule over the earth; thus disregarding the contradiction of this view in Apoc. xx., 9. And more correctly have the old Chiliasts viewed the chronological matter of the 1,000 years than Bengel, who thought he discovered two periods of 1,000 years each, the one beginning with the destruction of the beast and binding of Satan, the other with the letting loose of Satan and ending with the end of the world."

It is true, indeed—and we feel it so—that we "prophesy in part" and "know in part" now, and much of the future lies in shadow. An inspired apostle could say this. And where God has not spoken man may not speculate. Our intellectual mirror is not brighter than the gospel, or prophetic "glass," into which we look even now, as into a "riddle," *en ainigmati* (I. Cor. xiii. 12). But yet some splendors of the coming age are shimmering there, like some bright sea of glory in the distance; some grand outlines of "the glory ready to be apoclypsed in the last time." (I. Peter i. 5). Von Hofmann,

THAT EPOCH-MAKING SCHOLAR,

has clearly shown that Canaan, after which, made heavenly, the patriarchs sighed, will be physically transfigured at the coming of Christ, and Koch has triumphantly defended Hofmann's exegesis against Keil's great effort to disparage it, as also against Strobel's later strictures. It is bound up with our Lord's answer to the Sadducees, out of Moses, in proof of a literal resurrection of the dead, and has the closest connection with the promise of "the land" to Abraham himself and to his seed forever. (Exod. iii. 2, 6, 8; vi. 4, 8. Acts vii. 5. Matt. xxii. 23-33.) Lange insists upon "a gradual cosmical process of regeneration" beginning at the advent, when the glorifying spirit of God passes over, in His energy, at the resurrection, from the spiritual to the material side of the kingdom on earth, a process whose completion is crowned by the last mundane catastrophe, and issues in the "new heaven and earth," at the close of the 1000 years. Christlieb calls it "a grand and gradual progressive process of the world's renewal, ultimating in the new heaven and earth, it being God's will that His glory should dwell in the whole creation." Professor Volck, like Hofmann, Koch, and many others, rejects Keil's view, and teaches "a glorification of Palestine before the final judgment, the prelude of a future perfect transfiguration of the whole earth." "The earth, not heaven," says Luthardt, "is the abode of

THE GLORIFIED CHURCH.

There shall not be one part of the church, the gentile part, glorified in heaven, and another part, the Jewish part, glorified on earth. The church shall be one, with the Lord, returned to earth, and in her midst, as the sun and temple in the new Jerusalem. They who suffer with Christ here, shall reign with Him, upon the scene of their sufferings. The distinction still obtains between the glorified church gathered around her Lord, in her glorified place on earth, and the outer unglorified humanity still liable to sin and death, yet freed from Satanic dominion, and subject to the dominion of Christ and His church. Before her the nations shall bow in obedient recognition of the authority of Christ, during the millennial age; one of the great world-æons which belong to the kingdom of God." In like manner, Rothe says, "The apostles describe the coming kingdom on earth as a Sabbatism, a glorious rest for the people of God. James calls it a Basileia God has promised to the poor, rich in faith. Paul loves to picture it as "a reigning together with Christ" in the resurrection. The Apocalypse exhibits co-regency as the chief element of blessedness in the Chiliastic kingdom. The redeemed reign with Christ on His throne, have power over the nations, and participate in judgment of the enemies of their Lord."

The support this view has received

FROM SO MANY PRINCELY SCHOLARS

will justify, without trespass, in a theme so full of interest, a few words more from its defenders. That incisive exegete, Professor Schmid, of Tubingen, says "The judgment at the second coming of Christ must be distinguished from the one at the close of the 1,000 years. By means of the former, the "regeneration," (Matt. xix. 28), is brought about, which coincides with the commencement of the coming age, and the "redemption" of the creature in the sense of Rom. viii. 18-23, and the "restitution," Acts iii. 19-21, and "resurrection" unto life, the righteous shining in the kingdom, (Luke. xiv. 14, Matt. xiii. 43, Dan. xii. 1-3, I. Cor. xv. 40-57)." Stockmayer holds the same view, and, tenderly as beautifully says, "To see Jesus and behold His face—face to face—is the longing of all believing souls. A day is coming when this longing shall be stilled, in a way surpassing all human thought, the day of the wedding of the Lamb in glory, the ceremonial day of the Bridegroom with His loved and loving bride. The attainment of this end has for its presupposition the glorification of the bride through her resurrection and the transfiguration of the living saints. But the Lord comes, not only as a Bridegroom, but as a Warrior—King, the King of kings—to overthrow the whole anti-Christian power of the world, and

ESTABLISH HIS VISIBLE KINGDOM

on the earth, in which the risen saints shall reign with Him, 1,000 years, as priests of God and of Christ." Orelli, who has written so well on Messianic prophecy, has argued conclusively—as also Kuenen, who saw the matter, did—that Ezekiel's last eight chapters can not refer to the restoration of Israel from Babylonish captivity, nor to our present church-historical period, nor to the eternal state, but to a period intervening between the church-historical and the ultimate goal. And Hofmann holds that Jerusalem, the "Beloved City," Jerusalem made glorious at the coming of Christ, and increasingly glorified, passes over into the new heaven and earth at the close of the one thousand years. Still further, Volck has ably shown that this intervening age, described so gloriously by Ezekiel, corresponds to the one thousand years in the Apocalypse of John, and identical with the "multitude of days" in Isa. xxiv. 21-23, and the "many days" in Ezek. xxxviii. 8, bounded by precisely the same events, viz., the judgment on the Antichristian and Satanic powers at the beginning, and the judgment on Gog at the end, Israel's glory lying between. He says: "Ezekiel's prophecy differs from pre-exile prophecy in this, that while the glance of the latter reaches, as in Isa lxv. 17, to the nearest impending catastrophe behind which the glory centers, Ezekiel's glance not only reaches as far, but overshoots that entrance and stretches to a greater catastrophe

AND A RICHER GLORY

still more distant; so that what in pre-exile prophecy appear as the end of the world-course, appears in Ezekiel as the beginning of a new and final age. Ezekiel's prophecy throws great light on the partial obscurity in Isaiah's prediction (Isa lxv. 17, etc.), in so far as that oracle does not clearly show us the mode of transition from one phase of the complex end to the other, in the distant perspective, the mode of transition from the millennial age and Israel's glory, to the final and entire new heaven and earth, or the New Jerusalem in eternal glory. For since the judgment on Gog comes "after" Israel's re-establishment (Ezek. xxxvii. 1-28), and "many days after" the judgment on the nations which precedes that establishment (Ezek. xxxviii. 1 8), and so, lies on the other side of the world's course to which Israel belongs, we are obliged to recognize the judgmen on Gog as the mode of transition from the millennial age to the final new heaven and earth. That is the end of the *Rav Yamim* of Isa. xxiv. 30. And just as Ezekiel's Apocalypse was a further development of all pre-exile prophecy, so John's Apocalypse is a further and final development of all Old and New Testament prophecy preceding. It separates the ages and the ends by a clear and

INDUBITABLE LIGHT.

(Apoc. xx. 1-15). Keil's and Kliefoth's identification of these two different ages cannot be maintained, and we must hold to the view of Hofmann and others, as above stated. Heaven and earth are ever coming nearer, and one day will unite, God "all in all." Lister, Fellow of the Royal Geological Society of Great Britain, in his "Physico-Prophetical Essays," has endeavored to show the geological changes and convulsions that, according to the prophets will occur at the second coming of Christ, and make for the transformation of the Holy Land. What he teaches is in perfect harmony with what the venerable author of the above letter so beautifully says on Psal. lxviii, 16, viz, that in the day of future glorification the material will correspond to the spiritual, the outer reflect the inner, the phenomenal, the essential: "die Aussere dem Innern, die Erscheinung dem Wesen und Werthe, gleich!"

It will not be deemed out of place to say here that the millennial state is only a transition state, not the highest manifestation of the Spirit's energy and glory. So the early church fathers conceived it. Even for the risen saints an advancing splendor is reserved. They "shine," indeed, but their glory, even then, is progressive. Bindemann has called attention

TO THE PROFOUND THOUGHT

of that great man, Irenæus, who said that they who are counted worthy to attain to the resurrection of the just do not, at once, even in their transfiguration, reach the ultimate perfection of glory, or the eternal completion of their likeness to God, but gradually, by beholding the face of Jesus, though already changed into his likeness, yet increase more and more therein, as they gaze and take on the splendor of His image. It is a deep thought! It is a holy thought! Is it not a true thought?—"qui digni fuerint, paulatim assuescunt capere Deum, * * * crescentes ex visione Domini!" Even the righteous, raised from their graves, are unable, at once, to assume the overpowering and insufferable splendors of God!

The passages referring to the renovation and transformation of the Holy Land are: Joel iii. 16-21, ii. 18-21-27; Amos ix. 11-15; Micah, iv. 1-4, vii. 11-20; Isa. ii·2; xxiv. 19-25, xxxiv. 4, xxxv. 1-10, xl. 4, lvii. 16, lii. 1, liv. 11-17, lx. 1-22, lxii. 3-5, 11-12, lxv. 17-25, lxvi. 22; Ezek. xxxvi. 34-36, xl. 2, xlvii. 1, and the last 8 chapters; Jer. xxxi. 35-40; Zech. xiv. 4-11; Rom. viii. 18-23; II Pet. iii. 13; Heb. xi. 16, etc.

BISHOP W. R. NICHOLSON.

MESSIAH'S KINGLY GLORY.

In the devotional exercises opening the evening the Rev. Dr. J. S. Kennedy, of Abingdon, Va., led in prayer. The following address was delivered by Bishop W. R. Nicholson, pastor of Immanuel Reformed Episcopal Church, Philadelphia, his subject being "Messiah's Kingly Glory."

Messiah is King. Of all creation He is King, for He is the Eternal Son, the Logos of God, God. Of human hearts He is king, for He is Jesus; that is to say, Jehovah the Savior. Of all the interests of His mediatorship betwixt God and man He is king, for, in view of His sin-expiating sufferings as godman and His triumph in resurrection, the Father gave to Him "all power in heaven and in earth;" gave it to Him in the sense (for it already belonged to Him as God) of His using it for

ADMINISTERING THE SALVATION

so meritoriously wrought out, and for grounding the assurance to His people. "Lo, I am with you alway, even unto the end of the world." So Messiah is King. Nevertheless, in neither of these senses, nor in all of them combined, is he king as Messiah. Messiah or Christ is a kingly title with a definite sense, and used distinctively.

Let us define the Messianic kinghood.

His sovereignty as God Messiah has always had; whereas his sovereignty as the Messiah has ever been a subject of the Father's promise and is still in the future. His reigning in the hearts of His people and His wielding all power in heaven and on earth in the interests of His church are exercises now going on; whereas His reigning as the Christ will have been introduced only subsequently to certain events that are yet to occur. Messiah, or Christ, is God-king appointed to an earthly throne. He will come to His kindom only in pursuance of the fact that He became the Son of man in a lineage of human royalty. Successor He is to a man-predecessor. His throne He will take as man, though it be as God-man. His Kingdom as the Christ is not that He is God, but that, being God, He reigns in a man's position and a man's surroundings. This makes the Christship a most distinctive form of kinghood. The Queen of England is also

the Empress-Queen of India, but not that by reason of this. Messiah, King on

HIS EARTHLY THRONE,

is also King of the universe: but not by reason of this. The Christ he could not be, indeed, according as Christ is depicted in the Scriptures, without being God. Victoria was long Queen of England before she was Empress of India; on the contrary, the Christ-king is the Christ-king by reason of being God as well as man. On the other hand, God incarnate, the Savior, He might have been without being Christ the King. Deity, however, did not so will it. Son of God and Son of man, he is also Son of David; this last-mensioned sonship being the focus, as it were, in which concenter the other two. In this Davidic sonship he takes the kingdom that has descended to him, the earthly throne that he has inherited, reigning thereon in all essential attributes of our manhood, yet robed in the majesty of his Godhood. This His Davidic heirship will have been made available by reason of His accomplished atonement for the sins of men, and as a priest, as well as a king, He will sit on the throne of His glory. A theocracy, then, the kingdom of the Christ will be; a divine-human monarchy, wherein, as well as the Savior and the supreme object of worship, the world's supreme civil ruler He will be. Men shall see the King in His beauty: evangelist divine, society's regenerator, creation's master, "glorious in holiness, fearful in praises,

DOING WONDERS."

This is King Messiah as the Scriptures portray Him. And this is the gospel of the kingdom, and, we may add, the kingdom of the gospel. We have the gospel of sin-expiation in the blood of Jesus, the gospel of repentance and faith, of pardon and personal acceptance, the gospel of the believer being after death with Jesus. But, precious beyond telling as all that is, it comes short of the gospel of the kingdom. All that is essential to it, preparatory to it, but not the whole of it. The gospel of the kingdom is the good news of perfected salvation actually attained at the time of the kingdom; of justification by faith in the blood that saveth, and sanctification, and glorification, all completely applied; of the glorified joint heirs with Christ to regal authority and magnificence; of the human race, as such, delivered from sin, renewed, made holy to God, advanced; of earth, the home of the race, purified, renovated, illuminated; the good news of all this to be secured under a King, whose face and form, feelings and actions are those of a man, whose love is unfailing, and wisdom omniscient, and power almighty, whose effulgence fills the world, "The same yesterday, to-day, and forever." This gospel of the kingdom is the sum total of the word of God, and the sum total of the gospel of the kingdom is this

KINGDOM OF THE GOSPEL.

The Messianic kinghood, then, is but another name for glory; spiritual, intellectual, social, material, human, divine glory. The kingdom of this king will be mankind's one eternal hallelujah to God and the Lamb.

But I must defend my definition of Messiah's kingdom, else some will charge me with dreaming. Is the Christ, the anointed one, just as I have described him? "To the law and to the testimony." Our time will suffice for no more than a glance. Even so, however, we may become assured of some prominent proofs; just as the eye, in the first flash of vision, may detect in a landscape, and make sure of, hills and valleys, woods and waters, although it will have passed unnoticed many features of the scene.

A preliminary word as to the phraseology of the subject. The natural universal sovereignty of God is by no means ignored in His word, but for by far the most part the references are not to it. The expressions so often occurring, "the kingdom," "Thy kingdom," "My kingdom," when not referring to any then existing kingdom among men, designate, in almost every instance, a kingdom promised; and what kingdom was ever promised but that of the Christ? Again, "kingdom of heaven," "kingdom of God," especially the latter, are of frequent occurrence; and these two are one. Matthew says that Jesus preached

"THE KINGDOM OF HEAVEN

is at hand" (iv, 17), while Mark says he preached "The kingdom of God is at hand" (i, 15). Kingdom of heaven and kingdom of God, then, are one and the same kingdom; one that was said to be "at hand"—about to appear, but not as yet come; and what kingdom were the Jewish people looking for but that of the Christ? The three phrases, "kingdom of heaven," "kingdom of God," "kingdom of Christ," are one. Moreover, when Jesus said, before Pilate (John, xviii, 36), "I am a King," he added, "To this end was I born, and to this end came I into the world, that I might bear witness to the truth." He came, then, to proclaim his own kingdom. And yet, as we have seen, it was the kingdom of God he preached. "I must preach the kingdom of God," he said, "for therefore am I sent" (Luke iv. 43). He was sent to preach the kingdom of God, while yet he preached his own kingkom. The kingdom of heaven, the kingdom of God, the kingdom of Christ, all three are one. This consideration will help us forward in our argument.

Now, how do the Scriptures set forth the kingdom of the Christ? The Spirit of God in Isaiah said that a child should be born whose name should be The Mighty God, and yet that He should have His government on

THE THRONE OF DAVID,

to establish the kingdom of David with judgment and justice even for ever (viii. 6-7.). Weigh the words well. Messiah should sit on the throne of David, and the indentical kingdom of David is the one he should establish forever. How express, how definite. Equally express is the spirit in Jeremiah. Nay, that prophet in one place (Jer. xxx. 9), goes even so far as to give to Messiah, with reference to the time of his actually reigning, the very name, "David, their king;" precisely as successive Roman emperors were called Cæsar. Accordingly, in the annunciation to Mary, after saying to her that her son should be called Jesus, and also the Son of the Highest, Gabriel said: "The Lord God shall giue unto Him the throne of His father, David, and He shall reign over the house of Jacob forever; and of his kingdom there shall be no end," (Luke i. 32-33). Seven centuries had passed since Isaiah had uttered his sublime oracle; but this idea, so definitely stated, of Messiah's successorship to David in the kingdom of Israel was spanning the centuries, as with the rainbow's beauty and distinctiveness, and was the foremost thought of the angelic messenger from heaven. Indeed it is the favorite thought of heaven; for the message out of the opened heavens to the shepherds was this: "To you is born this day in the city of David a Savior, Christ the Lord." Thus, on

THE NIGHT OF HIS BIRTH,

and out of the sky, emphasis was given to His Davidic royalty, and then the angels sang, "Glory to God in the Highest."

These are but specimen passages from the word of God. Could you, with your most skilful pen, put in more positive language that which they state? That the Christ, although "the mighty God," "the Son of the Highest," should succeed to David's throne precisely as a son succeeds to his father: that he should succeed to it as being so identically David's throne, that He would have as the inherited subjects of His kingdom "the house of Jacob," or, as elsewhere expressed, Judah and Israel—the self-same people whom David ruled; that, therefore, He should be a visible king reigning on earth; this is what these Scriptures so plainly declare. Their grammatical sense, by universal concession, points in but one direction. Yes, but, after all, may they not be figurative? The throne of David—may it not stand for Christ's reign in the heart, or in the church, or in the third heaven? If so, how is it indicated? If the Holy Spirit had meant His words to be taken according to their normal sense, how more effectively might He have secured His purpose? Do you object that it strikes you as incongruous that the Son of God should be a visible king on earth? So Celsus, the infidel philosopher of

THE SECOND CENTURY,

thought it a shocking thing that the Son of God should be born of a woman. So the modern infidel scouts the truth that Jesus was virgin-born. Did not the prophesies of the first coming of the Christ realize in fulfillment their normal meaning? But is any one of the prophesies of the coming kingdom so improbable in itself as was that of the virgin-motherhood of Mary? And the idea of inheriting—of what is it a figure? If the Christ get not from David what David had—an earthly throne—does He get from David what David never had—the reigning in the human heart, or the headship over all things to the church, or the seat of power in the third heaven?

But consider this. The Jews, including the Lord's disciples, did believe that Messiah should succeed to the veritable kingdom of David, and be a visible King on an earthly throne. All the world admits it. Now Jesus commissioned His disciples to preach the Kingdom of God (Luke ix. 2) without even saying a word to set them right in their understanding of the kingdom. He never told them to preach something different from what had already been their belief. This alone, if there were nothing more to be said, proves the unfigurativeness of the prophecies

WE ARE CONSIDERING.

Furthermore, over and over it is declared that the saints shall share with Christ in the ruling power of His kingdom. They shall sit with Me, says Jesus, on My throne (Rev. iii. 21). If they, mere men, shall occupy the Messianic throne, then is it a human throne—verily David's own.

Besides, in view of the overthrow of David's kingdom, God said that He would build it again. "In that day will I raise up the tabernacle of David that is fallen, and close up the breaches thereof; and I will raise up his ruins, and I will build it as in the days of old" (Amos ix. 11). The very thing that had fallen, will He raise up. Yea, He will build it again "as in the days of old." Here there

Rt. Rev. W. R. NICHOLSON, D. D.,
BISHOP REF. EPISCOPAL CHURCH, PHILADELPHIA.

is no possibility of a figure. And for what will He build up that fallen kingdom but for a King in the Davidic lineage? Accordingly Isaiah saith, "The Lord will have mercy on Jacob, and will yet choose Israel, and set them in their own land," (xiv, 1), and Amos saith, "They shall no more be pulled up out of their land" (ix, 15). Without the restoration of that people the kingdom of David could not possibly re-appear. And what do we see? Here to-day are the Jews in perennial preservation; a people rooted up out of their land, scattered throughout the nations for long ages, without a government,

WITHOUT A COUNTRY,

peeled and slaughtered, the hundredth part of whose sufferings had sufficed to obliterate any other people from the face of the earth, yet kept by the power of God, the standing miracle of the ages. And for what? Is not God's providence harmonizing with God's prophecy? Although they have been a most rebellious people, yet will He not break His covenant with them (Lev. xxvi. 44). I will not cast off Israel for all that they have done, saith the Lord, for as surely as the sun shines, and the moon and the stars give light by night, the seed of Israel shall not cease from being a nation before me forever (Jer. xxxi. 35-37(. Thus the rehabilitation of David's own identical kingdom will be a fact, and Messiah will be its king.

If now we would gain for this truth a redundancy of confirmation, let us glance at the famous covenant of God with David, of which we read so much; the fountain head of the Davidic royalty of the Christ. It is contained in the seventh chapter of Second Samuel and the seventeenth of First Chronicles. The prophet Nathan, was sent to David to say, "The Lord telleth thee that He will make thee a house. I will set up thy seed after thee, which shall proceed out of thy bowels, and I will establish His kingdom and the throne of His kingdom forever. I will be

HIS FATHER,

and He shall be my Son. And thine house and thy kingdom shall be established forever." You will notice that God said to David, Thy house, thy kingdom; and that it shoulk be perpetuated by transmission from himself; that his own seed, that should come out of his bowels, should succeed to the kingdom. Now that seed is Messiah. The apostle in the Hebrews quotes from this covenant, and applies it to Christ (i. 5). Peter, in the Acts, does the same, and says it means that Christ should sit on David's throne (ii. 30). And so did David himself respond to the communication. "O Lord God," he said (I read in Bishop Horsley's translation). "O Lord God, Thou hast spoken of Thy servant's house for a great while to come, and hast regarded me in the arrangement about the Man that is to be from above, O God Jehovah." Or, as some translate, "the Adam from above, God Jehovah." Certain it is that the future personage of the covenant with David is Messiah. So the Apostles understood it. So David understood it.

One sentence, indeed, as it stands in our English version, has involved this covenant in confusion. "If He (David's seed) commit iniquity, I will chasten him with the rod of men." How can the Messiah be regarded as

COMMITTING INIQUITY?

Bishop Horsley gives it thus: "When guilt is laid upon him, I will chasten him with the rod of men." Dr. Adam Clarke reads it: "In his sufferings for iniquity, I will chasten," etc. Here, then, is the doctrine of the atonement: Chastened with the rod due to men because of guilt laid upon him. The application to Messiah is perfect.

The subject matter of this covenant is the perpetuity of the kingdom of David; of the self-same kingdom that was in existence at the time the covenant was made. And yet the subject-matter of it is the perpetuity of the kingdom of the Christ. And further, the subject matter of it is the perpetuity of the kingdom of God the Father; for a part of the covenant is in these words of the Father: "I will settle him (the Messiah) in Mine house and in My kingdom forever" (I. Chr. xvii. 14). The kingdom of David, the kingdom of Christ, the kingdom of God is one and the same kingdom. And this kingdom is to be for ever perpetuated by transmission from David; but not by an endless process of transmission, for the succession is to terminate in the Christ as being a successor never failing. "Once have I sworn by my holiness," says God, referring to this covenant, "that I will not lie to David. His seed shall endure forever, and his throne as the sun before Me" (Ps. lxxxix. 35-36). Is it possible to

CONSIDER THE COVENANT

with David and doubt that the same royal house that God founded in his person is to reappear and be continued in the person of the Savior of the world? We do know that Messiah is Prince of the House of David, and that His distinctive kinghood is the outcome of David's kinghood.

Where, then, is this kingdom? It is not yet. It will be inaugurated at Christ's second coming. For while, in His earlier ministry, the Lord Jesus offered to the Jewish people the kingdom of heaven as nigh at hand, yet, at a later date, and because of their rejecting Him, His preaching of the kingdom underwent a remarkable change. It was no longer nigh at hand; it had been postponed; then it was that, because the people thought the kingdom of God should immediately appear, he told them of the nobleman's going into a far country to receive a kingdom for himself, self and to return (Luke xvix., 11) To this fact of the postponement he recurred again and again. And yet did he not say: "The kingdom of God cometh not with observation, for, behold, the kingdom of God is within you?" (Luke xii., 20-21.) "Within you," however, is not to be taken in the sense of piety, for then the expression would not have suited the Pharisees, to whom he said it. The kingdom cometh not so as to be observed in its approach. They shall not say, Lo here! or Lo there! for, behold at once

THE KINGDOM

is among you. So suddenly shall its splendors break upon the world, even as a thief in the night. Again, He said to the Pharisees. "If I cast out devils by the spirit of God, then the kingdom of God is come unto you" (Matt. xii., 28). The word for "come," however, is not the word usually so translated, but means reaching toward, and is explained by what he instructed the seventy, whom he sent before him, to say to the same Pharisees, that notwithstanding their rejection of the message sent them, they might be sure that the kingdom of God is come nigh to them Luke x. 9-11). He said, also, "The kingdom of Heaven is like a sower," "like a grain of mustard seed," "like leaven," etc., and is understood by many to mean that the kingdom of heaven is present in this dispensation. On the contrary, those parables have to do with the qualifications for the kingdom, teaching certain truths pertaining to it, illustrating them by the whole series of circumstances detailed in each parable. As, in that of the sower, for instance, the truth that such alone will be ready to enter the kingdom who so receive the word of God as to bring forth the fruit thereof, and the truth that a large number of those to whom the gospel is preached, not so receiving it, shall not enter the kingdom. It is not the

PRESENCE OF THE KINGDOM

that is taught, but our present duties with reference to it. Still, has not Paul positively said of all converted persons, that "the Father did translate them into the kingdom of the Son of His love" (Col. i. 13)? Yes, but just as positively he has said, that "whom God justified He also glorified" (Rom. viii. 30). Now has every justified believer been already glorified? We see that the vivid present is substituted for the future. No; the kingdom of God is not now. "When the Son of man," said Jesus, "shall come in His glory, and all the holy angels with Him, then shall He sit on the throne of His glory" (Matt. xxv. 31). Then, and not till then; for the nobleman did not begin to exercise his functions as king till after his return fromthe far country, but did exercise them instantly at his return.

The present time, then, is an interregnum in the kingdom. Certain writers have sought to identify the Davidic throne with that of England. But, besides many other proofs of the falsity of that notion, the truth that the recovery of the down-fallen throne is inseparably united to the future coming of the Christ is demonstration enough. But the fact of the interregnum—will it not make against the Davidic sameness of the kingdom at the coming of the King? No more than the intervening of

CROMWELL'S PROTECTORATE

between the First and Second Charles of England invalidated the succession of the Second to the First. Still, this weary interval of so many centuries—is faith able to leap the chasm and seize the future? See! So much as a thousand years rolled away after the covenant with David before any part of it relating to the recovery of the ruined throne had come to pass; but there did come to pass the most important part of it, and by far the most incredible. The man from above—the Adam, God Jehovah—did actually appear. A virgin did conceive, and bear a son A child, a wondrous child! Gethsemane, Calvary, resurrection, the nobleman gone for his kingdom! This the fulfillment in part already historical is the acorn centaining the oak. He will come. Prom the Mount of Olives He went away, and on the Mount of Olives, saith Zechariah, His feet shall stand in that day. Our faith does jump this weary interval, and sees the same Jesus that was taken up into heaven coming in like manner as He went into heaven (Ac. i, 11.)

And so a theocracy will the Davidic kingdom be at the Lord's coming. In fact, the theocracy was instituted at Sinai, and with it the kingdom of David was subsequently identified. The Lord God of Israel had His royal palace, and in it His divine glory, and also, emblematically,

ALL APARTMENTS

complete of His domestication among them. Nothing was to be done, no laws made, no enterprises undertaken, without the authority of the resident King. And, correspondently to the signet ring of royalty among men, He made known His will in the flashing of Urim and Thummim on the breast of the High Priest, the minister of State. Now, of the very house and kingdom emphasized as David's God said, my house, my kingdom, (1 Chr. xvii 14); thus grounding the Kingdom of David upon a theocratic basis. It is this theocratic character of the kingdom that justifies the Godman's inheriting of it; as inheriting the royalty of David, He also inherits the theocracy whereon it stood. But in Him the theocratic character will have to take a more perfect form. He, and not the Son of Jesse, will be the Theocrat under the Father: and, therefore, while, as occupying David's throne, He will be as human, and as visible as was David, yet will He wield its power with the very hand of God. God in human form, on his earthly throne, and as well mankind's civil as religious ruler, "He will dwell with them, and they shall be His people, and God Himself shall be with them, and be their God." (Rev. xxi. 3).

Will any one meet the idea of this sublime consummation with the words carnal,

OF THE EARTH, EARTHY?

What, can not God decide whether or no a thing is carnal? And this word of His concerning the kingdom can you change for the better? Oh, but Jesus said, "My Kingdom is not of this world" (John xviii. 36). Yes, and He also said of His apostles, "They are not of the world" (John xvii. 14). Were the apostles, then, not on the earth, not visible, and not holy men? Not of the world, Jesus said. He did not say not in the world. Did not the Son of God inherit his humanity, yet without sin, from his mother? Wherein is his becoming man less degrading than, being man, is his visible reign among men? Solomon succeeded to David; but he erected a new and more gorgeous throne, built a new palace, instituted a different train of attendants, and varied in many features of administration. Was his kingdom, therefore, not the same as his father's? And may not the Christ's kingdom be Davidic, even though it be not a copy of David's imperfections, and be not fashioned according to this present evil world? The truth is that, while his kingdom shall emerge into view out of a royal lineage of earth, at the same time it shall be seen to have come from out of the heavens. It is as well God-derived and heavenly in origin as man-descended and of

A SUBLUNARY SPHERE.

While being in the earth, it will yet be the kingdom of heaven; or, as it always is in the Greek, the kingdom of the heavens.

And now we may see the greatness of the kingly glory of Messiah. Even if we did not know many of the constituents of this glory, we could still be independently sure of its magnificence and its preciousness. For the kingdom of the Christ will be the reward of his Godmanhood. He will come, not as at the first advent, as a sin-bearer, but without sin unto salvation (Heb. ix. 28); that is, unto perfected salvation, unto the ultimate results of His work. Hence his session at the right hand of the Majesty on high is but precedent to his inauguration as Messiah the king (Heb. xii. 2; Ps. cx. 1). It is the joy that was set before Him in all His work and shame in the expiation of sin wrought once for all; the proportionate requital of that wail of agony on the cross, "My God, my God why hast thou forsaken me?" Now, what might fittingly reward such an one for such a work—for that work of redemption, in comparison with which creation itself is but as the glow-worm to the sun in the heavens—who could adequately depict? Thus as seen from Gethsemane and Cavalry, and had we not one word to certify us of the make-up of its glory, the coming kingdom must needs be thought to surpass

OUR UTMOST IMAGININGS.

But we do know something of its glory. First, itself essential glory is our authorized conception of this prince of the House of David. The Brightness of the Father, the Lord of Creation, the Ruler of hearts, the man sinless and spotless, one with the constitution of our nature, overflowing with our sympathies; He, seated in the midst of mankind, reigning before their eyes, reigning audibly—the priest on his throne, administering his salvation, making his subjects willing in the day of his power—in mightiness absolute, in wisdom omniscient, in love divine—wearing the one crown of the world's monarchy, the supreme religious satisfaction of men; He—oh, this King in his beauty and his majesty! There is no glory by reason of the glory that excelleth.

Secondly, in his associate rulers He will be glorious. The saints of all the ages down to His second coming shall be exalted to kinghood with Him. "Joint-heirs with Christ," says Paul (Rom. viii. 17). "Heirs of the kingdom," says James, "which God hath promised to them that love Him" ii. (5). "Shall sit with Me on My throne," "Shall have power over and rule the nations," says Jesus (Rev. iii. 21 ii. 26-27). Isaiah says, "A king shall reign in righteousness, and princes shall rule in judgment" xxxii. (1).

"The saints," says Daniel, "shall possess the kingdom, and the

GREATNESS OF THE KINGDOM

under the whole heaven" vii. (22-27). Even the poor and the beggar among His saints, as Hannah sang, will He lift up from the dust and the dunghill, to set them among princes, and to make them inherit the throne of glory (I. Sam. ii. 8). For, just as in the ancient theocracy, although God had the supremacy, there were other rulers or judges appointed under him for administering the laws, so will Christ have His associate princes in the government.

This implies the resurrection of the saints at the coming of the Lord, for "flesh and blood can not inherit the kingdom of God." Mortal man could not carry the weight of partnership with Christ in his sovereignty. Accordingly we read, "The dead in Christ shall rise first. Then we which are alive and remain shall be caught up together with them in the clouds, to meet the Lord in the air." And so, fitted for their high destiny, they shall come back to the earth with Him, and "shall be forever with the Lord."

Priests, too, on their thrones shall those glorified rulers be. Every Christian now is a priest, officiating in the service of God. Every prince then will be a priest, blending the princely and priestly in discharging his functions of sovereignty. And while herein they shall be reflections of the King, devoutly will they feel His supremacy; that "He is anointed with

THE OIL OF GLADNESS

above His fellows" (Heb., i, 9); for they will "fall down before Him and cast their crowns before the throne, and their united attestations, as the sound of many waters, will be, "Thou hast made us unto our God kings and priests, and we shall reign on the earth" (Rev., iv, 10; v, 10).

How splendid will be that court of the King—Enoch, Abraham, David, Elijah, Elisha, Isaiah, Jeremiah, Daniel, John, Peter, Paul, and all the myriads out of the ages whom we can not name, all, as Jesus says, "shining as the sun in the kingdom of their Father" (Mat. xiii. 43). Yet, like diamonds in the sunlight, the brighter they shine as suns, the more will He, the central sun, refulgent be.

Thirdly, in the subjects of His kingdom He is glorious. Over Judah and Israel, regathered and restored, as king of the House of David he must needs reign. But what of other peoples? In fact, under the sway of the King, all mankind shall become Israel. It is alone by being grafted into the Abrahamic covenant, that any gentile believer is ever saved. "Christ hath redeemed us from the curse of the law, being made a curse for us, that the blessing of Abraham might come on the gentiles through Jesus Christ," and "if we are Christ's, then are we Abraham's seed, and heirs according to the promise" (Gal. iii. 13, 14, 29).

ALL GENTILE BELIEVERS

then are engrafted seed of Abraham; are themselves Israel by adoption. And, since the Davidic covenant is the outcome of the Abrahamic, so therefore are they also heirs according to the promise. This is why the risen gentile saints, equally with the risen saints of natural Israel, shall be sharers with Christ in the power of the kingdom. And, as gentile believers are adopted children of Abraham, so it is that all gentile peoples then in the flesh shall become Israel, and be embraced within the Dividic subjects of the kingdom. Wherefore, on and on evermore shall be fulfilling that promise to Abraham, "I will make thy seed as the dust of the earth, as the sand of the sea, as the stars that cannot be numbered for multitude." (Gen. xiii. 16; xv. 5; xxxii, 12).

4. Even an ocular demonstration of His glory has been vouchsafed us. A real exhibition of His kingdom we have in the scene of the transfiguration. Peter calls it "the power and coming of our Lord Jesus Christ," and says he was an eye-witness of his majesty and glory (2 Pet. i. 16-18). Jesus himself, referring to it by anticipation a few days before its occurrence, said: "There be some standing here which shall not taste of death till they see the Son of man coming in his kingdom" (Matt. xvi. 28). It was therefore an earnest of the kingdom;

A TOKEN

that more is yet to come of the same kind. And of what kind was it? Transfigured was the King; "His face did shine as the sun, and his raiment was white as the light" (Mat. xvii. 2). And associated with him were Moses and Elijah, both shining in the glory of the King, talking with Him; Moses, who had died, as representing the risen saints, Elijah, who was translated, as representing those that shall be caught up to meet the Lord. And Peter and James and John were there, representative of Israel in the flesh; witnessing the wonderful scene, transported with the heavenly splendor, foreshowing how the subjects of the kingdom shall be affected by the sight of the King and His companion princes. And over all the Father's voice coming out of the cloud, "This is my beloved Son in whom I am well pleased," thus echoing the words He spake in the covenant with David, "My house, my kingdom." Oh, verily, the kingdom of the Christ on David's throne will be the kingdom of heaven on earth.

5. In the results of His kingdom He is glorious.

There will be a world-wide experience of the gospel salvation. True, "the Lord Jesus shall be revealed from heaven in flaming fire, taking vengeance in them that know not God and

OBEY NOT THE GOSPEL"

(II. Thess. i. 7-8). That day shall burn as an oven (Mal. iv.), and the conflagration foretold by Peter shall do its work of vengeance (2 Pet. iii). But, besides the uniform teaching of all Scripture, both Peter himself and Isaiah explain [see note] that, terrible as shall be that fire, yet the earth will remain, and Israel will remain, and other peoples will remain. Nay, in words of the Divine oracles, it is even then that "the world shall be established, that it shall not be moved, the earth shall be glad, the field be joyful, the trees of the wood rejoice, the floods clap their hands, the hills be joyful together" (Psa. xcvi., xcviii.). And then it is that even they who through all the centuries have persisted as a people in their enmity to the gospel, and who, like Shylock, have never ceased to say, "I hate him because he is a Christian," that even Judah and Israel "shall teach no more every man his neighbor, saying, Know the Lord, for they shall all know Me, from the least of them to the greatest of them, saith the Lord, for I will forgive their iniquity, and I will remember their sin no more." (Jer. xxxi, 34). Not only this, but the Holy Spirit "shall be poured out upon all flesh." (Joel ii. 28). Not Israel alone, but, according to James in the Acts (xv. 16, 17, as the result of "the rebuilding of David's kingdom, the residue of men will seek after the Lord, even all the gentiles upon whom the Lord's name is called." The fruit of the Spirit shall fill the

FACE OF THE WORLD.

Again, there will be a renovation of physical nature. For creation, says Paul, is groaning in pain for redemption along with man, and shall be delivered from the bondage of corruption into the freedom of the glory of the children of God (Rom. viii. 19-22). "New heavens and a new earth." The light of the moon shall be as the light of the sun, and the light of the sun sevenfold, as the light of seven days" (Isa. xxx. 26). "Instead of the thorn shall come up the fir-tree, instead of the brier the myrtle-tree" (Isa. lv. 13). The wilderness shall be glad, and deserts rejoice and blossom like the rose (Isa. xxxv. 1). The ground shall yield its increase (Ps. lxvii. 6); as if its present fertility were no fertility at all. "I will answer the heavens, saith the Lord, and they shall answer the earth; and the earth shall answer the corn, and the wine, and the oil; and they shall answer Iezrael" (the seed of God) (Hosea ii. 21-22). Mountains shall drop down wine, hills flow with milk, the plowman overtake the reaper, the treader of grapes him that soweth seed (Joel iii. 18. Amos ix. 13). The animals too,—even the beasts of the field, the fowls of heaven, and the creeping things of the ground shall be under a covenant bond of the kingdom (Hos. ii. 18); the wolf and the lamb, the leopard and the kid, the calf and the young lion, all dwelling together, and a little child leading them: and children playing on

THE HOLE OF THE ASP

and on the cockatrice's den (Isa. xi. 6-9). Thus the curse removed from even the hated serpent:

"The mother sees,
And smiles to see, her infant's playful hand
Stretched forth to dally with the crested worm
To stroke his azure neck, or to receive
The lambent homage of his arrowy tongue."

---

*Note referred to above.

[Isaiah and Peter are speaking of the same time and the same series of events. The new heavens and the new earth, (Isa. lxv. 17; lxvi. 22; II. Peter iii. 13)

THE TERRIBLE FIRE

preceding. (Isa. lxvi. 15-17; II. Peter iii. 7-10-12). Now the prophet declares that after the devastation by the fire there will still be nations in the flesh, (lxvi. 19-24). Evidently, therefore, the apostle's language is to be interpreted in the light of the prophet; especially so, since the apostle expressly refers to the prophet (II. Peter iii. 13) and quotes from him the promise of the new heavens and the new earth. But the apostle himself throws around his language certain plainly intimated limitations. At the same time that he speaks of the burning of the earth at the coming of the Lord he also speaks of the earth having perished by means of the deluge (6). If, however, after having perished in the deluge the earth still remained, so may it remain after the stupendous conflagration shall have visited it. Again, he speaks of the object of the fire as being, not the sweeping away of all mankind, but "the perdition of ungodly men" (7): which perdition might be inflicted upon certain multitudes, while yet other multitudes might be spared. And this if just what Isaiah asserts will be the fact (lxvi. 19). Finally the apostle locates the conflagration at the coming of the Lord (10): at which time, however, in common with the other apostles and the Christians of his day, he believed that that the Davidic kingdom would be rebuilt. Prodigious, then, as may be the conflagration that he so terribly depicts, he does not mean to be understood as saying that it will burn up all men and all things in the earth.

[See propositions 149-150 in the Theocratic Kingdom, by the Rev. George N. H. Peters.]

And health shall bloom on every cheek. The inhabitant shall not say, I am sick (Isa. xxxii. 24). The leaves of the tree of life shall be for the healing of nations (Rev. xxii. 2), and as the days of a tree shall be the days of the people of the King (Isa. lxv. 22). In a thousand ways has sin turned nature into a minister of calamity against us; but the curse shall be lifted, and earth, regenerated, be ushered into the perfect service of the subjects of the King.

And again, what exuberant blessedness of mankind as a body politic. The government over them one: perfect in its unity, grand in its massiveness. Divine, yet human; committing no iniquity, making no mistakes, purely good. The king, the princes, and the subjects bound together in perfected redemption. And, according to the prophets, a mighty increase of population (Isa. xlix. 19-20, Jer. xxx. 18-20); yet no national jealousy, no cause of war, no civil disturbance. Swords beaten into plowshares, spears into pruning-hooks (Isa. ii. 4). Old men and old women, every man with

HIS STAFF IN HIS HAND

for very age, dwelling in Jerusalem, and the streets full of boys and girls playing therein (Zech. viii. 4-5). Riches increased; multitudes of camels, dromedaries of Midian and Ephah, flocks of Kedar, rams of Nebaioth, gold, incense, precious woods (Isa. lx). Satan-bound (Rev. xx. 3). All things used as consecrated to God (Isa. xxiii. 18; Zech. xiv. 20). Knowledge universally diffused (Isa. xxxii. 4). The forfeited unity of language restored (Zeph. iii. 9). Angels of God, ascending and descending, in communication with men (John i. 51). Sorrow and sighing fled away, joy and gladness prevailing, thanksgiving and the voice of melody (Isa. xxxv. 10-51-3. The image of God, reflected in the myriads of millions of mankind, overspreading the world with a moral glory, like dewdrops sparkling in the rays of the sun. And over them all the Christ, the Son of God, the Son of man, the Son of David, reigning in Mount Zion from henceforth, even for ever (Micah. iiii. 7).

We are not to suppose that these several classes of results of Messiah's kinghood shall, in their totality, be effected instantaneously. The prophecies imply that there shall be a thousand years of the purifying process. Some sin, some death, there will be during that millennium (Isa. lxv., Zech. xiv., Rev. xx. 14).
Especially at its close, Satan being loosed for

A LITTLE SEASON,

one prodigious outbreak of rebellion will burst forth on the part of the yet unsaved (Rev. xx. 8-9). Only for a little season, however; the final winding up of sin's history in connection with our earth. For "fire shall come down from God out of heaven and devour them," and the devil that deceived them shall be cast into the lake of fire (Rev. xx. 9-10). And then, death, the last enemy, having been destroyed, and all things subdued unto Christ (I. Cor. xv. 25-26, Rev. xx. 14), it will have become absolutely true that the "knowledge of the Lord covereth the earth as the waters cover the sea." Then will the dominion of the world have been delivered up to the Father, precisely in that it will have been delivered up to His Christ; for, as we have all along seen, the Kingdom of the Christ is expressly the Kingdom of the Father. For that passage in I. Cor. xv. 25-28 does not teach the giving up of the distinctive kingdom of the Christ. In Rev. xi. 15 we have substantially the same teaching as in that Corinthian text: "The kingdom (mark the singular number) of the world is become the kingdom of our Lord and of His Christ, and He shall reign unto the ages of the ages." It is the dominion of the world that is delivered up, and is delivered up at one and the same moment to both

THE FATHER AND HIS CHRIST.

Of Messiah's kingdom the angel said, "There shall be no end" (Luke i. 33). Daniel says, "It shall not pass away" (vii. 14); "His associate princes are expressly declared to possess the kingdom forever, even forever and ever" (Dan. vii. 18); and they possess it only as joint heirs with him. The statement that "then shall the Son also Himself be subject to the Father" means simply that then, also, then as now, even after all things have been subdued to him, he shall be subject to the Father. Accordingly, the Father saith to the Son, in express allusion to His Davidic royalty, "Thy throne O God, is for ever and ever" (Ps. xlv., Heb. i. 8, 9). All antagonisms will have ceased; the Godhead, Father, Son, and Spirit, will be all in all, and the Christ on David's throne, in joint heirship with His glorified brethren, the princes of the kingdom, and over happy subjects countless as the sands of the sea, shall reign "unto the ages of the ages."

Glory is it? What else is glory? Poets have dreamed of a golden age. Politicians build their Utopias. Social agitators are ever trying to make a paradise out of this present disordered world. But, all the same, history's stern recorder, Time, but chronicles wickedness, turbulence, misery. A candle's flame burns dull and dim in the

FLOOD-LIGHT OF NOONDAY,

and all unsanctified imaginings of political

regeneration are only abortions when looked at in the glory of Messiah's reign, wherein the will of God shall be done on earth as angels do it in heaven. And, best of all, the kingdom is a certainty.

Glory to God in the highest the angels sang when the Christ, David's son and heir, was born. Glory to God in the highest will be the heavenly music of the King and princes in David's kingdom. Glory to God in the highest the chorus of mankind when the moon shall be confounded and the sun ashamed in the light of the Lord of Hosts reigning in Jerusalem and before His ancients gloriously (Isa. xxiv., 23). And we in this dreary interregnum—we who are never so disenchanted of worldliness and so enchanted of godliness and watchfulness and diligence and communion with God, as when intelligently sympathizing with the kingdom of heaven on earth—do we not feel, "blessed is the people that know the joyful sound; they shall walk, O Lord, in the light of thy countenance (Ps. lxxxix. 15-3-35-36)? Oh, be this the jubilant Te Deum of our lives, "Thou art the king of glory, O Christ!" "Thou art able to present us faultless before the presence of Thy glory with exceeding joy. To Thee, the only wise God our Savior, be glory and majesty, dominion and power, both now and ever. Amen."

FIFTH DAY.

THE REV. DR. J. D. HERR.

IMPORTANCE OF PROPHETIC STUDY.

The opening paper of the morning meeting of the fifth and last day's session of the conference was read by the Rev. Dr. J. D. Herr, of the Grand Avenue Baptist Church, Milwaukee. After the usual devotional exercises, prayer being offered by the Rev. J. M. Orrock, of Boston, Dr. Herr read as follows on the subject, "Importance of Prophetic Study:"

God's word, in God's order, with God's emphasis, should be the watchword and spiritual war-cry of every diligent student of its inspired pages. The Bible is not a book of hobbies. It never emphasizes one truth at the expense of another. Neither does it deal in fragmentary truth. The book is a grand mosaic, divinely perfect in all its parts, and perfect in its divine completeness. The various truths contained in

THIS WONDERFUL BOOK

are set forth in the measure of their importance, and it behooves every careful student, not only to study God's truth in God's order, but also to observe closely the emphasis He places thereon. It is the most glaring lack of wisdom to select one or two passages of Scripture and isolate them from all the rest in order to prove any favorite dogma of our own. In the Bible there may be seeming parodoxes, but there can be no contradictions. Truth must never be diverted from its legitimate trend, no more than the currents of a river from their natural channels. Truth lies not in eddies, but in the onflow, in the massive bed of thought hewn out of the eternal word. God's order must therefore be closely followed, even though it be at the expense of preconceived opinions or the prejudices of faulty education. Not only must God's truth be taken in God's order, but also with God's emphasis. There are portions of the Bible upon which the Holy Spirit dwells with peculiar force; thus elevating such passages above the mountain peaks of thought around them in order that they may catch the eye, excite the intellect, and touch the heart of the devout student of the word. The first advent of our Lord runs like a golden thread from the Garden of Eden to the manger at Bethlehem. Each succeeding prophet threw more emphasis upon

THE WEIGHTY FACT

until Judean plains trembled with the thrilling glory of angelic testimony. The trend of thought upon this overwhelming subject accumulated in power and volume until the voice of the wilderness crier heralded the presence of the long-expected Messiah. The importance, therefore, of accepting the emphasis placed upon the various lines of God's word by the Holy Spirit can not well be overestimated by careful and diligent searchers after truth.

This emphasis is also seen in the large amount of Scripture sometimes given to a single theme. We judge wisely when we estimate the importance of a subject by the amount of space it occupies in the Book of God. The prophetical writings both of the Old and New Testaments constitute the major portion of the Bible. If we enumerate the books directly prophetical, together with the multitudinous passages touching on prophecy in other books, especially in the Psalms of David, and remember also the adumbrations of things to come contained within the character of much Scripture history, as well as in the ceremonial law, and also in the tabernacle service, we are forced to the conclusion that prophetic study ranks high in importance in the estimation of the Holy Spirit, and should also in the unprejudiced Christian mind.

Notwithstanding these plain facts, a strange hesitancy, and I might almost say timidity, has obtained

FOR MANY YEARS

among students of the Bible in relation to the earnest and persistent study of prophecy. This may be accounted for in various ways. The main reason perhaps, being the wild and unscriptural fancies springing from the brains of theorists and superficial thinkers.

The failures and follies of speculative writers upon prophecy have characterized every age of eclesiastical history. Just as men have wandered from the fundamental doctrines of the word of God, and "given

Rev. J. D. HERR, D. D.

heed to seducing spirits and doctrines of demons," so men through all ages have studied prophecy, not with a humble desire to find out the mind of God, but to build up some baseless fabric of their own fancy. These abnormal conditions of doctrine and prophetical research should in no possible way deter the faithful study and calm inquiry of an intelligent Christian mind. It was by "books" that Daniel understood the number of years that spanned the Babylonish captivity. As a scholar and statesman he stood peerless in pre-eminence over all others of his day. His life was so thoroughly saturated with divine impulses as to carry him beyond the reach of adverse criticism. Yet he did not think it unwise or unprofitable even up to old age to search with profound diligence

THE REALM OF PROPHECY.

God had made him a prince among prophets, yet he did not fail to devote himself to the study of "books," and especially of those containing the prophecies of Jeremiah, in order that he might solve to his own satisfaction the exact period when the Babylonish captivity should terminate. The effect of his study upon himself was a prostration in prayer and supplication before God, and a quickening of the spiritual pulses of his soul. Thus the reflex influence upon his life was most healthful, and brought him, a profound worshiper, to the feet of the Lord God Almighty.

The same may be said of Simeon and Anna, who were found daily in the Temple waiting for the "Consolation of Israel." Evidently they had been diligent students of the prophetic Scriptures, and God honored them with an actual vision of His long promised Son, in the person of "the holy child Jesus." Surely, then, we should not lightly esteem the importance of prophetic study and cast aside carelessly that portion of the Word upon which God has placed such peculiar emphasis. The Bible declares, and the history of nations and men corroborate the declaration, that the only safe pathways toward the future are along the inspired lines of prophecy. This is the massive telescope with lens sufficiently powerful to give the earnest observer an outline

OF FUTURE EVENTS

and in profound humility bring him a willing worshiper to the feet of our adorable Lord. Upon the threshold of thought before us the question comes: In what attitude should we assume the study of prophecy? The Bible is the infallible word of God. Therefore, to be rightly understood it requires an infallible interpreter. In the wondrous economy of grace such a teacher has been provided. The mission of the Holy Spirit to the earnest student of God's word is clearly set forth by Christ Himself. He declares the Spirit "will guide into all truth." "He shall receive of Mine," says Jesus, "and shall show unto you," "He shall show you things to come," "He shall abide with you and shall be in you." Thus provision is made for the devout student to secure a correct knowledge of God's intention toward man. "What things eye saw not and ear heard not, and in man's heart came not up, as many things as God prepared for those loving Him, to us, notwithstanding God revealed through the Spirit, for the Spirit searcheth all things, even the deep things of God." This same divine teacher instructed men of former ages: "For the prophecy came not in olden times by the will of man; but holy men of God spake, as moved by the Holy Ghost." Only holy men were permitted to know sufficient of the mind of God in relation to future events, to be made mouthpieces to the nations

THIS SPIRIT OF PROPHECY

rested without measure upon the Lord Jesus Christ. His emphatic corroborations of the testimony given in former times by holy men, together with the wonderful prophetic utterances falling from his own lips, were all promptings of the same Spirit. This line of thought runs through all the revelations of Paul to the churches, and also inspires the tongues of Peter, Jude, and John as they voice the prophetic teachings of the Holy Spirit. These thoughts crystalize into the fact that all true conceptions of future events came only to holy men who were in full sympathy with God, and only to them as they were enlightened and prompted by the Holy Spirit. If then all true prophecy be the direct product of the Holy Spirit then is it the province of the Holy Spirit alone to interpret prophecy. The Bible does not cater to the peculiar and favorite theories of men. No matter how intelligent and scholarly the student of prophecy may be, he will be wholly unfit to comprehend the mind of God in relation to the future unless he assumes the proper attitude of a devout inquirer after truth. Scholarship may understand the written word, but only the man taught and indwelt by the Holy Spirit can properly grasp the incarnate word. It is as true to-day as in former times that "the secret of the Lord is for them that fear Him, and He makes them know His covenant." "If perchance," says Christ, "any one be willing

TO DO HIS WILL,

he shall understand about the teaching whether it is of God, or I from myself am talking." Under these flashing lights of

Scripture prophetic study assumes an importance and dignity worthy the profoundest scholar as he bows to the leadership of the Holy Spirit. The student of prophecy requires more thorough equipment than can be secured by efficient scholarship or biblical criticism. The highest gifts and attainments must be sanctified and subordinated to the teachings of the divine Interpreter. When any man or any church assumes the prerogative of the Holy Spirit and becomes his own interpreter the result will always be disastrous. The dogma of infallibility promulgated by the Roman Catholic Church was the logical sequence of her sacreligious assumption of the interpretation of the word of God. By so doing she ignores the office work of the Holy Spirit and opens up pathways to ultimate and overwhelming ruin. With these thoughts in view permit me to notice some reasons why more attention should be paid to a calm and prayerful study of this important subject.

Anything relating to the mission and work of the Lord Jesus Christ should be of interest to His professed followers. All prophecy, from Eden to the close of Revelation; relates directly or indirectly to the Divine Redeemer. To this fact the Lord Jesus not only assented, but emphatically gave utterance. He said to the Jews,

"SEARCH THE SCRIPTURES,

for they are they which testify of Me." To the two disciples whom He met on their eventful journey He says: "O thoughtless and slow in your heart to repose faith in all things which the prophets spake! And beginning at Moses and from all the prophets He thoroughly explained to them in all the Scriptures the things concerning Himself." What Christ was to the prophecies relating to His first advent, He is to the yet unfulfilled prophecies concerning His second advent. The testimony of Jesus is the spirit of prophecy. No one therefore who is interested in the past history and ultimate triumphs of the Son of God can afford to ignore the study of prophecy. The unfolding of Christ as the World's Redeemer and our personal Savior is the foundation of all true spiritual knowledge. Upon this rock we are privileged to stand, and direct our vision toward the ultimate fulfillment of God's mighty purposes concerning His illustrious Son. The dignity of our calling as Christians embraces all the truths wrapped up in the wonderful events of the future. God never would have spread before us the sublime map of prophecy if He did not greatly desire us to carefully study its marvelous features. He never would have traced the exalted pathway of His son through the long aisles of the future did he not

CORDIALLY AND LOVINGLY

invite us with the eye of faith and profoundest research to follow. The invitation of Jesus to follow him not only relates to our moral uprightness and spiritual consecration, but to the unfoldments of His future achievements as our glorious King. He has already displayed Himself to us as our Prophet and Priest, but we look for the consummation of His matchless character, as the future will soon unfold His regal splendor as our King. This is the sheet anchor holding our faith and hope amid the skepticism and prevailing unbelief of the day. Just as God invited Abraham in respect to Canaan to "Arise, walk through the land, in the length of it, and in the breadth of it, for I will surely give it thee." So he invites those who through faith are to inherit the kingdom with His Son—to study the maps of prophecy lying before them in His holy word. When we accept this loving invitation and take a holy excursion through the wondrous land of prophetic promise, we find revealed to our enraptured vision glorious doctrines, precious promises, practical precepts, and the highest incentives to holy living. We also find that the full-tuned harp of prophecy fills the entire temple of revelation with awful and entrancing melody. So deep are its tones and far-reaching its

DIVINE HARMONIES

that we listen with ever-increasing reverence. As we gaze upon that majestic harp we are reminded that it was tuned by Jehovah Himself, to proclaim the magnificent triumphs of His only begotten Son. The strings of that harp have been touched by holy men of ancient days; by mighty kings who sat on Judah's throne; by inspired apostles as they were indwelt by the Holy Ghost, and by some of the tallest angels who walk the guardways of eternity. We are reminded also that its sweetest and most entrancing melodies have been awakened by the touch of His fingers whose peerless achievements are yet to fill the universe with the jubilant anthem of eternal thanksgiving. Shall we then depreciate such exalted companionship and rob ourselves of such spiritual enjoyment simply on the ground of an unwarranted prejudice against the study of prophetic truth?

It is only through prophecy we learn the true destiny of this present world. The history of the world as chronicled by eminent men of all ages is full of profoundest interest. The development, reign, and ultimate overthrow of vast empires, the rise of mighty warriors and able statesmen, the

TRANSMISSION OF POWER

from one nationality to another, the hereditary impulse to conquer and annex territory manifested by all nations, together with the solemn yet awful trend toward an evadeless crisis are to the student who puts his fingers on the feverish pulse of the world profoundly interesting. Watching the kaleidoscope of passing events we dare not forget that history is the dial-plate upon which the finger of God indicates the epochs of prophecy. It is God alone who "changeth the times and seasons; He removeth kings and setteth up kings; He giveth wisdom to the wise, and knowelge to them that have understanding; He revealeth the deep and secret things; He knoweth what is in the darkness, and the light dwelleth with Him." The march of the centuries is toward a legitimate future. Each revolution assists in advancing the world in its prophetic destiny. All things keep step along the lines of God's eternal purposes, and the Christian who fails to read history by the lamp of prophecy will find no other light to illumine the deep mysteries surrounding this earthly planet. It is impossible to close our eyes to the fact that dreamers and theorists, together with speculative teachers, have prophesied concerning events in the future pathway of this globe and its inhabitants. Scientists have attempted to demonstrate

THE PECULIAR METHODS

by which the present world is to be destroyed, together with the heavenly bodies beyond us. Yet no theory has ever been promulged receiving a hearty and unhesitating approval from intelligent thinkers. We are forced, therefore, to the conclusion that all speculative theories of the future, drawn from other sources than the word of God, are only conjectures and can not be relied upon with any degree of certainty. In the Bible alone do we find the sure word of prophecy: "Whereunto ye do well to take heed as unto a light that shineth in a dark place, until the day dawn, and the day-star arise in your hearts."

The certainty of prophecy should prompt us to careful study. Much of the prophecy of past ages has crystalized into history. The wonderful statements of the Bible stand or fall as the verdict of history is written. Prophecy is peculiar to the Bible, and distinguishes it from all other systems of faith. False religions deal very little with future events. Mahomet, in his public life, expressly disclaimed reliance on prophetic testimony. He was much too sagacions to lay the writings of the Koran open to the certain and unrelenting detection of history. What Mahomet and all other false systems of religion failed to do has been unhesitatingly and grandly assumed by the inspired word.

THE BIBLE CHALLENGES HISTORY

to detect a flaw in its marvelous assertions concerning the future.

If history to-day does not corroborate the "sure word of prophecy," so far as prophecy has become history, then the Bible is not the infallible word of God, and we have been following a cunningly devised fable. Eighteen hundred years have elapsed since the last book on prophecy was written, and during that long period the leading events of history have proven in a marvelous manner that "holy men of old spake, moved by the Holy Ghost." If the Bible will not stand the test of history then it dare not lay claims to divine inspiration. One hundred and nine predictions concerning Christ's first advent were literally fulfilled. If the famous doctors of Jewish law had been as faithful in the study of prophecy as they were in tithing "mint, annise, and cummin," they might have been daily in the temple with old Simeon and Anna the prophetess, waiting for the consolation of Israel. The earth on which we live bears the footprints of prophecy through all ages. Nations, cities, temples, and individuals have met their doom through the lips of inspired men, and the records of such doom are so plainly written on the brow of history as to be beyond any

CAVIL OF SKEPTIC.

The literal fulfillment of predictions which have passed into history should be to all an earnest for the future unfolding of those declarations yet lying in the womb of coming events.

The very certainty of prophecy should induce to its faithful study. "Hath He said and shall He not do it?" "These are the true sayings of God," declared the angel who opened the prophetic vision to John upon Patmos. The more fully we can become penetrated with the conviction of the certainty of prophecy the higher will be our elevation and enrichment. Nothing is so stimulating to the devout mind as to mark the footprints of God along the highways of the centuries and the distant uplands of coming ages. The Bible does not place any premium upon that mental indolence which ignores the major part of its wonderful teachings. The objection urged that it requires too careful and abstruse study to penetrate the mines of God's wondrous purposes, and gather the hidden jewels therein, is not in harmony with the dignified relationship and high calling of the child of God.

The importance of prophetic study is also seen in its practical effects on Christian life. Christian conduct is not moulded and regulated by mere ordinances and precepts. The law is "holy, just and good," but

WE ARE TOLD

that by it "no flesh can be justified before God." The Gospel points to redemption, not through ordinances, but through Christ. It unveils the sublime and precious truth, that "God was in Christ reconciling the world to Himself, not imputing their trespasses unto them." They who hear and heed the Gospel are set free; chains of prejudice and condemnation fall from the soul, and the light and liberty of the sons of God are realized. The soul thus disenthralled requires teaching in order properly to understand what is the "good, acceptable and perfect will of God." He must not only know what he is saved from, but what he is saved for. What are God's present and future purposes concerning me? Am I to go on to know the Lord? Or am I simply to stop at the initial step of salvation from sin and fail to inquire what God's will is in relation to myself personally? Am I to be satisfied by the "glittering generalities" and intangible conceptions of heaven as they come to me through the various avenues of theoretical Christian thought? Has Jesus Christ placed in my lips the wonderful petition, "Thy kingdom come," and given me no knowledge what that kingdom is to be? Has he excited in my breast a hope which is only to be fed by speculative fancy and strengthened through the fertile

RESOURCES OF IMAGINATION?

We all know that the tenor and drift of Christian life and conduct are controlled by the actual and real hopes animating the soul. Hope, to have a purifying tendency upon the human heart, must have a tangible and well-defined objective point. This objective point, to be correct, must be clearly taught in the word of God. If our lives are not governed by the true hope set before us in the gospel, then some lower hope is controlling us and the highest practical benefits are not reached. There are three steps in the onward grasp of hope and these three embrace the full ordered life of a child of God upon earth. Paul enumerates them in such concise manner as to startle us with the overwhelming thought. He says: "The grace of God that bringeth salvation hath appeared unto all men"—here we have the new birth—"teaching us that denying ungodliness and worldly lusts we should live soberly, righteously, and godly in this present world"—here we have the Christian life—"looking for that blessed hope, the glorious appearing of the great God, our Savior Jesus Christ." Here we have the true Christian hope. John climaxes this thought, and shows that

THE TRUE OUTGROWTH

of Gospel hope is a symmetrical Christian character. "Beloved now are we, the sons of God." It is not yet manifested what we shall be. We know that if He shall be manifested we shall be like him, for we shall see Him even as He is; and every one that has this hope set on Him purifyeth himself even as He is pure." "Wherefore, beloved, seeing that ye look for such things, be diligent, that ye may be found of Him in peace, without spot, and blameless.

But what is this hope, purifying and animating the Christian? Here again we see the importance of prophetic study, for prophecy alone reveals the ultimate triumphs of the Redeemer's kingdom and comes to the relief of an intelligent faith. A zeal worthy in its activities, yet lacking true Scriptural knowledge, has loudly proclaimed the disenthralldom of earth from satanic power simply through the reformatory efforts devised and executed by organized societies. We are urged to believe that the world, through these multiplied appliances of reform, will be compelled to submit to the higher laws of morality, and thus gradually assume the universal and glorious millennium reign. Beautiful as this theory is, it can not be sustained by the actual condition of things existing at

THE PRESENT TIME.

According to the most reliable statistics the world is advancing much more rapidly in population than the church in proportion to numbers. The prospect of a speedy change in this direction, when we study the moral conditions of society, is neither flattering nor even hopeful. From the plain teachings of the Bible we are led to believe that a day of universal peace and blessedness is yet to dawn upon this oppressed and groaning earth. How God shall usher in this day of gladness and joy can only be understood by careful study of prophetic scriptures. If the popular theory prevailing so extensively, that the present methods of promulgation of gospel truth would finally usher in the millennium, then surely we ought to have some tokens of it ere this. But where are such tokens to be found? Not among the missionaries in foreign fields, where sometimes a year is spent in securing one convert to Christianity. Not in the wide extension of infidelity gradually but surely darkening the nations of the earth. Not in the abundance of iniquity

ROLLING IN TIDAL WAVES

over the habitations of earth and causing the love of many to wax cold. Not in the advance of civilization, which carries ofttimes as much moral evil to heathen nations as good. Not in all these things do we see one token that would cause us to believe that the gospel as now promulged is to convert the world and bring in the reign of peace and righteousness a thousand years. We would not depreciate the progress of society and the march of intellect—the advance of science and the spread of modern ideas—the establishment of missions among the heathen and the planting of churches and Sunday schools in destitute places; these are all proper and right, and should be nurtured, fostered, sustained, nda carefully protected in every possible way; but each and all of these do not in any way argue in favor of the gospel converting the whole world. They are all necessary in holding the ground for truth and righteousness, and every honest, earnest heart should assist in promoting these holy interests. No hand should be idle, no purse should be closed, no tongue should be silent, when fields are white for the harvest. These are royal avenues through which the hosts of God can march in obedience to the divine mandate. But it is not by these means alone that Satan's kingdom is to be overthrown and the world delivered from

HIS HATEFUL SERVITUDE,

but by the coming of our Lord Jesus Christ on the clouds of heaven. This is the one grand event placed before us in "the sure word of prophecy." Here we can rest our faith and plant our hope amid the sad disasters and spiritual depressions constantly surrounding the walls of Zion. No seeming defeat of moral reform, no beating back of the armies of truth, no attempt to overthrow the bulwarks of Christianity, shakes our confidence or paralyzes our aggressive efforts. Beyond and above all these is seen the outshining of His power, and we wait in earnest expectancy and humble patience for the appearing of the great God and Savior Jesus Christ. Here we find the objective point of all prophecy. This is the star outshining in splendor the one followed by Eastern magi, and destined eventually to fill the universe with its effulgent rays. This is the true hope which gilds the darkest cloud with beams of holy light and comes to the relief of a calm and intelligent faith in the word of God.

With such a faith we can stand in the watch-tower and look through the lattice of prophecy for the coming of the royal bridegroom.

THE REV. G. H. N. PETERS.

ESSENTIAL RELATIONSHIP OF THE COVENANTS.

The devotional exercises of the afternoon meeting were conducted by B. F. Jacobs, of Chicago, prayer being offered by Professor Blanchard, of Wheaton College. The Rev. G. H. N. Peters, of Springfield, Ohio, read the following paper on the subject, "The Essential Relationship of the Covenants and the Supernatural to the Kingdom:"

It is desirable that in every assembly of this kind, intended for the advancement of Bible doctrine, the Abrahamic and Davidic covenants should be prominently presented. My heart has been deeply moved by the reference made to these covenants in the papers given by the brethren. These fundamental revelations of the divine will form the basis of our faith, firmly establish our hope, and direct us to our glorious inheritance. They are both the pledges and the guides to the glory that shall be revealed, giving to us the central points around which succeeding revelations cluster, which must, of necessity, correspond in their teaching. No one can possibly have a clear understanding of "the salvation" unless he comprehends the covenants, which embrace, in an epitomized but distinctive manner, the substance of the divine plan designed for completed redemption from the entailed curse. If we ever have the

UNSPEAKABLE HAPPINESS

to realize in our own experience what it is to be heirs of God and joint heirs with the

Christ, we inherit the promises made to Abraham, Isaac, and Jacob, and corroborated in "the sure mercies" covenanted to David. Blessed, indeed, is he who receives the covenanted blessings through the supernatural power of the covenanted seed and son of David; for that contains perfected salvation. A correct knowledge of these covenants and their fundamental relationship to the unity of revelation and the final outcome of the divine purpose, with faith in God's ability to fulfil them, is to be so rooted and grounded in the truth that, in view of its certainty, the future is realistic to our hope, imparting the needed comfort and support.

These covenants are confirmed by oath, distinguishing them above all other announcements, as if purposely to rebuke the prevailing unbelief in them, and to give believers the strongest possible assurance of their ultimate realization. The fulfilment is unfailing; for, however conditionality may apply to individuals in the acceptance of conditions in order to experience the same, the covenants themselves are unconditional as the oath of God attests. No matter, therefore, how long the purpose of God may be postponed, we have the absolute assurance given that these promises shall be verified. More than this, the oath of confirmation covers all the blessings enumerated in both covenants. Hence, we are not at liberty to accept of some and reject as unworthy of credence others, as the unbelief of many at the present day evidences. Now multitudes profess to receive these covenants, but only such portions as their own judgment considers reasonable. Thus, for example, the entire Davidic covenant is practically rejected, with the single exception of the Messiah's promised descent from David. The perpetuity and confirmation of the covenant, as a whole, is utterly ignored. The treatment received by the Abrahamic covenant is similar; while the blessing through Abraham to the families of the earth in his seed is partly acknowledged, yet the personality of the promises to him and his seed pertaining to inheritance, the

GREATNESS OF THE NATION,

and the multitude of his seed, the land of Canaan as "an everlasting possession," etc., are entirely rejected as unreasonable, or conditional, or to be spiritualized away from their grammatical meaning, notwithstanding the repeated confirmatory predictions of the prophets, the teachings of Jesus and His apostles (which to preserve unity must also be spiritualized by them). We insist upon it that the oath confirms not merely a portion of these covenants, but the whole. The inspired faith of the prophets informs us that the sun may refuse to shine, the moon and stars may depart, the sea may no longer roll its waves, day and night may not alternate, the ordinances of heaven may be repealed (Jer. xxxiii. 17-26, Isa. liv. 9, Jer. xxxi. 35, 36, Psl. lxxxix. 36, 37, etc.), but the promises of God shall not fail in their accomplishment; yea, a greater than these has declared (Matt. v. 17, 18): "Think not that I am come to destroy the law or the prophets; I am not come to destroy, but to fulfill. For verily I say unto you, 'Till heaven and earth pass, one jot or one title shall in no wise pass from the law till all be fulfilled." The belief of many to-day is that the mission of the Christ was not absolutely to destroy the law and the prophets, but so to change and modify them that a sort of fulfilment may be predicted of them to save their credit. Men may ridicule our faith which accepts of all these promises, because standing related in the same oath-bound covenanted purpose of God, but we stand firm in the same, seeing that God's word and honor are pledged, most solemnly and sacredly, to a full realization of not merely one, but all. We earnestly protest against that destructive process which either denies or fritters away promises of God pertaining to salvation, substantiated to us for acceptance by the oath of the Almighty and by the covenant name of Jehovah expressive of His unchangeableness, and hence indicative of the certainty of ultimate execution—for (Psalms xxxiii. 11) "the counsel of the Lord standeth forever."

A question of practical importance must first be decided, the answer to which will materially affect our reception and understanding of the covenants. It is this: Are we to

RECEIVE THE PROMISES

contained in them in their plain grammatical meaning, or are we at liberty after such a meaning is ascertained to engraft upon it another and different import under the plea of a higher spirituality? Pre-millenarians, of course, being firmly attached to the reception of the clear, unmistakable grammatical interpretation—of which Luther said: "The Christian should direct his efforts toward understanding the so-called literal sense of Scripture, which alone is the substance of faith and of Christian theology; which alone will sustain him in the hour of trouble and temptation, and which will triumph over sin, death and the gates of hell, to the praise and glory of God,"—accept of the covenant promises just as they are written, as shown in the able paper presented to this conference by Professor Lummis. That they are right, prudent and wise in so doing will be apparent in answering some questions that the subject suggests. If one party gives a promise of value to another party, is it not universally conceded that if such a promise is to be understood it must be interpreted according to the plain grammatical meaning contained in the language. Are the covenants an exception, so that some spiritual, mystical or typical meaning is to be sought out before they can be comprehended? Is it reasonable to suppose that God will attest by oath a sense which all admit is contained in these covenants, and yet that this meaning is to be discarded for one that is inferred? Is it in the nature of a covenant that embraces the vital interests of the Messiah, of believers, of the race, and the world, that it should be so constructed that, instead of conveying a decisive meaning clearly expressed in its wording, it presents a hidden or typical one which requires the revolution of centuries to develop through such men as Origen, Agustine, Swedenborg, and others? Would God, who said (Matt. vii. 9) "What man is there of you whom, if his son ask bread, will he give him a stone?" give a grammatical signification, accessible to all who read, that is

DECEPTIVE AND MISLEADING,

that fosters a faith which can never be attained, and that leads to hopes which can never be realized? Such questions might be multiplied, all indicating that God could not in justice to Himself, and did not in mercy to man, present covenants which in their grammatical sense would be delusive. Men, and even learned men, tell us that if we trust in the evident sense contained in the laws of language in the words that we are deceived, in gross error, satisfied with "husks" and heretical. The word of God speaks for itself, and is not dependant upon the dicta of men. It expressly cautions us against any alteration of its meaning, and predicts that such changes will be made that at the second advent of Jesus but little faith in the recorded promises of God will exist—a lack of faith brought about by the prevailing spiritualistic and typical theories with their multitudinous interpretations. Three facts alone are sufficient to set aside those speculations so dishonoring to God's word, and to indicate the correctness of our position. One is, that our opponents can not, and do not, make the whole of these covenants spiritual or typical, for in them they fully admit the grammatical sense pertaining to the seed, and correctly apply it to Jesus. Why admit that part is thus to be received and the remainder with other and differing senses? The reply is, that they are forced to such a partial recognition because of the initiatory preparation for the realization of the covenants in the first advent of Abraham's seed and David's Son, but they reject the other statements, because no fulfillment of the grammattical sense down to the present day justifies their reason or faith to accept of them. Whether consciously or unconsciously, they virtually assume the judgship of what is worthy of their belief. Another is that God has impressed the grammatical sense of the covenants to be the true one, by literally fulfilling a portion of them in the meaning expressed. A sufficiency is found in the

HISTORY OF THE MESSIAH,

in His descent and mission, to show us that the covenants contain a substantial verified grammatical sense. Hence we justly feel that it would evidence unbelief, should we change such a sense for something else. The third is, that God appeals to those covenants as to promises readily comprehended. This He could not do if the language in them was susceptible of meanings differing from the plain text, thus making them not subjects easy to understand, but intricate, conjectural, and mysterious.

Taking it for granted that every prophetic student is familiar with the engagements included in the two covenants (the Abrahamic in Gen. xii. 1-3-7, xiii. 14-17, xv. 4-21, xvii. 4-16, xxii. 15-18; the Davidic in II. Saml., vii. 10-16; I. Chron., xvii. 11-14), and their reference to the Jewish nation, believers and the Messiah as plainly given by the prophets, Jesus, and apostles, attention is directed to the demands that these promises make upon our faith. We freely admit that, owing to the present non-fulfillment of much that is recorded, we accept of them simply because God has granted them and most sacredly attested to their faithfulness by oath. We are not concerned respecting the difficulties of accomplishment, which cause the multitude to engraft other meanings upon these promises. For we hold that He who gave them has already evidenced in creation and in the provisionary arrangements for redemption, a power adequate to meet every emergency that may arise, and to crush all opposition that may be formed, seeing (Psl. lxxxix. 34) "My covenant will I not break, or alter the thing that has gone out of My lips." While it is true to-day as in the days of the ancients that "the just live by faith," it is also true that such faith is greatly sustained by contemplating the confirmatory statements of inspired writers, showing that our acceptance of the plain surface meaning is undoubtedly the correct one; and then by regarding the attested provision for their fulfilment. This is the more necessary, since our

FAITH IS DENOUNCED

as "carnal," "extravagant," and "fanatical" by many who only receive these covenants as perpetual after changing their grammatical meeting and substituting some other as more suitable, thus virtually doing what God Himself declares He will never do, viz.: "alter the thing that has gone out of My lips." We thank God that in an age abounding with unbelief in His promises, He gives us an abundance of testimony by which not only our own belief is supported, but we are able to be (I. Pet. iii. 15) "ready always to give an answer to every man that asketh you a reason of the hope that is in you." As illustrative that our confidence is intelligently placed, take the inheriting of the land as given personally to the patriarchs and to the seed. In view of our inheriting the promises with Abraham, Isaac, and Jacob, the Divine Spirit gives us a varied array of evidence to show us that our comprehension of the Word accords fully with the purpose of God. First, we are divinely assured that Abraham, Isaac, and Jacob did not personally inherit the land (Acts vii. 5), and that they died as "pilgrims and strangers," "not having received the promises" (Heb. ix. 8, 9, xi. 13-40). Next, seeing that this, owing to God's faithfulness, necessitates the resurrection, Jesus Himself teaches us (Luke xx. 37; Matt. xxii. 31; Mark xii. 26) that the covenanted memorial ("the Lord God of your fathers, the God of Abraham, the God of Isaac, the God of Jacob * * * this is My name forever, and this is My memorial unto all generations) implies the resurrection of the dead, for it is based upon the majestic attributes of a God, who (Mal. iii., 6) changes not, who (Numb. xxiii., 19) "is not a man that He should lie, neither the Son of man that He should repent;" who (Jer. xxxii., 17, Matt. xix., 26, Luke i., 37 and xviii., 27, Dan. iv., 35) does not allow His power to be limited by unbelief, because (Job xxiii., 13) "He is in one mind, and who can turn Him? and what His soul desireth, even that He doeth;" "For (Isa. xiv., 27) the Lord of Hosts purposed, and who shall disannul it?" Would to God that an Abrahamic faith would more and more

CHARACTERIZE BELIEVERS;

such a faith as caused Abraham to believe, as in Isaac's case (Heb. xi., 17-19), that the Almighty would be faithful in fulfilling His promises even if such a fulfillment required as an essential a resurrection from the grave. Next observe that as all believers are engrafted by faith and thus become the children of Abraham obtaining a personal interest in the covenanted promise of inheriting, the Scriptures in all their teachings corroborate the indisputable sense of the covenant by asserting that this earth, delivered from the curse and renewed under the all-providing creative hand of Him who will (Rev. xxi., 5) "make all things new," shall be "the everlasting possession" of the redeemed, verifying the declaration of Jesus (Matt. v., 5), "Blessed are the meek; for they shall inherit the earth" (Compare Psa. xxxvii.). With Irenœus (Ag. Her. ch. xxxii.) relying upon the covenant and God's faithfulness, we say: "It is fitting that the just, rising at the appearance of God, should in the renewed state receive the promise of inheritance which God covenanted to the Fathers, and should reign in it." This and this alone makes the Bible a unit in promise, beginning with the earthly paradise forfeited and ending with the same regained; thus enforcing as vital a perfect redemption from the curse, restoring that which was lost with added beauty, glory and blessedness. The consciousness that the living God is the Holy One who engaged himself must, in the very nature of the case, inspire faith and hope both in the patriarchs and in us that the future fulfillment thus presented will be performed. Abraham's faith is greater than ours, however impressed to look forward to "the day of the Christ," because the promises were given purposely in a form to test his trust in God's ability and faithfulness, which the actual presence and oath of the great Promiser materially aided to enliven. Our faith, indeed, like his, is tested by our utter inability to explain just how this and that promise is to be accomplished, leaving the Supernatural to fulfill His own engagements; but unbelief in us is inexcusable, seeing that to

THE WORD OF GOD

as given to the patriarchs we have added revelations with promises, added dispensations with their redemptive developments, and added means culminating in the Person of the Messiah, designed expressly for a verification of these promises. The past non-fulfillment has nothing whatever to do with the validity or the stability of covenant engagements. This stumbling-block to the multitude, causing either a rejection or modification of them, has no effect upon the intelligent believer, because the same Scriptures clearly teach not only the postponement, but also give the reasons why the long delay occurs, and exhort to patient waiting. Thus, likewise, we might take the seed, directly referred to the Christ (Gal. iii., 18) and trace the partial fulfillment, the developments, the promises attached to Him, all evidencing an omnipotence in Providence that is irresistable, a covenanted result in continuous prospect that must, in view of the means provided, manifest itself according to the will declared to Abraham and David; and also the loving personal interest that God takes in the unfolding of His purpose so that honor, praise and glory may ever be ascribed to Him by the inheritors of His marvelous grace. In brief, the entire analogy of Scripture and of faith evidences by a progressive testimony, bound together in a unity of design, such a harmonious plan, founded on the everlasting covenants, that we would be faithless not to accept of their promises as unchanging and irrevocable, "ordered in all things and sure" (II. Sam'l xxiii., 5). Let me appeal to your own experience, brethren, is it not true, that whenever in your personal study of the Scriptures they were read in the light afforded by covenant promises the result has been increased knowledge of redemptive mercy and grace, increased faith and hope, warming the heart with anticipated deliverance?

Our belief is finally established in these covenants by considering the means already provided for their ultimate fulfillment. We freely admit that which our opponents allege as a serious and even fatal objection, viz., that to have our faith and hope in such promises realized there must be, of necessity, a direct and special intervention of, and power exerted by, the supernatural. Why this shrinking back from this proffered aid, when the natural, as Paul testifies, must ever remain under its present

GROANING BONDAGE

without its assistance? Why, especially, do those who professedly accept of these covenants, object to our reliance upon, and our trust in, the supernatural to fulfill them, when the covenants themselves are the most sacredly specified utterances of the supernatural, hedged in by supernatural acts, and culminating in the supernatural birth and person of the seed, David's Son and Lord? From the day these covenants were given down to the present, the Lord God of the Fathers has warned us to put our trust only in Him for their realization. Ponder over the promises, their greatness, and comprehensiveness, and it must be admitted that they can never, never be experienced by either the patriarchs or by believers, unless God aids immediately by His omnipotence. The germal promises covenanted, as explained, enlarged, and enforced by the prophets and and apostles, fully corroborate this position. Thus, for example, they include, as the attestation of inspired men proves, the personal coming of Abraham's and David's seed to inherit; the resurrection from the dead; the inheriting of a renewed earth; the effectual removal of the curse in "the times of the restitution of all things;" the glorious theocratic reign of the seed and His co-heirs; the perpetual deliverance from sufferings, sickness, sorrow, tears, and death; the removal of the bondage under which nature labors with groanings; the restoration of all forfeited blessings with increased exaltation and happiness; and all these, as well as other promises still unfulfilled, embrace such radical and grand changes that the Bible uniformly, from beginning to ending, teaches that the personal intervention of Him, in whom all power is lodged, can alone produce results so far-reaching and magnificent. The Messiah is the peaceful instrumentality provided to bring about these astounding manifestations in heaven and earth, in nature and the creature, in the saints and the race, in the Holy Spirit and the Christ. Our faith grasping the things recorded of, and pertaining to, Him as the

MIGHTY RESTORER,

makes him pre-eminently "our hope" (I. Tim. i., 1), and His second coming, "the blessed hope" (Tit. ii., 13). Let us briefly contemplate a few particulars associated with our Messiah, and requisite to perform covenant purposes. It will cheer our hearts and urge us to increased "love for His appearing." The Old and New Testaments unite in the declaration that the mission of Jesus is to fulfill the covenants and related promises. The simple question for us to answer is this: As the supernatural is indispensibly necessary to accomplish their realization, does this Jesus possess the required supernatural power? The answer to this is overwhelmingly in the affirmative, leaving no apology for unbelief. The covenants, supernaturally given in the preparatory fulfillment evidence with a distinctness and force that can not be resisted, without the grossest disbelief, the possession of all power in the seed. It is impossible to be a believer either in the covenants or the Messiah, as the ordained Covenant-Fulfiller, without conceding this much. The conception of the seed was supernatural; the life and the works were supernatural; the death, resurrection, and ascension were supernatural. Eliminate these from Jesus and we have no longer a Savior able to save, a Restorer with strength to restore, and hope perishes under the heaviness and bondage of an entailed curse. When the Christ came at the first advent it was absolutely necessary that He should exhibit the actual possession of the needed power to consummate covenanted redemption. Thank God this, that is foolishness to unbelief but wisdom to the wise,

He did, and constantly appealed to its possession and manifestation as decided proof that He was the appointed seed, the Messiah with adequate authority and might to fulfill. The union of the supernatural with Him is His distinguishing excellency, and in His appeals forms the crowning characteristic inviting to belief. Behold His works! Is death to be removed to make inheriting possible? He has abundantly shown that he has authority over

DEATH AND THE GRAVE.

Is nature to be fashioned anew to effect its deliverance? He has sufficiently manifested his ability to control nature. Is glorification to be realized in order to enhance the blessedness of the inheritance? He has exhibited His astounding transformation power. Is Satan, the god of this world, to be eventually cast out and bound? He has proven His foreshadowing might and purpose over him. Are sickness and sorrow and tears to be banished; are blindness, lameness, deafness, and dumbness to be removed; are hunger, thirst, and famine to be expelled; are all the evils incident to a curse pressing so hard upon animate and inanimate creation to be repealed? He in the numerous attested miracles of healing, the removal of grief-producing causes, feeding, dominion over creatures, etc., has unmistakably testified to His amazing ability to complete redemption as covenanted. This extraordinary demonstration of the supernatural in Jesus is full of comfort and joy, for it points us on to the future when this same Jesus of supernatural origin and glorified in the supernatural shall return unto salvation; and then, as a thousand promises declare, shall exert His omnipotence in order to verify the truthfulness and faithfulness of covenants given specially under the auspices of a faithful God. This is the most reasonable and God-honoring faith, seeing that it makes the supernatural and miraculous indispensable adjuncts to the grand consummation intended. Hence, as various writers have correctly pointed out, the miracles of Jesus are called "signs;" signs of divine power lodged in Him to be used in securing the goal intended; signs of that future exertion of might to subserve the covenanted salvation; signs of the potent strength that will be exerted in re-creation: signs of that dominion that shall be enforced in behalf of the highest welfare and happiness of man and the race; signs of that

POWERFUL WILL.

"Working, whereby He is able to subdue all things to Himself" (Phil. iii. 21); signs that (Col. i. 16) "by Him were all things created, that are in heaven, and that are in earth, visible and invisible, whether they be thrones or dominions, principalities or powers, all things were created by Him and for Him; and He is before all, and by Him all things consist." Surely when such a mighty One challenges our acceptance of these signs as tokening the intended faithfulness, it indicates a deliberate, if not sinful, lack of faith if we refuse to make the designed application. In this day of unbelief and lowering of the majesty of Jesus, these words (Jno. x. 25) of His are significant: "The works that I do in My Father's name, they bear witness of Me:" (Jno. xiv. 10-11) "Believest thou not that I am in the Father, and the Father in Me? the words that I speak unto you I speak not of Myself; but the Father that dwelleth in Me, He doeth the works. Believe Me, that I am in the Father and the Father in Me; or else believe Me for the very work's sake." Yes, blessed Jesus, our hearts respond, we believe in Thee; we believe in Thy works of mercy and grace, stamping Thee as "the Anointed," "the Faithful Witness," "the Mighty God,' and "Immanuel," who will come again to perfect salvation, of which Thou hast given us abundant assurances to impart confidence and patient trust. The supernatural is essential in bestowing the plan of redemption, in providing the means requisite to its completeness, in giving the evidence of its existence and interest, and in bringing forth the glorious consummation.

The splendid prospect that the future presents under the guidance and controlling influence of the supernatural, may be illustrated by a reference to the person of the Redeemer. To obtain a correct view the Abrahamic and Davidic covenants—both everlasting—must be linked together, seeing (as the primitive branch so logically held) that the latter embraces the kingly instrumentality by which the former is to be eventually realized. This combination gives us at once a supernatural King, so majestic that he is the "King of Kings." The germal theocratic idea is already given in the Abrahamic covenant in the declaration, that God will be a god to Abraham, Isaac, and Jacob. This was developed in the establishment of a theocracy in which God Himself is the head. Foreseeing the withdrawal of the

THEOCRATIC GOVERNMENT

on account of the sins of the Jewish nation the Davidic covenant is purposely given so that we might have implicit confidence in God's theocratic purpose. Hence it is, to complete assurance, also attested (Psalm cxxxii., 11: lxxxix., 35; Acts ii., 30) by oath. David, by inspiration, directly foretold the overthrow of the theocracy, but expresses his unalterable faith in the realization of the covenant in the future. He describes this promised Seed who shall occupy the theocratic throne as "higher than the kings of the earth," as infinitely superior to Solomon, giving Him exaltation authority, dominion, immortality, and perpetuity of reign that would be folly to ascribe to a mere mortal king. In David's last words (II. Saul, xxiii., 5), filled with trust and foreseeing the great salvation attached to the reigh of this seed, he emphatically says: "He hath made with me an everlasting covenant ordered in all things and sure; for this is all my salvation and all my desire." Having already briefly looked at this King, and seen that the supernatural abided with Him, we are ready and willing to indorse and emulate David's faith and hope. We unhesitatingly accept of the claims put forth by this covenanted seed as required for salvation and attested to by earnests. We deeply feel that while the human is essential to redemption and the exaltation of humanity, the divine incorporated with it in the person of Jesus is likewise necessary, and the union of the two in Him forms the perfect Redeemer needed by sin and curse, by sinner and saint, by the dead and the living, by the race and the earth, imparting the most precious hope of God again dwelling with men, and being, in the theocratice sense, their God (Rev. xxi., 3), who gives the required validity, efficacy, and realization to His word. We do not see how anyone who receives the Scriptures in humble faith and has tested them by the most satisfactory of proofs, a personal reception of the Christ, can possibly object to such a vital and indispensible union of the human and supernatural in Jesus; now he can turn away from His oneness with the Father (John xv., 30), His claim of equal power with the Father (John v., 23), His declaration that the fulness of the Godhead bodily dwelleth in Him, (Col. ii. 9), hence making Himself equal with God, (Jno. v. 18; x. 36; xix. 7). This, this is the Savior that man, the race and the earth burdened under an all-pervading and

SORROW-PRODUCING CURSE

requires. His ability shines forth in the saying, "all things that the Father hath are mine;" (Jno. xvi. 15). His pre-eminent dignity and power to save appears in His being "the brightness of the Father's glory, and the express image of His person. (Heb. i. 3). So that it is true that He is the "Alpha and Omega, the beginning and the ending," (Rev. i. 8), and that it is a certainty that He is the One of whom Isaiah (liv. 5) predicts: Thy Redeemer, the Holy One of Israel, the God of the whole earth shall He be called."

Such a view of "the Coming One" is amply sufficient to establish the dignity, power, riches, honor, blessing, and glory, constituting Him "the All in all;" and hence leaving us inexcusable to reject or alter His covenant promises. How can we be faithless when this divine, human, this God-man has even sealed this covenant with His own precious blood, causing it to be possible, by the remission of our sins in His atoning blood, and the obtaining of those accounted worthy to inherit, to make these promises realities. Van Oosterzee (Ch. Dog. vol. 2, p. 471), utters a pregnant truth when he so aptly remarks: "We have learned to recognize the covenant of God with Abraham as the foundation of the entire revelation of salvation." Let us pray that every believer may attain to such learning, for then (Eph. i. 18) "the eyes of our understanding will be enlightened that we may know what is the hope of His calling, and what the riches of the glory of His inheritance in the saints." Misled by the word "new," which is employed in the Scriptures in the sense of "renewed" as in new moon, new heart, new creature, new heavens and earth, etc., many fail to grasp the weight and deep significance in the memorable words (Math. xxvi. 28), "this is my blood of the new testament, which is shed for many for the remission of sins." (Luke xxii. 20). "This cup is the new testament in my blood, which is shed for many." Now what is, as Paul (Heb. xiii. 20) calls it, this "everlasting covenant" ratified by His blood? The answer from hundreds of passages, the argument especially of Gal 3, Eph. 2, and of Hebrews, the general analogy and unity of Scripture, unmistakably teaches that it is the Abrahamic, for that contains the promises we inherit with Him, provided we through this blood become the children of Abraham, and thus come into covenanted relationship, by which we become heirs with the

PATRIARCHS AND CO-HEIRS

with the seed. If that covenant were disannulled, then there would be no salvation; if that covenant ever fails, then the blood of Jesus has lost its claimed sealing efficaciousness; if that covenant is not ratified by His blood, then the blessing of Abraham can not come upon us gentiles through Jesus, the Christ, that we might become Abraham's seed and heirs according to the promise (Gal. 3), and we can never hope to enter with the patriarchs the covenanted inheritance. We, however, have faith in that costly blood! Realizing its exceeding preciousness now in the spirit-imparted self-consciousness of sin forgiven, we possess the earnest that the promises of God contained in the covenants, and which we acquire by union with the Christ and adoption as Abraham's children, are not disannulled (Gal. iii. 17), can not possibly fail, but are confirmed of God in the Christ (Gal. iii. 15), who thus becomes the surety of "the promise of eternal inheritance." What a pledge of faithfulness and covenanted love, mercy, and grace is given in the shed blood of the agent appointed to bring to pass the accomplishment, seeing, also, that in all this His own inheritance and glory is involved. Hence, Paul, grounded in the covenants and believing in the Second Advent as the predicted period of realization, says (I Cor. xi. 26), in immediate connection with the ratification of the covenant in Jesus' blood: "For as often as ye eat this bread and drink this cup ye do show the Lord's death till He come." Hence the precious testimony of the venerable Dr. Bonar on this point in his letter read by the secretary. In the divine procedure this death is a prerequisite to a restoring to us the once forfeited but now covenanted blessings of an Edenic state. The resurrection associated with it is also vital, not only in showing us that the keys of death hang at His girdle, but in constituting Him the immortal, glorified son of David, thus meeting the very conditions imposed by the covenant. His ascension and exaltation are not merely an assurance of the acceptance of His work as in accordance with the Divine will, but they confirm the proposed work of the future. How then, in view of all these things, can we refuse to receive all the promises of God as written? It is faithless to set aside a part as

UNWORTHY OF BELIEF,

to limit a portion as demanded by so-called progress, to modify and change the plain grammatical sense to suit our reason and ideas of the fitness of things, for it is God that promises and God that fulfills. Brethren, is it not as true to-day as it was in the days of Christ and the apostles that salvation is of the Jews, and is not, therefore, Paul's warning (Rom. xi. 20), to the gentiles not to be "high minded" fairly applicable to the general unbelief of Jewish covenanted promises? Let us constantly keep in mind as a caution and help, that no portion of these covenants in their preparatory fulfillment ment were ever realized as the natural wisdom of man conceived, or in accord with the expectations and anticipations of the multitude, and this, as predicted, will be repeated.

Now combine the covenants and associated promises with this divine-human, supernatural King, and behold, the untold riches ascribed to Him, the splendor of the saints' destiny, the exaltation of the Jewish Nation, the blessings bestowed upon the race and the deliverance given to creation. We have a veritable theocratic King, God, himself, condescending to be an earthly ruler, thus giving us a perfect, infallible head, and securing stability and perpetuity to His kingdom. God manifested, in the person of One related to humanity, seated on the theocratic throne, restored with the grandeur due to so sublime a personage, the human and the divine united in identical rule, secures one determining will, a bulwark of supremacy, strength of execution, unity of purpose, the endless majestic relationship of headship over the race as the Second Adam, the filling and lighting up in glorification of the darkly glimmering chasm between the finite and the infinite, world-wide dominion, the highest possible spirituality and personal access so that we may behold the King in His beauty and royalty. We see the divine and political, the civil and the religious, the church and the State, the natural and the spiritual harmoniously combined, as of necessity they must be under such a rule that is truly theocratic, thus giving us God's own judgment of what constitutes the highest possible form of government; thus showing us that God's instructive

CONCEPTION OF GOVERNMENT

is not a failure, but will inevitably result in universal empire, thus evidencing that all things, without exception, will indeed be consecrated to the praise of God, and thus happily exemplifying that He is a priest forever as well as a King—a King-priest, who reigns over a redeemed and "a willing people," in whose behalf He will forever dispel the evils, clashing interests, jealousies, and wars of gentile domination. By faith we behold the theocratic relationship and blessings of the elect Jewish nation augmented in the regeneration and times of refreshing, when regrafted into its own olive tree by this "King of the Jews," thus constituting it "the holy nation," forming the nucleus of "the greatness of the kingdom under the whole heaven," introduced by the change of princes and leading to the heartfelt allegiance of the nations. By faith we see the marriage of the Lamb with the festal robes and supper, the victory over sin and death, the redemption of the body, the manifestation of the sons of God, the blessed meaning of adoption displayed in Christ-like fashioning, the kingship and priesthood of the saints, the overthrow of all enemies and the destruction of the works of the devil, the vindication of justice and mercy, holiness characteristic of the great and minute, the Holy Spirit so marvelously poured out that the supernatural abides continuously with power; the withdrawal of the glass through which we see darkly the new heavens and the new earth in which dwelleth righteousness, the perpetual wiping away of tears by the sympathizing hand of Omnipotence, the joyfulness in glory, the splendor and association of angels, the mighty increase of the kingdom, the creation under the plastic hand of this Ruler lavish with gifts and fatness, so that even the creature basks in the sunshine of renovation, and the new Jerusalem with God and the Lamb as its highest excellency, bestowing the priceless legacy of eternal fellowship with the Father, Son, and Holy Spirit.

Is it not then true (Col. i. 27), "Christ in us the hope of glory?" Is it not then a most prominent truth that the

SECOND COMING OF JESUS

unto salvation is "the blessed hope?" And is it not then pre-eminently true that our hope is (Jer. xvii. 13; Acts xxviii. 20) "the hope of Israel," "the hope of the promise made of God unto our fathers, unto which promise our twelve tribes, instantly serving God day and night, hope to come," so that when the long-delayed, long-desired "day of the Lord Jesus, the Christ," shall come (Isa. xxv. 9), "It shall be said in that day, Lo, this is our God; we have waited for Him, and He will save us; this is the Lord; we have waited for Him, we will be glad and rejoice in His salvation." O, come, speedily come, thou covenant-keeping God!

Blessed are the covenants; blessed are the oaths of the Almighty attesting the same; blessed are the provisionary means instituted toward fulfillment; blessed are the evidences of God's faithfulness and ability to verify them; blessed is the sealing blood; blessed is the all-powerful Agent ordained to perform the sublime work; and blessed, beyond description, is every one who shall have the unspeakable happiness of experiencing in his own person the transforming and glorifying hand of the covenant-fulfilling God! And let all true and enlightened believers say, "Amen!"

RESOLUTIONS ADOPTED

The concluding meeting of the conference, showing no decrease in good attendance, was presided over by Bishop Nicholson. Prayer was said by the Rev. Mr. Osler, of Providence. To confute all misrepresentations which might prevail concerning the purport and purpose of the conference, this body, on motion of the Rev. Mr. Parsons, adopted the following declaration of principles, the identical platform adopted, for similar reasons, by the New York conference eight years before. These resolutions express, in brief, the views of the large body of ministers who participated in, or were present to sympathize with, the proceedings.

1. We affirm our belief in the supreme and absolute authority on the written Word of God on all questions of doctrine and duty.

2. The prophetic words of the Old Testament Scriptures, concerning the first coming of our Lord Jesus Christ, were literally fulfilled in His birth, life, death, resurrection and ascension; and so the prophetic words of both the Old and the New Testaments concerning His second coming will be literally fulfilled in His visible bodily return to this earth in like manner as he went up into Heaven; and

THIS GLORIOUS EPIPHANY

of the great God, our Savior Jesus Christ, is the blessed hope of the believer and of the Church during this entire dispensation.

3. This second coming of the Lord Jesus is everywhere in the Scriptures represented as imminent, and may occur at any moment; yet the precise day and hour thereof is unknown to man, and only known to God.

4. The Scriptures nowhere teach that the whole world will be converted to God, and that there will be a reign of universal righteousness and peace before the return of the blessed Lord; but that only at and by His coming in power and glory will the prophecies concerning the progress of evil and the development of Antichrist, the times of the gentiles, and the ingathering of Israel, the resurrection of the dead in Christ, the transfiguration of His living saints, receive their fulfillment, and the period of millennial blessedness its inauguration.

5. The duty of, the church during the absence of the bridegroom is to watch and pray, to work and wait, to go into all the world and preach the Gospel to every creature, and thus hasten the coming of the day of God; and to His last promise, "surely I come quickly," to respond, in joyous hope, "even so; come Lord Jesus."

6. That the doctrine of our Lord's premillennial advent, instead of paralyzing evangelistic and missionary effort, is one of the mightiest incentives to earnestness in preaching the Gospel to every creature, until He comes.

The conference then

ADOPTED THE FOLLOWING:

1. *Resolved*, That our thanks are extended o the committee who have called us together for the interesting and profitable arrangement of subjects presented at this conference, and especially to the secretary for his indefatigable labors in respect to the details of this instructive and satisfactory meeting. The thanks of this conference are tendered to Mr. John Morrison, Chairman of the R. R. Committee, and the brethren

associated with him in their labors of love so helpful to the committee.

2. That we request the following brethren to act as an interim committee, with authority to act in our stead, in regard to any unfinished business connected with this meeting, and also to call a future meeting of this conference when it may be deemed expedient: The Rev. Dr. James H. Brooks, St. Louis; Bishop W. R. Nicholson, Philadelphia; Professor W. G. Moorhead, Xenia, Ohio; the Rev. Dr. A. J. Gordon, Boston; the Rev. S. H. Kellogg, Toronto, Ont.; the Rev. Dr. E. P. Goodwin, Chicago; the Rev. W. J. Erdman, Boston; and George C. Needham, Boston.

THE REV. A. J. FROST, D. D.

"Condition of the Church and World at Christ's Second Advent; or, Are the Church and World to Grow Better or Worse Until He Come?"

This question divides Christendom, nominal or real, into two classes. Postmillennialists hold that the church and the world are growing morally better, and that they will continue to improve until our Lord returns. Premillenialists maintain that the church and the world are destined

TO GROW MORALLY WORSE

until the end of the age. One class believes that the condition of the church and the world at Christ's second advent will be the culmination of millennial glory; while the other class as firmly believe that this dispensation will end in diabolical wickedness and well-nigh universal apostasy amid the crash of Apocalyptic thunder and the unparalleled judgments of God. One division of Christendom is looking for a millennium without a personal, visible Christ; the other division is looking for His coming to introduce that golden age. This question admits of no concessions, no compromises. If one division of Christendom is right the other division is wrong. Our appeal is to the infallible word of God. If the condition of the church and the world at Christ's second advent is shown by the sacred writers to be deplorable beyond conception, then the church and the world are to grow morally worse until He come.

I am fully aware that the mere suggestion of such a question is enough to rouse an emphatic protest both from the nominal church and the world. So accustomed are they to boast of the progress of the age, the advancement of science, and the spread of the gospel among all nations, that a proposition expressing the conviction that the church and the world are to grow morally worse instead of better, culminating in the downfall of all human institutions and the complete overthrow of the great world-powers, is likely to evoke the severest criticism from both the secular and the religious world. This proposition implies so much of rebuke that this proud, vaulting, God-denying, God-defying age will hardly tolerate it for a moment. We shall endeavor to show that the sacred writers in the Old and New Testament scriptures foretold this state of moral declension and religious apostasy. With unerring wisdom, through divine inspirations, they predicted that this dispensation, like all that had preceded it, would close in utter failure of man's hopes to redeem the world by the preaching of the gospel, and that

THE IMPENDING JUDGMENTS OF GOD

would fall upon a faithless church and a guilty world and thus close the scene. Dark and gloomy as this prediction may be, it becomes us to pause and consider this greatest and gravest question of the age. So much has been said by optimistic writers concerning the glory of the nineteenth century and the coming era, is it not time to listen to the other side?

1. What do past dispensations teach regarding man's faithfulness and responsibility. Both the human and divine nature being the same in all ages, past dispensations will throw light upon the present and the future. In every dispensation God is sovereign and man is free, and therefore the success or failure of a redemptive scheme is less or more contingent upon man's faithfulness and responsibility. The principles of divine government being the same in all ages, human nature being the same in all dispensations, we may derive much knowledge of the present tendency and the final outcome of this dispensation, by briefly considering those that are past. We shall not only find them analogous but identical in their underlying principles.

(a) The paradisaical dispensation. Never dispensation began with better oppotunities and more favorable prospects. Paradise, the garden of the Lord, the favored spot; Adam and Eve, God's image and masterpiece, the favored occupants; angels for companions, the triune God for counselor and guide, the "Tree of Life" for symbol and pledge of immortality; with natures immaculate, if not holy; temptation the least possible, reward the greatest conceivable, yet how did the Eden dispensation terminate? Man ruined, lost, driven out of paradise by his Maker, his entrance barred by cherubic sword melting into flame. Notwithstanding the

UNSULLIED MORAL BEAUTY.

the majesty and the glory with which that dispensation began, it ended in universal apostasy and the consequent judgment of Almighty God.

(b) The antediluvian dispensation. Adam and Eve in God-made vestments of sacrifice, outside the gates of paradise, stand at the head of a new dispensation. Cain and Abel represent the good and evil principles of the new era.

1. Good and evil forms of worship. Abel presents a sin offering, Cain a thank offering; one a sacrifice, the other a curse; one of faith, the other of works; one wins God's respect, the other His frown.

2. Good and evil results of such worship. Jealousy, hatred, murder, eternal death.

3. Good and evil alliances, sons of God in alliance with the daughters of men. Sethites and Cainites in wedlock. "Every imagination of the thoughts of man's heart was only evil continually. "All flesh was corrupt before God," "the whole earth was filled with violence."

4. Good and evil, in judgment by God's saints Abel, Seth, Enoch, and Noah, condemned the world. Perchance they were called pessimists, bigots, fanatics. Enoch, a premillennialist, who prophesied that the Lord would come with 10,000 of His saints to execute judgment upon a guilty world, walked so near heaven's gate that God reached out and took him in—first of the translation saints. Noah, a preacher of righteousness representative of the resurrection saints, is hid in the pavilion of the Almighty till the indignation is overpast.

We have it on the authority of Jesus Christ that, "As the days of Noah were, so shall also the coming of the Son of man be. For, as in the days that were before the flood, they were eating and drinking, marrying and giving in marriage, until the day Noah entered the Ark, and knew not till the flood came and took them all away. So shall also the coming of the Son of man be." Here is not only analogy, but identity in the ending of dispensations.

(c.) The Patriarchal dispensation teaches a similar lesson. Noah and his family stand beside God's altar at the head of a new dispensation. All God's waves and billows had passed over him unharmed. Good and evil are to have a new trial. We have neither time nor space to even summarize the underlying principles of this dispensation. We are to deal with the outcome of dispensations, the condition of things at the close of the present age. Two things claim attention, however, on this point. (1) The Patriarchal dispensation closed with the world lying in wickedness and God's chosen people in bondage. (2) The Lord Jesus represents the condition of the church and the world at the end of this age as far worse than that of

EGYPTIAN BONDAGE.

"As it was in the days of Lot, they did eat, they drank, they bought, they sold, they planted, they builded. But the same day that Lot went out of Sodom it rained fire and brimstone from heaven and destroyed them all. Even thus shall it be in the day when the Son of man is revealed." No method of exegesis can overthrow the fact that our Lord, in speaking of the condition of the world at His second advent, purposely selected the darkest period in both the Antediluvian and Patriarchal dispensations, as representing the coming apostasy and the retributive judgments of God. If the world is to grow better until Christ returns, if millennial glory is to flood the earth for a thousand years before His advent, then he should have said: "As it was in the days of paradise before sin entered, so shall it be in the day when the Son of man cometh." Or as it was in the days of Solomon, when peace spread her banners over all the kingdom; or, as it was in the days of Joshua, when all opposing kings were trodden in the dust, "so shall it be when the Son of man cometh."

(d) The Mosaic dispensation is not less explicit in regard to man's responsibility and faithfulness.

Let an inspired apostle speak of the exalted privileges of the Hebrew nation. "Who are Israelites; to whom pertaineth the adoption and the glory, and the covenant, and the giving of the law, and the service of God, and the promises? Whose are the fathers, of whom, as concerning the flesh, Christ came, who is over all, God-blessed forever?" What mighty deliverance from the bondage of a former dispensation, what revelations on Sinai, what magnificent ritual, what divinely appointed sacrifice, what unearthly glory of tabernacle and temple, what prophets, priests, and kings. What nation so exalted to heaven in privilege. And yet what idolatry and spiritual whoredom—what rebellion and hardness of heart. What wailing in Babylon. What judicial blindness for ages. What a Bethlehem, Gethsemane, and Calvary. What invocations: "His blood be upon us and our children." How has that imprecation been answered? "Without a king, and without a prince, and without a sacrifice, and without an image, and without an ephod, and without a teraphim." Thus ended the Mosaic dispensation in

APOSTASY AND JUDGMENT.

It may be replied that the Christian dispensation will not thus terminate, since it is the dispensation of the Spirit. Every dispensation has been blessed with the Holy Spirit. Eighty-eight times is the Holy Spirit mentioned in the Old Testament, so that "God is no respecter of persons; but in every nation, he that feareth Him and worketh righteousness is accepted with Him." Privilege, responsibility, apostasy, judgment, are the characteristics of all dispensations.

II. What do the great world powers teach concerning the condition of things at Christ's second advent?

Daniel's exposition of the king's vision of empire forever settles two things: (1.) That four universal monarchies in a divided form would not run their entire course until Christ comes to grind them to powder and set up a stone kingdom on the Rock of Ages which should fill the whole earth.

(2.) That these kingdoms were to deteriorate until the end. The gold of absolute monarchy, the silver of monarchical oligarchy, the brazen aristocracy, and the iron of democratic imperialism, were to end in iron mixed with clay. What a decadence of world power—from the precious metals of gold and silver to the worthless pottery of iron and clay! There is not a government on earth to-day within the limits of the old Roman Empire, that is not made of Roman iron and clay. Rome still rules the world by her iron laws, partly strong and partly brittle, by the ever changing will of the people. The condition of the world at Christ's second advent has been predicted by the nature of these four great gentile world-powers, which run their course until He come whose right it is to rule. The golden age of human government is past; we are already in the iron and the clay, of the earth earthy. Suddenly, with one awful crash, the stone kingdom is to destroy these gentile powers, and, mountain like, stand upon the granite of the globe forever. Instead of human government becoming ideally perfect for one thousand years before He comes, it is to grow weaker and worse until

HE REIGNS ON THE EARTH.

III. What do the eschatological parables of Christ teach regarding the church and the world at the end of the age? The parable of the sower does not teach that the trodden ground, the stony ground, and the thorny ground will all become good ground, yielding thirty, sixty, or a hundred fold when our Lord returns; on the other hand, the good ground is all oversown with tares according to the next parable, and both wheat and tares are to grow together until the harvest which is at the end of the age. But the final state is even worse, for it is a law of tares to outroot and outgrow wheat. Let anyone sow wheat and weeds and thistles on the same soil, and it is easy to see that the wheat will soon be almost wholly exterminated. Thorns and thistles will thrive without cultivation; wheat will not. The parable of the sheep and goats informs us that there will be whole nations on the earth at the time of Christ's second advent who have not ministered to Christ or to His brethren. The parable of the treasure hid in the field shows that it is the treasure and not the whole field that will be taken out of the world. The parable of the pearl shows that not the whole world, but a single pearl will be taken when Christ returns. The parable of the net teaches not that all the fish of the sea will be gathered, but only some of every kind, the good saved and the bad cast away. "So shall it be at the end of the age; the angels shall come forth and sever the wicked from among the just." Thus the eschatological parables of Christ all teach that this dispensation will end in vast and overwhelming wickedness.

IV. What do the eschatological prophecies of Christ and the apostles teach in regard to the final state of the church and the world?

There is not a prophecy in the Bible which teaches us that the last days are to be characterized by the universal

RECEPTION OF THE GOSPEL;

on the other hand, many passages inform us of a well nigh universal rejection of the gospel. "When the Son of man cometh, shall He find faith on the earth?" If Christ is to find a millennium on the earth, then He should have said, "When the Son of man cometh, shall He find unbelief on the earth?"

No possible exegesis can set aside the fact that Christ predicted almost universal unbelief at the time of His second advent.

"Now the Spirit speaketh expressly that in the latter times some shall depart from the faith, giving heed to seducing spirits, and doctrines of demons; speaking lies in hypocrisy; having their conscience seared with a hot iron."

"This know also, that in the last days perilous times shall come. For men shall be lovers of their own selves—covetous, boasters, proud, blasphemers, disobedient to parents, unthankful, unholy, without natural affection, truce-breakers, false accusers, incontinent, fierce, despisers of those that are good, traitors, heady, high-minded, lovers of pleasure more than lovers of God: Having the form of godliness, but denying the power thereof."

Such is an inspired description of the state of the church and the world when Christ comes to set up His visible kingdom at the end of the age.

At the very time of His appearing not one of the nations of the earth will be converted to God. "Behold, He cometh with clouds, and every eye shall see Him, and they also which pierced Him, and all kindreds of the earth shall wail because of Him" (Rev. i. 7). If the whole world is to be in the full blaze of a millennial glory when Christ appears with his saints, why should all kindreds of the earth wail because of Him? Christ also says: "And then shall appear the sign of the Son of man in heaven, and then shall the tribes of the earth mourn, and they shall see the Son of man coming in the clouds of heaven with power and great glory (Matt. xxiv. 30). Why should all the tribes of the earth mourn if they have all been converted to God a thousand years before His appearing? If the Jews have all been born of the Spirit

WHEN CHRIST RETURNS.

why does Zachariah (xii., 10-14) say, "and they shall look upon Me whom they have pierced, and they shall mourn for him as one mourneth for his only son, and shall be in bitterness for him as one that is in bitterness for his first born." Why will the Jews mourn, every family apart, and their wives apart, if they have all accepted Him as their Messiah? These predictions show that the state of the church and the world at Christ's second advent will be that of mourning and wailing. Suppose the world improve, as it certainly will outwardly in science, art, education, discovery, invention, commerce, and in certain worldly reforms; he is short-sighted, indeed, who does not see how superficial and deceitful is all such progress, how stimulating to all human pride, and therefore exalting human wisdom, whereas it is the wisdom of God that the world by wisdom shall not know God. And it is a fact of history that religious decline is the inevitable prelude to national ruin. Science, art, literature, jurisprudence have not the power to make a state strong if its religion is corrupt, its morals base and God ignored. The time of Christ's second advent will be a period of abounding apostasy and unbelief; a time of revolutionary troubles and political agitations and sufferings; a time when an awakening cry will go forth announcing His nearness, and yet a time when there shall be great skepticism and indifference on the subject by the nominal church. While Belshazzar was feasting with a thousand of his lords, and drinking wine from the vessels of God's sanctuary, while music and revelry were holding high carnival, the Medes and Persians had silently entered the city of Babylon. That night the king saw the handwriting on the wall, and that night was Belshazzar,

KING OF THE CHALDEANS,

slain. These also are days of the world's feasting and merriment, the captivity of God's people forgotten, the vessels of God's temple dishonored. Already God's finger is writing on the walls of the temples of earthly glory, "Mene, Mene, Tekel, Tekel." Such, according to the eschatological prophecies of Christ and his apostles, is to be the condition of the church and the world at the time of Christ's second advent. Not only will men not receive the truth and thus become really better, but they are represented as becoming so filled with themselves, their ease, and their comforts, that sudden destruction will overtake them at the very moment they are crying "peace and safety." We have no hesitation in saying if there is to be a millennium before the second advent of our Lord, then the prophetic Scriptures are false from beginning to end, since they predict the exact opposite. If the world should be converted by the preaching of the gospel, and all should know the Lord from the least to the greatest 1,000 years before his return, then the prophets of the Old and New Testaments have prophesied falsely, their moral characters are impeached, their inspiration is a false assumption, and the Bible has no claims upon our reason or faith. If Christ and his apostles foretold apostasy, and unparalleled wickedness as characteristic of the last times, such must be the condition of the church and the world, or Christ and His apostles

DECEIVED US.

V. What do the letters to the seven churches of Asia teach concerning the final state of this dispensation? There is the highest exegetical authority for believing that the seven churches of Asia represent seven successive pages of church history, and that the Laodicean Church accurately portrays the condition of nominal Christendom at the end of this dispensation. I am aware that I touch the most sensitive nerve of post-millennialists, nevertheless final and well nigh universal apostasy of Christendom is repeatedly foretold in the Scriptures. This dispensation, like all that have preceded it, will end in the most fearful apostasy this world has ever known, to be immediately followed by the overwhelming judgments of God. Paul speaks of this "falling away." "Let no man deceive you by any means; for that day shall not come except there come a falling away first, and that man of sin be revealed, the son of perdition" (II. Thess. 2-3). "For the time will come when they will not endure sound doctrine; but after their own lusts shall they heap to themselves teachers having itching ears; and they shall turn away their ears from the truth and shall be turned unto fables" (II Tim. iv. 3-4). "Knowing this first, that there shall come in the last days scoffers walking after their own lusts, and saying: Where is the promise of his coming? For since the fathers fell asleep, all things continue as they were from the

BEGINNING OF THE CREATION"

(II Pet. iii. 3-4). Christ warned us that "many false prophets shall rise, and shall deceive many. And because iniquity shall abound, the love of many shall wax cold" (Matt. xxiv. 11-12). In the Laodicean age of the church we find indifference and lukewarmness, a most nauseating condition, with Christ standing outside his own professed church knocking for admission, while those within say. "I am rich and increased with goods, and have need of nothing;" but they know not that they are wretched, and miserable, and poor, and blind, and naked. At this stage, nearly all Christendom will be leavened with false doctrine; it is already rapidly working. The nominal Christian world will be one vast mass of baptized profession, "a corrupt, mysterious mixture, a spiritual malformation, a masterpiece of Satan, the corruption of the truth of God, and the destroyer of the souls of men, a trap, a snare, a stumbling block, the darkest moral blot in the universe of God. It is the corruption of the very best thing, and, therefore, the worst kind of corruptions. It is that thing which Satan has made of professing Christianity. It is worse by far than Judaism, worse by far than all the darkest forms of paganism, because it has had higher light and richer privileges, made the very highest profession, and occupied the loftiest platform. Finally, it is that awful apostasy for which is reserved the very heaviest judgments of God,

THE MOST BITTER DREGS

in the cup of His righteous wrath." Few persons realize what nominal Christendom is to-day, and the inevitable doom which awaits it. But our Lord gave abundant warnings of the degeneracy of the professing church, and the Spirit of God testified against early corruption—the first workings of the mystery of iniquity—and fortold the failure and abuses which shall ripen into complete apostasy, and which shall call down the judgments of God on Christendom. The great Apostle also warned the church if she did not continue in the goodness of God, she should also be cut off.

On the day of Pentecost, the church was Christendom, and Christendom was the church—they were identical. Are they so to-day? Has the church continued in the goodness of God? Has not every dispensation, so far as man's responsibility is concerned, been a failure? Under the Christian dispensation, man's privileges and responsibilities are as high as heaven, yet he himself will sink to hell through faithlessness. The Loadicean age of lukewarmness is upon us. Christ, the judge, stands at the door, while "spiritual declension and indifferentism are widespread, inveterate and increasing."

VI. What does the coming Antichrist foreshadow as to the condition of the world at the close of this dispensation? John tells us that "the spirit of Antichrist" was "already in the world" in his day. He also says "even now have there arisen

MANY ANTICHRISTS

whereby we know that it is the last hour." But there is an Antichrist to come; he is the coming man of sin. A brief glance at his character and work will tell us the condition of the church and the world at the close of this age.

1. His character is sufficiently indicated by his names. He is called "The Beast," "The King of Fierce Countenance," "The Little Horn," "The Prince that shall come," "Lucifer," "The Man of Sin," "The Son of Perdition." The dragon is anti-God, the beast is Antichrist, and his false prophet is anti-Holy Ghost. Such his character.

2. His work is plainly foretold in the word of God. "He speaks great words against the Most High" (Dan. vii. 25). "He opens his mouth in blasphemy against God to blaspheme His name, and His tabernacle, and them that dwell in heaven" (Rev. xiii. 6). "He makes war with the saints and overcomes them" (Rev. xiii. 7). "He causes the sacrifice and oblation to cease" (Dan. ix. 27).

3. The reign of Antichrist will be at its height when Christ comes in power and great glory; hence the condition of the church and the world at Christ's second advent can not be that of the universal reception of the gospel and millennial glory. For He "shall prevail until the Ancient of days came, and judgment is given to the saints of the Most High; and the time came that the saints possessed the kingdom" (Dan. vii. 22). "And then shall that wicked

BE REVEALED,

whom the Lord shall consume with the spirit of His mouth, and shall destroy with the brightness of His coming" (II. Thess. ii. 8). One thing is certain, if Christ does not destroy Antichrist until the close of the millennium, then the reign of the dragon, the Antichrist, and the false prophet takes place during the millennium! Strange millennium that!

But Satan is bound during the millennium, and the Antichrist and false prophet are cast into the lake of fire before the millennium, hence Christ could not destroy Antichrist by the brightness of his appearing after the millennium. The irresistible alternative remains that the whole world will wonder after the beast, and they will be under his sway when Christ appears with his saints. Such will be the condition of things at Christ's second advent.

VII. What do the Apocalyptic judgments teach concerning the condition of the church and the world at Christ's second advent?

The church proper will be taken away before the seals are broken, the trumpets sound, or the bowls of God's wrath are poured out upon the earth. From the close of the Laodicean age, in Revelation, third chapter, the church is not mentioned until the last chapter of the Apocalypse.

The nominal church, with a baptized profession, and a form of godliness, will pass into, if not through, the great tribulation period, and with the whole world will drink of the cup of the fierceness of the wrath of God Almighty. If any one desires to know the condition of

THE NOMINAL CHURCH

and the world at Christ's second advent, let him read with blanched cheek and bated breath from the fifth to the twentieth chapter of Revelation. With God's own hand the portrait is drawn. The hand that was nailed to the cross breaks the seven judgment seals and all nature trembles, all mountains from their firm base are moved, all islands flee, all seas disturbed, the sun is black, the moon is blood, all nations in the winepress of the wrath of God.

The seven judgment trumpets sound and "there followed hail and fire mingled with blood," burning mountains cast into the sea, waters of wormwood, heavens darkened, bottomless pit opened, the seven thunders rolled a universal elemental war, "the great day of his wrath is come and who shall be able to stand?" The seven judgment bowls are poured out upon the earth, all nature reels with signs of woe, the earth quakes in all her parts, and the cities of the nations fall—Rome falls, Chicago falls, God has arisen to shake terribly the earth. Satan's wrath is great, his time is short, the nations blaspheme, the squadrons are gathering in the valley of Armageddon. God and anti-God, Christ and anti-Christ have come—it is "the battle of the great day of God Almighty." The beast and the false prophet are cast into the lake of fire, Satan is bound for a thousand years, and the millennium has begun. Such, my brethren will be the condition of church nominal and the world when Christ comes with all His saints to take to himself his

GREAT POWER AND REIGN.

This dispensation, like those that have preceded it, will certainly end in the unparalleled judgments of God. Already are we entering the penumbra of that awful eclipse; already men's "hearts are failing them for fear, and for looking after those things which are coming on the earth."

But we are informed by our post-millennial brethren that "the earth shall be full of the knowledge of the Lord, as the waters cover the sea;" they forget, however, that this very passage is preceded by the words: "He shall smite the earth with the rod of His mouth, and with the breath of His lips shall He slay the wicked" (Isa. xi. 9-4). They tell us that "the wilderness and the solitary place shall be glad, and the desert shall rejoice and blossom as the rose;" but they forget that the context informs us, "Behold your God shall come with vengeance; even God with a recompense He will come and save you" (Isa. xxxv. 1-4). We are reminded also that God has said to His Son: "Ask of me, and I shall give Thee the heathen for Thine inheritance, and the uttermost parts of the earth for Thy possession;" but they ignore the fact that this world-wide salvation of the heathen does not take place until "The kings of the earth set themselves, and the rulers take counsel together against the Lord and against His anointed, saying, 'Let us break their bands asunder and cast away their cords from us. Thou shalt break them with a rod of iron (the kings of the earth, not the heathen). Thou shalt dash them in pieces like

A POTTER'S VESSEL;"

and hence he says: "Be wise now therefore, O ye kings; be instructed ye judges of the earth" (Ps. ii., 2-3-8-9-10). Is not this a plain allusion to the battle of the great day of God Almighty. But we are again told that "the God of heaven shall set up a kingdom that shall never be destroyed." Very true, but not till the stone cut out of the mountain without hands shall smite the great world-kingdoms and they become "like the chaff of the summer-thrashing floor." Then shall the stone-kingdom "become a great mountain and fill the whole earth." They tell us that all nations are to be converted by the present system of missions, and that "the kingdom and dominion and the greatness of the kingdom under the whole heaven shall be given to the saints of the Most High;" but they are to recall the fact that this does not take place until the Ancient of days "shall come and a fiery stream issued before Him, thousand thousands ministered unto Him and ten thousand times ten thousand stand before Him, the judgment was set and the books were opened. I beheld even till the beast was slain, and his body destroyed and given to the burning flame" (Dan. vii., 27. 9, 10, 11). How often in missionary addresses we hear it said "this gospel must be preached until the kingdoms of this world are become the kingdoms of our Lord and His Christ," but they seem to forget that there is no such command or assurance in the Bible, while we are informed that this transfer of kingly dominion will not take place till "the time of the dead, that they should be judged," etc. (Rev. xi. 15-18). Thus we might multiply passages showing that the conversion of the world takes place after the

PERSONAL, VISIBLE RETURN

of our Lord. There is not a passage in the Bible which teaches that the nations are to be converted during the present dispensation. The Holy Spirit carefully guarded every sacred writer from so much as hinting such a thing; on the other hand He directed that whenever the conversion of the world was mentioned the immediate context should contain some allusion to his premillennial advent, and to the pouring out of his judgments upon an apostate church, or the Antichristian world powers.

VIII. What do the "signs of the times" teach in regard to this solemn subject?

"Ye can discern the face of the sky, can ye not discern the signs of the times?"

We have pursued thus far seven lines of argument, any one of which is sufficient to establish the fact that the condition of the church and the world at Christ's second advent will be deplorable beyond description, while the cumulative weight of these seven independent propositions seems to us convincing and overwhelming. If, then, the condition of the church and the world at the close of this dispensation is to be that of well nigh universal apostasy and judgment, does it not follow that the nominal church and the world are certain to grow worse and worse. What do "the signs of the times" indicate in regard to this question? Do they point in the direction of the foregoing arguments?

1. What is the religious condition of the world to-day, after eighteen hundred years of gospel preaching? There are in the world to-day 856,000,000 heathen, 170,000,000 Mohammedans, 190,000,000 Roman Catholics, 84,000,000 Greek Catholics; 8,000,000 Jews, and 116,000,000 Protestants. Out of the 390,000,000 nominal Christian population, about one-half are Roman Catholics; one-quarter Greek Catholics, and

ONE-QUARTER PROTESTANTS.

There are only 30,000,000 Protestant church members in the world, and about 86,000,000 Protestant non-church members. About 1,000,000 of the 30,000,000 Protestant communicants are in unevangelic communions, leaving 29,000,000 in evangelic communions. Such is the religious population of the world to-day. Protestants regard the 1,300,000,000 outside themselves as without God and without hope in the world, with perhaps few exceptions among the Catholics. But what of the 116,000,000 Protestants? This includes the Protestant population, not the church membership merely, much less the regenerated church membership. Does any one believe that more than one-half of Protestant church members have ever been born of God? Is there any evidence that more than one in a thousand Roman or Greek Catholics know anything of experimental religion? Are there 15,000,000 persons in the world to-day who give any token by their fruits that they are saved? God alone must judge. But Christ also told his disciples how to judge of these things: "By their fruits ye shall know them." Brethren in the ministry, have you never been pained—nay, overwhelmed—to think how many members in all our Protestant as well as Catholic churches are going down to hell? How many ministers of the gospel will finally say, "Have we not prophesied in Thy name, and in Thy name done many wonderful works? And then will I profess unto them, I never knew you; depart from me, ye that work iniquity." There are more unconverted persons in the world to-day than ever before. So long as

SINNERS INCREASE

far more rapidly than saints, will some one tell how long it will take to convert the world? At the rate of advancement for the last eighteen hundred years the endless cycles of eternity would not be sufficient to furnish the requisite ages for the conversion of the world, whereas the evangelization of the world might be accomplished in a very few years. If Christ is not to return until this world is converted by the preaching of the gospel He will never return until eternal ages roll away. "Dark picture, this," you say. True, but you gave me a dark subject. "Evil seducers shall wax worse and worse." Every sinner is an evil seducer, and so long as sinners by far outnumber the saints, and multiply with greater rapidity, it is easy to see that the world is growing religiously worse instead of better.

The Eden dispensation grew worse instead

of better, and ended in death. The Antediluvian dispensation increased in wickedness to its close; the patriarchal dispensation waxed worse and worse; the Mosaic dispensation murdered its own Messiah saying, "His blood be upon us and our children." The Christian dispensation has more light than all that have preceded it, yet when that light becomes darkness by apostasy, how great will be that darkness! This dispensation is destined to grow worse and worse; a remnant will be saved out of it—and only a remnant. Take our own fair land, where Christianity has had the best possible opportunity for development, and what do "the signs of

THE TIMES" INDICATE?

There are millions on millions more unconverted people in these United States to-day than ever before, and they are increasing more rapidly than Protestants and Catholics combined. In the year 1800 there were in the United States 4,836,000 non-church members; in 1850, there were 19,-047,012; in 1870, there were 27,284,704; while in 1880, there were in this country 34,000,000 non-church members, and only 10,000,000 Protestants and 6,000,000 Catholics. The non-church membership class is more than twice as large as the Protestant and Catholic combined, and that class is increasing far more rapidly than all religious denominations put together. Reduce the church membership class down to those who give any evikence of regeneration, and the outlook is still more apalling. The same is true of the foreign field. The Rev. James Johnston, in a work entitled, "A Century of Protestant Missions," which will be published in England this month, estimates that while 3,000,000 converts have been added to the church, there are now 200,000,000 more heathen in the world than there were when Protestant missions began, a hundred years ago. There are only 1,650,000 heathen converted in the whole world to-day—leaving over 854,000,000 unconverted heathen.

"The signs of the times" in regard to the progress of Christianity in the United States and the world at large is ominous. It is precisely as our Lord predicted of the last days, "And because iniquity shall abound, the love of many shall wax cold," the world more wicked, the church more cold. Instead of the church converting the world, the world is

CONVERTING THE CHURCH.

An eminent American writer has said: "When we survey the charateristics of our times, the unrighteousness, the avarice, the lustfulness, the untruthfulness, the hypocrisy, the impiety, the crime, the hollow-heartedness, and the untold hidden iniquities which prevail, in all circles of church business and State; when we consider the wickednesses which are perpetrated by people who call themselves Christians, and the shameless, worldliness of professors of religion, and the wreck of all distinctive doctrinal belief, and the prostitutions of the House of God, and the sacred desk itself, to vanity, politics, selfishness, sensuality, and base trickery in the name of Jesus; when we look at the insubornation which is left to run riot in the great majority of so-called Christian families, and the secret vices and concealed blood-guilty crimes of so-called Christian husbands and wives, and of the utter moral emptiness, headiness, and incontinence of the most of the busiest and noisiest modern religionists; when we contemplate the goings forth of sin in these days, like Death on the pale horse with hell following in its train, and come to count up the names of those in our congregations whom we can confidently set down as true and thorough saints of God—we are sometimes tempted, with the Psalmist, to say, 'All men are liars,' and to doubt whether God has not resigned His dominion over mankind, and abandoned them to be drifted by the whirlwinds of their own passions to irremedial ruin." When we consider that four-fifths of our population seldom, if ever, frequent the

HOUSE OF GOD

on the Sabbath day, that over 95 per cent of the young men of our land belong to no religious organization whatever, leaving less than 5 per cent of our young men who even profess the Christian religion; when we consider that the greatest of all curses, the sum of all villainies, which sends fifty thousand men to a drunkard's grave, and a drunkard's hell every year, is actually upheld by the suffrages of the church, Catholic and Protestant; when we consider that "the vicious class are Christian born, that this Christendom has authorized by law and sanction of the State, the creation of this frightful pest gang; that it has provided for its creation; that it is here not in opposition to, but of her will; that by formal and deliberate legislation, brought about by Christian votes, she has opened in all her towns and cities, slaughter-houses of men, women, and children, and of all virtue, and employs a million minions to do this dreadful work; that she has done this, and continues to do it with her eyes open, and with full knowledge and purpose; that she has prepared, and planned, and deliberated in government chambers, for the production of these classes;" when we consider these gigantic evils in the very heart of Christendom, we are not only led to believe that Satan is the god of this world, and that the whole world lieth in the wicked one, but we are impelled to say, "Come out of her my people, that ye be not partakers of her sins, and that ye receive not of her plagues. For her sins have

REACHED UNTO HEAVEN

and God hath remembered her iniquities." A ship recently sailed from Boston to the Congo region of Africa. It had on board one hundred thousand gallons of rum, and one missionary. How long will it take such a Christendom as we have described to convert the world?

But is there not more consecrated wealth in the church to-day than ever before? Yes, and more unconsecrated wealth; more temperance in the church, and more intemperance in the world; a more wholesale condemnation of the liquor traffic, and more liquor made and sold than ever before; more evangelism, and more diabolism; more theism, and more atheism; more religion, and more religiosity; more piety, and more impiety; more of the spirit of godliness, and more who have the form of godliness without the power thereof; more zeal without knowledge, and more knowledge without zeal; never so many who honor the Christian name, and never so many who disgrace it; never was the church so alive to missions, never was the mystery of iniquity so full of amazing energy; never so much of the spirit of Christ, and of Antichrist.

What do "the signs of the times" teach in regard to the leaven of false doctrine in the church and out of it?

Two-thirds of nominal Christendom is one vast overshadowing hierarchy, a system of Mariolatry, if not of idolatry, with a false ritualism, and a grossly materialistic sacramentarianism, while the remaining third of the professed church is sadly

COMPROMISED BY RATIONALISM

in its theology, and humanitarianism in its Christology. Outside the church and within, spiritualism enrolls its millions; annihilationism and second probationism, a kind of "incipient, theological dry rot," boast their thousands, hundreds of whom stand in so-called orthodox pulpits, and openly proclaim these false doctrines, or secretly entertain them. The latter day delusions are sapping the very life of multitudes of professedly Christian people.

Both the church and the world are rapidly becoming ripe for Antichrist.

The leaven of false doctrine and hypocrisy is spreading world-wide, and the indications are that it is to wax worse and worse. There is not so much as a hint in the word of God that the world is to grow morally better until Christ comes, and that the millennium will be ushered in by the preaching of the gospel in this dispensation, nor do "the signs of the times" indicate any such religious progress to-day. It is very doubtful if the gospel is so universally preached to-day as it was during the first century of the Christian era, or if there are as many regenerated persons in proportion to the population of the world. Both post and premillennialists have committed the great error of spending ages to educate and Christianize a part of the world instead of evangelizing the whole world. Deep are the shadows that gather about the church and the world to-day. What mean these forebodings of the near and solemn future? What mean these great upheavals and

CONVULSIONS OF SOCIETY?

What mean these seething, surging, riotous masses of the dangerous classes of the ground tier? What mean these armies marching and countermarching with banners on which are emblazoned dynamite, anarchism, communism, nihilism? What means this ominous tramp of gathering legions? What mean these lowering clouds, dark and tempestuous, all around the horizon? What mean these earthquakes in divers places? What means the fig tree when it putteth forth leaves? During the great eclipse in 1806, a certain Legislature in New England was in session. All at once noon became night. Darkness terrified the members. One man arose, and moved to "adjourn for the day of judgment has come." The Governor arose and said: "Gentlemen, either the day of judgment has come or it has not. If it has not come we have no need to fear; if it has come I desire to be found at the post of duty. Bring lights! Bring lights." So, my brethren, in these dark and degenerate days, when gross darkness seems settling down upon the people, bring the "sure word of prophecy whereunto ye do well that ye take heed as unto a light that shineth in a dark place until the day dawn and the day star arise in your hearts."

2. What is the *moral* condition of the church and the world to-day? We believe it to be growing worse and worse. The condition of wheat and tares is always worse and worse. If the religious condition is such as I have endeavored to show, then by necessity the moral condition is still lower. Take the two

OLDEST INSTITUTIONS

in the world—the Sabbath and the family. These two institutions are the foundation of all good society. They epitomize the two tables of the law. No one will question that the Sabbath is more and more disregarded and desecrated all over the Christian world, with its Sunday trains, Sunday papers, Sunday beer gardens, Sunday theaters, and Sunday trade; and as for the marriage relation, it is rapidly becoming more like the days before the flood when men "took to themselves wives of all which they chose." In the State of Massachusetts the number of divorces in proportion to marriages is one to fifteen; in Vermont, one to thirteen; in Rhode Island and Connecticut, one to nine; in England, one to 300; in Belgium, one to 200; in France, not allowed until recently. Will some one tell us how the moral condition of christendom is growing better when the two oldest and most sacred moral institutions in the world are growing into a condition worse and worse? If reverence for God and the family relation, the two foundation-stones of all morality, are settling lower and lower, as the "signs of the times" most abundantly prove, how is the morality of society becoming higher and higher? How long will it take to usher in the millennium at this rate of progpess? There never will be a millennium on this earth until Christ returns the second time without sin unto salvation. "Even so come Lord Jesus. Come quickly."

We are also living in a boastful age. On great anniversary occasions it is quite common to hear representatives of

RELIGIOUS DENOMINATIONS

boasting with the materialist and the demagogue of the progress of the age, its increased morality and its unparalleled social and religious advancement. Let us for a moment longer look at the morality of the two foremost Christian nations on the globe, Great Britain and the United States. A recent writer in the *Christian at Work* has the following significant paragraph: He says, "It ought to humble our national pride and boastfulness to make solemn note of the fact that the United States leads all other countries in the commission of crime. Carefully collected statistics force upon us the reluctant conclusion that we are the most violent and bloodthirsty people. Here is evidence from 'Dr Mulhalt's Statistical Dictionary' in regard to the proportion of murders to the population: England, 237 murders to 10,000,000 of population; Belgium, 240; France, 265; Scandinavia, 266; Germany, 279; Ireland, 294; Austria, 310; Russia, 325; Italy, 504; Spain, 533; the United States, 850, murders for every 10,000,000 of people or 4,510 murders every year! From these figures it appears that nearly four times as many murders are committed among the same number of people here as in England; while in Italy once prominent as the land of assassins, and in Spain equally notorious for bloody affrays ending in death, fewer persons are now slain with malice prepense, in the ratio of population than in our self-lauded Christian and Protestant country. And at the same time the mania for suicide as fearful as it is common. As an illustration of this mania it may be mentioned that the other day a boy of twelve years of age hung himself becouse he had been chastised by his mother, while an old man of seventy-five ended his life because he had been harshly addressed. Does any one ask the cause of this awful record of murder and suicide? The answer is we think three-fold; viz., infidel doctrines, cheap fictitious sentimental literature and the decadence of family training. This state of things is shocking beyond expression. It reveals glimpses like

LURID FLASHES OF LIGHTNING

over a rock-bound and storm-beaten coast, of wild dangers and unspeakable miseries." When we consider that most of these tragedies occur in cities, and that one-fifth of our population reside in the great commercial centers, which are fast becoming plague-spots of moral and political leprosy, the hotbeds of lawlessness and crime our outlook for the futnre as a Nation is appalling. Such is the social morality of boasting Protesting America! How is it in England, Protestant England, who sits as a queen and no widow upon her emerald throne? In answer to the question, "Are we better than we should be?" a recent number of the *Pall Mall Gazette* gives us what it styles a pictorial view of English morals.

It is well known that the hideous revelation of social evil in the foremost nation of Christendom during the past year has shocked the civilized and the uncivilized world! The number of indecent assaults in England and Wales in the year 1861 were 280; in 1881 they were 270; in 1884, 510. The apprehensions for drunkenness and on charges of being drunk and disorderly for England and Walas in 1861 were 82,196; in 1884 they numbered 198,274, the increase being steady and far more rapid than the population. Had the increase only kept pace with the natural growth of population, the figures for 1884 would have been 108,000 instead of 198,274. The people of the United Kingdom paid for drink in 1861 nearly £95,000,000. In 1876 they should have paid, according to natural increase, about £108,000, whereas they actually paid the enormous sum of £148,000,000. Since then the drink bill has declined to £125,000,000 in 1883, but it should have been only £115,000,000.

In 1861 there were 263 petitions filed in the divorce courts of England and Wales; in 1884 there were 703, although, according to population, there should have been only 350. In 1861 there were 1,553. Suicides in

ENGLAND AND WALES:

In 1884 the number had increased to 3,312, though it should have been not more than 2,000. In 1861 there were 39,647 lunatics, idiots, and persons of unsound mind in England and Wales. Since then the number has increased with remarkable regularity until, in 1883, it was 76,765, whereas, in proportion to the increase of population, it should have been only 53,000. These facts all show that drunkenness, immorality, and idiocy are increasing in Great Britain at a rate out of all proportion to the growth of the population." A recent writer in the *Fortnightly Review* for October, 1886, in an article entitled "The Statistics of Morality," shows that the most highly cultivated State of continental Europe is at the same time the most degraded by the social evil, even as the golden age of Greek and Roman literature was also the era of its greatest moral corruption. And yet Christian men in all our religious denominations are boasting of the moral and religious progress of the age, whereas the two foremost Christian nations on the globe are every day sinking lower and lower in immorality and crime, and out of all proportion to the increase of population. It is also a singular fact that these so-called optimists who paint the nineteenth century in roseate hues show us but one side of the picture. They tell us in glowing eloquence how much has been expended for missions, but they do not tell us how many millions on millions more these same Christian nations spent to ruin the bodies and souls of men. They tell us how many have been saved by the gospel of Christ in the past year. They do not tell us how many have gone down to hell during the same time on account of the lethargy of Christendom. They tell us of the labors of Judson and Carey and hundreds of other missionaries

ON FOREIGN FIELDS,

but they do not tell us that Protestant England and America have sent more souls to perdition through forcing upon unwilling heathen the demons of opium and rum than all the converts of all the missionary societies of the world a hundred times over.

Satan is still the god of this world, the whole world lith in the wicked one, and there is laughter in hell when so-called optimists tell us that Satan's kingdom is rapidly being overthrown and the gates of perdition effectually closed. Perhaps there are anniversaries in Hades and jubilees in the underworld. Perchance they have on record so many lost souls the past year, so many who profess and so few who possess Christianity, so many who have abandoned the old theology and have at our suggestions accepted the "New Theology," so many who have come down out of all the churches of Christendom to people the dark regions of dispair, so many whose names have been transferred from the church roll to the black page of Satan's minions. So much for the immorality of Christendom. But suppose the morality of every person on the globe were equal to that of the Scribes and Pharisees, not one of them would enter the kingdom of heaven. Morality divorced from Christianity is more fatal to the souls of men than immorality—since it blinds the possessor both to Christ's righteousness and to his own unrighteousness.

The publicans and the harlots will go into the kingdom of God before the Scribes and the Pharisees. "O Christ, the only true morality is love of Thee!" The self-righteous moralist no more fears God nor regards man, than the most depraved.

Whether you regard the world, therefore, in its morality or immorality, there is no difference as before God. If there is to be a millennium 1,000 years before Christ comes, it surely ought to begin to dawn after 1,800 years of gospel preaching, but there is

NOT A CONTINENT,

a State, a city, a town, a family, or an individual in which Satan is bound, while there are thousands of places where Christianity has become entirely extinct. A very good man was once asked if he enjoyed much religion. His significant reply was, "None to boast of." We are living in a boastful age. Neither Christ nor His apostles ever boasted of the spread of the gospel or the progress of the age. On the other hand God's ancient prophets were always warning the people against apostacy; Christ and his apostles inform us that when we have done all we are unprofitable servants. My brethren, there is not one-half so much Christianity in this world as is generally supposed. In these degenerate days we need to "cry aloud and spare not to lift up our voices like a tempest and show the people their transgressions and the house of Jacob their sins."

Not long ago a Baptist clergyman, crossing the Atlantic on a very stormy passage, noticed the Captain walking the hurricane deck with a very anxious and troubled countenance. He approached him and said: "Captain, you seem very much agitated. Is anything wrong, sir?"

The Captain replied: "We are on a terrible sea; nor sun nor stars have appeared for many days, and we are drifting, sir; we are drifting far out of our course." All day long the Captain walked that stormy deck with sextant in hand to make his observations and take his bearings. How eagerly he watched for the Northern star; how he prayed for one gleam of light! All night long he was drifting on that open sea, with its deceitful currents, saying, "I am lost; I know not where I am." At last there was a rift in the cloud. Instantly he took his bearings and exclaimed to those on board, "We are one hundred and seventy-five miles out of our course." Men to-day are on the wide, open sea of doubt; darkness overshadows them; they are drifting away from the Bible. A thousand pulpits are drifting from the

DOCTRINE OF INSPIRATION,

the deity of Christ, the vicarious atonement, the resurrection of the body, and eternal retribution. Nearly the whole church, Catholic and Protestant, in the United States has drifted away from the apostolic doctrine of Christ's premillennial advent. This doctrine is the pole-star of the church, the only doctrine in the Bible that enables us to take our bearings and tell where we are; the only doctrine that throws any light upon our future course. The accredited scholarship of the world is on the side of premillennialism, but the rank and file in this country are against us. There is hardly a commentator in Great Britain or on the continent that is not with us, but in the United States the churches have drifted far out of their course. Wanted, a premillennial chair in every theological seminary in our land! Wanted, a professor in each institution to teach the Bible, the whole Bible, and nothing but the Bible! Wanted, a man in all our religious schools to teach the entire system of prophetic and dispensational truth! Wanted, great, energetical leaders who with the Bible in hand can take observations and show the theological drift of the age. Some of us remember what an electric light was thrown upon the sacred page when the doctrine of Christ's premillennial advent flashed upon us.

Dark and foreboding is our theme, yet not half so black as revelation paints it. Still premillennialism presents a far brighter prospect for the future of the race than postmillennialism as it really is. The one believes that if Christ were to return to-day and raise the righteous dead and change the righteous living, after a brief tribulation period he would bind Satan for one thousand years, set up his visible kingdom on earth, convert whole nations in a day, and the whole world would be brought into subjection to his sway. All would know the Lord, from the

LEAST TO THE GREATEST.

Christ's heavenly people would be as the stars of heaven for multitude, and His earthly people from generation to generation forever be as the sand of the seashore, innumerable enough to fill all worlds that roll in the great Creator's space, the lost being to the saved as a drop in the vast ocean. Such is the optimism of premillenianism.

The other theory which vainly hopes for a millennium without Christ would require eternal ages for the conversion of the world, and the saved to the lost would be only as a grain of sand to the whole earth. Such is the pessimism of post-millennialism. We have a brighter hope, a more glorious prospect, a Savior coming the second time without sin unto salvation—the almost immediate salvation of the whole world, instead of the dreary ages of heathenism and everlasting destruction.

While we believe that the Scriptures are altogether on our side of this question, it is gratifying to have the late Dean Alford say, "The weight of the scholarship both as regards the number and the character of interpreters, is on the side of premillennialism."

At the conclusion of the meeting the conference unanimously voted, on motion of the Rev. Dr. Pierson, that the committee on conference provide that a conference shall be held at least once in every three years. After a hymn Bishop Nicholson pronounced the benediction.

PROFESSOR JOHN T. DUFFIELD.

THE APOSTOLIC CHURCH WAS PREMILLENARIAN.

One of the appointments for Friday's session was that of Professor John T. Duffield, of Princeton College, New Jersey. Professor Duffield could not attend, but forwarded his paper on the subject, "The Apostolic Church Was Premillenarian." The paper is as follows:

If asked for a concise and conclusive argument for premillenarianism, we reply, the Apostolic Church was premillenarian. We are aware of the apparent anachronism in the statement that the church was premillenarian before the apocalyptic prediction that "Satan should be bound a thousand years, and should be cast into the bottomless pit, and deceive the nations no more until the thousand years should be fulfilled." The anachronism is only in name, not in fact. It is a common yet wholly erroneous impression that our pre-millennial faith is based mainly, if not solely, on a disputed passage in the Apocalypse. In a recent work in

DEFENSE OF POST-MILLENARIANISM.

the writer manifests his misapprehension and misappreciation of the doctrine he is opposing, by the statement that "the twentieth chapter of the Revelation is at once the birth-place and the Gibraltar of premillennialism." The fact is, the main question at issue in what is now known as the millenarian controversy, antedates the Apocalypse, and would have been a question of no less interest and importance throughout this dispensation if the Apocalypse had not been written.

What is the main question at issue? The Scriptures contain distinct predictions, yet unfulfilled, of two events of momentous importance:

1. The return of our Lord Jesus Christ to this earth. The "same Jesus" whom the apostles beheld taken up into heaven shall come again, in the glory of His Father, and with His holy angels.

2. Throughout Old Testament prophecy the prediction is prominent of an era of universal righteousness and peace on earth under the reign of the Messiah. "He shall have dominion from sea to sea, and from the river to the ends of the earth. All kings shall fall down before Him, all nations shall serve Him, all nations shall call him blessed" (Ps. lxxii. 8, 11, 17). "They shall beat their swords into plow-shares, and their spears into pruning-hooks; nation shall not lift up

THE SWORD AGAINST NATION,

neither shall they learn war any more. The earth shall be full of the knowledge of the Lord as the waters cover the sea" (Isaiah ii, 14, xi., 9). "They shall teach no more every man his neighbor, and every man his brother, saying, know the Lord; for they shall all know me, from the least of them unto the greatest of them, saith the Lord" (Jer. xxxi. 34). "I saw in the night visions, and behold, one like the Son of man came with the clouds of heaven, and came to the Ancient of days, and they brought him near before Him. And there was given him dominion and glory and a kingdom, that all people, nations, and languages should serve Him; His dominion is an everlasting dominion, which shall not pass away, and His kingdom that which shall not be destroyed." "The kingdom and dominion and the greatness of the kingdom under the whole heaven shall be given to the people of the saints of the Most High" (Dan. vii. 13, 14, 27).

The question relates to these, and similar, Old Testament predictions, and the issue is, *whether this era of universal righteousness and peace on earth—the [Mes]sianic kingdom of prophecy—will precede or follow the second coming of the Lord Jesus?* As the prediction in the Apocalypse of

THE BINDING OF SATAN

for 1,000 years, seems to refer to the era of righteousness and peace or earth under the reign of the Messiah, the term "Millennium" has been appropriated to designate the Messianic kingdom of old Testament prophecy, and the word should be so understood in any discussion of the subject at issue.

It is in point here to remark that much labored argument has been expended to prove that Christ is now a king; that "all power in heaven and on earth" has been given unto Him; that He rules in the hearts of His people; that He is head and sovereign of His blood-bought Church. All this is true, but it is wholly irrelevant to the question at issue between premilenarians and postmillenarians. This question has reference exclusively to the predicted Messianic kingdom. Unless the language of Scripture is meaningless, the prophecies above referred to have never yet been fulfilled, and the question is, whether their fulfillment is to precede or to follow the Second Advent? It is with reference to this question that we assert, that the Apostolic Church, including the apostles themselves, was premillenarian.

God's covenant people, to whom "were committed the oracles of God," and to whom pertained not only "the giving of the law," but "the promises," expected the fulfilment of the predictions of the Messianic kingdom at the first advent of the Messiah.

THE APOSTLES

undoubtedly cherished this expectation, and probably did not entirely abandon it until they beheld His ascension and heard the annunciation of the heavenly messengers. But a few days before His crucifixion He spake to them a parable, "because they thought that the kingdom of God should immediately appear." As He was about to be parted from them and taken up into heaven, their last inquiry was, "Wilt Thou at this time restore the kingdom to Israel?" After His departure and their baptism by the Holy Ghost, whom Jesus had promised "to shew them things to come, and to bring to their remembrance whatsoever He had said to them," the truth, both as to the coming and the kingdom, was distinctly apprehended. They now remembered and understood the parable—"A certain nobleman went into a far country to receive for himself a kingdom, and to return." They now remembered and understood what He had so recently taught men as to the state of the church and of the world between the time of His departure and His return—"wars and rumors of wars, famines, pestilences, and earthquakes; false prophets, whereby many should be deceived; abounding iniquity, whereby the love of many should wax cold"—but no intimation of an era of righteousness and peace—no Messianic kingdom—before the advent. "The Gospel of the Kingdom"—the

GLAD TIDINGS

of its coming and of the way by which citizenship therein might be attained was to be preached unto all nations "for a witness," and then should the end come.

He foretold "the coming of the Son of Man in the clouds of heaven with power and great glory," and having mentioned signs of this coming, He spake a parable: "Behold the fig tree, and all the trees; when they now shoot forth ye know that summer is nigh. So when ye see these things come to pass know ye that the kingdom of God is nigh at hand."

So instructed by the Master and enlightened by the Holy Ghost the apostles taught that the Lord Jesus would return again to the earth, but that "the heaven must receive him until the times of restitution of all things which God hath spoken by the mouth of all His holy prophets since the world began." What can be here referred to, if not the prominent theme of all Old Testament prophecy—the reign on earth of the Messiah? As this kingdom was to be manifested at and not before the advent, the advent became the immediate object of desire and expectation—the "blessed hope"—of the apostles, and through them, of the Apostolic Church.

The fact of special interest and importance in its bearing on the question under consideration is, the apostles not only taught that Christ

WOULD CERTAINLY RETURN,

but that the event was possibly near at hand—that it might occur in their day—and hence was to be "looked for" with expectation and preparation. They would recall, and now appreciate as they did not before His departure, Christ's repeated injunction in his memorable discourse on the *Parousia*, "Watch, for ye know not what hour your Lord cometh." They would recall and now appreciate how He had illustrated and enforced this injunction by reminding them that if the good man of the house had known at what hour the thief would come he would have watched; by commending the faithful servant who lived in expectation of his master's coming, and by the parable of the ten virgins with the accompanying interpretation, "Watch, therefore, for ye know neither the day nor the hour when the Son of Man cometh." Whatever questions have been raised as to the meaning of this injunction, by interpreters of Scripture in these latter days, there could have been no doubt as to its meaning in the minds of the apostles. When he spoke of "the coming of the Son of man in the clouds of heaven with power and great glory, and he shall send his angels with a great

SOUND OF A TRUMPET

and they shall gather together his elect from the four winds, from one end of heaven to the other," the apostles could never have imagined—what many at the present day not only imagine, but teach—that the coming here referred to was His coming to each one at death, or a spiritual coming, as on the day of Pentecost, or a providential coming, as at the destruction of Jerusalem. They could not but understand Him to mean His personal, visible return to this earth, in the glory of His Father, and with His holy angels." And as to the duty enjoined, of "watching" for the coming, the apostles could never have imagined—what some at the present day imagine and teach—that the duty would be fulfilled by believing that the Lord would certainly return, but in the distant future. The apostles could not but understand the Savior to mean that they were to regard his return as an event possibly near at hand for which they were to watch—as virgins for the coming of the bridegroom—as faithful servants for the return of their master.

So undoubtedly the apostles did understand the injunction, and accordingly believed and taught the possible nearness of the advent—that for aught that was revealed Christ might come in their day. They did not—as is sometimes alleged—believe or teach that Christ would certainly come in their day, but

THAT HE MIGHT COME

—and that in that sense His coming was to be regarded as ever near.

The proof that the apostles so taught is two-fold—first, their language does not fairly admit of any other interpretation; and, second, the Apostolic Church understood the apostles so to teach.

1. As to the language of the apostles in reference to the advent, Paul writes to the Thessalonians: "We which are alive and remain unto the coming of the Lord shall not prevent them that are asleep. * * * We which are alive and remain shall be caught up with them in the clouds to meet the Lord in the air. * * * Of the times and the seasons ye have no need that I write unto you, for yourselves know perfectly that the day of the Lord so cometh as a thief in the night. * * * But ye, brethren, are not in darkness that that day should overtake you as a thief. * * * Therefore let us not

sleep as do others, but let us watch and be sober" (I. Thess. iv. 15; v. 6). To the Phillipians he writes: "Our conversation is in heaven, from whence also we look for the Savior, the Lord Jesus Christ" (iii. 20). "Let your moderation be known unto all men, the Lord is at hand" (iv. 5).

To the Romans he writes: "The night is far spent, the day is at hand; let us therefore put off the works of darkness, and let us put on the armor of light" (xiii. 12).

So Peter in his first epistle: "The end of all things is at hand, be ye therefore sober and watch unto prayer" (iv. 7).

So James exhorts those who were enduring affliction:

"BE PATIENT,

brethren, unto the coming of the Lord." "Be ye patient, stablish your hearts, for the coming of the Lord draweth nigh" (v. 7-8).

These and other similar passages that might be quoted it should be observed are not exhortations to duty, based on the certainty of Christ's coming, they are exhortations to watchfulness and patience and holy living in view of *the uncertainty as to the time*, and hence the possible nearness—uncertain, not of course in the divine purpose, but to human foresight. To suppose that the apostles did not intend to teach that for aught that was revealed, the Lord might come before the generation then living had passed away, would be to make the reason on which the exhortation was based inapplicable to the very persons to whom the epistles were immediately addressed.

The only passage in the apostolic epistles which seems to teach that the day of the Lord was not at hand is in the second to the Thessalonians, ii. 2. Paul there exhorts the Thessalonians that they "be not soon shaken in mind, or be troubled, neither by spirit, nor by word, nor by letter as from us, as that the day of Christ is at hand." What Paul is here represented as teaching does undoubtedly contradict in terms what he and Peter and James had elsewhere repeatedly and distinctly taught. By this seemingly anomalous passage our post-millenarian brethren insist that all other scriptures which expressly teach the nearness of the advent must be interpreted.

The simple explanation of the apparent anomaly is, that there are in the original two

ENTIRELY DIFFERENT EXPRESSIONS

that in our common English version are translated "at hand." The precise meaning of one of these expressions is, "is near." The precise meaning of the other is, "is present." Now the former is that which the apostles uniformly use when they are represented in our translation as teaching that the day of Christ is "at hand." The latter is that used by Paul in II. Thessalonians, where he is represented as teaching that the day of Christ is not "at hand." To the Romans (xiii. 12) Paul writes: "The day of the Lord is near" (*eeggiken*). To the Phillipians (iv. 4) he writes: "The Lord is near" (*eggus*). So Peter writes (I. iv. 7): "The end of all things is near" (*eggus*). So James (v. 8): "The coming of the Lord is near" (*eeg. ke*). In the second epistle to the Thessalonians (ii. 2) the language is: "Be not soon shaken in mind or troubled, as that the day of Christ is present (*enesteeken*). That this is its precise meaning is established beyond all controversy by its unquestionable meaning in other connexions in Paul's epistles, as in Rom. viii. 38, and I. Cor. iii. 22, where the participle of the same verb and tense (*enestoota*) is used to denote "things present" as contrasted with "things to come;" in I. Cor. vii. 26, "the present (*enestoosan*) distress;" in Gal. i. 4. "This pres- (*enestootos*) evil world;" Hebrew ix. 9. "The time then present (*enesteekota*). However, Paul's language in regard to the nearness of the advent, in different epistles, is to be interpreted, he is not chargeable with a contradiction in terms.

As to the meaning of the passage, Bishop Ellicot suggests—and not without reason—"Probably the form which

THE FALSE DOCTRINE

was beginning to take was that the day of the Lord had already set in, thus confusing the whole idea of a personal, visible advent, just as at a later period Hymeneus and Philetus confused the true doctrine of the resurrection, by affirming that it was already past." This interpretation is favored—if not indeed required—not only by the express language "The day of Christ is present," but also by the intimation that the Thessalonians were in danger of being "shaken in mind" and "troubled"—literally "frightened"—by the erronneous doctrine referred to. Christians in apostolic days were not so affected by the prospect of the nearness of Christ's coming. It was to them a "blessed hope," and they "looked for" it and "hasted unto" it with longing and expectation. In his first epistle to the Thessalonians, written probably within the previous year, Paul commended them in that they were "waiting for the Son of God from heaven." If, however, they were subsequently taught, as some interpreters of God's word at the present day teach, that by the *parousia* of our Lord they were not to understand a personal advent, but a spiritual coming, or a providential coming, and that this coming had already occurred, we can readily understand why Paul should beseech them to be "not shaken in mind," or "troubled" with doubts and fears as to the certainty of what he had previously taught them, both orally and in his first epistle, the literal

PERSONAL COMING

of the Lord. This interpretation is confirmed by the subsequent exhortation in the same chapter: "Brethren, stand fast, and hold the traditions which ye have been taught, whether by word or our epistle."

In the passage in question Paul undoubtedly teaches that the advent of the Lord was not immediately at hand. This, however, is not in conflict with anything he or the other apostles had elsewhere taught. He reminds them that when he was yet with them he had told them that before the day of Christ "there should first come a falling away"—an apostasy—that then "the man of sin" should be revealed, and that then the Lord would come to "consume him with the spirit of His mouth and destroy him with the brightness of His coming." An apostasy, and the revelation of the man of sin, before the advent is predicted, but the time within which these events would occur is left wholly uncertain. As if to guard them against assuming that for the occurrence of these events a long period must necessarily intervene before the advent, he tells them that "the mystery of iniquity doth already work;" that they knew "what withholdeth" the revelation of the man of sin; that as soon as this restraining power was "taken out of the way" that wicked one would be revealed; and that then the Lord would come for his destruction. Is there anything here inconsistent with what is repeatedly and

EXPLICITLY TAUGHT

elsewhere—the possible nearness of the advent? In his commentary on this passage, Meyer says: "It is incontestable, as the result of correct exegesis, that Paul not only considered Antichrist as directly preceding the advent, but also regarded the advent as so near, that he himself might then be alive." "The events which he predicted were for him so near, that he even thought that he himself would survive them.

As conclusive that Paul himself did not regard the events predicted as inconsistent with the possible nearness of the advent is the fact that the epistle to the Romans and that to the Philippians, in which he expressly declares "the day of the Lord is near," were written subsequently to this epistle to the Thessalonians.

Whatever questions may be raised as to the interpretation of this notable passage, on the main point at issue between premillenarians and postmillenarians its teaching, or rather what it does not teach, would seem to be indubitable and decisive. Paul is here foretelling what would occur between the time then present and the advent. He mentions an apostasy, he mentions the revelation of the man of sin, but he makes no mention or intimation of a millennial era of righteousness and peace on earth, such as the Old Testament prophets predict of the Messianic kingdom. Now is it credible that Paul would have omitted all allusion to the Messianic kingdom had he believed that it would

PRECEDE THE ADVENT.

2. That we have not misapprehended the teaching of the apostles is confirmed by the fact that the apostolic church believed that Christ might come before the generation then living had passed away, and accordingly "looked for" the glorious appearing with longing and expectation. Of the many eminent authorities for this assertion that might be referred to, we select the following:

In Lange's Commentary on I. Cor. i. 7, it is said, "The constant expectation of our Lord's second coming is one of the characteristic features of primitive Christianity; hence the clause has been taken as a simple paraphrase of the word, Christians."

On the same passage, Dr. Hodge says, "The second advent of Christ, so clearly predicted by Himself and His apostles, was the object of longing expectation to all the early Christians."

On the same passage, Mr. Barnes says, "The earnest expectation of the Lord Jesus became one of the marks of early Christian piety."

On the same passage, Bishop Ellicott says, "Waiting for the revelation"—that is the second visible appearance—"of our Lord Jesus Christ"—which the early church expected would soon occur."

In Conybeare and Howson's Life of St. Paul, it is said, "The early church, and even the apostles themselves, expected the Lord to come again in that very generation. St. Paul himself shared in that expectation."

In Professor Fisher's "Beginnings of Christianity," it is said, the expectation (of the personal coming of the Lord) is expressed by all the apostles in terms which fairly admit of no other interpretation. It is found in Paul, (Rom. xiii. 11-12; I. Cor. vii. 29-31, 10-11, Phil. iv. 5, I. Tim. vi. 14.) The same expectation is expressed in Heb. x. 25; Jas. v. 3-8, I. Peter iv. 7, II. Peter iii. 3, Jude v. 18, I. John ii. 18, The Apocalypse i. 1, iii. 2, xxii. 7, 20-22.) To put

ANY OTHER CONSTRUCTION

on these passages, as if the Parousia to which they refer were anything else than the second advent of the Lord to judgment, would introduce a dangerous license in interpretation, and one which might be employed to subvert the principal doctrines of the Christian system."

It is needless to extend these quotations. In regard to many important facts and doctrines of our holy religion, devout and intelligent students of God's word differ. As to the premillennial faith of the apostolic church there is, so far as we are aware, entire agreement. We cannot but regard this acknowledged fact as establishing beyond question our interpretation of the teaching of the apostles. If the matter were one of minor importance, or referred to but incidentally or obscurely, the belief of the church might not be regarded as authoritative and final as to the faith of their teachers. The second coming of the Lord, however, is a subject referred to by the apostles prominently and repeatedly; it is presented as a matter of the highest practical moment; it is referred to in terms which imply that it was a subject familiarly known and well understood. In regard to such a theme and so presented, is it not simply incredible that after all, not merely here and there an ignorant believer, but that the whole body of believers—the church in which dwells the spirit promised as a guide to truth—should have misapprehended the meaning of their inspired teachers? Is it not still more incredible that if by any possibility this were the case, they should have been commended by the apostles for their misapprehension?

That the apostolic church—including the apostles themselves—was premillenarian, we cannot but regard as established beyond the possibility of a reasonable doubt. If this be true, each one for himself can make the application.

SUNDAY DISCOURSES.

THE REV. DR. P. S. HENSON.

PRAYER.

At the First Baptist Church, the Rev. Dr. P. S. Henson preached in the morning, his subject being "Prayer." He took for his text:

What profit should we have if we pray unto Him.—*Job xxi*, 15.

The oldest book in the Bible is the one from which my text is taken. Two things this Scripture indubitably proves. One is that from the earliest ages man has felt impelled to pray; and the other is that, even when the world was young, and when men presumably were predisposed to religious superstition, there were not a few to be found who utterly disbelieved in the efficacy of prayer and scoffed at those who offered it as being absurd fanatics. "What is the Almighty that we should serve Him? And what profit should we have if we pray unto Him?" These are questions that are supposed to be the outcome of the "advanced thought" of this the foremost age of human history, and yet they were as scornfully propounded 3,000 years ago as they are to-day by scientific cavilers. They are questions, indeed, that ought to be asked and ought to be answered, if answer be possible, for they go down to the very roots of life and up to the very gates of heaven.

The question of prayer, with which, on this occasion, we are especially concerned, is the pivotal point of all religion. If that be a previous reality, then all else follows; but if prayer be only as empty form, "then is our preaching vain,

YOUR FAITH IS ALSO VAIN,"

the whole Bible is a tissue of lies, and we are left without God and without hope in the world. It is not without reason, therefore, that the earnest-minded Christian men who have associated themselves together in a Bible and Prophetic Conference, held last week in this city, should have emphasized this fundamental feature of the Christan system, and should have urged its presentation in a special discourse. I could very heartily wish that its preparation might have been entrusted to abler hands than mine.

Praying God that I may worthily deal with a theme which is alike most precious and most profound, I invite your attention to the nature, power, and privilege of prayer.

I. The Nature of Prayer—(1) It is not a matter of locality, for God is "within no walls confined." And He who in this, as also in all things else, is the only infallible teacher, said 1800 years ago to a woman of Samaria, under the shadow of Mount Gerizin, "Believe Me, the hour cometh, when ye shall neither in this mountain, nor yet at Jerusalem, worship the Father, but the true worshipers shall worship the Father in spirit and in truth." In magnificent cathedral, or in lowliest cottage home, in the midst of a vast worshipful multitude, or all alone in the darkness of the night or the solitude of the desert, it matters not where on earth the prayer be offered, only so it be devout.

(2) Nor is it a matter of bodily attitude. A man may stand

LIKE THE PENITENT PUBLICAN,

or kneel like the godly Daniel, or prostrate himself in the dust like the devout Isaiah—the Lord of Hosts cares not for the posture of the body so the spirit be sincere and the heart beat loyally. And yet it deserves to be said that the man who affects to pray, but who, out of pure indolence or sinful irreverance, declines to worship God with his body, by its decorous prostration at a throne of grace, deserves to be spurned by the Sovereign he has insulted.

(3) Nor is it merely a form of words. A great deal of the grandilaquence that in public assemblies purports to be addressed to God, but which in point of fact is ambitiously addressed to men, so far from deserving the name of prayer is a blasphemous pretence that God Almighty hates.

We believe in the use of words in prayer—they classify thought and intensify desire. We do not believe in those sublimated saints who have reached such an altitude that they no longer need to voice their minds, but deem it sufficient silently to exhale their sentimental piety. It will, we fear, be commonly found that the process of exhaling has gone so far as to leave their souls exceeding dry. Most wisely did the prophet Hosea write, "Take with you words and turn to the

Lord;" and when the Christ would teach His disciples to pray He did not exhort them to exhale their emotions silently, but gave them instead a form of words, the most simple and sublime that ever were breathed by human lips.

Prayer in its very essence is the devout

COMMUNION OF THE SOUL

with God. And to such communion faith is ever a prime condition, for "he that cometh unto God must believe that He is, and that he is a rewarder of them that diligently seek Him." To the man of the world such communion is incredible, if not utterly inconceivable, for "the natural man knoweth not the things of the spirit of God, neither can he know them because they are spiritually discerned."

And yet this communion is most real, and of all things most precious. I speak to a multitude of men and women who know God, who have walked with Him as did Enoch, and talked with Him as did Moses, face to face, as a man talks with his friend. This hidden communion of the soul with God—this is prayer. The soul may pour itself out in adoration, or in thanksgiving, or in confession, or in supplication—all these are prayer—and none of them are to be neglected. We cannot sufficiently adore God's infinite and excellent attributes. And no request for future blessings will ever be granted unless there be grateful appreciation of blessings already bestowed. "Let all your requests be made known by prayer and supplication, with thanksgiving unto God and the peace of God which passeth all understanding shall keep your hearts and minds through Jesus Christ."

And confession is made an absolute prerequisite to the forgiveness of sins, and accordingly we knew that "if we confess our sins, God is

FAITHFUL AND JUST TO FORGIVE

us our sins and to cleanse us from all unrighteousness." But it is not of prayer in these several forms that we propose, at present, to speak, but of prayer in the sense of supplication made to God for the bestowment upon us of such things as we need. Does such prayer profit? And is it possible for human lips and human hearts, by presenting their requests to God, to achieve results that shall affect the outer world, as well as the inner life, that shall bring bread as well as spiritual blessing, healing for the body no less than for the soul; and be practically potential in the determination of the destiny, both of individuals and nationalities? This is one of the burning questions of our time and upon its decision hang issues the most tremendous. And so we come to the consideration of

II. Prayer as a Power.—We do not propose, in this discourse, to deal at all with atheists and infidels. To them all forms of prayer are silly superstitions, only believed in by fanatics and fools. Our present argument is not for them, but for reverent believers in a personal God, and in the Bible He has given a revelation of His will. All such, of course, believe in prayer, but with very varying degrees of faith as to the sphere of its operation, and the measure of its power. And not a few are painfully perplexed by what appears to them to be a contradiction between the teachings of Scripture and the deductions of science. There ought not to be contradiction, for

THE BIBLE IS GOD'S WORD,

and the universe is God's work, and yet in the light of the latest research it does seem almost impossible to reconcile the promises of the one with the [illegible] of the other. And hence there are not a few earnest souls groping about in deepening darkness "feeling after God if haply they may find Him," and as to prayer especially are losing the grip of simple faith, and so, though they still retain the forms of prayer it has lost for them all conscious power. A graceful, appropriate, and æsthetically beautiful exercise it may be for a creature to present himself in worshipful attitude before the Great Creator. Its reflex influence upon the soul of the worshiper can not fail to be most helpful. It is a health lift that develops one's spiritual life. It is the tug of the soul at the invisible cable that links our lives to the other shore, and hence by the aid of it we draw ourselves nearer to our God and heaven. All this seems natural and explicable.

But to suppose that prayer can operate as a material force to alter physical results, to suppose that prayer can still a storm, can bring a rain, can heal disease, can win a battle; to suppose that by some subtle, spiritual telegraph by way of the throne of God in heaven we can touch the heart of Asia, or accomplish results

IN THE VALLEY OF THE CONGO;

All this we are assured is preposterous and impossible.

We may concede, indeed, that God may touch the hearts of men, and in the realm of spirit may be still allowed some sway, but from things material he is absolutely barred, for over them is the reign of law, stern, hard, inexorable law. Fire will burn, water will drown, poison will kill, beasts will devour, and we vainly make our tearful protests or lift our pleading hands in prayer. God made the world originally, impressed upon it immutable laws, and then launched it and left it, or else stands impassively by, watching the grinding of the mighty machine with

Rev. P. S. HENSON, D. D.,
PASTOR FIRST BAPTIST CHURCH, CHICAGO.

iron wheels and cruel cogs, glutted with gore and quivering flesh; but He may not touch the things that He has made, for they are under the dominion of irrevocable law—brainless, soulless, heartless law—and this is practically an orphan world, from which God is banished and the laws of nature have taken his place, like a herd of Molochs, "horned gods besmeared with blood," and at the sound of the cornet, harp, sackbut, dulcimer, and all kinds of instruments of music, as played upon by our modern philosophers, we must fall down and worship or else be consigned to a furnace of criticism hotter than that material fire that was kindled by a heathen king for three redoubtable Hebrew children that dared to carry their heads erect and

WORSHIP ONLY THE LIVING GOD.

What are these new found deities that have taken the places of their venerable ancestors in the Parthenon of modern science? I approach them, I examine them—I dare to, for they are dead. "They have mouths, but they speak not; eyes have they, but they see not; they have ears, but they hear not: noses have they, but they smell not; they have hands, but they handle not: feet have they, but they walk not; neither speak they through their throat." Who are they that they should take the place of God Almighty? What is a law of nature, anyhow? What on earth did it ever do? What is it but an order of sequence, an order of proceeding? And where there is an order of proceeding there there must be somebody to proceed. And whose footsteps are they that echo through the universe and go sounding down the ages but those of the High and Holy One that inhabiteth eternity? He is imminent in nature and "upholdeth all things by the word of His power," and "worketh all things after the counsels of His will."

Ordinarily He works in uniform ways, and beneficent and beautiful is this same uniformity, for in consequence of it, in consequence of the orderly succession of day and night, and of recurring seasons, and of all those processes through which nature passes, we are able to forecast the future, and

ADJUST OUR LIVES IN HARMONY

with our surroundings. But it does not follow that the God of nature is shut up to any slavish uniformity. Shall scientists wall in the material universe with their philosophy, and then post a placard on the wall, "No trespassing allowed," so as to warn off the Almighty Maker from teaching the things which His hands have made?

May He not, if He please, depart from His uniform method in nature, and by that very departure make manifest to doubting men the might of His arm, and the love of His heart?

While the electric current flows on with uninterrupted circuit, there is no manifestation of its presence and its power, but let there be a break in the circuit, and there is a gleam of the electric light, whose palpable reality no man can dispute. Even so, ever and anon, God makes a break in the ordinary course of providential administration, that men may know that there is a God, enthroned in heaven, but still ruling over all the earth.

Why should it be thought a thing incredible for God sometimes to interpose directly in answer to His people's prayers?

A man may interpose his own personality, to arrest the action of what we are pleased to call a law of nature. A little child is in the act of falling—it is my child. It is falling in accordance with the law of gravitation.

I EXTEND MY ARMS

to break its fall. Do I then unwarrantably break a law, because, forsooth, I break a fall by the interposition of my personality? May a man do that? And may not God, who is not only a divine person, but an infinitely loving and almighty Father? Must he alone be barred from the universe just because he made it? That were to show that in the universe, at least for the present, man is more of a god than is God himself. This is the very insanity of intellectuality—the very blasphemy of proud impiety.

That God did answer prayer in the earlier ages of human history—that by the power of prayer was "subdued kingdoms, wrought righteousness, stopped the mouth of lions, quenched the violence of fire, escaped the edge of the sword, waxed valiant in fight, turned to flight the armies of the aliens"—while thrones were overturned, and even the dead were raised up from their graves—is all so clearly written in the Book of God that to deny it is to renounce the book itself, with all its previous legacy of everlasting love.

And has God gone because philosophy has come? Do his footsteps ignominiously retreat with the dawning of the day? Then better give us back the night with its throbbing stars and the beaming of God's face through the darkness and the

WHISPERS OF GOD'S LOVE.

But God is not gone. He is still a very present help in trouble. His word is all ablaze with exceeding great and precious promises, and none shall find his promises fail. Such is the teaching of revelation, and the highest reason evermore comes back into accord with the Scriptural revelation. Ever and anon it looks, indeed, as if man's reason were swinging away to the farthest extremity of opposition to the word of God. But only wait—the foundation of God standeth sure—and we have only to appeal from Philip drunk to Philip sober—poor man, intoxicated with a little knowledge, to man grown clear and calm by wider knowledge and profounder thought. Well has the poet written:

"A little learning is a dangerous thing,
Drink deep or taste not the Pierian spring;
For shallow draughts intoxicate the brain,
While drinking deeper sobers us again."

The little child, standing beneath heaven's cope and looking up at its celestial splendors, with eyes dilated with large wonder cries:

"Twinkle, twinkle, little star,
How I wonder what you are
Up above the world so high,
Like a diamond in the sky."

By and by the child has grown to be a young collegian, full of undigested knowledge, and fuller still of insufferable conceit. He knows about the stars. He can confound you with his learned discourse about Galileo, and Kepler, and Granhaber, and the Spectrum.

HE KNOWS IT ALL.

He has plucked out the heart of the stellar mysteries. But by-and-by when he is older grown, and has become a philosopher worthy of the name, he comes back to the starting point of wonder, and awe, and reverence, and conscious ignorance; and again, as he stands beneath the open heavens, I hear him whispering as in childhood's unsophisticated hours,

"Twinkle, twinkle little star,
How I wonder what you are."

So we begin life with simple-hearted faith in prayer. In our childish ignorance we suppose that the thing to do is to go to God as to a loving and almighty Father, and that He will graciously hear us, and do for us precisely the things that we desire. Latter, when we have attained to a smattering of philosophy, and have obtained some glimpses of the laws of natures, we come to think that even God is held in leash and that prayer is a thing of no avail. But when we have really launched out into the depths, and have come to know how little we know, and to realize something of the infinite majesty of that awful presence which is in nature, and under nature, and over nature—even the presence of Him who is God over all blessed forevermore—then we return to childhood's simple and beautiful faith, and feel that the thing to do is to go to Him in humble prayer, and spread our wants before Him, and expect that he will do for us "exceeding abundantly," according to the greatness of

THE WORKS OF HIS GRACE.

In conclusion, I beg your attention to a few thoughts relating to III. *Prayer as a privilege.* We are tired of hearing the changes rung forever more on duty. Duty is all well enough in its way. It is a sort of fly-wheel, with a reservoir of power in it to carry us past the dead points when the stimulus of motion fails us; but for all that it is a cold, hard, joyless, loveless thing. There are things that only a stern sense of duty would ever prompt us to do. To reprove the faults of a friend is not a pleasant task, at least not for a noble and sensitive soul. To preach of hell is not a thing to take delight in, though there be some who preach as if it were. No true minister of Jesus Christ will ever preach it except from stern constraint of duty.

But there are some things in respect to which considerations of duty should never be needed to furnish a spur. And prayer has been belittled and degraded by dwelling upon it as a duty to be done instead of a privilege to be enjoyed.

I pity the man who simply prays because he must, scourged to his duty like a galley-slave, instead of flying joyfully to a throne of grace, as a weary wanderer to love's embrace. Oh, brethren, if our God be the King of kings and Lord of lords

THEN ACCESS TO HIS PRESENCE

and assurance of gracious audience is a privilege of supremest honor. If he be an infinitely tender-hearted Father their prayer is a privilege of sweetest joy. If he be an omnipotent ruler who can guide us in perplexity, who can give us light in darkness, comfort in tribulation, bread for our hunger, healing for our diseases, salvation for our souls, salvation for our friends, who can smooth all earth's rugged pathway for us, and prepare us for Him and give us an abundant entrance—then prayer is a privilege of grandest opportunity.

"Give me a place where to stand and a lever long enough and I will move the world," cried the great philosopher of Syracuse. We have the place where to stand—in the promises of God—and we have that mighty lever in the power of prayer. Let us in simple faith lay hold of the power, and we shall move the world with the might of God.

THE REV. JOHN F. KENDALL.

SANCTIFICATION.

At the First Congregational Church, the Rev. Dr. John F. Kendall, of Laporte, Ind., occupied Dr. Goodwin's pulpit in the morning, preaching on the subject of "Sanctification." He spoke as follows:

In our human relations conduct and character are the result of condition. The Prince of Wales is the prospective king, and the condition of kingship into which he was born regulates his conduct and molds his character. The resident of Zululand or of the Congo Free State will develop character quite in accordance with the condition which surrounds his birth; similar condition will result in similar conduct, and similar conduct will harden into similar character. Improve the condition into which one enters at birth and you secure at once improved character. Every ascending step in the one will be marked by corresponding ascent in the other.

The rule, like all, is not without exception. One in a thousand, a Socrates or a Keshub Chunder Sen, may have his eyes enlightened to see the deep degradation of national character and conduct, and may strike out a new and higher path for himself, or one born to higher purpose, may grovel a debase himself; but the rule will be.

Character Corresponds to Condition.—In like manner, all holy living and holy character flow from a sanctified condition. God first gives something and then he makes his demand. The law says, "do and live;" God says, "live and do." His order is, "I make you alive; now live and act accordingly." Whence these scriptural facts and demands: "Ye are dead," therefore be dead to sin and all this world, "mortify (make dead) your members, which are upon the earth" (Col. iii. 5). Ye are "buried with Him," therefore "crucify the flesh with the affections and lusts" (Gal. v. 24). Ye are "risen with Christ," therefore "seek those things which are above" (Col. iii. 1). Ye are seated with Him, in the heavenlies, therefore, "set your affection" on heavenly objects. Thus it will be found that every exhortation to personal holiness, in the Bible,

IS BASED UPON A SALVATION,

already possessed and enjoyed. The question of salvation is no longer open, but, as saved and "sanctified in Christ Jesus," the believer hears his Lord's demands for holy living. "I beseech you, therefore, brethren," "beloved of God, called saints," "by the mercies of God, that ye present your bodies, a living sacrifice, holy, acceptable unto God, which is your reasonable service" (Rom. xii. 1), the reasonable service of one who has been redeemed, and for whom, "walking not after the flesh, but after the spirit," "there is therefore now no condemnation" (Rom. viii. 8). Paul having assured the Ephesians that they had been chosen in Christ before a founding of a world, and that, in time, they had been quickened out of their death in sin, having taught them that they were already saved by grace, through faith, then demands of them that they "walk worthy of the vocation wherewith they were called" (Eph. iv. 1). "Now are ye light in the Lord: walk as children of light" (Eph. v. 8).

In a word, ye are "sanctified in Christ Jesus," therefore be sanctified in your character and conduct. See that character corresponds to the condition into which grace has brought you. God makes no demand till He first gives something, on the basis of which His demand may have easy compliance. How can a depraved, sin-loving man obey the demand of the Lord, "Be ye holy;" how can a sinner exhibit saintly living? He can not till a change is wrought in his nature which only God can work. That change God accomplishes; He makes the sinner a saint, and then calls him to saintly living.

It will be the purpose of this study to show that the teaching of the Scripture plainly is that there is first, a

SANCTIFIED CONDITION,

into which the believer is introduced, solely by the grace of God, and there is then a holy life, flowing from and consequent upon that; and these may not be confounded, but especially may their order not be reversed without serious spiritual harm. The reversal of order lands one at once in the bonds of legalism, and he seeks to assure himself of his sanctified condition by means of his holy acts. On the contrary, it is a fact that no attainment in holy living can add one iota to that sanctification, which is the immediate and exclusive gift of the grace of God.

We will seek first the Scripture meaning of our term.

Sanctification.—The one root-word from which spring all the words which are translated "hallowed," "sanctify," "holiness," "sanctification," is the word, adopted from the profane Greek *hagios*. The nearest thought to "holiness," of which the profane Greek was capable, was "the sublime," "the consecrated," "the venerable." The moral element was utterly wanting, to his thought. In adopting this word, therefore, for use in the Scripture, it had to be "filled and coined afresh with a new meaning."

Using the term "holy," in its highest sense, as applied to God, Professor Cremer, of Greifswald (Theo. Lexicon, p. 39), defines it as "what deserves and claims moral and religious reverence." The same authority defines holiness as "that element in the divine nature which lies at the basis of, determines, and molds the reverence which is due from man toward God" (p. 35). There is that in God which makes it fitting, and demands that men approaching shall, with bared, bowed heads, exclaim, "holy and reverent is His name" (Ps. iii. 9). The distance between this thought and "the sublime"

OF THE PROFANE GREEK

is measureless. The point of departure from his low idea to the supernal conception of the Scripture, is that definition, in classic Greek, which makes our word mean "devoted to the gods." Anything devoted to the gods—an animal for sacrifice, a house for worship, a vessel for sacred use, a garment for priestly wear, a man for service—becomes, by such destination, holy. It is at once perceived that, in this early meaning, the thought of personal character, has not found place. A person or thing was denominated "holy" by reason of being separated from secular uses, and devoted or set apart to sacred purposes or to the service of God. While this is the lowest thought concerning holiness it gives occasion for the use of such terms as "holy city," "holy place," "holy Jerusalem," "holy garments," "holy vessels," and others. All these are termed holy, not from any intrinsic character of their own, but because they stand in certain relations to God and His person, His character or His service, and each, "in their degree, participate in the divine holiness and embody and manifest it" (Theo. Lexicon, p. 42). This is very important and helps us to understand the force of such scriptures as this: "Jehovah shall establish thee an holy people to Himself * * * and all the people of the earth shall see that the name of Jehovah is named upon thee" (Deut. xxviii., 9-10); and this: "Holy men of God spake, as they were moved by the Holy Ghost" (II. Pet. i., 21). In their personal characters Moses, David, Solomon, even Jeremiah, exhibited traits and tempers which would detract much from the ascription to them of holy lives; but in their relations to God, which was the only light in which He could view them, they were "partakers of the Divine nature" (II. Pet. i., 14), "partakers of Christ" (Heb. iii. 14), and were "complete in Him," holy. In all instances sanctification implies this setting apart for God and separation from the world, both in their own intent and in the calling of God. Thus the Lord said unto Moses: "Sanctify unto me all the first-born;" "thou shalt set apart unto the Lord all that openeth the matrix" (Ex. xiii. 2, 12); "I hallowed unto me all the first-born in Israel, both man and beast" (Num. iii. 13).

AS SEPARATED, DEVOTED ONES

these were "saints," and they were called to a saintship which was not yet theirs. We may not and we do not identify the setting apart and the saintly living. We only assert that God calls that holy or sanctified which is set apart for himself, and that then he demands a holiness which "is the perfect purity of God," a holiness which only himself can impart. "It makes no difference whether it be the children of Israel, the Sabbath, the temple, the priesthood that are called holy; in every relation of communion based upon election the object of the election participates, according to its degree in the holiness."

From the thought of being set apart or devoted to God the passage is thus easy to the higher idea of personal, holy character. This is the thought whenever we speak of the Holy Spirit, the holy angels, the holy God. And holiness, is only and always, "likeness to God, to Him who is the holy one of Israel, to him whom they laud in Heaven, as holy, holy, holy * * * so that we are dead to sin but alive to God, alive to righteousness, having died and risen in Him, whose blood has made us what we are, saints, holy ones." The final demand of the sanctified condition is a holiness, nothing inferior to the holiness of God.

Two texts of scripture will now show us, that, according to the divine plan, all believers have been thus set apart for a holy purpose, to holy ends. "According as He hath chosen us in Him, before the foundation of the world, that we should be holy and without blame, before Him in love" (Eph. 1-4), and "elect, according to the foreknowledge of God, the Father, in sanctification of the spirit" (1 Peter, 1-2).

Having thus discovered the first thought in holiness, the holy destination, and the final thought, the holy life, we proceed now to show that

WE HAVE A SANCTIFICATION

directly from God, and being from Him, it must be complete and perfect from the start. And this is something entirely apart from personal holiness of life. The evidence of its completeness is found in the fact that it is spoken of in the present and past tenses, but never in the future. Look at such texts as these: "Unto the church of God, which is at Corinth, to them that are sanctified in Christ Jesus, called saints" (I. Cor. i. 2). Speaking of thieves, covetous, drunkards, revilers, Paul says: "And such were some of you, but ye are washed, but ye are sanctified, but, ye are justified, in the name of the Lord Jesus and by the spirit of our God" I. Cor. vi. 11). And the revision puts these all in the past tense, "but ye were washed, ye were sanctified," etc. Now, to say, as some do, that "this denotes the progressive and advancing process of purifying which succeeds regeneration," is to violate the plainest and simplest principles of grammatical construction. It is to say that the Apostle Paul and the Holy Spirit did not know what they wanted to say, or to affirm that they made egregious blunder, in saying it. The washing, the sanctification, the justification are alike complete, all "in the name of the Lord Jesus and by the spirit of our God." In God's view, that is to say, we are already sanctified, for in this, he verily "seeth not as man seeth."

Consider again, the words of Paul: "Lo, I come," said Christ, "to do Thy will, O, God;" and the and the apostle immediately adds, "in which will we are sanctified (R. V. have been sanctified) through the offering of the body of Jesus Christ once for all." "For by one offering He hath perfected forever them that are sanctified" (Heb. x. 9, 10, 14). On the first of these passages, Winer, (N. T. Gram, p. 387) who certainly can not be actuated

BY ANY THEOLOGICAL BIAS,

says: "It is founded in the will of God that we are sanctified through Christ's sacrificial death." And it is plainly a work already completed, wholly apart from human striving. "We are sanctified through the offering of the body of Jesus Christ." His offering is divinely and eternally perfect, nothing can ever be added to it; on the basis of that, a sanctification has been wrought, and it must be finished, and complete."

Other passages have a similar import. "Both He that sanctifieth, and they who are sanctified are all of one." (Heb ii. 11). Christ Jesus, "of God, is made unto us, wisdom, and righteousness, and sanctification, and redemption" (I. Cor. i. 30). Who shall assume, or dare to say, that the Divine One "is made" to us, matchless, wisdom, perfect righteousness, complete redemption; but before we possess full sanctification, we must add, to what our Lord has wrought, and "is made," some pitiable and worthless human efforts and strivings? No, all our completeness is "in Him." And all that we have in Him, must be complete. It is of this spiritual nature, that the Apostle assures us, "whosoever is born of God, doth not commit sin * * * and he can not sin, because he is born of God" (I John, 3. 9). In other words, "that which is born of the spirit is spirit," it partakes of the nature of its origin. The sanctified one, is a participator, by reason of his heavenly birth, in God's holiness; abiding in Him, in whom is no sin, he sinneth not. The believer has been received into fellowship, with the redeeming God, that is, the God who has chosen him "to salvation through sanctification of the spirit. (II Thess. 2. 13). The work of His sanctification is accomplished in Christ, apart from creature striving, by the blood of Christ.

AND IT SHOULD BE NOTED

that the passages which have been cited teach that the sanctification has already taken place, though the self-sanctification and offering of Christ, who says: "For their sakes, I sanctify myself, that they also might be sanctified through the truth" (John xvii. 19).

It has been said, in a word, in passing, that this sanctification is wholly apart from personal holiness of life. In proof, consider the Corinthian believers. They are not sanctified because of personal attainment. They have not been battling with sin till they have overcome and are now personally holy. For, but a few sentences after Paul had called them "sanctified in Christ Jesus," he says, "I hear that there are contentions among you" (I. Cor. i., 11), and his letter is largely filled with stern rebuke for great defects in individual character and Christian living.

It deserves our notice also that this blessing of santification was not for the few, but for the many. Christ suffered "that he might sanctify the people" (Heb. xiii., 12), not a few of them, not those of eminent attainments, but "the people." And Paul says of all the Hebrew Christians. "We have been sanctified" (Heb. x., 10). And to the Corinthians he writes "unto the church of God, which is at Corinth, to them that are sanctified" (I. Cor. i., 2). The sanctification of which we speak is thus the common lot of the "called saints."

Puzzling questions may perplex many minds when we begin to inquire, "how can these things be?" How can those be said to be sanctified who are so manifestly imperfect? A sufficient answer would be that

THE PUZZLE IS NOT OURS,

but God's, who settles all with the affirmation, "My thoughts are higher than your thoughts" (Isa. lv. 9.) It is all a part of God's eternal plan, and in the line of His eternal purposes, and we may speak of God's purposes as of no other. It is no violence to language or to truth to say that all God's purposes are accomplished purposes, not because we actually see their accomplishment, but because, "declaring the end from the beginning, and from ancient times, the things that are not yet done, saying, my counsel shall stand, and I will do all my pleasure" (Isa. xlvi. 10), He thus does. Whatsoever He purposes He will bring about, because able to bring it about. He sees the end from the beginning. There can be no thwarting, in the end, of His purpose formed in the beginning. We have been seeing God's accomplished purpose toward us; we shall presently see how His purpose is accomplished in us. To Him our sanctification is already accomplished by the blood of Christ. And He reckons according to facts as they will finally appear, while we judge according to facts, as they appear to-day. "We can not count a man worthy or meet for a place till we know that he is meet for it. But when God calls a man to any position He accounts him meet for it beforehand, be cause He can make him so." Says Paul: "I thank Jesus Christ, our Lord, who hath enabled me, for that He counted me faithful, putting me into the ministry." (1 Tim. i. 12.) Saul of Tarsus was thoroughly bad, but beforehand God reckoned him faithful, and then he

MADE HIS RECKONING GOOD.

Precisely so on the point before us. "God hath not called us unto uncleanness, but unto holiness." (1 Thess. iv. 7.) "Be ye holy, for I am holy." (1 Pet. i. 16.) And He begins with calling us holy "saints," "sanctified in Christ Jesus;" and as He now reckons us, so will He finally make us. From the moment they believe, all believers "being viewed by God according to the value of Christ's sacrifice, and according to what they are in Him, are 'called saints,' 'sanctified in Christ Jesus,' and are 'clean every whit.'" Thus it appears that, as children of God, we have from Him a sanctification which is complete from the start.

We now approach that portion of our subject which is of most eminent importance for its practical bearings. It may be expressed in these terms: The sanctified condition demands holiness of life and leads to it. The sanctification, of which we have spoken, does not convey moral qualities, but it does imperiously demand them. The one, who is already, "in the will of God," "sanctified in Christ Jesus," may be very far wanting in practical holiness of life, as is clearly manifest in the Corinthian believers, but he may not be content to remain so. The Antinomian would pervert our doctrine, and would say, "I have Christ, I am sanctified, I may live as I will." But the Christian apostle replies, "As ye have, therefore, received Christ Jesus the Lord, so walk ye in Him, rooted and built up, in Him" (Col. ii. 6-7).

THE DOCTRINE YOU PREACH

leads to carelessness in life, one says. But we reply: Before all others, "he that saith," with unqualified and unwavering assurance, "he abideth in Him, ought himself also so to walk, even as He walked (I. John, ii. 6), who has left us "an example that we should follow His steps." (I. Peter ii. 21). If there is a man on the face of the earth who ought, by every motive, whether of common gratitude or of the fitness of things, that he may seem not unworthy his "high calling" to live a holy life, it is he who most fully realizes that he belongs to the number of those whom Jesus designates as "sanctified by faith that is in me." (Acts xxvi. 13). And the apostle who teaches most clearly our sanctified condition is the one who most insists on the holy life. Look for a moment at the letter to the Ephesians. In the first half Paul sets forth with wonderful force and clearness the believer's standing. He is "blessed with all spiritual blessings * * * in Christ." God's eternal purpose of love chose us in Christ before the foundation of the world. His final thought for us was "that we should be holy and without blame before Him in love." Our adoption, forgiveness, redemption, present salvation by grace, and many other blessings, are already the possession of the "sanctified in Christ Jesus."

Then, having assured the believer of his place and standing in the love of God, he devotes the last half of the epistle to the most earnest and importunate exhortation in reference to the believer's life. "I, therefore," he says, "the prisoner of the Lord, beseech you that ye walk worthy of the vocation, wherewith ye are called." (Eph. iv. 1). Ye are chosen, ye are called "to be holy, and without blame before Him," who chose and called you; now live up to that. Five times, in two chapters the apostle exhorts the Ephesians, to consider their "walk." They are to

"WALK WORTHY OF THE VOCATION,"

to "walk in love," to "walk circumspectly," to "walk as children of light," to "walk, not as other gentiles walk." Being all that God has made them, there must now follow warfare to the end, and to the death, against Satan and all his hosts. The doctrine does not lead to carelessness of life, either in the divine thought, or in any valid Christian experience. God's own holiness is the basis of the demand, for his people's holiness. "Be ye holy, for I am holy." And what is more, his holiness brings about their holiness. "I am Jehovah that doth sanctify you." Ex. xxxi. 13). By reason of the fact, that believers "are born of God," and are "partakers of the divine nature," "God's holiness leads on to the sanctifying of his people." Hence such scriptures as these. "I will be sanctified in you. Ye shall know that I am Jehovah when I have wrought with you, for my name's sake." (Ezek. xxi. 41-44). "The heathen shall know that I am Jehoviah, saith the Lord God, when I shall be sanctified in you, before their eyes. For I will take you * * * and will gather you out of all countries. * * * Then will I sprinkle clean water upon you, and ye shall be clean: from all your filthiness, and from all your idols, will I cleanse you. * * * I will also save you from all your uncleannesses * * * and ye shall loath yourselves in your own sight, for your iniquities and for your abominations" (Ezek. xxxvi. 23-33). These scriptures, with many others which might be quoted, show that God, having brought his people first into a sanctified condition, then proceeds, by means within his own power, by judgment, cleansing, by teaching and by His spirit, to make them

WHAT HE CALLS THEM, "HOLY."

This teaching does not lead to carelessness of life. In the beginning of the twenty-seventh chapter of Isaiah we find account of God's care for his people and his defence against their enemies. In the fifth verse we read: "Let him (i. e., the enemy) take hold of my strength, that he may make peace with me, and he shall make peace with me." An English clergyman relates the following incident illustrative of the thought of this text: "One of my little children," he says, "had committed a fault, for which I thought it my duty to chastise him. I called him to me, explained to him the evil of what he had done, and told him how grieved I was that I must punish him for it. He heard me in silence and then rushed into my arms and burst into tears. I could sooner have cut off my right arm than have struck him for his fault. He had taken hold of my strength and he had made peace with me." The grief of the father that he must punish was to the child the token of the grace which reigned

IN THE FATHER'S HEART.

The sight of that grace overcame the child's rebellion, and he cast himself helplessly upon the father's grace and was saved.

What effect had the father's forgiveness upon the future conduct of the child? It could have but one—to make him more obedient and faithful. The grace of the father wrought righteousness in the child.

Let us now notice that this is the constant requirement of the word, both in the old testament and in the new. To the priests, specially set apart, and consecrated to his service, the command comes: "Let the priests also, which come near to the Lord, sanctify themselves, lest the Lord break forth upon them." (Ex. 19-22). The days of King Hezekiah were a time of deep degradation and sin in Israel. The king summoned the people to keep the passover, "and the priests and the Levites were ashamed, and sanctified themselves" (2 Chron. xxx. 15). The voice of Hezekiah, calling to the passover, was to them the voice of God, proclaiming, "Be ye clean that bear the vessels of the Lord" (Isa. lii. 11). As soon as they became conscious of the sanctified condition into which grace had called them, they heard, clearly, the call to holiness of life. Precisely such was Hezekiah's requirement. For, having assembled the priests and Levites, he said unto them, "Hear me, ye Levites; sanctify now yourselves, and sanctify the house of the Lord God of your fathers, and carry forth the filthiness out of the holy place" (2 Chron. xxix. 5).

YE ARE HOLY, THEREFORE BE HOLY.

With equally explicit and emphatic demand does the Lord call upon all His people, "I am the Lord your God; ye shall therefore sanctify yourselves, and ye shall be holy, for I am holy. * * * I am the Lord that bringeth you up out of the land of Egypt to be your God; ye shall therefore be holy, for I am holy" (Lev. xi. 44-45). The very purpose for which he had redeemed them out of Egypt was that they might be separated from other people and be holy unto Himself.

How easy, now, the transition to the requirements of the New Testament. "I beseech you, therefore, brethren, by the mercies of God, that you present your bodies a living sacrifice, holy, acceptable to God, which is your reasonable service" (Rom. xii., 1). And another apostle: "As He which hath called you is holy, so be ye holy in all manner of conversation, because it is written, Be ye holy, for I am holy" (1 Pet. i., 15-16). Who will say, in the face of these Scriptures, "I am saved, therefore may I live as I list?" Listen: "He hath chosen us in Him, before the foundation of the world, that we should be holy and without blame before Him in love" (Eph. i., 4). Believers are not originally distinguished from other men by any merits or excellencies, but it is the will of God that they should become distinguished from all. "This is the will of God, even your sanctification, that ye should abstain from fornication, that every one should know how to possess his vessel in sanctification and honor. * * * For God hath not called us unto uncleanness, but unto holiness" (I Thess. iv., 3-4-7.) "I may live as I list;" the thought

SHOWS UTTER PERVERSITY

of wickedness, and ignorance of the power and demand of grace. We are called unto holiness. "Follow * * * holiness, without which no man shall see the Lord" (Heb. vii. 14). We are to "be like Him," when "we shall see Him as He is;" and how will that agree with living as a sinful man may list? God's word requires be ye "holy in all manner of living." The end of all things approaching, "what manner of persons ought ye to be in all holy living and godliness?" (2 Pet. iii. 11.) This, and this only, is the high demand of a sanctified condition, viz., a holy life, practical holiness, proceeding from a holy state. "Know ye not that your body is the temple of the Holy Ghost, which is in you, which ye have of God, and ye are not your own? For ye are bought with a price; therefore glorify God in your body" (1 Cor. vi. 19, 20). What right has the redeemed man to use his redeemed powers in any other way than as his Redeemer shall list? Or "who can live, in the calm sense of oneness with Jesus, and not war against sin? Who can delight in His love and not obey?" Who can go from day to day saying "I belong to the sanctified in Christ Jesus," and not then add, "So must I walk, even as He walked?" This is the divine order, and the divine requirement. God puts our hearts at rest from anxiety that our hands may be free for His service. Man says:

"Do holy things, that you may be sanctified." God says, "Ye are sanctified, now do holy things." Saints should strive for saintliness. A holy life is therefore to be looked for as the legitimate fruit of a sanctified condition. And

SUCH HOLY LIFE SHOULD BE

the object of constant, earnest striving on the part of every believer. Sanctified already "in the name of the Lord Jesus, and by the spirit of our God" (1. Cor. vi. 11), there is certainly no room for any contribution of creature performance, so far as our standing in God's sight is concerned. But while thus "perfected forever" in the estimation of Him who sees us only in the face of Jesus Christ, our ever serious question should be am I "meet for the Master's use" (II. Tim. ii. 21) as priest, vessel, house, implement was required to be kept clean for holy service? Whence such exhortations as these: "Having, therefore, these promises, dearly beloved"—the promises to "saints," to those who have an assured dwelling on high—"let us cleanse ourselves from all filthiness of the flesh and spirit, perfecting holiness in the fear of God." (2 Cor. vii. 1). The "saints," the "sanctified in Christ Jesus," have not, in their practical experience, attained to perfect holiness, and they need, like the apostle, who exhorts them, to "follow after that they may apprehend that for which also they are apprehended of Christ Jesus." There is ever a higher mark in attainment. The end of striving will never be obtained, the need of striving will never cease, until there is in all our lives a practical compliance with the requirement, "be ye holy." What are the means of

THIS PRACTICAL SANCTIFICATION?

We shall find them, appointed in the word, even as our sanctification in Jesus is there declared. Says the Apostle Peter, "Ye have purified your souls in obeying the truth." (1 Pet. i. 22). "What is truth?" "Thy word is truth." Thus shall we be driven continually to the word of the Lord, with absolutely obedient heart, which ever says: "Speak, Lord, for thy servant heareth" (1 Sam. iii. 9). In obeying the truth a practical work shall go on in our own souls, with which our Lord shall be well pleased, as He holds therein the accomplishment of His own will, even our sanctification. This obedience will find its expression in every day and every act of our earthly life. The word will enlighten our understanding, it will foster the growth of heavenly affections, it will prepare us unto every good work, and cause us to abound therein. The word of the apostle will have heed: "Dearly beloved, I beseech you * * * abstain from fleshly lusts, which war against the soul, having your behavior seemly among the gentiles" (1 Pet. ii. 11-12). "Hating even the garments spotted with the flesh" (Jude xxiii.). And the word of another apostle: "Casting down imaginations, and every high thing that exalteth itself against the knowledge of God, and bringing into captivity every thought to the obedience of Christ" (2 Cor. x. 5). How many unhallowed imaginations in hearts where flesh lusteth against spirit, how many thoughts,

UNWORTHY THE CHRISTIAN NAME

and profession, and especially, how many that are not harmonious with a state of advancing holiness. By the grace of God, we would lay restraining hand on every lewd or unhallowed imagination; we would capture every unholy thought and bind it fast within the restraints of holy living; we would struggle ever upward towards that state in which spirit, soul and body shall be first blameless and then faultless before the Lord. For this we may walk in no energy of the flesh, but in the energy of the thrice Holy One. Just in proportion as we do that shall we lead holy lives, and walk as He walked. Thus the word becomes the efficient means of personal holiness. "Sanctify them through thy truth; thy word is truth." (John xvii., 17.)

And equally prayer will aid in this attainment. "If ye abide in Me, and My words abide in you, ye shall ask what ye will, and it shall be done unto you." (John xv., 7.) "If ye shall ask anything in My name, I will do it." (John xiv., 14.) Thus, when the prayer of Jesus "sanctify them, through thy truth," becomes the believer's own, and he prays "sanctify me through Thy truth," that prayer, offered sincerely and in faith, is in process of swift answer.

Another topic, not less important than the others, remains to be considered, and it concerns the measure of practical holiness after which we are required to strive.

HOW HOLY OUGHT WE TO BE?

What attainments should be ours? There have been theories, concerning spiritual attainment in our time, which, while the end was altogether worthy, have been lamentable failures. When any would bring holiness down from what holiness is, and, reaching some point, should then say, "I am holy," that is no scriptural sanctification. Sanctification does not consist in lowering the demand. This the late President Finney did, in these words: "The law does not require that we should love God as we might do, had we always improved our time, or had we never sinned. It does not suppose that our powers are in a perfect state. The service required is regulated by our ability." Similarly, President Mahan lowers the demand in saying: "Perfection does not imply that we love God as the saints do in heaven, but merely that we love Him, as far as practicable, with our present powers." Even Mr. Wesley says: "Mistakes and infirmities are not sins. These are, indeed, deviations from the perfect law, and consequently need atonement. Yet they are not properly sins. A person filled with the love of God is still liable to these involuntary transgressions. Such transgressions you may call sins, if you please, I do not." Up to such a standard it may be easy for some to come. But how does such attainment agree with the divine word, "Whatever is not of faith is sin" (Rom. xiv. 23); and with this: "The very God of peace sanctify you wholly; and I pray God your whole spirit and soul and body be preserved blameless unto the coming of our Lord Jesus Christ" (1 Thess. v. 23). Sanctification does not consist

IN DENYING OUR FAILURES.

We are no nearer to practical holiness by seeking after something which is not holiness.

Some who long for holiness say plainly they do not expect or strive for Adamic or angelic perfection, but for something less than these, and so say we, not for either of these do we strive, for these are not the scriptural standard; for the Scripture nowhere says, "Be ye holy as Adam," "or be ye holy as Gabriel," but distinctly and emphatically, "be ye therefore perfect, even as your Father which is in heaven is perfect." The standard of holiness to which God calls us is none other than the holiness of God. Nothing below that can satisfy him. Nothing below that can satisfy anyone who has a true apprehension of the demand of the sanctified condition. We want that high attainment which is according to the Divine mind, and not some inferior attainment, which lets us keep our mistakes and infirmities and involuntary transgressions. We must see all these swept away before we dare to call ourselves holy with the "holiness of the thrice Holy One."

But this is

IMPOSSIBLE OF ATTAINMENT.

No, rather, not yet attained; in the holiest life, as yet, far short of attainment. But because an end is not yet attained there is no necessary inference that it cannot be attained. There is the constant demand for high endeavor. The goal of to-day is no place at which we may sit down and congratulate ourselves on our success; it is only the starting point of to-morrow. "Behold what manner of love the Father hath bestowed upon us, that we should be called the sons of God; and we are" (I. John iii. 1), and "He that spared not His own son, but delivered him up for us all, how shall He not, with Him, also, freely give us all things?" (Rom. viii. 12). He will give us all. "Beloved, now are we the sons of God, and it doth not yet appear what we shall be, but we know"—blessed knowledge founded on the unfailing word of God—"we know that when He shall appear, we shall be like Him, for we shall see Him as He is. And every man that hath this hope in Him purifieth himself, even as He is pure" (I. John iii. 2-3). No other apprehension of the demand is correct save that of the Psalmist: "As for me, I will behold Thy face in righteousness; I shall be satisfied when I awake with Thy likeness" (Ps. xvii. 15). Hence, though continually obliged to confess failure, we are not thereby discouraged, for "the battle is

NOT OURS BUT GOD'S"

(2 Chr. xx. 15), and we are "confident of this very thing, that He which hath begun a good work in us, will perform it, until the day of Jesus Christ" (Phil. i. 16). "This is the will of God, even your sanctification," perfect and complete; and "n ught can withstand His will." The standard, which is placed before us, is that of absolute perfection. We will not lower the standard, and we will not deny our failures. These might well discourage us, if it were not for the calling, "unto holiness," the "high calling of God in Christ Jesus." But with this, and with the assurance of needed help, we

must surely "follow after, if that we may apprehend that for which also, we are apprehended of Christ Jesus." And we will ever "press toward the mark" (Phil. iii. 12-14). The sanctified condition, into which grace has introduced us, requires nothing less than absolute holiness of life. As yet, we attain it not; but, in spite of frequent failure, we are not "utterly cast down."

W. E. BLACKSTONE.

MISSIONS.

The Prophetic Conference resolved itself into a general mission meeting at 3 o'clock Sunday at Farwell Hall. A large audience listened to the following address by W. E. Blackstone, of Oak Park:

"Lift up your eyes and look on the fields."—John iv. 35.

Jesus sat by the well. To the east was the little plain of the cornfields. To the west was the multitude, coming forth from the Samaritan city, filled with desire to see the Man of whom the woman had said, "Is not this the Christ?"

To his wondering disciples Jesus said: "Lift up your eyes and look on the fields." It was not the cornfield, from which no harvest would be reaped for four months, but on this company of human beings, with many repentant hearts, that the Lord asked his disciples to look. To these same disciples he also said, "the field is the world." With these two texts before us let our thoughts reach out beyond our immediate surroundings, beyond our State, beyond our Nation, and get one wide sweep of the whole world, with all the teeming millions; and as we bring it up to our minds may the Holy Spirit bring it into our hearts. Let us consider first the

NUMBERS OF MANKIND,

and to aid us in this, this chart has been prepared. See chart on page 204. There are 1,434 squares, each representing 1,000,000 souls, divided as shown according to the prevailing religions: Christian—Protestants, 136; Greek and Oriental, 85; Roman Catholic, 195; total Christians, 416; Jews, 8; Mohammedans, 175; Heathen, 835; total, 1,434.

It is difficult to comprehend such numbers. Into one square we could put Chicago and its suburbs, and have a quarter of it left. New York and its suburbs would go into two squares. From the bottom we could cut off sixty squares, and hardly miss the entire population of

THE UNITED STATES.

An audience of 500 people, if proportionately represented on the chart, would not cover one-sixteenth of the intersection of the white lines, and 10,000 people could, on the same scale, stand in the eye of a fine cambric needle. Now, if this chart was enlarged to three feet by four feet, it would represent the entire number of human beings from the days of Adam to the end of 6,000 years; possibly 180,000,000,000. How insignificant the individual appears in the presence of such multitudes, and how little a part we form of the vast congregation of humanity who are even now traveling with us toward the grave and the judgment? But while the multitudes of earth are almost incomprehensibly great in our sight, they are very small in the sight of the Creator. Behold the nations are as a drop of a bucket, and are counted as the small dust of the balance" (Isa. xl. 15). Possibly we may get some conception of this if we consider how small a space the

RACE WOULD OCCUPY

if all were gathered together. Very few have any proper idea of the area they would require to stand or sit upon. Indeed it has been argued against the literal resurrection, that if all were raised from the dead they would cover the entire earth, and some have even said, "yes, three deep." But this is like many of the foolish assertions against the truth of God's word, all of which vanish into oblivion when candidly considered. The fact is, all the race now living could stand or sit upon 206¼ square miles, or less than six ordinary townships. "I don't believe it," says one. Well, let us compute it. The figures will not lie. An average sitting is 18 by 30 inches, or 540 inches, nearly four square feet. The latest estimated population of the world is 1,437,000,000. This multiplied by four equals 5,748,000,000 square feet. Divide by 27,878,400 square feet in a square mile, the result is 206¼ square miles, a surface 10 by 21 miles, or a circle 16¼ miles in diameter. The little Isle of Man would accommodate them all and have room to spare. They could all stand in the city of Philadelphia. How easily they can all be gathered before the Son of man, where He sits in the throne of His glory, (Mat. xxv. 31-32). From Mount Tabor He could

VIEW THEM ALL

in the little plain of Esdraelon and surrounding hillsides, or they could be easily marshalled on the plain of Sharon. Again all the population of the earth for 6,000 years from Adam could stand on the Island of Tasmania, and have room to spare. "Prove that," says one, "I can't believe it." Well, suppose we average each generation at forty years; this gives 150 generations in 6,000 years. Suppose each generation to have 1,200,000,000 souls. This is doubtless far too large on estimate, as the race began with two in Adam's generation, and there were only eight in Noah's time, but we want to make the estimate very liberal. Multiply 1,200,000,000 by 150; the result is 180,000,000,000; four square feet to each equal 720,000,000,000 square feet; divide by 27,878,400 square feet in a square mile, and we have 25,826 square miles. Tasmania has 26,215 square miles, and Hayti 28,000. So we see either isle would have room to spare. Oh, skeptic! remember that God will sometime gather all the dead (who have not had part in the first resurrection) before the great white throne. What a mighty gathering that will be, and yet the human eye, looking from one of the foothills of the Rockies, could measure the whole multitude on Colorado's plains. God grant that when we see them there may be

NO BLOOD REQUIRED

at our hands (Ezek. iii. 18). This mass of humanity is distributed upon the earth according to the prevailing religions, as shown by the map.

(An immense map of the world, in two hemispheres, expressly prepared in colors to show the religions, having the mission stations in gilt, so as to be easily distinguished by a large audience, was used for this purpose.) The pagans and heathen, in black, are seen to be in Africa, India, China, Japan, Australia, some islands, and a mixture of natives in America and Siberia. The Mohammedans, in green, are principally in India, Persia, Turkey, Arabia, North Africa, and some islands. The Jews are sown like seed through a sieve, among all nations (Amos ix. 9). The Catholics, in scarlet, are in Europe, Mexico, and South America, and scattered in many nations. The Greek and Oriental Christians, shown in brown, in Russia, Siberia, Turkey, and Abyssinia. The Protestants, in yellow, are found in Great Britain, part of Europe, United States, Australia, Madagascar, and many islands.

It was into these masses that the Lord Jesus gave command to His disciples, Go ye and preach the gospel. It was His last command, and

SHOULD BE TREASURED

as dearly as the last words of our departing friends, and obeyed in sincere reverence to our ascended Lord and Savior. The early disciples did obey, and went everywhere preaching the word.

But, at the conversion of Constantine the church was deluded into the error that the kingdom had come on the earth, and a long era of dark ages followed.

The true missionary spirit began to dawn again upon the earth about 100 years ago, and men like Gutzlaff, Morrison, Carey, Duff and Judson soon knocked at the doors of heathenism. But lo, Satan had locked and barred the doors, and so impregnable did the wall of darkness appear to be that one cried out in despair, "Oh, rock, when wilt thou open?" But they toiled on and the church prayed on till the rusty bolts are drawn and the hinges creak as the heavy doors slowly swing, one after another, until all the world is open except the little province of Thibet.

Africa, sealed for two millenniums, is pierced in every direction by explorers, and all opened up to

POSSIBLE EVANGELIZATION.

India already has 125,000 Christians, with gospel light in every part. In China the prudent missionary may go where he will. In Turkey, Persia, Japan, Burmah, Siam, Madagascar, and the islands the work of evangelization moves grandly forward. Even hermit Korea has joined the family of nations, and several missions have already been planted there. Only Thibet, the present home of Buddhism, with the Grand Lama living in the city Lassa, and the subordinate Lamas controlling the country, remains locked against the gospel message. The Moravians have long essayed to enter from the province of Nepaul, in India, where they patiently waited and translated the Bible into the Thibetan language. Again they tried via Cashmere and Bod, on the west. The China Inland Mission has scouted the eastern border through China, but thus far all efforts have been in vain. But, lo! the English Government in India is negotiating for a political mission to enter Thibet, and we thank God, for wherever the English go, the Christian missionary can soon follow. And this last little spot held in the clutches of Satan shall see the great light that is shining among the nations. With such an outlook and such opportunities what should be the

ATTITUDE OF THE CHURCH?

Surely it should be that of enthusiastic endeavor. With the command behind her, Providence leading her, and marvelous success attending all efforts, she should obediently and resolutely prosecute the work her Lord has left her to do. Every member should consecrate self and substance to the proclamation of the gospel.

Bought with His blood, born of His Spirit, filled with His love, and stirred by His presence, oh! how she should obey His command in fidelity and power. The very thought of maternity and fatherhood, the nursing of children, their development, training, and education at home, in Sunday school and church should all be for the object and purpose of making them soldiers of the cross. The preaching of the gospel, all the means of grace, our schools and theological institutes should have for their sole object the winning of converts and training them as an army to obey our Captain's marching orders. It thrills the soul to think what could be accomplished with such consecration and devotion. But alas! alas! what is the attitude of the church? As a whole, Protestantism is now

WORLD-CONFORMING

and easy living. Even evangelical churches are simply playing at missions. Look at some of the facts. Out of the 6,093 churches in the Presbyterian denomination, North, 2,267, or over one-third, gave nothing for foreign missions in 1885. Of 1,742 Congregational churches in the District of the Interior, embracing thirteen States and Territories, 902 churches, over one-half, gave nothing for foreign missions in 1885. The Methodists, North, make a better showing in this respect, for out of 19,728 churches, thousands of which are in the South among the colored people, only 872 churches report nothing for missions, and 140 of these are mission churches in foreign lands. There is an impropriety in averaging congregations which give nothing, or only a trifle, with those which are giving as the Lord hath prospered; and yet for the sake of comparison we give the following average per member: Presbytrians, North, $1.08; Congregationalists, $1.53; Baptists, North, 54 cents; Methodists, North, including Woman's Society and Bishop Taylor's work, 35 cents; Baptists, South, 7½ cents; Disciples, 7 cents; Protestant Episcopals, 40½ cents. Think of it. Protestants, even evangelical Protestants, are not giving an average of 50 cents each per year for

THE WORLD'S EVANGELIZATION!

Some are doing their best. Many are doing well, but thousands upon thousands are doing nothing. What are the reasons for this spirit of disobedience in the army of the Lord? First of all, we believe that a lack of genuine spiritual life lies at the root of the matter. The cares of the world, the deceitfulness of riches and the lust of other things entering in have choked the Word until it has become unfruitful in multitudes of professedly Christian hearts. Self and substance are not consecrated to the work, and consequently there is little interest in it; indeed, not enough to stimulate the desire for information. They do not care to read the news from the outposts of the Lord's army. Very few missionary periodicals are self-supporting. Most of them have to be subsidized from the

GENERAL COLLECTIONS

of the societies. A notable exception to this is *The Heathen Woman's Friend*, which not only pays it way, but has considerable surplus for the Zevana paper and other publications. Why is this? Simply because it has an interested constituency among the 100,000 women of the W. F. M. S. Why does the secular press need no subsidy? Because the people are interested in the news, the markets, and, alas! even in the sensational stuff printed therein. How it would please the Lord if His disciples were thus interested in the news from His army, in the tidings from the skirmish line, where brave soldiers are meeting Satan's forces in the strongholds of darkness.

2. This want of information about the condition of the heathen and evangelistic work among them leads to an utter neglect of their claims upon us, and we hear it said, "There are heathen enough at home; let us stay here till these are converted," and thus an attitude is assumed which is utterly opposed to the spirit of the gospel and the plainest commands of the Master.

The work of evangelization was to be from Jerusalem out among all nations. The disciples were

TO BE WITNESSES

in Judea, Samaria, and unto the uttermost parts of the earth (Acts i.). Not a word was spoken that they should remain in any place until all were converted. Indeed, there is no Scripture statement that all would be converted. On the contrary, the testimony is directly the opposite.

In Matt. vii. 13 the wide gate, broad way, and many are contrasted to the straight gate, narrow way, and few.

The parable of the sower in Matt. xiii. shows how few are fruitful, and the words in Luke xviii. 8 show how few will be faithful Christians at the last.

The parable of the tares and the teaching of I. Tim. iv., II. Tim. iii., II. Pet. iii. show how evil men and wickedness will increase to the end. The lawlessness of II. Thes. ii. 7, 12, Satan's masterpiece, is only brought to an end by the coming of our Lord. Jesus did not set any such example. He hastened on that he might preach in the other towns and cities also (Mark i. 38, Luke iv. 43). His followers were to go and make disciples of all nations. At the first apostolic council it was declared to be the express purpose of God in this dispensation "to take out of" the nations a people to His name (Acts xv. 13-17). Hence we see that our business is to carry the gospel into all the world with the assurance that it will be the power of God unto salvation, both at home and abroad to the few who will believe. Where should we be if missionaries had stayed at home? Dancing around the Druid fires of our ancestors.

Another most important reason results from the erroneous statements concerning the progress of Christianity and the condition of the world. Very much is said and written about the progress of Christianity. The progress of Christianity is stated to be as follows: 1000, A. D., 50,000,000; 1500, A. D., 100,000,000; 1700, A. D., 155,000,000; 1800, A. D. 200,000,000; 1885, A. D., 416,000,000. These are divided as shown upon the chart, viz: Protestants, 136,000,000; Greeks and Oriental churches, 85,000,000; Roman Catholics, 195,000,000; total, 416,000,000. And it is exultingly claimed that at this ratio of increase all mankind will be Christians in less than 100 years. It is also claimed that the ratio of increase of population under Christian governments is even greater, viz: 1500, A. D., 100,000,000; 1700, A. D., 155,000,000; 1830, A. D., 387,788,000; 1876, A. D., 685,459,411; the latter being divided as follows: Roman Catholic governments, 181,000,000; Greek Church governments, 96,000,000; Protestant governments, 408,000,000. At the same rate of progress all would be under

CHRISTIAN GOVERNMENTS

in less than fifty years more. These figures are so enchanting that we hear much about Christians "capturing a planet" and "bringing the world to Christ," and often the "progress" is painted in such glowing colors that the millennium seems to have really dawned upon us, and the mass of the church settles back upon the lees, scarcely thinking it necessary to help push the "car of salvation" that appears to be so grandly rolling on. Progress in art, science, invention, commerce, material wealth, civilization, and refinement are all arrayed to help swell the delusion. We say delusion, for there never was a greater deception than such wholesale figures to represent true Christians and christian influences. It is a miserable opiate lulling the church to sleep in the arms of false security. Let us analyze these figures. We will not begin with the Catholics, who put the church and the Pope in the place of Christ, prohibit the Bible from the people, practice idolatry in the worship of Mary and the saints; a church that was once pure and the mother of us all, but is now recognized as mission ground; nor with the

GREEK AND ORIENTAL

churches permeated with formalism and political power. But let us consider the Protestants about whom we ought to know the most, and upon whose "progress" the greatest stress is laid. Where are these 136,000,000 Protestants? Dr. Dorchester gives the total of Baptists, Congregationalists, Methodists, Moravians, Presbyterians, and New Jerusalemites in all the world in 1880, at 11,530,979; all others in the United States, 1,675,214; add sundry small denominations in Great Britain and Europe, estimated at 2,000,000; Church of England, total estimated population, 21,000,000: Lutherans in the world (see Stall's Year Book), 47,451,136, and we have a total of 83,647,329. Where are the rest to come from? We must put in nominal Christians, as follows, who make no profession of Christ and belong to no church, and yet are counted in to swell the numbers of "evangelical" population: In the United States, 25,000,000; Great Britain, 4,000,000; Germany, 1,000,000; Holland, 2,600,000; Switzerland, 1,557,000; total population of Australia, Van Dieman's Land, and New Zealand, not enumerated above, 2,000,000; Canada, 3,000,000; Madagascar, 2,000,000; and now we must scrape up from somewhere, and not even imagination can tell where, a balance of 11,185,671, to make the total of 136,000,000.

If the number of Protestants be called 160,000,000, as shown on the diagram published by the American Baptist Mission Union, then this balance from nowhere would reach the enormous number of 35,185,671.

Over 108,000,000 of nominal Christians are counted into this mass. Are not such figures deceiving the church into an imagined prosperity? The truth is that, if we reckon one in four of the Church of England population and one in seven of the

LUTHERAN POPULATION

as actual church members, we have a total church membership in all Protestantism of 27,039,526. And when we consider that this includes Universalists, Unitarians, and Swedenborgians, as well as the vast number of those whose Christianity consists only in a name on the church record, shall we not regard 12,500,000 to be a large estimate of the number of Protestant consecrated disciples of the Lord Jesus? What do the other 123,500,000 belong to? Jesus said, "He that is not with me is against me" (Matt. xii. 30). Now let us set over against this 12,500,000 consecrated Protestants, the solemn fact that this world's population is increasing every year about 14,000,000 souls, or more, in two years, than the entire Protestant Church membership in the world!

The portion of the earth's population under Christian governments in 1876 is given as follows: Under Catholic governments, 180,787,905; Greek Church, 96,101,894; Protestants, 408,569,612; total, 685,459,411. And these figures are said to "demonstrate

THE RAPID EXTENSION

of Christian influences and the Christian subjugation of the world." If "Christian subjugation" here means subjugation to Christ, then is it not fair to assume that Christian governments ought to be serving Christ? Mohammedan governments are faithful to Mohammed. Are Christian governments faithful to the King of kings? Let us take the United States for example. First as to population. The census of 1880 gives the total population at 50,145,783, which we find divided as follows: Protestant church members, 8,953,870. Over against this we have the Catholics, 6,174,202; nominals, 35,027,801.

Who are the people serving? It is pretty fair to judge of a nation's fealty by the way it spends its money. Hence we make the following comparison: For the annual support of the gospel, education, and charities—Sixty-five thousand clergymen,* $1,000 each, $65,000,000; public schools, $103,949,528; universities and colleges,† $5,124,189; charities, estimated, $24,426,283; missions, home and foreign, $5,500,000; total, $204,000,000.

Thousands of ministers in the West and South do not receive $200 apiece, and it is

A LITTLE QUESTIONABLE

about including public schools, in many of which the Bible is prohibited; but we wish to make the total liberal and large, and $204,000,000 does seem a grand sum to be annually expended in the service of Christ. But look at the other side.

Our nation spends for liquor, $900,000,000; for tobacco, $600,000,000; luxuries and frivolities, $100,000,000, the latter including $25,000,000 for kid gloves and $5,000,000 for ostrich feathers, making a total of $1,600,000,000. One dollar for Christ to $8 for self and Satan! But let us look at an aggregate for ninety years. Dr. Dorchester gives the total receipts of all foreign missionary societies in the United States since their origin until 1880 at $57,628,946; home missionary societies, $72,676,801; religious publication houses, including Sunday school and tract societies, $109,483,436; support of clergymen and churches for ninety years, $3,154,950,000; total, $3,394,339,183. This is a very great sum, and it might fill us with admiration for the Christian consecration of our nation. But behold the appalling sum on the other side!

Dr. Dorchester, who is corroborated by other

PROMINENT STATISTICIANS,

gives the amount spent in the United States in ninety years for liquor alone at $78,899,943,864, a sum greater by half than the present real and personal value of all land and property of the whole Nation. Oh! what waste, what destruction, what anguish, sin, and misery, what a multitude of hopeless souls, what a throng of widows and orphans, what squandered fortunes, ruined homes and blasted lives are represented by this tremendous sum. Yet the fearful traffic is licensed by our government, and a large portion of its revenue derived therefrom.

Whose is this government. Christ's or Satan's?

"Know ye not, that to whom ye yield yourselves servants to obey, his servants ye are to whom ye obey" (Rom. vi. 16).

Multiply the above totals by three, and we have the approximate expenditure in Protestant nations, or by seven would give us, perhaps, the total expenditure in all "Christian" governments. One is overwhelmed by such

INCOMPREHENSIBLE SUMS.

Christian nations are said to have spent for war in this nineteenth century over $15,000,000,000, and for missions $300,000,000. One dollar for the sword of the Spirit to $50 for the gods of war!

It is in "Christian nations" that we find communism, socialism, and nihilism. Atheistic anarchists are here preaching and practising the diabolical doctrines of lawlessness, and they may be the forerunners of that "lawless one" of 2 Thes. ii. 8-12 The evil influence of so-called Christians in heathen lands is one of the greatest obstacles to missionary work. One ship from a Christian land to the Congo took one missionary and 100,000 gallons of rum. The government of Great Britain, the chief of Christian nations, for "the love of money" monopolizes the opium trade, raises the poppy, manufactures the drug, ships it to China, and at the mouth of the cannon forces it upon that helpless heathen nation. God have mercy on our mother land. If there is one crying evil under heaven this must be it, this total eclipse of national righteousness. Oh, Christian governments, who shall deliver you from the wrath to come. The degree of light is the basis of responsibility. Remember that the

AWFUL DENUNCIATIONS

of Jesus were not against the heathen, but against Israel and her rulers, who had the light but walked not in it. "Ye are of your father, the devil" (John viii. 44). "Ye serpents, ye generation of vipers, how can ye escape the damnation of gehenna" (Mat. xxiii. 33), are his awful words. Rather would I be a kind hearted Brahmin or Confucianist, than a "nominal Christian,"

*Including Catholic priests. See p. 203.

†See American Almanac 1886. p. 46.

rejecting the gospel of the grace of God in a favored Christian land. Of what value, in the sight of heaven, is this nominal Christianity? And of what avail if the whole world should be converted to such a Christianity? This is not to Christ. A secular paper in Japan is said to have lately advocated the adoption of Christianity as a state religion, not for the service of Christ, but in order to be on a better footing with the Western Christian nations. A world conforming, power denying form of godliness may prevail, but not sound doctrine and holiness. For the simple fact is, Christian nations are not serving Christ.

There has come to be a great difference between Christ and Christianity. Christianity is a term which now embraces more than 100,000,000 of Protestants and 250,000,000 of Greeks, Orientals, and Catholics, who profess no change of heart, but simply because they are not Mohammedans or Buddhists, are regarded as servants of Christ. Surely this is Satan's arithmetic. The true Christians of all denominations are a comparatively little handful of witnessing disciples, "holding forth the word of life," in the midst of the world's masses who are plunging on the broad

ROAD TO DESTRUCTION.

"Ah! what a dark picture," says one. Indeed it is, but it's true, for it was painted by Jesus in answer to the question, "Are there few that be saved?" (See Luke xiii. 23-24 and Mat. vii. 13-14.) Ever since sin entered in the garden separation from God, moral darkness and spiritual death have followed. The whole history of the race has been one mighty panorama, showing that "the wages of sin is death." Each dispensation has ended in judgment—Eden in the expulsion, Antediluvian in the flood, Post-diluvian in Sodom, Patriarchal in the Red Sea, Mosaic in the cross and destruction of Jerusalem. So will this Christian dispensation end in the judgment. Fifty-nine centuries, and still it is night! Satan is still deceiving the nations; yea, he is even deceiving the church into a blind confidence that "things are going well" and the world is waxing better. God help us to dispel this delusion. "We know," said the beloved John, "that we are of God, and the whole world lieth in the wicked one" (I. John v. 19, N. V.), lieth like a child asleep in the

ARMS OF SATAN.

Oh! beloved, ye Christians, beware! beware lest ye sleep also (I. Thes. v. 6). Awake! awake! and gaze upon the multitudes of those who are in the gall of bitterness and bonds of iniquity. While Christian missions in 100 years have gained 600,000 converts from Mohammedans and heathens, representing with their families a possible population of 3,000,000, the population of the latter has increased 200,000,000, or about 70 to 1. Think, as you read your Holy Bible, that every chapter, nay every verse, nay every letter, stands for over 230 of the heathen. What a throng of aching hearts one single precious promise would thus represent. It's an awful fact that in these closing years of the nineteenth century 15,000,000, possibly 30,000,000, are serving Christ, while 1,200,000,000 are serving Satan—"children of the devil taken captive at his will." And so it has been in past generations. Every thirty-three years a new host floods the road to darkness. Ah, you say this is discouraging! So it is in the false assumption that all living are to be converted in this dispensation. How long; how long at this rate shall we be in "bringing the world to Christ?"

Beloved! We are not bringing the world to Christ. We were not told to do it. What we are doing, what we were told to do, is to

TAKE THE GOSPEL

to the world. And God by His blessed Spirit is taking out of the nations "a people for His name" (Acts xv. 14).

Is there then no hope? Ah, yes, indeed. Through this red sea of sin, sorrow, and darkness, in the fullness of faith and hope, we see the coming kingdom. There is to be an era of peace and holiness. "The earth shall be full of the knowledge of the Lord as the waters cover the sea." "Behold a king shall reign in righteousness." Jesus said: "Fear not little flock, for it is your Father's good pleasure to give you the kingdom." God lifted the curtain to that grand old prophet Daniel, and let him see the great, beastly empires of earth, with all their destroying power, wearing out the saints of the Most High. But thanks be to God, He let him see farther on, until "the judgment shall sit and the kingdom and dominion, and the greatness of the kingdom under the whole heaven shall be given to the people of the saints of the Most High."

But notice; they do not possess the kingdom until after the judgment. It is not in this dispensation, but in that which is coming.

JESUS AND THE APOSTLE

make a plain distinction between this eon and that which is coming. (See Mat. xii. 32, Luke xx. 34-35, Eph. i. 21). The present is called an "evil eon, (Gal. i. 4), and we are not to be conformed to it (Rom. xii. 2), nor love it (II. Tim. iv. 10). The wisdom of this eon, the princes of this eon and the god of this eon are all evil (see I. Cor. ii. 6-8, 2 Cor. iv. 4). It is the power and glory of the coming eon which we are to seek (see Heb. vi. 5, and Tit. ii. 12-13).

This word eon, in the Greek, is a measure of time just as distinct as a century, though, unlike centuries, eons are not of equal duration. Each eon has an end (see Mat. xiii., 39-40-49, Mat. xxiv. 3), and as another follows, it must have a beginning. It is best rendered dispensation, as the word age has become too indefinite, although originally derived from eon. We believe there is no key to Scripture more potent than this. There have been many eons in the past (Eph. iii. 9, Gr., and Col. i. 26), and there are to be many in the future (Eph. ii. 7). Jesus is the King of the eons (1 Tim. 17, Gr.), and they are all arranged according to a plan (Eph. iii. 11, Gr.). Several of these eons, possibly seven, compose a great eon, so that we have eons of eons (Gal. i. 5, Phil. iv. 20, N. V. Marg.), like the week of weeks. The subject is enchanting, and opens up to us these great

MEASURES OF TIME

as the hours of eternity. But we only touch upon it to show how clearly the Scriptures distinguish these dispensations, both past and future. Throughout them God is working out a great plan of salvation, and though only a small portion of the race have been His servants, He has surely accomplished His plan in the past dispensations, and He is also accomplishing it in this present "evil" dispensation, though there be but few that are saved. Let us then reverently enquire what is God's plan or purpose in this dispensation? If we can discover this our hope will be brightened just in proportion as we see how nearly the purpose is accomplished. We answer then, in the words of Jesus Himself, "This gospel of the kingdom shall be preached in all the world for a witness to all nations; then shall the end come." (Matt. xxiv., 14.)

This world is to be evangelized. All nations are to hear the good news of the coming kingdom, and while men proclaim it God, by it, gathers the bride for His Son. He selects out from all who hear the gospel such as believe, who by His spirit are born from above, justified and sanctified, and are cleaned with the washing of the water of the word, that Jesus may present them to himself, as his bride, a glorious church

WITHOUT SPOT, WRINKLE,

or any such thing (Eph v. 25-32; 1 Thes. iv.: 16-18; Rev. xxi. 9-27). To be a member of this bride of Christ; to be joined to Him in holy wedlock, and to reign with Him over His kingdom, is the very pinnacle of human exaltation. It is throughout the eons to come God's unparalleled object lesson to the universe of the exceeding riches of His grace (II Cor. xi. 2; Rom. viii. 17; I Cor. vi. 3; 2 Tim. ii. 12; Eph. ii. 7). Now whatever salvation God may have for the heathen by the law of conscience, as stated in Rom. ii. 14-15, none of them can become members of this body or bride of Christ without hearing the gospel. This is clearly stated in Rom. x. 14. "How shall they call on Him in Whom they have not believed? and how shall they believe in Him of Whom they have not heard? and how shall they hear without a preacher? Let none excuse their remissness by imagining that God will whitewash the heathen into this body of Christ. Nay! Nay! Nothing will avail but regeneration by the Holy Spirit, (John, iii. 5), a new creature in Christ Jesus. (Gal. vi. 5, Tit. iii. 5). It is God's plan that we shall preach the gospel to them as a witness. Then shall the end come—the end of the dispensation, or eon, about which the disciples had asked in verse 3. The end of this "evil eon," the end of the overflowing of sin and sorrow and the end of Satan's dominion. God hasten it, and He will if we are obedient, for we can hasten it if we will. (See II. Pet., iii. 12, margin). He will cut it short in righteousness. What is a witness? The original word signifies testimony, and it is so translated in the new version. This testimony, then, is the Word of God and the testimony of the believer, or, in other words, the open Bible and the preacher or proclaimer. Go! said Jesus, "ye shall be witnesses unto the uttermost parts of the earth." To take the gospel to all nations is the business He has given the church. Oh! if we could only realize this, what an inspiration it would be to our zeal and hopes. For it is not

A HOPELESS TASK,

like an attempt to convert all the people in a single city, but it is something we can accomplish. We can translate the Bible into the mother tongue of every tribe, and we can give them the living preacher, and then, oh, joy of joys! He hath said it, the end shall come! Our Lord shall appear, and Satan, rising in the might of his power, and putting forth his masterpiece, the Lawless One shall be paralyzed, bound, and cast into the pit, that he may not deceive the nations, and the multitudes of earth shall turn to seek after God (II Thes. ii. 8; Rev. xx. 2; Acts xv. 16, 17). What a blessing to hasten such an end as this.

Now let us see how great things God hath accomplished even with the feeble efforts that hath been put forth. First, we notice that the Protestant courses of evangelization are in the United States and part of Europe. In these there are now organized eighty-seven missionary societies, with

5,835 male and female missionaries and 29,-091 native preachers and helpers. The Bible

HAS BEEN TRANSLATED

into 287 languages and dialects, and two of these, the Wenli of China and the Arabic, can each be read by 100,000,000 of people, and altogether these languages comprise the speech of nine-tenths of the inhabitants of the world. And now we turn to the map again to show to what a wide extent the mission stations have been planted throughout the world. [Here the large map was used, upon which the mission stations of all societies are shown in bright gilt spots.] The Russo-Greek Church does give give the Bible to the people, and a Bible society exists in St. Petersburg and there is considerable active evangelistic work in Russian countries. In these we have no mission stations. But in Catholic countries, where the Bible is prohibited by the apostate church, we have many mission stations, as also in Mohammedan and heathen lands.

The stations shown are only the central or principal ones, and in many cases several societies have missions at the same stations. Around these there are large numbers of out-stations, as, for instance, around the one Presbyterian station of Tamsui, in Formosa, there are thirty-four out-stations, and aronnd the five Methodist stations in the Foo Choo district, in China, there are forty-five out-stations.

THE AMERICAN BOARD

in 1885 had eighty-three stations and 826 out-stations. If all these out-stations were put on the map it would indeed make a blaze of light. Again, to this must be added the journeyings of missionaries and colporteurs, like Sir Henry Lansdell in Siberia and Central Asia, and Cameron, the Livingstone of China, and especially those avant couriers, the Bible Society agents, who have threaded back and forth through the distant fields of the unevangelized, distributing the Word to the people in their own tongue. It would be impossible to show these journeys on the map distinctly, as in some countries it would be an indistinguishable maze.

But how hopeful we ought to be as we thus look upon the present state of the world's evangelization. Again, consider for a moment the helpful agencies of our day. The Postal Union and the avenues of commerce have covered the seas and the continents with highways for transportation and communication. The spread of the Anglo-Saxon race and of the English language are marvelous providences to help forward the work.

In short, only let us substitute the Scriptural idea of the world's evangelization in place of the papal idea of its conversion, and we join hands with the most

SANGUINE OPTIMIST

in hearty thanksgiving for the heaven-ordained helpful agencies now at our command. And just here we note that in all the range of evangelizing forces we know of none so hopeful as the present organized work of women. Beginning in the gentleness and weakness which usually characterizes God's great undertakings, it has spread from heart to heart until 100,000 praying women in the Methodist church alone, and over 200,000 in other churches are now banded together for the work of proclaiming the gospel. It is a grand fulfillment of the Psalmist's prophecy, "The Lord giveth the word. The women that publish the tidings are a great host." (Ps. lxviii, 11-12, N. V). And the most hopeful feature lies in the fact that these women, meeting from month to month in their little circles, are not only praying, but are systematically studying the whole subject of missions and mission fields. There is many a mother, despite her busy cares, who knows far more of Japan, China, and Africa than her good husband, who spends his leisure moments in the daily paper. And this knowledge accounts for the increasing total of

THEIR YEARLY GIFTS,

which in some societies even now excel the regular contributions of the churches to which they belong, and in some have already passed not only the one, but the two million dollar line.

If the husbands and brothers were only thus organized; nay, if even the pastors were all thus interested, what a mighty ground swell of missionary zeal and labor we should see! But, alas! how few pastors hold a monthly missionary prayer-meeting. How few comparatively take their own church missionary periodicals. If but the pastors patronized the missionary literature of their own church societies there would be no deficiency in the publication fund. Can we expect the stream to rise higher than the fountain? Will the flocks follow unless the shepherds lead them?

Oh, that we might have a Pentecostal baptism upon the pulpit and the pew, and that the genuine primitive missionary spirit might enter and possess every disciple's heart. Then should we have

AN EASY TASK

to enter Mongolia, Thibet, Turkestan, Arabia, Tripoli, Central Africa, the Soudan, and the Gallas, Venezuela, Ecquador, the Valley of the Amazon, and the Islands, and to translate the Bible into the remaining languages.

Given 10,000,000 consecrated Christians,

and the whole world could be easily evangelized in twenty years. Think of it! All the millions of the unevangelized might hear the gospel in twelve months if there were only preachers to declare it. Praise God for the increasing interest, and the scores who have obediently gone to the front. But the cry comes from nearly every mission field, "Give us more men and more women." Will we do it? We can if we will. Oh, ye Christian business men! there is no investment that will pay so well as to give yourselves and your substance to Jesus for this work. Heap no longer treasure for yourselves in these last days, but think, plan, and execute, for the proclamation of the gospel. The time is short. What is done must be done quickly, for the night cometh when no man can work. We want men and we want women who can go and bear their own expense, and who will esteem it a privilege thus to do it. The work must and it shall be done. It is the era of

UNIVERSAL MISSIONS.

One grand determined effort is demanded. Duty demands it—obey the marching orders—the last words. Gratitute demands it; Jesus has saved us, shall we save our kindred? The Hindoos are our own blood relation, the other arm of the great Aryan race. Sympathy demands it. All the sorrow and anguish of a Godless, benighted, hopeless, household; multiplied by hundreds of millions, appeals to our hearts in agonizing tones. "Why didn't you come before?" said a poor old Chinese woman to Mrs. Crawford; "My mother would like to have heard of this Jesus, but she is dead." These fellow-beings for whom Christ has died are dying, dying, dying, over sixty every minute. Will there be any blood on our souls when we meet them at the judgment? And now, beloved, while we remember that it is said unto us, "Ye shall be witnesses unto me," it is also said unto Israel, "Ye are my witness," and let us not forget that after God takes away the church (Acts xv.) He will build again the tabernacle of David, which is fallen down, that the residue of men may seek after the Lord. Therefore it may be converted Israel who shall complete the witness, to all the nations, of the coming kingdom. Hence we have no event to stand, as a sign, between us and the coming of the Lord. We are to live with

OUR LOINS GIRDED

and our lights burning like unto men that wait for their Lord. For the Son of man cometh at an hour when ye think not. Herein lies the grandest incentive to be minute-men for Jesus. There are to be three great gatherings of mankind, in one of which every mortal shall appear before God.

The first is when the saints, both those who sleep and those who wake, shall be caught up together to meet the Lord in the air. (I. Thes. iv.) The second is when Jesus has come down to earth, and, with saints, shall sit in the throne of His glory, and before Him shall be gathered all the nations. (Matt. xxv.) The third is when all the dead are gathered before the great white throne. (Rev. xx.) Beloved, in which of these gatherings shall you and I assemble? Heed the admonition of Jesus against the cares of this life. Watch at every season, making supplication that ye may prevail to escape all these things that shall come to pass, and to stand before the Son of man.

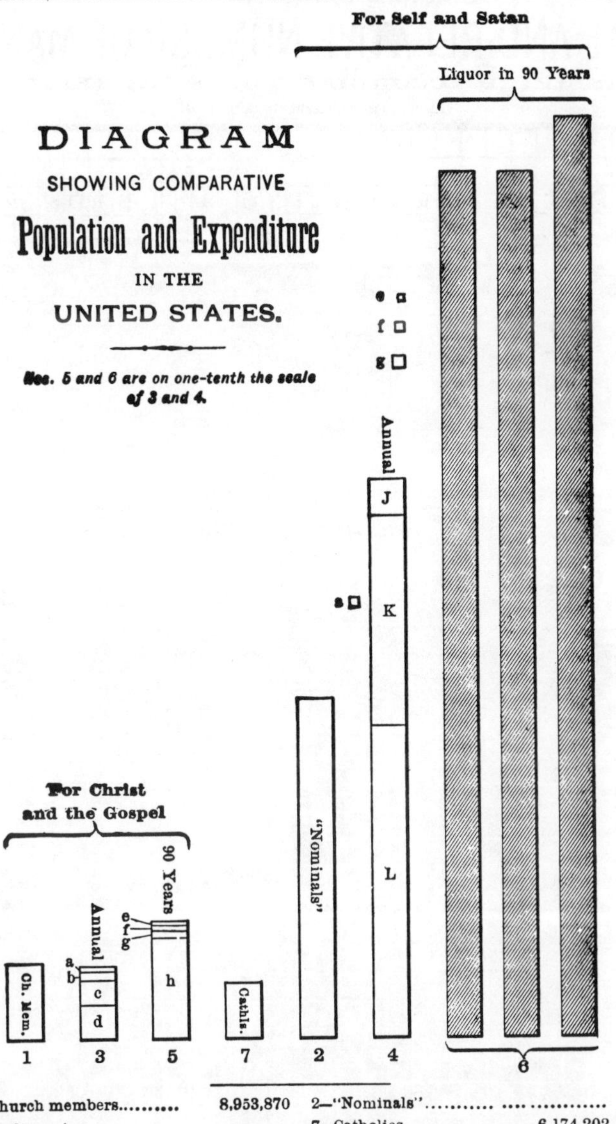

1—Protestant Church members..........	8,953,870
3—Annual expenditure for:	
(a) Home and Foreign Missions......	5,500,000
(b) Charities..............................	24,426,283
(c) Clergymen, 65,000 at $1,000......	65,000,000
(d) Public schools, universities, and colleges..........................	109,073,717
Total..........................	204,000,000
5—Expenditure in 90 years for:	
(e) Foreign mission societies since their organization..............	57,628,946
(f) Home mission societies since their organization..............	72,276,801
(g) Religious publication houses....	109,483,436
(h) Clergymen and churches, $1,000 each per year....................	3,154,950,000
Total................................	3,394,339,183

2—"Nominals"............................		35,027,801
7—Catholics....................	6,174,202	
4—Annual expenditure for:		
(J) Luxuries and frivolities..........		100,000,000
(K) Tobacco............................		600,000,000
(L) Liquors		900,000,000
Total..................................		1,600,000,000
6—Liquor alone in 90 years (see Liquor Problem by Dr. Dorchester)...		78,899,943,864

DIAGRAM EXHIBITING THE

ACTUAL AND RELATIVE NUMBER OF MANKIND

CLASSIFIED ACCORDING TO THEIR RELIGION.

Each square represents 1,000,000 souls.

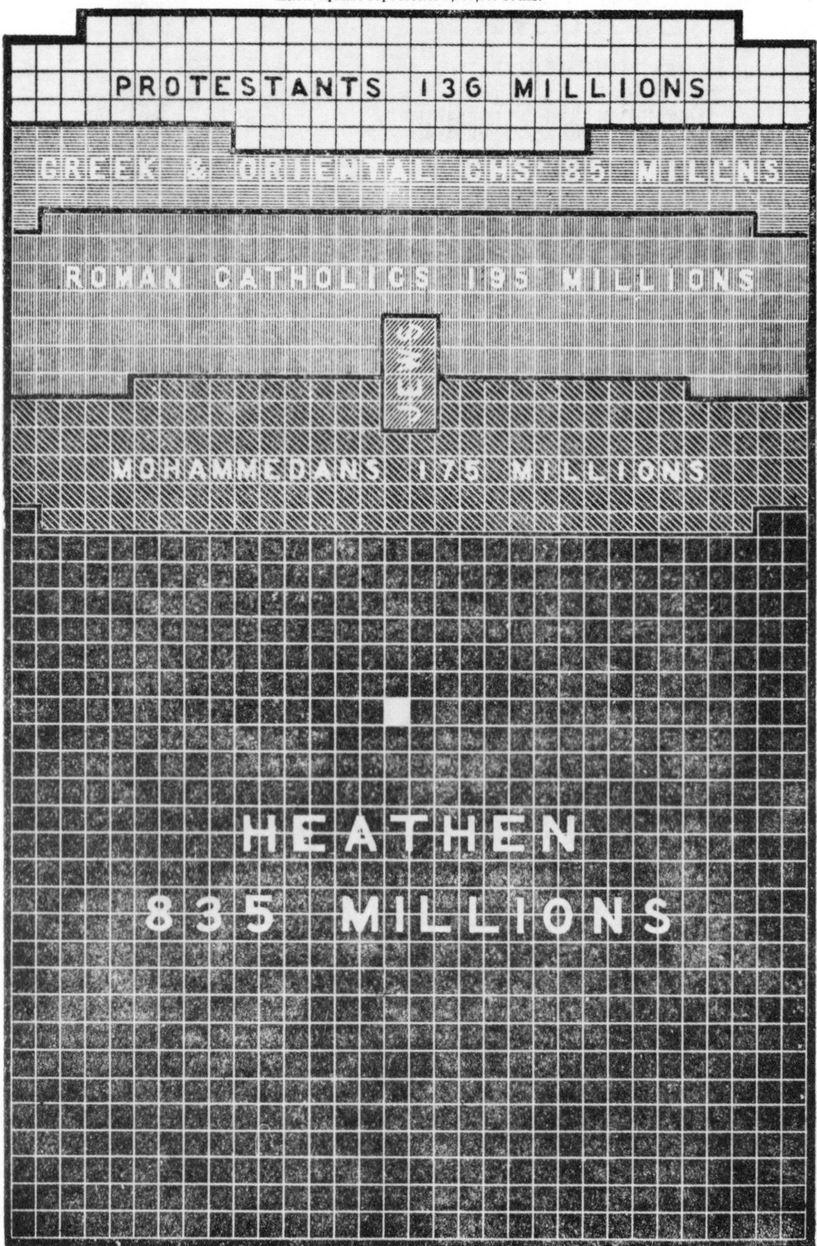

The one white square in the black indicates converts from Heathenism.

In 100 years the Heathen and Mohammedan population has increased 200,000,000.

PROFESSOR J. G. PRINCELL.

WAITING, WATCHING, WORKING.

The remarks of Professor J. G. Princell, of Chicago, until lately President of the Swedish-American Ausgari College at Knoxville, Ill., formed the last of Saturday afternoon's exercises. Professor Princell's remarks were extemporaneous, and he occupied but thirty-five minutes in speaking upon the subject, "Waiting, Watching, Working." The address, somewhat abbreviated, is as follows:

Several parables, as well as direct teaching of our Lord, inculate the lessons which the three words of my subject are intended to suggest. Thus He says in Luke xii. 3-37: "Let your loins be girded about, and your lights burning; and be ye yourselves like unto men that wait for their Lord, when he will return from the wedding, that when he cometh and knocketh they may open unto him immediately. Blessed are those servants whom the Lord, when He cometh, shall find watching."

And the parable in Luke xix., 11-27, about the ten servants and the ten pounds, with the ringing command, "Occupy till I come," teaches plainly that the Lord's disciples should be waiting for and expecting His return; that they should be watching and eagerly looking out for His coming, and that in the meanwhile they should faithfully serve Him, making good use of the gifts, the powers, the position afforded them by Him. Other words and other parables of His bring out the same thoughts which, in terms a little differing from those of my subject, may be thus expressed:

1. Patient waiting, or the exercising of that attitude of mind by which a person stays or rests in expectation of something, here of the literal, personal, bodily, visible coming again of Jesus Christ, who

WAS ONCE ON THIS EARTH,

lived, taught, worked miracles, was despised, rejected, crucified by His enemies, died but rose alive from the grave and from or out of the midst of the dead, and then ascended into heaven. We should thus be expecting that he will return to this earth again for great, glorious, and, on the whole, most beneficial purposes.

2. Eager looking for that Christ's return—i. e., we should be in such a state of mind as continually to be attentive to or observant of any indications of His coming, earnestly desiring and always ready for that great event; watching being opposed to inattention and indifference, watchfulness opposed to sleepiness or carelessness.

3. Faithful service in the meantime, or between the present moment and the actual coming of the Lord, i. e., we should be earnestly, joyfully, obediently engaged in some effort for Him, be it by teaching, testifying, giving, sacrificing, suffering, using mind, hands, feet, whatever we have and whatever we can for His honor and for making Him and His will known among men for their welfare.

All this, I apprehend, is embraced in waiting, watching, and working for our dear Savior. Of course more or less of this has been presented in different forms and in different connection by several or all of the speakers on prophetic subjects, especially those who have pointed out the direct practical bearings of these subjects on Christian life and work. But it may not be amiss to try to bring together under one view what belongs practically to these parts of the great prophetic field.

I will begin by calling attention to the waiting. Having hinted at what waiting is, and the word "wait," for which there are several different words, more or less strong, in the Hebrew and the Greek is used in the Bible in no more different or peculiar sense than it is

USED IN COMMON LANGUAGE

or everyday speech, as we say "waiting for rain," "waiting for snow," "waiting for a friend," "waiting for this or that change." etc. Now, having hinted at what waiting is, I will ask, what, according to the Bible, are we thus to wait for?

We are not to wait for death. There is not in the New Testament a single exhortation to wait for or be looking for death. On the contrary, death is always regarded as an enemy, as one that will be destroyed after Christ has come. True, death can not harm the true believer in Christ; still he is a separator, a destroyer, a severer of the most tender ties. Christ is a uniter of what properly belongs together. Some writers exalt death; the Biblical writers exult over death: "O death, where is thy victory? O death, where is thy sting? * * * Thanks be to God which giveth us the victory through our Lord Jesus Christ." There is nothing inspiring about death; death is indeed an expiration, not an inspiration. Dr. Waldenstrom, the great leader in the free church movement in Sweden at present, related once at a large public meeting a little story about one of his children. "Mama," said a bright little boy of 5 or 6 summers, "when will Jesus come to earth again?" "I do not know, my child," answered the mother. "Does the catechism say when Jesus will come?" "No, it does not." "Does papa know when Jesus will come?" "No, he can not know that, for the Bible does not say when Jesus will come." "Does it not stand in the Bible? But does not the Bible say He may come any time?" "Yes, my darling, the Bible says He may come any time." "Well, then, mother, I wish Jesus would come while we all are living, for then I and you and papa and my brothers and sisters would not have to die." In relating this story the good and learned Doctor added: "That was an apostolic way of thinking."

AGAIN, WE ARE NOT TO WAIT

for the conversion of the whole world to Christ, nor even for the general preaching of the gospel in all the world before Christ comes. This idea, which is quite generally entertained, is based on an erroneous view of Matt. xxiv. 14, "This gospel of the kingdom shall be preached in the whole world for a testimony unto all the nations; and then shall the end come." Most surely this shall happen, but Christ will come before the end comes, as is clearly proved by I. Cor. xv. 23-28: "Each in his own order: Christ the first fruits; then they that are Christ's at His coming. Then cometh the end, when He shall deliver up the kingdom to God, even the Father. * * * But He must reign until He hath put all His enemies under His feet." Then, and not before then, will "the end" come. By that time, indeed, "the gospel of the kingdom" shall have been reached in the whole world. By that time shall have been fulfilled the great commission: "Go ye and make disciples of all nations." By that time the great promise to Abraham shall have become a literal fact: "In thy seed shall all the nations of the earth be blessed." These and all similar promises and declarations of God shall most truly be accomplished; but the loving parting promise of Christ to His sorrowing disciples will precede and ante-date them all in fulfillment: "I come again, and will receive you unto myself."

Then, again, we are not to wait for great upheavals or catastrophes in nature, extraordinary signs and wonders in the heavens, in sun, moon, and stars, nor for unusually calamitous occurrences on earth. Though such things are predicted in the wonderful Word, and though they will without doubt and without fail come to pass, they will not precede the coming of the Lord for the purpose of gathering and taking unto Himself His own people

FOR THEIR PROTECTION

and eternal security. Hear the word of the Lord about this. In Isaiah xxvi., after the Lord has spoken of the resurrection of the dead of His people, He says: "Come, my people, enter thou into thy chambers, and shut thy doors about thee; hide thyself for a little moment until the indignation be overpast. For, behold, the Lord cometh forth out of His place to punish the inhabitants of the earth for their iniquity." Of this escape of God's people before a single one of those predicted blows at this old creation is struck, both Christ (in Luke xxi., 36) and Paul (in I. Thess., iv. 16-17) testify.

Further, we are not to wait for the general gathering of Israel into their own land, Canaan, and their establishing a kingdom there. No doubt that will happen; it is absolutely foretold in the sacred Scriptures. In a measure this event may be even now in these days beginning, but no general fulfillment of the prophecies in this regard may be expected before Jesus Himself shall have come and removed His people of the present age or dispensation, and, after that, shall commence to deal with that ancient people of God which once rejected Him.

Then, again, we are not to wait for the fall of the Turkish or Mohammedan power, nor for the reconstruction of the old Roman Empire, nor in fact for any great political change. It is true that there will be, very likely in the near future, great political changes on the map of the world, especially in the old, historic world. But at least the main part of these changes or revolutions belongs to a time subsequent to the coming of the Christ Himself. This is plain from the connection of the great historic latter-day pictures in the book of Revelation.

Again, we are not to wait for the rise of the Antichrist, with his lying words and wonders.

THAT STRANGE, FEARFUL PERSONAGE,

the very man of sin, will not dare to raise his head as long as "the anointing of the Holy One" is here, according to I. John ii. 18-22, for through this anointing the true believers "know all things" concerning that execrable individual, and would, if he dared to turn the electric light of God's truth on him, disclosing him to the horrified gaze of mankind, causing him to hide himself for shame. The Christ of God must, therefore, first come and take to Himself His anointed ones before that Antichrist of the devil will show himself.

Finally, we are not to wait for that great and general apostacy spoken of by Christ and Paul (Matt. xxiv., 2 Thess. ii.), nor for that fearful persecution and that dire tribulation which especially Jeremiah, Daniel, our Lord Himself, and John have pictured in such red colors. There will come "a time of trouble" unparalleled in all history and every age, affecting at first Israel, but gradually all who then may yet be holding on to faith in the true, personal God, and in Jesus of Nazareth as the only true Christ. But the true church of Christ, especially that part of it living on earth at the time of Christ's coming, has the particular promise of being exempt from those awful calamities; it has the promise of escape from all these things by being previously "caught up in the clouds to meet the Lord in the air;" it is to be "kept from [or out of that is spared] the hour of trial;" it is to have "rest, not tribulation, at the revelation of the Lord Jesus from heaven with the angels of His power." If it were otherwise; if we, believers now living on this earth, have to expect a general apostacy and a terrible tribulation, unlike anything that has ever hitherto befallen the people of God; if we were to await any such dreadful things before the coming of our Lord in person, how could we, or how can we "comfort one another" with the words, "The Lord Himself shall descend from heaven with a shout, with the voice of the archangel, and

WITH THE TRUMP OF GOD?"

Should we not rather wish to fall asleep, to die, before that terrible event comes to pass, so that we thus might be spared from coming into that fearful whirlpool of possible disasters to ourselves and others?" Oh, it is this dreadful misapprehension, yea, this frightful misrepresentation of the Lord's coming that has so sadly put that glorious event aside and in the shade, in the feelings, thoughts, and beliefs of thousands of dear Christians. Thus represented to them, they dread and can not love their Lord's coming; they prefer to die before that happens; and so, naturally enough, they have put death in the place of the Lord, and have toned down and watered that real personal coming into a sentimentally sweet, vapory, spiritual coming—just as if He had ever been spiritually away or broken His own dear promise: "Lo, I am with you alway." No, no, dear Lord, Thou hast never left; no, never forsaken us. We will not, we dare not accuse Thee of having, even for a single moment, broken Thy parting pledge. We cling to that; and we cling, also, to that other oft-repeated parting pledge of Thine: "I will come again and receive you unto Myself. Yea, I come quickly." And we send the answer back to heaven: "Amen. Come Lord Jesus."

Thus, then, we see what or rather whom we are to wait for; it is our Lord and Savior Jesus Christ, the Bridegroom of our souls, our heavenly Elder Brother, our dearest friend, the benefactor of the whole world, the rightful king of all the earth, the remover of all wrong, sin and misery, the great restorer of all creation to ideal order, beauty and loveliness. It is He Himself whom we are to await every day and night, and expect to come at any moment. He whose coming, at its first stage, will not be with outward pomp and manifestation, visible to the whole world; but silently as a thief comes. He will come to catch up His people, snatching them away from coming disasters and judgments; after that "every eye shall see Him."

NOT NECESSARILY AT ONCE,

but some at one time, some at another, some in one place, some in another. (Several Bible passages were here read, showing how the Scriptures speak of the waiting under consideration; such passages were I. Thess., i. 9, 10; I. Cor., i. 7; Rom., viii. 19, 23, 25; Phil., iii. 20; Heb. ix., 28. The revised version was quoted throughout.)

Truly, there is a rich, beautiful benediction on all true waiters for the Lord: "Blessed are all they that wait for Him."—(Is., xxx. 18.)

Some of the most important conditions or requisites of true waiting are: 1. Knowledge of and living personal faith in Jesus Christ. 2. Knowledge of and real faith in what He and His accredited witnesses have said concerning His return. 3. Desire and hope for this His return. 4. Intense love of Christ as a personal Saviour and Friend. 5. Freedom from entanglement with the world: its evil ways, thoughts, societies, its dishonest business, its selfish pharasaical Laodicean religion, its corrupt politics. Or many, even professed believers, would be greatly surprised if their Lord should now, immediately appear.

"If He cometh to-day, your Lord and your God,
Would gladness or anguish o'erwhelm you."

Among the reasons for waiting for the coming of Jesus, the following may be urged: 1. His own word, and the words of His inspired witnesses declare that He will surely come again. 2. What He has done for the world, and for each one of us personally, all this will ripen into its full, perfect, everlasting fruit, only when He comes again. 3. His love for us, and our love for Him; it is good for us that He is with us where we live, and as long as we live, but it will be better for us to be with Him where He lives, and as long as He lives, that is always. 4. What He will do for us and the whole world when He comes back; what an inheritance "the heirs of God and joint-heirs of Jesus Christ" will then receive and take possession of! What bettering of all conditions, of all classes, of everything social, religious, political, material in all creation there will then be! The good time which prophets have foretold, and of which poets have sung, will, indeed, then come.

WATCHING.

As regards watching for the Lord, it may be defined as that eager looking for or frequently (not to say continual) thinking about our Lord's return, by which state of mind we are constantly attentive to the notice of any indications of His coming. There is in general no great difference between waiting and watching; yet in particular there is some quite distinct difference. Watching is the stronger of the two terms; watching is more intense than waiting. We may be waiting for a friend, yet not be watching for him. We are not only to wait for Jesus, we are to watch for Him.

Watching is the very "watch-word" of the Bible in regard to all the truths concerning our Lord's coming. Our blessed Master did constantly urge His disciples to watch, particularly with reference to His return. Seven times the word occurs in His discourse about the last things. (The following passages were quoted and commented upon: Luke xxi., 3 6; Mark xiii., 33-35-37; Matt. xxiv: 42, 43; xxv., 13; I. Thess. v. 6, 10; Rev. iii., 3; xvi-15). It is remarkable to note, as lexicographers tell us, that the original Greek word used in most of these passages is one that occurs nowhere in all extant Greek literature outside of the New Testament and the Septuagint translation of the Old Testament. It is *gregoreo*, I watch, from a word meaning to awaken. From it is derived the strictly Christian proper name Gregorius or Gregory, one who watches, a watcher. We should, therefore, be awake, be on the alert, be looking out for the coming of our Lord.

Why? 1. Because we have so much to watch over, we have so many valuable things, the grace and peace of God, the word of God, "precious and exceeding great promises," title deeds of our inheritance, the spirit of God as "an earnest of our inheritance." A watchman over coffers full of gold, or jewels, or other valuables, will be more likely and careful to watch, well armed, than a tramp will be over an empty old bag. 2. Because we are sojourners and pilgrims through a strange land, full of enemies and various dangers, such as worldliness, formalism, love of ease, proneness to run down, get low or cold in spiritual life, or, on the other hand, fanaticism, religious egotism and the like. Nothing will so much help us to be sober, to watch and pray as having our Lord's near appearance before our eyes, revolving it with all its consequences constantly in our minds.

As an incentive to and aid in watching comes naturally earnest, faithful

WORKING

for the Master. "Trade ye herewith till I come." "Glory and honor and peace to every man that worketh good." "Give diligence to present thyself approved unto God, a workman that needeth not be ashamed." These are ringing, significant words, like trumpet calls. True, earnest, unselfish, self-sacrificing, spiritual, Christian work is needed everywhere—within us, near us, around us, and away beyond our horizon—individual and united work, work in thousand different ways, work by the learned, the talented, the rich, the old, the young, the poor, the unlearned; work till the Master comes. But how can active Christian work agree with eager watching and longing for Christ's speedy coming? Very well. There is the same connection between waiting and watching for the Lord's return on one hand, and working for the saving of the lost or for any other direct Christian object on the other hand, as there is generally between faith and works. It is certain, and has been demonstrated innumerable times, that where there is the greatest faith the most implicit, childlike, loving faith in God, in Christ, in the Divine Spirit, in God's word, in its commands and promises, there is the greatest, most faithful, most earnest, most joyful, most successful Christian work. And thus it is here. One who most lovingly and hopefully believes in and expects his dear Lord's near advent, that one will be most actively, buoyantly, faithfully and wakefully engaged in some work for his adorable Master. Because he is awake and watching for the coming of his Lord, he will be the more watchful for souls. Because he believes more of the word of the Lord, he will use it more, teach it more, press it home more on the consciences of sinners. He has the cross of Christ in one hand with which to fish out poor sinners from the mire of the world, and in the other he has the title deeds of a full, undefiled inheritance and of several glittering crowns that the new convert may obtain just as soon as Christ comes, and the sooner He does come the better. The Christian worker who believes in and rightly uses both the advents of Christ, the past and the future, has the true two-edged sword, with which to fight most valiantly the battles of the Lord.

Which think you would be the more encouraging and inspiring to work faithfully on the part of a company of

SERVANTS OF A PRINCE,

if that prince with his servants should stand by a seashore and say to his servants: "Now, I am going away for a while; you go to work and empty that ocean, and save the water (transfer it to other quarters), and when you have done that, then I will come back and reward you." Well, they would go to work and get out a good deal of water, but, oh, the idea of emptying that ocean! How it would overpower them! How they would find excuses, and discuss methods, and invent machinery, and theorize about the chances of the water finding some underground passage in order to be saved. No wonder if they are saying: "Our Lord delayeth his coming." But on the other hand, suppose the prince says to his servants, "I am going away from you so that you will not see me for a while, but still I'll be with you; my thoughts and my mind will be with you; everything you need I'll supply you with. Now you know that big sea there is unhealthy, and is generally not what it ought to be; you go to work and get out all the water you can, filter it, distill it; it will be put to special use. I am going to turn it into something wonderful, and when I find you have done all that is needed in this respect then I will come back and atttend to the rest of this old stinking ocean, and it is going to be all right by and by."

Now, judge for yourselves, dear friends, which of these different orders would in the inspiring for the servants of the prince to supposed case be the most encouraging and work diligently and enthusiastically? Well, we, all believers in Jesus, are His servants; the ocean is the world of humanity; the water now taken out and filtered and purified for special uses is "the church of the first-born who are enrolled in heaven," and here we are to work till Jesus comes.

The more that are gathered unto Him the sooner will his church be full grown, and He will come and take her home, and the angels will publish the marriage banns, and there will be a "high life" wedding in "high places." Thus, if we love our Lord and His church, we will have the experience of Jacob, who "served seven years for Rachael, and they seemed to him but a few days for the love he had to her."

"My soul crieth out for a jubilee song!
There is joy in my heart, let me praise with my tongue;
For I know though the darkness of Egypt still lowers,
That the time of release is not ages, but hours."

BISHOP MAURICE BALDWIN.

THE POWER OF THIS TRUTH TO STIMULATE THE WORK OF EVANGELIZATION.

My Christian friends, I have been asked to speak on the subject of the bearing of the doctrine of Christ's premillennial coming on the subject of missions, and, I may add, of our daily Christian life. There are many indications, no doubt, of the speedy coming of our Lord and master Jesus Christ, but among the most tangible is this, the awakening interest in the cause of missions. Wherever we see members of the church of Christ we see awakening interest in the great work of missionary labor. Not a hundred years ago there was the utmost apathy and indifference everywhere upon the subject, and many of you are aware of the reception which Carey met with when he preached to the people on his going to India to proclaim the gospel of the grace of God. The subject was met with ridicule, sarcasm, and scorn. It was derided on every hand. But where, I ask, to-day is there any representative of the Church of Christ who will stand up in a public assembly to ridicule the great work of missions? Such an one could not be found. There has been a most tremendous growth upon the subject, and the fact of this great growth is one indication, at least to my mind, of the speedy coming of our Lord.

Let us observe the following facts: Our Lord tells us in the 24th of Matthew, that His gospel was "to be preached in all the world for a witness unto all nations, and then shall the end come." It seems to me clear and definite that the instruction given to us in this passage is that our Lord intends that His gospel is to be preached in every land for a witness.

Now, a hundred and fifty years ago people might have folded their arms and said that that idea of Christ's coming was, to say the least, intensely remote. And what was the state of the whole church at that time? There was great laxity and indifference. And I can say as a member of the Church of England that the growth of that church has been in direct ratio to her advancement of the cause of missions, and I will further say that never was there a time of deeper spiritual life—never was there a time of intenser earnestness than there is to-day, and if we ask what reason may be assigned for this, it is that there has been this increased blessing in the work of advancing the gospel of Jesus Christ. Great missionary societies have arisen. They are constantly developing and expanding in their work, so that to-day there is scarcely to be found a nation not willing, to a greater or less extent, to receive the heralds of the cross. The world is to-day interpenetrated by missions. India, from the mountains of Himalaya to the Cape Comorin is receiving the word of truth, and away into Tartary and Thibet, the Lord Jesus is sending out His messengers, glad precursors of that blessed morning when He shall come to take His bride to be with Himself; to be forever with Him in His presence.

I would state in the next place, that our Lord is further preparing for His advent by stirring up his people so that they have learned this truth, that whilst the whole work must be advanced,—whilst the millions which lie about their own doors must be seen to, yet there is the paramount duty which we cannot divest ourselves of, to spread the gospel "till like a sea of glory it spreads from pole to pole." We see, however, that in this dispensation there are limitations. Christ says (using a Greek word) "this gospel must be preached for a witness." He does not say till every nation is converted. He does not say until every person is brought into direct and positive subjection to His perfect sway. He tells us that it is for a witness, and we are told distinctly that His coming is to gather out from the nations His ecclesia. That gathering is going on to-day.

The subject before me is the power of this truth to encourage and stimulate the church in and to the work of evangelization, and I therefore pass on to state in the next place that there has often been brought to my mind the objection that so little is apparently done. The enemies of missions have risen and said, Where are the results which we might have anticipated? Where are the nations born in a day? Where are the unconverted millions that are bowing down at His feet to worship and serve him? In answer I would state, the Lord's purposes unfold slowly but surely, and we look forward through the darkness to the brighter morning before us. There was an able paper read this morning upon the Second Coming of Christ as Related to Israel, and I might first add that, amongst the many blessings which are in future store for the world, is this restoration, the conversion of the ancient people of Israel. It is just one of those grand majestic steps, the heighth, and the depth, the length and the breadth of which our finite minds have not yet fully grasped. Sufficient however to say, that the subject was just touched upon, and may be developed this afternoon concerning the effects which flow from the restoration of God's ancient people.

The apostle says. "If their rejection be the reconciling of the world, what shall their acceptation be but life from the dead?" Now does that mean something absolutely figurative? Is it to be related to the domain of metaphor? I do not think so. We find that the rejection of Israel was the preaching of the gospel to us gentiles. The apostle said, "Since you count yourselves unworthy of eternal life, lo, we turn to the gentiles." Well, now we gentiles have been receiving the gospel for so many hundred years, I may say that we have not been as faithful as we should have been, and the apostle distinctly states that there was the fear lest, if God spared not the natural branches, He would not spare the wild olive tree. But we learn from Scripture that there is an end of the church of the first born, that it, the church of the first born, is to be caught up to meet the Lord in the air, and that in this blessed milenial glory which is to follow Israel is to take its place as the great and mighty priestly nation for the advancing of the gospel of God's eternal love.

Now I draw your attention to the fact there is a line of prophecies concerning Israel which, under no mode of interpretation, can be claimed to have been already fulfilled. Take the wondrous prophecy concerning Israel commencing with the sixtieth chapter of Isaiah. No one can say that this has ever as yet met with its fulfillment. In the tenth verse: "And the sons of strangers shall build up thy walls, and their kings shall minister unto them; for in my wrath I smote thee, but in my favor have I had mercy on thee." Twelfth verse: "For the nation and the kingdom that will not serve thee shall perish, yea those nations shall be utterly wasted." There are so many besides these that might be quoted that I would consume too much of your time were I to read them. I may say, however, that they point to the time when Jerusalem shall be the moral center of the earth. It shall be neither London, nor Paris, nor New York, but the kingly glory—the center of God's mighty operations, shall be the Holy City, and Israel being restored and converted shall become the great nation to extend the gospel throughout all quarters of the earth. In the 20th chapter of the same prophet, and at the 26th verse, the sublime language is used, "Moreover the light of the moon shall be as the light of the sun, and the light of the sun shall be sevenfold, as the light of seven days, in the day that the Lord bindeth up the breach of His people, and healeth the stroke of their wound." The church of the first born having been removed to be at the side of the Heavenly Bridegroom, the millennial glory shall be the great time of missions. It will be the time when the light of the moon shall be as the light of the sun. It will be the time when nations shall be born in a day. It will be the time when Israel's people shall be righteous, and men shall know them as the ministers of God.

Let us note in the next place, that therefore we are to pray that the Lord will speedily come. Then at his coming, living waters shall flow out of Jerusalem for the healing of the people. Therefore it is our duty, our blessed, glorious privilege, to know that Christ is coming, and to cry continually, "Come, Lord Jesus, come quickly" to thy waiting, waiting church.

Now, these truths must have the greatest power upon our Christian life. They are doctrines which must affect us. As some people hold that there is no personal coming, it seems to me to take away the brightest sight that the eye can rest upon. A pleasant thing it is for the eye to see the light, but a pleasanter thing for the soul to look upon Jesus Christ, and to know that our dear Lord is coming, coming soon to take His bride to be forever with Him; and therefore if we believe that Christ is coming, and if, in the second place, we believe that coming to be contingent upon the diffusion of the gospel of Jesus Christ, does it not follow, as a necessary consequence, that those who are permeated with such views will want to do everything that lies in their power to advance the cause of missions? It is His cause, not ours. We see Christ in struggling missions, we see His glory in the feeblest of them. There is a mistaken idea in this world about what are the great movements. People suppose that when great nations sign declarations of war against other nations that these are the great events, but as I look at it the great events of life are the going forth of groups of missionaries with the gospel in their hands, to proclaim God's love to dying men. The great event waits the work of these men. This gospel must be preached to every nation, and then shall the end come. Then in view of this ought we not—and this seems as practical as the other—to be more ready than we are to lay down our silver and our gold—to consecrate our means to the blessed cause of Jesus Christ, that this work may be accomplished and that the bride may soon look up and say, "Behold he cometh leaping upon the mountains, skipping upon the hills."

The next point I have to speak about is, that in considering the subject of our Lord's coming and its bearing on missions, we can not but notice that the whole subject of revelation is only now being slowly examined into. I do not underrate the labors of earnest men in the past. I am only speaking of the general fact in the case. The book of the Revelation has been practically sealed. Now I do not wonder at the fact. Let us understand that the Scripture clearly points out that Satan is the god of the world. It indicates that Satan has had a great deal to do upon the earth. He caused the failure of our first parents, and this book is the book which tells his doom. It shows him bound, and thrown into the lake of fire. It shows us the fulfillment of the statement of the dear Lord. "I saw Satan as lightning fall from heaven." It shows us the final end, the holy foot of Jesus Christ upon the neck of our great foe, and his being hurled into that bottomless pit, from which he is never to rise. Is it likely that he would promote the study of the book of Revelation? No, it is not likely. It is more likely that he would induce people to consider that it is so dark, so mysterious, so utterly incomprehensible, that the safest, the wisest, and the most judicious course was to leave it absolutely unread; but at the very threshold of the book lies the statement, "Blessed is he that readeth, and they that hear the words of this prophecy, and keep those things which are written therein, for the time is at hand."

Now if we go to the study of the book of Revelation we find that it is just that which the grace of God indicates we should do. In the epistle of Paul to Titus there are three effects noted of the grace of God. One is that it teaches us to deny ungodliness and worldly lusts; secondly, that we should live soberly, righteously, and godly in this present world. The one is the negative, the other the positive, and the third is that we should "look for that blessed hope, the glorious appearing of our great God and Saviour, Jesus Christ." I would say that these three effects ought to be kept together, the negative, denying ungodliness: the positive, living soberly; and thirdly, looking for the blessed coming. Thus we live in hope, however bright the day may be, and howevor joyous we may be if we are looking for His coming, it makes the day go swifter. The thought that in a moment we may stand face to face with Him, how it helps us to bear the sorrows of this troubled life. To stand amidst the duties of every day and look through the dark and thickening air, and feel that the coming of the Lord draweth swiftly nigh. It is the grace of God within the heart that makes us look up from things temporal to things eternal.

Now, the next point is the statement of the Apostle Paul as to our present position. His language is very remarkable. He says that our commonwealth is where Christ is. If we turn to the Epistle to the Philippians, third chapter, twentieth verse, we find the apostle stating—as it is in the old version—"our conversation is in heaven." Now that word means more than that; it is our commonwealth, our state is in heaven. We are to live there; that is, we do not live there as regards the body. We do not live there as regards things temporal, but the apostle, in his epistle to the Ephesians, tells us that this is our commonwealth, that place where Christ is and from which we expect our Lord to issue; we are to live there. And I would say, how much more nobly would we walk and live if we realized more the pilgrim character of those that are expecting the coming Christ. The sandals then would always be upon our feet, and the staff would ever be in our hands, and our faces would be towards the city of the great King. We would use the things of this world as not abusing them. We would fill the time of our sojourn with happy, joyous service, seeking to improve each moment, that we might advance the glory of our blessed God.

Another point I would draw you attention to is a very remarkable one concerning this subject. That just in proportion as we expect our Lord's coming, and look for that coming, do we grow in divine life. In the third chapter of the second epistle to the Corinthians, eighteenth verse, the apostle

RT. REV. MAURICE BALDWIN, D. D.,
BISHOP OF HURON.

says: "We all with open face beholding as in a glass the glory of the Lord, are changed into the same image from glory to glory, even as by the spirit of the Lord." Now I gather that however difficult this passage may be, and however many interpretations have been given as to its proper meaning, that it simply teaches us that the view of Christ transfigures us. That just as a man going into the state where people are below him and inferior to him in education, inferior to him in life, and he to go among them and adopt their modes of living and expression, loses his high position by going down to them—he sinks, whereas if we look at Christ, the apostle says, gazing at Him, setting the Lord always before us, from sunrise to sunset, we are changed into His image from glory to glory. There is elevating power in the study of the coming of the Lord. None of us deny for one moment that people have taken up unscriptural ground on the subject. That people have run into wild excess, and have brought the subject in the eyes of many into discredit, but the truth is here. It is before us, and just as we keep Christ before us, and His coming glory do we, ourselves, becomes changed into the likeness of His image, so that if He tarries, and we have fallen asleep, we shall awake satisfied with His likeness. We shall see Him when this corruptible shall have been exchanged for the incorruptible, and this mortal shall be changed into the immortal, and we know not what we shall be, but we know that when He shall appear we shall be like Him, for we shall see Him as He is.

Again, I might speak too of the comfort of this doctrine. We are sometimes called to comfort those who mourn, and I think that so often whilst people comfort the mourner with whatever doctrine they have at their command, they fail to see the mode in which the apostle Paul would comfort those that weep the loss of friends. So often people get no further than the language of David when he said, the child could not come to him, but he could go to the child. True, but we go to the house of mourning with the apostle and say, at least we try to say, that there is a strong consolation, that that body which represents the home of a sleeping saint is just laid—perchance for a little while to rest there—perhaps only a day, a week, a month, a year, and then Christ shall come, and the dead in Christ shall rise first. We point them to the fact that the believer's falling asleep is, as it were, momentary; that that body is precious to God. That it has been redeemed as well as the soul. That the Lord knows its resting-place, and that He shall call it forth again, purified, beautified, and made meet for the eternal home. "Comfort one another with these words." Tell them that the night is far spent, and that the day is at hand. In the day of mourning people are told to bear their sorrows, and it is most proper and most true; but there is this further to be said that while we do bear our sorrow, and whilst we mourn, it is not of those who have no hope; that we know it is only for a little while. If I am called to go to the bedside, and afterward to follow to the grave, one who has sunk without hope, what can I say? I say, I know he shall rise, but I know not when; the Lord knoweth. There is a darkness and a gloom, but that darkness and that gloom does not rest on the believer's hope—it is bright. It is "the Lord shall come again."

Two other points, and I conclude. First, the apostle says there is a crown for those that love His appearing. In the second epistle to Timothy, fourth chapter and eighth verse, we read: "Henceforth there is laid up for me a crown of righteousness, which the Lord, the righteous Judge, shall give me at that day, and not to me only, but unto all them also that love His appearing." Have you ever thought that that crown is for all who love His appearing? It is for those who are looking for it. The Greek verb signifies the waiting for His coming. That crown is not spoken of as being given to those who have achieved great results. Not even to those that even the church have thought the most worthy, but to those who love His appearing. To those who through good and evil report have waited, and with the cry, "Come, Lord Jesus, come quickly."

The next thought is with reference to the gifts. In I. Corinthians first chapter and seventh verse is the remarkable statement. The apostle says that they, the Corinthians, come behind in no gift, waiting for the coming of the "Lord Jesus Christ." In other words, that just as they waited they were endowed with the various gifts of the Holy Ghost. Now just as the gospel of Christ is proclaimed with the Holy Ghost is with power and the men who, anterior to Christ's first advent, proclaimed that Christ would come, were men of power. They were the great and mighty of Israel—the men who, like Isaiah and Jeremiah, Ezekiel, Daniel, and the minor prophets, lifted up their voices and said that Messiah cometh. They were men of power, having the gifts of the Holy Ghost. Now, then, we come to our day, and I gather that the apostle's teaching is this: That the men who to-day proclaim the second advent shall have the especial *charisma* which belong to the Church of Christ. That, in other words, the Holy Ghost will endow with special powers those that boldly, fearlessly, and emphatically make known the hope of the church in the speedy coming of Christ.

Those true servants in Corinth came behind in no gift. I might expatiate onthe subject, but I will only say that these gifts of the Holy Ghost were to dwell in the church, and just as this truth of the second advent is brought forward the servant of Christ may expect power.

In conclusion, there are several subjects on which I might speak; but I will conclude with the following: If the cause of missions be brought before us, let us cease from looking at the subject from the human stand point and rather identify the cause wholly with the personal, living Christ. Second, let us bear in mind the words of Christ, "Pray ye therefore the Lord of the harvest, that he may send forth more laborers into the vineyard." I do think that each day we should pray for the cause of missions; we should pray that the faith of those in the work may be stronger, that mightier success may be given them; and let us remember that on their success is dependent the coming of our risen and exalted Lord. Let us, therefore, live very near to our Divine Master, in abiding, holy, blessed union, for "he that abideth in me, and I him, the same bringeth forth much fruit." Christ in me bringeth forth much fruit, and the whole effect of this blessed doctrine is to bring us into closer personal union with Jesus Christ. It is that we may die and He live. Oh, that we shall learn more and more the power of our daily death and His daily life.

In the next place, it will lead us to be more earnest in the reclamation of those that have wandered away. It will make us more in earnest in trying to win the lost and erring souls to the Lord Jesus. It will make us preach with more fervor, more earnestness the gospel of love to sinners. It will make us feel as Frances Ridley Havergal said she felt, that sainted woman who fell asleep so recently, "I try to see my Lord in every person I meet, and I try to minister to every one, that I may minister in every one to my Lord and Master Jesus Christ."

And, dear fellow Christions, let this Lord dwell richly in you. Let Him be the Alpha and He the Omega. Let Him come with many crowns upon His head into your heart, and let Him sit upon the throne, and you lie low at His feet. Let Him speak, and do you obey, and just as you dwell in this attitude you will find His yoke is easy and His burden is light, and you will get faith each day to hasten His blessed coming.

IMPORTANT EXEGETICAL PAPERS.

VOICES OF EUROPEAN PROFESSORS.

NOTE.—The important letters appearing on pages 135 to 138, from old-world professors of the first standing and scholarship, in addition to the one from Professor Godet, of Neuchatel, Switzerland (pages 121-122), were laid before the conference by Dr. West, who had, with much pains, secured and prepared them in translated form for this occasion. A brief note from Professor Luthardt, of Leipzig, expressing his regret at inability to write any communication, and referring to the forthcoming new edition of his work on the "Last Things," was not read. As for these professors, their names are household words with multitudes of our American scholars, and of great authority. Drs. Godet, Delitzsch, and Luthardt are known so well by their great scholarship, piety, and Biblical labors that it is unnecessary to say anything more. Pastor Koch, of Bardewisch, Oldenburg, Saxony, is one of the most powerful critics of the age, and, like Professor Volck, has vigorously defended the early church faith. Both, like many others in Germany, have answered, with effect, the spiritualizing commentaries of Keil and Hengstenberg on the prophets and the Apocalypse. Professor Volck, of the University of Dorpat, Russia, is unsurpassed, as an exegete, to-day, and his name appears as in the list of eminent contributors to Zockler's "Hand Book of Theological Sciences." Among his colleagues are Kurtz, the church historian, and Christiani, both strong Chiliasts. The celebrated Martensen, recently deceased, was of the same university.

REASONS FOR HOLDING THE BIBLE AND PROPHETIC CONFERENCE.

BY GEORGE C. NEEDHAM.

Before the adjournment of this precious meeting I wish to summarize a few of the reasons for its existence:

1. To give prominence to neglected truth. This is simply history repeating itself. God, who is jealous for all portions of His word, compels His servants to give each part its due place. Hence when any doctrine falls into disuse He moves in a single heart, as in the heart of Luther, who gave the needed emphasis to "justification by faith," or He draws together for counsel and action a number of Christians who become a unit in their utterance of a lost or forgotten testimony. Nor will any servant of our Lord escape reproach who persistently determines to rescue from oblivion any or every item of God's complete and revealed will.

It is a universally acknowledged fact that unfulfilled prophecy has, for centuries, been relegated to the theologian's grave. But truth is life and power. It leaps from its sepulchre soon as the stone is rolled away. In every age willing hands are found to do this work; in every century Bible students have come to the front, not shrinking from the stigma put upon them because of their zeal in endeavoring to bring Scripture prophecy out into the open

SUNLIGHT OF CRITICISM

and publicity. Let none, however, be intimidated by scoffs nor be deceived by sophisms. Formerly the cry was raised that prophetic study bred fanaticism; now it is the siren song that materialistic theology is alone attractive, and eschatology is both unpractical and non-essential.

If this be so how singularly unpracticable was our Lord, who gave so much prominence in his teaching to future events, and how short-sighted was the Divine spirit, the author of scripture, who inspired holy men of old to write so largely of things to come. "The testimony of Jesus is the spirit of prophecy." Is it not libelous, irreverent, nay infamous to charge the living God with folly? Does it not, to say the least, betray a heart far removed from fellowship with God in His eternal purposes for any to dare affirm there is anything non-essential in the Bible? The object, then, of the conference has been to make prominent teachings of God's word which have been so greatly neglected; teachings both powerful in motive and practical in every detail of life.

2. Another object of the conference has been to emphasize the true principles of Scripture interpretation. The figurizing theory has made sad havoc of Bible prophecy. Its advocates are compelled to violate their own principle in every case of fulfilled prophecy. Where is the consistency of saying the prophecies concerning our Lord's first advent must be literally interpreted, while those relating to

HIS SECOND ADVENT

are purely metaphorical? In Zech. ix. it is prophesied that our Lord should come meek and lowly, riding upon an ass; but in chapter xiv. it is said He will come again, and His feet shall stand upon the Mount of Olives. The ass, say those who figurize, means an ass, but the Mount of Olives is the broken heart of the penitent sinner, who is now close to Jerusalem, that is the church.

The true principles of interpretation have been made prominent by several speakers throughout the conference, viz.: That where no figure is intended, the word of God is to be interpreted in its plain, literal, and grammatical sense. Hence prophetic truth is to be received, as every other truth, by faith; "with the heart man believeth unto righteousness." The faith which rests on divine testimony concerning any doctrine of the Bible is the same kind of faith which believes in the same Word concerning things to come..

3. Another object the conference had in view was the awakening of Christians from slumber. We are living in an enchanted age, and are passing over Bunyan's enchanted ground. The air is heavy, and the spiritual senses of the King's pilgrims are

ever in danger of stupefaction. We have need to meet together and exhort one another, in view of

THE APPROACHING DAY.

Sleep is for sons of night; "Let us not sleep as do others, but let us watch and be sober." As the hour of our completed salvation draws near "is it not high time to awake out of sleep?" By every consideration, of the heathen abroad and at home; of the present intensity of sin and the philosophical forms of wickedness; of the unregenerate state of our neighbors, our sons and our daughters, our husbands and wives; of the drunken and debauched state of society, and the benumbed and paralyzed condition of Christendom, we appeal to you, to the church of God, to all who name the name of Jesus, to arouse you from slumber. Nay more, our divine Lord Himself appeals to you: "Awake thou that sleepest and arise from among the dead."

4. Again, the conference presents the most majestic of all motives for world-wide evangelism. Both earnestly and powerfully the hope of our Lord's glorious return has been presented. And this present meeting, the final session of the conference, has convened for the purpose of bringing before us the harrowing need of the world, our grave responsibilities in relation to its dark moral condition, and the divine incentive, the stimulating motive for immediate and persistent action. Oh! let not the heathen nations rebuke us as pagan sailors rebuked the renegade prophet: "What meanest thou, O, sleeper? Arise, call upon thy God, if so be that God will think upon us, that we perish not."

5. This Bible and Prophetic Conference calls attention to the doctrine of "last things" as

A BULWARK

against the skepticism of modern theology. Two hundred years ago old Manton wrote: "All new light is old darkness revived; it is neither new nor light." The gentlemen at Andover feel deeply aggrieved that their smoky and sulphurous match-light of mongrel Ayrian-German rationalism is not readily utilized by those who walk in the undimmed sunlight of divine revelation as it shines in every verse, word, and letter from Gen. i. to Rev. xxii. Brethren, premillenarianism pure and simple forms a breakwater against every advancing tide which would throw upon the clean beach of a God-given theology the jelly-fish theories evolved out of man's erratic consciousness, pride, and self-will.

"Waiting for the Son from heaven" is an antidote against the feverishness of the age, as shown in its excited race after theological novelties.

6. I could furnish you with other weighty reasons why this important conference should be held. But I mention only one more. Thousands of our Lord's dear saints who love His appearing and kingdom, many of whom live in isolated places, are hereby brought into nearer fellowship one with another. How gratifying has been our meeting together, how blessedly helpful to each and all who have for the first time greeted one another within these walls. We have met; we now part; but the warm grasp of the hand, the

TONES OF THE VOICE,

the form and features of brethren hitherto unknown will abide with us in memory and in influence. Our oneness in Christ is made more real and precious because of this present communion.

Let me not, however, be misunderstood. We are no clique or party coterie—no exclusive company of self-admiring Pharisees. Thank God, we can and do say, with tender emotion, "Grace be with all who love our Lord Jesus Christ in sincerity." Our love in the Lord, our fellowship in service, our companionship in tribulation, embrace the friends of Jesus who, though not one with us in prophetic study, are one with us in eternal union, redeemed with the same blood, indwelt by the same spirit, having become heirs together of the grace of life.

Beloved, the brotherly fellowship we have so sweetly enjoyed during the days we have been together will not be severed, though necessarily interrupted, as we now part one from another. But

"The memory, so precious of hallowed delight,
Shall strengthen our faith and equip for the fight.
When severed in presence there still doth remain
Our oneness in hope of His coming again.

"We go to the fields where our lot has been thrown,
Where soil must be turned and where seed must sown,
That sinners may hear of the Lamb who was slain,
And saints be prepared for His coming again."

"*Our God shall come.*"—Ps. 50:3.

ADDRESSES

—ON—

The Second Coming of the Lord.

DELIVERED AT

The Prophetic Conference,

ALLEGHENY, PA.

December 3—6, 1895.

"*Even so, come, Lord Jesus.*"—Rev. 22:20.

PITTSBURGH:

W. W. WATERS,

706 Penn Avenue.

PRINTED BY

WM. G. JOHNSTON & CO.,

Cr. Penn Avenue and Ninth Street.

Pittsburgh, Pa.

CONTENTS.

PREFACE.

A meeting of those who believe in the premillennial coming of the Lord Jesus Christ was held July 15, 1895, in the parlors of the Young Men's Christian Association, Pittsburgh, and it was then decided to call a Conference for the study of the prophecies relating to the second coming of the Lord, to meet in Allegheny, Pa., December 3–6, 1895, and the following named as a General Committee of Arrangements:

Rev. Joseph Kyle, D. D.,	Rev. B. F. Woodburn, D. D.,
Thos. J. Gillespie,	Sam'l P. Harbison, Chairman,
Henry W. Fulton, M. D.,	Geo. M. Paden, Treasurer,
M. W. Callender,	Rev. William S. Miller, Sec'y.

Together with Prof. W. G. Moorehead, D. D., and Rev. W. J. Erdman, D. D., as advisory members.

Invitations for holding the sessions of the Conference were received from the Fourth United Presbyterian Church, Arch street and Montgomery avenue, Rev. Jos. Kyle, D. D., pastor, and from the First Presbyterian Church, on Arch street, Rev. D. S. Kennedy, D. D., pastor.

The Conference met on Tuesday evening, December 3, 1895, 7.30 o'clock, in the Fourth United Presbyterian Church, and held three sessions there on Wednesday.

Thursday and Friday three sessions each were held, in the First Presbyterian Church.

The attendance was very large, and great interest was shown in the study of God's Word, and great blessing attended each service.

It was felt that such testimony as was given to those who were privileged to be there should have a wider circulation, and to stimulate imitation of the Bereans of old, to "Search the Scriptures daily whether those things were so," these addresses have been published and are now sent forth, with the prayer that the Holy Spirit, who was so manifestly present in the Conference and opened eyes to see the "truth as it is in Jesus," will bless these pages to every reader and help us all "grow in grace and in the knowledge of our Lord and Saviour Jesus Christ," "looking for the blessed hope and appearing of the glory of our Great God and Saviour Jesus Christ."

And may we ever join in the prayer of the Apostle John, "Even so, come, Lord Jesus."

JOSEPH KYLE.
WILLIAM S. MILLER.

THE FINAL ISSUE OF THE AGE.

PROF. REV. W. G. MOOREHEAD, D. D.,

Professor in United Presbyterian Seminary, Xenia, Ohio.

I speak to you of the Final Issue of the Age. By *the age*, of course, is meant the present dispensation. It is the period during which the Gospel is proclaimed to the world for the obedience of faith, and in which the church, which is Christ's body, is being gathered. It began its course when the people of Israel rejected and crucified the Messiah, and were themselves in turn rejected and sent forth into an exile that still endures. It began with the resurrection and ascension of our Lord and the marvels of Pentecost. During this age, God's work of salvation is mainly confined to Gentile peoples, an elect remnant only of Israel sharing in its glories. For in the significant and profound words of the Lord Jesus, these are the "times of the Gentiles," the times in which divine favor is shown them, and the gifts and graces of God are richly bestowed upon them. The sovereignty of the world is in their hands. God's goodness flows out to them in unmeasured abundance. In the meantime Jerusalem lies prostrate in the dust, the chosen people a dismembered and dispersed nation. Partial blindness has smitten Israel. The solemn words in which Paul closed his interview with the heads of the Jewish colony at Rome have had ample fulfilment in subsequent times: "Be it known therefore unto you, that the salvation of God is sent unto the Gentiles, and that they will hear it," (Acts 28:28). This state of things will continue until the fulness of the Gentiles is come in, *i. e.* until the full complement of the chosen and called from among the Gentiles shall have been gathered to the Lord Jesus Christ, and then all Israel shall be saved, and once more assume their place as the covenanted people of God. Rom. 11.

The history of this age has been a most eventful one; its achievements have been gigantic, its disasters stupendous. In the earlier centuries of it Christianity won its most marvellous victories, when it confronted a hostile world and defeated it. It encountered the huge Roman Empire and conquered it. Met the savage Gaul and Briton, and subdued them. It traveled northward to the homes of that strange, wild people, the Norsemen, and from the fierce and brutal sea-kings they were, it transformed them into humane and tender Christians. It has changed the face of the world. Nor have the failures and crimes of the age been less conspicuous. Its guilt has been something enormous. Perversion of the truth, lust of power, rebellion against God, treason against human liberty, apostasy and persecution are only some of the counts in the indictment against this age. Declension and recovery, corruption and reformation, liberty and license, Smyrna faithful in the fire and the prison, and Thyatira with the woman Jezebel not only tolerated but teaching, Philadelphia with a feeble few holding fast the word of Christ's patience, and Laodicea lukewarm and latitudinarian—such has been the long, sorrowful story. Our own times offer a fair portrait of the chief features of the entire age. The evidences are not wanting that the people of God at this present exhibit a faithfulness and zeal unsurpassed in the annals of the age. There are multitudes who live and labor for God with a self-sacrificing devotion that must fill and thrill every true heart with gladness. Never since the Reformation of the Sixteenth century has the Bible commanded such attention as now; never has it been read and studied and expounded as now. Even its more mysterious part, its marvellous prophecies, are investigated and grappled with by the acutest minds of the civilized world. The words of the revealing angel to the prophet Daniel are now receiving a literal fulfilment; "Many shall run to and fro," shall eagerly and industriously turn over and re-turn these prophetic pages, shall dig and delve and mine into them and so shall the knowledge of them be increased. Missionary activity is one of the marvels of our day. Never since apostolic times has the Gospel been preached to the nations of the world as now. Nor are martyrs lacking. In China, in Africa, in the Isles of the sea, the heralds and heroes of the Cross *die* if need be for the name of the Son of God. But there is a reverse side of this hopeful picture, and it is dark and dreadful enough. The ship that carries the missionary carries rum and gin and opium and fire-arms, whereby the so-called Christian nations are destroying a hundred souls where the church saves one. The printing press, which scatters the Bible in more than three hundred tongues, is flooding the world with infidel and impure literature. The thousands of devout and reverent students of the Scriptures are offset by men in the highest places of trust and influence, heads of literary institutions, professors in Theological Seminaries, occupants of commanding pulpits, Christian teachers at least in name, men of the broadest cultivation and the widest reading—who are striving to slit the leaves of the Holy Book into strips with their Jehoiakim penknives, and to burn them in the braziers at their feet. Hear the illustration of our beloved brother, lately gone to his rest, Dr. A. J. Gordon: "What progress has there been made in lighting our homes within a single century: from the rude tallow candle of our forefathers, through the sperm-oil wick and the rock-oil lamp and the jet of burning gas, till we have reached the electric light so surpassingly brilliant that I cannot see it without beholding a startling emblem of 'that light into which no man can approach.' But look at the shadows which this electric light throws upon the pavement at night! Was there ever such blackness of darkness—such a dense and almost tangible concentration of night? Our times display a splendor of light perhaps never before surpassed. But the shadows it casts are correspondingly black."

Such is our age—an age which for nearly nineteen centuries has been characterized by a mixture of good and evil, now the one, now the other in the ascendancy—an age in which God visits the Gentiles to take out of them a people for his name, (Acts 15:14) an age in which wheat and tares grow side by side, in which the children of God and the Devil's brood struggle for the mastery, an age whose God is Satan, Paul assures us, (2 Cor. 4:4), and which he accordingly describes as "this present evil age," (Gal. 1:4). The fathers, who saw as deeply into the tendencies of the times as we, said, two antagonistic forces will be seen deepening and intensifying as the age hurries to its close: the activity of the righteous who witness against the evil and who spread the knowledge of the truth far and wide, and the activity of the wicked, who obstruct the good, propagate the evil, and combine and mass for the final conflict. These two, working side by side, running neck and neck, will distinguish the End time.

The question that is now to occupy our attention is this: What is to be the final issue of this age? What will be its consummation? The conversion of the world? The establishment of that kingdom of righteousness and peace which the prophets announce in such glowing terms? Multitudes of honest and faithful men make answer in the affirmative. They believe and teach that worldwide evangelism means ultimately worldwide conversion, and the in-bringing of Millennial blessedness. An increasing number of men make answer in the negative. They believe and teach that during this age God's work is elective. They hold that it is not the divine purpose to introduce the promised blessing for the whole earth by the agencies and instrumentalities now at work. The universal offer of the Gospel does not mean its universal acceptance. It is not a question of power, but of purpose, and the revealed purpose is to gather out of the nations a people for God's name. But there is a dispensation when the earth shall be filled with the knowledge of the glory of the Lord as the waters cover the sea, when preaching and teaching will no longer be required, for all shall know him from the least to the greatest. This dispensation therefore cannot be the last, for the effects stated in *that* are not contemplated in the instructions and the results of *this*. The aim of this paper is not to determine which party is right in this contention, but to discover if we can the final outcome of this age, what its end is to be. To this one point we unflinchingly adhere. The testimony of Scripture must be our only guide in this investigation.

What testimony does the Bible render touching the end of the age? We do not hesitate to reply, that on any fair principle of interpretation God's word represents this age as terminating with the coming of Christ in judgment, in the overthrow of every form of wickedness, and in the establishment of the predicted kingdom of righteousness and peace. Both Testaments, the Old and the New alike, witness to this central truth. To a very limited portion of this testimony can reference now be made.

1. Joel 3. The prophet himself affirms that the mighty scenes he announces transpire in "the day of the Lord." Five times in his book Joel employs this phrase, a phrase which in its full import

always means the last day, the day of judgment, the time of the end. The prophet foretells seven stupendous events that occur in the day of the Lord. *First*, Restoration of Judah and Jerusalem. "For, behold, in those days and at that time when I shall bring again the captivity of Judah and Jerusalem." *Second*, Assembly of hostile nations at the holy city and their judgment and overthrow. "I will also gather all nations, and will bring them down into the valley of Jehoshaphat, and will plead with them there for my people and for my heritage Israel, whom they have scattered among nations, and parted my land." *Third*, Signs and wonders in the heavens. "The sun and the moon shall be darkened, and the stars withdraw their shining." *Fourth*, The Lord's intervention in overwhelming majesty and power. "And the Lord shall roar out of Zion and utter his voice from Jerusalem; and the heavens and the earth shall shake." *Fifth*, Jehovah's reign in Zion. "So shall ye know that I am the Lord your God dwelling in Zion, my holy mountain; then Jerusalem shall be holy." *Sixth*, Universal prosperity and blessing ensuing. "And it shall come to pass in that day, that the mountains shall drop down new wine, and the hills shall flow down with milk, and all the rivers of Judah shall flow with waters, and a fountain shall come forth of the house of the Lord, and shall water the valley of Shittim." *Seventh*, Judah and Jerusalem's perpetual duration. "But Judah shall abide forever, and Jerusalem from generation to generation." Such is the brief but graphic picture of the Day of the Lord, and of what follows it, by one of the oldest of the prophets. Its details are filled in by almost every subsequent prophet, by Isaiah, Jeremiah, Ezekiel, Daniel, Micah, Zechariah, and by our Lord and his servants Paul and John. Nothing in the history of the chosen people has since occurred to which Joel's great prediction can be properly applied. It finds no fulfilment in the capture of Jerusalem by Nebuchadnezzar, B. C. 606; nor in the return from Babylonian exile, B. C. 536; nor in the destruction of the holy city by Titus, A. D. 70. Its complete accomplishment awaits the future.

2. Zechariah 14. In this chapter events are announced almost identical in every particular with those of Joel. The time is the Day of the Lord; the place, Jerusalem; the occasion, a siege by hostile nations. The Lord Himself comes; His feet stand in that day on the Mount of Olives; cosmic convulsions follow; the judg-

ment of the nations, the deliverance of Israel, and the Lord's reign over the whole earth succeed His glorious presence. Nothing since Zechariah's time has happened that in any adequate sense can be deemed the fulfilment of this prophecy. If we spiritualize it, and substitute some other place for Jerusalem, and some other people for Israel, then we may adjust it to any event we please, may make it mean whatever we wish. But if the prophet says what he means, and means what he says, then this great prediction marks the end of the age, and the advent of the Lord. Delitzsch's rule of Biblical exegesis is golden; the deep word of Delitzsch should be remembered; "Interpretation is one, application is manifold."

3. Daniel 2. Nebuchadnezzar's Dream. It was a huge image or statue the king saw. Its form was that of a gigantic man, resplendent with brightness, imposing in attitude, and terrible in appearance. Unlike any work of art with which the king was familiar, this colossal man was composite; the head of gold; the breast and arms of silver; the body of brass; the legs of iron; the feet and toes of iron and clay. As the king gazed on the lofty statue, suddenly a stone, extra-human and super-human in its origin, struck the image with crushing force on its iron-clay feet and ground the entire Colossus into powder.

That the revelation made to the heathen monarch was intended to foretell the course and end of Gentile supremacy, the chapter itself declares: "Thou art this head of gold," said the prophet to Nebuchadnezzar; "and after thee shall arise another kingdom inferior to thee, and another third kingdom of brass, which shall bear rule over all the earth. And the fourth kingdom shall be strong as iron," (vers. 30–40).

Four great Gentile Empires were to succeed each other as World-powers, and only four. We know what they were: Chaldean, Persian, Greek, Roman. It is with the action of the Stone we are now specially concerned. Christ is frequently called in Scripture a *Stone.* In Matt. 21:44, we are told that "on whomsoever it shall fall, it will grind him to powder." Now mark, the Stone smites the image, not on the head, nor the breast, nor the body, nor yet the legs, but on the feet and toes. The destruction of the World-power takes place when it has reached its final form, its last stage. Not when Babylon fell, nor when Persia was overthrown, nor when the Greek empire went down, nor when Jesus was born, nor even yet, has the Colossus been crushed. It still exists. The sceptre of the world is yet in Gentile hands. But when history shall have descended to this last stage, to the feet and the toes, then the destruction of the World-power ensues. And it is after the Colossus has been ground to dust that the Stone becomes a mountain and fills the whole earth. It is then the Kingdom of God in its outward manifestation and glorious supremacy is established. Mark, also, that the action of the Stone is *judicial*, not one of grace or mercy. Demolition is not conversion; destruction is not salvation. Gentiles times end in judgment, and are followed by the unending Kingdom of God.

4. Daniel 7. The Vision of the Four Wild Beasts. The subject here is the same as that of chapter 2 of this book, seen from another and a different point of view. Man's view of Gentile sovereignty is, that it is one of splendor, the concentration of all material civilization, wealth and power. God's view of the same World-power is, that it is rapacious, cruel and beastly. The interest of this vision concentrates on the fourth beast, the anonymous monster with ten horns. It is with its doom the prophet is specially concerned. He thus describes it: "I saw, in the night, visions, and behold, one like the Son of man came with the clouds of heaven"—the beast was slain and his body given to the burning flame. But, let us not fail to note, that it is when the beast has ten horns—*i. e.* in its final form of existence, that it is flung to the devouring flame. These horns answer to the ten toes of the image, as Auberlen has clearly shown. Precisely the same peculiarity is seen in the Revelation; the beast there has also ten horns, when the mighty Conqueror from heaven casts him, together with his prime minister, the false prophet, alive into the lake of fire. That it is Rome which is meant is almost universally conceded. The final stage of this God-opposed power will be ten confederate kingdoms with Antichrist at their head. The Spirit looks forward to the *crisis* rather than at the *course* of its history. Under it, in its pagan state, the Son of God was crucified and untold multitudes of Christians were put to death; and more under its papal form. The world is not yet done with it, nor is God. "It was, it is not, it shall be present again," is John's marvellous word about it; and when it reappears, it will be a ten-kingdom power that shall receive

its doom at the coming of Christ. Daniel tells us, that upon the destruction of this beast, the glorious kingdom of God is set up.

Here, then, are four great prophecies of the Old Testament, which deal with the events in the Day of the Lord, the time of the end. The chief events are: 1. The Coming of the Lord. 2. Judgment of the nations. 3. Deliverance of Israel. 4. The establishment of the Kingdom of God over the entire earth. The prophets have but one main theme—viz: the Kingdom of God, and its final victory over all opposing forces. But that final and supreme triumph is to be realized at the coming of the Lord Jesus Christ in power and great glory.

It deals with the steps and stages that lead on to the end, but it centers in and dwells on the End-time itself; and the supreme End is the coming of the Lord, the judgment of enemies, and the manifestation of the glorious kingdom.

It will be said, May not these and the like predictions of the Old Testament pertain to New Testament times, to the blessings under the Gospel, and to the triumphs of Christianity? In reply, we turn to three great predictions of the New Testament itself, and we shall find that nothing different from the former prophets are the expectations and the utterances of the latter.

1. Matt., 13:24–43. The Parable of the Wheat and Tares. Happily we are not left to conjecture the meaning of this parable. We enjoy the immense advantage of having our Lord's own interpretation of it, an interpretation that needs no explanation. Here it is: "And his disciples came unto him saying, Declare unto us the parable of the tares of the field. He answered and said unto them, He that soweth the good seed is the Son of man; the field is the world; the good seed are the children of the kingdom, but the tares are the children of the wicked one; the enemy that sowed them is the Devil; the harvest is the end of the world, and the reapers are the angels. As, therefore, the tares are gathered and burned in the fire, so shall it be in the end of this world. The Son of man shall send forth his angels, and they shall gather out of his kingdom all things that offend and them that do iniquity, and shall cast them into a furnace of fire: there shall be wailing and gnashing of teeth. Then shall the righteous shine forth as the sun in the kingdom of their Father." (Matt., 13:36–43.)

Certain facts of immense importance emerge from this divine teaching: 1. The parable covers the whole period of our dispensation. The Sower is Christ Himself. He began the good work; He opened the new era. 2. The field is the world, the globe. Christ's work of redemption is no longer confined to a single nation as once; it contemplates the race. 3. His people are the good seed, begotten by His word and Spirit, and born into His kingdom. 4. The Devil is also a sower. He is the foul imitator and counterfeiter of God's work. He sowed the tares. 5. The tares are not wicked men in general, but a particular class of wicked, brought into close and contaminating association with the people of God. "Within the territory of the visible church the tares are sown," says Dr. David Brown. It is the corruption of Christendom that is meant, a gigantic fact to which we cannot shut our eyes. 6. The mischief, once done, cannot be corrected. "Let both grow together till the harvest." Christendom once corrupted remains so to the end. 7. The harvest is the end of the age. Twice our Lord assures us this is the final culmination of the dispensation; it terminates in the judgment of the Son of God.

Here, then, we have the beginning, progress and consummation of our age. Christ Himself introduced it in purity and power. But the glorious system of truth and salvation was marred by the cunning craftiness of the adversary, Satan. No after-vigilance or earnestness on the part of the servants can repair their fatal sleep. They are forbidden to attempt to eject the tares. The expulsion of these is left for angels' hands in the day of the harvest.

What a perfect picture of our age does this parable offer! In every feature and lineament touched by it, in its whole color and contour and character, the portrait is infinitely exact. A Zizanian field is what Christendom has been and is now, and Christ assures us such it will continue to be to the end. No matter what form the professing church takes on itself—*over* the State, dominating the State, as in the Middle Ages; *under* the State, dominated by the State, as in Europe since the Reformation; separate *from* the State, as in our country—it is essentially the same, wheat and tares growing together. In Roman Catholicism, in Greek Orthodoxy, what a vast field of tares, with only here and there a stinted, struggling spear of wheat! In Protestantism far more wheat is found, but how abundant also the tare crop! Worldliness, lawlessness, ritualism, sacerdotalism, indifference to the truth, perversion of the truth, denial of the faith, rationalism, incipient apostasy—who can furnish a complete catalogue? And to reflect that, in spite of all efforts to correct and reform, the corruption of Christendom remains, nay, grows apace! "For every handful of good grain sowed by the servants of Christ, that great missionary, the Devil, sows a hundred." To expel the tares of Popery, the tares of Rationalism, Unitarianism, Universalism, Annihilationism, Second Probation, and the whole immense crop of false teachers and false doctrines, is now, as it has been for centuries, an impossibility. Christ's solemn word steadily holds down to the end, "Let both grow together till the harvest." Then, and not till then, the separation takes place, and the righteous shine in the glorious kingdom.

2. Luke, 19 : 11–27. Parable of the Pounds. Jesus was on His last journey to Jerusalem, and near the city. The multitude was eager, expectant. They supposed the kingdom of God was immediately to appear. The parable was spoken to correct this mistake and to reveal some of the events connected with the manifestation of the kingdom. "A certain nobleman went into a far country to receive for himself a kingdom, and to return; and he called his ten servants and delivered them ten pounds, and said unto them, Occupy till I come. But his citizens hated him and sent a message after him, saying, We will not have this man to reign over us. And it came to pass that when he was returned, having received the kingdom, then he commanded these servants to be called unto him, to whom he had given the money, that he might know how much every man had gained by trading." There is little difficulty in apprehending the aim and scope of this suggestive narrative. The nobleman is Christ Himself; the far country, heaven; the kingdom is the Messianic Kingdom, whose immediate appearance was the exultant expectation of the crowd around him that day; the kingdom predicted by the prophets; the kingdom for which all God's people hope and long, for which we still pray, Thy Kingdom Come. The servants are those who sustain a special relation of responsibility to Christ because of the trust committed to them. The rebellious citizens are not only those who now refuse subjection to Christ, but those who will openly defy Him in the last days of our age, for, as Trench well says, "the

parable will find its full accomplishment when the wickedness of the apostate world shall receive its final doom in the destruction of Antichrist," when the Lord Jesus shall return in His glory. The parable spans the whole period between the first and second advents. It measures across our entire age. It tells of Christ's going away, describes the conduct of His servants and citizens during His absence, His return, and the reckoning which is to follow.

But let us note an expression which in our rapid reading may not be seen in its force and depth. It is this: "And it came to pass, when he was returned, *having received the kingdom.*" It is in heaven He receives the investiture of the kingdom. It is on earth He administers it. The phrase, "having received the kingdom," cannot by any torture of exegesis be made to designate the end of time nor the end of the Millennium, for instead of His receiving the kingdom at that time, it is then He delivers it up to God, even the Father, (1 Cor. 15:24-28). It is on His receiving the kingdom that He returns to reckon with His servants, punish His enemies, and establish His glorious reign.

Here again, as so often before, we have the mighty events connected with the close of our age clearly traced and sharply defined; their chronological order and sequence designated. 1. The mixture of good and evil among Christ's own followers during the entire period between His ascension and His Second Coming: some of His servants true to Him in His absence, some false and disobedient; while the world goes on in unbelief and enmity down to the very end. 2. The Advent of the Lord. 3. The judgment; reward of faithful servants, punishment of the unfaithful, and destruction of the rebels who defiantly spurned His authority. 4. Establishment of the Kingdom.

In these six great predictions we have merely glanced at one central idea which predominates, viz.: the Coming of the Lord and its supreme consequences. One would imagine the six furnish sufficient proof to demonstrate our proposition. But we are slow of heart to believe even the testimony of the prophets. To one other Scripture, therefore, the seventh and last one, we turn: 2 Thess. 2:1-12. The apostle is here disabusing the minds of the saints who had been led to think through a letter forged in Paul's name, that the Day of the Lord had already set in. He tells them "that day shall not come except there come a falling away first, and that man of sin be revealed, the son of perdition, who opposeth and exalteth himself against all that is called God, or that is worshipped; so that he sitteth in the temple of God, setting himself forth as God. Remember ye not that when I was yet with you I told you these things? And now ye know that which restraineth, to the end that he may be revealed in his own season. For the mystery of lawlessness doth already work: only there is one that restraineth now, until he be taken out of the way. And then shall be revealed the lawless one, whom the Lord Jesus shall slay with the breath of his mouth, and bring to nought by the manifestation of his coming; even him whose coming is after the working of Satan with all power and signs and lying wonders, and with all deceit of unrighteousness for them that perish; because they received not the love of the truth, that they might be saved."

This passage foretells the appearing of an enemy of God and of all good, whose extraordinary character, unparalleled wickedness, sudden and awful doom he so vividly portrays; the conditions of whose coming he so carefully explains. Let us attend to this prophecy, for it sheds no small light on the final issue of our age.

First, note the names and titles given this enemy. 1. "Man of Sin." He is one of whom sin is the distinguishing feature; whose inner element and outer characteristic is sin, and nothing but sin; who has his being, plans, and activity in sin and in nothing else; who, as the living embodiment of it, is known and recognized as the Man of Sin.

2. "The son of perdition." Perdition is no less distinctive of him than sin. He not only leads others to perdition, he goes thither himself; it is his portion and heritage. To one other alone in all the Bible is this frightful designation given, Judas Iscariot, and who like his great prototype, the Man of Sin, "went to his own place." 3. The antagonist of God: "Who opposeth and exalteth himself against all that is called God, or that is worshipped." He is God's opponent, who, Titan-like, uplifts himself against whatever, Divine or human, has hitherto challenged the adoration and obedience of mankind. *Treason against God*, is his uncommon crime. This is none other than Antichrist, of whom Daniel and John so solemnly prophecy, of whom John tells us, "He is the Antichrist, even he that denieth the Father and the Son," (1 Jno. 2:22). 4. "The lawless one." He is one who is impatient of

every restraint, hostile to all authority, the enemy of all order, who puts himself above law, or outside of law, or against law—the lawless one.

Second, note the amazing powers which are ascribed to him. His "coming is according to the working of Satan with all power and signs and lying wonders, and with all deceit of unrighteousness." In Daniel he has "eyes like the eyes of a man," "he understands dark sentences," "he practices and prospers." In the Revelation, by his prime minister the false prophet, "he doeth great wonders, so that he maketh fire come down from heaven on the earth in the sight of men, and deceiveth them that dwell on the earth." He has horns, and horns are the symbols of power. He has diadems on his horns, and diadems are the badges of regal dominion.

He is described as "the deceiver" and the "liar;" as one who shall intoxicate men with a "strong delusion," and daze them with his majestic signs and powers and lying wonders. He is represented as being a consummate flatterer, a brilliant diplomatist, a superb strategist, a sublime hypocrite. For he is the Antichrist, the Vice-Christ, *alter Christus*, the rival of the Son of God and His adversary. He assumes and presumes to be God, shows himself as God; and he takes this blasphemous place through the strange witchery of his stupendous powers. For he is one to whom Satan will give his power and throne and great authority. (Rev. 13: 2).

Third, the conditions of the appearing of this Man of Sin. Two things precede and condition his coming. The *first* is the apostasy: "It cannot come except there be a falling away first, and the Man of Sin be revealed." Obviously, the falling away is a defection from the truth of God and from the faith of Christ. It is religious, not political or social apostasy that is meant. In the incipient stage it was present in Paul's day; for "the mystery of iniquity," in malignant counteraction of the mystery of godliness, was already working, and it would continue to work until it should issue in the apostasy and Man of Sin. The falling away is not the result of the presence of the Antichrist. It precedes and prepares the way for his advent. The *second* thing is, a certain hindrance which must be removed before he can appear. Paul speaks of it as both masculine and neuter, "that which withholdeth," and "he that withholdeth." Without stopping to inquire what this is, let it be noted that upon its removal, whatever it is, the great adversary makes his appearance. I once asked a very competent scholar this question, Is the removal of the check gradual, or sudden? His answer was, "Sudden, undoubtedly; for the Antichrist in this passage is declared to have both a *parousia*, coming, and an apocalypse, like the Son of God Himself." No mortal knows when the obstruction will be taken away—*that* is kept within the secrets of the divine mind. But the moment it goes, then comes the Man of Sin. The restraining influence holds only until it is taken out of the way, and then the tide of godlessness, with Antichrist at its head, sweeps in.

Fourth. His Destruction: "Whom the Lord Jesus shall slay with the breath of his mouth, and shall destroy with the manifestation of his coming." The two words, *epiphaneia* and *parousia*, which elsewhere are used separately to denote the coming of Christ, are here both employed. Why both? Let that prince of New Testament grammarians, Winer, answer: "Redundant structure includes fulness of expression, by which the writer aims...at graphic vividness," and he cites this very language, "the appearing of his coming," as an example. The coming, therefore, that is here meant, can only be the coming spoken of throughout both these epistles, the great, second, personal coming of the Lord to judgment. Duffield is right when he says: "Human language is utterly incapable of being interpreted on any fixed and definite principles whatever, if it be not literal and personal coming." Right, also, is Seiss: "Either of these words is held sufficient in other passages to prove the real and personal presence. And when both are united, as in the case before us, how is it possible that they should mean anything else than the literal, real, and personal arrival and presence of Jesus, with reference to whom they are used?"

Thus, in this prophecy we have the beginning, progress and end of the whole period lying between the first and second Advents of the Saviour. Incipient apostasy had begun in Paul's time; it would continue, deepening and intensifying, until it would issue in the revelation of the Man of Sin, the son of perdition, whom Christ shall bring to nought by His coming.

Two supreme inferences spring from this passage: 1. Our age will close with the personal appearing of the Lord Jesus Christ, and with the judgment of the wicked. 2. There can be no Millennium this side the Advent. It cannot come before the falling away, because the mystery of iniquity was secretly at work in the apostolic times. The epistles detect the presence of the deadly virus. It is the testimony of all the apostles. They disclose its latent activity, and announce its huge development. The principles of lawlessness then working would gather into them kindred elements, would combine and ripen into the apostasy. But may not the falling away take place, be arrested, the Millennium ensue, and after *that* the Man of Sin appear? No, for the culmination of the falling away is the revelation of the Antichrist. But may not the Antichrist have his day, be destroyed by the light of truth, the gospel of the blessed God, the Millennium follow, and the Lord come at the final close of all things, the end of time? No, for the Antichrist is brought to nought by the manifestation of the Coming of the Lord. Thus we are shut up to the conclusion that there can be no kingdom of universal righteousness and peace, no filling of the earth with the knowledge of the glory of the Lord, until Christ shall come again. It is for this reason that such prominence and pre-eminence is given the Advent in the word of God. Three hundred and eighteen times it is mentioned in the New Testament. One verse out of every thirty is occupied with it. It is found shining with a glad hope in the very first epistle Paul ever wrote, the first to the Thessalonians. It is found in the last he ever wrote, the second to Timothy, gleaming with the bright and blessed anticipation of the crown he was to receive at the Redeemer's appearing. James quickens the flagging courage, and reanimates the drooping spirits of believers with this trumpet peal: "Be ye also patient; stablish your hearts: for the coming of the Lord draweth nigh," (v. 8). Peter exhorts to all holy conversation and godliness by the same motive: "Looking for and hastening unto the coming of the day of God." (2 Peter, 3 : 12). Amid the deepening gloom and the gathering storms of the last days of our age, Jude cheers us with the words of Enoch, the seventh from Adam, "Behold, the Lord cometh with ten thousands of his saints, to execute judgment upon the ungodly." And John closes the canon with the majestic book of the Revelation of Jesus Christ, with His Coming in the clouds of heaven—the mighty Conqueror—who arrests the beast, and hurls him and his false prophet, alive and in their bodies, into the lake of fire; who arrests Satan, the prime cause and mover of all evil, chains and shuts him up in the bottomless pit, and inaugurates the kingdom. These inspired men know there can be no reign of universal righteousness, no deliverance of groaning creation, no redemption of the body, no binding of Satan, and no millennium, while the tares grow side by side with the wheat, while the ungodly world flings its defiant shout toward the nobleman, "We will not have this man to reign over us"—while the road for Antichrist is getting ready, and while Satan, that strong fierce spirit, loose in this age, tempts, deceives, leads captive, devours and ruins as he lists. And therefore they turn to the Coming of the Lord with a passionate longing and joyous assurance of nearing deliverance and victory that seem an exaggeration, or a dream to our mercantile and materialistic times! And we, instead, have forgotten the Hope; ignore it in our teaching, and have substituted death for the Coming. We delude ourselves with the fond belief that by advancing civilization, the spread of culture, the achievements of science, the marvels of invention, and the work of the church, the world will be subdued, the evils suppressed, the antagonisms destroyed, the devil bound, and the golden age be introduced. Busy, enormously busy, with social, financial, educational, and religious problems; engrossed with questions of reform, with plans for the extirpation of the evils that we feel, with the erection of barriers against the greater evils that we fear; there is little disposition and less time reverently to inquire into these things. Accordingly, the doctrine of the Lord's coming, so prominent in the early church that Gibbon names it as one of the chief causes for the triumphs of Christianity; that Harnack, the greatest living patristic scholar, says was a test of orthodoxy in the martyr church, is quietly thrust aside in our day, or becomes, what it never was intended to be—a theme of controversy and a subject of acrid debate. Heedless of the tremendous fact, that 1800 years of advancing Christian endeavor have been powerless to avert, and powerless to extirpate the wrongs and oppressions of the world, the wickedness of Heathendom, the bundled crimes of Christendom; blind to the fact that, as Thiersch asserts, "Not one nation yet, in its general mass, has accepted Christianity, but only individuals, and, relatively to the population, few"—we comfort ourselves with the optimistic notion that the world is fast becoming Christian, the Millennium is almost in sight! And this in spite of Christ's own testimony, that Christendom once corrupted remains corrupted down to the harvest; in spite of Paul's solemn witness, that there lie before this age the apostasy, the Man of Sin, and the Coming of the Lord.

The advent of the Man of Sin : *that* lies before us. So Daniel, John and Paul declare. But who is this Man of Sin, or what? Has there appeared in the field of history any person or any system that verifies the description? Many sober-minded interpreters find the fulfilment of this great prophecy in Popery, gathered up into the person of the Pope, or in the Papal hierarchy, the head of which is the occupant of the Papal chair. The Reformers as a body entertained this view. It was held by some even in pre-Reformation times ; and there is no little verisimilitude in it. The marks of correspondence between the prediction and the Papacy are extraordinary, almost conclusive. In its marvellous origin and history ; in its near relation to the old Roman Empire as its heir and successor—for as Wylie says, "the Papacy is the ghost of Peter crowned with the shadowy diadem of the old Cæsars ;" in its wide departure from the truth ; in its idolatry, persecuting spirit, daring assumptions and blasphemous pretensions, the Papacy, it must be confessed, strikingly resembles the Man of Sin. No one can compare the two without feeling the force of Richard Baxter's quaint remark, "If the Pope be not Antichrist, he has bad luck to be so like him." But, wonderful as the parallelism is, and traceable to almost any length, nevertheless the Papacy does not fill up nor complete the titanic portrait of the final adversary which the prophetic word furnishes us. Rather this system belongs to the apostasy which precedes and issues in the revelation of Antichrist, and is identified with Babylon of the Apocalypse. That a revival of its influence and power is now going on, Germany, Britain and the United States attest. And this is in exact accord with the predictions about its last days. The final view which the Spirit of prophecy gives us of Babylon the harlot, the apostate church, presents her as throned upon the Seven Hills, as seated on the Beast, controlling and using the world-power for the accomplishment of her own purposes. (Rev. 17). But she is not alone. Babylon is a mother, Babylon has daughters. Who would venture to deny that there are signs of a falling away from the truth of God in Protestantism itself? A scarcely disguised infidelity dominating the great schools of Germany; an "open and organized movement toward Rome, numbering hundreds and thousands of clerical and lay adherents," in the Church of England; doctrines held and taught in Evangelical churches which, as one well says, "thirty years ago would have ranked a man as an infidel"—things now said of Christ's *Kenosis*, or humiliation, that Adolph Saphir asserts "none of the old Socinians would have dared or wished to say;" and the churches of Scotland, once the bulwark of truth, and faithful even to the suffering the loss of worldly place and maintenance, now unwilling or unable to deal with the growing unbelief and rationalism of the most gifted and influential teachers—with all this, and much more than this, clear as the noonday sun to those who have eyes to see, who will venture to deny there are unmistakable signs of growing apostasy in the bosom of Protestantism itself? It is in view of this state of things that many thoughtful men fear, and have reason to fear, that the road for the coming of the Man of Sin is rapidly preparing.

Two great forms of iniquity constitute the burden of prophetic warning. Ecclesiastical corruption and apostasy form the one, the revolt of the civil power against God is the other. The first culminates in Babylon, the blood drunken harlot. The second finds its horrible climax in the Man of Sin, the Antichrist. The first, we solemnly believe, is now here, though greater depths of wickedness, no doubt, will yet be reached. The second is still to come. And these two form the gigantic figures of the End-time of our age. Concerning the latter of the two, some observations are submitted.

1. The Antichrist is a person, an individual man, the man of prophecy. Whatever in human speech betokens personality and personal action is employed by the prophets to designate a man, a single being. According to Daniel, he is the "king" who overthrows three other kings, obtains the supremacy over the fourth kingdom, exalts and magnifies himself above all, speaks stout words against the Most High, persecutes the saints, and thinks to change the times and the law. According to Paul, he is the man of sin, the son of perdition, names which at once fasten on him

the idea of a person. "The terse personal language of Paul," writes John Eadie, "fore-pictures one man, one human being, as really as the phrase 'son of perdition' described from the lips of our Lord the fate of Judas, the traitor." This man, made of sin, is the personal antagonist of Jesus Christ, is the counter-Christ. Both are individual persons, both are revealed, both have a *parousia*, a coming. The one, Christ, has life and glory to bestow; the other, ruin and perdition.

2. The Antichrist is the supreme head of the World-power in its final form. This is evident from the composition of John's stupendous symbol. Daniel's beasts are successive empires—Chaldean, Persian, Macedonian, Roman. But the lion, the bear, the leopard and the ten-horned nameless monster, each distinct in Daniel, are all united in one by John, in Revelation 13. It is upon this God-opposing power that the judgment of heaven falls. The Antichrist is cast into the lake of fire, and his armies and adherents experience the wrath of the Son of God. Precisely the same fate marks the huge image of Daniel 2, for while the blow falls on the feet and toes, the whole statue, with all its component parts—clay, iron, brass, silver and gold—share in the overwhelming destruction.

Moreover, John saw one of the heads of the nameless monster smitten unto death, but he saw also that the death-wound was healed. No doubt it is the Roman Empire, the fourth of the beasts, that is thus characterized, but it is the empire in its final form, its last stage. Rome has an extraordinary history, according to prophecy, a history that is divided into three stages of existence. "It was, is not, and shall come," or as the Sinai Codex reads, "shall be present again." "It was." In John's time it existed in the plenitude of its power, and the world lay helpless at its feet. With beak of brass and talons of steel the great Eagle of Rome had grappled and overcome the whole race of the prophetic earth, and men trembled when from his seven-hilled eyrie he flapped his wings of thunder. "It was." There came a second stage, that of non-existence. Beneath the deadly sword-wound of the Barbarians, imperial Rome sank and died. "It is not." From that time to the present, a universal dominion centered in one grand emperor, there has not been. Ambitious soldiers have once and again attempted to found one homogeneous worldwide kingdom, but in vain. Charlemagne tried it, the first Napoleon likewise, but they failed. Still "It is not." A third stage arrives, and the sovereign colossus reappears. "It shall be present again." "The deadly wound was healed." And at its head stands the peerless man, the Satan-inspired man, the man in military genius, executive capacity, intellectual brilliancy, and savage ferocity, surpassing Alexander of Macedon, Augustus of Rome, Antiochus Epiphanes of Syria. It is the Man of Sin, the Antichrist, from whom the stupendous confederacy takes its name and its laws, to whose will it bows, whose sway it owns—the Beast! It is the time of the end, the closing scenes of our age; for the Man of Sin goes to perdition as his own and proper place by the irresistible might of the Son of God. It was a saying in the olden times, that Rome would endure to the end of the world. The age terminates, indeed, when the Beast is here, and when the mighty Conqueror flashes down from the opening sky, and the Beast is hurled into the lake of fire! It is then that the kingdoms of this world become the kingdoms of our Lord and of His Christ.

3. The origin of the Antichrist is mysterious, apparently supernatural. Twice in the Apocalypse it is said that he "ascends out of the bottomless pit." (Rev. 11:7; 17:8). In Rev. 13:2 it is declared that the Dragon, *i. e.* Satan, gives him "his power, and his throne, and great authority." In 2 Thess. 2:9, he is declared to have a *parousia*, like Christ Himself. Many of the great Fathers of the primitive Church believed he would be a satanic incarnation. Hyppolitus calls him "a son of the devil, a vessel of Satan." Irenæus speaks of him as "taking on himself all the power and all the delusion of the devil." Origen describes him as "the child of the devil, and the counterpart of Christ." Lactantius thinks he will be "a king begotten by an evil spirit." Theodoret believes the devil will be "incarnate in him," and Theophylact, that he will be "a man who will carry Satan about with him." Augustine says he will be born as other men, "but that the devil will descend on his mother, and fill her, totally, surround her totally, hold her totally, and possess her totally, within and without, and the thing that shall be born of her shall be altogether sinful, altogether damned." Is it objected that all this is extravagant language, and unjustifiable? Perhaps so. We are distinctly informed, however, that Antichrist will come from "the bottomless pit," from the

abyss, the identical place where Satan is shut up and sealed during the thousand years. Assuredly, there is something ominous in these words, "he cometh up out of the abyss," "whose *parousia* is according to the working of Satan"—something altogether aside from the ordinary way of men's appearing in the world. Nevertheless, we cannot believe they import the return to earth of one who has long been dead, as Nero or the First Napoleon, nor yet a demoniacal incarnation. They mean, or seem to mean, that, to accomplish his fell purpose, Satan will transfer to Antichrist his power and his throne, and fill him from head to heel with his infernal and appalling energy. As he entered into the heart of Judas, the son of perdition, so he will take possession of the Man of Sin, the other son of perdition, and inspire him with power, intensify his malignity, and dower him with extra-human craft and pride, till he shall attempt self-deification.

Is this to be the final issue of the age? The science, discoveries, culture; the energy, activity, and achievements of our modern era—are they all to terminate in worldwide godlessness and the Man of Sin? A forbidding outlook, you say; one utterly repugnant to all our anticipations and our hopes. One whose love for man is deathless, whose power is matchless, has said: "As it was in the days of Noah, so shall it be in the days of the Son of man." (Luke 17:26). How was it in the days of Noah? The whole world in revolt against God, and true piety reduced to a family of eight souls! "The flood came, and destroyed them all." "Likewise also as it was in the days of Lot;" and how was it then? Corruption had culminated, godlessness was at the flood. "But the same day that Lot went out of Sodom it rained fire and brimstone from heaven, and destroyed them all: after the same manner shall it be in the day that the Son of man is revealed." (Luke 17:28-30). Another, guided by the Spirit of God in every word he wrote, has said: "But know this, that in the last days grievous times shall come. For men shall be lovers of self, lovers of money, boastful, haughty, railers, disobedient to parents, unthankful, unholy, without natural affection, implacable, slanderers, without self-control, fierce, no lovers of good, traitors, headstrong, puffed up, lovers of pleasure rather than lovers of God; holding a form of godliness, but having denied the power thereof." (2 Tim. 3:1-5). That is the picture, the tremendous picture, drawn by the pen of divine inspiration, of the "last days," the closing days of our age. Impossible to be realized in our enlightened times, is it said? We have but to remember that little more than one hundred years ago, in the most highly cultivated and intellectual country of Europe, in France, society was so wrecked, and atheism was exalted to such a height of proud impiety that the world witnessed the audacious spectacle of a prostitute enthroned on the high altar of Notre Dame, and enthusiastically saluted as the "Goddess of Reason." We have but to remember that at this very hour there resides in the city of Rome a man who one-half of Christendom itself honors and adores as the vicar of Christ, the vice-gerent of God, infallible, the sole possessor of the keys of the kingdom of heaven—a man who is borne along "in solemn procession on the shoulders of consecrated priests, whilst sacred incense fumes before him, and blest peacocks' feathers full of eyes wave beside his moving throne, and every mortal near uncovers, bows and silently adores." Impossible to be realized in our times? For an ordinary man impossible, certainly, but not for an extraordinary man. Talent is influential, but circumscribed. Its sway is bounded by well defined limitations. Genius is commanding, possesses a sort of universality. Let one appear upon the scene of action in our day of transcendent genius, of supreme abilities, with the mental grasp of Cæsar, the towering ambition of Napoleon, the defiant self-assertion of Nero, the colossal egotism of Caligula; let him be, as the Man of Sin will be, the recipient of all Satan's energy and craft and power; and John's word about him would have a literal and immediate fulfilment: "And all the world wondered after the Beast." (Rev. 13:3). The unbelieving world, in spite of its culture, nay, because of its very culture, would be on its knees before such a man!

There are principles at work in modern society which, if left unchecked, will soon make the advent of the Antichrist not only possible but certain. The lawless drift is already on us, precursor of worse to come. Who does not perceive that the forces are already loose which tend to the disintegration of the whole social fabric! Who does not perceive that the axe is already aimed at the chief hoops which bind together the staves of the civil polity? The restlessness under restraint, the revolt against authority and law, the spread of Socialism, the growth of agnosticism, the prevalance of materialism, fostered as it largely is by both the science and the politics of our time, the enormous greed of those who have and who want still more, the deep, ominous growl of those who have not, and who want and will have—all this, and much more than this, betokens the breaking down of the barriers, the overthrow of the restraining influences, and the speedy advent of the great adversary. The Frenchman spoke well, perhaps better than he knew, who lately said, "I think I hear the galloping of the man on horseback!"

We have only to suppose the portentous movements of the times to grow and gather head until the hindrance is gone, the breakwater is down—and then—yes, what then? Then cometh the Man of Sin, the world-deceiver, whom the Lord shall slay with the breath of His mouth, and shall bring to nought by the appearing of His Coming. Then the kingdoms of this world shall become the kingdoms of our Lord and of His Christ, and He shall reign for ever and ever.

THE SECOND COMING OF THE LORD.

PERSONAL AND PRE-MILLENNIAL.

REV. E. P. GOODWIN, D. D.

All believers in the Scriptures hold to some doctrine of the Lord's return to this world. They differ as to the time and manner of that return. Some think that coming took place at the capture and destruction of Jerusalem by Titus. Others say the Lord comes to believers when they die. Another class hold that this coming was first fulfilled in the descent of the Holy Spirit at Pentecost, and, since then, has been many times fulfilled in repeated manifestations of the Spirit's power, as in great revivals. Probably the most popular view of the Lord's Coming is that which associates and identifies it with the spread of the Gospel, by which, as by a continual coming, the Lord manifests His power, and is ultimately to convert and possess the world. And all these different classes would quite heartily concur in this, that when the Lord personally comes, if indeed He ever does so come, as to which there is a diversity of belief, it will be at the end of the thousand years mentioned in the twentieth chapter of Revelation.

When, therefore, one takes the ground which I do, and the brethren of this conference, that the Lord's coming is to be personal, visible, and prior to the thousand years, there is a very marked contrast of belief between us and the brethren who hold the other view, and it becomes a question of importance to know where the truth lies. The great bulk of the church sees nothing important about it; is very much inclined to think the question one of no practical significance, a matter speculative or theological, and as to which it is of very little consequence which view is held.

But the disciples of Christ are called to be His witnesses, the revealers of His truth to men. But to what truths shall they bear witness? Shall they have nothing to say about the teaching upon which He dwelt so often, and with such peculiar emphasis? He certainly put His future coming into the very foreground of His instructions to His disciples as the chiefest and most important event of all the future. Upon that coming was to hinge their resurrection, their glorification and their future reward for faithfulness in service. It would seem, then, as if we ought to have here, if anywhere, clear and positive convictions. Furthermore, it is easy to see that upon right Scriptural views on this doctrine will of necessity depend right Scriptural views as to others. The true understanding of Scripture, as to the resurrection of believers, the judgment of rewards, the future of the Jewish nation, the establishment of the Messianic Kingdom depend on this doctrine of the Lord's return. We ought, therefore, to carefully and prayerfully search God's word as to its teachings upon this subject. Moreover, since our Lord, in His promise of the Spirit, said, and with undoubted inclusion of this very matter—if not with specific reference to it—"When he, the Spirit of truth, is come, he will guide you into all truth: and he will *show you things to come*," we are most certainly warranted in expecting as full and clear light upon this as upon any other truth of the word.

Let me emphasize, then, this point—that the question before us is purely a question of Scripture. Outside of these sacred writings we know and can know nothing whatever on this subject. Speculation, philosophy, the learning, the logic of the schools has no part nor lot in this discussion. Not, what ought these witnesses to say? What would it be rational for them to say? What would harmonize best with science, with advanced thought, with enlarged conceptions of God and improved conceptions of man? Nothing of this, but simply what, fairly taken, as we read and understand language elsewhere, do these men, speaking as they are moved by the Holy Ghost, say as to the manner of the Lord's return. Some latter-day theorists upon this subject quite overlook this. They raise objections based upon what they conceive to be certain impossibilities connected with the appearing of the Lord in a personal, visible way, and therefore, declare the doctrine cannot be taught.

But all such reasonings and speculations have no value whatever in determining what the truth is. As well say the creation of the world out of nothing is irrational and inconceivable, and hence the first chapter of Genesis is a fiction. As well say it is utterly irrational and inconceivable that a human and divine soul could dwell together in one person, and that person could be born both of the Holy Spirit and of the Virgin Mary, and therefore, deny the twofold nature of the supernatural birth of Jesus Christ; or again, it is irrational and inconceivable that bodies once turned to dust and scattered perhaps to the ends of the earth, should be reconstructed and made to reinvest the spirits that once dwelt therein, and, therefore, scout the doctrine of the resurrection. That is precisely the method of reasoning by which some excellent people explain away the doctrine of an expiatory atonement, and others the doctrine of miracles, and others still the imprecatory psalms, and all such stories as the deluge, and the destruction of Sodom, and Jonah and the whale. There is no trouble in having a Bible exactly according to our mind, when we set up this modern principle or canon of authority which so many adopt, that only that is true which in its own pet phrase "finds me," or carries the assent of my inner consciousness.

But that is not what settles questions according to this book. This claims to be of God, to voice His thoughts, to reveal His will. And the men who made this book did not write down what they thought, or imagined, or presumed, or reasoned out; not what would accord with other men's thoughts or reasonings or speculations; not what would seem wise or beneficent, but what God thought and chose to say, and what He commanded them—the writers of the book—to say. "Holy men of old spake as they were moved by the Holy Ghost," and our attitude before their testimony is simply that of accepting and obeying what they declare as the truth of God. We have no option whatever and no right of speculation or debate as respects the things revealed. We are as law students before the statutes of the State. The only question for us is, what do these authorities, these books of God's revealed will teach? No matter whether we can understand or explain, or harmonize their teachings with our views of things or not. They give us what God says, and we believe them because of that, and not because of our ability to explain or expound them.

There can be no unity of faith until the standard of authority is fixed, and it is idle without that to raise any such questions as this programme involves. We might as well engage in seeing who could blow the most brilliant soap bubbles. But once agree that human speculation, opinion, and reasoning have no more to do in settling what we shall receive and believe as students of this divine word than they had in determining what the people of old should receive and believe when Moses came out from his closetings with Jehovah on the cloud-wrapt mountain top and declared the message with which he was charged, and then there is an end of controversy. And this, I repeat, is where I stand. *I assume the absolute, infallible authority of this book as the word of God.* And on that basis, believing that on this subject in hand, as upon all others essential to the right understanding of the plan of God in redeeming lost man, the Holy Spirit has given clear and decisive testimony, I propose to ask what saith the Scripture on the question of the manner of the Lord's return.

What the belief of the early church was as to the teaching of Scripture I need not stay to consider. It is sufficient to say, without taking time for the citations that could easily be made, that not a single authority in church history pretends that for two hundred and fifty years at least, the early disciples, apart from the heretical sects, held any other view than that of the Lord's literal, personal, and pre-millennial return. It is agreed on all hands that as to this there is not among apostles, apostolic fathers, or apologists down to Origen, a single dissenting voice.

And it may almost be said that, taking the church as a whole, this early belief has never been lost nor modified. The faith-symbols of every branch of the Christian household have most clearly and emphatically put forward this doctrine. What need, then, of arguing for it in such a conference as this? Simply because in this day of so-called advanced thought and of new departures, men set to be teachers of the Lord's people in pulpits and editorial and theological chairs, have abandoned the faith of the fathers. Or rather, they have, as they claim, improved upon that faith by taking out of it the hyper-literalistic element and so making it accord with the figurative and spiritualistic way of putting truth, which, as they affirm, is a prime characteristic of the Scriptures. The pulpit of our day, and not in any one denomination, is leavened with such rationalistic teachings. And a great multitude of disciples, if they do not share such doubts, are at least in a great maze as to what to believe. It will be ample reward for this undertaking if it shall help any student of theology to stand fast by the old historic faith, and any perplexed child of God to cling steadily to that ancient, blessed hope of one day seeing the Lord face to face and of being from the hour of that beholding forever with him and forever like him.

1. First, then, the language of Scripture gives as much reason for believing in a literal, personal, visible second coming of the Lord as in such a first coming. If it was intended by the Holy Spirit that there should be a distinction made between these comings, that one should be taken literally and the other figuratively, obviously there would have been a difference in the use of the language setting them forth. But there is nothing of the kind. The same personality underlies the testimony in both cases. "Occupy till I come." "If I will that he tarry till I come, what is that to thee?" "Judge nothing till the Lord come." "Ye do shew the Lord's will till He come." "Waiting for the coming of our Lord Jesus Christ." "When Christ, who is our life, shall appear, then shall ye also appear with Him in glory." "And to wait for His Son from heaven whom he raised from the dead, even Jesus, who delivered us from the wrath to come." These are representative passages. And no one, it is safe to say, reading them without previous bias in favor of preconceived opinions, would ever think of their meaning anything else than the literal return of the Lord. So everywhere in the Word. The most superficial reader of the Scriptures cannot fail to have noted how particularly the prophecies set forth the facts concerning the first coming of Christ, the place and circumstances of His birth, His mother, His name, His character, life, sufferings, death, and resurrection. It is almost like having His life history written, or one might say photographed, in advance. But the same kind of particularity precisely characterizes the prophecies of His second coming. Indeed, by so much as the incidents of that coming are grander and more royal than the former one, by so much are they set forth in fuller statement, in more vivid and imposing imagery, and profounder emphasis. Whatever principle of interpretation we apply to one part of His career, obviously we must apply to the other. If we take the first set of prophecies to be literally fulfilled, and this we know to be the fact, we must needs, upon the very ground of such fulfilment, look for a like literalness as to the fulfilment of what remain. It is impossible to divide the testimonies of the sacred Word concerning our Lord at His resurrection, and say that all those preceding that are to be taken as they read, the foreshowings of literal facts; but that those relating to events subsequent to the resurrection, though given by the same prophet, and side by side with the other declarations, are to be taken symbolically, figuratively, not as they read. Take as an illustration the familiar passage in Luke 1: 31–33, the word of the angel to Mary: "And behold thou shalt conceive in thy womb, and bring forth a son, and shall call his name Jesus. He shall be great, and shall be called the Son of the Highest; and there shall be given unto Him the throne of His father David, and He shall reign over the house of Jacob forever; and of His kingdom there shall be no end." No one questions that there is taught here a literal birth, a literal name for the child, and a literal greatness to be His portion as the Son of the Highest. By what principle, then, can the exegetical dagger be made to stab the literalness of the second part, so that there shall be no literal throne of David; no literal reign; no literal house of Jacob; no literal personal, visible manifestation of the Son of the Highest in His glory? But all attempts to dissolve out of these Scriptures the literalness of the Lord's return and His Kingship as related thereto, and to keep in the literalness of His humiliation, His sufferings, are faced with precisely such absurdity.

2. *But again, the words which are especially used in setting forth the Lord's return require it to be personal and visible.* There are three of these in the Greek, *apocalypsis*, *epiphaneia* and *parousia.* The first signifies an unveiling, a disclosure, a manifestation, and would suggest naturally to every Greek scholar when coupled with a person, the idea of some visible, external appearance. 2 Thes. 1: 7, is a good example. "When the Lord Jesus shall be revealed with His mighty angels." Angels, we know, have forms, and when they are "revealed" are literal, visible personalties. And like their revelation or disclosure, will be that of the Lord Jesus. This is the natural meaning and use of the word as applied to persons.

The second word, *epiphaneia,* is still more emphatic in its witness. It is a word which is never used except of some external, visible and imposing manifestation. It is used five times in connection with our Lord; once as to His first advent, and four times as to His second. And in each instance it denotes His personal manifestation. Titus 2 : 13, is a good example: "Looking for that blessed hope and the glorious appearing of the great God and our Saviour Jesus Christ;" or, as the revised version gives it: "Looking for the blessed hope and appearing of the glory of our great God and Saviour Jesus Christ." As Professor Kellogg well says: "It would be impossible to find in the New Testament Greek any word which should more precisely and unambiguously denote the visible, bodily appearing of the Lord."

But the word oftenest used is *parousia*. This occurs in twenty-four passages. In two of these it is rendered "presence," and in the rest "coming." The revisers have left the translation unchanged, but in the margin of the twenty-two passages having the word coming, have put the word presence. Seventeen of these passages refer to the coming of the Lord. The root idea of the word, according to the lexicographers is, to be there, as indicating the arrival of one that has been absent. As, when Paul says (1 Cor. 16 : 17), "I am glad of the coming of Stephanas, and Fortunatus, and Achaicus;" and (2 Cor. 7 : 6) "Nevertheless God comforted us by the coming of Titus." Or as when he speaks of himself to the Philippian Christians, (1 : 26) "That your rejoicing may be more abundant in Christ Jesus for me, by my coming to you again." So when he speaks of his bodily presence (*parousia*) being weak (2 Cor. 10 : 10) and exhorts the Philippians to obey, not as in his presence (*parousia*) only, but much more in his absence (Phil. 2 : 12). Exactly corresponding to these are the passages respecting the future coming or presence of Christ. (Matt. 24 : 3.) "What shall be the sign of the coming and of the end of the age?" (1 Cor. 15 : 23.) "But every man in his own order: Christ the first fruits. Afterward they that are Christ's at His coming." (1 Thes. 2 : 19.) "For what is our hope, or joy, or crown of rejoicing? Are not even ye in the presence of our Lord Jesus Christ at His coming?" These are merely representative texts. It is simply impossible to read out of them everything objective, real, visible. Whoever can do that with this word that in every instance denotes a literal, personal presence, can make his Bible mean anything he chooses, and there is an end to all authority.

3. But let us advance the argument. *I affirm, then, that the Lord's return must be literal, personal, visible, because He must needs return as a true and proper man.* That He was such when He was upon earth, and as truly such subsequent, as prior to His resurrection, admits of no doubt. It was as the man Christ Jesus that He appeared to Mary Magdalene and the other women, to Peter, to the disciples on the way to Emmaus; to the eleven when Thomas' doubts were removed; to the five hundred in Galilee; to the little company that saw Him ascend from the slopes of Olivet into the clouds of heaven. Up to that vanishing point we know past a peradventure that our Lord was a true and perfect man, and that He took with Him into the heavens a true and literal, though glorified, human body. What I say now is, that He will return with that same body, a body that can be seen and touched, and personal fellowship as true and real, and loving and blessed, be had with Him who wears it, as in the days of His dwelling upon the earth. This is exactly what, if there had sprung up no men wiser than the men who wrote these Scriptures, every one would say was what the angels meant, when after the ascension they said to the wondering disciples, "Why stand ye gazing up into heaven? This same Jesus which is taken up from you into heaven, shall so come in like manner as ye have seen Him go into heaven."—(Acts 1 : 11.) The point of the angels' message is not only the fact of the return but also the *manner* of it. This same Jesus is to come as he departed, in the air, in the clouds of heaven. The rationalizers may refine upon the phrase "in like manner," and seek to make it agree with the spread of Christianity or the destruction of Jerusalem, or the manifestation of the Spirit in the heart, but there will still confront them this unquestionable fact, that in the minds of those to whom the angels spoke these words they had an altogether different meaning. They went forth looking for the return of the "same Jesus" whom they had seen depart, and for His coming in the clouds. And the best scholarship of all the ages is agreed that this is what the language signifies. Says Professor Hackett: "The expression, 'in like manner,' is never employed to affirm merely the certainty of one event as compared with another. It signifies 'in what manner;' *i. e.*, visibly, and in the air." So Bengel, De Vette, Meyer, Olshausen, Lange, Alford, etc.

But how do we know, it may be asked, that He has not laid aside His humanity, and so will return in a spiritual way? I answer, in the nature of things He cannot lay aside His human nature, but must keep it forever. There is much loose and unscriptural thinking and speculation among Christian people here. Jesus Christ, when He was born of the Virgin and entered this world as the incarnate Son of God, took upon Him our nature. He was not a make-believe man, God disguised in a human form, as some have held from the earliest ages, but a literal and true man. He was as truly man as if He were not God; as truly man as He was truly God. So that as He was God of God, very God of very God, He was man of man, very man of very man. That is, He had a true, rational, human soul and a true flesh and blood body. And "it behooved Him" to be made thus; "forasmuch as the children are partakers of flesh and blood"—*i. e.*, the race He came to save—"He also Himself likewise took part of the same." He must needs become one with those whom He would rescue, must in the most literal sense be identified with their nature. But having taken on Himself the seed of Abraham by being born of the Virgin, by that fact He made Himself thenceforth forever a true and literal man. We talk loosely and lightly about our bodies. We seem to think they are the mere houses in which for a time we dwell; or they are related to us as the casket to the jewel, or the shell to the seed which it encloses. Not so the Scriptures. In their view man is a complex being. The body is not the man, nor is the soul the man, nor the soul and the spirit. He is made up of all these factors, and neither of them can be left out, and the true, complete man remain. As in the divine idea of the tabernacle, the shechinah glory and the tent in which it dwelt were to be inseparable, so the divinely bestowed soul and the humanly created body, which constitutes a man, were never to be divorced. The law of God concerns both factors; sin concerns both; redemption concerns both. Their future destiny for weal or woe is, according to Scripture, indissolubly linked.

When, therefore, Jesus the Christ was born, He took our nature to keep it. The indispensable condition of His becoming our Redeemer was that He should become our kinsman according to the flesh, and that He should remain such forevermore. And rightly speaking, philosophically speaking, as well as Scripturally, He could no more lay aside His humanity than we can lay aside ours. In the language of the early time, the time of the great councils that shaped the faith of the church virtually for all the centuries. Christ was on His human side consubstantial with men, and on the divine side consubstantial with God. Hence He was and continues to be both God and man in two distinct natures and one person forever. (Councils of Chalcedon and Constantinople, Hodge Sys. Theol. vol. 3, p. 651, also vol. 2, p. 388.)

And the Scriptures emphasize this permanency of our Lord's human nature. They make it the basis of His intercessorship. "For verily He took not on Him the nature of angels; but He took on Him the seed of Abraham. Wherefore in all things it behooved Him to be made like unto His brethren, that he might be a merciful and faithful High Priest in things pertaining to God, to make reconciliation for the sins of the people." Heb. 2 : 16, 17. "For we have not an High Priest which cannot be touched with the feeling of our infirmities; but was in all points tempted like as we are, yet without sin. Let us *therefore* come boldly unto the throne of grace, that we may obtain mercy, and find grace to help in time of need." Heb. 4 : 15, 16. So long then as men need a mediator through whom to approach God, so long at least must Jesus Christ as one who shares our nature and thereby knows and sympathizes with our needs, retain His perfect humanity. Paul says in Acts 17 : 30, 31 : "And the times of men's ignorance God winked at, but now commandeth all men everywhere to repent; because He hath appointed a day in which He will judge the world in righteousness, by that *man* whom He hath ordained; whereof He hath given assurance unto all men, in that He hath raised Him from the dead." Up to the hour of the judgment, then, we have the express witness of the word that Jesus Christ retains His perfect humanity. Then it is affirmed of Him—Jesus, the Christ—names both of them applied to Him in relation to His human nature—that He is "*the same, yesterday, to-day, and forever.*" (Heb. 13 : 8.) And among the last testimonies of this book, speaking of the fellowship with their Lord which His redeemed and glorified people shall enjoy after the judgment is passed, and the new heavens and new earth are come, and the holy city descended out of heaven to earth, it is said: "And His servants shall serve Him, and they shall see His face, and shall reign (with Him) for ever and ever." Such language by any ordinary rules of interpretation would certainly seem decisive as to the unchangeable and everlasting humanity of our Lord.

4. *But there is stronger ground than the necessity which attaches to the abiding humanity of Christ for affirming such a literal, personal, visible return. The Scriptures set the seal of a divine certainty upon it, in the doctrine of the resurrection.* Modern theorizings, some with Swedenborg and some with German rationalism to lead the way, have attacked the literalness of the resurrection. A part teach that the resurrection takes place at death; that then we drop the material body, but that our immaterial—or psychical—body, in which the soul dwells, passes into another state of existence. Others say all this language about resurrection is figurative, only an intense form of expression to emphasize the wonderful transformation the soul experiences when it is set free from the bondage of its earthly body. It rises up, breaks forth into a new life, just as the soul does when the touch of God first comes upon it to quicken it when dead in its trespasses and sins. That is called a resurrection, and what occurs at death, or after death, is only a more pronounced form of the same experience.

But neither of these views is what the Scriptures teach concerning this great truth. They set forth unequivocally and emphatically the doctrine of a resurrection of the body. No language could be more clear and decisive than the language they use. It is the bodies, not the souls of men that are to rise again. "*They that are in the graves* shall hear His voice, and shall come forth." (John 5:28, 29). "He that raised up Christ from the dead shall also quicken your *mortal bodies* by His Spirit that dwelleth in you." (Rom. 8:11). "Who shall fashion the *body* of our humiliation, that it may be conformed to the body of His 'glory.'" (Phil. 3:21, Rev. Ver.). Then the mighty argument of the great apostle in that wonderful resurrection chapter, 1 Corinthians, 15, of itself ends all debate. The whole pith and force of it turns on the fact that Paul is speaking on the resurrection of *the body.* The seed that is put into the ground has a body, and that new growth which is developed therefrom has a body, and every seed has its own body—*i. e.*, a growth-form peculiar to itself and given to it of God. There are also celestial bodies and bodies terrestrial, and each with its appropriate and divinely appointed glory. So also is the resurrection of the dead. It is sown a natural body; it is raised a spiritual body. "It"—the natural body—"is sown in corruption;" "it"—the spiritual body—"is raised in incorruption;" "it"—the natural body—"is sown in dishonor;" "it"—the spiritual body—"is raised in glory;" "it"—the natural body—"is sown in weakness;" "it"—the spiritual body—"is raised in power." The argument hangs absolutely upon the literalness of a bodily resurrection. It is this mortal that puts on immortality, this corruption that puts on incorruption. It is not some awakening of the soul as from a sleep, nor some sudden development of it into a larger activity, nor some mystical dropping of its gross outer enswarthment and a passing into a freer and higher state of existence. What these Scriptures teach is, that the same body that is put into the ground is the body that is to be raised. Just as truly and literally of our bodies, and more, as it was of the body of the Lord Jesus Christ. He was the first fruits, and the harvest must needs be identical in kind with the first sheaf. He was the first born from the dead of God's great redeemed family, and the rest of the household of faith must needs be like Him. And this they clearly cannot be except by the literal resurrection of the body. I do not pause here to consider what constitutes identity, and how that may be secured. I simply say that this doctrine holds no matter what the difficulties involved may be, difficulties as to bodies burned and their ashes scattered to the four winds, or as to bodies drowned and devoured by the fishes of the sea, or as to bodies buried, turned to dust, and their elements incorporated into trees, animals, or other human beings. These are God's questions, not ours. With Him nothing is impossible, and the resources of omnipotence are as ample now as when they availed, however unphilosophically, or in contravention of natural law, to create a universe out of nothing, and make the original man out of the dust of the earth. Of one thing we may rest assured, whatever the pledges of this word, God will make them good in every jot and tittle. Our concern is not with the difficulties of the word, but with its teachings. And these compel us to hold that these bodies are to be resurrected, and that in the resurrection, although transformed and ineffably glorified, they will be just as identical with what they now are as was the body of our risen Lord with the body laid in the tomb of Joseph. They will be literal, visible, glorious, just as His was, and because His was.

You have anticipated, no doubt, the force of this as related to the subject under discussion. The doctrine of resurrection not only makes our future bodily existence certain, but it conditions that future estate upon the bodily existence and return of our Lord. It is at "His coming" that the righteous dead are to be raised, and with believers then living are to be caught up to meet Him in the air, and, as in the twinkling of an eye, changed into His image. I need not stop to read the passages so familiar to all upon this point (1 Cor. 15 : 23–52 ; 1 Thes. 4 : 14–17 ; Phil. 3 : 20, 21). But you will notice this : that the resurrection of the bodies of saints who have died and the transformation of saints who are living when He comes, is conditioned not only upon the fact that our Lord actually rose from the dead and that He is actually to return, but that at His coming He shall possess still His body, the identical body with which He left the tomb. For only so can the bodies of our humiliation be conformed unto the body of His glory. Only so can we see Him as He is, and therefore be like Him. Only so can we meet Him in the air, and in our transformed and glorified bodies, the likeness of His own, abide with Him forevermore. It is therefore the clear necessity of the Scripture teaching as to the resurrection that our Lord's return should be literal, personal, visible. And this is precisely what we know it must be from other testimonies of the word; for these require that He should come "in the clouds of heaven ;" that "men shall see Him," that "they that pierced Him shall look upon Him," and that He shall "come as the Redeemer to Zion," take the "throne of David" and "reign over the house of Jacob forever." (Matt. 25 : 30 ; Rev. 1 : 7; Zech. 12 : 10; Is. 59 : 20; Luke 1 : 32).

Standing now on the ground of this argument, there is a swift and decisive answer furnished to all theories as to the Lord's return which do away with this literalness. There is just one trouble with them all. They are, some of them, very learned, very philosophical, very satisfying to men's reason ; but they lack *one thing—the authority of God's word.* Take the view *e. g.* that seeks to identify the Lord's return with the destruction of Jerusalem. These Scriptures declare that at that time "shall all the tribes of the earth mourn," that "men shall see the Son of man coming in the clouds of heaven with power and great glory," that then "He shall send His angels with a great sound of a trumpet, and they shall gather His elect from the four winds, from one end of heaven to the other." (Matt. 24 : 29–33). Not taking into account now the manifest absurdity of making an idolatrous Roman General the representative of our Lord, and his heathen legions the type of holy angels, the facts do not agree with these prophetic testimonies. For all the tribes of the earth did not then mourn, nor was the Son of man seen coming in the clouds of heaven, nor were the elect gathered from the four winds. More than that, the gospel was not preached in all the world as a witness, the voice of the archangel was not heard, nor the trump of God, nor were the righteous dead raised, and living believers caught up to meet the Lord in the air; all which events are explicitly declared to be the accompaniments of the coming of the Lord. Only an exegesis which is bound to make Scripture harmonize with its prearranged conclusions can possibly construe these prophetic utterances as aimed at setting forth the destruction of Jerusalem.

Take, again, the view which identifies the Lord's coming with the death of believers. This, like the theory just considered, is without Scripture warrant. Its favorite passage, "I go to prepare a place for you, and if I go and prepare a place for you, I will come again and receive you unto Myself," has no reference to death. Our Lord nowhere taught His disciples that He would come for them at death, and nowhere else in Scripture is the doctrine taught. The teaching of the word is, that when the believer dies, he departs to be with Christ, and his longing is to be absent from the body and present with the Lord. Hence, Stephen, when the mob were stoning him to death, saw the "heavens opened," and the Son of man not come down to earth, but "standing on the right hand of God." And a little later he said, "Lord Jesus, receive my spirit," and passed into the presence of his Lord, waiting to give him glad welcome in the skies. It was a company of angels, not the Lord, that came for Lazarus when he died; and perhaps they often come to convey God's children home in triumph when their work is done. But the Lord himself is never represented as coming with them, nor bearing them away. Nor did His disciples so understand Him to teach. They very clearly understood that He did not so come at death. For when He made answer to Peter concerning John—"If I will that he tarry till I come, what is that to thee?" John adds, very significantly, "Then went this saying abroad among the brethren, that that disciple should not die." So far were they from supposing that our Lord meant death by His coming, that they imagined Him to mean that the beloved disciple should *not* die, but should tarry till the Lord returned, or possibly before that be caught up into heaven. Hence the tradition that prevailed in the early church that John did not die, but, like Enoch and Elijah, was translated. The true Scripture idea is that death is our great, relentless foe, and that the mighty adversary of our souls, to the utmost of his power, seeks to invest it with terrors. Its coming never ought to be in a believer's mind made the same thing as the coming of the Lord. He who rides upon the pale horse, and who goes forth to kill with the sword, and with hunger and with death, and with the beasts of the earth, is surely not to be confounded with Him who rides upon the white horse, wearing many crowns, called Faithful and True, and followed by the armies of heaven! He that has redeemed us has indeed conquered death, and pledges us victory likewise. But we must face the grim foe as He did, and be prepared to feel to the last hour all the pangs his malignity can inflict. We may indeed see our Lord's face beaming on us in the struggle, and catch even His word of cheer. But it will be as with Stephen, with the Blessed One standing not on earth, but at the right hand of God, and waiting to receive us there. We have the best of rights to say over the caskets of God's chosen, "Blessed are the dead that die in the Lord," and "where is thy sting, O death, and where thy victory, O grave." Yet this largely over the final release from long continued torture, and the faith-discerned issues of the struggle which even the king of terrors cannot shut out from the soul. But a day is coming when this mighty shout of triumph shall burst from ten thousand times ten thousand lips, because when He for whose appearing we watch, and toil, and pray shall come, the sacred dust of all the ages shall catch the trumpet's sound and recognize its Lord and spring to meet Him, clothed in immortal beauty like His own. And then, and not till then, will there roll round the world as the mighty pean of this uprisen host, "Death is swallowed up in victory!"

But one other view—and the favorite view with many—must not be overlooked. That which identifies the Lord's coming with the work of the Spirit in the hearts of believers, and in the hearts of men to convert them to Christ. All quickened spiritual experiences, all conversions, and all revivals are regarded as a true coming of the Lord. And this view, it is held, puts honor upon the Holy Spirit, while that of the Lord's personal return does Him dishonor by belittling His competency to save man. As Dr. Lyman Abbott puts it: "Far better for Christian work and Christian character is the universal presence (the Holy Spirit) than the localized one; the invisible Christ than the visible one." "It would be difficult to conceive anything more disastrous to the healthful and moral activity of the Christian church than a return of Christ to the earth to reign in the flesh in Jerusalem." (*Christian Union*, Sept. 2, 1886.) And similarly Dr. Bushnell. "There is nothing, I must frankly say, that would be so nearly a dead loss of Christ to any disciple who knows Him in the dear companionship of faith, as to have Him come in visible show. Nothing could be more inexpedient, or a profounder affliction, than a locally descended, permanently visible Saviour." (Christ and His Salvation, pp. 334–336.)

This is strong language. If these brethren are right, I am most certainly wrong in this presentation. But to the law and the testimony. Is this theory of the coming of the Spirit as identical with the coming of Christ, what the Scriptures teach as to the Lord's return? Far from it. They never confound the gift and indwelling or work of the Spirit with the coming of the Lord. The Spirit is *another* comforter. His office is to glorify Christ by taking the things of Christ and showing them to His disciples. He is the representative of Christ, taking his place in the world, and doing His work. It is true that through Him Jesus Christ is spiritually with and in believers, is their life, has His image formed within them. But all this not as personally present with them in the same sense in which He is personally at the right hand of God, but in the same sense in which God the Father is so present in their hearts. (John 14 : 23, and 17 : 21–23.) That is to say, Christ is potentially in the hearts of His disciples, there by His Spirit to teach, guide, admonish, comfort, help, purify, empower for service. This is what the Spirit was sent into the world for by our Lord after the ascension, while He remained at the right hand of God clothed in His glorified human body, and personally visible there as our High Priest, our Intercessor.

And just here is where those who hold to the theory of the coming of Christ in the Spirit seem to halt in their readings of the word. They recognize the office of Christ as advocate, and the work of the Spirit as dwelling in the hearts of believers and accompanying the preaching of the word and making it the power of God to save souls. And they seem to forget that according to the Scriptures all this looks to something further on. They seem never to ask whether, beyond the gift of the Spirit, there was any ulterior purpose in the Lord's going away. Whereas the testimony abounds, and that of the plainest sort, that He went away in order that He might come again. This is what parable after parable is specifically aimed to teach. This is what He says Himself when He gives the promise of the Spirit, and this, be it noted, is the continual witness of the Spirit when he has taken the Lord's place in the church, and is teaching truth and managing everything according to His own supreme wish and will. It is He that testifies that when the times of restitution of all things shall come, Jesus Christ will come to set up His throne and fill the world with His glory. It is He that testifies of that coming day when the Lord shall descend from Heaven with a shout, and the dead in Christ shall rise, and the living saints shall be caught up to meet Him in the air, and hence are to comfort one another in this hope. It is He that exhorts believers to be patient, because the coming of the Lord draweth nigh ; to live soberly, righteously, and godly in this present world, looking for that blessed hope and the glorious appearing of the great God and our Saviour Jesus Christ. Surely, if this doctrine of the literal, personal, visible return were one that puts dishonor on the Spirit, this is strange testimony for the Spirit to bear concerning it! To keep it always in the foreground, to emphasize and magnify it as the one especial secret of realizing closest fellowship with Him, highest allegiance to the Lord Jesus, and fullest measures of the peace and joy and power to love others that He Himself could impart!

One other division of my subject remains to be considered, viz: *that the Lord's coming will be pre-millennial.* I have left myself no time for a full presentation of the argument and must be content with a comparatively brief outline of the proof upon which it stands.

1. *It is a most weighty fact that this was the undoubted view of the early church.* I mean, of course, of all orthodox believers. The gnostics rejected it, and so did some of the other heretical sects. But generally it was the accepted and joyful faith of the early Christians. This is not, of course, infallible proof of the truth of the doctrine. Good men in that age were liable, as are good men in all ages, to make mistakes and misread Scripture. But these early disciples were but a brief remove from apostolic days and apostolic teaching. Until the first century closed they had the teaching of supernaturally inspired men. Later than that, they had for instructors those who received the truths they taught from the lips of these inspired apostles. It is agreed on all hands that so universal and ardent was the belief and feeling of these early disciples, that they were watching eagerly for the Lord's return in their day. And Paul has been charged by the critics with holding and teaching this in his earlier ministry, and then in later years seeing his mistake and changing his instruction. However, the churches so held, and John, the beloved disciple, fresh from personal communion with his risen and glorified Lord, and filled with the Spirit, expresses this common faith and longing when, at the end of the apocalypse, he pictures the majesty and glory that mark his Lord's return and the establishment of His kingdom and prays, "even so, Lord Jesus, come quickly."

It is a strong confirmation of this early belief that in that document discovered a few years since, and known as the "Teaching of the Apostles," and which is conceded to go back to 160 and possibly 120 A. D., we find this testimony : that in the days of Antichrist "the heavens will open, the trumpet will sound, and there shall be a resurrection of the dead—not however of all—but as it is written, the Lord shall come and all His saints with Him."

2. *Further: if this belief of the earliest Christians was a mistake, and the coming of Christ is to be post-millennial, we should look to see this mistake pointed out and some very positive teaching given to the contrary.* Whereas there is nothing of the kind, not a word about any error in this matter nor a word of different teaching. Paul did indeed tell the Thessalonian brethren who were troubled by the teaching of some that the Lord had already come, that this was a mistake, and that He could not come till the

man of sin, the antichrist, should be revealed. And he told them further, that when He did come, this man of sin would be destroyed by the brightness, the supreme splendors and consuming glory of His coming.

If now the apostle wanted these brethren to know that the Lord would not come till the world was converted, this of all places was the very one in which to tell them so. That would have cleared up all their doubts and fears and made the truth simple and plain. Indeed, it is inconceivable that not only should this great apostle and instructor of the churches say nothing about any mistake in their pre-millennial belief, but on the contrary affirm that there was to be, not the world's conversion before the Lord should come, but a prodigious manifestation of evil, the man of sin welcomed and even worshipped as God.

I do not forget that the parables of the mustard seed and the leaven, are claimed to set forth the doctrine of the world's conversion, by the gradual spread of the Gospel. These parables have had to do large duty as supporters of this doctrine, being the only Scriptures that have even a look toward such a consummation. To my mind they were not designed to so teach. I may not understand them. But this much would seem clear, that in order to fulfil the post-millennial idea, the mustard seed should be the counterpart of the stone cut out of the mountain without hands and attain to a growth that should spread its branches over the whole earth. Failing of that, the mustard seed simply stands for the wonderful greatness of results that are to be realized in Gospel work from insignificant beginnings. A single testimony, a sentence of Scripture, a prayer, how often it has been the little seed that has come to a mighty fruitage first in a soul saved, and then through that soul multiplied itself a thousand times, possibly in revivals like that wrought through Peter at Pentecost, or that through Philip at Samaria, or those of which we have known through Mr. Moody and his fellow evangelists.

Or, keeping to the thought of the kingdom, first, the helpless Babe of Bethlehem, and in the fullness of time the King of kings in His resplendent glory. And it is this wonderful contrast between the beginning and the results, the apparent nothingness of the one and the mightiness of the other, and not the law of development that it is meant here to emphasize. And the parable of the leaven, to say nothing of the fact that throughout Scripture the word is invariably used in a bad sense and never as representing the work of grace, goes no further, in my judgment, than to symbolize that noiseless and imperceptible way in which transformations are wrought in the heart through the divine power of the Gospel. That it cannot be meant for a gradual transformation of the race that shall ultimately bring all men into the kingdom, is proved by the other parables that are coupled with it, the tares and the wheat, the good and bad fish. These teach emphatically that when the Lord returns there will be a mixed state of things; on the one hand those who have accepted the truth and who will be gathered by the angels as wheat into the garner: and on the other hand those who will be gathered into bundles by the angels as tares and cast into the fire to be burned. And with these agree all those teachings of our Lord which represent the world at His coming in such a moral condition as it was in the days of Noah and Lot, when fearful judgments were visited upon the ungodly. And other Scriptures accord with this. For their testimony is that in that day of the Lord's return, there will be believers even without oil in their lamps, and who will fail of admission to the marriage feast; professed disciples who will discover that they were never known; and those upon whom vengeance will be taken as those that know not God and obey not the Gospel of the Lord Jesus Christ.

3. *Again, the teaching of the Scriptures as to the Jewish people require the pre-millennial coming of the Lord.* I cannot take time to go fully into the testimony of the word upon this point. It is very full and very decisive. Doubtless in the discussion as to the Jews, which comes further on in the programme, there will be a full presentation. I shall therefore content myself with a single passage. In Acts 15: 14–17, we have the witness of the Apostle James at the Council called at Jerusalem to consider whether believers should be required to conform to the Mosaic ritual. After Peter had told how wonderfully the preaching of the Gospel had been owned among the Gentiles and how the Holy Ghost had come in fullness upon them, even as upon Jewish converts, James says: "*Simeon hath declared how God at first did visit the Gentiles to take out of them a people for His name. And to this agree the words of the prophets; as it is written, After this I will return, and will build*

You have anticipated, no doubt, the force of this as related to the subject under discussion. The doctrine of resurrection not only makes our future bodily existence certain, but it conditions that future estate upon the bodily existence and return of our Lord. It is at "His coming" that the righteous dead are to be raised, and with believers then living are to be caught up to meet Him in the air, and, as in the twinkling of an eye, changed into His image. I need not stop to read the passages so familiar to all upon this point (1 Cor. 15:23–52; 1 Thes. 4:14–17; Phil. 3:20, 21). But you will notice this: that the resurrection of the bodies of saints who have died and the transformation of saints who are living when He comes, is conditioned not only upon the fact that our Lord actually rose from the dead and that He is actually to return, but that at His coming He shall possess still His body, the identical body with which He left the tomb. For only so can the bodies of our humiliation be conformed unto the body of His glory. Only so can we see Him as He is, and therefore be like Him. Only so can we meet Him in the air, and in our transformed and glorified bodies, the likeness of His own, abide with Him forevermore. It is therefore the clear necessity of the Scripture teaching as to the resurrection that our Lord's return should be literal, personal, visible. And this is precisely what we know it must be from other testimonies of the word; for these require that He should come "in the clouds of heaven;" that "men shall see Him," that "they that pierced Him shall look upon Him," and that He shall "come as the Redeemer to Zion," take the "throne of David" and "reign over the house of Jacob forever." (Matt. 25:30; Rev. 1:7; Zech. 12:10; Is. 59:20; Luke 1:32).

Standing now on the ground of this argument, there is a swift and decisive answer furnished to all theories as to the Lord's return which do away with this literalness. There is just one trouble with them all. They are, some of them, very learned, very philosophical, very satisfying to men's reason; but they lack *one thing—the authority of God's word.* Take the view *e. g.* that seeks to identify the Lord's return with the destruction of Jerusalem. These Scriptures declare that at that time "shall all the tribes of the earth mourn," that "men shall see the Son of man coming in the clouds of heaven with power and great glory," that then "He shall send His angels with a great sound of a trumpet, and they shall gather His

4. I name only one other proof of this pre-millennial coming of Christ, but that, in my judgment, the most conclusive one of all, viz: *the Scripture doctrine of the resurrection of believers.* I cannot enter into the discussion which this involves. Nor is it needful, for the whole matter is to be fully presented in a paper this afternoon. I can only say that I regard it as impossible to fairly interpret the Scriptures and not admit that two resurrections are taught, the resurrection of believers at the beginning of the thousand years of Rev. 20, and the resurrection of unbelievers at the end. I believe that all attempts to explain the first resurrection here taught as figurative and spiritual, and the second as literal, are a clear perversion of the Scripture and only possible by a forced and unnatural exegesis. According to the Scripture use of language both by the writer of this book of Revelation and by others, the word souls means persons. But these are not the only ones included in this first resurrection. The Greek text plainly implies, and so does the revised version, that there are others who shared in it, all those who "had not worshipped the beast, nor received his mark." This would include all true believers. And these all, martyrs and others, as John says, lived and reigned with Christ a thousand years. Then followed the resurrection of the rest of the dead, those who had died in unbelief. I hold with Dean Alford, that "no legitimate treatment of the text will extort what is known as the spiritual interpretation now in fashion. If in such a passage the first resurrection may be understood to mean *spiritual* rising with Christ, while the second means *literal* rising from the grave, then there is an end of all significance in language, and Scripture is wiped out as a definite testimony to anything." Standing then on this doctrine of two resurrections, the pre-millennial coming of the Lord Jesus becomes an incontrovertible fact. For we have this explicit statement in 1 Thes. 4 : 13–17. "*For if we believe that Jesus died and rose again, even so them also which sleep in Jesus will God bring with him. For the Lord himself shall descend from heaven with a shout, with the voice of the archangel and with the trump of God, and the dead in Christ shall rise first: then we which are alive and remain shall be caught up together with them in the clouds, to meet the Lord in the air, and so shall we ever be with the Lord.*"

There are other arguments that might be adduced, but I pause here. For myself I have only to say that the conclusion involved in what has now been presented, seems irresistible. The faith of the early church, so clear and intense and inspiring; the lack of any positive testimony to the contrary anywhere in the word; the emphatic teaching of many Scriptures as to a mixed state of things and a very great prevalence of iniquity instead of a converted world, to meet the Lord at His return; the express teaching as to the conversion of the Jews after His return and conditioned upon it; and finally, the decisive teaching as to the two resurrections and the Lord's coming as contemporaneous with the first, and as conditioning it—make it impossible for me to do otherwise than believe that the longed for return of our absent Lord, the blessed hope that filled the hearts of believers in the early days with inexpressible joy, is to be at the beginning and not the end of the thousand years during which Satan is bound and truth, righteousness and peace comparatively prevail in the earth.

And I give it as my profound conviction that no greater blessing could come to the church of Christ, than a revival of this ancient faith. I believe it would, as in that early day, exalt these Scriptures as the divine and infallible word of God. It would make them, and not the speculations and theories of men, the law of Christian living, the abounding source of cheer and comfort, the unfailing secret of spiritual growth and fruitfulness. It would magnify every doctrine of grace. It would make sin not a foible, a misjudgment, an undeveloped and crude form of good; but instead a conscious, wilful disobedience to God. It would set the Cross of Calvary in the foreground of all true faith and make salvation through the blood there shed the one vital doctrine of the church, the one only hope of a lost world. It would exalt the personality and divinity of the Holy Spirit. It would inspire all hearts with Paul's ambition to count all things but loss that they might know Christ and be found in Him. It would put great emphasis on prayer. It would separate the church from the world. It would make the things not seen real and glorious and the things seen perishable and mean. It would lay upon God's people the burden of these unevangelized millions of the race, and give them no rest till the Gospel should be preached to every people and kindred and tongue under the whole heaven. It would, in a word, fasten all eyes on the promise of the Lord's return and by day and night keep His disciples toiling, praying, waiting with ever increasing earnestness and longing till the flash of His resplendent coming shall burst athwart the sky. And it would hasten mightily that coming and the in-bringing of that kingdom which is the one hope of this poor, groaning, sin cursed world. Would we might all lead on our lives as if with that last message of our glorified Lord sounding in our ears: "Surely I come quickly," and with that last prayer of Scripture ever on our lips, "even so, come, Lord Jesus."

THE SCRIPTURAL DOCTRINE OF THE RESURRECTIONS.

REV. H. M. PARSONS, D. D.,
Pastor of Knox Presbyterian Church, Toronto, Ont.

The fact of the resurrection of Jesus Christ from the grave, is as well attested historically, as any other event of the past. The importance of this doctrine on the destinies of men, is also verified in the history of civilization. Apart from revelation, the doctrine of the resurrection from the dead, based upon the fact of the resurrection of Jesus Christ, has been the source of hope and comfort to the human race, beyond any other distinctive truth of religion.

But the doctrine in its spiritual power and influence, is entirely one of revelation by the Spirit of God.

In the Old Testament, it was predicted of the Messiah that was to come—as we learn from the testimony of Acts 2 : 30, 31, when as a prophet, David "knowing that God had sworn with an oath to him, that of the fruit of his loins, according to the flesh, he would raise up Christ to sit on his throne; he seeing this before, spake of the resurrection of the Christ, that, neither was he left in hades, nor did his flesh see corruption" (quoted from Ps. 16 : 10). The apostles add their own testimony. Verse 32. "This Jesus hath God raised up, whereof we all are witnesses." As the keystone of the arch of Christian doctrines, constituting the foundation of the Christian religion—this truth is the basal rock upon which the temple of God is built. "He rose again the third day, according to the Scriptures." "If there be no resurrection of the dead, then is Christ not risen." "If Christ be not risen, then is our preaching vain, and your faith is also vain." 1 Cor. 15 : 4-13-14. Upon this sure basis the fabric of Christian doctrine throughout the

Scriptures is founded. Accordingly the doctrine of the resurrections is purely one of revelation and utterly beyond the power of the natural man to conceive or to comprehend.

1st. *What is meant by the resurrection of the body?*

This truth seemed incredible to the Athenians and to Felix, when Paul declared it in his famous sermon on Mars Hill, and before the Roman governor. Equally it is denied by the unbeliever of our own day. Though many who profess the name of Christ accept his resurrection as an historical fact, upon credible evidence, yet in their hearts they deny it, and no sensible influence from it is felt or seen in their lives.

Our bodies now have a life adapted to our present environment, and subject to the requirements and conditions of this present state. When our life here closes, the body returns to dust, and the personal identity of each body is preserved for the resurrection life, imparted when the dead arise, as in the body now it is recognized through the various stages of growth from birth to old age. There is no greater mystery in the resurrection body, than in the fact that the infant, when an old man, is the same person.

That this body will be a material one, is evident from the example of our Lord, and the assertion of the Holy Spirit, that "we shall be like him."

The description given of our Lord's body of glory, reveals the fact of the real corporeal form, and adaptation to the environment of the spiritual body. When our Lord arose from the dead, he invited the disciple who doubted, to verify his real presence by actual touch.

This is also clearly taught by the Apostle Paul in the parable of the grain. "Thou sowest not that body that shall be, but a bare grain." "But God giveth it a body, even as it pleased Him, and to each seed a body of its own." (Revision.) Thus, the BODY OF GLORY, will be adapted to the celestial environment, which will be its eternal abode: and the BODY OF SHAME will be adapted to its chosen residence forever.

2d. *This resurrection of all the bodies of the dead will be universal.*

Our Lord teaches in John 5:28, that "All that are in the tombs shall hear his voice, and shall come forth," and the argument of the apostle before Felix affirms his own faith, as also that of the Jews who opposed him, in "hope that there shall be a resurrection of the dead, both of the just and of the unjust." This has been the general faith of all the children of God, in the present dispensation. When our Lord made a new revelation at the death of Lazarus, Martha confessed the belief of the resurrection of the body at the last day, as then prevalent among the Jews. This meant, at the end of all the ages, when judgment would be given, and the dissolution of all things would occur. In that view, resurrection was universal, instantaneous, and simultaneous.

This view is still held by many Christians. Jesus at that time declared advanced truth for the acceptance of His followers. He specially announced and proved His power over death, saying, "I am the resurrection and the life."

3d. *There is a resurrection unto life, of the bodies of all who have died in Christ.*

Before this, the doctrine of the Scriptures was, a resurrection from the dead, general and comprehensive. Now, a specific resurrection of a certain class is affirmed by the Lord, and the positive question added, "Believest thou this?"—To the sorrowing sisters the Lord discloses His mighty love.

"He that believeth in Me, though he were dead, yet shall he live." "I am the resurrection of the dead" body. And, in connection with this wonderful truth, He adds the translation of the mortal bodies of believers who are alive on the earth, at the moment of the resurrection of this specific company.

"Whosoever liveth and believeth on me, shall never die." "I am the life"—of the living and mortal body.

An element of time is introduced here, by the connection of the dead and living believers.

Revelation concerning this is more explicit in the fuller details recorded in 1 Corinthians, 15th chapter. We have there, resurrection of the dead, in its universal completeness, and in its definite order. Ver. 22. "For as in Adam all die, even so, in Christ, shall all be made alive." Ver. 23. "But every man in his own order." (Company or band.) "Christ the first fruits: then they that are Christ's at His coming, then the end, when He shall have delivered up the kingdom to God, even the Father: when He shall have put down all rule, and all authority and power." In the same chapter, the close connection of the resurrection and translation of believers, at the same time, makes the coming of Christ the second time the moment for the mighty transformation. Thus in ver. 51, "Behold, I show you a mystery: we shall not all sleep, but we shall all be changed in a moment, in the twinkling of an eye, at the last trump: for the trumpet shall sound, and the dead shall be raised incorruptible, and we shall be changed."

Our Lord describes death as a sleep, when speaking of Lazarus to His disciples. So in this connection it is repeated, "we shall not all sleep."

But with stronger emphasis this mystery is repeated in 1 Thes. 4 : 14, 15, 16, 17. "If we believe that Jesus died and rose again, even so them also which sleep in Jesus, will God bring with him." "We say unto you, by the word of the Lord, that we which are alive, and remain unto the coming of the Lord, shall not prevent them which are asleep." "For the Lord himself shall descend from heaven with a shout, with the voice of the archangel, and with the trump of God: and the dead in Christ shall rise first." "Then we which are alive and remain, shall be caught up together with them in the clouds, to meet the Lord in the air: and so shall we be forever with the Lord."

This resurrection of the righteous dead, is thus connected with the translation of the living saints, and definitely described in the process of ascent from the earth and the descent of the Lord from heaven above, to the meeting place in the air. None but those in Christ are included in this resurrection. It is predicted in Dan. 12 : 2, "as awaking from the dust of earth, to 'everlasting' life." In Luke 14 : 14, it is named "the resurrection of the just," and in John 5 : 29, it is called "the resurrection of life."

4th. *There is a resurrection unto "shame and everlasting contempt," of all who die in unbelief.* Dan. 12 : 2, represents two companies arising from the sleepers in the dust. The one party "some" to "the resurrection of life," and after them, the other "some" "to shame and everlasting contempt." We need to notice the distinction of Scripture in regard to the term LIFE, as applied to resurrection-being. A clear statement of this is given by Mr. B. W. Newton in his work on the "Prospects of the Ten Kingdoms." (pp. 170, 171). We know from other parts of Scripture, that all the righteous dead will then awake to life, "life," and not "awake," being the word which implies the possession and exercise of the power of resurrection-being. The souls of the departed saints, whilst in a disembodied state, although in Paradise, and perfectly conscious of their blessing, are not in the exercise of the functions of life, those functions requiring the presence of the body. Hence our Lord, in his reply to the Sadducees, who denied the resurrection of the body, proves it by saying that, if there were no resurrection, God would not be called the God of Abraham, for that He is not the God of the dead, but of the living. The soul of Abraham is now consciously receiving blessings from God, but Abraham will not be able to live *unto* God until he again receives his body; and in this sense is still regarded as dead, not as living.

So also, the departed wicked are not represented in Scripture as living, although their souls exist in torment. Hence it is said, "The rest of the dead lived not (*ouk ezesan*) until the thousand years were finished," "live" being here used, not in the sense of "exist," but as denoting the exercise of the functions of life. Man, therefore, is not said to "live," *i. e.* in the sense of exercising the functions of life, either when he is dispossessed of his body, or when having his body, he is placed in the second death. Thus, the reality of the "resurrection to shame and everlasting contempt," is as surely taught in Scripture as the "resurrection of the just," or, as it is termed in Rev. 20 : 5, "resurrection the first."

5th. *These two resurrections are utterly diverse in CHARACTER and in DESTINY.*

We have noticed the distinction made in the prophecy of Daniel, one is unto LIFE, including all that the word implies of worth and esteem in character: the other to exactly the opposite—"shame and everlasting contempt," a state of death, or eternal separation from God, in character and destiny.

The same facts are contained in the word of our Saviour, in John 5 : 29, where the preceding life and character are defined, and assigned to each resurrection. "They that have done good, unto the resurrection of life; and they that have done evil, unto the resurrection of judgment." (Rev.)

Still more clearly we find the difference of the two marked in the twentieth chapter of Revelation. The apostle saw the souls of martyred saints live again, necessarily in their bodies, because the souls had never died, and their actions in their former bodies are described. They were "Beheaded for the testimony of Jesus, and for the word of God, and which had not worshipped the Beast, neither his image, neither had received his mark upon their foreheads, or in their hands." These lived and reigned with Christ a thousand years. After this resurrection there is another for those not raised at this time. Books had been kept of their conduct. These books were opened. In order to have absolute justice, the Book of Life was opened. This judgment of those now raised from the dead, and standing before God, was of things recorded in the book, and according to their works, whether done for the glory of God, or for the glory of man. All the dead remaining after the first resurrection in their graves, in the sea or on the land, were judged according to their works, as designating character, and if not found written in the book of life, were cast into the lake of fire, and this, for them, is called "the second death." There is no intimation in Scripture that this first issue of their case is ever changed. If the results of the first resurrection are everlasting, the results of this must endure forever. If those who have refused and resisted the grace of God, enforced by the pleading of the Holy Ghost, before their first death was experienced, have voluntarily taken the risk, and chosen the ways of sin—there is no reasonable ground for supposing that they will choose to change their character and state, when all the needed resources for such choice and change have been withdrawn. This resurrection of souls remaining through the thousand years, in their own place, will certainly be the assumption of bodies adapted to the requirement of their spiritual state, under the final sentence. And, so far as revelation pronounces upon the duration of the sentence, it is for the ages upon ages of eternity.

6th. *These two resurrections are separate, both as to place and as to time.*

The first is from the earth to the judgment seat in the air—above the earth, and for the purpose of rewards and appointments in the kingdom of God. The works of each one are scrutinized to determine the place of honor and glory in the firmament above the throne. "One star differeth from another in glory." The second resurrection is unto judgment, before the great white throne, upon which the judge is seated, "from whose face the earth and the heaven fled away: and there was found no place for them." All the remaining dead of the earth will stand before this throne, to be judged as to their character by their works.

As to time, the two resurrections are separated by a thousand years. The day of the Lord is a peculiar expression of the Scripture, in regard to the coming again of Jesus Christ, and the assumption of political sway over the nations. A clear statement of this peculiar period is found in 2 Peter 3 : 10, in which the morning and evening of the day are tersely described. "The day of the Lord will come as a thief in the night." The beginning or dawn will be almost imperceptible, as the first rays of the morning dawn ; its advance rapid, sudden, stealthy, and as the tread of the midnight thief. The advance and close will be notable;" in the which the heavens shall pass away with a great noise, and the elements shall be dissolved with fervent heat, and the earth and the works that are therein, shall be burned up."

The pen of inspiration, with a single rapid sweep, often sketches an whole dispensation of the earth—fulfilling that other statement of this epistle, "one day is with the Lord as a thousand years, and a thousand years as one day." (3 : 8.) The opening of this day synchronises with the first resurrection. Definitely the word of God places it at this point of time. "They that are Christ's at his coming," and of all such, it is written in 2 Cor. 5 : 10, that "they must be manifested before the judgment seat of Christ, that every one may receive the things in his body, according to that he hath done, whether good or bad." These deeds, according as done in the energy of the spirit, or of the flesh, shall receive the due meed of praise and reward, or shall be cast away as refuse, because not enduring the test applied to each one. The order of the resurrections of the righteous, is followed by an interval between Christ and his members. The word "then" (*epeita*) marks this interval, and the same word is used between the rising of the saints and the last company or band, in this minute and clear statement of the resurrection of God's people. A careful examination of the words used in the revelation of this doctrine will show in every case, this distinction of time. Thus in John 5 : 29, the two companies are defined in regard to character and destiny. "They that have done good, unto the resurrection of life; and they that have done evil, unto the resurrection of judgment." Nothing is here said of the time. And nothing said, prevents an interval of time between the two events. If we turn to the context of this passage, we find a reference to time, that is suggestive as to duration of the period. Our Lord, speaking of man's spiritual death, which was and is universal, says, verse 25, "The hour is coming and now is, when the dead shall hear the voice of the Son of God, and they that hear shall live." That "hour" has now lasted eighteen hundred and sixty years, and surely there is room for one thousand years between the two resurrections.

We have, however, definite testimony that when the righteous dead arise, the rest of the dead will be left in their graves.

The Apostle Paul, in his letter to the Philippians 3:11, expresses strong desire to be with Christ, and to be like him in this way: "If by any means I might attain unto the resurrection from the dead." The literal meaning of the Greek makes the bearing of this passage on the point before us, most emphatic. He desires "to attain," to reach, to come upon, "the out-resurrection, the one from among the dead." Indicating plainly that many of those who are in the dust, are left behind in this resurrection.

The Greek word here used "*exanastasis*" is found nowhere else, and is most clearly used to signify this out-resurrection—a "resurrection out from"—which, joined with the definite article and "*nekron*" following—"the one from among the dead"—requires the assumption that a portion are left in the graves. The force of these repeated statements of diverse companies, with diverse characters and destinies, prepares us for the direct declaration found in Revelation 20 : 5, in connection with the fourth verse.

After the binding of Satan, the Seer of Patmos saw the souls of martyr witnesses, alive in bodies, reigning with Christ for one thousand years. And he adds in verse 5, "This, the resurrection first." He further adds, "But the rest of the dead lived not again, till the one thousand years were finished."

If this interpretation be received, then the resurrection of the wicked, "according to the Scriptures," takes place in the evening of the day of the Lord, at the close of the millennial age.

Dean Alford, on this text says: "No legitimate treatment of it will extort what is known as the spiritual interpretation now in fashion. If in a passage where two resurrections are mentioned, when certain souls lived at the first, and the rest of the dead lived only at the end of a specified period after that first—if in such a passage the first resurrection may be understood to mean SPIRITUAL rising with Christ, while the second means LITERAL rising from the grave :—then there is an end of all significance in language, and Scripture is wiped out as a definite testimony to anything.

If the first resurrection is spiritual, then so is the second, which I suppose none will be hardy enough to maintain; but if the second is literal, so is the first:—which, in common with the whole primitive church, and many of the best modern expositors, I do maintain, and receive as an article of faith and hope." (Alford Com., Rev. 20 : 6.)

7th. *The practical importance of this doctrine.*

It will be found to have large influence on the present life, when held in its relations to the future life.

Just as the resurrection of Jesus Christ is realized by faith, so will the resurrection of the bodies of saints, and of sinners, affect the present responsibilities of both believers and unbelievers. If risen with Christ by faith, we shall long to be formed anew in that body of glory which He has promised. And so the fact of the terrible future before the unsaved, must quicken all our sensibilities to the pressing obligation upon us of seeking to save the lost, by the immediate presentation of the Gospel to every creature.

And, for self-judgment in the daily life, nothing will more stimulate the obedience of faith than the momentous thought, "for which resurrection am I preparing to-day?" In one or the other, I must appear. Shall it be in the morning, or in the evening of the "Day of the Lord?"

"Blessed and holy is he that hath part in the first resurrection, on such the second death hath no power." Rev. 20 : 6.

"Whosoever was not found written in the book of life, was cast into the lake of fire. This is the second death." Rev. 20: 14, 15.

THE SECOND ADVENT ERA IN BIBLE PERSPECTIVE.

By the Rev. J. A. Owen, A. M.

Of St. James Methodist Episcopal Church, Elizabeth, N. J.

"Perspective" is defined as "the art of representing natural objects upon a plane surface, in such a manner that the representation shall affect the eye in the same way as the objects themselves." It is of three kinds : linear, aerial and isometric.

Linear perspective, as its name indicates, is the accurate delineation of the LINES of a picture. These lines are three: 1, the BASE line, from and upon which the whole picture is built up, and which limits the sketch towards the operator (even though He be the Holy Spirit); 2, the HORIZONTAL line, in which the earth and sky apparently meet; 3, the VERTICAL or VANISHING line, which is drawn from the supposed position of the sketcher, perpendicular to the base and horizontal lines, and which meets the horizontal line in a point which is called the point of sight—the view point, or center of the picture. This, more fully, is THAT POINT IN THE HORIZON LINE WHICH IS OPPOSITE THE EYE, OR SUPPOSED POSITION OF THE SKETCHER, AND TOWARDS WHICH AND ON WHICH THE VERTICAL OR VANISHING LINES OF THE PICTURE ALL CONVERGE.

This is the heart of perspective proper; being the indispensable condition of due PROPORTION throughout the picture. Prophesying "according to the proportion of faith," or, "rightly dividing the word of truth," is largely a lost art in the modern pulpit, owing to the neglect of the Bible Point of Sight.

There is a Bible perspective. Or rather, the BIBLE ITSELF IS THE CELESTIAL PERSPECTIVE OF THE KINGDOM OF GOD, sketched with faultless accuracy and completeness and finish by the pencil of the Holy Ghost.

Linear perspective determined the whole OUTLINE of the Bible picture of the kingdom of God. Its BASE line, the very GROUND on which the whole picture is built on, is SIN; man's sin, not silliness; man's wickedness, not weakness; man's fall downward, not upward; man's guilt, needing atonement and forgiveness through divine judgment. Hence the BLOOD RED HUE of the BASE line of the Bible picture as the Holy Spirit has drawn it. Unitarianism ignores the very base line of the Bible picture of redemption. Therefore it is self-blinded to every other line of the picture. Therefore it has no "Gospel." Therefore it is LAW, without mercy. "Save THOU thyself, or be damned" is its colorless and freezing message. Therefore it is falling into the cold, dead deism of Rabbinic orthodoxy, instead of being lifted into the warm, living monotheism of the Scripture.

Not one line in the massive sketch can be discerned; not one object in the grand panorama of redemption can be clearly seen OUT OF ITS RELATION to this base line of man's sin, sin in the sense of guilt and desert of judgment. But, discerning this, we cannot help seeing the second line in the Bible sketch of the kingdom of God, viz:

2. The HORIZONTAL line, in which the moral earth and sky appear to meet.

This line, in the Bible picture of redemption, is the DIVINE-HUMAN HOLINESS OF JESUS CHRIST. Not the DIVINE holiness of the Son of God alone. Sinful man never could have met the Holy God on that line alone. Our "earth" never could have moved up to his sky had not his "sky" condescended to our earth. Nor is it the mere HUMAN righteousness of the Son of man that constitutes the horizon line of the Bible picture of the kingdom of God. The Holy God never could have moved down to meet sinful man in peace, blessing and glory on the line of first Adam, or old-creation, righteousness. It is the TWO TOGETHER, the divine DIVINE *and the* HUMAN human, the SON OF GOD *and* the SON OF MAN in real, however mysterious, union, that constitute the horizon line of the Bible picture. The sky and earth MUST MEET, to form the horizon line of true redemption. God's holiness must bend to "the likeness of sinful flesh" (Rom. 8:2); man's righteousness must rise through moral discipline from mere innocence to divine holiness, (the visible IMAGE OF GOD on earth); and WHERE THEY MEET, melting into one, there, and nowhere else, is the horizon line of the Bible picture of the kingdom of God.

But what of the VIEW POINT, or POINT OF SIGHT, in this horizon line? This is THAT POINT IN THE HORIZON LINE TOWARDS WHICH, AND ON WHICH, THE VANISHING LINES OF THE PICTURE ALL CONVERGE. These vanishing lines, being DRAWN FROM THE SUPPOSED POSITION OF THE SKETCHER, OR BEHOLDER, are as NUMEROUS, of course, in the Bible sketch as are the OBJECTS that are painted into the Bible picture. They may START from the Fall of Man, or from the Victory of Armageddon; from the Ascent of Babel, or from the Descent of the New Jerusalem; from the Captivity in Babylon, or from the Captivity in Pilate's Judgment Hall; etc.; but, from whichever point they START, these vanishing lines of the Bible picture, I repeat it, ALL RUN UP INTO, AND CONVERGE ON THAT ONE POINT IN THE HORIZON LINE which we call the VIEW POINT, OR POINT OF SIGHT, of the Bible picture of the kingdom of God.

What this view point, in my judgment, is, the theme of my paper hints. IT IS THE SECOND ADVENT ERA OF THE SON OF MAN, opening with the Fall of Mystical Babylon and the Rapture of the Church, centering in the Millennial Kingdom in and through Israel, and issuing in the Eternal State; that glad era when the moral "sky" and "earth" will melt into one, when the divine-human holiness of Jesus Christ will be PERFECTLY REALIZED AND MANIFESTED, FIRST FOR HIMSELF, THEN FOR HIS BODY, THE CHURCH, THEN FOR HIS COVENANT EARTH-PEOPLE, ISRAEL, THEN FOR THE NATIONS; IN ONE WORD, FOR THE WHOLE HUMAN RACE AS A SOLIDARITY, AND FINALLY FOR THAT "GROANING CREATION" of which man is the divinely-ordained-head.

But what of the first advent era? it will be asked. Was it not then that the divine-human holiness of Jesus Christ was built up through moral discipline, and prepared through death, resurrection and ascension as God's free gift to sinners, whether of the Jews or the Gentiles?

Yes, I answer, it was then that all this was done.

But, it will then be asked, if the divine-human holiness of Jesus Christ BE THE HORIZON LINE of the Bible picture of redemption; and if that horizon line was thus PROJECTED IN THE FIRST advent era, does not this, in all fairness, mean that the FIRST ADVENT ERA IS THE TRUE POINT OF SIGHT in the horizon line of the Bible picture?

Not necessarily, I reply. To see this it is only needful to recall WHAT IT IS THAT CONSTITUTES AND DETERMINES, BOTH THE HORIZON LINE ITSELF, AND THE POINT OF SIGHT in that horizon. This is not the ERA WHEN the horizon line was projected, whether the first or the second advent era. The horizon line of the Bible picture is the divine-human holiness of Jesus Christ WITHOUT REGARD TO THE TIME WHEN such holiness was projected.

And what determines the TRUE POINT OF SIGHT in that horizon line is NOT THE TIME WHEN the horizon line was laid, but the CONVERGENCE TOWARDS AND ON THAT POINT OF WHAT ARE CALLED THE VANISHING LINES of the Bible picture. The test question, therefore, is this: TOWARDS WHICH, AND ON WHICH, ADVENT ERA, DO THE VANISHING LINES OF THE BIBLE PICTURE CONVERGE, THE FIRST, OR THE SECOND ADVENT ERA? And on this, the real point at issue, our appeal must be to Scripture.

I believe that the true point of sight in the horizon line of the Bible picture of the Kingdom of, God is the SECOND ADVENT ERA, and not the first. Will a critical examination of the Bible picture from the standpoint of perspective confirm my belief? I believe that it will. Let us see.

The criterion is this: WHERE, AT WHAT POINT, in the horizon line do the VANISHING LINES OF THE BIBLE PICTURE CONVERGE; in the FIRST, or in the SECOND advent era? These vanishing lines, let it be repeated, are drawn from the supposed POSITION of the sketcher and beholder, which, of course, is THAT OF THE EVENTS, OR PERSONS, OR GROUPS of events or persons, painted into the Bible picture, and which we happen to be inspecting; they may even include the PRINCIPLES OF ARRANGING AND GROUPING such events and persons: but whatever the OBJECT from which they start, these vanishing lines run straight up from the base line of the picture, sin, and MEET IN ONE POINT in the horizon line, which we call the view point, or point of sight.

This definition gives us a simple test for determining both WHAT these vanishing lines are, and which are the MOST IMPORTANT. It furnishes at least seven broad groups or classes of vanishing lines, as follows: 1. The Logical lines; 2. The Historical lines; 3. The Dispensational lines; 4. The Chronological lines; 5. The (Astronomic) Cyclical lines; 6. The Doctrinal lines; 7. The Practical or Missionary lines.

1. Consider first, the broadest of such vanishing lines. I mean the PRINCIPLES OF GROUPING the different objects that are painted into the Bible picture. These are the LOGICAL divisions of the Bible as an organic body of truth, the THOUGHT PLAN, OR STRUCTURE, of the Bible as a whole. This is admirably conceived and expressed by Dr. Monroe Gibson's Analysis of the Bible, presented some years since in the Bible School at Northfield, Mass. The logical lines of division of the Bible are four:

OLD TESTAMENT.		NEW TESTAMENT.
	1. MANIFESTATION.	
Pentateuch.		Four Gospels.
	2. APPLICATION.	
Historical Books.		Book of Acts.
	3. EXPERIENCE.	
Poetical Books.		The Epistles.
	4. OUTLOOK.	
Major and Minor Prophets.		The Revelation.

This analysis is only BROADLY true. Rigidly viewed, each of these sections of the Bible exhibit all four of the principles named. But not to the same degree; there is MORE of the one principle in each section than of any other.

Glance, now, at these broad vanishing lines of the Bible picture, the lines of logical division. They start from the base line, man's sin and guilt. But WHITHER do they run? WHERE do they END? TOWARDS WHAT POINT, and ON WHAT POINT, do they all CONVERGE? What, in other words, is their true POINT OF SIGHT? The answer is inevitable: THE SECOND ADVENT ERA OF THE SON OF MAN. The logical links that bind us to this conclusion are mainly two:

(1) That the FINAL PRINCIPLE, INTO WHICH ALL OTHER PRINCIPLES RUN UP, AND FIND THEIR FULFILMENT, IS THAT OF OUTLOOK, OR PROPHECY. Such manifestation as is found in Pentateuch and Gospels is not FINAL. Nor is the application into which such manifestation runs in the historical books FINAL, etc. The lines keep running on and up UNTIL THEY END IN OUTLOOK, *i. e.*, the outlook of inspired PROPHECY, from the then present on to that august age, the Second Advent

Era. Only in such OUTLOOK can the FINAL "manifestation," and the FINAL "application," and the FINAL "experience" be found.

(2) That the ONE POINT ON WHICH THE MAIN LINES OF THE OLD AND NEW TESTAMENT "OUTLOOK" ALL CONVERGE, IS THE SECOND ADVENT ERA, not the first.

(Our limits will confine us, from this point, to a bare outline of the argument).

(1) We have the dictum of the Holy Ghost by the mouth of Peter, that THE CENTRAL THEME OF OLD TESTAMENT PROPHECY IS "THE TIMES OF RESTITUTION OF ALL THINGS," [identical, as other Scriptures show (Matthew 19 : 28; Rom. 8 : 18–25; Rev. 21 : 5,) with the SECOND ADVENT ERA], Acts 3 : 20, 21.

(2) This dictum is CONFIRMED BY AN EXAMINATION OF THE OLD TESTAMENT ITSELF, WHICH SHOWS TEN TIMES AS MANY REFERENCES TO MESSIAH'S GLORIOUS REIGN IN ISRAEL OVER THE WORLD (*i. e.*, to His Second Advent Era) as there are references to His HUMILATION in Israel, (*i. e.* to His FIRST Advent Era).

(3) These arguments are clinched BY WHAT THE HOLY SPIRIT DOGMATICALLY TEACHES IN THE NEW TESTAMENT, CONCERNING ISRAEL AND THE CHURCH.

Concerning ISRAEL, He dogmatically declares, (*a*) That the FIRST Advent Era, from beginning to end, is an AWFUL GAP, during which "Jerusalem shall be TRODDEN DOWN OF THE GENTILES UNTIL (no longer) the times of the Gentiles be fulfilled." (Luke 21 : 24; Rom. 11 : 25); (*b*) That, in spite of this BREAK in the predestined thread of Israel's history, GOD's gifts (to Israel of the land, and of earth pre-eminence among the nations (Gen. 12:2, 3; Gen. 27:29; Numb. 28:9, etc.) AND CALLING (of Israel to be a prophetic priest-king-nation under their Messiah) IS WITHOUT REPENTANCE (or permanent change of purpose) (Rom. 11 : 28, 29); (*c*) That the PRESENT GAP in His covenant people's history SHALL BE FOLLOWED BY A GLORIOUS FULFILMENT OF JEHOVAH'S PROMISES TO THEIR FATHERS AT AND BY THE SECOND ADVENT ERA OF THEIR PREDESTINED MESSIAH KING, (Rom. 11 : 25, 26; Acts 15: 15–17; Luke 12 : 24, etc.) Concerning the CHURCH, the Holy Spirit dogmatically declares: (*a*) That it is "THE MYSTERY O Christ," a SECRET purpose of God in Christ, ONLY NOW made known to men by His apostles, and NOT TO BE FOUND IN THE OLD TESTAMENT AT ALL (save, of course, in TYPE, which does not PROVE doctrine, but simply illustrates a doctrine otherwise proved). (See Eph. 3 : 2–5; Rom. 16 : 25, 26; Col. 1 : 26); (*b*) That its NATURE IS ENTIRELY HEAVENLY, OR SPIRITUAL, having its true "CITIZENSHIP IN HEAVEN" (Philipp. 3: 20, 21), not in the earth "Canaan" of God's covenant people—Israel; (*c*) That its PLACE, in God's plan of the ages, is to ONLY TEMPORARILY fill the gap in Israel's history, as identified with the kingdom of God. (Matt. 21 : 43; compared with Luke 21 : 24; Rom. 11 : 25, 26; Acts 15 : 15–17); (*d*) That its DESTINY, when the fullness of the Gentiles has come in, is the RAPTURE out of this earth-sphere into heavenly glory by the POWER AND COMING OF ITS DIVINE HEAD, the Lord Jesus Christ. (John 14: 3; 1 Thes. 4: 13–18; 1 Cor. 15: 23; Rev. 20: 4–6; Compare Rom. 8: 18–25).

What an impeachment of the wisdom of the Holy Spirit, to make THAT (the FIRST Advent Era) THE VIEW POINT OF ISRAEL'S HISTORY, WHICH HE HIMSELF AGAIN AND AGAIN DECLARES TO BE AN AWFUL GAP in Israel's history, filled with clouds of divine judgment, in their dispersion among, and oppression by, the Gentiles! What a double impeachment of the wisdom of the Holy Spirit, to make THAT (the CHURCH) THE CENTER OF THE OLD TESTAMENT PICTURE WHICH HE HIMSELF AGAIN AND AGAIN DECLARES TO HAVE NO PLACE IN THE OLD TESTAMENT! The main lines of Old Testament outlook, it thus appears, do, and can, *converge on* NO OTHER POINT OF SIGHT THAN THE SECOND ADVENT ERA.

That the NEW TESTAMENT point of sight is the SECOND ADVENT ERA is proved by the same method. (*i*) We have the dictum of the Holy Spirit by the pen of Paul that the PREDESTINED DRIFT even of that spiritual salvation to which the church are called, the VIEW POINT even in our heavenly citizenship, is NOTHING ELSE OR LESS THAN THE BLESSED HOPE AND APPEARING OF THE GREAT GOD AND OUR SAVIOUR, JESUS CHRIST. Such dictum is found in Rom. 8 : 24. "For IN HOPE WERE we saved;" the meaning being admirably expressed by Conybeare & Howson's free rendering: "For the salvation whereto we were called (at conversion) LIES IN HOPE; *i. e.*, finds its predestined crown and completion in THAT FUTURE GLORIFICATION OF THE CHURCH WHICH IS CONDITIONED BY THE FUTURE GLORIOUS APPEARING OF THE CHURCH'S HEAD, JESUS CHRIST. (See the context, Rom. 8 : 18–25.)

(*ii*) This dictum is confirmed by AN EXAMINATION OF THE NEW TESTAMENT ITSELF, which shows

(*a*) That the Second Appearing of Jesus Christ is the CENTRAL THEME OF THE TWO (CHRONOLOGICALLY) EARLIEST BOOKS OF THE NEW TESTAMENT, First and Second Thessalonians; (*b*) that the Second Advent Era is the CENTRAL THEME (or Point of Sight) OF THE LATEST BOOK OF THE NEW TESTAMENT, Revelation; (*c*) that WHOLE CHAPTERS OF THE FIRST THREE GOSPELS ARE ENTIRELY OCCUPIED WITH THE TRUTH OF THE SECOND ADVENT; and (*d*) that the ENTIRE NEW TESTAMENT IS THREADED ALL THE WAY THROUGH WITH DISTINCT REFERENCES TO THE SECOND APPEARING OF JESUS CHRIST, there being about THREE HUNDRED such references to that august event as the true hope of the church, and ONLY THREE distinct references to that *Earth-millennium* which Post-millennialism filches from Israel in order to misappropriate to the church. Against such CHANGE OF VIEW POINT the entire New Testament is a divine protest! And the MORAL and HISTORICAL RESULTS TO THE CHURCH of such change of view point are PROVIDENTIAL SEALS TO THAT DIVINE PROTEST. The MORAL result, notoriously, is a perfect DELIRIUM OF THAT VERY GENTILE CONCEIT against which the Holy Spirit warned the Roman Church in vain! (Rom. 11:25.) And the HISTORICAL result? Behold it in ROMANISM, "making a drag-net of its sacraments," on the one hand, and LATITUDINARIANISM, erasing all distinctions between the church and the world, on the other hand; the APOSTATE CHURCH of the Papacy on the one side, and the CIVIC CHURCH of William E. Stead on the other side!

The lines of NEW TESTAMENT PROPHECY, it thus appears, all CONVERGE ON THE SECOND ADVENT ERA AS THEIR TRUE POINT OF SIGHT.

Summing up our first GROUP OF LINES then, we may fairly claim that the entire BIBLE, VIEWED IN ITS LOGICAL STRUCTURE, IS THE PERSPECTIVE, IN WHICH THE SECOND ADVENT ERA STANDS OUT AS THE TRUE POINT OF SIGHT.

II. Consider next the HISTORICAL LINES OF DIVISION of the Bible, in proof of our hypothesis that the Second Advent Era is the true point of sight of the Bible picture of the Kingdom of God.

To see this, it is only needful to remember, as we examine these historical divisions of the Bible, the THREE LIMITS WHICH, as previously shown, THE HOLY SPIRIT HAS RIGIDLY FIXED IN THE

INTERPRETATION OF ALL SCRIPTURE, both of Old and New Testaments: (1) That the FIRST ADVENT ERA IS, FROM BEGINNING TO END, AN AWFUL GAP IN ISRAEL'S HISTORY (and cannot, therefore, be the true view point of Old Testament history, which has to do with Israel exclusively); (2) that the broken thread of Israel's history WILL BE AGAIN TAKEN UP, AND CARRIED TO ITS PREDESTINED END, IN THE SECOND ADVENT ERA of their Messiah King; and (3) that the DOCTRINE OF THE CHURCH, or mystical body of Christ, IS NOT REVEALED IN THE OLD TESTAMENT AT ALL, its nature, place, work and destiny being something entirely NEW, AND DISTINCT FROM THOSE OF ISRAEL.

With these three points in the perspective plan thus firmly fixed by the Holy Spirit, we would expect, *a priori*, to find that all the BROAD LINES OF HISTORICAL DEVELOPMENT OF THE KINGDOM OF GOD, in both Old and New Testaments, MEET IN NO OTHER POINT THAN THE SECOND ADVENT ERA. That they do meet there, and nowhere else, will appear from a scrutiny of the following outlines of the stages of development of the Kingdom of God.

STAGES in the Development of the Kingdom of God (*as Laid in the Second Adam.*)

I. *Initial* or Germinal Development of the Kingdom—Genesis—2369 years.

(1) The need of such Kingdom of God—as Laid in the Second Adam. (Genesis 1 : 11–26.)

(i) Failure of First Adam—Without "Law"—the Flood—Genesis 1 : vii. (1656 years)—Adam to Noah.

(ii) Wider Failure of First Adam—Under Civil Law—Dispersion. (Genesis viii–xi. 9.)

(2) The open *Beginning* of God's Kingdom in the Second Adam. (Genesis xi. 10–l.—305 years.)

(i) Foundation of such Kingdom Laid in the Choice and Training of Abram. (Genesis xi. 10–xx.)

(ii) Development of such Kingdom in the Election and Training of "The Patriarchs." Isaac—Jacob. (Genesis xxi–xxxvi.)

(3) Final Germinal Development of such Kingdom in the Training of the Twelve Sons (Tribes) of Israel, especially of *Joseph*, in Egypt. (By Separation from the Canaanites, by Servitude and Suffering, issuing *in Glory.*)

II. *Typical* Development of the Kingdom of God. From the Founding of the *Elect Nation* (Israel) to Birth of the Promised "SEED." (Jesus Christ.)

(1) *Development* of the Kingdom of God Under the Guidance of *Prophets.* (Moses—Samuel.)

(2) Development of the Kingdom of God Under the Rule of *Kings.* (Saul—Captivity in Babylon.)

(3) Development of the Kingdom of God Under the Guidance of *High Priests.* (Ezra—Jesus Christ.)

III. Mystical Development of the Kingdom of God (Mystery of the CHURCH.)

(1) Vindication of this Unexpected (because non-foretold (see Rom. 16 : 25, 26; Eph. 3 : 3-5; Col. 1 : 26,) Development of God's Secret Purpose by ISRAEL'S *Rejection* of the MANIFESTED Kingdom. (From Birth of Christ to His Crucifixion.)

(2) FOUNDATION of the Mystical Kingdom, (as of the Manifested and the Eternal Kingdom), Laid in the Death, Resurrection and Ascension of Jesus Christ. (From the Cross to the Ascension.)

(3) Founding and Development of the Mystical Kingdom—the Church, (FROM THE PENTECOST TO THE SECOND COMING OF CHRIST AND RAPTURE OF THE CHURCH.)

IV. Manifested, or Externally Realized, Development of the Kingdom of God (Upon Earth,) or THE SECOND ADVENT ERA.

(1) The Fall of Mystical Babylon. Rev. xviii.

(2) The First Resurrection (of the Saints.) Rev. xix. 6–9.

(3) The Glorious Appearing of Christ and His Saints. Rev. xix. 11.

(4) The Conversion of Israel, by the Power and Coming of their Messiah King. Acts xv. 16, 17; Rom. xi. 25-27, etc.

(5) The Final (Armageddon) Conflict and Victory. Rev. xix. 17–21.

(6) The Binding of Satan for a Little Season. Rev. xx. 1–3.

(7) The MILLENNIAL BEING OF CHRIST AND HIS SAINTS. Rev. xx. 4–6.

(8) The Loosing of Satan for a Little Season. Rev. xx. 7, 8.

(9) The Post-millennial Apostasy and Its Judgment. Rev. xx. 9.

(10) The Final Destruction of Satan. Rev. xx. 10.

(11) The Final Judgment of the Wicked Dead—the Great WHITE THRONE. Rev. xx. 12, 13.

(12) The Destruction of the Last Enemy—Death. Rev. xx. 14.

(13) THE SURRENDER OF THE KINGDOM by the Son to the FATHER (1 Cor. xv. 18,) issuing in THE ETERNAL KINGDOM OF GOD. Rev. xx–xxi. 5. (See Guinness' Light for the Last Days, pp. 543–4.)

Now, in what point, if any, do the vanishing lines of the first three stages, thus outlined, converge?

Scrutinize the initial, or germinal stage, of the Kingdom.

It *begins* in the Garden-promise "of the SEED of the woman" of Gen. 3:15. It is God's promise of the "Second Adam," the Lord Jesus Christ. To whom was the promise given? To Shem, Ham, or Japheth, or to any of their respective seeds? No; there were *no* such family distinctions; all three families were yet *one race* in the loins of the first Adam. The promise, accordingly, was given to the HUMAN RACE as a solidarity, and therefore can find its only real fulfilment *in the* HUMAN RACE AS A SOLIDARITY. Now, *when*, at what point in the unfolding Kingdom of God, will that promise be realized? When will the "SEED of the woman," the "Second Adam," crush the head of " that old Serpent;" and that, not for Jew alone, nor for Gentile alone, nor yet for the church, BUT FOR THE HUMAN RACE AS A SOLIDARITY? The answer to this test question leads us straight to the very CENTE R F THE SECOND ADVENT ERA—IN THE BINDING AND FINAL DESTRUCTION OF SATAN. (Rev. 20:1–3, 10.)

It is admitted and emphasized that the promise had its INCIPIENT AND POTENTIAL fulfilment in the Cross of the First Advent. But that, as history and Old Testament Scripture both show, was a "bruising of Satan's head" which was not effectuated, and not meant to be effectuated, either for Israel as the Covenant Nation, or for the human race as a solidarity. Its only immediate bearing, and that but a partial one, was upon the mystical Kingdom—a secret purpose of God not revealed in Old Testament Scripture. The true point of sight in the very beginning of this initial stage, therefore, is the Second Advent Era.

So with the close of this first sub-section of that initial stage, the flood of judgment, with the deliverance through such judgment of the faithful remnant, or family of Noah. This also points, according to Christ's own authority (Matt. 24 : 36–41 ; Luke 17 : 22–27), to the same august period, the Second Advent Era, only on its negative side.

So with the next sub-section of the initial stage of the Kingdom. Its opening and closing events are both clearly typical (being explicitly referred to as such in Holy Writ) of Jehovah's dealings with the SAVED JEWISH REMNANT and with the builders of the mystical Babylon, in the *last days—i. e.*, at the Second Advent Era. This sub-section opens with Jehovah's ASSUAGING THE WATERS OF THE FLOOD and His PROMISE TO NOAH THAT THEY SHOULD NEVER AGAIN COVER THE EARTH, the very event by which, in Isaiah 54 : 9, Jehovah confirms his oath *to the saved Jewish remnant of the last days* that there shall be no return of the deluge of His wrath upon Israel. The section closes, more than 300 years later, with Jehovah's JUDGMENT OF CONFUSION AND DISPERSION UPON THE BUILDERS OF BABEL (the world kingdom as opposed to the Kingdom of God.)

How unmistakably that judgment points forward to the JUDGMENT OF THE LAST DAYS, depicted in Rev. 18, as falling upon Mystical Babylon, whose blasphemous pride and God-defiance, like that of its prototype, "reached unto heaven," let the sober and scholarly Edersheim tell : "Such words read singularly like those which a Nimrod would employ, and they breathe the spirit of 'Babylon' in all ages. Assuredly their meaning is : 'Let us rebel,'—for not only would the divine purpose of peopling the earth have been thus frustrated, but such a world-empire would in the nature of it have been a defiance to God and to the Kingdom of God, even as its motive was pride and ambition." A German critic has seen in the words, 'Let us make a name,' in Hebrew, *sheen*—a kind of counterfeit of the SHEM in whom the promises of God centered, or, if one might so express it, the setting up of an ANTICHRIST OF WORLDLY POWER. Something of the kind seems certainly indicated in what God says of the attempt (ver. 6) "And this they BEGIN to do ; and now nothing will be restrained from them which they have imagined to do." These words seem to imply that the building of Babel was only intended as the commencement of a further course of rebellion. The gathering of all material forces into one common center would have led to universal despotism and to universal idolatry, in short, to the full development of what AS ANTICHRIST IS RESERVED FOR THE JUDGMENT OF THE LAST DAYS." (Biblical History, pp. I. 61, 62.)

Glance now at the second and last great period in this initial stage of the development of the Kingdom of God, viz, the ACTUAL AND OPEN BEGINNING of God's special work in the second Adam on behalf of mankind, "The Patriarchal Dispensation," as it is commonly called. It covers a period of about three centuries, beginning with the election and call of Abram, and closing with the exaltation of Joseph.

Does anybody need to be told how directly both these "vanishing lines" run up into the one point of sight—the second advent era?

The election of Abram: What was its divinely avowed purpose and motive—its final cause, in the terms of logic? The WORLD-WIDE and MANIFESTED Kingdom of God to be established in Abraham's "SEED," Israel—as headed-up in, and administered by, the second Adam and seed of Abraham, the Lord Jesus Christ. What was the PROMISE of God which rewarded Abram's faith? Millennial blessing through Israel to all nations; "in *thee* shall *all families of the earth* be blessed." (Gen. 12 : 1-3). This, remember, was the SECOND and effectual call of Abram. "By faith" Abram had left the then—only—civil protection of his home, his family, his country, and his people, in Ur of the Chaldees. "By faith" he had waited until the death of his father Terah in Haran. "By faith" he had now entered Canaan—the high school of faith's training through future ages. A new *mode* of God's self-revelation marks this crisis of the world's history. Formerly, God had SPOKEN to man; now he *appeared* to Abram in the person of the Angel of the Jehovah. This PERSONAL revelation of Jehovah, as Edersheim shows, marked each of the four critical stages in the history of Abraham. Each stage in the training of Abram's faith, moreover, was marked by Jehovah's PROMISE of EARTHLY SUPREMACY to the natural seed of Abraham—Israel—or of MILLENNIAL blessing, or of Canaan as a perpetual possession (Gen. 17 : 8), confirmed, at last, by the tremendous oath of Jehovah's self-existence. (Gen. 22 : 16).

Now to what does this divine promise to Abram point? To the dispensation of the law? No; for that ended in the murder of the second Adam by the natural seed of Abraham, and in their uprooting from the promised land by the judgment of Jehovah. To this church-age? No; for the Holy Spirit repeatedly tells us that "the church, which is His body," was not foretold in Old Testament at all (save in type, which proves no doctrine.) (Rom. 16 : 25, 26; Eph. 3 : 3-5; Col. 1 : 26). The "church" are again and again declared to be an "heavenly people" and so were not in God's thoughts when he promised *earthly Canaan* to the seed of Abraham "for an EVERLASTING possession." The church in its distinctive character as a spiritual, or heavenly, body, composed of Jews and Gentiles ON PRECISELY THE SAME LEVEL, can nowhere be found in Old Testament Scripture, at least by a reverent exegesis. It needs the *eis-agesus* of "Higher (or 'Babel') Criticism," either in its germ of post-millennial warping, or in its full flower of German rationalism, to do that.

The "church" is the "*pleroma*" of the Gentiles, literally "that which is put in to fill up" the AWFUL GAP between the sad chapter of Israel's history in the past and the glorious chapter of Israel's history in the future. Therefore "the church" is not pointed to by this divine promise to Abraham, "that he and his seed should be the *heir* of the world." (Rom. 4 : 13.) (1)

What *is* pointed to by that colossal promise is the equally colossal Kingdom of God in MANIFESTATION: that realization on this sad earth and through this "groaning creation" of the divine-human holiness of the second Adam, whose glorious POINT OF SIGHT IS THE SECOND ADVENT ERA.

Glance at the closing feature of this initial stage of the Kingdom of God. It is the glorious exaltation of Joseph, after a long period of persecution and rejection by his Israelitish brethren, and of suffering from the Egyptians; exaltation, be it remembered, OVER both the world ("Egypt") and "all Israel" (the sons of Jacob)!

To what other POINT OF SIGHT, I ask, can this magnificent painting of the WORLD GLORY OF ISRAEL'S ONCE REJECTED, BUT NOW ENTHRONED MESSIAH point us than to the Second Advent Era, in which alone Jehovah will fulfill his promise to Abraham and his "SEED" of the land, of earthly supremacy, and of universal blessing to the Gentile world? (See Rom. 11 : 25, 26; Acts 15 : 16, 17, etc.)

Is it without significance in this connection that Stephen, in his grand historical sketch of Jehovah's progressive revelation, and of Israel's progressive disobedience thereto, should leap over the centuries between Abraham and Joseph; that he should fix upon the murderous jealousy of the *patriarchs against Joseph* as the first outbreak of that rebellious spirit which had just culminated in their murderous rejection of their Messiah, and that he should then remind the Sanhedrim that "*at the second time* (not the first) Joseph was made known to his brethren" (Israel)?

And again, what means it that, in the grand apocalyptic picture of the arrest of judgment in order to the sealing of the twelve tribes of Israel, "Dan," Jacob's child, not by Rachel, but by Zillah, Rachel's maid; "Dan," the fruit of fleshly unbelief; "Dan," the "serpent" of dying Jacob's forecast of Israel's future history (Gen. 29 : 17); "Dan," the source, historically, of Israel's apostasy of the golden calf (Compare Judges, 18, and 1 Kings 12 : 29); "Dan," the "Antichrist" of ancient conjecture, is dropped out of the list of the tribes of Israel, and "Joseph," the child of promise and of faith, and the self-attested type of Christ in the glory of His Second Advent Era, takes His place?

II. Glance now along the main lines of the second great stage of the development of the Kingdom of God, the typical development of that Kingdom, which extends from the *founding of the elect nation*, Israel, to the birth of the promised "SEED" in its ideal personal sense.

Edersheim divides this whole period into three subordinate stages: 1. Israel's history UNDER THE GUIDANCE OF PROPHETS (from Moses to Samuel.) 2. That UNDER THE RULE OF KINGS (from Saul to the Babylonish Captivity;) and 3. That UNDER THE REIGN OF HIGH PRIESTS (from Ezra to the birth of Jesus Christ.)

He rightly characterizes it as the "typical" development of the kingdom of God, on the ground that Israel's history during this period was genuinely TYPICAL of what Israel's history was meant to be, and will be, in the second advent era, when the true, *i. e.*, divinely ordained, or ideal theocracy, will be realized in Israel under the peaceful and glorious rule of their predestined PROPHET, PRIEST AND KING, JESUS CHRIST.

Edersheim emphasizes the historical character of Old Testament prophecy, as interpreted by Peter, Stephen, and Paul, the writer to the Hebrews. He also shows that *Israel's history itself is prophetic*, that it is divinely intended to be PROPHETIC, as *really prophetic* as Israel's *Institutions* of Prophetism, Priesthood and Royalty, and what we more narrowly call "PREDICTION."

"Canaan is a prophetic land, and Israel a prophetic people, of whom God says to the world: 'Touch not mine anointed and do my prophets no harm.'" And their *whole history* IS PROPHETIC. It is not merely one or another special prediction that is Messianic: everything, every event and institution, is prophetic and Messianico-prophetic, and what we one-sidedly call special predictions (although there are such, having no basis in the then-present) are only special points on which the golden light rests, and from which it is reflected. And it is in this sense that we understood and adopt the fundamental principles of the Synagogue, repeated in every variety of form, that every event in Israel's history and every prophecy pointed forward to the Messiah, and that every trait and fact of the past, whether of history or miracle, would be re-enacted more fully, nay, in complete fullness in the times of the Messiah ("the *Acherith hayyamim*, or latter days" of the Second Advent Era)......This Messianic idea is the moving spring of the Old Testament. It is also its sole *raison d'etre*, viewed as a revelation......Hebrewism, if it had any divine meaning, was the religion OF THE FUTURE, and Israel embodied for the world the religious idea which in its universal application, is the kingdom of God. (Prophecy and History, lecture IV, pp. 130 and 136.) And again, "ultimately ALL PROPHECY points to the latter days," or the "end of days" (the *Acherith hayyamim*.) This was to be the GOAL of the religious development of Israel. Thus we read in the prophecy of Hosea (3 : 5,) that after many days in which Israel would be without King or Sacrifices—true or false—they would return and seek Jehovah and his goodness IN THE LATTER DAYS (The *Acherith hayyamim*.) It was NOT *for a gradual development into a more spiritual worship that the prophets looked : their gaze was bent on the Acherith hayyamim*. They expected not a religious reformation, but a renovation, not the cessation of sacrifices, but the fulfilment of their prophetic idea in the latter days, which WERE THOSE OF THE EXPECTED MESSIAH AND OF HIS KINGDOM." (Lecture VI, pp. 172, 173.

Now what is all this, but to say that the true POINT OF SIGHT of Israel's history is, not the first, but the second advent era? The FIRST ADVENT ERA, so far at it bore on Israel at all, was marked by the proffer, rejection, and temporary withdrawal of the kingdom of God. History, as divinely interpreted by the inspired theodicy of God's dealings with Israel—the eleventh of Romans—proves this. The first advent era, therefore, was and is an awful blank, or gap, in Israel's history—so far as concerns the divine ideal in Israel, the realization of the prophetic idea of the kingdom of God. That first advent era, in the terms of perspective, was only the *visible* POINT OF SIGHT, in the *near*, or *sensible* horizon, enveloped in choking mists and thunderous clouds. The TRUE point of sight in the REAL horizon of Israel's historic progress is the "latter days" of the second advent era. On the edge of that horizon "Canaan" lies, bathed in the celestial sunlight of the realized kingdom of God.

For proof of this statement glance along the three main lines of the typical development of the theocracy in Israel, as drawn by Edersheim: 1. The development of the theocracy UNDER THE GUIDANCE OF PROPHETS, from Moses to Samuel; 2. That UNDER THE RULE OF KINGS, from Saul to the Captivity in Babylon; and 3, that UNDER THE REIGN OF THE HIGH PRIESTS, from Ezra to the birth of Christ—the "near" horizon of Israel's progress.

Now who can fail to see that all of the *vanishing lines* in this fifteen century perspective of Israel's history run up into, and *meet together*, IN ONE POINT ONLY—and that, no other point than the Second Advent Era, that august period when, according to the unanimous testimony of the Old Testament prophets, and the uniform witness of Jesus and His apostles, Israel's age-long travail shall issue in the realized kingdom of God upon earth, under their predestined Messiah—who is at once and altogether, Prophet, Priest and King.

No other true point of sight *can* be discerned by one who views Israel's history as itself *prophetic*, having its moving spring in the MESSIANIC IDEA, and all prophecy as pointing from the then-present, on and on to "the latter days."

To stop those vanishing lines at the First Advent Era, centering them in the "church," is to deny the testimony of the Holy Spirit to two facts: (1) that "the mystery of the church" is not revealed in the Old Testament at all. (Rom. 16:25, 26; Eph. 3: 2–5; Col. 1:26); (2) that the present awful gap in Israel's history has NOT cut the thread of God's purpose in and through Israel FOREVER, but that "the gifts (of God to Israel, the land and holy supremacy in the earth) and the calling (of God for Israel, to be a kingdom of priest-prophets to the nations) is without repentance" (or permanent change of mind).

III. So with the vanishing lines of the third main stage of the development of the kingdom of God. They all meet in no other point than the Second Advent Era. We designate this as the mystical development of the kingdom, because its vital center is the "mystery of Christ"—the church, whose distinctive marks have been already noted: (1) It is "THE BODY of Christ," organized by the indwelling Holy Spirit out of Jews and Gentiles, with "no difference," or earthly distinction whatever; (2) Its nature is entirely heavenly, or spiritual, having its true "citizenship in heaven," not in the "Canaan" of earth (Philipp. 3:20, 21); (3) Its PLACE in God's plan of the ages is to TEMPORARILY fill the gap in Israel's history; (4) Its DESTINY, when "the fullness of the Gentiles has come in, is the RAPTURE" out of this earth into heavenly glory by the power and COMING OF THEIR DIVINE HEAD—THE SON OF GOD.

Who, that reads the Old Testament with an opened, reverent eye, needs to be told that NO SUCH IDEA as this can be found therein, from Genesis to Malachi? Who, again, needs to be assured that the Holy Spirit's dictum, by the mouth of Paul, is absolutely true, that such a "mystery" had been "hid from all ages and generations, but is NOW (and only now) made manifest to his saints—by the prophetic writings" (of the New Testament apostles) (Col. 1 : 26; Rom. 16 : 25, 26)?

See, now, how the vanishing lines of the Church-age run up into the Second Advent Era as the true point of sight. First comes the PROFFER of the kingdom to Israel, the REJECTION of that kingdom by Israel, and the divine, although temporary, WITHDRAWAL of the kingdom from Israel. This stage extended from the birth of Jesus to His crucifixion at the hands of Israel's leaders.

It both vindicated and prepared the way for God's temporary withdrawal of the earthly kingdom from Israel IN SPITE OF HIS

OATH AND COVENANT with the fathers, and the *revelation for the first time* of HIS SECRET PURPOSE of the "Church," the *pleroma* of the Gentiles which was to fill the foreseen and foretold gap in Israel's history "until (no longer) the times of the Gentiles be fulfilled." (Luke 21 : 24.) Its manifest DRIFT, therefore, is towards the Second Advent Era. On what other point can its lines converge? For *Carnal* Israel—the Nation as a Mass—it was a—*blank!* so far as positive results were concerned. "He came unto His own; and His own received Him not." For *Spiritual* Israel—the faithful Remnant who, as the first believers in Jesus as the Christ, constituted "the organic root and basis" of the Christian Church, the Christ "after-the-flesh" of this period (that is, the Christ upon Whom death and resurrection had not passed,) was of *no avail* for the "new-creation" to which *they* were destined! (Compare 2 Cor. v. 14–17 and John vi. 63).

Glance at the second line of development in the church age, the foundation of the mystical (as also of the manifested) kingdom, laid in the atoning death, the glorious resurrection and the exaltation of Jesus Christ. This stage bore equally, although not so immediately, upon Israel's manifested kingdom in the future, and upon the church, or mystical kingdom, of the then-immediate present. Hence its double aspect as depicted in the gospels—an earthly and Jewish aspect (the synoptic gospels), and a heavenly and a church aspect (John). But in both aspects the lines run up into the Second Advent Era as the true point of sight. To what did Jesus point the Jewish scribes, Pharisees and Sanhedrim as THEIR *true point of sight?* "Behold your house (the kingdom as constituted in Israel) is left unto you desolate. For I say unto you, ye shall not SEE ME HENCEFORTH, till ye shall say, Blessed is He that COMETH IN THE NAME OF THE LORD." (Israel's final homage to their predestined Messiah King. Matt. 24 : 38, 39.) Again, "Henceforth ye shall see the Son of man sitting on the right hand of power, and COMING IN THE CLOUDS OF HEAVEN." (Matt. 26 : 64.)

And to what did Jesus, even in this early stage, point His Jewish disciples (the foundation of His church) as *their* true point of sight, the point in which all lines of witness, of suffering, and of work would finally meet? Listen: "If I go to prepare a place for you (in the Father's house) *I will come* again *and receive you unto myself.* (John 14 : 3). "Father, I will that they also whom Thou hast given Me *be with Me* WHERE I AM: THAT THEY MAY BEHOLD MY GLORY WHICH THOU HAST GIVEN ME." (John 17:24). And again, "If I WILL THAT HE [JOHN] TARRY TILL I COME, WHAT IS THAT TO THEE?" (John 21 : 22).

So with the final period of the mystical development of the kingdom, which extends from the Ascension of Christ to the rapture of the church, or end of the present Church-age. The vanishing lines of this period all run straight up into, and converge on, the Second Advent Era, as their true point of sight.

The period opened with the Ascension, which itself was signalized by the angel promise: "This same Jesus WHICH IS TAKEN UP FROM YOU INTO HEAVEN, SHALL SO COME IN LIKE MANNER AS YE HAVE SEEN HIM GO INTO HEAVEN." (Acts 1 : 11).

It closes with the Rapture of the church by the POWER and COMING of the Lord, which is the church's only blessed hope during the long night of the present dispensation, and which is the true point of sight in the New Testament picture of the Kingdom of God. The only needed proof of this is the fact, already used in another connection, that the New Testament contains some *three hundred references* to the coming of the Lord as the church's true hope, and *only three* references to that millennium, or manifested Kingdom, which constitutes the heart of the second advent era, and the hope of Israel as distinct from the church.

What but that very Gentile "conceit," against which the Spirit solemnly warned the church (Rom. 11 :25), could inspire the daring attempt to *alter the view point* of the New Testament picture of the mystical Kingdom of God, putting that in the background which the Holy Spirit has painted into the foreground, and bringing into the foreground that which He has painted into the background?

The post-millennial "perspective" of the mystical Kingdom of God, it needs to be said with emphasis, is NOT the perspective sketched by the pencil of the Holy Spirit.

It thus appears from this review of the *history* of the Kingdom of God that THE ENTIRE BIBLE, VIEWED IN ITS HISTORICAL DIVISIONS, IS THE PERSPECTIVE IN WHICH THE SECOND ADVENT ERA STANDS OUT AS THE TRUE POINT OF SIGHT.

NOTE.—The limits of this paper, as fixed by the volume of which it forms an humble part, are already passed. The further development of the argument is therefore reserved for another form and time.

THE COMING OF THE LORD.

THE DOCTRINAL CENTER OF THE BIBLE.

REV. ARTHUR T. PIERSON, D. D., OF BROOKLYN, N. Y.

My Beloved Friends:

It was a remark of Aristotle that truth is what an object is in itself; secondly, in its relations, and thirdly, in the medium through which it is viewed. It may seem a trifling maxim, but I venture to utter it: that nothing is so necessary to us and nothing is so unusual in us, as an absolutely candid mind. To be willing to lay aside bias, prejudice, prepossession, and admit that we may have been in serious error, that, in fact, the whole system which we may have embraced may have as its foundation a fundamental mistake—is a very rare experience with any man, yet it is sometimes the very beginning of a true search and research.

I have been very much impressed, of late, with the opening expression of the seventh chapter of the Acts of the Apostles. The witnesses had just borne their testimony against Stephen, the first of the martyrs:—that he had made the astounding declaration that Jesus of Nazareth should destroy the existing customs of the Jews, and should even bring to destruction the whole Jewish order. That was an idea that probably had never entered into the mind of the members of the Jewish Council, who represented the learning and the wisdom of the Jewish nation.

Now will you remark what was that peculiar but simple question which begins the book of the Acts, 7th chapter:—"Then said the High Priest: Are these things so?" A very simple question. The high priests of many a modern synagogue would do well to ask the same question. Not: Do these things tally with my previous notions, or with the system or doctrine which I have embraced, or with the peculiar ideas which I have been accustomed to cherish, but, "Are these things so?" We have first to do, not with fancies but with facts; not to do first with philosophy but with facts, and, in the examination of the word of God, we have to do with divine facts and with a divine philosophy—not with divine facts and a human philosophy, but with divine facts and a divine philosophy.

I have more than once had my doubts about what we call "Systematic Theology." Theology is a science, and every science is arranged about a center. Botany is arranged about the cellular law of growth; Zoology about a type of structure; Geology about an order of strata. Now, the difficulty is, that we are apt to arrange our Theological science about some preconceived center, and anything that does not fall into our plan of crystallization we reject. I like a Biblical theology that does not start with the superficial Aristotlian method of reason, that does not begin with an hypothesis, and then warp the facts and the philosophy to fit the crook of our dogma, but a Baconian system, which first gathers the teachings of the word of God, and then seeks to deduce some general law upon which those facts can be arranged. I had a little fear of coming to Allegheny that I might be drowned in systematic theology, (laughter) and I had a very special desire that I might be grounded in a Biblical theology which is honored to be in such a deluge of learning.

Now, beloved friends, I have said that the first question is one of facts and the second question is one, not of a human philosophy but of a divine philosophy. You all remember, when Kepler was making his investigation of the planetary and the stellar worlds and was seeking to discover what is the true law of planetary motion, that he made seventeen successive experiments before the eighteenth and successful experiment, which disclosed what is the true path of a planet's orbit. That is to say, he had endeavored to unlock the mysteries of planetary motion, he had tried seventeen different keys and they would not work, but at last he tried this key. He said: "I will suppose the path of the planet around the sun to be not a circle but an ellipse, with the sun at one of the foci of the ellipse." He put that key in the lock and the bolts were thrown back, the doors that had been shut for millenniums went open, and he flung up his hands in rapture and said: "Oh, Almighty God, I am thinking Thy thoughts after

Thee," and he knew not how to hold his divine rapture. That is the way to study the Bible. Take the Biblical facts, acknowledge that there is mystery in the word of God, that nothing but a divine philosophy can unlock that mystery, and then seek to find God's key. When you have found God's key and it perfectly unlocks God's mysteries, do not go hunting around for a human locksmith—even though you may find him in a theological seminary, to explain the mystery.

Now you will permit me to say, after this modest introduction, (laughter) that for many years I was very much in doubt and difficulty with regard to certain teachings of the word of God. I had been brought up in a peculiar school of teaching. I had, what I thought at that time was a pretty perfect system of theology, and my system of theology made very little account of the Lord's second coming. I could not be very well satisfied with any system that left out so very prominent a fact in the landscape of Scripture truth and I began to study and to pray, if so be that I might find some key that unlocked what had hitherto been to me a very difficult question.

I found the key; it absolutely unlocked all my difficulties. Two-thirds of the Bible which had been previously a closed chapter to me I have been permitted to walk in, as in marvelous apartments, for fifteen years, and I am not hunting around for any locksmith to make me a new key. I simply come, very humbly, modestly—notwithstanding you laugh at my modesty—I have come very humbly and modestly just to give you the key, and, if it does not unlock the mystery for you, all I have to say is: there is not any charge. It is perfectly free; it is a suggestion, but it has been so blest to me that I cannot but hope it may be equally blest to some of you.

I have thought that I would use a blackboard for a few moments, though it is not a necessary feature of the very informal, simple and conversational talk which I have to make, but it may perhaps serve to indicate the relation of these two great events, the first and the second coming of the Lord. I lay no claim to being an artist, and therefore, if what I put on the board possesses no artistic features you are perfectly welcome to come up and improve the artistic features.

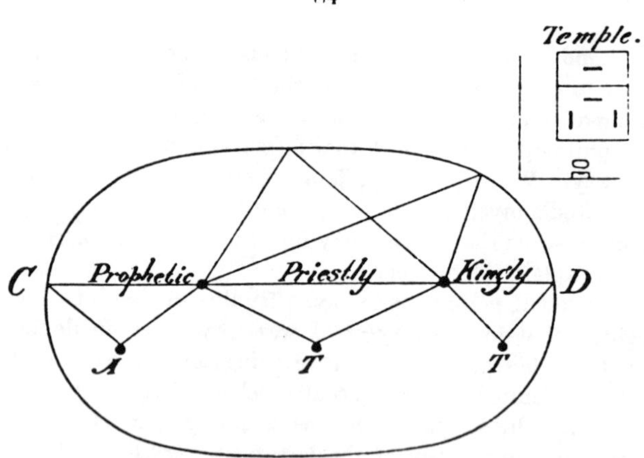

What I want to do is to give you a rough outline of an ellipse. We will put in the middle a medium line touching from side to side, indicating on this line as near as may be the focal points of this ellipse. Now this figure is exceedingly happy—or it would be if it were artistically drawn—to illustrate exactly what I want to illustrate. We have been accustomed to think that a circle was the most perfect form, but for the illustration of many truths a circle is a very imperfect form, for a circle allows of but one center where an ellipse allows of a twin center. You know what the law of the ellipse is, and if we were going to draw an ellipse accurately, we would put a nail at each of these foci, take a cord reaching from this nail to this, with proper opportunity for play, put the chalk within the cord, begin here and so follow around. That is to say, availing ourselves at each point of the total length of the cord, we will call this (I) our Lord's first advent and this (II) our Lord's second advent. Let this be the creation of man marked C, and this be the delivering up of the kingdom to God and the Father, which we will indicate by D. Then this ellipse will serve to give us the entire range and scope of Christ's mediatorial work, reaching from the fall of Adam backward from His incarnation, and to the conclusion of His mediatorial work when He surrenders the kingdom up to God and the Father.

I would have you notice that between creation and the incarnation of Christ, there is one small but important object, an altar of sacrifice, which we will indicate by A. Between the first coming and the second coming is another small object, which we will indicate by the letter T, the table of the Lord. This altar of sacrifice refers back to the creation and fall of man, forward to the incarnation and grace of Christ. Every victim that bled upon the altar reminded men of their sin in Adam's fall and the disaster that overtook the race, pointing forward to the Lamb of God that should take away the sin of the world. So we may unite those two points in that fashion (by a line) and every time we sit down at the Lord's table, the body and blood of our Lord, as represented in the bread and the cup, point back to His grace and forward to His second coming. "As often as ye eat this bread and drink this cup ye do show the Lord's death till He come." So we may unite these also (drawing line).

Now between this second coming of our Lord and the delivery up of the kingdom to God and the Father, as given us in the 15th chapter of 1st Corinthians, we have one other object. Let me call it a throne; that points back to the assumption of the throne at His second coming and forward to the delivering up of the kingdom to God the Father that he may be all in all at the end, and so we may connect these three.

I want you to notice, that here we have not only a philosophy of theology but we have a philosophy of history. You will observe that the entire ellipse embraces the mediatorial work of Jesus Christ, which reaches back to the creation of man and fall of man, and forward to the final delivering up of the kingdom to God and the Father when the mediatorial work ceases. I will have you notice another thing. There are three great offices of Jesus Christ, the prophetic, the priestly and the kingly, and there are three great periods of human history embraced within this mediatorial scope. The first is the prophetic, which reaches mainly from the fall of Adam to the cross of Jesus Christ. There is then the priestly, which reaches mainly from the incarnation of Jesus Christ to His second coming. There is third, the kingly, which reaches from His second coming to His delivery up of the kingdom to God and the Father. Now during this prophetic period there was a shadowing forth of the priestly office of Christ in the sacrifices of the temple. During the priestly period there is a shadowing forth of the kingship of Christ in the individual surrender to His sway, whereby you and I become members of His kingdom, though the kingdom is now invisible and individual and not visible and collective. So we have in the prophetic period the foreshadowing of the priestly, in the priestly the foreshadowing of the kingly, and in the kingly the foreshadowing of that period where in the eternal ages God shall be all in all.

Observe how many things are embraced in this plan. Adam fell. The mediatorial work of Christ must begin with Adam's fall, and immediately after the fall we read, "the seed of the woman shall bruise the serpent's head." That is a simple prophecy? It is a compound prophecy. We often say that that is a single prediction. but my friends, there are at least six predictions in that. In the first place the woman is to have a seed. Second, it is to be peculiarly the woman's seed, not the man's seed. Third, it is to bruise the serpent. Fourth, it is to bruise the serpent on his head. Fifth, it is to be attended with the bruising of his own heel, and, Sixth, it implies a work for the race, for it is the woman's seed as a generic thing. So you have in that simple prophecy a sixfold prediction.

Now notice there must be a prophetic, priestly and kingly office if Christ is to be a perfect mediator, for when man fell he lost the quickness of his conscience, he lost the guidance of his moral and spiritual sensibility, he lost that divine sympathy with God which made him able to understand the will of God, and not only so but probably made him able prophetically to indicate the will of God in the absence of a direct revelation. Just as soon as he fell, losing these faculties, he needed now a teacher and guide. Often the conscience itself is not a perfectly safe guide. The conscience sustains to the will of God the same relation that the eye sustains to any work that we have to do. Suppose you are building a wall and you sight the wall by your eye. Your eye may be very accurate but I wouldn't trust you to build a wall if you have no dependence but your eye, for the wall might lean from the perpendicular or incline from the horizontal. What do you do? You drop the level, the plumb-line, and lay the level upon your work, and then the united action of eye, plumb-line and level, helps you to make a perfect wall. Your eye is the fallible conscience; the plumb-line and level the revealed will of God, and the action of the two together enable you to make work that is according to the will of God. Christ had to come as the prophet to supply us with the plumb-line and level. "Righteousness will I lay to the line and judgment to the plummet"—that is God giving us the prophetic standard. You are to take your conscience and reason and powers as a man and in connection with these the receptive powers; with the declarative powers of the Holy Ghost in the word of God you are to be able to know the will of God. So you have to have a prophet to make up for the loss of the prophetic faculty, and inasmuch as man had become a sinner by the fall, he must have a sacrifice; inasmuch as man had the dominion given unto him when he was created and lost it when he fell, there must be one like unto the Son of man as Himself the last Adam, that shall recover the sceptre that he lost in the fall. So we have Christ supplying the prophetic office in view of Adam's loss of prophetic faculty; Christ supplying the priestly office in view of Adam's sin; Christ becoming the human king, the king over many men, to make up for the loss of the sceptre in Adam, and inasmuch as Adam's sin was a stroke against the dominion of God, Christ must end it by giving up the dominion that He, as the Son of man, held, into the hands of God the Father, and then all the ruin and wreck of the fall is restored. Now if you don't see that, so much the worse for you.

I would have you notice again, with regard especially to the kingly office, for that is the intensely interesting point of this whole discussion, that there is no indication in the word of God that Christ has ever yet assumed the kingship. I challenge any man to confute that testimony, and yet you will find, that through the entire range of this ellipse there runs the one conception of kingdom. Please follow me here, for otherwise what I shall say will have very little effect. The whole conception of mediatorial work rests upon the basis of a kingdom.

Now mark. When Adam was created what do we read? God said: "Let us make man in our own image and let them have dominion." The sceptre was given into the hands of Adam at the very first. Right on the scene of creation comes one who disputes the sovereignty with Adam and wrests the sceptre out of his hand. He brings successfully to bear a diabolical temptation. Adam loses the sceptre, and observe, he (Satan) becomes the prince of this world. All along through the Old Testament there is no kingdom proper among men, it is a theocracy, a divine kingdom. When the Israelities clamored for a king God said: "Ye have rejected me. I am the only king!" I want you to observe that in studying this great scheme of redemption you must not follow worldly history, for the Bible is a blank and has nothing to do with worldly history—it is the history of God's chosen people. You cannot make out the 490 years if you do not leave out even the periods of their captivities or apostasy, for God does not count in the divine chronology any time that is not spent in His service. It is all a blank as to that. You should understand that if you are going to study church history, if you are going to study the religious history, as we call it, with a term that I do not like to use, if you are going to study the history of the spiritual development of the race, you have to look up along the lines of the human chronology or of the divine chronology and notice how God's clock ticks and strikes for the fullness of time. Following this history you will notice, that when the Israelites pressed for a king God gives them one, but he gives them his own disapprobation, and when Saul is an utter failure he says, "I have chosen me a man after mine own heart; his kingdom shall be a perpetual kingdom, and even if his sons forsake my law I will not take my loving kindness from him, but there shall sit on the throne of David a prince of whose kingdom there shall be no end." Here we have the idea of the kingdom adopted by God—not adopted by God, for he never had any other idea. It was kingdom all the way through, only he transmutes the human opinion of kingdom into the theocratic opinion of kingdom. The Jews themselves did not understand this, but we can understand it for we have the open eye.

When Jesus Christ came to this world the first proclamation of John the Baptist was, "Repent, for the kingdom of heaven is at hand." Make ready for the king, he is coming. When Jesus Christ began his ministry it was the same proclamation, "Repent, for the kingdom of heaven is at hand." When He sent forth the Seventy they announced, "The kingdom of heaven is at hand." When He sent forth the Twelve they also said, "The kingdom of heaven is at hand." What did it all mean? Look in the 21st chapter of Matthew, see Zachariah's prophecy fulfilled, "Behold, thy King cometh unto thee." When Jesus Christ entered Jerusalem, exactly in the manner prophesied, the king came to the Jews. He made the offer of the kingdom to the Jews exactly as had been indicated in prophecy and the people said, "Hosannah;

Blessed is the king that cometh in the name of the Lord. Blessed be the kingdom of our father David." Mark 11. Little children shouted "Hosannah," but the rulers of the Jews, the chief priests, scribes and pharisees and the members of the sanhedrim—the theological professors of that day—said, "We won't have this man to reign over us." What is the consequence? I want you to notice what the consequence was. The offer of the kingdom was suspended from that time and has never yet been renewed. What did Jesus Christ say? "How often would I have gathered thy children together, even as a hen gathereth her brood under her wings, but ye would not;" and, "Verily I say unto you, ye shall not see me henceforth," etc. I want you to notice, those of you who are students of the Greek, that the emphatic word in that passage is not the emphatic word ordinarily rendered in the reading of it. It is the word 'Ye.' "I say unto you, YE shall not see me henceforth until YE shall say," just as the people and the children have said, "Blessed is He that cometh in the name of the Lord."

Notice another thing, that from that time you hear no more of the kingdom. Up to that time "The kingdom of heaven is at hand" by the forerunner of the kingdom, by the Messiah, by the Seventy, by the Twelve, but from that time forth no more mention of "kingdom." In fact Christ himself says: "The kingdom shall be taken away from you." "The kingdom of heaven is as a nobleman that goes into a far country to receive for himself a kingdom, and to return." And what have we now? Adam loses dominion and Satan gains it. Christ in the temptation regains the sceptre from Satan, and the proclamation goes out "The kingdom of heaven is at hand." Christ moves into the city of Jerusalem, exactly as it had been indicated in the prophecy he would, and makes an offer of the kingdom. It is rejected by the elders of the Jews and the offer of the kingdom is suspended and remains in suspense to this day. This is the times of the Gentiles and the kingdom is suspended, but Jesus Christ is coming and the Jews are going to say, "Blessed is he that cometh in the name of the Lord," and take up the acclamations of the little children in the temple, of which they were once jealous, and then the King of Israel will sit on the throne of his father David and the kingdom will be recognized.

When, after many many years of study I found that key and saw these mysteries unlocked for me, I felt just as Kepler did, I wanted to throw up my hands in adoration and say: "Oh, Almighty God, a little child like myself is thinking God's thoughts after God," and the things that have been inexplicable to me are now unraveled. My one object in coming to Pittsburgh was, if possible, to put that key into the hand of some one that during these years may, like myself, have been vainly seeking for something that is going to be satisfactory.

Well, let us go on and see if we find confirmation of this divine philosophy of history. I have spoken of the prophetic office of Jesus Christ. I have spoken of the priestly very briefly, and let me now return to the priestly. There were four things that the priests did. I am surprised that I went so long without understanding these four things. First of all, they sacrificed at the altar. Second, they served in the holy place where were the golden candlestick, table of shew bread and altar of incense. Third, they interceded in the holiest of all, and the fourth, what is very seldom mentioned, they blessed the congregation. Perhaps you will allow me to give you another very simple figure, because I think every Christian man and woman ought to have this impressed on the mind so that it stands before them as the alphabet does. (Drawing figure). The outer court of the tabernacle and the inner court consisting of two parts, a perfect cube, and another portion in front of it twice as long as it was broad. Here stood an altar of burnt offering (indicating it on figure) here a laver, here the golden candlestick, here the table of shew bread, here an altar of sacrifice. Sacrifice performed here, service there, benediction here, and you will see these things if you look in the 9th chapter of Hebrews. Let me read a few verses, for I like to confirm everything I say by the testimony of the word of God. What I think is of no sort of consequence, but what the Bible thinks you put away from you at your peril. Ninth chapter of Hebrews: "Now when these things were thus ordained the priests went always into the first tabernacle (that is the holy place) accomplishing the service of God," 6th verse. See the 23d verse: "It was therefore necessary that the patterns of things in the heavens should be purified with these; but the heavenly things themselves with better sacrifices than these." Twenty-fourth verse: "For Christ is not entered into the holy places made with hands, which are the figures of the true; but into heaven itself, now to appear in the presence of God for us." That is intercession. Now look at the end: "So Christ was once offered to bear the sins of many; and unto them that look for him shall he appear the second time without sin unto salvation." That is benediction.

Observe, the High Priest began here (indicating on the blackboard) He took the blood and went into the holy place and accomplished the service. He went from there, with the blood, into the holiest of all, and performed intercession, the people mutely waiting outside to see if the atonement was accepted. Then he returns, not now in the white garments of humiliation, but in the garments of glory and beauty, stands before the people and lifting his hands—says: "The Lord bless thee and keep thee; the Lord make His face to shine upon thee and be gracious unto thee: the Lord lift up His countenance unto thee, and give thee peace;" and then the day of atonement was through. Once in 49 years the trumpet sounded and the year of jubilee was inaugurated. The sacrifices were not complete until the benediction was pronounced, and I venture to say to you, that the priestly office of Jesus Christ will not be complete until He comes the second time, and, with the same beloved hands with which He left us, still uplifted in blessing, shall bestow upon us the fullness of the divinely accomplished salvation!

Another beautiful thing: the High Priest began his sacrifice not with service in the holy place, because he had sins of his own to atone for, and the people had sins to atone for, but when Christ came He began with service and not sacrifice. "Wist ye not that I must be about My Father's business?" He began with thirty years of service in His Father's business, then, having been in the holy place and given substance and time and heart's devotion to God, He comes back to the brazen altar, and because there is no other victim that would answer He became priest and victim and gave Himself for our sins. Now He has gone into the holiest place of all to appear in the presence of God for us, and, my friends, His priestly work is not done until He comes out from the presence of God and appears once more to those that are anxiously looking for Him, no longer to be a sin offering, or made sin for us, but to bring us the fullness and the glory of His salvation.

This is only the beginning of a great and marvelous theme. I want you to notice not only that the prophetic office and the priestly office and the kingly office all find their solution in this very simple plan, by which we make the first and second coming of Christ co-ordinate centers for the drawing of this ellipse which gives us the range and scope of His mediatorial work, but I want you to notice the progression that runs through the ages. Never a backward step, not once. The prophet unites with the priest, and both with the king—prophet, priest and king, in one person, accomplishes the glorious redemption, and we priests and kings with Him unto God and the Father. Satan here loose and dominant; Satan here loose but restrained by a new power, the power of the Holy Ghost. I should have said, Satan here loose and toward the end of this era restrained by the power of the Holy Ghost. But after Christ accomplishes His priestly work, what do we find? In the millennial era Satan bound, and beyond, Satan burnt, cast into the lake of fire. You see the regular progression all the way through. Satan's power being subjected to more and more and more restraint until in some marvelous way, we know not what, evil is eliminated in the government of God.

Again, most of you, I suppose, believe in the doctrine of election. How about that? See the method of election. Here an elect family out of all the families of the earth; here an elect church out of all the nations of the earth; here a kingdom in which the nations of the earth form factors and beyond here the universal empire of God. Never is there a backward step. Failure at every point, but man's failure only, never God's failure. People say: "How about making this dispensation end in failure?" Every dispensation has ended in failure, and will end in failure. Why? Because God is going to be all in all, and the only way to be all in all is that man should get to the end of himself, for only then he gets to the beginning of God. Impress that thought upon your minds. God has been making experiments, is making them still, and every experiment is a greater advantage to God, but every experiment turns out in man's failure.

Look at the experiment before Christ came. A family gathered out from the families of the earth. Prophets given to them and priests with typical sacrifices, at first an oral and then a written law of the Old Testament. Man fails. The whole dispensation ends in awful disaster and wreck. Here another experiment and what comes of it? In the first place new light in the Holy Spirit's descent among men, as well as in Christ's personal appearance and teaching and work among men. Then the full Bible, the New Testament added to the Old, and so, with these additional privileges and opportunities, man starts on a second career. At the end of the period comes disaster, a falling away, an -apostasy, even teachers who do not know what they say or whereof they affirm, evil men and seducers waxing worse and worse, deceiving and being deceived. Now here we start on a new experiment still—on the personal belief that as the Holy Ghost came here in the earlier rain He is coming here in the latter rain; that as He here descended on all believers He is here to descend on all flesh and that Cæsarea was the type of that outpouring where the Holy Ghost fell on unbelievers for the first time in history, as pentecostal Jerusalem was the type of this dispensation of the Holy Ghost. Jesus Christ will be here in the person of the Holy Ghost in the latter rain. In addition to all, Satan will be bound; yet even the millennium ends in disaster. Did you ever think of that? It ends in disaster. When Satan is loose he goes out into all the world, the four corners of the earth, and gathers together the enemies of God, the number of them being as the sand of the sea, and the most tremendous revolt that has ever been, or will be known, since the creation of God, will be the finishing up of the awful drama of the millennial.

What is all this for? It is, as I said, that men should see demonstrated by the course of thousands of years of history, that with every chance given him of God, first by prophets and typical sacrifices and the Old Testament gospel, then by the person of Christ and the descent of the Holy Ghost, the Old and New Testaments combined; then in the very personal reign of Christ with the latter rain of the Holy Ghost as well as the completed gospels and the converted nation of Israel for evangelists, and Satan bound—with all this he is still apostate and rebellious. Then, having learned, that except as he is lost in God he never can stand, no longer compromising with the world, the flesh and the devil, having lost all confidence in himself, having fallen over and over again into increasing disaster, with increasing light and privilege, man will have lost himself in God and God will be all in all. That is the security that sin is not going to enter the eternal estate of man, that man has learned the lesson of the ages, that he must be vitally united with God; that the only hope is, that his will shall be merged in God's will, his heart in God's heart, his thought in God's thought, his life in God's life.

Beloved, if you think that this is any matter of polemic interest to me you have entirely mistaken the speaker of this evening. This is to me a vital subject. I long have studied the Holy Scriptures in the original tongue, availed myself of every human help that I could find and, as I have said, the whole of this word of God was largely an unlocked chamber. When I found the blessed truths that I have been putting on this board, as briefly and as simply as I could, I found the key that unlocked my perplexities. You cannot take that key from me and there is no use of your trying.

Now will you allow me to say in conclusion, that in my judgment this matter of the coming of the Lord is a complex subject, not a single subject. It involves, in my opinion, seven things, which I desire very briefly as I close to put before you, for I am aiming to make this address as absolutely simple as it may be and not embarrass it with any technicalities or learned disquisitions—even if I were able to. There are seven things that I pray you to associate with the doctrine of the Lord's coming.

First of all, the session of Jesus Christ at the right hand of God. It is a common and superficial interpretation, that when Jesus Christ ascended up on high he took his place on his throne, and hence a great many people say to us: What's the use of your talking to us about the kingdom of Christ as something that is to come, Jesus Christ is already king. Well, you haven't any place in the word of God where it says so. I haven't found it, but I will tell you what I have found, beloved, that when Jesus Christ had accomplished his great victory over death and ascended up on high God said to him "Come and sit with me on my throne." Jesus Christ is not an enthroned king. Jesus Christ is a prince, that is to say, an expectant heir of the throne. He is seated not on his own throne but on his Father's throne. Waiting for what? Till his enemies are made his footstool and until on the necks of his enemies he mounts his own throne. Look what he says in the 3d chapter of Revelation "To him that overcometh will I grant to sit with me on my throne." I pray you to notice this exactly. "Will I grant to sit with me on my throne, as I also have overcome and am sit down with my Father on his throne." What of your systematic theology that has to adopt a tortuous system of exegesis to get rid of such a text as that?

I have read within the last 24 hours an article by one of the most distinguished men abroad who does not hold the views we hold—and I am very sorry for him, not because they are my views, but because I am as thoroughly satisfied that they are Scripture as I am that the Bible teaches blood atonement. He has been endeavoring to discuss the matter of the prophecies about the Jews and the kingship of Christ, without admitting that Christ is not yet a king but that He is coming as a king. Notice what he says: "It is perfect nonsense for us verifying the prophecies about Israel to any literal facts about their regathering and restoration; that they are all spiritually to be interpreted; that Israel is the church and that all the prophecies about Israel refer to the church." That is on one page. Turning over to the other page what do you find? You would think the man had lost his mind. Listen: "After the fullness of the Gentiles shall have been gathered in, all Israel shall be saved." On one page Israel is the church, on the next page Israel is separate from the church and suspended are its privileges, but after the fullness of the Gentiles have been gathered in, Israel is going to be saved. He says this in the same article. Listen: "If these prophecies about the kingship of Christ are to be literally interpreted then Jesus Christ has never come, for he certainly did not come as an earthly king." That is to say, because he did not come in the first place as an earthly king and the prophecies indicate that he shall be an earthly king, therefore he will not come at all if these prophecies are to be literally interpreted. Suppose this man had got hold of this key; suppose he had seen that he did not come here as an earthly king, but is coming here as an earthly king, he would not have been obliged to resort to such a terribly destructive method of exegesis as that. That is the first factor of the seven.

Then, there are four that pertain to the church. The first is: The doctrine that the church is an out-going body—ecclesia, called out. Archibald A. Hodge, whom most of the theologians in this vicinity think is one of the saints that ought to be canonized for the soundness of his theology, says: "That ecclesia always implies a minority"—a Daniel come to judgment, you see. Now mark that, ecclesia always implies a minority, hence, during this period the ecclesia, of which this is the period, is always to be in the minority. What do you think of that? It is a fatal admission unless you accept some such interpretation of Scripture as I have humbly tried to put before you. That is the first of the things about the church, that it is to be a minority, called out from the world to be the body of Christ.

The second thing about the church is this:

It is to be a witness to the world, and throughout the whole world, until the end of the age. That is to say, witnessing includes everything that tends to put before human souls the grandeur and dignity of Christ as the Lord. It does not mean jumping on a horse, and rushing into a place and trumpeting forth the doctrine that the man who believes shall be saved, and he that don't shall be damned, and then hurrying to some other village. It means the calling out of the world the body of Christ, and the business of the church is not to stop to convert the world but to go through the world to evangelize it.

The third thing is: The church itself is going to end in apostasy. There is going to be a falling away; some will be true to God, some will not be true to God, and there is going to be an alarming defection in the very church itself toward the end of the age. I even wonder whether the apostasy is not begun while I am speaking. There are men who are teaching in some of the theological schools—east of Allegheny and Pittsburgh—that would not have been tolerated at the Lord's table twenty-five years ago, but who would have been classed with infidels. There are preachers—east of Allegheny and Pittsburgh (laughter)—who are teaching doctrines that intermit blood atonement, inspiration of the Holy Scripture, and everything else that is vital to the gospel of the New Testament. I want to say, for it may be the last time I shall ever speak to this audience or in this place to the same body of people, my beloved friends, the center of this religion of ours is not Jesus Christ but it is the word of God. Why? Because what do you know about Jesus Christ except what you know through the word of God or the experience that has been begotten through the word of God? Mark, the enemy of souls strikes first of all at this Bible, because if you disintegrate this Bible, and scatter it to the winds, your Christianity is gone. You may talk about a *Christo-centric* theology, instead of a Biblical theology, but I tell you your theology is bound up in this book and if you lose this book you have lost your Christ. I want to say that, because it is not said as it ought to be said in these days. My knowledge of this blessed Christ, the living Word, comes through this written word, the four Gospels and the Epistles and the Book of the Revelation. If you tear from my heart that book, or you make that book no longer an inspired book to me, what becomes of Christ to this dying world? The enemy is concentrating his attacks on this book. He is wise to do it, and the wisest thing the devil ever did is to get respectable men to do his fighting for him. If he took none but a profligate we should turn away from him, but when he gets men that we cannot but respect as Christian men and gets them to teach his doctrines, what a triumph there is and what a jubilee in hell. Now we have three things about the church: first, it is ecclesia, it is a called-out body, always in the minority. Second, a body that witnesses to the world. The whole field is to be sown with the seed of the kingdom, and I am not to wait at the one corner of the world and let the rest of the world go to destruction. Third, there is going to be an apostasy even in the church itself.

Fourth.—There is going to be a resurrection of dead saints out from the body of the dead when Jesus Christ appears from glory. Those are the four things about the church, and that makes five.

Sixth.—The doctrine of the restoration of Israel. That the gifts and calling of God are without repentance; that when God makes a covenant with His own people and they do not fulfill it, He is going to make another in which He is to be the one contracting party and Jesus Christ is to be the other contracting party on behalf of men. Look in the Epistle to the Hebrews, "Inasmuch as they regarded not my covenant, saith the Lord, I will make a new covenant with the house of Israel after those days. I will put my law in their midst and in their hearts will I reward them, and their sins and iniquities will I remember no more." Man has broken every covenant he has ever made and God has gotten tired of their covenants. Jesus Christ now says, I will make a covenant and I will be responsible for these poor frail human believers; they can't keep a covenant, but I can. So God makes a covenant with Jesus Christ on behalf of His people, and your unfaithfulness or mine never can void that contract.

Seventh.—The man of sin. All the systems of the earth that have been opposed to God represent Antichrist, but I believe there is to be an Antichrist in whom all these false systems are to head out finally. These are the seven things that are connected with the Lord's coming.

It is a simple question, so simple that a little child can understand it. Jesus Christ came down to earth to fulfill what Moses said about His being a prophet, to start on His priestly work, to ascend and carry on His priestly work until the end of the dispensation. Then He comes to set up His kingdom, and He reigns until he has put all enemies under His feet and until the last enemy is destroyed, then He gives up the kingdom to God and the Father. Having begun His priestly work of service, then sacrifice, then having gone to appear in the presence of God, He is coming forth to appear the second time, no longer with a sin offering, but with full salvation, and then you and I who have trusted and believed on Him shall be exalted with Him to share the dignity and glory of His throne.

Beloved, the time is short. God keep us from dishonoring the truth by shutting our eyes to that which we cannot make tally without simple, defective, human philosophy. I met a man on the train last night, and as he occupied the same section with myself before we went to bed I got into conversation with him, as I like to do in traveling. We pass this way perhaps but once, why shouldn't we seek to be a blessing to other people? I found that young man in the deepest doubt. He was a follower of Ingersoll. He had been reading everything against the Christian religion and nothing in favor of it. The Bible his mother had given him years ago had lain in his trunk neglected. He hadn't read a page of it for ten years. As we got into conversation he began to say to me, "I am not going to believe anything that I cannot understand." Well, I at once attacked him. I said: "Can you understand how your arm is lifted when you will to lift it? You say that the will influences the nerve, the nerve the muscle, the muscle the sinew and the sinew the bone. You know the facts but of the philosophy of this thing you are absolutely ignorant." I gave that young man the principle, and I beg to give you the principle as I sit down to-night. It has been an immense help to me in all the years of a life that began in a skeptical frame of mind, and until I found the precious truth I am going now to enunciate I kept along in a skeptical method of thought.

I said this to him, and I say it to you. The thing to do is, first for you, on rational grounds, to find out that the Bible is the word of God. Take, for instance, the seal of pardon; see the 333 particulars in the Old Testament. When you have determined on rational evidence that you have the word of God in your possession, you are prepared to expect to find in it things that transcend your reason. Why not? If I can understand everything about my watch—why it is made of the metal it is, why the jewels are in the places they are, why various metals are in it, why the different proportions between the wheels—give me the time and material and I will make a watch; but as long as there is something in this watch that transcends my mental power to understand, it shows that the man who made the watch knows more than I do. If you take everything out of this Bible that you cannot understand, you have taken the divine things out of it. There is mystery in this word, of course, because it is the workmanship of the Almighty. The range, the scope of it is terrible. It is like the wheels that Ezekiel saw in his vision. They mount from earth to heaven; they are full of eyes before and behind; they are complicated, the wheel within the wheel; they move in one direction, because they fulfill the purpose of God; but you cannot fathom this divine mechanism. The more I find of mystery in this word the more I am compelled to bow before it as the word of God. But observe, mystery never once touches duty. There are some things that belong to the Lord our God, but there are things revealed that belong to us and to our children.

With the reason you are to decide that this is the word of God, on rational evidence, and then you are to make the venture of faith. If there be something about the future purposes of God, something about punishment in the future that you do not understand; something about the elective purposes of God, the consistency of it with the freedom of man, that you do not understand; something about the immutability on the part of God, about the doctrine of prayer that claims to move the arm and move the world—if you cannot understand these apparent paradoxes, lay it to the weakness of your vision or to the obscurity of the medium through which you are looking, instead of laying it to contradiction in God Himself. One reason why we stumble over this doctrine of the Lord's second coming is because we try to bring down the things of heaven to the atmosphere and level of earth. When Jesus Christ comes again it will be on a scale of grandeur and magnificence for which our human experience furnishes no adequate dialect. When God wants to express celestial things he uses a human dialect, but it is necessarily imperfect, because God cannot frame any words for the human understanding of what is above the level of human experience. We have only to accept the facts and the divine philosophy and wait for the day to unfold and reveal wondrous things that eye hath not seen, ear hath not heard, and human imagination not conceived, which before the Holy Ghost can but partly reveal to us, because our eyes are yet inadequate to discern fully spiritual things.

And now, may the Lord bless thee and keep thee; the Lord make His face to shine upon thee and be gracious unto thee; the Lord lift up the light of His countenance unto thee and give thee peace.

NOTE.—The addresses of Dr. Pierson were delivered extempore, and reported by a stenographer. They have been carefully revised, but did not have the advantage of the author's revision, on account of his having sailed for England.

THE COMING OF THE LORD.

THE PRACTICAL CENTER OF THE BIBLE.

REV. ARTHUR T. PIERSON, D. D., OF BROOKLYN, N. Y.

My Beloved Friends:

This really is nothing but the second part of an address which I had the pleasure to deliver last evening, and can perhaps be but imperfectly understood by those who did not hear that address. In the Holy Scriptures doctrine and practice are inseparably united. God does not reveal truth to satisfy human curiosity, or even to gratify intellectual thirst after knowledge. Truth is in order to duty. We must hold the faith in love; we must understand the truth by obedience. It is one of the great truths of the word of God that obedience is the great organ of spiritual perception. "If any man will do his will, he shall know of the doctrine." (John 7:17). In human schools we can get a second lesson without mastering the first, but our Divine teacher never permits us to get a second lesson until we have mastered the first. It is round by round that we ascend the ladder and you can never pass from one round to reach a second until you learn the first lesson, and then you ascend to the level of the next. So that doctrinal and practical truth are intimately and inseparably united.

If, therefore, the Lord's coming as it was presented last evening, and has been presented in other sessions of this conference, is important, as a center of Biblical doctrine, it must, *ipso facto*, be the center of a Biblical practice. Now, perhaps, it will be well for me to avail myself of the same diagram that I used last night, which was simply a way of presenting a truth to the eye as well as to the ear. We have the advantage of the two sense channels, vision and hearing, at the same time. I will therefore draw, if you please, a crude ellipse. We will endeavor to discard the entire line of truth which I pursued last night, but avail myself of the same general pictorial exhibition. (Drawing an ellipse.) We

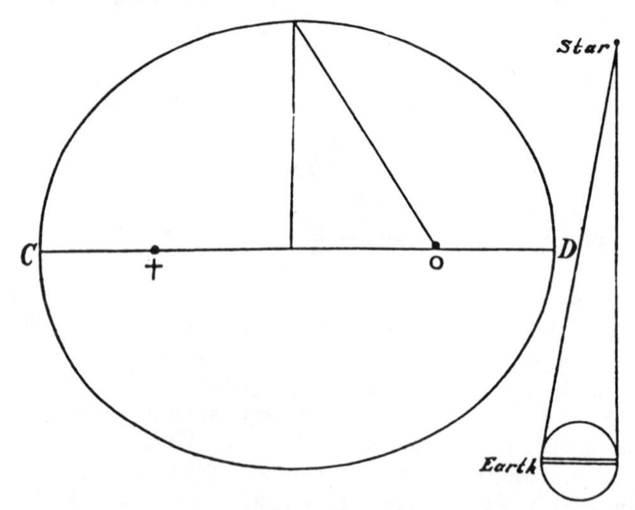

will suppose this to be an ellipse, and we will let these two dots on the medium line represent the foci. The first will stand for the incarnation, which I will represent by a cross ; the second, for Christ's second coming, which, if you please, I will represent by a circle, making a crown. This will stand, as it did last night, for the creation of Adam, and this for the delivering up of the kingdom to God and the Father at the close of the mediatorial work of Christ, and the whole ellipse will represent the scope and range of that mediatorial work. The point in the middle may stand for the view point of the believer, the point, if you please, at which we now stand. You will observe by this figure, as I showed last night, every point in this circumference or curve bears a relation to each of these foci, a proportionate relation. It is the beauty of this curve that a line drawn from this focus to any point in the circumference, and then to the other focus will represent, with its corresponding line, precisely the same length. Another thing that helps me to illustrate the part of the subject I am now going to speak of is, that the moment we take in this curve as a colossal curve, entering into the very infinities of God, you will see at once that to the observer here any point in this circumference, though it may be toward the right or toward the left, will not vary essentially in its relative position on account of its great height. You know in astronomy what parallax means, and you all understand when you have the base line for a circle here on the earth, and extend the lines up to the stars, although this base line here may be a thousand miles, the angle which these lines subtend is a very acute angle. "One day is with the Lord as a thousand years." The base line is broad, but how narrow is the angle that the line subtends. So, the comparative remoteness of our Lord's period of coming from the time of His incarnation, though the base line here which it subtends may be 2000 years or more, the angle between the lines that ascend from these two different points, is a very acute angle. The space seems long to us, but it is nothing to God. You want to get that conception, and the ellipse helps to understand it.

Suppose I draw a line from this supposed position of the observer to a point in this circumference and then down to this point. This will represent now the upward look of the believer towards Christ, and this will represent the descent of Christ toward the earth at His second coming. That is the simple diagram that I want to keep before your minds.

Now let me use two words and explain their importance with reference to my thought. The Lord's coming is in the New Testatment especially, to which I now confine myself. The Old Testament would of itself absorb more time than is allowable this afternoon. I want to say specifically here, that the doctrines we are proclaiming rest on no human authority. I would like to say to my beloved brother, whose courteous words of greeting and recognition began this service this afternoon, that I would not have him attach the slightest importance to anything that is said here because of any authority of man that is back of it. We want this doctrine searched by the Holy Scriptures, and we do not want to be met by any amount of authority on the other side, no matter how conservative the men are nor how pious ; we wouldn't give a snap of our finger for the whole of them put together.

The only question is this : Is this doctrine taught in the word of God? If it is and my philosophy does not tally with that doctrine, then so much the worse for my philosophy. Let us understand, brethren, that we are appealing simply to the word of God; personally, we have no philosophy on this subject. What are the divine facts, and what are the divine philosophies of the facts? That is all we care anything about. Human authority in this matter is of no use, whether it be on the one side or on the other, and if any of my brethren do not approve, that I am speaking just what they would say, I wish them to rise and say so now, because I want it understood just what our position is.

I think the great mischief about this whole question is, that we have not been turning to the word of God for the final settlement of it. The traditions of the elders, and the notions that have prevailed in the church, have been continually confronting us, as a reason why this or that view should be accepted. The opinion of men in this question is of no consequence whatever. It is simply what does God teach, and if anything that I shall say this afternoon is not established by the word of God, I beg you to pay no attention to it whatsoever, but if it is established by the word of God, then it is at your peril that you do not receive it.

With regard to this doctrine of the Lord's coming, there are just two thoughts that I desire first of all to present: *Imminence* and *eminence*. The imminence of the Lord's coming consists in two things; its certainty as a revealed fact and its uncertainty as to time. Imminence consists of certainty as to the revealed fact. "The Lord is coming" and uncertainty as to the time, "of the day and the hour knows no man; not the angels in heaven, but my Father only." It constitutes therefore an overhanging fact, liable always to occur. The object of imminence is that we might be perpetually looking for and waiting for, the coming of the Lord. If the time of it had been revealed we could not, in the nature of the case, be perpetually looking for it. The mischief of the doctrine that interposes a millennial era between the first and second coming of the Lord is, it makes impossible this posture of perpetually looking. This is enough to condemn it. The imminence of the Lord's coming is destroyed the moment that you locate between the first and second coming of our Lord any period of time whatsoever that is a definite period, whether 10, 100 or 1,000 years. I cannot look for a thing as an imminent event which I know is not going to take place for ten years to come. Therefore all the warnings of Christ and all the warnings of the Holy Ghost touching the imminence of the Lord's coming, become not only absurd but farcical if the Lord's coming is not to introduce the millennial but to end it. If I appear dogmatic it is dogmatism of a positive conviction that does not allow of anything to shake it, because there is not anything that can shake it. As I have said, we must not turn the warnings of our Lord into a great farce, and we are doing so if we dispute the imminence of the Lord's coming. Its certainty is a fact and its uncertainty as to time.

Now as to eminence. Eminence means prominence; something that rises above all else. I challenge denial of the statement that, in the New Testament the coming of the Lord is the one transcendent, eminent event, that rises in dignity and importance over every other event mentioned—even the incarnation of Christ and the coming of the Holy Ghost. There is nothing that is made so prominent, so eminent, as the Lord's coming, and this little diagram will give you both the imminence and the eminence. From the point of this observer, looking up into the infinite heights, Christ here is an eminent object, and His coming, which is linked with His presence above us as the object of our hope, we have eminence by the very height to which He is exalted; we have imminence by the very fact that to the observer this point is always in his zenith. However long the base line is here, it does not alter the relative position of the object so high in exaltation as this; it always occupies the zenith. You walk a hundred miles here on earth and it does not change the position of the pole star to you, it is always at the pole just the same. You walk a thousand miles on the earth and it does not change, relatively, the position of the star in your zenith.

Jesus Christ is the star in my zenith and it does not make any difference to me whether he waits 100, 500 or 1,000 years before He comes, he can be in the zenith of every year that stands between me and His coming. That is imminence and eminence both. The eminence also depends upon this: that the Lord's coming is the hinge upon which everything turns in this new, great dispensation of the Holy Ghost.

Now I want to verify these statements. We are to speak this afternoon of the Lord's coming in its relation to Christian living, the practical center of the Bible. If you have read carefully the New Testament, you will have observed that there are five representative authors in it. There are five representative departments that have to do with practical, holy living. There are three great Christian graces, faith, hope and love. Then there is the conception of holy living in external conduct, which we call good works; then there is the danger of the decay of faith, hope and love, and the destruction of the external, dutiful conduct, and that is apostasy. In the New Testament we have one representative writer for every one of these five departments. Paul, the great apostle of faith; Peter, the great apostle of hope; John, the great apostle of love; James, the great apostle of good works, and Jude, the great apostle of the apostasy. Every department of practical, holy living, is treated by one distinct and representative author in the New Testament Scriptures, or, let me say rather, is treated by the one great Author through five of His selected human agents.

Now if this doctrine has a predominant influence upon holy living, we shall expect to find that every one of these representative authors, or agents of the great Author, makes that great second coming of the Lord the one great, dominant argument in his writing. How is it? My beloved friends, I have been perfectly surprised to see how long my eyes were holden to the prominence and eminence of this doctrine of the New Testament. Suppose I take just one representative passage from each of these five writers, beginning with Paul, the apostle of faith. I would to God that you all had open Bibles, that you might see this thing is not dependent upon any man's testimony. It is the united, harmonious, consistent, accumulating testimony of the word of God.

In the Epistle of Paul to Titus, 2d chapter, beginning with the 11th verse, these words will be found, and I think this is simply the most remarkable of all the passages in Paul's writings, though it is only one of about four hundred: "For the grace of God that bringeth salvation hath appeared to all men, teaching us that, denying ungodliness and worldly lusts, we should live soberly, righteously and godly in this present world, (this present age,) looking for that blessed hope, and the glorious appearing of the great God and our Saviour Jesus Christ, who gave himself for us, that he might redeem us from all iniquity and purify unto himself a peculiar people, zealous of good works." You will not think me pedantic if I venture upon a little different translation of this passage to bring out the power of one phrase. The word translated "appearing" is epiphany, and that means a coming out from obscuration. For instance, Paul, in connection with the shipwreck in the Mediterranean, gives us this record, "that when neither sun nor stars had, after many days, had their epiphany." There was a long period of cloud, of obscuration, and the sun had not yet come out from this obscuration. "For the grace of God that bringeth salvation hath had its epiphany (that is, here), teaching us that denying ungodliness and worldly lusts," we shall live soberly, as to self, righteously as to our fellow men, godly unto God, in this present evil age, that subtends this whole arc, and the whole period from this point to that, looking for that blessed hope and for the glorious appearing of the great God and our Saviour Jesus Christ. That is the upward look of the believer to this descending Christ. There you have it all.

When the apostle Paul wants to give us the comprehensive scheme of redemption he says: there is the epiphany of Christ, that is past; there is the epiphany of glory to come, that is future, and there is a present intermediate time, this present evil age. Looking back to this epiphany of Christ, as the foundation of my salvation and the completed work of Christ, and looking forward to the epiphany of glory as the consummation of my salvation in the returning Lord, I am to be enabled to live soberly, maintaining my whole equilibrium; righteously, honoring all my relations with my fellow men; godly, honoring all my duties and obligations to my God. Now, answer me this question: If the motive in holy living is drawn from the epiphany of Christ, why does Paul insist that we must have the epiphany of glory to look forward to in order to have this double motive for holy living supplied? That is Paul.

Take Peter, the apostle of hope, and see what he has to say about it: 1st Peter, 1st chapter, and let me read a few verses, beginning with the 3d verse. "Blessed be the God and Father of our Lord Jesus Christ, which according to his abundant mercy hath begotten us again unto a lively hope by the resurrection of Jesus Christ from the dead, to an inheritance incorruptible, undefiled, and that fadeth not away, reserved in heaven for you, who are kept by the power of God through faith unto salvation ready to be revealed in the last time." Notice those words. It is not a salvation that is already revealed, but it is ready to be revealed in the last time. And again (7), "That the trial of your faith, being much more precious than of gold that perisheth, though it be tried with fire, might be found unto praise and honor and glory at the appearing of Jesus Christ. Whom, having not seen, ye love; in whom, though now ye see him not, yet believing, ye rejoice with joy unspeakable and full of glory. Receiving (this by way of expansion) the end (the consummation) of your faith, even the salvation of your souls." Now isn't that astounding teaching? Does Peter say anything about a salvation that was completed there?. Not at all. The resurrection of Jesus Christ from the dead only started that salvation for us; that was the beginning. Is a child matured when he is born? Not at all. The resurrection of Jesus Christ was only our begetting into the lively hope, and what is that hope centered on? A salvation reserved in heaven for us that are reserved for that salvation, and that salvation is ready to be revealed in the last time. We are to receive the end of our faith, even the salvation of our souls, at the appearing of Jesus Christ, whom, during this period of obscuration having not seen because he is hidden behind the cloud, yet believing in him, we rejoice with joy unspeakable and full of glory. That upward look is such a look in its prophetic character that, by it, we are enabled to receive even in the present life that consummated salvation that is coming when he returns.

Now I do not claim to be an exegete at all, but it seems to me that is sound exegesis. It is very simple. It doesn't take much brains to get at sound exegesis when you have such a broad Biblical basis. But look a little farther, in the 13th verse, "Wherefore gird up the loins of your mind, be sober, and hope to the end for the grace that is to be brought unto you at the revelation of Jesus Christ," and that expression, "revelation of Jesus Christ," implies that this was not a revelation at all. We sometimes say that when Christ became incarnate he was revealed. No, my friends, he was disguised. He came in disguise. He was a king in essential character, but he had the disguise of humanity and it was only once in a while when this disguise was swept aside that men saw the star of empire gleaming on his breast. When he comes again he is not coming in disguise. In the glory of his Father, with the holy angels, as becomes such a personage as he is, and that is the revelation of Jesus Christ. There has never been a revelation of Jesus Christ yet; the incarnation was not a revelation. Notice again, "the grace that is to be brought unto you at the revelation of Jesus Christ" implies that grace has never been brought to you yet, you only have had a little foretaste of it. If you want to know what grace is, you will have to wait to that day until the grace is brought unto you. That is what Peter thought about it. I think Peter is a greater authority than modern theological professors, or even than the gentlemen who are teaching in this conference, and Peter evidently thought that the Lord's coming was a mighty factor in the development of hope.

Now let us look at the apostle of love and see what John has to say about it. 1 John, 3d chapter, 2d verse, and we are just taking two or three passages at random. "Beloved, now are we the sons of God, and it doth not yet appear what we shall be; but we know that when he shall appear we shall be like him, for we shall see him as he is. And every man that hath this hope in him (not in himself) purifieth himself, even as he is pure." Now in the opinion of the apostle John, and I think he also knew more than any of us do, there was nothing that helped to the personal purification of character like this blessed hope set on the appearing of Jesus Christ. Look a little farther in the 3d chapter and let me read three verses from the 15th on: "Whosoever shall confess that Jesus is the Son of God, God dwelleth in him and he in God. Herein is our love made perfect, that we may have boldness in the day of judgment, because as he is so are we in this world. There is no fear in love, but perfect love casteth out fear, because fear hath torment." There is a marvelous argument here. Evidently the apostle John is referring to those mysterious words of Christ in the gospel of Matthew where he says: "Whosoever shall confess me before men, him will I confess before my Father and the holy angels." John says: "Whoso confesseth that Jesus is the Son of God, God dwelleth in him and he in God. Herein is our love made perfect, that we may have boldness in the day of judgment," because as he is yonder, so are we in this world. What is the thought? You, in this world, confess Christ in the face of a gainsaying world, perhaps a persecuting world, an opposing age. You stand forth and say: Treat Jesus Christ as you will, I am identified with Him; He is my master and Lord, I am His apostle and servant and I will stand by Him to the death. That is confession. When this world is dissolving, the heavens melting with fervent heat, and you are looking about in the universe to find a solid standing place, lo, the Son of God appears and says: That disciple confessed me in the face of a gainsaying world, I confess him before my Father and the holy angels. John tells us that the man who has his eye fixed on Christ Jesus and His second coming, who has the boldness to confess Him in the face of a gainsaying world, in view of what he is and what he is in his identification, that that disciple, in the day of final judgment, shall have boldness. Why? Because he is part and parcel of Jesus Christ. As He is there we are here ; we are one with Him.

Let us look farther and see what the apostle of good works has to say on the subject. James 2 : 5 : "Hath not God chosen the poor of this world rich in faith, and heirs of the kingdom which he hath promised to them that love Him?" There were these men giving up all things for Christ's sake, taking joyfully the spoiling of their goods. He said : God has chosen those who are in this world poor, but rich in faith, to be the heirs of the kingdom that he hath promised to them that love him. Their gaze again is fixed on the coming of Christ when the kingdom is set up, and those that have been poor in this world shall inherit the kingdom ; those that have shared Christ's humiliation shall share the glory of the day of reconstruction. 5 : 7. "Be patient therefore, brethren, unto the coming of the Lord. Behold, the husbandman waiteth for the precious fruit of the earth, and hath long patience for it until he receive the early and latter rain. Be ye also patient, stablish your hearts, for the coming of the Lord draweth nigh." What is the figure? Just as when a man steeps his seed in tears and plants it, waters it, cares for it, and through the long period of doubt and difficulty watches over the germs and the development of the plant life, and waiting for the golden harvest. So the apostle says : In all your labors be patient. The harvest will not come till the Lord himself comes, so that the Lord's coming is the day of harvesting. I am not to look for the fruits of my labor till the Lord comes. I am never to be discouraged, whatever may be the difficulties of my present position and the apparent fruitlessness of my labor. I am to look for Christ's coming as the day of the harvest, as the day of my reward.

How about the prophet of the apostasy? Let us see what Jude has to say, and I regret the necessity of passing over these passages so rapidly, because any one of them might take an afternoon for its proper exposition. Jude 20 and 21: "But ye, beloved, building up yourselves on your most holy faith, praying in the Holy Ghost, keep yourselves in the love of God, looking for the mercy of our Lord Jesus Christ unto eternal life." Keep yourselves in the love of God. Now I propound this question to this audience: Whether there is anything that is more vital to spiritual life than that I should keep myself in the love of God—not in my love to God, but in God's love to me; just as a plant needs to keep in the sunshine in order to keep to its growth.

How am I to keep myself in the love of God? First, I must build up myself on my most holy faith by a growing knowledge of the Holy Scriptures. Second, that I should live in the Holy Ghost as in the atmosphere or element in which I live. Third, associated with the other two as a necessary part of Christian culture, "looking for the mercy of our Lord Jesus Christ unto eternal life"—not looking back at what Christ did at the cross, but looking forward to the mercy that is to be revealed unto eternal life when He comes. So we have Paul, Peter, James, John and Jude, all presenting to us, as the consummate, transcendental, eminent point that is to fix our vision for the cultivation of our faith, our hope, our love, our good works, and for the prevention of all possibilities of apostasy, the one transcendent point, eminent above all others, the coming of the Lord.

Now let me say farther, in the conception of some of the thoughts which I have barely suggested, take for instance faith, which is used in the New Testament in a twofold sense. In the first place, of the acceptance of truth, and, second, of the bond of union with Jesus Christ. When you get a true conception of the second coming of the Lord as related to your spiritual life, your faith is vitalized, energized and quickened. Now faith, of course, is partially an intellectual process. It is a process of the reception of revealed truth, and all intellectual processes of reception depend very largely upon clearness of apprehension. If the subject is vague, is indistinct, is obscure, it becomes proportionately difficult to receive it, but if it becomes clear and obvious, and all the intervening atmosphere of cloud and mist may be removed, so that we have a medium that is transparent through which to look at the object, it becomes correspondingly easy to believe and our reception becomes correspondingly satisfactory.

Now it seems to me that the doctrine of the second coming of the Lord as it is presented in this conference substantially, of course we do not care about minute details, but the great, surpassing truth, is the thing about which we are intensely in earnest, that that conception of the Lord's coming clears the atmosphere, casting the mists and clouds out of our way; presenting before us something that is easily apprehended and therefore simple to the faith of a little child. Last night I tried to show how the prophetic period reaches from the creation of man to the cross of Christ, the priestly period from the cross of Christ to His second coming, the kingly period from His second coming to the delivery up of the kingdom to God and the Father. That the prophetic period anticipates in type the priestly because sacrifices were then ordained, that the priestly anticipates in type the kingly in that conception of each willing and obedient soul to the rule and reign of Jesus Christ, and how the period of the kingship anticipates the period of the eternal ages when God shall be all and in all.

I should, perhaps, have said that all these periods are closely related to Jesus Christ. Take the prophetic period, what does Peter say, "That the spirit of Christ, which was in these prophets, testified beforehand of the sufferings of Christ and the glory that shall follow." Notice the language, "the spirit of Christ which was in them," so that this period of prophecy, before He came, belongs to His mediatorial work, although He hadn't yet been manifested on the earth, as a prophet Himself, although He had not yet become incarnate. It was His spirit in the prophets that testified beforehand the sufferings of Christ and the glory that shall follow. So that this first period belongs as much to Him as the second or third.

How about the priesthood itself? Was not He, the Lamb of God, slain from the foundation of the world, but manifested in these latter times for you who, by Him, do believe in God, that raised Him up and gave Him the glory, that your faith and hope might be in God? So you see, I trust you see, and I think many of you do see, that this scheme, which is simply a presentation on the application of the essential truths as presented in the word of

God; this little scheme of the salvation that is in Jesus Christ, of the whole scope of the mediatorial work of Christ, symbolizes the whole subject, relieves it from difficulty, takes away mist which is often confounded with mystery, and removes the clouds. I cannot express the joy that came to me when these clouds passed away in my apprehension, and at last truth came out, after long obscuration, and shone down upon my soul. I know what it is to walk in this light, in the light through this truth; it makes me intensely earnest in the advocacy of it, and the desire that others should be enabled to see it somewhat in the same blessedly luminous view.

Now, to show a few things which are simplified by this doctrine of the Lord's second coming, I pray you, beloved friends, always to observe in your own thinking and in your own reading of the Scripture, a very grand distinction of which the Bible never once loses sight. I want you particularly to remember this, because it will help greatly, I think, in the understanding of the word of God. There are four terms that never should be confused, for they never once mean the same thing: the whole creation; the Gentiles or the nations, sometimes called the world; the Jews or Israel, not that those two words absolutely mean the same thing, but I group them together for convenience, and, the Church of God. The Church of God never means Israel, and Israel never means the Church of God, not once. The Gentiles never means the Church, and the Gentiles never means Israel; the whole creation never means either of them; it is the most all-embracing term. It embraces, as I believe, even the lower orders of the animals, literally the created world itself, the world of matter. 1 Corinthians, 10:32, "Give none offense, neither to the Jews nor to the Gentiles, nor to the church of God."

If these things were not distinct, what did Paul want to distinguish them for? He was not fond of making discriminations where no ground of discrimination existed. If Israel means the Church of God, why did Paul make a distinction between these two? Then we will again make a careful distinction between matter worlds and time worlds. It is one of the vices of our most excellent and beautiful translation that it does fail to distinguish oftentimes the word "age" from the word "world." There are three equivalents for the word "world," but the word "age" is the word *aion*, from which comes the word *eon*, meaning an indefinite period of time. Oftentimes this word "age" is translated "world," when all confusion possible is introduced into the Bible reading on account of it. When we read in Hebrews of "those that have tasted the powers of the world to come," the Greek word is *aion*—they have tasted the powers of the "age to come," they are in the present evangelistic age and yet standing here between the first and second coming of our Lord, they are anticipating the glory of the "age," that is, the millennial age. Christ gave Himself for our sins that He might deliver us—not from this present evil world, but from this present evil age. "I will be with you even unto the end of the world"—not that, but unto the end of the age. So we want to distinguish between the matter world and the time worlds. In Hebrews we are told that He made the worlds—it is the word ages again; that He framed the world—ages. What is the idea? That just as God made matter into worlds, so God took out of eternity, as it were, the idea that does not belong to eternity at all, the succession of time; He constructed time as He constructed worlds and built up the ages as He built up the worlds, an age above an age, in which everything gathers into one, in Christ, just as all the lines of a pyramid meet in the apex.

Then a third thing I pray you to notice, by which I think your faith will be simplified and the objects of your faith will be readily and simply received by you, getting the cloud mist out from between you and the objects of vision—that is, the distinction between three resurrections. We sometimes talk of two resurrections, but there are three: The resurrection of Jesus Christ here, the resurrection of the dead saints there, and the resurrection that occurs at the end, a thousand years after. Let us see what the Bible has to say about this, for human testimony is of no account. 1 Corinthians 15: 22, and I want my brethren here particularly to observe this, for it is a very remarkable passage. "For as in Adam all die, even so in Christ shall all be made alive" or, (For as all in Adam die, so all in the Christ shall be made alive.) "But every man in his own order: Christ the first fruits; afterwards they that are Christ's at his coming. Then the end, when he shall have delivered up the kingdom to God and the Father—to God even the Father." Mark, "every man in his own order" or military rank. Greek scholars that are present will remember that there are two words *epeita* and *eita* and they are correlative terms, like now and then.

Now I want to ask this question: If the *epeita* covers already 2,000 years between Christ's resurrection and the resurrection of the dead saints that has not yet taken place, why should we find any difficulty in the *eita* covering at least 1,000 years between the raising of the dead saints and the raising of the rest of the dead? That we may know that the *eita* does cover that, let us look at Revelation 20: "And they lived and reigned with Christ a thousand years (that is, those that have been raised from the dead at his coming) but the rest of the dead lived not again until the thousand years were finished." There you have the resurrection of Christ, the first fruits, *epeita*, afterwards them that are Christ's at his coming, *eita*, then the end after the thousand years when the rest of the dead live again. Three resurrections, separated by these intervals of time.

Now we understand, I think, what Paul means when, in the Epistle to the Philippians he uses the word which, if I remember rightly, is only used here, the only use of this word that I remember in the New Testament. In Phil. 3:11 he says: "That I may know him in the power of his resurrection, and the fellowship of his suffering, being made conformable unto his death. If by any means I might attain to the *ex-anastasis*—not resurrection, but the *ex-anastasis*, a resurrection from the body of the dead. When Christ arose it was an *ex-anastasis*, the whole of the dead did not rise. He himself rose out from the multitude of the dead, and Paul says: I am willing to count everything but loss that I may be conformed to His sufferings and know the power of His resurrection, and that I may attain to the *ex-anastasis*. Not the *anastasis* but the *ex-anastasis*.

Now didn't Paul know that he was going to rise? As a matter of course he did; there was no question whatsoever with regard to resurrection, but what he wanted was the resurrection when the saints at Christ's coming rise to take their part with him, reigning on thrones and wielding sceptres during the millennial period. So he says: I am willing to count all things but loss if I may be permitted, not to attain the resurrection which every man will attain whether he be good or bad, just or unjust, but that

I may be counted worthy to attain that resurrection; just as Christ says, you remember, "Them that are counted worthy to attain that world and the resurrection from among the dead."

Now with regard to faith as a bond of union between ourselves and Jesus Christ, and I will not detain you much longer, beloved friends. Faith is not only an intellectual process of the apprehension and reception of truth, bnt it is a bond of fellowship and union between Jesus Christ and me. How does the Lord's coming affect this bond of union? Do you know, beloved friends, that the most important verse in the New Testament is a verse of two little words? *In Christo*, in Christ; that it is the solution of every epistle of the New Testament? Romans justified 'in Christ,' Corinthians sanctified 'in Christ,' Ephesians united 'in Christ,' Galatians complete 'in Christ,' Philippians satisfied 'in Christ,' Thessalonians glorified 'in Christ.' Every epistle in the New Testament depends and hinges upon that little expression 'in Christ.' What is the idea of being in Christ? As soon as I believe I enter into Christ and become part of His mystical body, everything that Christ did in His representative life on earth I am considered by God as having done in Him. In His birth I was new born; in His circumcision I was separated from the sins of the flesh; in His crucifixion I was crucified; in His burial I was buried; in his resurrection I rose; in His ascension I went up to be seated with Him in heaven and when He comes again I shall come with him in the glory. It is an identification between Jesus Christ and myself, and the coming of Christ is the consummation of that union. No wonder that it appeals to faith as the bond of fellowship between me and Jesus Christ. Jesus Christ looks forward to it as His consummation and the consummation of His saints, and I believe we may reverently say, that the joy of Jesus Christ in that day is not the joy of His own exaltation; it is the joy of the exaltation of His saints when He presents them faultless before the presence of His Father and the glory of His Father.

How about hope? Hope depends for its inspiration upon three things. First, that it shall be a sublime hope; second, the authority of Scripture back of it, and third, confirmed by facts. When you set your hope on the second coming of the Lord Jesus Christ in glory, you have the sublimest hope that can possibly engage your attention. If you look back to the cross you have a sublime hope, a crucified Saviour, but when you look forward to Christ's coming you have the crucified Saviour still, only risen, ascended, glorified, crowned, coming again in garments of glory and beauty; all you saw that was beautiful at the cross is in Him when He comes with the crown, but all that is glorious in Him in His coronation, was not in Him visibly and manifestedly, in His crucifixion. Whatever there was in the prophetic period or the priestly period that occupied your attention and engrossed and absorbed your heart, you shall have it all when He comes again, and added to it regal glory and dignity, the consummated likeness of Jesus Christ. Find me a sublimer object than that if you can, upon which to fix hope! No wonder it is called, over and over again in the New Testament, "the blessed hope," as though there were no other hope that were blessed.

Now, if hope depends upon the authority of Holy Scriptures you have this hope most eminently supported by multitudinous passages, both of the Old and New Testaments, and in closing I want to say a word about the confirmation of this hope. You remember in Proverbs we are told that "hope deferred maketh the heart sick." There are two phases of this subject, as I think my brethren who have been laboring in this conference will agree. One is, that the church is in the world to convert the world; that the church is going to grow like the mustard seed, spreading its branches far and near until it covers the whole face of the globe, and that the world is going to be assimilated to the church. That the church perhaps is like the dough that the woman makes, and this lump of dough is going to increase and grow bigger and bigger and bigger and bigger, until it fills the whole sphere of humanity. They forget that the dough expands by gases on the inside, that gases represent corruption, and that leaven is always the symbol of corruption in the word of God without one single exception, so far as I am aware.

This is one doctrine; what is the other?

If the world is not converted we begin to charge the church with guilt; it is not pushing its work with sufficient energy; must reform itself, increase its fervor and enthusiasm. The notion is, that the church is here to convert the world, if the world is not converted it is the church's fault, and therefore the church must be reconstructed.

The other view is: That the church is in the world to gather out God's believing body of people from the nations; that the church is here to attract to itself all the elements in this world that are regenerated by the Holy Ghost and associate them in one mystical body of Jesus Christ. That the church is not going to convert the world but she is going to witness to the world, bear her testimony in all parts of the earth. Then the Lord will come; and that as soon as this body of Christ is gathered out from the nations so that it becomes complete, then the head will appear and the body will be associated with Him in glory.

I began my ministry with the idea that the church was going to convert the world. I expected I was going to do my part in the conversion of the world, and I preached with a great deal of enthusiasm, ardor and conviction. I expected to see my whole congregation converted. It was not; here and there there was one gathered out, and it has been so all through the years of my ministry. I have seen many souls converted under my preaching, but I have never yet seen a whole congregation brought to Christ, and if any of you brethren have it is a very exceptional case. I would like to take a pilgrimage to see where a whole congregation has been brought to Christ.

We have been preaching 1,900 years. There are 40,000,000 Protestant communicants in the world. Mr. Mueller, of Bristol, says: "It is a wonderful thing that not more than 10,000,000 out of that 40,000,000 know what conversion is, what regeneration is." Here are 10,000,000 of people after 19 centuries have passed and the total population of the world is very close to 1,500,000,000 of souls. Heathenism is growing more rapidly by birth than the church is growing by the new birth. My friends, I put this question to you: If hope deferred makes the heart sick, how heart sick must brethren be who have been laboring all through their lives expecting to see the world converted—yet they turn about and look, and with melancholy cadences confess, that the great proportion of the human race does not even know about Christ thus far and that the great majority of the church of Jesus Christ know nothing about the regenerating power of the Holy Ghost.

But, if the hope of this dispensation is not the conversion of the world but its evangelization, and if I am going forth into the world, as my Saviour did, to bear my witness and gather those whom the Father hath given to Christ into the mystical body of Christ, then my hope is not defeated, then it is not deferred; then my heart is not made sick, and I know that I have a Scriptural hope, because I find the confirmation of that Scriptural hope in my experience. If, on the other hand, I think I have a Scriptural hope, and the facts do not confirm my hope, what is the consequence? I either begin to say that there is doubt in the Holy Scriptures, and perhaps doubt the inspiration of Scripture itself, or else, I get despairing and disheartened by the confidence being destroyed that I am a true messenger of Christ.

I hope I shall not be misunderstood in saying this, but I believe that any doctrine, save the doctrine I am trying to present this afternoon, so disappoints hope that it is a natural source of infidelity, because, if my hope is perpetually baffled, I begin to doubt the inspiration of Scripture. Have I been building on something that was a promise of the word of God, and that promise is not fulfilled, then, how do I know this is the word of God? Remember, when the disciples went out from the presence of the Council they said, "And now, Lord, behold their threatenings, and grant unto thy servants, that with all boldness they may speak thy word, by stretching forth thy hand to heal." My brethren, we have a right to challenge Almighty God to put new iron into our blood, and new courage into our soul, by standing by us in the fulfilment of His promises. That is the only way I can keep bold in my Master's service, by having my hope confirmed from time to time by being met with results. If I have an unscriptural hope, it is baffled, it is disappointed, and I have either to learn what the Scriptural hope is, or, I am beginning to doubt that this word is infallible, the inspired word of God. I do not know that you see this, but it is perfectly plain to me, and I bless God that, from the day when I saw that the hope of the church through this generation was to gather out the body of Christ from the Gentiles; that I was not to expect to see the world converted, and therefore, was not to be disappointed if I did not see it converted, but simply expect to see Christ's body gathered out from the nations—the moment I found that Scripture hope, new courage came into my soul, new iron came into my blood, and I have been laboring under this divinely inspired expectation, and it is not baffled, it is not disappointed, it is not turned to confusion.

Now a word in regard to the hope of reward. This blessed doctrine of our Lord's coming puts rewards where they belong, at the coming of the Lord. "Behold I come quickly, and my reward is with me, to give every man according as his works shall be." You are not to expect your reward till Christ comes, and then the reward is going to be wonderful, glorious, abundant. 1 Corinthians 3 : 11. "Other foundation can no man lay than that is laid, which is Jesus Christ. Now if any man build upon this foundation gold, silver, precious stones, wood, hay, stubble; Every man's work shall be made manifest, for the day shall declare it, because it shall be revealed by fire; and the fire shall try every man's work of what sort it is." What is the thought? You are building on Jesus Christ. Look out what kind of material you build. Is it precious material, consistent with the foundation? Will it stand the ordeal of fire, or is it like wood and hay and stubble, like those cottages, hovels, that were built round about the temple of Ephesus, which are swept away with the conflagration almost in an instant of time? What kind of material are you building? When the Lord comes he is going to try your work. If you have built on that foundation you will be saved, though like a man fleeing out of a burning house with the timbers falling around him; you will be saved so as by fire; but, if you have built on that foundation material that is appropriate to the foundation and like unto the foundation, when the ordeal of fire tries that building it will stand; it will glow with lustre like precious gems when the light of the fire shines upon them and the rainbow hues are irradiated from a thousand facets. That is the doctrine of reward. What did Jesus Christ say to his dicsiples when Peter said "Lo, we have left all and followed thee, what shall we have?" Jesus said, "Them which have followed me in the days of my humiliation, in the regeneration or reconstruction (notice when) when the Son of man shall sit on the throne of his glory, they also shall sit on twelve thrones judging the twelve tribes of Israel."

Beloved, the hope, the blessed hope, is the hope of reward. You may preach the gospel now and be persecuted, as Jonathan Edwards preached it in Northampton when he preached against the policy of compromising with the world that prevailed in that day. They thrust the godliest man of that age out of the pulpit and he died in comparative poverty, if not in actual starvation.

The godliest man of his century cast out, as though to be trodden under the foot of men, because he dared to be loyal to the word of God. You may be cast out as he was, but do not be discouraged. Your reward is when Jesus Christ comes. Do not study to show yourselves approved unto men, be content to be approved unto God. Do not seek to gather your rewards here, either in compensation to your purse or compensation to your person, but look for the coming of the Lord, wait for His coming and be willing to have the crown of righteousness and the crown of glory deferred until the Saviour is crowned. What have I to do with wearing a crown before the coronation of the Lord Himself? That is the time for the coronation, when the Lord Himself leads the way as the crowned king. That is the hope of reward.

We have seen the effect on faith, the effect on hope, and now what shall we say of the effect on love? My beloved friends, as you stand here keeping your eye fixed on your Master, the eminent personage, the Son of God, on that most eminent event, His second coming, how it quickens your love. It could not help but quicken your love. Remember what it is to be in Christ; remember that He is coming again for your sake and He cannot be satisfied until that consummation when the bride is to sit with Him on His throne. What husband ever was satisfied to have a blessing that his wife did not share, and how can you imagine the head crowned if the body is not on the throne when the head is enthroned and encrowned. I do not know anything that ever quickened my love for my Master like this, that He looks forward to His coming as my coronation; that He proposes to present me faultless, blameless, holy, incorruptible, so that the omniscient eye of God can look upon me and its penetrating glance shall not be able to find in me the slightest remnant of the sins of my youth, the sins of my manhood, the sins of my old age. For this consummation Jesus Christ gave Himself, and He will never ascend His throne until He gets you ready to ascend with Him. He will never wear His crown until He gets you ready for the crown, and He will never take the consummated glories of His empire until His bride is ready to sit with Him on her companion throne. If you can think of such things as that, my beloved, and not have your love quickened to the Lord Jesus Christ, have you any love at all!

During the progress of our war there was a curious sight occurred in Denver. The day was very dark and cloudy, and the rain had been descending in torrents. The people looked to the mountain that exalts itself outside the city and saw a very strange sight. Right on the brow of the mountain the American flag was waving in the midst of the only gleam of sunshine that lightened the landscape. The clouds had parted at such a point, with reference to the sun, as that the only rift in the clouds opened the way for the sunbeams to rest on the nation's insignia. The people stood admiring and wondering. There was the flag, waving in the breeze, but how it came to be planted there was a mystery. An exploring party of the United States had gone up on some measurements of the mountain heights, and they happened to have set the American flag there, at the precise moment when that rift in the clouds permitted the sunbeam to rest upon it. That very day, Fort Donelson was taken and the war for the Union turned its awful crisis.

My brethren, thick darkness covers the firmament. There are many clouds about us and there are severe storms that sweep across our landscape, but, blessed be God, there is a rift in the clouds, a golden sunbeam, and it rests upon that blessed hope of the Lord's second coming. If you will keep your eye on that blessed hope you will turn the crisis of your life gloriously; you will be patient in sorrow and suffering; patient in unrewarded and unrequited toil; patient under the unrecognized and unappreciated service and serving that you render to humanity. Your faith will be quickened, your hope will be transfixed, your love enlarged and glorified. Keep your eye on that waving insignia, and may the Lord hasten His coming in His time.

THE PROPHETIC MOLD OF THE PRESENT DISPENSATION.

REV. W. J. ERDMAN, D. D., OF PHILADELPHIA, PA.

The design of this study is to show that certain prophetic Scriptures of the early apostolic day form the mold of the history of Christendom and until the Messianic age begins. Only a few, however, will be considered, but these will show the great outlines and reveal the peculiar character of the present dispensation. Before taking up the specific theme it may be shown, in general, that divine prophecy is the mold of human history.

The *very earliest prediction*, that of enmity between the seed of the serpent and the seed of the woman, comprises within its vast and shadowy outlines the whole of human history from the fall of man to the final perfection of the kingdom of God. Gen. 3: 15; 1 Cor. 15: 28.

The prophetic word of Noah touching his sons foretold, in its far-reaching import, the future of the great races of the world; of the Japhetic, characterized by the genius of civilization and culture; and of the Shemitic, by a religious enthusiasm whose cultus would find its source and form in the revelation of the God of Shem. Gen. 9: 26, 27.

In Leviticus and Deuteronomy are predictions that most clearly and exactly reveal the divine purpose and the historic mold of the career of Israel, the most illustrious people of Shemitic blood. Therein are seen the sadly monotonous experiences of curse and captivity of past and present centuries, and the future restoration and world-wide blessings in the days of the Messiah and His glory.

Especially in the "*Song of Moses*" is given, to use the words of Delitsch, "the compendious outline and the common key to all prophecy." Deut. 32 : 1-43. Therein Israel is seen according to the unchangeable purpose of God as the fore-ordained head and center of the race, and the peculiar portion of Jehovah. And accordingly, to this day, the nations as dismembered parts of an organic whole, are waiting to be gathered together in one under Israel as their imperial head. In this "song" we hear of the prolonged apostasy of the chosen people of God and the contemporaneous dominion of Gentiles over them; in it, how Jehovah at last will avenge His people in their final great trouble by the destruction of their arrogant, ungodly enemies; and in it also that the residue of the Gentiles shall share at last in the blessings of Israel after the judgment of the nations.

Finally, in *the visions of the prophet Daniel*, the great empires and kingdoms under which the chosen people of Shem and Abraham are captive and dispersed, appear in succession above the prophetic horizon, and moving through their predestined course disappear in disastrous eclipse and one consummate ruin to give place to the everlasting kingdom of God, whose heir is Israel regenerate and holy. Daniel, chapters 2 and 7.

In all these predictions only two great divisions of the race are known, Israel and the nations, but into these "times of the Gentiles" during which Jerusalem is trodden by them under foot, into this great problem of the goal and outcome of human history, there entered nearly 1900 years ago, another force and factor, *the "Church of God."* Its appearance brought new matter into the prophetic outlines, and postponed by a long interval the final fulfilments of Messianic prophecy. The "times of the Gentiles," beginning with the Babylonian day instead of ending with the first advent of the Messiah, were prolonged to His second. It is with this interval the present discussion has to do.

THE INTERVAL. A hint of such prolongation and delay is now clearly seen in the message of the angel Gabriel to Daniel. *An interval* is intimated between the advent of a rejected Messiah and the advent of an accepted Anti-Messiah; an interval of war and desolation for city, temple and people until Messiah come again, to destroy the oppressor, deliver the "holy people," and on the ruins of ungodly, unrighteous Gentile governments establish His kingdom of everlasting righteousness and peace. Dan. 9 : 24-27.

The same interval had also been foretold by the Lord to *the prophet Isaiah*, how to Israel would come a time of blind eyes and deaf ears and hard hearts, of a forsaken and desolate land, its people removed far away, the prey of the nations, the outcast of the world.

In conformity with this very word of prophecy in Isaiah, *the Gospel of Matthew* is framed, this prediction being quoted at the point of transition from the preaching of the Kingdom to an obdurate Israel, to the scattering of the seed of the Word throughout the world of nations. *In John, likewise,* the same prediction is quoted at the final hiding of Jesus from the unbelieving Jews and His turning to reveal His innermost truth to the chosen disciples, the representatives of "the church."

In the Acts, finally, the mirror of the world, of "Jews, Gentiles and the Church of God," during this interval, Paul testifying to the Jews in Rome, again comes to such transitional point and quoting the same prediction to the unbelieving Jews turns to the Gentiles to preach salvation to them.

The transaction, in each instance, of Jesus and of Paul, became a permanent parable of the interval that now is. Is. 6:1–13; Matt. 13:14, 15; John 12:35–41; Acts 28:17–29.

Even after the Lord Jesus had been rejected and crucified, *another offer of the kingdom* was made to the house of Israel by Him, risen and glorified. The preaching of the apostles with the Holy Ghost sent down from heaven was at first to the Jewish people only and to prepare them for the return of the Messiah. "Repent ye, therefore," said Peter to the people, "and turn again that your sins may be blotted out, that so there may come seasons of refreshing from the presence of the Lord, and that he may send you the Christ, who hath been appointed for you, even Jesus; whom the heavens must receive until the times of restoration of all things, whereof God spake by the mouth of His holy prophets since the world began." Acts 3:19–21 [R. V.]

But all the preaching and mighty miracles attesting it were in vain. The nation stumbled against the stone and rock of offense —a Messiah crucified—and was broken. Its impenitence and unbelief were consummated in a formal representative act, the stoning of Stephen. The conversion of a Paul and of a Cornelius soon followed; and this national rejection opened the way for the preaching of the Gospel to the whole world, according to the once hidden purpose of gathering out of all nations a new and heavenly people of God to be added to the Jewish nucleus, and according to a fresh revelation of unspeakable mercy to Gentiles. Had Israel as a people repented, the course of history would long ago have been conformed to the mold of Messianic prophecy, which has to do only with Israel and the nations, but their disobedience postponed such fulfilment to the future, but to a future that now, in the light of present events, seems to be not very far off.

All these forementioned predictions, beginning with the first uttered in Paradise, sketch in broad outlines the course of human history to its goal in the perfected kingdom of God; each in succession, as with all prophetic words, reveals a new element or more fully and clearly sets forth those already revealed. The details become many and various, but although given centuries apart, harmonize with the great and earliest predictions that inclose and subordinate all.

Many such details and other parts large and dominant might be considered in relation to our special theme THE PROPHETIC MOLD OF THE PRESENT DISPENSATION, the period from Pentecost to the Messianic kingdom, but overlooking the dark and judicial and punitive aspects of this period, we shall confine the study to *the three great events of salvation' that belong to it* and especially to its close, and to the inauguration of the kingdom. These three events are : 1. The fulness of the Gentiles. 2. The fulness of Israel; and 3. The conversion of the world. These are the three to which all the movements of the present age tend; they shape and mold this whole period preceding and preparatory to the establishment of the kingdom of God on earth.

The Scriptures also that describe these fundamental forms of a present and future historic experience are many, but the explanation of a few and the most significant is all that will be attempted.

I. THE SCRIPTURES. 1.—The first passage to be examined is as follows: "For I would not, brethren, that ye should be ignorant of this mystery, lest ye should be wise in your own conceits; that blindness in part is happened to Israel, until the fulness of the Gentiles be come in." Rom. 11 : 25.

Whatever meaning may be given to this "fulness" it is evident that, until it is come in, the "blindness" will continue. In passing, it may be said, such "fulness of the Gentiles" signifies, in the light of the context, and of the argunent preceding, and of grammatical usage, the full number, the totality of Gentiles in the church, when complete at the return of Christ. This complement of Gentiles, with the elect remnant of Israel gathered out during the present centuries, together compose the body of Christ to be glorified with Him at His coming.

The "fulness of the Gentiles," or of "the nations," cannot be "the conversion of the world," for then the whole argument of Paul is aimless. As will be seen, he is discussing not two events, the conversion of the world and the conversion of Israel, but three events. To teach that the conversion of the world takes place before the conversion of Israel is to contradict every word of Old Testament prediction. No Jewish scholar, "orthodox" or "reformed," has ever given any other interpretation than this, (for the word is too plain) that the nations are to be blessed *after* Israel according to the "orthodox," or *through* Israel according to the "heterodox;" in either case, it was a new thing and most perplexing to the early Jewish Christians, though intimated here and there in the Old Testament, that Gentiles should be blessed by the God of Israel *before* Israel itself as a people is blessed. Paul well knew all this when in sorrow of heart he discussed the question Hath God cast away his people? and so we turn with him to the next passage in his great argument: "And so all Israel shall be saved;" "so," on this wise, after the fulness of the Gentiles is come in; "as it is written, There shall come out of Sion the Deliverer, and shall turn away ungodliness from Jacob." 11 : 26.

2. This is the second great event of salvation; this conversion of Israel as a nation. The phrase "all Israel" is explained in a previous passage, "Now if the fall of them (Israel) be the riches of the world, and the diminishing of them the riches of the Gentiles; how much more their fulness?" 11 : 12.

This "fulness of Israel" corresponds to the "all Israel" saved at the second coming of the Redeemer. But it is evident that in this argument is involved a third event, the "conversion of the world;" the great result of their fulness.

The argument is very pointed; what untold blessing will yet come to the world of nations when this fulness of Israel has come in. If the world is all converted before Israel turns to God, if all Messianic blessings have already come, what mean these words? They clearly point to the conversion of the world *after* Israel's conversion, according to the tenor of all Messianic prophecy. In brief, the unbelief and rejection of Israel as a nation made possible a fulness of Gentiles out of all nations with all the attendant blessings of Christendom, but a fulness of Israel will be followed by blessings coextensive with the race, when *all nations* shall turn to God. When Israel sings from the heart,

> "God be merciful unto us and bless us,
> And cause His face to shine upon us,
> That Thy way may be known upon earth,
> Thy saving health among all nations;"

then shall the time come for all peoples to praise God, then "all the ends of the earth shall fear him." Ps. 67.

3. This, the third great event of salvation, is the conversion of the world. The order of these events is never changed in any psalm or predictive word.

And therefore Paul, taking for granted that such order and such connection between cause and effect was ackowledged by his readers who knew the Scripture of the Old Testament, again returns to his brief argument and repeats it in a parallel but deeper, more significant form. "For if the casting away of them be the reconciling of the world, what shall the receiving of them be, but life from the dead?" 11 : 15. Israel's rejection resulting in a world's reconciliation to be followed by Israel's reception and a world's revivification! Yea more, "life from the dead" involves not only a world wide conversion corresponding to the reconciliation, but also, the bodily resurrection from the dead of Israel's righteous, inseparable from the coming of the mighty Redeemer of Jacob.

> "He will swallow up death in victory.
> Thy dead shall live, my dead body
> they shall arise."
> "And many of them that sleep in the
> dust of the earth shall awake."

AN ORDER OF TIME.—That *an order of time* is indicated by these predictions is self evident. The fulness of the Gentiles and the national blindness of Israel are contemporaneous and come first in order; they are facts to-day; the fulness of Israel and the Coming of the Redeemer are contemporaneous, and belong to the future; and the conversion of the world is subsequent to all. By no laws of language or of exegesis can one be confounded with the other. As sure as "one, two, three," follow each other in the counting of a child and in the calculations of an astronomer, so "one," "the fulness of the Gentiles," cannot be "three," "the conversion of the world," much less can it be "two," "the fulness of Israel." Neither can number "two" be dropped out, and Israel be no longer Israel, and "the miracle of history," the Jew, come to a pointless conclusion. If the three chapters, the ninth, tenth and eleventh of Romans, refer not to Israel as distinct from both the Church and the Gentiles, why were they written? On the contrary, the divine order will be maintained to the end of the age, "For the gifts and calling of God are without repentance." He must fulfil His word to the fathers; "I am Jehovah." Rom. 11 : 29.

And this very parenthesis of these chapters of the great epistle corresponds to this parenthesis of the historic period of the blindness of Israel and the fulness of the Gentiles. But, according to the popular theory, which ignores the Jew and expects now the conversion of the world, if these chapters should drop out of the epistle, they would never be missed.

II. One more Scripture, and of three parts, casting human history in a similar mold with the foregoing, will be considered.

At the Council of Jerusalem, James set forth the same three great events of salvation, and in the same order of succession: 1. "Simeon hath declared how God at the first did visit the Gentiles to take out of them a people for his name. 2. And to this agree (symphonize) the words of the prophets; as it is written, After this I will return and will build again the tabernacle of David, which is fallen down; and I will build again the ruins thereof, and I will set it up. 3. That the residue of men might seek after the Lord, and all the Gentiles upon whom My name is called, saith the Lord, who doeth all these things. Known unto God are all His works from the beginning of the world." Acts 15 : 13–18.

Here again, it is to be noted, are three points: 1. The visiting of the Gentiles is not for universal conversion, but for taking out a people for His name, an election corresponding to the fulness of the Gentiles; 2. This election will be followed by the re-establishment of David's throne at the return of the Lord, this corresponding to the time of the fulness of Israel at the coming of the Deliverer out of Zion ; and, 3. The return to God of the spared nations, after the Lord's coming and Israel's salvation, corresponds to the conversion of the world.

The facts are the same, the order is the same.

2. It should also be remarked, that to this prophecy of Amos there is added by James, not only the preface concerning the election of Gentiles going on then and now, but also the phrase "After this I will return" is put in the place of the "In that day" found in Amos. On consulting the context of the prediction of Amos, it is seen that a time of Israel's dispersion and punishment precedes the restoration of David's tabernacle, so corresponding exactly to this present time of Israel's blindness as preceding Israel's future fulness. Accordingly, the statement "After this I will return" is an inspired note of time, a very key to the interpretation of the chronological order of prophetic fulfilment.

Had the words of Amos, "In that day," been used instead, the prophecy might have been quoted to prove only that Gentiles too would turn to the Lord; but by the change, "After this I will return," an order of events is given, not of two, Israel and the Gentiles, but of three, "the Jews, the Gentiles, and the Church of God." That Gentiles would turn to the Lord in the latter days was well known by these Jewish Christians, but they were not prepared for this parenthetic, elective body of Gentiles, and they were reconciled only by the argument of James assuring them from Scripture that when the Messiah returned then the Kingdom would be restored to Israel, and then, after such return, all the Gentiles would be converted, so fulfilling the prophetic Scriptures of the Old Testament and in the order they clearly taught.

3. Amos also locates such restoration of David's throne at a time of a return from captivity and dispersion, of which it is said, "And I will plant them upon their land, and they shall no more be pulled up out of their land which I have given them, saith the Lord thy God." Amos 9 : 8–15.

Such a final and permanent restoration of Israel, followed by the turning to God of all nations, has not taken place since the time of James, and therefore, the visitation of the Gentiles of which he speaks as coming before the return of the Lord and before the restoration of Israel, cannot be the same as the conversion of the nations after such return and after such permanent restoration. Gathering together the elements of these several predictions, the complete idea concerning the three fulfilments of salvation may be stated as follows:

1. In *the song of Moses* there is a hint of this time of Gentile election in these words quoted by Paul: "they have moved me to jealousy with that which is not God ("a no-God") they have provoked me to anger with their vanities, and I will move them to jealousy with those which art not a people ("a no-people") I will provoke them to anger with a foolish nation." Deut. 32 : 21; Rom. 10 : 19. This threat is significantly found in a context predicting a long time of national punishment and hardness of heart. This "no nation," this "not a people" is most surely the body of Gentile believers existing in this historic interval while God is hiding his face from the house of Jacob. Is. 8 : 14-18.

But this blessing on the "no-people" of the nations predicted in the *heart* of "the song" is clearly distinguished from the blessing and rejoicing of the nations predicted at the *close* of "the song," and to occur when the day of Israel's salvation has at last come at the return of Israel's God. Deut. 32 : 21-43.

The former Gentile blessedness is during the time of Jewish blindness, the latter Gentile rejoicing with Israel is after the Gentiles, once the tools of divine judgment on Israel, have themselves been smitten in the day of God's wrath. 32 : 40-43.

2. With this word of Moses agrees that of Amos concerning the sifting of the house of Israel among all nations, but Amos speaks also of the restoration of the Tabernacle of David and as preceding the conversion of all the Gentiles.

To this of Amos there is added by James the new fact of a Gentile election and the announcement of a *second* coming of the Messiah. And to this of James is added by Paul the fact of an elect remnant of Israel as existing during the centuries of national blindness, and who with the elect of the Gentiles form the body of Christ, and to be discriminated as a heavenly glorified people both from a later fulness of Israel and from the conversion of all nations. Each prediction in turn adds some new feature to the prophetic portraiture until it is complete. Much of it we can recognize as characteristic of our own day. The interval, as such, must needs be a time of unrest and conflict, the old is still mingled with the new, the evil with the good.

As parenthetic and transitional no institutions of the present centuries, civil or ecclesiastical, can be permanent; the turbid sea of human misery in ceaseless ebb and flow cannot rock itself to rest; the voice is not now on land or sea to say "peace: be still." To understand the times we go to the prophetic word as to a lamp shining in a dusky place; it illumines all, even as it determines all, conforms all, fixes all.

III. THE CONCLUSION.—In conclusion, some questions may be asked.

1. First, can the foregoing prophecy be at all verified by so much of it as has become history? If it can, as has been already intimated it can, then such present fulfilment is a sure pledge of the fulfilment of the remainder; and especially of the return of the Lord Jesus before the conversion of the world.

But it does not require argument; mere statement is sufficient. The conflict between the seed of Satan and the seed of the woman is still going on; that prediction cannot be gainsayed; the Japhetic and Shemitic races have ruled the world and still rule, each in its own predicted way; that prophetic word is true, we are its witnesses; Israel, with its alternate blessing and curse, has outlived the empires and kingdoms which oppressed it; lived to see its Messiah and to reject Him, and ever since in blindness and hardness of heart has been a wanderer among the nations; that prediction is a daily fact; the church whose nucleus and foundation was of Jews, has for centuries been filling up its vaster complement of Gentiles; and we Gentile believers should acknowledge it with profoundest humility; and Christendom, enriched with countless blessings through Israel's trespass and rejection, is even now filled with predicted self-conceited wisdom and highmindedness, and is bringing into strong relief the prophesied characteristics of the last days both in the church and in the world; and Christendom may well be filled with foreboding fear of coming doom. All these present and past fulfilments are the pledge of all future. The condition of Christendom to-day is a continuous contradiction of the optimistic views of modern enthusiasts. If they had lived in the apostolic age and with nineteen centuries before them, they would have predicted far different times, even of universal peace and righteousness. But if, contemporary with the completing of the fulness of the Gentiles, there can exist such consummate form and outcome of ecclesiastical pride and arrogance as "Babylon the Great," then it should be no hard matter to believe that in the deepest darkness of a hardened Israel will appear its false Messiah, and at the height of Gentile civilization, humanistic and man-exalting, should be revealed the "Man of Sin," "the Beast" self-deifying and demoniac.

On the other hand, the better things will also most surely appear; a present believing remnant of Jews is a sure pledge of the national fulness to come; "if the first fruit be holy, the lump is also holy;" and a present fulness of Gentiles does not exhaust all prophecy concerning the conversion of the nations; some Jews and many Gentiles are saved after the first coming of Christ, many Jews and all nations at His second coming. Above all, there is assured the blessed hope of the personal second coming of the Redeemer as an event inseparable from the three great events; then will the church be glorified, Israel saved, the world converted.

2. *But, second, then Christendom is on trial before God and the end is failure and judgment?*

To this solemn aspect of Gentile history our attention will be for a moment directed. The answer is, Israel was once on trial both for itself as to law and for the nations as their teacher and bringer of divine blessings, and failing in both, its long time of punishment began.

With the Gospel and the Church, the nations entered into a time of probation to know whether they would be brought into "the obedience of faith," and by righteousness and showing mercy unto the poor lengthen a tranquil existence, the true ground of prolongation of national life during "these times of the Gentiles." Dan. 4:27; Rom. 16:26.

That they have not done so to the full requirements of the divine plan is self-evident to-day in the ominous signs of the times in church and state, in camp and court, in city and hamlet, and all this after nearly nineteen centuries of the gospel of the grace of God. It is only the true church, the salt of the earth, the light of the world, that illumines the darkness and restrains the increasing lawlessness and corruption. Judgment is impending, and is even to begin at the house of God, if the Epistles are to be viewed as a perpetual mirror of what is possible for each and every generation of the church until the Lord comes.

Even from the days of Moses to those of Paul a note of foreboding import for Gentiles is heard mingling in the predictions of woes and blessings to Israel.

In the Song of Moses *the nations are punished* with terrific judgments for their unmeasured evil treatment of Israel, and just before the blessings come upon the latter ; in the prophecy of Amos, foretelling that they shall "possess the remnant of Edom," the very name Edom suggests how this inveterate foe of Jacob is typical of all his enemies in the latter day ; in the quotation of James the phrase "remnant of Edom" is changed to the "residue," or remnant, "of men" (Edom to Adam)—Jacob's enemy becomes the whole world of anti-Semitic nations—but in both instances the word "remnant" implies and confirms all prophecy that only fragments of the great anti-Christian nations, enemies of Israel and of God, survive the judgments of the great day of God Almighty ; and in the solemn argument of Paul the warning is lifted against Gentile Christendom and its possible apostasy, "Behold, therefore, the goodness and severity of God—on them which fell, severity ; but towards thee, goodness, if thou continue in His goodness ; otherwise *thou* also shalt be cut off." Rom. 11 : 22.

3. There is, then, we may say, in the third and last place, according to Paul's word of warning, *no room for Gentile boasting and self-conceit, but great reason for fear.*

The optimistic expectations of progress to a state of permanent peace and prosperity are in direct contradiction to all the Scriptures we have quoted, and to others that speak of apostasy and "perilous times in the last days."

Such Scriptures do not accord with the eloquent orations of statesmen and the sonorous sonnets of poets urging on the hosts of freedom to "take the world" for—humanity! Much less do they agree with the fervid, confident predictions of preachers whose specific theory of salvation as elective is wholly inconsistent with such expectations, and who forget that "prophecy is predestination." Such desires and expectations—even all the desirable things of the most magnificent civilization—shall indeed be realized at last, in noblest, purest forms, in the Messianic age to come, but these cannot be developed out of the elements and institutions of the present. The civilization of the natural man, at its best, is but as the glory of the grass that fadeth and falleth away; and, at its worst, a gorgeous poison-flower whose fragrant exhalations intoxicating men unto pride and arrogance, and stupefying in them the sense of the divine presence and power, shall itself be shriveled and consumed, at last, in the fiery wrath of the great day.

And the strangest, saddest evidence of the deceitful power of the spirit of the world is the treatment of these divine predictions, by many who handle the Word of God as if they were, like the fabled prophecies of a Cassandra, true, but not to be believed. But, as sure as the fashion of this world passeth away, they shall most surely be fulfilled.

Man may devise and plan and work for other ends, but all in vain. The work of all good men, who wrought for God, will be builded into the divine structure, even though they knew not the plan of the Divine Architect, or misconstrued it; their work will count, not their theory. God overrules, also, all those who work against Him and those who work without Him. His eternal and gracious purpose gives "the form and pressure" of each nation's life and experience. He overlooks much, forgives more, and is "long suffering, not willing that any should perish, but that all should come to repentance."

Even long before Christ came, it was true of God, "He made of one every nation of men for to dwell on all the face of the earth, having determined their appointed seasons, and the bounds of their habitation, *that they should seek God.*" Acts 17 : 26.

However dark and perilous the way through which the nations pass to the age of righteousness and peace beyond, it is assured, by the word of God, that when He appears again, they, in spite of themselves, will be given greater blessings to enjoy than those of the present or of any future fabled by the heart of man. The race walks not with aimless feet. "Known *unto God* are all His works from the beginning *of the world.*" Acts 15 : 18.

THE SECOND COMING OF CHRIST IN RELATION TO ISRAEL.

By E. F. Stroeter.

Careful observation leaves no room for doubt that recent years have brought a change of attitude both in the Jewish mind toward the Gospel of Christ, and in the Christian mind toward the Jew. Increasing numbers of that strange people are reading eagerly the New Testament accounts of Jesus of Nazareth, and are willing to listen quietly to the Gospel of a crucified Redeemer. And God's Spirit is manifestly laying Israel's paramount claim to our most earnest efforts at evangelization upon the hearts of God's children, and is causing them to acknowledge, as never before, Israel's birthright to covenanted blessings which the future still holds in store for that despised and downtrodden people. This does not mean that we are to look presently for wholesale conversions of the Jews to the Gospel of the Son of God; nor does it mean that anti-Semitism and Jew-hatred is a thing of the past in Christendom. The greatest and most awful foe and destroyer of that wonderful people is still to arise. The time of Jacob's greatest trouble is still to come.

But we may well hail with gladness the fact that the blasted and withered fig tree is showing unmistakable signs of returning life, and is giving promise of a speedy budding forth into renewed fruitfulness for the blessing of the nations. And we give thanks unto God for the other fact as well, that believers are awakening to a deeper sense of their obligation and responsibility toward the long despised and neglected Jew, and to a readiness to know the mind of the Lord and His purposes with His covenant people Israel. This to us is a sure indication that the Spirit of the Lord is hastening the special preparation of Christ's own body for the consummation of His approaching manifestation in glory.

Israel's position in the divine plan of the ages can never be understood except in the light of that central truth of revelation, the glorious appearing of the Son of man from heaven. And this blessed truth, in turn, finds its richest setting in the marvelous dealings of God, in grace and in judgment, with that people which he foreknew, and whom he has all concluded in unbelief that he might have mercy upon all. Rom. **11** : 2–32. "For Zion shall be redeemed with judgment and they that return of her with righteousness." Isa. **1** : 27 (margin.) "And I will place salvation in Zion for Israel, my glory, saith the Lord." Isa. **46** : 13.

Of all the varied relations, then, in which we may consider the central fact of the *Coming of the Lord, its relation to Israel* is eminently calculated to bring into view the depth of the riches both of the wisdom and knowledge of God, whose judgments are unsearchable, and his ways past finding out. Rom. **11** : 33.

I desire to present for your thoughtful and prayerful consideration these three propositions :

I. God's dealings with Israel in the past are unintelligible and self-contradictory apart from the assurance of the return of Israel's Messiah, even our Lord Jesus Christ.

II Israel's present-age attitude of hostility toward the Gospel of Christ is caused chiefly by the failure of the Gentile church to believe and to preach the second coming of our Lord and Israel's Deliverer.

III Israel's future glory as a nation is assured at and by the return of Jesus, the son and heir of David, the King of the Jews, the desire of all nations.

I.

Israel's history is unique. No other people on earth ever did or ever will stand as Israel does, in covenant relation with the God of heaven and earth. Greek and Roman, American and Chinaman, may, in Christ Jesus, approach that same God and call Him Abba, Father ; but God has never undertaken to be the God of Americans or of the Chinese as He has to be the God of Israel, of Abraham, of Isaac, and of Jacob. "Thus saith the Lord that created thee, O Jacob, and He that formed thee, O Israel : Fear not, for I have redeemed thee ; I have called thee by thy name ; thou art mine."

Isa. **43** : 1. And again, "This people have I formed for Myself; they shall show forth my praise, saith the Lord." v. 21. "He hath not dealt so with any nation." Psalm **147** : 20. But God's dealings with his covenant people have not been continuous. From the Exodus, when the nation was born in a day, as it were, until the destruction of their city and sanctuary by the Romans, Israel has stood in actual covenant relation with the God of their fathers in the promised land. God spake and dealt with them for 1,500 years, through priests and kings and prophets, and finally through His own Son, whom, like all God's messengers, they rejected, and killed. Ever since that awful catastrophe, when God "sent forth His armies and destroyed those murderers and burned up their city" Matt. **22** : 7, they have been scattered and driven among all the nations of the earth, and Jerusalem has been trodden down of Roman, Saracen, Crusader and Turk, even unto this day. This forms the second period of Israel's history, already longer by 300 years than the first; and while the brief night of the 70 years' exile in Babylon was made resplendent by three of the greatest prophets God ever sent to his people—Jeremiah, Ezekiel, Daniel—during these last eighteen centuries the voice of the Lord has been silent in Israel. Since the death of Jesus of Nazareth no prophet has arisen to lighten the gloom of Israel's second and greater dispersion. Surely He was that prophet of whom Moses spake. Deut. **18** : 15–18. His name for all these centuries has been a benediction and a joy among the nations of the earth. Wherever proclaimed and believed it has brought life and light and peace. Only in Israel it still brings out awful maledictions and blasphemies. They still hate Him without cause. No wonder the question rises to our lips again and again, with strange persistency, Hath not God, after all, cast away this people? Have they not sinned away their day of grace?

But here he is, the imperishable, ubiquitous, irrepressible Jew, the most conspicuous and emphatic figure of all history. The Jew, without a king or a government of his own, has seen the mightiest empires rise and has attended their funeral. An exile from his own land, he has witnessed every civilized country of the Old World change ownership over and over. No nation has ever prospered in his land, the land that flowed with milk and honey while he dwelt there; he has prospered in every land, under every clime. He receives no hearty welcome, no legislative favors, no social advantages anywhere, hardly justice; but in the race for wealth, for success and for honors in art and science and literature he leads everywhere. He has been branded with infamy, loaded with unutterable contempt; behold him, the cringing, crouching, unresisting object of pity!

But a few brief hours of genial sunshine, a few decades of emancipation and equal rights, and behold the unbearably proud, and loud and obnoxious modern Jew, whose race-pride will yet fan the slumbering embers of inbred Gentile anti-Semitism into furious flame.

Talk of Egyptian Sphynxes and of Gordian knots—the greatest riddle, the one unsolvable mystery of all the ages, is the Jew. His very existence and preservation is an unanswerable challenge to the human mind for a rational explanation. No philosophy was yet equal to the task. Let us look more closely at the striking contrast, the inexplicable discrepancy, between those two great periods of Jewish history, and see what riddles, what apparently hopeless contradictions we discover from the standpoint of God's own dealings with that nation.

1. *The history of Israel is the history of divine revelation.* God might have caused the story of the antediluvian world to be written by an Enoch or a Noah, and the records might have been safely carried over the flood in the Ark. But God waited for the Jew Moses to give us the inspired account of the creation and of His subsequent dealings with the race. And when, centuries after Moses, that mystery was brought out, which God had kept hidden from the ages, when the church was born, and believing Gentiles became fellow-heirs in that body with believing Israelites, there was no lack of consecrated talent of Gentile extraction to whom an equal share might have been given also in the composition of the New Testament canon. But not so. Let Greek and Roman classic charm the world, if you please. But, to feed and upbuild the church, the body of the glorified Son of God, the Spirit again selects as penmen none but sons of Jacob. Open your New Testament at the first chapter of Matthew, and these are the words you read: "The book of the generation of Jesus Christ, the son of David, the son of Abraham." Turn to the closing book, the Apocalypse, and you will find its language, symbolism and

imagery all intensely Jewish. Take the heart of your New Testament, the Epistle to the Romans, and examine its innermost heart again, the chapters **9**, **10** and **11**, it is Paul's testimony concerning Israel.

And now look at the strange discrepancy in the attitude of that people to whom were committed the oracles of God and to whom pertaineth the adoption, and the glory, and the covenants and the promises (Roms. **3**: 2; **9**: 4) toward these same oracles of God which have been committed to them. For unquestioning faith in the absolute divine authority and infallibility of the Old Testament Canon the orthodox Jew (and he is in the majority, the world over,) is not behind any, and far ahead of a great many Christian teachers and professors. For two-thirds of this Bible we, who still believe in the integrity of the old book, have in the Jew the staunchest ally against all the insidious attacks of infidelity upon it. But when you wish to take the Jew from Malachi right into Matthew, John and Paul, he turns away. Yet these are all men of his own race, of his own faith; men who never renounced, much less denounced Judaism, whose every word breathes the same Spirit that spake through Moses and Isaiah, who never weary of unfolding the riches of divine grace and truth as laid down in the Law and the Prophets!

What is the meaning of this? It is all very well to cry out: Oh, the blindness, the perverseness of the Jew! He will not see that this Bible of ours is one great, organic whole. Yes, sadly true enough. But, what of the God of Israel? What of His committing all His oracles exclusively to this one people, and then this people of His own choosing for more than eighteen centuries turning a deaf ear to its own prophets of the New Testament? Is the history of revelation to end in such a signal failure? Is the symphony of divine revelation to break off in an unbearable discord? Will that greatest, matchless prophet of Israel, the Word made flesh, never hear the hosannahs of His own people? Will they never obey His perfect law and herald it forth from Jerusalem into all the earth abroad?

2. *Again, secondly, the history of Israel is the history of redemption.* Salvation is from the Jews. John **4**: 22. All the appointments of Israel's national life, their worship, their social and economic laws, have one supreme object, of which the epistle to the Hebrews

is an exponent—to shadow forth the wonderful purposes of God in redemption for the human race. That nation was born, delivered, guided, ordered, smitten and kept of the Lord, in order to be God's age-lasting object lesson in grace and in judgment, for all time to come. More than this. They are they of whom, as concerning the flesh, Christ came, who is over all, God blessed forever. Rom. **9** : 5. There is not a principle or phase of salvation but God exemplified and illustrated it in Israel. There is not a fact of salvation but God gave it expression in Jewish form. The Saviour of the world lived, and suffered, and died a Jew. And when the Holy Spirit, the promise of the Father, came, as announced by the Son when about to ascend, he fell upon none but Jewish believers at the first. For the fulness of life and salvation in the glorified Christ the Spirit of Christ sought and found its first (and perhaps best and purest) expression in that body of Christ-believing Jews in Jerusalem. For several years the church of Christ was without Gentile elements. And now, for eighteen centuries, this same people have been the unwilling witnesses of the world-wide power of Jesus' name over men's hearts and lives in every nation under heaven. They have seen innumerable Dagons fall helpless before the ark of the New Covenant, which is Christ, the son of Mary. They have seen untold blessings come to families, and tribes, and kindreds of every description, through the despised Nazarene. They have seen the honor given to their brother Joseph among the Gentiles—and yet they have not known him. While they, who have been God's only vessels of blessing to the nations, have been cast aside, unfruitful, withered branches.

Again you cry: Behold the blindness of the Jew ! Ah, yes, but again, what of the God of Israel? What of His choice for heirs of the covenanted blessings? What of His choice for channels of salvation to the ends of the earth? Was, then, salvation to be only from the Jews, and not also for that people? Hath God cast away His people? God forbid. God hath not cast away His people which He foreknew. Rom. **11** : 2.

"There shall come out of Sion a Deliverer and shall turn away ungodliness from Jacob: for this is My covenant unto them when I shall take away their sins." Rom. **11** : 26, 27.

3. *The history of Israel is the history of the kingdom of God on earth.*

There never was, in any age, or in any nation, a pure theocracy, except in Israel. Over that people, Jehovah Himself did exercise the functions of lawgiver, judge and king. Of this fact and of the mind of the Lord, His own word leaves no doubt.

When Samuel, the prophet of the Lord, was old, and his sons walked not in his ways, the elders of Israel said unto him: Now make us a king to judge us like all the nations. And the thing displeased Samuel, and he prayed unto the Lord. And the Lord said unto Samuel, "Hearken unto the voice of the people, for they have not rejected thee, but they have rejected Me, that I should not reign (*i. e.*, be King) over them." 1 Sam. **8** : 7. Then Saul became the first king over Israel, a man after the people's heart. But this first king, who lifted up his heart in rebellion and witchcraft against the Lord, was followed by a second, a man after God's own heart in matters of the Kingdom. David always recognized his true position as the human representative of King Jehovah over God's people Israel. He says: "And of all my sons (for the Lord hath given me many sons) He hath chosen Solomon, my son, to sit upon the throne of the kingdom of the Lord over Israel." 1 Chron. **28** : 5. And thus it is recorded later on of this Solomon, the typical son of David: "Then Solomon sat on the throne of the Lord as king, instead of David, his father." 1 Chron. **29** : 23. And this is the word of the Lord unto David, by Nathan, the prophet: "Thus saith the Lord of hosts, I took thee from the sheep-cote that thou shouldest be ruler over My (not thy) people Israel. Also I will ordain a place for My people Israel, and will plant them, and they shall dwell in their place and shall be moved no more. * * * And it shall come to pass, when thy days be expired, * * * that I will raise up thy seed after thee, which shall be of thy son, and I will establish his kingdom forever. * * * I will settle Him in Mine house and in My kingdom forever, and His throne shall be established forevermore." 1 Chron. **17** : 7–14.

Here, then, is the only authentic and Scriptural definition of that much abused term, the Kingdom of God. It evidently means just what it says, an actual, personal Kingship, in history, of the Lord God of Hosts over His people Israel, through the human personality of Him who is to be the seed of David according to the flesh. To this explanation of the Scripture term "Kingdom of God" we submit without hesitation. God Himself has given actual, historical demonstration of its correctness. Nor has He ever said a word about a change or a radical departure from His original conception of it as set forth in the Davidic theocracy.

Several facts in this connection are very patent:

1. That this promise to David, confirmed by an oath (Psalm **89**: 3, 4), has not found its adequate fulfilment in Solomon, for these reasons: (*a*) Solomon was established as rightful heir on his father's throne *before* David's death. The Lord speaks to David of what He will do *after* David's days be expired. (*b*) Solomon's kingdom was not established forever. Solomon himself went down in idolatry and abominations, and his misrule brought on the speedy disruption, under his son Rehoboam, of the kingdom of Israel into two kingdoms, a breach that has never yet been healed unto this day. (*c*) Moreover, David himself clearly understood that the word of the Lord was not to be limited in its application to Solomon when he says: "For Thou hast also spoken of Thy servant's house for a great while to come," or, as Luther renders it, "of the far-distant future." 1 Chron. **17**: 17.

2. That God's people Israel have never yet seen the fulfilment of that distinct and unconditional promise, coupled with God's oath to David: "I will plant them, and they shall dwell in their place, and they shall be moved no more; neither shall the children of wickedness waste them any more."

3. That the tabernacle of David is still in ruins. God's people Israel have not had a son of David to rule over them on the throne of the kingdom of the Lord for 2,000 years. It is worse than idle to make out that the exaltation of Jesus, the son of Mary, to the throne of the Majesty on high, constitutes in any sense a re-establishment of David's throne. At the announcement of His birth to His Virgin mother the angel clearly distinguishes the two events. "He shall be great, and shall be called the Son of the Highest." This covers His exaltation in resurrection, ascension and consequent outpouring of the Spirit with power. Then the angel proceeds: "And the Lord God shall give unto Him the throne of His father David, and He shall reign over the house of Jacob forever, and of His kingdom there shall be no end." Luke **1**: 32, 33. Nothing in the experience of Jesus of Nazareth corresponds to a fulfilment of this Scripture in its plain, obvious sense.

Again, years after Christ's ascension and the birth of the church, James, through the Holy Spirit, with the assembled apostles and elders of the church at Jerusalem, still considered that the tabernacle of David was yet in ruins. Acts **15**: 16. This disposes effectually of the unscriptural and confusing notion, that Jesus, by going up on high, entered upon the inheritance of His father David. The simple truth is, that Jesus then returned to that glory which He had with His Heavenly Father before the world was. (John **17**: 5.) The inheritance of His earthly father David He has never yet received. For David never reigned either in heaven nor over the hearts of believers in Christ.

And now look at the condition of that people again, whom God, even where He shows them to Ezekiel as very dry bones, calls once and again: "Oh, my people!" Exhaust your powers of invective in upbraiding the sons of Jacob for their utter failure to enter into the mind of the Lord concerning His kingdom over Israel—you can only echo what God, through the mouth of His holy prophets, has foretold of them long before it came to pass. You cannot add one feather's weight to the terrible condemnation which God Himself has pronounced upon them. He knew what a wretched failure they would be. And yet—answer me, "Why has not the Jewish race perished from the earth long ago?" Has not the fury of God's anger been upon them? Have they not been burned, put to the sword, tortured, cast into wells and rivers and seas? Yes, but fire will not consume them, nor water destroy them. Here they are, twelve million strong, more numerous than in the palmy days of David and Solomon. Why will they not succumb to the ravages of plague and pestilence? Have they not been impaled in the ghettoes of three continents? Yes, but here they are, with the third lowest mortality rate in the Jewish ghetto of New York City, where over nine hundred souls are huddled together on an acre. Answer me, what has kept them? What wonderful spell has sustained them? Do not ask the easy-going, free-thinking, liberal Jew of our western cities for an answer. Go and ask the generations of those whose only signs of life for centuries have been cries of agony, and streams of blood wrung out from them by the most atrocious cruelty and oppression of Christian and Moslem alike. Ask them: they will answer you. It is the never dying hope of a coming Messiah and Deliverer, the

Son of David, who shall save them from the hands of all that oppressed them. And this hope has been kept alive and nourished by the ever living streams of God's sure word of prophecy.

You may make bold to doubt or to deny, if you please, that the glowing promises given to Israel of a gracious restoration, as a people, to divine favor and to great glory under Messiah their king, in their own land, can or will ever find an actual literal fulfilment in history. You may labor long and earnestly and finally prove to your own complete satisfaction that it is the mark of a very carnal mind to believe that God's word to Israel means just what it says, in blessing as in cursing, but you cannot, you dare not deny the tremendous fact, that the words of Moses, and of Isaiah and Ezekiel, and Zechariah, do bear on their very face that meaning to which orthodox Judaism, the world over, has clung through eighteen centuries of unparalleled trial by fire. And the closing decade of this nineteenth century has brought an awakening of the national spirit and a revival of national hopes and aspirations—not indeed in Reform Judaism, but among the downtrodden masses of Jews in Eastern Europe, which only waits for the breath of favorable opportunity to burst forth in a blaze of unquenchable enthusiasm that will startle the world.

Are you a mere philosopher? Do you believe only in the inexorable laws of nature? In the law of the survival of the fittest? Very well, test your philosophy on the Jew. He has survived persecution and oppression, before one half of which any other race of men would have utterly perished.

But if you believe in the God of Abraham and of Isaac and of Jacob, the God and Father of our Lord Jesus Christ, the son of David, the son of Abraham, then do not say that the miraculous preservation of this wonderful people, by the hope drawn from a literal reading of God's own holy oracles, is nothing but an exhibition of the implacable anger of God toward His chosen people! Then do not say that their immortal hope of seeing David's Son on David's throne ruling his people Israel in truth and righteousness, is never to be for them anything but one stupendous, age-lasting mockery.

II.

Israel's present-age attitude of hostility toward the Gospel of Christ is caused chiefly by the failure of the Gentile church to believe and to preach the second coming of our Lord and Israel's Messiah.

There can be no question as to the facts here brought together. The Jews do not conceal their hostility toward him whom we call their Messiah and our Saviour. The Gentile church at large is openly congratulating herself that she has succeeded in relegating that belief in Messiah's visible return to restore Israel and to establish His kingdom on David's throne in Jerusalem—which in the early church was a very test of orthodoxy—to the limbo of exploded theories and theological curiosities. The only serious question that may be raised is, do these two patent facts stand in the relation of cause and effect to each other, as indicated in the proposition?

1. We have the most abundant evidence to the character of apostolic preaching on this subject. Turn to Acts **3**:19–21, Peter's second recorded sermon after Pentecost. Does he make light of his nation's sin? Hear him: "Ye denied the Holy One and the Just, and desired a murderer to be granted unto you, and killed the prince of life." (**3**: 14, 15.) But what follows? Ye are therefore hopelessly rejected as a nation, there never will be any restoration? Not so: But, "repent ye, therefore, and be converted, that your sins may be blotted out, that so there may come seasons of refreshing from the presence of the Lord, and that He may send the Christ who hath been appointed for you, even Jesus: whom the heaven must receive until the times of restoration of all things, whereof God spake by the mouth of His holy prophets from of old." (R. V.)

Turn to Paul, the great apostle to the Gentiles. Does he rightly appreciate Israel's sin? Hear him: "according as it is written, God hath given them the spirit of slumber, eyes that they should not see, and ears that they should not hear, unto this day...Let their table be made a snare, and a trap, and a stumbling block, and a recompense unto them." Rom. **11**: 8–10. But, what are his conclusions?

1 If their fall be the riches of the world, how much more their fulness? v. 12.
2 If the casting away of them be the reconciling of the world, the receiving of them will be life from the dead. v. 15.
3 If the first fruit be holy, the lump is holy. v. 16. (And the early church were first fruits from the Jewish nation, exclusively.)
4 God is able to graff them in again. v. 23.
5 If thou from the wild (Gentile) olive tree, wert graffed, contrary to nature, into the good olive tree (Israel), how much more shall these natural branches be graffed into their own olive tree? v. 24.
6 The mystery: blindness but in part to Israel; not forever, only until the fulness of the Gentiles be come in—all Israel saved—the Deliverer out of Zion—their sins taken away. v. 25–27.
7 As ye (Gentiles) in times past have not believed God, yet have now obtained mercy through their unbelief, even so have these also now not believed, that through your mercy they also may obtain mercy. v. 31.

These words are from that boasted foundation epistle of the churches of the reformation. This was inspired, apostolic teaching on Israel's restoration long after their rejection of Jesus the Messiah at His first appearing.

On the other hand, a careful study of the Acts of the Apostles, and of the experiences of Paul, especially, will show clearly, that Jewish antagonism in those days was not aroused nearly so much by the presentation of the claims of the Crucified One to the Messiahship, as by the announcement that the hated and despised "Gentile dogs" should be admitted into the divine family of God's children, through faith in Christ Jesus, on the same plane exactly—free grace—with the descendants of Jacob. That was the sharp sting in Jewish animosity toward apostolic preaching. Acts **22** : 21, 22; 1 Thess. **2** : 16.

Things have changed. The Gentiles are turning the tables on the children of the promises with a vengeance.

2. There is no need of bringing much evidence as to the totally different character of present day teaching and preaching on these points. The claims of God's chosen people to a literal

fulfilment to them, as a nation, of God's oath-bound covenants with Abraham and with David are simply ignored. The boast is made openly, by a majority of the teachers of Christianity of to-day, that the theology of the church has, at length, cast off the husks and shackles of a carnal, Judaistic chiliasm which is claimed to have been hampering the preaching of the apostles and early fathers.

And now to the question: Why do the Jews reject Christ? Here is their own answer, clearly and concisely put in the *Reformer and Jewish Times* of Dec. 6, 1877:

"The Jews reject the belief in Jesus as the Messiah because his coming did not fulfill the prophecies of the Bible in regard to the real Messiah; because these prophecies have not since been fulfilled; because, of the important events that were to accompany the coming of the Messiah, not one has come to pass......When these prophecies are fulfilled the Jews will believe that Messiah has come. They will not believe that he has come until God's promises have been fulfilled, for God is not a man that he should lie, or the son of man that he should repent; but what he says he will do, and what he speaks he will perform." Num. **23**:19.

This is the general statement. How does present-day evangelical theology meet this? Let us examine a few points in detail. Says the Jew: The promised Messiah was to bring universal peace, as it is written: In his (Messiah's) days shall the righteous flourish and abundance of peace so long as the moon endureth. Ps. **72**:7. Hezek. **34**:25. But your Jesus himself has said: "Think not I am come to bring peace: I came not to bring peace, but the sword." Matt. **10**:34.

Fifteen centuries of Christian history, during which the professed followers of Jesus have shed more Jewish blood alone than Titus and Epiphanes combined, accentuate the Jew's objection. All the answer he gets are pitiable attempts of Christian teachers, in the face of Jesus' own words, to make themselves and others believe that Christ's first coming meant not only peace for the believer's heart through faith in his blood, which it does, but also peace to the nations on earth, which it does not, and which only his second coming will secure.

Again, the Jew objects: Those prophecies, obviously and explicitly given to the Jewish people, the land of Israel and the city of Jerusalem, have not, since Jesus came, and died, been fulfilled. Very true, he is told, these prophecies have never yet found an historical fulfilment for your people, or your land and city: and, *take our word for it, they never will.* Your conceptions of God's promises are altogether too grossly sensual and carnal. They have been, and are even now being spiritually fulfilled in the church, which is spiritual Israel, Jerusalem and Zion.

And if the Jew should turn and ask: But what about the literal, historical fulfilment of all those awful judgments of God upon my people and land and holy city? Ah yes, he is told, that is all right; you are so awfully wicked; your ancestors have crucified our Lord; you must bear all those awful curses—and we appropriate all the blessings.

Let our brethren of the spiritualizing school of interpreting prophecy beware. The Jew is very blind spiritually, to be sure. But he is not very dull, intellectually. He is not slow to discover that the most effective way to dispose of the really unpleasant fact of the historical Christ is to borrow from these good and learned Christian teachers their patent invention of a spiritual interpretation of prophecy and to apply it—backwards. We can see him turn with fine scorn upon the would-be evangelical theologian: "Away, sir, with your too grossly carnal conception of the Eternal Jehovah, away with your low and degrading idea of a real, literal flesh and blood incarnation of the Deity in the womb of a Jewish girl. The true spiritual conception of the Messiah is the idea of humanity, exemplified in the suffering, yet eternal, Jewish race." Modern reformed Judaism has made the practical application of spiritualizing methods to Messianic prophecy backwards.

Do you marvel that the God-fearing and pious orthodox Jews should not take very kindly to that sort of Christian teaching which coldly denies to them the only thing which has made age-long and unspeakable suffering endurable to them, the hope of a coming glorious Deliverer?

3. The practice of the Gentile Christian church of our day, even where a genuine desire has been awakened by God's Spirit to reach out and go after the lost sheep of the house of Israel, has been in sad harmony with such pernicious teaching. We can only sketch a few of the salient points in connection with the principles applied in Jewish missions.

a. The Jew as an object of missionary activity is put on a level with the heathen. There is no recognition of the divine truth: this people shall not be reckoned among the nations. Much less of apostolic practice: to the Jew first. The Saviour's own words are forgotten: the bread for the children. Who are the children? It is as good as forgotten, that Christianity is the legitimate daughter of Biblical Judaism; that in all the essentials of a supernatural, revealed religion the orthodox Jew is our elder brother, not a heathen who imagines vain things and worships devils.

b. Again, no heathen is expected to renounce his nationality on accepting the gospel of Christ. Nobody finds it inconsistent to be an American, or a Chinaman, and a Christian also. But the Jew is expected forthwith, on becoming a Christian, to strip himself of all national feelings, hopes, aspirations or expectations. And the Jews are the only everlasting nation God's word knows.

c. The Jew is supposed to be so very blind, of course, that he does not see the glaring inconsistency of professing Christianity in all this; *e. g.*, the Jew has a way of reckoning his day that is as old as creation: And it was evening and it was morning, the first day, etc. The enlightened Gentile Christian who claims to regulate his whole life by God's word, begins his day in heathen midnight darkness, and of course ends there, too.

The Jew had an ordering of his year given him by Jehovah and to it he still adheres. The Gentile Christian expects his Jewish brother to forsake all this and to exchange it for the so-styled Christian calendar, in which the very names of months and week days are still fragrant with the memories of heathen abominations and the worship of demons.

The Jew is even now watching millions of Christians preparing to celebrate Christmas, their Saviour's birthday, in a more or less heathenish manner. Not one of these millions could tell him on what Scriptural authority they do this, for there is none, absolutely. But these same millions will lift up their hands in holy horror at the mere suggestion: might not a Christ-believing Jew continue to observe the divinely appointed feasts of his nation in perpetual remembrance of God's wonderful deliverances in the past, and in joyful anticipation of still more glorious things to come with the Coming One?

Is it any marvel, that observing, thinking Jews should come to the conclusion, which has often filled our hearts with unutterable sadness, as we heard them say: Your Jesus may be the Messiah of the Gentiles; but He cannot be the Messiah of our people. Gentile Christian teaching and practice have so completely unjewed the Jewish Messiah, that He is to His own people almost beyond recognition.

On the other hand, I know that I am only voicing the common experience of all true Scriptural chiliasts, when I say, that the loving and believing acceptance, with the heart, of that great central truth, the Lord's return from heaven to establish His glorious, theocratic kingdom on the earth, has for its legitimate fruit a loving recognition of poor Israel's paramount claim on us as "beloved for the Father's sake," and a deep and ever deepening interest in their welfare and future, second only to that in the future manifestation of the Son of David himself.

I would also bear witness, from personal observation and experience, that even to-day, in spite of the cruel denial, for centuries, to the Jewish nation as such, on the part of the Gentile church, of any hope in the second coming of King Messiah—the eager attention of earnest, God-fearing Jews can be gained and held by nothing more readily than by preaching to them, as Peter did by the Holy Ghost: Repent and be converted—for God will send back this same Jesus to usher in the seasons of refreshing and the times of restoration.

III.

Israel's future glory as a nation is assured at and by the return of Jesus, the Son and Heir of David, the King of the Jews, the desire of all nations.

All we desire to present in support of this proposition, is God's own word. If allowed to mean just what it says, it will overwhelm the careful reader and student with the abundance of grace and glory vouchsafed to poor, downtrodden Israel. The world has never yet witnessed anything like the demonstration of God's unbounded mercy in restoring, healing and sanctifying a whole nation, after most awful judgments, such as is most plainly and clearly foretold in God's sure word of prophecy.

Our list of prophetic passages is not exhaustive; but it is complete enough to remove the last lingering shadow of a doubt as to Israel's national future, in righteousness and peace and blessing, from the mind of any who have ears to hear, and who have learned to take God simply at His word.

1. *Israel is to be a nation forever.*

Jeremiah **31** : 35–37 :

"35. Thus saith the LORD, which giveth the sun for a light by day, *and* the ordinances of the moon and of the stars for a light by night, which divideth the sea when the waves thereof roar; The LORD of hosts is his name:

"36. If those ordinances depart from before me, saith the LORD, *then* the seed of Israel also shall cease from being a nation before me for ever.

"37. Thus saith the LORD; If heaven above can be measured, and the foundations of the earth searched out beneath, I will also cast off all the seed of Israel for all that they have done, saith the LORD."

Also, Isaiah **41** : 8, 14 ; **43** : 1, 4, 21 ; **44** : 21 ; **46** : 3, 4.

Jeremiah **33** : 23, 26 ; **46** : 27, 28.

Romans **11** : 1, 2, 29.

2. *The children of Israel are to be gathered from among all the nations of the earth, and to be re-established forever in their own city and in the promised land. The latter is to be restored to its former, and even greater, fruitfulness.*

Jeremiah **16** : 14–16 :

"14. Therefore, behold the days come, saith the LORD, that it shall no more be said, The LORD liveth that brought up the children of Israel out of the land of Egypt:

"15. But, the LORD liveth that brought up the children of Israel from the land of the north, and from all the lands whither he had driven them: and I will bring them again into their land that I gave unto their fathers.

"16. Behold, I will send for many fishers, saith the LORD, and they shall fish them; and after will I send for many hunters, and they shall hunt them from every mountain, and from every hill, and out of the holes of the rocks."

Jeremiah **31** : 10–12 :

"10. Hear the word of the LORD, O ye nations, and declare *it* in the isles afar off, and say, He that scattered Israel will gather him, and keep him, as a shepherd *doth* his flock.

"11. For the LORD hath redeemed Jacob, and ransomed him from the hand of *him that was* stronger than he.

"12. Therefore they shall come and sing in the height of Zion, and shall flow together to the goodness of the LORD, for wheat, and for wine, and for oil, and for the young of the flock and of the herd : and their soul shall be as a watered garden ; and they shall not sorrow any more at all."

Also, Isaiah **14** : 1, 3 ; **27** : 12, 13 ; **30** : 23, 26 ; **35** : 1–10 ; **43** : 5, 6 ; **44** : 26 ; **49** : 7–12, 22, 23 ; **51** : 11–16 ; **60** ; **61** : 4, 6 ; **62** : 4 ; **65** : 18–23.

Jeremiah **3** : 16, 18 ; **13** : 14, 15 ; **23** : 7, 8 ; **30** : 1, 3, 10, 11, 17, 19 ; **31** : 8, 23, 24, 27, 38, 40 ; **32** : 36–44 ; **33** : 10–13 ; **50** : 19.

Ezekiel **11** : 17 ; **20** : 33–44 ; **28** : 25, 26 ; **34** : 11–16, 22–31 ; **36** : 8–15, 22–24, 28–30, 33–35, 38 ; **37** : 1–14, 21, 22, 25 ; 47 : 13–23.

Hosea **1** : 10.

Joel **2** : 21–27 ; **3** : 1–7. 18, 20.

Amos **9** : 13, 15.

Micah **2** : 12.

Zephaniah **2** : 7.

Zechariah **1** : 14, 17 ; **2** : 4, 5, 12 ; **8** : 4–8, 11, 12 ; **9** : 16, 17 ; **12** : 6 ; **14** : 10, 11.

3. *The twelve tribes (two houses, Israel and Judah) are to be re-united into one kingdom, under a Davidic theocracy.*

Ezekiel **37** : 21–25 :

"21. And say unto them, Thus saith the Lord GOD ; Behold, I will take the children of Israel from among the heathen, whither they be gone, and will gather them on every side, and bring them into their own land :

"22. And I will make them one nation in the land upon the mountains of Israel ; and one king shall be king to them all : and they shall be no more two nations, neither shall they be divided into two kingdoms any more at all :

"23. Neither shall they defile themselves any more with their idols, nor with their detestable things, nor with any of their transgressions: but I will save them out of all their dwelling places, wherein they have sinned, and will cleanse them: so shall they be my people, and I will be their God.

"24. And David my servant *shall be* king over them; and they all shall have one shepherd: they shall also walk in my judgments, and observe my statutes, and do them.

"25. And they shall dwell in the land that I have given unto Jacob my servant, wherein your fathers have dwelt, and they shall dwell therein, *even* they, and their children, and their children's children for ever: and my servant David *shall be* their prince for ever."

Also, Isaiah **9** : 6, 7; **11** : 11–13.

Jeremiah **3** : 18; **23** : 5, 6; **30** : 7, 9; **31** : 1, 6; **33** : 14–26; **50** : 4, 5, 33.

Ezekiel **34** : 23, 24; **37** : 15–28; **47** : 13.

Hosea **1** : 11; **3** : 5.

Amos **9** : 11.

Micah **4** : 8; **5** : 2–5.

Zechariah **10** : 6–12; **12** : 7–10; **13** : 1.

Matthew **19** : 28.

Luke **1** : 32, 33.

Acts **15** : 16.

(Compare Psalm **72**; Acts **26** : 6, 7; James **1** : 1; Revelation **7** : 4; **21** : 12.

4. *The whole nation is to be redeemed, converted and cleansed.*

Jeremiah **33** : 6–9:

"6. Behold, I will bring it health and cure, and I will cure them, and will reveal unto them the abundance of peace and truth.

"7. And I will cause the captivity of Judah and the captivity of Israel to return, and will build them, as at the first.

"8. And I will cleanse them from all their iniquity, whereby they have sinned against me; and I will pardon all their iniquities, whereby they have sinned, and whereby they have transgressed against me.

"9. And it shall be to me a name of joy, a praise and an honor before all the nations of the earth, which shall hear all the good that I do unto them; and they shall fear and tremble for all the goodness and for all the prosperity that I procure unto it."

Romans **2** : 25–27 :

"25. For I would not, brethren, that ye should be ignorant of this mystery, lest ye should be wise in your own conceits, that blindness in part is happened to Israel, until the fulness of the Gentiles be come in.

"26. And so all Israel shall be saved: as it is written, There shall come out of Sion the Deliverer, and shall turn away ungodliness from Jacob:

"27. For this *is* my covenant unto them, when I shall take away their sins."

Also, Isaiah **1** : 25, 27 ; **4** : 3, 4 ; **29** : 22, 24 ; **30** : 18, 19 ; **32** : 14–17 ; **41** : 8–16 ; **43** : 25 ; **44** : 1–5, 22 ; **45** : 17 ; **46** : 12, 13 ; **52** : 1–6, 9, 10 ; **54** : 11–17 ; **60** : 18–22 ; **62.**

Jeremiah **31** : 31–34 ; **32** : 38–40 ; **50** : 20.

Ezekiel **11** : 18–20 ; **16** : 60–63 ; **36** : 21–38.

Hosea **2** : 14–23 ; **6** : 1–3 ; **14** : 4–9.

Joel **2** : 28–32 ; **3** : 21.

Obadiah **17** : 21

Micah **7** : 18–20.

Nahum **1** : 13, 15.

Zechariah **12** : 10 ; **13** : 1–5 ; **14** : 20, 21.

5. *They will then be a blessing to all the nations of the earth.*

Isaiah **27** : 6 :

"6. He shall cause them that come of Jacob to take root: Israel shall blossom and bud, and fill the face of the world with fruit."

Isaiah **52** : 9, 10 :

"9. Break forth into joy, sing together, ye waste places of Jerusalem : for the LORD hath comforted his people, he hath redeemed Jerusalem.

"10. The LORD hath made bare his holy arm in the eyes of all the nations ; and all the ends of the earth shall see the salvation of our God."

Isaiah **66** : 10–13 :

"10. Rejoice ye with Jerusalem, and be glad with her, all ye that love her : rejoice for joy with her, all ye that mourn for her :

"11. That ye may suck, and be satisfied with the breasts of her consolations ; that ye may milk out, and be delighted with the abundance of her glory.

"12. For thus saith the LORD, Behold, I will extend peace to her like a river, and the glory of the Gentiles like a flowing stream : then shall ye suck, ye shall be borne upon *her* sides, and be dandled upon *her* knees.

"13. As one whom his mother comforteth, so will I comfort you ; and ye shall be comforted in Jerusalem."

Also, Isaiah **2** : 2–5 ; **11** : 10 ; **14** : 7 ; **19** : 23, 25 ; **25** : 6, 9 ; **49** : 13–18 ; **60** ; **61** : 9–11 ; **62** : 2, 7.

Jeremiah **12** : 16, 17 ; **31** : 10 ; **33** : 9.

Ezekiel **36** : 36 ; **37** : 28.

Micah **4** : 5–7.

Zephaniah **3** : 19, 20.

Zechariah **2** : 11 ; **8** : 13, 20–23.

Romans **11** : 12, 15.

(Compare Psalm **67**.)

6. *The Lord Himself (Jehovah-Jesus) will be in the midst of His redeemed people.*

Joel 3 : 16, 17.

"16. The LORD also shall roar out of Zion, and utter his voice from Jerusalem ; and the heavens and the earth shall shake : but the LORD *will be* the hope of his people, and the strength of the children of Israel.

"17. So shall ye know that I *am* the LORD your God dwelling in Zion, my holy mountain : then shall Jerusalem be holy, and there shall no strangers pass through her any more."

Matthew **23** : 39 :

"39. For I say unto you, Ye shall not see me henceforth, till ye shall say, Blessed *is* he that cometh in the name of the Lord."

Also, Isaiah **12** : 2, 6 ; **24** : 23 ; **33** : 20–22 ; **35** : 4 ; **40** : 5, 9, 11 ; **60** : 19, 20.

Jeremiah **3** : 17.

Micah **4** : 7.

Zechariah **2** : 5, 10–13 ; **8** : 3 ; **9** : 9, 10 ; **13** : 6 ; : 3, 4.

THE SECOND COMING AND CHRISTIAN DOCTRINE.

By Prof. J. M. Stifler, D. D.,
Crozer Theological Seminary, Chester, Pa.

The weight of learned opinion in favor of the doctrine of the premillennial return of the Lord amounts well nigh to a *concensus*. With Delitzsch and Düsterdieck, DeWette and Bleek, Alford and Elliott, Bengel, Luthardt and John Wesley, and a score more equally eminent whose names can be cited, the doctrine cannot be said to be without scholarship on its side.

The coming of the Lord is the prominent, if not the central, doctrine of the Bible. From the day that God promised that the seed of the woman should bruise the serpent's head to the last word in the book—"even so, come, Lord Jesus"—the eyes of the faithful have been fixed on the future. The apostolic churches had this blessed hope before them; they looked for no converted world, no rest and no resurrection until the Lord's return. And they looked for that return along with the signs of it, immediately preceding, as the next thing to happen. Paul exhorts the Romans, "that knowing the time, that now it is high time to awake out of sleep, for now is our salvation nearer than when we believed; the night is far spent, the day is at hand: let us therefore cast off the works of darkness and let us put on the armor of light, let us walk honestly as in the day." (Rom. 13: 11–13.) He comforts them with the assurance that the very creation, now subject to bondage and groaning and travailing in pain, is awaiting their manifestation in the glory of the Lord, for the creation itself shall be delivered from the bondage of corruption into the glorious liberty of the children of God. The Romans were waiting for the Lord's return. To the Corinthians he writes: "Ye came behind in no gift, waiting for the coming of our Lord Jesus." (1: 7) To the Philippians he writes: "Our citizenship is in heaven, from whence also we look for a Saviour who shall change the body of our humiliation that it may be fashioned like unto His glorious body." (3:20, 21.) In writing to the Thessalonians, he gives their whole religious history, past, present and future in the verse: "How ye turned from God to idols," their past, "to serve the living and true God," their present, "and to wait for His Son from heaven," their hope for the future. Again he writes to them a second letter: "We ourselves glory in you in the churches of God for your patience and faith in all your persecutions and tribulations that ye endure; which is a manifest token of the righteous judgment of God, that ye may be counted worthy of the kingdom of God, for which ye also suffer: seeing it is a righteous thing with God to recompense tribulation to them that trouble you; and to you who are troubled rest with us, when the Lord Jesus shall be revealed from heaven with His mighty angels, in flaming fire taking vengeance on them that know not God, and that obey not the Gospel of our Lord Jesus Christ: who shall be punished with everlasting destruction from the presence of the Lord, and from the glory of His power; when He shall come to be glorified in His saints, and to be admired in all them that believe (because our testimony among you was believed) in that day." There are some who inconsiderately say that Paul wrote this letter to correct some mistakes into which he fell about the advent in his first letter. But in this second letter he says: "Remember ye not that when I was with you I was telling you these things?" The Thessalonians fell into error, Paul did not.

Peter tells his hearers to be "sober and hope to the end for the grace that is to be brought unto you at the revelation of Jesus Christ." (I. 1:13.) He had already given the contents of this awaited grace in saying that "we are begotten again unto a lively hope by the resurrection of Jesus Christ from the dead, begotten to an inheritance incorruptible and undefiled and that fadeth not away, reserved in heaven for you who are kept by the power of God through faith unto salvation ready to be revealed at the last time, wherein ye greatly rejoice." (I. 1:3–6.) The inheritance was kept for them and they were kept for the inheritance, and even in Peter's day it was "ready" to be revealed. Hence, he writes in his second epistle: "We according to his promise look for new heavens and a new earth wherein dwelleth righteousness. (II. 3: 13.) The epistle to the Hebrews, the epistles of John and Jude, show that those to whom they were directed lived in the expectation of the Lord's return. Of the Epistle to the Hebrews, Prof. Gilmore said in the Brooklyn Conference five years ago. "Of the 303 verses into which the epistle is divided, thirty-six, or nearly one verse in every eight, has reference to the coming of the Lord, or to events that are closely connected with his re-appearing." "The proportion of such verses in the entire New Testament is said to be one in every twenty-five."

And then, the apostolic church had that last book of the New Testament. And we have it, but unread. It is the most neglected book in the New Testament to-day. The opinion prevails that it cannot be understood. Why is it considered difficult and why is it not read? difficult, and yet it is a revelation, and neglected, although it promises a blessing on him who reads and on him who hears. Why difficult and why unread? Because post-millennialism rules in our churches, and post-millennialism never can explain that book. Its seals remain unbroken to him who will not accept the coming of the Lord as the next great event awaiting this world. But Dr. Luthardt, of Leipsic, in his book says of the interpretation of the revelation, "It is not as difficult as it appears at the first glance."[1] Now with this expectation of the Lord's return pervading and saturating the Bible; with this expectation filling the hearts of men to whom prophets and apostles wrote, how can any one rightly understand the book if he rejects this prominent doctrine? Delitzsch, a man as eminent for his piety and good works as for his colossal learning, has given his judgment on this point in language that is almost severe. He says: "No interpretation of prophecy, on sound principles, is any longer possible from the standpoint of anti-chiliasm, inasmuch as the anti-chiliasts twist the words in the mouths of the prophets, and through their perversion of Scripture shake the foundation of all doctrines, every one of which rests on the simple interpretation of the words of revelation."

Paul, and one of the greatest of his interpreters must go, unless they can find a bulwark in the pre-millennial doctrine. In many

[1] Das ist aber nicht so schwer als es fuer den ersten Anblick scheint.—*Die Lehre von den Letzten Dingen*, p. 174, 2d ed.

quarters they are already out. Said a brilliant and cultured young minister to me, on the sad morning that brought the news of Spurgeon's death, "He was a magnificent preacher, but what a pity that his theology was two hundred years behind the times." Spurgeon was nothing if he was not a Calvinist. In an authoritatively printed sermon by one of America's greatest preachers recently deceased, I find this sentiment: "Every human being, in very virtue of birth into the redeemed world, is a potential member of the Christian church. I cannot tell you, my dear friends, how strongly this view takes hold of me the longer I live. I cannot think, I will not think about the Christian church as though it were a selection out of humanity. In its idea, it is humanity." The most popular, the most widely read theological works to-day are those which emasculate the Pauline doctrines and declare that the Apostles misinterpreted Christ, and were themselves mistaken about the second coming. Dr. Horton, in a work recently republished in this country, kindly says: "Paul, rightly understood, is not in conflict with Jesus." But understood as Dr. Horton understands him and Jesus is no longer Jesus, and Paul is no longer Paul. He takes out the apostle's grace given spine and refills the cavity with a long, limp cotton string. And neither does Dr. Horton understand Jesus. The difference between the teaching of Jesus and the teaching of Paul is the difference between the fountain and the crystal stream that flows from it.

It would be absurd to say that the doctrine of an eternal hell, the doctrine of electing grace, the doctrine of justification only by the blood of Jesus—it would be absurd to say that these are going by the board because the post-millennial theory prevails. The thing to be said is that no pre-millennialist can refuse to hold the strong and distinctive doctrines of the Bible. He accepts its teaching of election. He cannot believe in salvation by character. He trembles at the fact that sinners are eternally consciously lost. Those who call themselves Adventists, and teach annihilation of the wicked—it reminds one of what Paul wrote to Timothy about those who desire to be teachers of the law, "they understand neither what they say nor whereof they affirm." A man who knows nothing but the doctrine of the second advent, does not know anything. A man who sees nothing in the Bible but the second advent and can preach and teach about nothing else—why, a rough fellow in the police court said that his business was that of a cabinet maker. The judge looked doubtful. "What part of the work do you do?" "The circular work." "And what is that?" "I turn the grindstone, your honor." This mechanic was not the crank, but he wasn't far from it. The ignorant advocacy of any doctrine is Satan's swiftest way to discredit it. The demons knew Jesus and tried to testify to his divinity, but he stopped their mouths.

Pre-millennialism is not so much a doctrine, it is not a scheme of the future; it is, first of all, an attitude toward Christ and toward His Word. From the man who proposes to tell me the character of the millennium, who can map out all the changing events at the time of the advent and thereafter—from such an one I can learn nothing. A man never knows so much about a thing as when he knows nothing about it.

Pre-millennialism is not a scheme. A man cannot be made a Pre-millennialist, or a Baptist, or a Presbyterian, or anything else by proof-texts. It is a habit of mind, a tendency, an attitude toward the whole book and toward Christ. It is that attitude which reads the Bible exegetically rather than doctrinally, that accepts its plain statements in a common-sense fashion. It was written in large part by men of culture, high culture—Moses, Daniel, Isaiah, Luke, Paul, John. If you assign the Epistle to the Hebrews to Paul, he and Luke wrote just about two-thirds of the New Testament. If Hebrews has some other author, the proportion is slightly less. Being written by men trained in thinking, it is exceeding plain. Being written to plain men to accomplish an end sought at that time, it was made plain, unless, like the Hebrews, men were in the wrong attitude toward Christ and His coming. It was the unlearned and the unstable which wrested some things hard to be understood in Paul to their own destruction. What was John after; what could he accomplish in writing to the seven churches of Asia if they understood his Revelation no better than men of to-day? They must have understood him, and we may if we will take their attitude, an attitude which the book from beginning to end asserts, "Behold, He cometh with clouds, and every eye shall see Him, and they also which pierced Him, and all kindreds of the earth shall wail because of Him. Even so. Amen." Here is an open, visible coming, that every eye may see. It is a coming before there is a converted earth or even one converted nation, for "all kindreds of the earth shall wail because of Him." Many of the difficulties of the Bible are not in it. They are brought to it by a wrong point of view.

The New Testament does not ask us to believe that this is the last dispensation, or even next to the last. It teaches rather that this is the dispensation of the rejection of Jesus and of His followers. He taught His disciples thus: "If they have called the Master of the house Beelzebub, how much more them of His household." He said: "If they have persecuted Me, they will persecute you also." And all down the centuries the course of the true church is clearly traced by its own blood-stains in the inhospitable earth. It is not the last dispensation. The Jew's fatal error was in thinking his was the last. May we be saved from a similar mistake! That which bounds this dispensation is the coming of the Lord. "This same Jesus shall so come again." And meanwhile His servants occupy their pounds waiting for His return. They are not waiting for a converted world, not waiting for the triumph of the Cross, as it is called, but looking for Him to usher in a better state of things, looking, "according to His promise, for new heavens and a new earth, wherein dwelleth righteousness."

That the world moral, the world spiritual and the world physical is to be redeemed from sin and Satan, and made more than Edenic in glory and splendor, is as certain as the promises of God that it shall be so, as certain as that Christ, who died to redeem the earth, cannot fail. That none of this happens in this age, in this dispensation, is as certain as it is that not one sentence and not one syllable in the New Testament promises it. Jesus said of this dispensation, "Wide is the gate and broad is the way that leadeth unto destruction, and many there be which go in thereat, because straight is the gate and narrow is the way that leadeth unto life, and few there be that find it." When was all this changed? When will it be changed? When will men lift up holy hands and say, O Lord, blessed be Thy name; the wide gate is closed and the grass is growing in the broad way, with no feet to tread it down? When will this come? When He comes who alone can alter His own word.

To the Thessalonians, mistakenly fearing lest they were already in the terrors of the day of the Lord, Paul writes that that day cannot come before the apostasy and the coming of the man of sin. "And now ye know what withholdeth that He might be revealed in his own time. For the mystery of iniquity doth already work, only he who now restraineth will restrain until he be taken out of the way. And then shall that lawless one be revealed, whom the Lord * * * shall destroy with the brightness of His coming." For two thousand years this iniquitous mystery has been smouldering because under restraint—under restraint only until the time for the lawless one's revelation shall come. How can there come in on top of this continually threatening danger any settled peace, any sure righteousness for the world? They might as well build a hotel on the crater of Vesuvius. The volcano is quiescent now, but its internal fires are only asleep, they have not died out. Society, government, the church and family have no promise of security in this age. The man of sin is coming, and after him the glory of the reign of the son of David on His own throne.

And that is the core of pre-millennialism, that this is not the final age, but only leading up to a better. James, in the Council at Jerusalem, gave the order of events. God is now "visiting the nations to take out of them a people for His name." "*After this*"—after the selection from the nations—God says, "I will return and rear up the tabernacle of David, that the residue of men may seek the Lord and *all* the Gentiles;" no longer an election. Now, what follows? Every doctrine of the New Testament and every line of the Bible falls into its right place.

Election! Why it is not only terrible but impossible on the post-millennial theory. No wonder that Paul who teaches it is tabooed, and the man who holds it to-day is said to be two hundred years behind the times, and that Calvin is classed with the enemies of the race. But there is election on every page. Jesus taught it with the clearness of the lightning flash. To condemn Paul is to condemn his Master. We may dispute about the ground of election, and yet the pre-millennialist has little trouble here—but dispute as we may, there it stands in the book so clear that simple candor cannot dispute it. "No man can come unto Me except the Father draw him." "As many as were ordained unto eternal life believed." "Chosen in Christ Jesus before the foundation of the world."

"Predestinated according to the purpose of Him who worketh all things after the counsel of His own will." Now how is any one to reconcile our age of election with a converted world? How can *election* ever take *all?* That is the post-millennarian's dilemma. If he holds to election, there is no converted world. If he claims that Christ must become King of kings and Lord of lords, then election must go. And it is going, and so the plain utterance of the New Testament is trampled under foot.

To the believer in the Lord's coming not at the end of all things, but at the end of this age to inaugurate another, all is plain. In the millenniums past, God elected, among the nations of the world, the least and most unpromising one, in order to keep alive the memory of his name until the time should come to spread the savor of that name among all peoples. Israel was an elect nation, and the rest were allowed to go their own way. We see, now, the wisdom of that. In a lost world, God's name could be preserved only by isolation, and by terrible discipline of that nation. It is so now. God has elected a spiritual nation from among all the people looking to that good time when He shall save the world. Judaism was not an end, but a magnificent means, that to it the Christ might come. New Testament election is not an end but a means toward the second coming. The Jews were a national election, an election of the flesh, that to them might come Christ after the flesh. Election to-day, election to life serves, that to it may come He who is the life. The first advent was to the Jews, by Jesus as a Jew. The second advent will be to the elect church endowed with resurrection life, an advent by Him who was raised from the dead.

Election loses its terror and its horror, when looked at as such a means to a glorious end. He who objects to it from this, which is the true point of view, must, to be consistent, object to God's plan to give the world a Saviour through the elect nation of the Jews.

And the doctrine of an endless hell—"the smoke of their torment ascending up for ever and ever!" It is not because men are wicked that this doctrine is secretly disbelieved in many pulpits to-day, and preached in none. But there it stands in the New Testament. And for this word "hell" Paul cannot be blamed. That dreadful syllable fell from no lips except the lips that prayed

"Father, forgive them; they know not what they do." Neither John, nor Paul, nor Luke, nor Peter—no one of the apostles ever used it, except James in one single instance, and that metaphoric. Jesus taught it. And now, if this is the long last age, stretching out, no one knows how long—men execute leases to-day for 999 years—what occurs? Just what has occurred, the wresting of the Scriptures, or with coarser minds, the assertion that God is a monster. But if this is not the last age, if there are scores and scores of millenniums before the race, if there are ages of ages in which all shall know the Lord from the least unto the greatest, then—why, then the proportion of the lost will be absolutely many, but relatively not one in ten million. "God sent not His Son into the world to condemn the world, but that the world through Him *might be saved*." (John 3:17.) What do these precious words of His own mean in such an age as this when "broad is the road that leads to destruction and many there be that go in thereat," in this age with four-fifths of the world in guilty heathenism? Has God's mission of the Son failed? Must we not say so if after well nigh two thousand years the world has not been brought to Christ? Has not the age proved its character—an age which began with rejecting Jesus and murdering His ministers, and will not hear them now. If this is to go on to the end, redemption is a failure and perdition leaves to heaven but the poor gleanings of earth's sad harvest. "Sent His own Son that the world through Him might be saved!" His work has not begun. We are "filling up that which is behind of the sufferings of Christ;" (Col. 1: 24,) the glory is to follow. There is every Scriptural reason for saying that, when His work is done, the relative number of the lost shall be so few that it can be triumphantly said, "The *world* was saved by Him."

Pre-millennialism by its comprehensive view conserves the whole providence of God for the salvation of the race. It conserves the whole Bible and makes it the simple, plain book that it is. Narrowness, narrowness is the bane of Bible study.

It was said to Joseph, hesitating to marry Mary, "She shall bring forth a son and thou shalt call His name Jesus, for he shall save his people from their sins." Here is the key to the mystery of godliness. What does this mean—"save His people from their sins?" The Old Testament begins with the first Adam, the

New Testament with the last Adam. They are counterparts. We understand one in understanding the other. The malign instincts of infidelity are right in always attacking the first pages of Genesis. The necessary counterpart of Christ's mission lies there. And if the outside is taken away the inside generally follows.

What was the fall? First, Adam tremblingly cries, "I heard thy voice in the garden, and I was afraid because I was naked, and I hid myself." Guilt, guilt, man afraid of his creator, and affrighted at the sound of his wooing voice. Secondly, "in the day thou eatest thereof thou shalt surely die." He that was made in God's incorruptible image was smitten with mortality, and humanity became a pilgrimage to the grave. Thirdly, "cursed is the ground for thy sake. Thorns also and thistles shall it bring forth unto thee. In the sweat of thy face shalt thou eat bread." Instead of earth henceforth being thy home, on which to rest, it shall be thy master to drive with lash and spur to painful daily toil. Fourthly, to the woman he said: "I will greatly multiply thy sorrow and thy conception; in sorrow shalt thou bring forth children and thy desire shall be to thy husband, and he shall rule over thee." The new woman can never change the judgment of God. But Christ will. And fifthly, to the serpent he said: "I will put enmity between thee and the woman, between thy seed and her seed; it shall bruise thy head and thou shalt bruise his heel." Five woes of sin, guilt, mortality, a groaning, thistle bearing earth, a sorrowing woman and a triumphant devil. The church has dropped, if ever it took up, four of these, and has confined itself to the first—"Thou shalt call His name Jesus, for He shall save His people" from the guilt of their sins. That's all. O, it is very blessed, very blessed to be saved from the guilt of sin, but Jesus saves from the whole terrible round of Satan's destructive work at the beginning. "Thou shalt call His name Jesus, for He shall save from the guilt of sin;" Jesus, for He shall save from the death of sin, "Christ, the first fruit of the resurrection, afterward they that are Christ's at His coming;" call Him Jesus, for He takes the curse from the ground, "and the meek shall inherit the earth;" Jesus, for He shall solve the woman question coming ever more and more to the front. Adam was not deceived, but the woman being deceived was in the transgression. "But she shall be saved through the child bearing if they continue in faith and love." After more than a quarter of a century I can vividly recollect how my dear old New Testament Professor wrestled with that Scripture one day in class, and gave it up. He was a post-millennialist. Fifth, "Thou shalt call His name Jesus," for He shall bruise the serpent's head, lay hold on the dragon, that old serpent who is the Devil and Satan, that deceived the nations, and bind him, and ultimately cast him into the pit, that he deceive the nations no more. Thou shalt call His name Jesus, for He shall save, save from all the fivefold ruin of the fall—"that the world might be saved through Him," not that a few elect ones out of a few favored nations might die in Jesus and go to heaven, but that the world in the fullest, simplest sense of the term, might be saved in Jesus, the last Adam.

Now what can post-millennialism say to this? It is clear on Jesus being Saviour from the guilt of sin. Thank God for that, for that is the great point after all. But there it stops, and darkens hope and loses two-thirds of the Bible, or explains it in a way that would not for a moment be tolerated in any other plain book. Death ! Why men will die right along, they say, until the end of time, and death will cease only with the ceasing of the race. How then does Jesus *save* the world from death ? And where is there a line to show that the race will ever cease to be on this planet? The last note of the blessed prophecy is that the nations shall walk in the light of the New Jerusalem, "and the kings of the earth do bring their glory and honor into it." Rev. 21 : 24.

As to the resurrection, it is so far off to the anti-chiliasts that hope of it is given up and men are said to be raised when they die! To look for a Saviour from heaven who shall change the body of our humiliation that it may be fashioned like unto the body of His glory, does not mean what it says, and the fifteenth of 1st Corinthians will not come into use for a thousand years, and it will be no use then for they will all have been raised from the dead, long before, when they died ! Since post-millennialism cannot well preserve the doctrine of the resurrection of the saints body, the error will react, and we shall have a clouding, it is to be feared, of the resurrection of Jesus' body.

As for Satan, the doctrine of a personal Devil, "the prince of the power of the air," "the God of this agé," (2 Cor. 14 : 4), "the spirit that now works in the children of disobedience," against whom we are so solemnly warned in many, many places in the New Testament; Satan, who occupies so large a place in the last book of the Bible, why, his name has become a mere jest, and is mostly used to give rhetorical emphasis, or pungency to an otherwise flat sentence. And yet he is a being of awful and malignant might, who holds the world in his clutch and who can never be expelled, which means the world can never have any happiness until Christ comes and binds him.

Now with this simple view that Christ *is a Saviour*, a Saviour from all earth's real and root ills, and that he is coming to save and plant salvation in the earth, in this view both the Old and the New Testament can be easily read. It is not only some hard nuts here and there that are cracked: "In the regeneration when the Son of man shall sit on the throne of his glory, ye also shall sit on twelve thrones." That's one. "What," says Paul, to the Corinthians, "know ye not that the saints shall judge the earth? The saints shall judge angels." That's another: "Hymenaes and Philetus I have delivered unto Satan," says Paul, "that they may learn not to blaspheme." That's a third. But it is not merely such isolated passages, and they are many, that are made plain by the pre-millennial point of view, but the whole book is illumined, its scope is seen, and everything falls into its right plane. Look at the beginning of Luke's Gospel. All is plain when we remember that the faithful Jew was looking for vastly more than a Saviour from the guilt of sin. This he had already. If that were all, David would never have prayed for him, for his description of the blessedness of the forgiven man is so clear that it becomes one of the texts of Paul's Epistle to the Romans. Hear old Zacharias, the father of John, as he speaks of the Saviour: "Blessed be the Lord God of Israel; for he hath visited and redeemed his people, and hath raised up an horn of salvation for us in the house of his servant David; as he spake by the mouth of his holy prophets, which have been since the world began: that we should be saved from our enemies, and from the hand of all that hate us; to perform the mercy promised to our fathers, and to remember his holy covenant; the oath which he sware to our father Abraham, that he would grant unto us, that we being delivered out of the hands of our enemies might serve him without fear, in holiness and righteousness before him, all the days of our life." Hear

Simeon, as he took the blessed babe in his arms: "A light to lighten the Gentiles and the glory of thy people Israel." Little light have the Gentiles in this age, and less glory has Israel. But it is coming.

Open Matthew. What is the first thing after Jesus enters his ministry? A triple contest with the Devil, in which the evil one offers then and there to give Him that for which He came—the nations of the earth, if he would worship Satan. What comes next, after the sermon on the mount, the principles of the kingdom? Why, two chapters of miracles, logically arranged, in which he heals the sick, stills the storm, cures a woman of a twelve years chronic complaint, raises the dead, and the series concludes with the casting out of a demon. He shows Himself the master of sickness, the Lord of nature, and the conqueror of death and the Devil. Do these miracles show no more than His almightiness? Yes, vastly more. They are generally used in apologetics to show that He was divine, and this they do, but if we use them for no more, much is lost. They show that He was just exactly answering to the Old Testament prediction of the fivefold Saviour. And so Isaiah is quoted in the midst of these miracles and is to be taken in a simply literal fashion: "Himself took our infirmities and bare our sicknesses." That he is a sacrificial, vicarious offering for sin is scarce even hinted at in the Gospels. You do not reach that until you reach Paul. Acts 20: 28 is the first instance. And so men set Paul against Jesus because they understand neither. They think Jesus ought to have been teaching blood atonement for the guilt of sin, as if this were the whole of his salvation. The gospels offer him in the other particulars of the glorious word. And so when we come to Matthew 12, and He is rejected, and His disciples are troubled that He does not set up the kingdom, He enters on a new course of instruction to them, privately. He pronounces seven parables logically arranged, the great one of which is the parable of the tares, showing to them that their enemies would not be overthrown in this age, that the wheat and the tares must grow together until harvest time, that the children of the kingdom and the children of the wicked one must exist side by side in the world until the end of the age, and then the latter would be overthrown, and the righteous shine forth like the sun in the kingdom of their Father.

It is impossible to interpret these or most of the parables in any simply natural way except on the pre-millennial theory. He offered himself as the Messiah of the Old Testament. He was rejected and then taught His followers that the Old Testament hope could not be realized till this age of rejection and election was at an end. The church was a new thing, occupying the long interval, a new thing of which the Old Testament never lisps. Over and over and over the New Testament declares this, and to read Old or New Testament it must be heeded.

For when one goes to the Old Testament, what does he find its few simple leading features? It glows with the promise of a Saviour. It exults in the blessings which he shall bring: "And there shall come forth a rod out of the stem of Jesse, and a branch shall grow out of his roots: and the spirit of the Lord shall rest upon him, the spirit of wisdom and understanding, the spirit of counsel and might, the spirit of knowledge and of the fear of the Lord; and shall make him of quick understanding in the fear of the Lord: and he shall not judge after the sight of his eyes, neither reprove after the hearing of his ears: but with righteousness shall he judge the poor, and reprove with equity for the meek of the earth: (the first coming) and he shall smite the earth with the rod of his mouth, and with the breath of his lips shall he slay the wicked (the second coming.) And righteousness shall be the girdle of his loins, and faithfulness the girdle of his reins. The wolf also shall dwell with the lamb, and the leopard shall lie down with the kid; and the calf and the young lion and the fatling together; and a little child shall lead them. And the cow and the bear shall feed, their young ones shall lie down together: and the lion shall eat straw like the ox. And the sucking child shall play on the hole of the asp, and the weaned child shall put his hand on the cockatrice den. They shall not hurt nor destroy in all my holy mountain: for the earth shall be full of the knowledge of the Lord, as the waters cover the sea. And in that day there shall be a root of Jesse, which shall stand for an ensign of the people; to it shall the Gentiles seek: and his rest shall be glorious." (the millennium) Isa. 11:1–10.

This is its uniform language, a regenerate earth, blossoming as the rose, the Jewish people always in the lead, the nations all walking in subordination, but in the fear of God, and sorrow and sighing having fled away. It knows absolutely nothing of an equality without distinctions, such as marks the church; it knows nothing of elect individuals; it knows nothing of heaven, dying and going to heaven for blessedness; it knows nothing of the saints' cross bearing; it does know of resurrection, but a resurrection to stand in one's lot on the earth in the latter day. Dan. 12.

Now to read the Old Testament into this new dispensation, and to try to identify its leading features in our age, is to confound confusion, is to make the Old Testament an enigma, instead of a plain simple book throwing clear light on the age still to come. It is worse; it is to leave it the prey of the destructive higher critic, who by referring it to this age can easily show its utter inappropriateness. But if this is the last age, if there is none beyond, then I for one give it up. The Old Testament is a riddle, and there is absolutely no rational interpretation of it.

And this is my first and great interest in pre-millennialism. I can read God's word by it. I can understand His blessed purposes for the world. I see his Fatherly heart yearning over a lost race, that was put on the earth to the praise of the glory of his grace, and to stay here. The future is not misty and unreal, but palpable and tangible, peopled with whole nations and cities of real men and women in the image of God. The Saviour is indescribably magnificent, the Wonderful, Counsellor, the Mighty God, the everlasting Father, Prince of Peace. Isa. 9 : 6. "This also cometh forth from the Lord of hosts which is wonderful in counsel and excellent in working." It was exactly in sight of this glorious view of the future that Paul cries : "O the depth of the riches, both of the wisdom and knowledge of God; how unsearchable are His judgments and His ways past finding out." Rom. 11 : 33. Pre-millennialism makes God great and His doctrines great. It converts a man into an exulting, praising optimist, and stimulates him to pray for the good time to come—"Thy Kingdom Come."

Who says we are hastening to the end? We may be near the end of the age. No matter. The sooner the less sorrow for the poor world that cannot be better but must grow more wretched while it rejects Jesus. But the end of all things? Near that? Never. We are not yet at the beginning. God has all eternity to work out the glory of His grace. We are not yet in the coming twilight.

For what says Peter about prophecy : "Whereunto ye do well to take heed as unto a light that shineth in a dark place until the day dawn, and the day star arise in your hearts." The night is dark but the light of His word shines clear to show the way. May we soon hail the rising of the blessed morning star that ushers in the everlasting day with the glorious sunshine.

THE PROPHETIC SIGNIFICANCE OF THE APOCALYPTIC RAINBOW.

By Bishop Wm. R. Nicholson, D. D.,
Pastor St. Paul's Reformed Episcopal Church, Philadelphia, Pa.

The feature of the revelation of which I am to speak is the prophetic significance of the apocalyptic rainbow. The passage for exposition is Revelation, fourth chapter and third verse: "And there was a rainbow round about the throne, in sight like unto an emerald."

A rainbow—a rainbow round about the throne—a rainbow in sight like unto an emerald. The rainbow of the apocalyptic vision. A rainbow, then, with a prophetic significance. God's message to us concerning the future; something He deems important for us to know.

First, let us get a good look at this rainbow. All rainbows are remarkable, but this one is the remarkable of remarkables. The usual rainbow is in nature; this rainbow is in vision. That is in our atmosphere; this is in heaven. That is a material phenomenon; this is an ideal phenomenon. That has its curve among the clouds; this is around the throne of God. That is a semi-circle; this is a circle. That is made up of the seven prismatic colors—violet, indigo, blue, green, yellow, orange, red—all blending in equal suffusion; this has one color dominating the others—green like an emerald.

In a word, this rainbow is a picture. But is it, therefore, a dream of the fancy? On the contrary, it is the word of God. He spread before the prophet the wonders of the apocalyptic sky. A picture, indeed, but a picture of God's making, and, seeing it is named a rainbow, is representative of the bow in nature, although, according as the occasion required, differing from it in certain circumstances, even as the throne in the same vision, though peculiar in its pictorial setting forth, represented the true throne of God. A picture, then, which, as reminding of the bow in nature, is predictive of what may be called a rainbow condition of things in the future.

And now, in the second place, having taken this look at it, we are prepared to listen to the message it brings us. The rainbow is God's appointed sign of His covenant with Noah. To the promises of that covenant the bow in the cloud is God's signature. This has been its significance for thousands of years, and shall be, as God has said, so long as the earth endureth. As often as we see it we are reminded that God is reminded of those His covenant engagements, namely, that nevermore shall the earth be overwhelmed by a deluge, that nevermore shall a calamity of any kind be so destructive to men and animals, that nevermore shall cease seedtime and harvest, winter and summer, cold and heat, day and night—nevermore to perpetual generations, so long as the world endureth. God has said it, every word of it. And so, whenever and wherever seen, whether it span the sublunary heavens or lay its beauteous arch in the heaven of God's presence, the rainbow has but one meaning: it is the office-bearer of the Noachian covenant, the Almighty's pledge of His earth-preserving care.

Now the bow in nature, with its meaning thus fixed, is yet affected in its impressiveness by its surroundings. If it overspread field and grove and hill and valley, it is beauty in the midst of beauty, a feature of a landscape scene; its very beauty shadowing forth the covenant promises of God's preserving care upon ground and growth and grain and harvest. Or if it bend its colors over a city, homes of men, busy streets, it is beauty amid human life; shining the promises into the seething mass of men's thoughts and feelings, picturing God's watchful interest in the course of human society, pledging His preserving care against an universal destruction of mankind, as from storms of rain, so, as is implied in His preserving the earth for the use of the human race, from storms of anarchy as well. At its every recurrence, the bow in nature speaks forth its covenant promises as they are accented by its local relations. What, then, were the relations of this apocalyptic bow?

It lay around the throne of God in heaven, and Him that sat on the throne, and the Lamb hidden in the throne. Meanwhile out of the throne came thunders and lightnings. And before the throne were glorified men, singing the song of perfected redemption to the Lamb who had been slain; the assembly of the Church of the First-born from among the dead, the redeemed gathered in their destined glory. Such was the scene. The presence there of the rainbow indicated that the promises of the Noachian Covenant were to be upheld and administered at the time referred to in the scene. The time referred to was indicated in the fact of the gathered Church in glory; which gathering shall have been effected, as we know from the Scriptures, just after the First Resurrection, and just as the Lord Jesus will be about to descend to the earth with his glorified Church following him. Wherefore we see that this rainbow is associated with the Second Coming of Christ. And lo, a storm is raging; the throne of God is uttering its thunders and shooting out its lightnings; for the Lord cometh to smite the earth for its wickednesses. But there shines the rainbow, curling its radiant green round the angry throne, and so making that very throne the guardian of those earth-blessing promises, while yet the throne is launching its bolts of destruction upon whatever is "proud and lofty, the cedars of Lebanon, the oaks of Bashan, the high towers, and the fenced walls." Such were the relations of this rainbow. It is beauty and mercy and preservation amid the "hailstones and coals of fire" of the Second Advent of the Lord from heaven.

That such is the right assignment of this rainbow is further shown in a subsequent vision, wherein the prophet saw the Lord Jesus "come down from heaven," with "a rainbow on his head," and cry "with a loud voice as when a lion roareth," with "seven thunders uttering their voices," and "set his right foot upon the sea and his left upon the earth," and "lifting up his hand to heaven, swear Delay shall be no longer." He had come to let fly his arrows of righteous vengeance. And yet he came not except as with a rainbow: "*the* rainbow" the prophet says; that is, the one he had seen in the earlier vision. Then it was around the throne of God; now it had been transferred to the head of the Son of man at his coming to the earth. Then it enwrapped the throne with the promises made to Noah, as with an adamantine chain of sweetness, and so held in check the Divine capabilities of righteous wrath ; now with the same promises it was shading and softening the wrath of the Lamb—that supernatural wrath, the *wrath* of a *lamb;* for he had come to wield the lightnings of the thunderous throne. Thus wearing its official dignity amid the terrors of the Lord's coming, it shed the sweet glories of its mercy as visibly as when the patriarch's eyes first greeted it as the sign of the Covenant.

Both these visions were but rehearsals of what, even in these days of ours, is yet future. This rainbow tells us, then, that beyond the Lord's return the earth shall continue to be, and shall go on revolving on its axis and pursuing its journey round the sun ; that day and night, twin children of the revolving earth, shall still by turns enliven and soothe the world, and seedtime and harvest, twin children of its annual orbit, still crown the year with fatness ; that therefore those witnessing the Lord's revelation from heaven shall not be the last generation of mankind, but waves of generations shall still flow on over the earth.

"Knowledge is pleasant to the soul." If this knowledge had been dug up out of some old Assyrian or Egyptian ruins, how the world would ring with the fame of it ; but it is not the less interesting for being in the word of God. And it is knowledge comforting ; for the rainbow round about the throne lightens the gloom and limits the storm.

Few things are worthier of our serious consideration, than that the closing chapters of this present dispensation are forewritten in fire and blood. Its final scenes will be the hour and power of darkness. On the one hand, the Harlot and the False Prophet and the Antichrist will have developed such wickedness as till then will never have been seen. On the other hand, the powers of the heavens shall be shaken, and the smitten earth reel like a drunkard : signs in the sun, the moon, and the stars, mountains and islands moving out of their places, the sea roaring, men's hearts failing them for fear, apostate men calling on rocks and mountains to fall and bury them from the wrath of the Lamb, the conflagration of Isaiah and Peter kindling over the world, the Son of man coming with the clouds of heaven, overwhelming the kingdoms of the world and giving them to the burning flame, taking vengeance upon them that know not God and obey not the gospel. Now to know that the world's civilization will issue in wickedness so flagitious, and pull down upon itself punishment so signal, concerns us much, since the effect should be to put us on our guard against the seductions of the present worldliness.

But see, there is a rainbow in the sky, suggestive of the shining of the sun and the retiring of the storm. The forces of the tempest are held in check. Terrific will be the punishment, yet not exterminating ; nothing to compare with the ruin of the deluge. Mankind shall not be so obliterated, nor the earth rendered unusable, nor the industries of society be abolished. "The Lord my God shall come," says Zechariah, "and his feet shall stand in that day upon the Mount of Olives.........but it shall come to pass that at evening time it shall be light;" which is to say, that the supernatural terrors of the Lord's descent having passed, after a day which he says shall be neither day nor night, upon the earth at rest again the stars shall twinkle down their light. And thenceforward, for the rainbow is in the sky, shall move on in regular steps the laws of nature and the interests of mankind; the clockwork of time running steadily, seed sprouting, harvests ripening, business humming, boys and girls playing in the streets, old men and women abounding, men laughing for joy. It is no fancy sketch. It is the rainbow's message. It is God's covenant with Noah. It is what prophecy plainly declares.

And now, thirdly, listen again to this message of the rainbow with special regard to the double emphasis under which it speaks.

Green like an emerald. No doubt, seeing it was a rainbow, all the colors of the prism were there, but the all-suffusing tone of the forefront was green. Why this difference from the ordinary bow? This emerald emphasis, what does it say to us?

When is it that a forest is most attractive? In its foliage of green. To a jaded eye what color is most restful? Green. Now the emerald splendor lay around Him who sat on tbe throne. It was that which was before the eye of God; the prevailing refreshing green. And did He not say to Noah, When I see the bow I will remember my covenant with thee and with all flesh for perpetual generations? Thus His ancient earth-blessing, man-loving promises were refreshing and delighting His infinite heart. It is only man's sins that call down the devastating judgments of the eternal throne. But when, as it were, His eye is weary in looking at men's sins, the preciousness of His covenant rests and delights Him. That emerald beauty in the vision was the sign of His immeasurable force of interest in taking care of the earth at the close of this dispensation.

And another truth is shining out from under this emerald emphasis—that in the operation of nature's laws after the Lord's return there shall be an improvement of the principle of life. In vegetative nature which is the leading life-color? A sere and yellow leaf and a green leaf, which is the living leaf?

In spring when the principle of vegetation is at work, and in summer when it reaches its maturity of expression, green are the hills and valleys; but in autumn when the principle is exhausted, and is subsiding into the sleep of winter, the foliage is not green, but brown or yellow or red. Green, then, is the life color. Now in the rainbow in the vision there was a great increase of the green, as compared with the ordinary bow. But the pledge of the ordinary bow is simply that there shall be continued the regular operation of nature's laws. Therefore the bow in the vision, by its predominance of green, indicated that, subsequently to the great day of wrath, the laws of nature shall operate in the power of a vastly improved principle of life; that the earth-blessing promises shall have a richer fulfilment than ever before. The emerald is the imagery of the perfection of working of the covenant with Noah.

We are not throwing the reins upon the neck of conjecture. Paul says the earth shall be delivered from her groan. What is her groan? Saith Joel, "The land mourneth, the corn is wasted, the new wine is dried up, the oil languisheth, the beasts of the field cry." Her thorns and thistles, her earthquakes, her volcanoes, her storms, the wildness of her winds, "the poisoned vegetation round peopled cities, the blazing prairie, the desolated forest, frustrated growth, and retarded progress." But she shall be delivered from her groan. "Thou renewest the face of the earth." The wastes disappear. "Deserts blossom as the rose." "The wilderness becomes a fruitful field, and the fruitful field is counted for a forest." "I will hear," saith the Lord, "I will hear the heavens, and they shall hear the earth, and the earth shall hear the corn and the wine and the oil, and they shall hear Jezreel." "The earth yieldeth her increase," as though she had never yielded it before. "The plowman overtaketh the reaper, and the treader of grapes him that soweth seed." "The light of the moon as the light of the sun, the light of the sun as the light of seven days." "The floods clap their hands, the hills are joyful together." Yea, the animals too, for God made his covenant with them as well: "the wolf dwelleth with the lamb, the leopard lieth down with the kid, the calf and the young lion and the fatling together, and a little child leadeth them, and the sucking child playeth on the hole of the asp." And man's life: "the inhabitant shall not say I am sick," "the youth a hundred years old," "for as the days of a tree shall be the days of my people, and my chosen shall long enjoy the work of their hands."

Transporting prospect! An improved principle of life! Competent is the covenant, for its green is not of an inferior sort, but of a precious stone—an emerald; a radiant green, resplendent, never flickering, unfading. Fitting token at once of the new life-power and of God's unbounded delight of good-will. And so the covenant huggeth God's throne of thunder with its emerald arms, to make all things glisten in the sheen of its green.

The other emphasis of the rainbow's message to us is its peculiar form. It lay *around* the throne. Not a semi-circle, but a circle. This difference from the ordinary bow—this circle-emphasis—what does it say?

In the vision, while God the Father was sitting on the throne, "in the midst of the throne stood a Lamb as it had been slain;" the Lamb that taketh away the sins of the world, the Lamb once slain but now standing, living again, the Risen Christ, the triumphant sacrifice for our sins. He was in the midst of the throne, and the rainbow circled the throne; thus was he, with the Father, the center of the rainbow's majestic sweep, as if the sparkling emerald had radiated from him. And now the symbolism discharges a sublimer function, as though the emerald were deepening its tint, and gleaming in a greener glow of glory. For it is not simply that the Almighty will speak, and the groaning earth shall cease to groan, but that he will thus speak, and thus effectuate what he speaks, because of the redemption in Christ Jesus. There had been no earth-preserving covenant, had there not been the soul-saving gospel covenant. For how should God minister to men the blessings of nature, if no provision be made for cancelling their guilt? The Better Covenant, therefore, is to the Noachian as cause to effect. On the other hand, how should such provision of mercy have room for action, if earth and man be not preserved? The Noachian, therefore, is to the Better Covenant as the bed of a river to the river. There had been no rainbow around the throne' had there not been the Lamb in the midst of the throne; and the Lamb being in the midst of it, the rainbow must needs be around it. It is by reason of the Christ that thus far along the ages creation has been sustained; the very laws of nature being no less than expressions of the fact that there is salvation in Christ for men. Day and night, seedtime and harvest, the industries of society, all are a chorus choir to the Lamb within the rainbow. Meantime, as saith Paul, "the earnest expectation of creation waiteth" for its deliverance from the curse. For man the sinner's sake the ground was cursed, the winds and waves were cursed, man's life was cursed, man's labor cursed, the earth cursed, and ever since the creation has been groaning and travailing in pain together, repressed and held back from the full burst of creative glory. That curse can be lifted only in Christ, and it will be lifted at the period of the apocalyptic rainbow; for, in the vision, the prophet heard all things on the earth, and under the earth, and in the sea, giving glory to the Lamb for their regenerated condition, at the very time the rainbow was reposing around the throne. The then brighter sun, the more abounding fruitfulness, and, in Edward Irving's phrase, "the richer dew than ever came from the eyelids of the morning," the reconciled animals too, and the ruddier vigor and more delicious bloom of human health, all that emerald splendor will have beamed from the power of redeeming blood at the center of the rainbow circle.

Wherefore the gospel salvation of mankind is as sure of eventual triumph, as of their continuance are the laws of nature. "As I have sworn," saith God, "that the waters of Noah shall no more go over the earth, so have I sworn that the covenant of my peace shall not be removed." That the will of God shall be done on earth as in heaven is as certain as that reaping follows plowing. Here the King in his beauty shall be. Here peace shall flow like rivers; here righteousness like waves of the sea. Here myriads of myriads of the human race sunning themselves in the brightness of the kingdom of heaven on earth.

And forasmuch as, in this rainbow vision, were assembled the Church of the first-born in their glory, so is it taught, as the Scriptures elsewhere teach, that they shall be here with their Lord and Saviour—our own departed in Christ, ourselves, if we are Christ's, all the risen saints; as much enjoying the new life of things, and earth's heavenly prosperity, as their brethren then as yet unglorified; visible to men in the flesh, regal in their appointments, bright with the jasper and the sardius of God's own Person, executives of God's will, with the six-winged swiftness now here and now there, and with eyes of intuition glancing before and behind. And here the angels; not as now merely secret ministering spirits, but visible and audible; for they also were in the vision, echoing in their own dialect, and with loud voice, the church's song of redemption.

Oh, what a world it will be. Shall you be there? Shall I? Are we Christ's?

Bow of Promise, the Emerald Bow!
Brothers, its saving truth do you know?
Throne-encircling,
Christ-enclosing,
God-refreshing,
Thunder-hushing,
Earth-preserving,
Man-consoling.

Amen!

THE RELATION OF THE HOPE TO HOLINESS.

REV. JAMES M. GRAY, Boston.

I have been asked to prepare a paper for this conference on the Relation of the Hope to Holiness. Of course the Hope referred to is that "blessed Hope and appearing of the glory of our Great God and Saviour Jesus Christ." What is the present and practical utility of this Hope? Why should it be proposed as a special theme of Biblical inquiry or emphasized as a working doctrine in the Christian pulpit? How does it affect the spiritual life of believers? What influence does it exercise in the production of right living and in the furtherance of the process of sanctification? My answer to this inquiry will be drawn first from the standpoint of experience and history, secondly from that of the Scriptures and thirdly, from that of the philosophy or the nature of the case.

Referring to the answer from experience and history, I recall the remark of a pastor of considerable experience who, in referring to worldly-minded church members, said in my hearing that he had never known a believer in the Lord's coming to be a frequenter of the *theatre*. I cannot say with what exactness he desired the remark to be understood, but it set me thinking nevertheless, and I began an examination of my own flock from that point of view. Of course it is not difficult to find illustrations of a principle like this when your heart is set on finding them, and the results of my examination will be taken with that allowance, and yet as far as recollection served me in the review of a pastorate of fifteen years, my testimony must entirely agree with the remark of the brother referred to. The members of my church on whose hearts the premillennial coming of Christ had really made any sensible impression, were those who were the separated ones from that whole system of worldliness of which theatre-going is only a single symptom. They were, for the most part, the working force of my church along spiritual lines, and the most intelligent Bible students. They manifested the greatest power in prayer, they were the most self-denying givers, they lived the most even and consistent lives, they were the most deeply interested in home and foreign missions, especially the latter, and more than others they opened their hearts to the reception of the deeper truths concerning the Holy Ghost with the spiritual results certain to follow in such a case. I would not press the results of this investigation beyond a certain point. I would not insinuate, for example, that all these graces were always absent from those who did not possess this Hope, neither would I aver that all who *professed* the Hope were examples of these graces, but speaking of the subject in general terms, my testimony is true.

From the examination of my flock I began that of my own life, and if I refer to its results it is not to exploit any peculiar experience or theory of personal holiness, as though I had something different from my brethren in that regard, but only as in the other case to bear testimony to facts. There are one or two things about myself that I know, and of which I am willing to speak to the glory of the Gospel of God's grace. I know that I am a different man to-day from what I was twenty-five years ago, prior to my conversion to Jesus Christ, and I attribute the change to that conversion; and I know I am a different *Christian* to-day from what I was say ten or twelve years ago, when the doctrine of our Lord's coming began to take hold of my spiritual consciousness, and I attribute the latter change to that fact. There are at least five things which (through the operation of the Holy Ghost) this hope has effected in my life, and as to the practical value and relation of them in the production of personal holiness you must judge—it has awakened a real love and enthusiasm for the study of every part of God's word; it has very sensibly quickened my zeal in Christian service, especially in the direction of foreign missions; it has delivered, or is delivering, my mind from the bondage of an overweening ambition for worldly success and the praise of men in my public ministry; it has developed, and is developing, an element of patience and quietness in the face of unjust treatment and attack to which previously I had been a stranger; and finally it has broken the bands of covetousness and set me free to give of my substance to the Lord. I could readily explain the philosophy of these changes as they stand related to the doctrine did I not fear to entirely overstep the limits of good taste and judgment in personal allusions.

But following the examination of my own life, I undertook that of the lives of others who were more conspicuous and abler exponents of this doctrine in our own time—Krummacher of Germany, the Bonars of Scotland, Spurgeon and Müeller of England, Andrew Murray of South Africa, J Hudson Taylor of the China Inland Mission, the late A. J. Gordon of Boston, of beloved memory at these conferences, and others of that class, with whom, of course, I do not compare or even associate myself, but who were men of special anointing, possessing extraordinary spiritual gifts, living exceptionally holy lives, conducting their churches or other Christian enterprises on spiritual lines, and generally looked up to by us all as leaders in the life of consecration to God's service. What made these men what they were, or are? Is it assuming to connect the peculiar spiritual experiences they enjoyed, or the spiritual fruits they produced, with their belief in the Coming of the Lord? No one who is familiar with their own utterances on this theme or who knew any of them personally, will affirm this. Time forbids my quoting their testimony on the question which, however, would be simply overwhelming.

But we have nobler and surer witness still in the inspired apostles and writers of the New Testament. It will appear later, for the benefit of those not already acquainted with the fact, how large a place in their spiritual horoscope was occupied with the hope of the speedy return to this earth of our blessed Lord. The language of Professor Hackett is none too strong when he affirms that it filled their circle of view, that it was the great consummation on which their strongest hopes were fixed, that they lived in expectation of it and labored to be prepared for it. But what kind of men, especially what kind of *Christians* did it make of Paul, and James, and Peter, and John and Jude? Let any reader of the New Testament answer this question for himself.

And finally, from the writers of the epistles of the New Testament we may turn to the churches to which those epistles were addressed. We know that they were not perfect churches, and admit that they had to be rebuked, but we know that they are the ideals constantly set before the churches of our own day. What gives them such a character? Not to anticipate the argument from Scripture, let us hear the testimony of the historian of the Decline and Fall of the Roman Empire. Edward Gibbon, it must be remembered, does not write as a friend of Christianity. In the language of Dean Milman, the best editor of his works, his imagination is dead to its moral dignity, and he seeks to keep it down by a general tone of jealous disparagement, or to neutralize it by a painfully elaborate exposition of its darker and degenerate periods. For this reason therefore, there is a peculiar value in his declaration that in the ancient church the influence of truth was very greatly strengthened by the universal belief that the kingdom of heaven was at hand and that it produced the most salutary effects on the faith and practice of the Christians. Without, therefore, proceeding further along the line of experience and history, enough has been hinted at least to indicate that there is a very close and practical relation between this blessed Hope and the personal holiness of one who embraces it.

Let us now turn our attention to the word of God. The argument from this source is the weightiest which can be presented, and has been treated in previous conferences of this character with far more completeness than present circumstances will permit. But the matter lies in my thought somewhat like this: What are the elements of holiness in the Christian, and what method do our Lord and His inspired apostles employ to produce them? In replying to the question I shall omit all reference to the book of Revelation, since many object to its use in such a manner on account of its highly wrought symbolism, and limit my attention in their order to the Gospels, the Pauline and then the Catholic epistles. To take a single illustration from the Gospels where at least twenty are offered to select from, let me inquire whether the crucifixion of self is an element of holiness in a Christian? If it will not be denied that it is, then let me call your attention to the fact that our Lord seeks to inculcate this grace in His disciples by the employment of the Hope of His second coming, saying: (Matt. 16: 25–27.) "Whosoever will save his life shall lose it; and whosoever will lose his life for My sake shall find it. * * * For the Son of man shall come in the glory of His Father with His angels; and then shall He reward every man according to his works." The context of these words is very important as adding to the significance of this application of them. Peter had just confessed Jesus to be the Messiah, the Son of the living God, and following that confession our Lord, for the first time, announced to His disciples His approaching sufferings and death at Jerusalem. They are astounded at the information. Peter especially is nonplussed. The disappointment is almost unbearable. There must be some mistake about it, and the impetuous disciple takes our Lord aside to expostulate with Him concerning it. Remember that Peter's solicitude is for himself—for what he shall lose, quite as much as it is for Jesus—for what he shall suffer. Like all the other disciples at this early period, his motives and desires are selfish and worldly to a great extent. If Jesus were Messiah then would He soon seize the reins of government and sit upon the throne of His father David. Who would be nearest to Him in His hour of triumph save those who had shared that place in His period of obscurity? Were these expectations to be destroyed? Were He not the One to redeem Israel? Had they left all to follow Him for naught? I know not which impresses me the more in Jesus' treatment of His disciples at this crisis in their history, the hope which He still holds out to them, or the tenderness and consideration with which He stoops to their human weakness in indicating the way in which it must be obtained.

He does not discourage them. He does not rebuke them for having such a hope. *He does not contradict their expectations*, and this especially is necessary to be emphasized. He does not say "your desires, and ambitions and anticipations are all sinful and radically wrong." He says rather "they will all come to pass, only somewhat later on in time, and by a different process to that which you contemplate." "If any man will come after Me, *let him deny himself, and take up his cross*, and follow Me. For whosoever will save his life shall lose it; and whosoever will lose his life for My sake shall find it. * * * * For the Son of man shall come in the glory of His father with His angels; *and then*, (not now, but then,) He shall reward every man according to his works." Could the relation of this Hope to the personal holiness of the believer be stated in clearer terms than these? Were not the disciples to have what they expected, and far more, indeed? And were not their expectations to be realized only when their

Lord should come again, not before, but certainly then? And were they not to enter upon a process of self-crucifixion in view of their attainment? Nor is this all. Some six days after this instruction our Lord takes Peter, James and John, and bringeth them up into an high mountain apart, and is transfigured before them. He condescends to give them a foretaste of the coming glory; He strengthens their conviction as to the truth of what He promised by a kind of first installment of its fulfilment; and so satisfied is even Peter, so refined and purified are, in consequence, the desires and ambitions of his heart already, that he is willing to remain upon Mt. Tabor, and forego anything he had in mind concerning Zion. Behold what the hope has done for him! It was the turning point in his whole career; it was the most impressive lesson, with a single exception, perhaps, that he ever learned in the whole of his earthly fellowship with Jesus. When the apostle is an old man, and in the near expectancy of putting off his tabernacle, would say his final word to those who had obtained like precious faith with him, it is to recall this scene, and say: "We have not followed cunningly devised fables, when we made known unto you *the power and coming of our Lord Jesus Christ*, but were eye witnesses of His Majesty. * * * * * When we were with Him in the holy mount."

If I have dwelt so long upon a single passage from the gospels it is not because there are not many others of a like character, as already intimated, but only in the hope that one illustration sought to be particularly impressed may have greater weight than a larger number cursorily referred to. Moreover, if the principle is established in this one case, it is as firmly rooted as though it were established by a hundred others.

And yet, for the sake of variety in the treatment of the topic, I will employ the opposite course in appealing to the testimony of Paul, and select several passages for briefer treatment instead of one to be dealt with more elaborately. Let us not lose sight of the point in view, viz: What are the elements of holiness in a Christian and by what means do our Lord and His inspired apostles seek to awaken them? For example, there can be no doubt that the subduing of the grosser fleshly appetites is such an element; but Paul, in writing to the Colossians, insists upon that duty in the light of the second coming, saying: "When Christ who is our life shall appear, then shall ye also appear with Him in glory; therefore mortify your members which are upon the earth, fornication, uncleanness, passion, evil desire, and covetousness which is idolatry (Col. 3 : 4, 5.) See also Titus 2 : 11–13. There can be no question that refrainment from hasty and uncharitable judgment is such an element, but Paul exhorts the Corinthians to "judge nothing before the time, until the Lord come, for He will bring to light the hidden things of darkness and make manifest the counsels of the hearts." (I. Cor. 4 : 5.) Gentleness and patience are certainly elements of holiness, but the Philippians are urged to cultivate them and let their "forbearance be known unto all men," because "the Lord is at hand." (Phil. 4 : 5.) Fidelity in Christian service is such an element, but that which spurred on the apostle in its exercise was the thought of the crown of righteousness which the Lord, the righteous judge, would give him at that day, and not to him only, "but also to all them that love His appearing." (II. Tim. 4 : 8.) It will not be questioned that brotherly love is such an element, and indeed Paul delares as much when he prays for the Thessalonians that they may increase and abound in love one toward another, to the end that God may establish their hearts unblamable in holiness before our God and Father at the coming of our Lord Jesus Christ with all His saints." (I. Thess. 3: 12, 13.) Here are only five epistles touched upon out of thirteen, and only a single reference from each of these, and yet in every instance a different Christian virtue is alluded to and its propagation insisted on and urged with reference to that one event, the coming of the Lord. This testimony from Paul might be multiplied many times were more required to show the relation of this Hope to holiness.

But let us examine very briefly the contents of the Catholic epistles. Peter, as might have been expected, is especially rich in his allusions to this blessed Hope. Indeed the Lord's coming is the keynote of both of his epistles, it is the pivot on which their interpretation turns, and singularly enough every allusion which he makes to that doctrine is intimately connected with and used to emphasize the duty of personal holiness. You recall the opening of the first epistle, where he blesses God and the Father of our Lord Jesus Christ, who "hath begotten us again unto a lively hope, * * * * * to an inheritance, incorruptible and undefiled, reserved in heaven for you who are kept by the power of God, through faith, unto the salvation ready to be revealed in the last time." But when is the last time? What is the period to which the apostle refers as that of this revelation? He himself explains it to be that of the appearing of Jesus Christ. It is at His coming and when His glory shall be revealed, so Peter represents it, that we are to receive the end, the consummation of our faith, that is, the full and complete "salvation of our souls." Nothing can be plainer than his teaching upon this point. But now, as based upon and growing out of this Hope, the "strangers" whom he addressed are exhorted not only to gird up the loins of their mind, be sober, and hope to the end for the grace thus to be brought to them at the revelation or appearing of Jesus Christ, but especially to be *holy*, as their Father in heaven is holy; to lay aside all malice, and all guile, and hypocrisies and evil speakings; to have their conversation honest among the Gentiles; and to submit themselves to every ordinance of man. Servants are besought on this account to be subject to their masters, and wives to their husbands. Husbands are called upon for the same reason to give honor to their wives, and all indeed to be compassionate one of another, loving, pitiful and courteous. A special appeal is made to ministers, the elders of the flock, to feed the same "not by constraint but willingly, not for filthy lucre but of a ready mind, not as lords over God's heritage but ensamples to the flock," that "*when the Chief Shepherd shall appear*" they may "receive a crown of glory that fadeth not away." The second epistle, the briefer, is of the same character as the first. There the subject of false teachers and their false teaching is treated of, but it is evident from the third chapter that the latter concerned the promise of the Lord's coming. Time was passing, and all things were continuing as they had been from the beginning, so that it appeared to some as if He would never come. But they are reminded of the scoffers in the days of Noah, and taught that God does not count time as men count it; and then with a final asseveration that He will come as a thief in the night, the apostle climaxes with an appeal most thoroughly in harmony with the proposition of this paper, saying, "What manner of persons ought ye to be in all holy conversation and godliness, looking for and earnestly desiring the coming of the day of God?"

The other Catholic epistles, those of James, Peter and Jude, are equally as plain if not as prolific in their teachings on this subject as those of Peter, but we must leave the argument from Scripture at this point, in order to refer very briefly to that from the philosophy or the nature of the case.

For example, we have now seen that as a matter of fact there *is* a close and practical relationship between this blessed Hope and the personal holiness of the one who truly entertains it. This has been shown from experience and history, and has been proved conclusively, I think, from the Holy Scriptures ; but it remains to ask, How do we account for it ? What is the reason of it ? For example, the apostle John says :—"Beloved, now are we the sons of God, and it doth not yet appear what we shall be ; but we know that when He shall appear, we shall be like Him, for we shall see Him as He is. *And every one that hath this Hope in Him purifieth himself even as He (Christ) is pure.*" (3 : 2, 3). The question is, Why does he do this ? It may be said that he does this because he is a son of God. Holiness is his already in the germ, and by a certain law of spiritual development it must continue to progress towards complete maturity. But this does not fully meet the case, since such a reason is just as applicable to other doctrines of the New Testament as that of our Lord's coming, and yet the latter, so particularly associated with the production of holiness, would seem to demand a particular reason to account for it. What if we say that such a reason is found in its tangibility and imminence? In its appeal to our senses, to something which we can readily understand, as well as to the possibility of its realization at any time? The hope of heaven, for example, is a blessed hope indeed, but it is vague and indefinite in comparison with this. It is difficult, if not altogether impossible for the average Christian to conceive of heaven—of its whereabouts or the manner of its life. In speaking of its felicity and reward the idea of rest occupies the foreground ; but rest is a negative blessing and lacks the impulse for overcoming sin and producing holiness which is found elsewhere. Moreover there are some Christians who, however we may disagree with them, believe that the Scriptures teach the unconsciousness of the soul after death and until the resurrection ; while among those who most strenuously oppose that opinion there are many again who cannot satisfy themselves that the believer at death goes immediately to be with Christ. And then, even if all these theories are set aside, as I believe they ought to be, it still remains that Christians die and go to heaven without their *bodies*, and there can be no complete felicity or reward until these are raised and glorified like unto Christ's glorious body. This last thought, indeed, seems absolutely necessary also to any firm conviction of the recognition and reunion of earthly friends in the world to come, which has so much to do with the happiness of its anticipation. But now compare with this common and popular hope of heaven that other Hope so constantly set before us in the New Testament as the stimulant as well as the comfort of the Christian—the Hope of our Lord's return. How much there is in its imagery to give form and substance to it. Think of His personal and visible appearing in the clouds, the raising of the bodies of the saints, the rapture of the church, the sitting upon thrones and judging, the regathering of Israel, the millennial glory upon the earth! How strongly calculated is all this to enkindle hope, to arouse ambition, and to aid in the formation of a correct estimate of the things of the present time in contrast with those that are to come; so that these lose their power to conform us to their mould as those increase in power in the opposite direction! And if it be said that, after all, this is only imagery and nothing more; if it be said that the teaching it represents is to be figuratively interpreted, it matters not. The argument of this paper is not affected by that hypothesis. It were easy to refute such an objection, but we are under no necessity so to do. This Hope may at the end prove to have been altogether fanciful and delusive, if such a conception be possible to one, and yet it remains true that it has been, and that it is, the greatest incentive to personal holiness, For this reason I recommend it to my brethren in the Christian ministry as a working doctrine of the pulpit, and to every disciple of Jesus Christ as a spiritual lever by which, through the operation of the Holy Ghost, he will be lifted to a higher plane of holiness, without which no man shall see the Lord.

NOTE.—Rev. Mr. Gray was not able to be present at the Conference, but has kindly furnished his paper for the printed reports.

"THE KINGDOM OF GOD."

PROF. J. M. STIFLER, D. D.
Of Crozer Theological Seminary, Chester, Pa.

The kingdom of heaven is spiritual in its origin,[1] in its constituency,[2] and in its aim.[3] The Bible therefore is our sole source of information concerning it. But it gives us no definition. It is for this reason that we are at sea, and that more than eighteen definitions have been found by a recent writer[4] in searching the commentaries for information.

The Bible knows of but one desirable kingdom, called for the most part kingdom of the heavens, kingdom of God, but also the kingdom of His dear Son, the kingdom, etc. We shall not stop to prove that these all refer to one and the same thing.[5] But beside the more than one hundred and forty passages in the New Testa-

1. John xviii : 36 ; II Tim. iv : 18.
2. John iii : 3.
3. Matt. xxi : 43 ; Rom. xiv : 17.
4. Professor E. F. Stroeter, Denver University, in *Truth*, Vol. XIX, Nos. 8, 9.
5. See Dr. James S. Candlish's *The Kingdom of God*. Appendix, Note K, pp. 371-375 ; also long note in Kuinoel's *Com. on Matt.*, Chap. iii : 2. *De formulis regnum caelorum et regnum Christi*. He gives many of the older authorities.

"We have to note then at the outset that he has two formulæ for his great idea—'the kingdom of heaven' and 'the kingdom of God.' These are used with a slight difference of meaning, and each is best understood through its antithesis. The kingdom of heaven stands opposed to the kingdoms of the earth, the great world empires that lived and ruled by the strength of their armies. The kingdom of God has as its opposite the kingdom of evil, or Satan, the great empire of anarchy and darkness creative of misery and death to man."—*Studies in the Life of Christ*, by *Rev. A. M. Fairbairn, D. D.* The difference between the two phrases must be very "slight" in view of Satan's claim in the temptation that he owned and controlled the kingdoms of this world, Luke iv : 5, 6, and in view of the fact that his malign power is manifest through them. Rev. xx : 3.

ment which name the Kingdom, there is a vast body of other Scripture bearing directly on the subject. Inspiration is concerned with little else than the kingdom. The Gospels open with the declaration that it is at hand. The Revelation shows its consummation.

1. The name itself indicates what the Kingdom is.[6] When God is called Father or Judge, or Christ is called the Good Shepherd, we learn the meaning of these words from the similar relations among men. The word Kingdom is significant.[1] Definition must begin with this word. A kingdom implies first of all and most of all a king. And Jesus declared Himself a King,[2] and He reigns.[3] It implies subjects, and Jesus taught in many places, and the Scriptures show who are without Christ, aliens from the commonwealth of Israel, and who are fellow-citizens with the saints.[4] A kingdom has a realm. It is not difficult to say what Christ's ought to be or what it will be—He is to be King of kings;[5] but what is it now? It can surely be said it is spiritual.[6] It is not terrestrial, and since his kingship is violently disputed, it is not universal. A kingdom must have some foundation on which to build, some power that secures to it immunity and existence. Christ's kingdom is built on the ransom price of His blood—redeemed * * * with the precious blood of Christ as of a lamb without blemish and without spot.[7] In the same hour in which He said, "I appoint unto you a kingdom as my Father hath appointed unto me,"[8] He also took the cup and said, "This cup is the new testament in my

---

6. "He who has penetrated its meaning knows what Christ came to do; he who has not done so has yet to know the Christ."—*Studies in Life of Christ. Fairbairn, p. 102.*

---

1. "The name (kingdom) is not a mere figure of speech, but the appropriate designation of a great reality."—*Candlish, p. 199.*

2. John xviii: 37.

3. I Cor. xv: 25.

4. Eph. ii: 12, 19.

5. I Tim. vi: 15.

6. "It is spiritual in the sense that it is the work of God's Spirit. * * * The progress of the kingdom is the constant product and manifestation of the ever-present and prevailing energy of the Holy Spirit."—*Prof. Harris in Bib. Sac., Vol. XXIX, p. 459.*

7. I Pet. i: 18, 19.

8. Luke xxii: 29.

blood which is shed for you."[9] The foundation of Christ's kingdom is not ethical, but sacrificial.

A kingdom must have a polity. It may be said in one word, the polity of the kingdom of heaven is righteousness.

But the earthly kingdom is but the type. Here the Jew made his mistake. He expected the Messiah to be but a larger, better David. A type is often the very opposite of its antitype. The convex of the baser metaled die gives its intent in the concave of the golden coin. So it is here. The earthly king is served. Heaven's king serves.[1] "I am among you as one that serves." He washed their feet with water; He washed them in His blood.[2] He gained headship by the very principle which He gave His disciples for the same purpose—by service.[3] In the earthly kingdom the subject gives to the king.[4] But God is not understood until He is known as a giver. He gave His Son :[5] how shall He not with Him freely give us all things?[6]

He gave the Holy Spirit.[1] "He gives to all men liberally and upbraids not."[2] "What hast thou that thou didst not receive?"[3] And the kingdom is a pure matter of gift.[4] The subjects do not win and maintain it for the sovereign. He wins it and gives it to them.[5] Everything essential to the kingdom is as purely a matter of gift as is the King Himself, and it is as unearthly as He is.

When it comes to the subjects of the kingdom, these are the antipodes of the earthly. The latter are natural men, born according to nature. The subjects of the kingdom are spiritual,[6]

---

9. Luke xxii : 20.

---

1. Luke xxii : 27.
2. John xiii : 8, 10; I Cor. vi : 11; Rev. i : 5.
3. Mark ix : 35.
4. I Sam. viii : 10–18.
5. John iii : 16.
6. Rom. viii : 32

---

1. Acts i : 4, 5.
2. James i : 5.
3. I Cor. iv : 7.
4. Luke xii : 32.
5. Luke xix : 11–27.
6. Rom. viii : 9.

and born from above.[7] In the earthly kingdom there is not necessarily any family tie between subject and sovereign. In the heavenly, every man is brother of his Lord, born to Him.[1]

As to the realm—this is necessarily variable. Ultimately, it embraces the whole world. One of the parables declares the field is the world.[2] This notion is given in various places, both in the Old Testament and in the New.[3] But the references are always to the kingdom in its triumph. The realm of the kingdom at any given time is variable, for it is subject to growth and so is larger in its scope at one time than at another. In the matter of realm the contrast to the earthly kingdom is not so apparent.

But when it comes to the foundation the antithesis is complete. In the kingdoms of this world the authority is gained for the king by the blood of the subject. In the kingdom of heaven the King gives His life for the subject. In the former, "the sheep dies for the shepherd." In the latter, "the shepherd dies for the sheep."[1] Every earthly kingdom is after all a misnomer. Whatever the name or form, the people rule. The governor bears sway only by consent of the governed. And rightly so. They redeem and preserve the kingdom by their own lives. And earth's most potent king was never anything more than the embodiment of the public will. In Christ's kingdom His will is supreme; and He is a real King because the kingdom is built on Him. He purchased it with His own blood, and it rests on Him. Its polity is love. "We love Him because He first loved us."[1]

As then darkness is the opposite of light and we know light by means of darkness; as the outside takes its shape and form from the obverse inside, so we learn what the heavenly kingdom is by its antithetic earthly type.

---

7. John iii : 5.

---

1. Rom. viii : 15–17.
2. Matt. xiii : 38.
3. Isa. ii : 4; Rev. xi : 15.

---

1. John x : 15.

---

1. I John iv : 19.

2. To some extent the Lord's Prayer shows what the kingdom is.[2] The phrase "Thy kingdom come" is explained by its appositive, "Thy will be done on earth as it is in heaven."[3] (a) Its existence and its certainty are unmistakably implied, for otherwise His disciples would not be appointed to pray for its advent.[1] (b) Its sphere is earth. It comes hither.[2] (c) It consists in a likeness in holiness of earth to heaven. "Thy will be done on earth *as* in heaven." The *as* refers both to the degree and the manner.[1] His will is not law, but love exhibited completely. To do God's will is to be like Him. The requirement of the law is nothing short of a holy man.[2] The answer to this prayer, the sigh of all ages, and who doubts that it will be answered, must bring paradise to earth. (d) The kingdom has its seasons. It was future when the prayer was given : it did come in the lifetime of the men who first uttered this prayer;[1] it is yet to come at a time unknown.[2] The advent of the Spirit may be a means to the kingdom, but it is not the kingdom."[3]

---

2. "The Lord's Prayer in Matt. has seven petitions, the first three relating to God, co-ordinate, co-equal: the last four relating to man joined by particles of sequence."—*The Gospel accord. to Matt., by H. G. Weston, page 77.*

3. "But how shall the coming of the Father's kingdom be brought about? Evidently by the doing of the Father's will perfectly." *Boardman Stud. in the Mount. Instruct., page 234.*

---

1. John xv : 16.

2. The prayer is not, Thy will be done *over* the earth, but on the earth. It is not *epi ten gen* but *epi tes ges.* The latter phrase alone is suited to its immediateness when first offered.

---

1. See *Witsius' Disser. on the Lord's Prayer. T. & T. Clark*, pp. 255–6. Witsius acutely distinguishes between the will of God and law—"free from the restraints of law which do not exist in heaven." *Ibid.*

2. Rom. viii : 4.

---

1. Mark ix : 1; Luke ix : 27.

2. Since God's will never has been done on earth, the kingdom is yet to come if the prayer is to be answered. After the resurrection, when the disciples inquired about its advent, the answer was, "It is not for you to know times or seasons which the Father has set within His own authority." Acts i : 7, on which *Baumgarten* tersely remarks : "For as Bengel observes no less briefly than forcibly, *res ipsa firma est : alias nullum ejus esset tempus.*" —*Baumgarten Acts, page 17, T. & T. Clark.*

3. In Acts i : 6–8, the advent of the Spirit and that of the kingdom are clearly distinguished, when Jesus told them that the *time* of the kingdom was not matter of their concern, but that they should receive the Spirit *not many days hence.*

The Lord's Prayer put in the mouth of His disciples shows the reality of the kingdom; its sphere which is earth; its character—it differs generically from all earthly kingdoms in being holy; its times; it is and it is to come.

3. The sermon on the mount gives light on the question, What is the kingdom? Here we have (a) the sevenfold characteristics of its constituents or members.[4] These are the poor in spirit, the mourners, the meek, the earnest after righteousness, the merciful, the heart-pure, and the peacemakers. (b) The joy with which the members of the kingdom must receive the persecution of the world because they are unlike it.[1] (c) The duties or responsibilities of the members of the kingdom toward the world. They are "salt." They are "light." These two terms can be misunderstood. Ten righteous men would have been salt sufficient to preserve Sodom.[1] Paul was once salt enough in the hour of shipwreck to save a company of criminals.[2] In Noah's day the salt was reduced to one family and the world was destroyed.[3] The salt of the kingdom saves by being in the world, rather than by effecting any change. The wheat saved the tares until the harvest. But tares did not become wheat.

As the light, it shines like a lamp at the street corner. It makes clear the danger in the path, but it does not change the path. The light shineth in the darkness and the darkness comprehended it not.[4] It is only of the members of the kingdom that it is said the darkness is passing away.[5] All others remain in darkness[1] with the light shining that they may see if they will.[2] (d) We have an exposition of the new righteousness in contrast with that of the law.[3] First of all is the general statement, that

---

4. Matt. v: 3–9.

---

1. Matt. v: 10–12.

---

1. Gen. xviii: 32.
2. Acts xxvii: 42, 43.
3. Gen. vii: 1.
4. John i: 5.
5. I John ii: 9. (R. V.)

---

1. I John ii: 11.
2. Acts xxvi: 18.
3. Matt. v: 17–48.

the new does not destroy but rather fulfils the old.[4] The teaching about murder,[5] adultery,[6] divorce,[7] oaths,[8] retaliation[9] and love[10] follows. These seven statements come logically after the seven beatitudes, culminating in the word love. They do not point to ethical acts, but to ethical essence, as is shown at the close, where He does not say "do" but "be," "be the children of your Father," "be ye therefore perfect, even as your Father which is in heaven is perfect." (e) After a general statement[11] about daily religious duties, three are specified; alms-giving,[1] prayer,[2] fasting.[3] That which is common to these three is such faith in God that His reward and His alone is sought in them.[4] Of the seven petitions of the model prayer, one is made conspicuous. The children of the kingdom must forgive others as the Father forgives them.[5] To forgive like God is possible only where there is a spirit like God's.

(f) Next, the aim of life in the kingdom, the true philosophy of living is presented.[6] Having looked just now at the religious activities of men of the kingdom, we note next the secular side of their life, its work[7] and its worry.[8] In work men are not to seek treasures below, but above; a doctrine enforced by weighty reasons. As to anxiety about food and raiment, it is utterly unworthy of the sons of the kingdom, because it is heathenish—

---

4. Matt. v: 17.
5. Matt. v: 21-26.
6. Matt. v: 27-30.
7. Matt. v: 31-32.
8. Matt. v: 33-37.
9. Matt. v: 38-42.
10. Matt. v: 43-48.

---

11. Matt. vi: 1.

---

1. Matt. vi: 2-4.
2. Matt. vi: 5-15.
3. Matt. vi: 16-18.
4. Matt. vi: 4, 6, 18.
5. Matt. vi: 14, 15.
6. Matt. vi: 19-34.
7. Matt. vi: 19-24.
8. Matt. vi: 25-34.

"after all these things do the Gentiles seek,"[1] and shows distrust of the Father's care. In secular matters the kingdom must be sought first, in which order everything necessary to life is promised.

(g) There follow the social relations, "our conduct toward other men."[2] This demands acute discernment and spiritual discrimination. If men judge not, it is because they see—rare gift of vision—that they are condemnable.[3] If they dispense their pearls wisely, it is because they know what a pearl is, and who are clean and who unclean.[1] And if prayer is next mentioned and enforced under this head,[1] what else can it mean, since the subject has already been comprehensively treated in the sermon,[2] except that this discernment can be gained in no other way—not by asking for discernment, but by asking in general, and learning by the Father's treatment of us, how we should treat others? In giving prayer here this connection, we make vital the conclusion to the whole that comes with a significant, deductive "therefore"—"therefore all things whatsoever ye would that men should do to you, do ye even so to them."[3] We can only learn how to "do" for men, in learning through a life of prayer how God does for us. The sociologist must be a man of prayer, whose experience is gained in God's dealings with him.

(h) Following this matter of discrimination, comes logically the care about entering the kingdom.[4] First there is to be care in

1. Matt. vi: 32.
2. *Alford Com. in loc.* Matt. vii: 12.
3. Matt. vii: 1–5; Phil. ii: 3; Rom. ii: 1.

1. Matt. vii: 6. Jesus exercises this power of discrimination again and again, as when he did not "commit Himself unto men," John ii: 24. when He was silent before Herod, Luke xxiii: 8–12, and Pilate, John xix: 9. and before the Sanhedrin, Matt. xxvi: 62. Paul shows it when he withheld the holy "meat" from the "carnal" Corinthians, I Cor. iii: 1, 2, and gave them instead milk. The author of the epistle to the Hebrews has this discrimination in view when he speaks of those who, by reason of use, have their senses exercised to discern both good and evil. The connection shows that this is radically different from mere discrimination between right and wrong morally.

1. Matt. vii: 7–12.
2. Matt. vi: 5–15.
3. Matt. vii: 12.
4. Matt. vii: 13–20.

reference to the entrance, whose narrowness limits the sons of the kingdom to a "few"[5] in number;[6] and false guides are to be discerned and shunned.[7] The false prophet's fruits are seen in his followers, not in their number, but in their character.

(i) The next point is the radical one.[8] No mere profession and no abundance and greatness of work will give a man a title to the kingdom. The excluding sentence, "I never knew you,"[9] shows that the members of the kingdom are only those whom He knows.[1] When speaking of the kingdom under the figure of a sheepfold, He said, "I know my sheep and am known of mine."[2]

(k) The last thing in the sermon is the test, which becomes also an exhortation.[3] "He that heareth these sayings of mine and doeth them." "To do," here means to produce or exhibit. For how could a man "do" most of the beatitudes? How could one "do" the discrimination required in the matter of false prophets? It is the same word which is used of a tree "bringing forth" good fruit.[4]

---

5. On the ground of His own experience of the reception of the Gospel on the part of men, He was certainly aware that it would always be comparatively few, only the minority, who would take the way to life (Matt. vii : 13f.; cf. Mark iv: 2-9); and He plainly foresaw that His disciples, like Himself, would always be hated and persecuted for the sake of the Gospel (Matt. x : 24 f.; cf. Mark xiii : 13). But yet His trust in a further increase of the kingdom of God, surprisingly great in relation to its very small beginning, was not precluded by this knowledge. *Wendt's Teach. of Jesus, Vol. II, p. 346.*

6. Matt. vii : 13-14.

7. Matt. vii : 15-20.

8. Matt. vii: 21-23.

9. Matt. vii : 23.

---

1. Christ's sentence that He does not know these persons means much more than a denial of acquaintance. He was well acquainted with them, for He speaks to them as "ye that work iniquity." The word know implies fellowship. What one knows he has made his own. To know "frequently implies a personal relation between the person knowing and the object known." "Christ here denies that the basis of union, and so the union itself, exists." See *Cremer's Biblico-Theol. Lex., pp. 154, 155.*

2. John x : 14.

3. Matt. vii : 24-27.

4. Matt. iii : 10.

The righteousness of the sermon on the mount is radically different from the most exalted natural goodness. It implies a character that no man has naturally. It demands exercises that are impossible to the flesh. It asks for faith in God and union with Christ, and teaches that on account of the unearthly holiness required only "a few" find the kingdom.[5]

4. In seeking a definite notion of the kingdom of God, it is found to be different from God's universal kingdom, or kingdom of nature. "The Lord hath prepared His throne in the heavens, and His kingdom ruleth over all."[6] Nebuchadnezzar recognized this when he said, "His kingdom is from generation to generation."[7] In this kingdom God is also Father—"fatherhood is itself kinghood;"[1] and in a sense, too, which means more than creator.[2] But He is not such a father as He is to those in Christ's kingdom.[3] Abraham was the father of both the older Ishmael and the younger Isaac. The mothers differed. And Paul makes a point of this in defining the spiritual sons. "So, then, brethren, we are not children of the bond woman but of the free."[4] The children of the natural kingdom come into it by natural means. The sons of the kingdom are the product of grace, born again, and having such a character as is described in the sermon on the mount.

---

5. "He had first to impress upon them those spiritual relations between God and men which He now perceived as the essential foundation of the kingdom of God. He had also to produce in them the conviction that where this relation had come to exist, there the kingdom of God was realized. He could then mature in their minds the self-evident truth that He was the Messiah, the perfect founder of the kingdom of God, and that in union with Him men must become genuine citizens of this kingdom."—*Wendt's Teach. of Jesus. Vol. I, p. 181. Chas. Scribner's Sons.*

6. Ps. ciii : 19.

7. Daniel iv : 34, 35.

---

1. *Boardman's Mount. Inst., p. 233.*

2. Acts xvii; 28, 29.

3. Rom. viii: 15, 16.

4. Gal. iv: 22-31.

The New Testament kingdom is to be distinguished from the Old. The two are intimately related and yet different. The Old was more than a type and more than a civil theocracy. It differed principally in that the cohesive power and motive were outward[5] rather than inward. It was temporary.[6]

The kingdom is to be distinguished from civilization.[7] Civilization is a natural product of intelligence. It existed before Christ. It may or it may not influence the progress of the kingdom. The kingdom may or it may not affect civilization. The kingdom can flourish in Africa or in India, as well as in England, Germany or America.[8] There is a Christian civilization, but strictly speaking, the phrase is a contradiction of terms. Says Prof. Harris, "Christianity is not necessary to create civilization. If preached to a barbarous people, it finds the capacity of civilization and develops it; but other agencies without Christianity might have developed it. Usually some form of civilization has existed before Christianity is brought to a people."[1] Civilization inheres in the state to which the principles of the kingdom cannot possibly be applied. It is made up of unregenerate men that hate the king with his sons,[2] and that cannot obey the principles of the kingdom.[3] Jesus did not teach and live and die to make men good and righteous, in the worldly sense of the term.[4] His ministry and career

5. Heb. viii: 6–13.

6. The kingdom of God (N. T.) is distinguished not only from the *universal* kingdom, or kingdom of *nature*, which is always the same; but from the *special* kingdom of God, as it existed under the Old Testament. At that time it was a *civil* kingdom, accommodated to the character of a single nation—a *ceremonial* kingdom, abounding in figurative representations and a spiritual kingdom, though "in bondage under the elements of the world." (Gal. iv: 3.) But now it has nothing human—no rulers or elders who might seem to share with the heavenly King in the government of the church—nothing worldly—no *worldly sanctuary*. It is in every respect the kingdom of God and the kingdom of the heavens.—*Witsius' Sacred Dissertations on the Lord's Prayer, p. 219.*

7. Civilization is not a product of Christianity, but has an independent existence.—*Prof. Harris, Bib. Sac. Vol. XXIX, p. 602.*

8. Matt. xi: 20–24.

1 Bib. Sac., XXIX, p. 603.

2. Matt. x: 16–18; John xv: 18, 19.

3. Rom. viii: 7.

4. Gal. v: 22–25. Natural goodness in a high degree existed before Christ came. The goodness, in a word, the *love* of the kingdom is born of the Spirit.

did not change the current of the Jewish state one iota. The same was true in the Roman world after His day. What Rome was at the beginning of the first century it was at the beginning of the third, only now, so many had become sons of the kingdom that the state changed its religion without apparently growing much better, while the church grew worse.[1] Jesus came for just one definite, clear object—"to save His people from their sins."[2] And He saves them only as they come into the kingdom, not one soul outside of it. The kingdom and the state are both God's creatures.[3] But they radically differ. The one is natural, the other spiritual. But the kingdom can embrace every natural tie and every real human relation existing in the state.

Again, to know what the kingdom is, we must know its opposite, Satan's kingdom in the world.[1] To say that Christ is now the king of nations, the king of trade, the king of the social fabric, is to confound the world and His kingdom. It is worse; it puts darkness for light.[1] Jesus taught that Satan is prince of this world.[2] Paul calls him the God of this world[3] who has blinded every unbeliever. He describes his own work comprehensively as that of turning men from the power of Satan to God.[4] He declares that the "course" of the world is guided by Satan[5]

---

1. The vigor of its life departed as persecutions ceased, and when Christianity began to sway the civil power, this was regarded as the victory the Millennium had promised. The middle age perpetuated this great error.—*Semisch, Herzog, Real-Ency. I, 659.*
2. Matt. i: 21 ; John x : 10.
3. Rom. xiii : 1–7.

---

1. The kingdom of darkness is always in antagonism to the kingdom of light. It is founded and perpetuated in selfishness. *Prof. Harris, Bib. Sac. Vol. XXIX, p. 471.*

---

1. There is a marked difference between the position of Satan in this Gospel (Matt.) and that which he holds in Luke and John. Here he is the official head of a kingdom in conflict with the kingdom of Christ; there his individual dealings with individuals are essential elements in the history (Luke xxii : 3, 31; xiii : 16; John xiii : 27).—*The Gos. accord. to Matt. by Henry G. Weston, p. 39.*
2. John xiv : 30.
3. II Cor. iv : 4.
4. Acts xxvi : 18.
5. Eph. ii : 2.

and John asserts that it "lies in him."[6] Jesus came to destroy Satan.[7] Jesus described him as the world's "strong man,"[8] holding it in his grasp. Jesus declared that all who were not with Him were on Satan's side.[9] The New Testament opens with Satan's offer of the world's kingdoms to Jesus;[10] it closes only when he is stripped of his power over them.[11] The ugliest fact in the world is the devil. He is its most powerful factor for evil. All others would be nothing but for him. To be saved is to get out of the world,[12] it is to be translated out of his dominion of darkness into the kingdom of God's dear Son.[13] And to be excluded from the kingdom is to be remanded to Satan's power.[14] The trouble with the world is not that it is bad and needs to be made better. It is in chains to Satan, and needs to be delivered.[15] The kingdom is the beacon light on the shore, shining over the dark sweeping flood, but not changing it, only showing the shipwrecked sailor how to escape and get to land.

Again, the kingdom, in so far as its religion is concerned, differs radically from all the great world religions in that it is not a religion at all. It is a life. It has no place in the World's Parliament of Religions. Religion means law, and the sons of the kingdom are not under law.[1] Its products are fruits[2] which are impossible without life. Christ's words are not legal; they are life.[3] He cares much for morals and benevolent deeds, but since the kingdom's benevolence is fruit and not acts[4] He cares for something else vastly more—vital union with Himself. He made heal-

---

6. I John v : 19, R. V.
7. Heb. ii : 14.
8. Mark iii : 27.
9. Matt. xii : 30.
10. Luke iv : 5, 6.
11. Rev. xx : 8, 10.
12. Gal. i : 4.
13. Col. i : 13.
14. I Cor. v : 5; I Tim. i : 20.
15. Luke iv : 18.

---

1. Rom. vi : 14; viii : 2.
2. John xv : 16; Rom. vii : 4–6.
3. John vi : 63.
4. "Where righteousness is real, the kingdom is realized." *Fairbairn, p. 106.*

ing secondary.[5] He taught: "This is the work of God, that ye believe on Him whom He hath sent."[6] In His scale of morals the bad man who came to Him was good, the good man who came not was bad.[7] The noble Nicodemus is condemned;[8] the sinful woman at Simon's feast is justified.[9] Hence to make Him known was His followers' first work. Peter would not abandon His testimony even to feed hungry widows.[10] The preaching of the Gospel is the highest benevolence. And to win men for the kingdom is the highest honor.[11]

5. No definition can compass the kingdom. It has often been attempted.[12] For the present it embraces a limited number of elect[13] persons, united together only as they are vitally connected in Christ. The union is brought about and maintained by a belief of God's word under the power of the Holy Spirit. The members of the kingdom are members of the church, but the church as it exists to-day and as it has existed since the hour Paul wept over its many false members,[1] does not belong to the kingdom. The church is a credal organization; the kingdom is a vital unity having no head but Christ[2] and no bond but the

---

5. Luke iv: 43; Mark iii: 9; John iv: 48. The four men who let the paralytic down through the roof to be healed found that Jesus gave him first what he needed most—"Son, thy sins be forgiven thee" (Mark ii: 1-11). He ordained the twelve (*a*) that they might be *with Him*; (*b*) that He might send them forth to preach; (*c*) to have power to heal sickness, etc. (Mark iii: 14, 15.)

6. John vi: 29.

7. Matt. xxii: 10.

8. John iii: 18.

9. Luke vii: 37; Matt. xxi: 31.

10. Acts vi: 2, 4.

11. Dan. xii: 3; I Thess. ii: 19, 20; Eph. iii: 8.

12. The following may be taken as a basis at least of the exposition of the idea: "The gathering together of men, under God's eternal law of righteous love by the vital power of His redeeming love in Jesus Christ brought to bear upon them through His Holy Spirit."—*The King. of God, by J. A. Candlish (Cunningham Lec.) p. 197.* This author gives also (pp. 392-396, Note 2) a number of definitions by others, among the rest, that by Prof. Harris, several times quoted in this paper.

13. Matt. xxii: 14.

---

1. Phil. iii: 18, 19.

2. Eph. i: 22, 23.

Spirit.[3] As to this world, it is in it, but not of it.[4] Its presence necessarily makes the world better and brighter, like a lamp in a cellar, but its business is not to reform the world, but next to worshiping God its chief aim is to persuade men to come into the kingdom.[5] The promises to its sons for the present time accord exactly with the treatment given its head. He was called Beelzebub; so shall they be;[6] if they have persecuted me, they will persecute you also.[7] The world "hates" the sons of the kingdom.[8] On this account there can be no hope in this era of vital, lasting reform.[9]

The Scriptures declare that Satan and the mystery of iniquity will persevere to the very end.[10] Says Hoffman: "The church may succeed in making a worldly caricature of the kingdom, but let us never allow ourselves to dream that by thus forming herself according to her model in the midst of the world, the secret and continuing increase of the world kingdom and power, with its fatal influence, is interrupted."[1] Says Auberlen: "Let us guard against the notion that it is either possible or destined that Christianity will Christianize, in any real spiritual sense, the world in this

---

3. Eph. iv: 3.
4. John xvii: 15, 16.
5. Matt. xxviii: 19.
6. Matt. x: 25.
7. John xv: 20.
8. John xv: 19.
9. "The view that Christianity will expand in this age to a world-religion and bring the golden time as the product of its historical development is *fundamentally false* and opposed to the word of God. It rests upon a false ground—the identification of the inner life of the church with her outward extension. Its consequences are the struggle after secular power, *national* churches, *national* creeds, *national* confessions, *national* patronage, *national* legislation, *propagandism*, and passion for *union*, fatal to the true life and mission of the church. We need only remember Constantine's time and the nominal conversion of the masses, mere *name Christians*. The hope of a Christian state ending in a Millennium is deceiving. According to the word of God, the outcome of the development of the Christian church in this age is a great apostasy, through which Christianity itself is forced back into the Great Tribulation."—*Kliefoth. Christliche Eschatologie, 196, 197.*
10. II Thess. ii: 4-10.

---

1. Weisagg. un Erfull. II, 295.

present age."[2] Yet a work remains for the sons of the kingdom, a work that would bring joy to an angel's heart,[3] when by the use of all means[4] they may save some.[5] It is greater to save one passenger than to save the ship.

6. The true notion of this kingdom of heaven must harmonize every statement about it in the Scriptures.[6] In the New Testament there are more than one hundred and forty of these. It is said to be "at hand."[7] Directions are given how to "enter"[1] it; many parables tell, as in a picture, what it is

---

2. *Auberlen's* Daniel, 288.

3. Luke xv : 10.

4. I Cor. ix : 22.

5. "The divine action in redemption is directed primarily upon individuals, and not upon organizations and institutions. It is not a diffused daylight, an all-pervading electricity, acting equally and indefinitely on society as such, through institutions, public sentiment, and the spirit of the age, and lifting society in mass to a higher level. Its aim is not primarily the promotion of general culture, and refinement, and the advancement of civilization. It is the direct action of God on individuals to bring them into reconciliation with Himself. Redemption aims to save souls. It is becoming fashionable in some circles to ridicule this phrase. A writer in a leading Review has even said that the idea of missions 'to save souls' is becoming obsolete. The phrase, like any other, may degenerate into cant. But rightly understood, it is the doctrine of Christianity, that redeeming grace is acting in human history to save souls. Christ came 'to save the lost.' The faithful saying, and worthy of all acceptation, is that Christ came 'to save sinners.' They who are offended at this are offended at Christianity itself." —*Prof. Harris in Bib. Sac., Vol. XXIX, pg. 117.*

6. "In its fullness it is past, it is present, it is to come; it is inward and spiritual, existing now; it is outward and visible, yet to exist; it is heavenly; it is a kingdom of grace; it is a kingdom of glory; it is earthly; it is temporal; it is everlasting. In its *forms* it is many, in its *essence* it is one. It has various dispensations. It is above, it is below, and its highest consummation is the realization of the Will of God on earth as it now is realized in heaven, a consummation begun now, developed in the age to come, and completed in the Eternal State." *John Wesley and Premill. Nath. West, pg. 46.* (*Hunt & Eaton.*)

7. Matt. iii : 2, iii : 17, x : 7, xii: 28; Mark i :15, ix : i, xii : 34; Luke x : 9, x : 11, xi: 20, xxi : 31.

---

1. Matt. v : 20, vii : 21, xvi ; 19, xviii : 3, xix : 23, 24, xxi. 31, xxiii : 13; Mark ix : 47, x : 11, 23, x : 24, 25; Luke xviii : 24, 25; John iii : 5; Acts xiv : 1; Col. 1 : 3.

"like";[2] we are told who are "in"[3] it, and their standing there, great or small. Christ and His apostles "preached"[4] the kingdom; many passages go to show the character of those to whom it belongs—"theirs"[5] is the kingdom. Though "at hand" and "entered," it is declared to be "future"[6] also; sacrifices are made "for its sake."[7] It is to be "sought."[8] Being supernatural, it has its mysteries.[9] Its spiritual character is indicated when we are told it is "within you," or told whence it is and what it is or is not.[10] The "word"[11] of the kingdom occurs just once. It is the Gospel. The kingdom suffers "violence"[12] at the hands of evil men. And finally, beside the mention of "human kingdoms,"[13] we have both John and Christ speak of "Satan's kingdom."[14] A synthetic view of these fourteen classes of Scripture passages enter into a true conception of the kingdom.

7. Finally the parables teach what the kingdom is. A parable is a comparison—a picture. It is an analogy from nature or from human affairs. Matthew, the gospel of the kingdom, gives seven

---

2. Matt. xiii: 24. xiii: 31, 33, 44, 45, 47, xviii: 23, xx: 1, xxii: 2, xxv: 1; Mark iv: 26, 30, xiii: 18, 20.

3. Matt. v: 19, bis. viii: 11, xi 11, xiii: 41, xvi: 28, xviii: 1, 4, xx: 21, xxvi: 29; Mark xiv: 25; Luke vii: 28, xiii: 28, 29, xiv: 15, xxii: 16, 30, xxiii: 42; Eph. v: 5; Rev. i: 9.

4. Matt. iv: 23, ix: 35, xiii: 52, xxiv: 14; Mark i: 14; Luke iv: 43. viii: 1, ix: 2, 60, xvi: 16; Acts i: 3, viii: 12, xix: 8, xx: 25, xxviii: 23, 31; Col. iv: 11.

5. Matt. v: 3, 10, vi: 13, viii: 12, xiii: 38, xix: 14, xxi: 43 xxv: 34; Mark x: 14; Luke vi: 20, ix: 62, xii: 32, xviii: 16, 17, xxii: 29; Acts i; 6; I Cor. vi: 9, 10. xv: 50: Gal. v: 21; I Thess. ii: 12; II Thess. i: 5; Heb. xii: 28; II Pet. i: 11; Rev. xii: 10.

6. Matt. vi: 10; Mark xi: 10, xv: 43; Luke i, 33, ix: 27, xi: 2, xvii: 20, bis, xix: 11, 12, 15, xxii: 18, xxiii: 51; I Cor. xv: 24; II Tim. iv: 1, 18.

7. Matt. xix: 12; Luke xviii: 29.

8. Matt. vi: 33; Luke xii: 31; John iii: 3.

9. Matt. xiii: 11; Mark iv: 11: Luke viii: 10.

10. Luke xvii: 21; John xviii; 36, bis, Rom. xiv: 17. I Cor. iv: 20; Heb. i: 18.

11. Matt. xiii: 19.

12. Matt. xi: 12.

13. Matt. iv: 8, xxiv: 7; Mark iii: 24, vi: 23, xiii: 8; Luke iv: 5, xi: 17, xxi: 10; Heb. xi: 33; Rev. xi: 15.

14. Luke xi: 18; Rev. xvi: 10, xvii: 12, 17, 18.

in one group.[1] The parable of the sower[2] shows the effect of the soil on the good seed, the word of the kingdom. In the general sowing only one kind of ground in four proves effective. The parable of the tares[3] of the field taught His disciples primarily that good and bad would exist side by side in the world to the very end, and that the devil is the author of evil. We have the same in the parable in Luke, the man going into the far country.[4] The husbandman says they cannot remove the tares without destroying the wheat. This is the very point of the parable.[5] Here, his servants' duty is negative. In the corresponding parable in Luke we have the positive side. The servants must attend to their pounds among the citizens who continue their hate to the end. The parable of the talents[6] is concerned only with his followers. The scope of these parables covers the whole period of the kingdom, from its inception to the consummation of the age. The parable of the mustard seed[7] teaches the expansiveness of the kingdom. Its branches spread to all the earth, but the evil attending it is not forgotten. The fowls of the air that lodge in its branches, are identified in the parable of the sower, as the wicked one who devoured the wayside seed.[8] The leaven hid in the meal shows the danger to the kingdom as it appears in the world, a danger long ago realized. False doctrines, admitted in the early centuries in the church, leavened the whole mass, so that the Lord only knows to-day where His Kingdom is.[9] In Mark there is the parable of the seed growing secretly;[10] coming in between that of the sower and that of the mustard seed, teaching the silent, mysterious growth of the kingdom by means known not to man

1. "The first four are from the human side—the kingdom in its historical development, as man beholds it; the last three are inherent, essential—the kingdom, as seen by Christ, who joyfully sells all that He has, that He may buy the pearl of priceless value and the field in which the treasure is hidden." *The Gosp. accord. to Matt., Henry G. Weston, p. 17.*
2. Matt. xiii: 3 fg.
3. Matt. xiii: 24.
4. Luke xix: 11 fg.
5. Matt. xiii: 28–30.
6. Matt. xxv: 14 fg.
7. Matt. xiii: 31; Mark iv: 31.
8. Matt. xiii: 19.
9. II Tim. ii: 19.
10. Mark iv: 26 fg.

but to God alone. This parable warns against three things: first, against expecting a harvest without the seed of the kingdom; secondly, against any attempt to force the growth beyond the speed provided by the secret laws which control it, and thirdly, against hoping for ripened grain before the harvest time. The husbandman's business is just definitely one thing—to put in seed. He can do no more but to wait hopefully. Let him sow. The harvest will not disappoint him.

These parables were necessary for the disciples then; they are needed to-day. The Gospel seed about a crucified and risen Saviour must be sowed. It will not overcome all evil.

The tares grow too. The kingdom will spread over the earth. It is threatened with the greatest dangers, but in its secret growth it will finally be ready for the sickle of the harvester. Such is the kingdom phenomenally. As God sees it, it is a treasure hid in the field,[1] for the sake of which Christ redeems the whole field. As it is in itself, it is a pearl[2] worth more than all others. As to its outcome, God will, at the end, gather His own to Himself, no longer to be mingled with the evil, as good and bad fish in a net.[3] Other parables, with perhaps two exceptions,[4] teach about the moral features of the kingdom, and especially of the professed followers, in their judgment, at the end.[5] Every one shows false professors. The virgins all went to meet Him. Only half were prepared.

The parables, especially in Matthew, are clear pictures of the kingdom, teaching what it is, especially in its relation to evil, and what we may expect.

---

1. Matt. xiii: 44.
2. Matt. xiii: 45.
3. Matt. xiii: 48.
4. Matt. xx: 1; Luke xviii: 1.
5. Matt. xxv: fg.

ADDRESSES

At the Closing Session, Friday Evening, December 6, 1895.
First Presbyterian Church, Allegheny, Pa.

REV. WILLIAM S. MILLER.

As we come now to the last session of this conference, bear with me just a single moment or two before we take up the order of the evening. I believe we all realize somewhat of the feelings of the disciples when they stood on that ground and had glimpses of the glorified King, when Peter said "Master, it is good to be here." During all the sessions of this conference, since we gathered last Tuesday night, again and again, as we have looked into the face of our coming Lord and thought of the crown rights of our Jesus, have our hearts glowed as the Scriptures have been unfolded; again and again we have said "Master, it is good to be here."

We have gathered here during these sessions with but one object, let us exalt His name together. We have gathered that we might know more and more of the wonderful teachings of this book. There has been but one aim and one object. It is, no man, Jesus only. In this closing hour let our eyes be lifted unto Him. We rejoice and are exceeding glad for what we have realized of His presence; for the numbers that have been gathered to hear the truth we give Him all the praise. As we come to the last night of the feast, God grant it may be the best night; that the Holy Ghost may rest mightily upon us, filling us, opening our eyes to see more and more of Jesus, and making our hearts burn within us.

As announced this afternoon, on account of sickness our beloved brother, Dr. Brooks, whom we had expected, is not able to be with us, but a number of the brethren will occupy this evening and it will be a very delightful service. Prof. Stifler will speak to us first, on the Kingdom of God.

REV. DR. W. J. ERDMAN.

My brief remarks are suggested by the wish of Mr. Kennedy, who so kindly has given us the use of this building, when he said he would like to have had here discussed the relation of the Holy Spirit to this great theme upon which we have been engaged these past few days.

Very briefly, therefore, let me make that twofold. The greatest blessing promised in the Old Testament was that of the gift of the Holy Spirit at the coming of the Messiah. On the day of Pentecost when the Holy Spirit was poured out, Peter said, not exactly what Joel said in the original Scripture but with a modification. He does not say, This is the fulfilment of Joel's prophecy, but, This is what Joel said. Then again I go back to Joel and I look at the context of Joel's prediction and I strike a law of interpretation, which is this:

Eighteen hundred and more years ago there was poured out a gift of the Holy Spirit. Prophecy tells us there is to be a second outpouring of the Holy Spirit. The first outpouring was upon a body of Jews, the second outpouring is to be upon a body of Jews. At the first outpouring there was gradually added after awhile Gentile believers to that Jewish nucleus. At the second outpouring there will be added Gentiles to the fullness of Israel and who together constitute the future Messianic kingdom.

Looking at the context there comes in this law of interpretation: Nothing in the Old Testament has been fulfilled completely of any prediction until the context itself is also fulfilled. To illustrate: I read in Joel of the outpouring of the Holy Spirit upon all flesh. I read the context and it is at a time when there has been a great tribulation, then a great deliverance, national, by the appearing of the Messiah; then a great salvation in the form of the forgiveness of sins, turning away ungodliness from Jacob, and, fourthly, the pouring out of the Holy Spirit. Four events. First, a trouble very great; second, a national deliverance; third, a national forgiveness of sins, and, fourth, the outpouring of the Holy Spirit. But what is the context in Joel? The restoration of Israel, a siege of Jerusalem, of nations anti-Semitic in their feeling gathered against Jerusalem. This is the context and when that context is again fulfilled then will be the second outpouring of the Holy Spirit.

Turning to the 59th chapter of Isaiah I read: There will be a time of great trouble, but the Redeemer will come to Zion and then there will be the fulfilment of the covenant made with the fathers and holy men, and they shall receive the Holy Spirit. He will put His spirit and words within them. What is the context? A great trouble, a great deliverer, then the outpouring of the Holy Spirit according to the covenants.

Turning to the latter part of the 43d and the forepart of the 44th chapter of Isaiah we again find the same context. What is it? Forgiveness of sins of Israel, then a pouring out of the Holy Spirit under the emblem of water upon all that are thirsty ; then follows what we Anglo-Saxons do not love to hear, a prediction that when the Spirit is poured out again upon Israel, Israel will be like willows overtopping the little Gentile grass along the water brooks ; then from all nations of the earth, one after the other, will subscribe himself with the name of Jacob, with the name of Israel and with the name of Jehovah; the second outpouring of the Holy Spirit followed by a fulfilment of the context which is according to the eternal purpose of God.

I turn to the 32d chapter of Isaiah and now, while in all the other places the word 'pour' translates the same Hebrew word, in this chapter the word 'pour' translates a different Hebrew word and means this : to pour out of a vessel until the bottom of the vessel is seen; a second exhaustive outpouring of the Holy Spirit. But what is the context? Our Lord quotes that passage when He says in this wise "Tarry ye in the City of Jerusalem until ye be endowed with power from on high." Turning to the chapter in Isaiah I find that the "from on high" there has this context : that the land of Israel would be a wilderness, filled with solitary cities, desolate places, "until the Spirit be poured out upon us from on high," then shall the land become one beautiful paradise. Has the context been fulfilled? When the second outpouring of the Holy Spirit takes place, then that context will be fulfilled.

So I might go on and show that there is to be a second outpouring upon Israelites at the opening of the next dispensation when the Messianic kingdom is to be established. In conclusion, the

Holy Spirit acts according to the dispensation in which he is given. He acts now by gathering together out of all nations into one body, believers, called the church, linked to the Son of God, the head in glory. That is, he is gathering out of all the nations the rulers of that future Messianic kingdom. He is not gathering out the subjects now. He is gathering out the priests of that marvelous kingdom, the co-reigners of the Lord Jesus Christ, the body that is to be glorified by that Spirit of glory. He will act as I have said, to draw into the kingdom of which we have heard to-night, the nations of the earth through the preaching of the Gospel, through the operation of his mighty power, but he will then act for that specific end as he is now acting for the present specific end, uniting us and all here to-night into that Son of God in Glory.

In brief, gathering together a great deal of New Testament Scripture we can say this: That when that body is complete, of which we, by faith, in spirit form a part, God in advance tells us that he writes over that body just one name, the Son of God; all saints of God together under the headship of the Son of God; one body. Another name, the Christ; as in I. Cor. 12 : 12. Another name, the Son of man; one with the Son of man as brethren of whose flesh and blood he partook, and under whose feet he is going to place the world to come.

All we to-night have, as Gentiles, most marvelous reasons for thanksgiving to God, that he has stooped down to those who never had a promise given to him as Israel, has stooped down to their depth of misery and degradation and lifted them up to the very throne of the Messiah, making them one with him. In view of that fact let the Holy Spirit move in us as never before, remembering our holy, high and heavenly calling, and then we will be fitted to do the work that God has given us, to preach the Gospel to every creature, that as quickly as possible he may complete the numbers of the sons of God.

BISHOP W. R. NICHOLSON.

We have listened with very great interest and pleasure to the remarks made by Prof. Stifler on the Kingdom of God or the Kingdom of Christ. I desire to call your attention to one phase of the subject which I think my reverend brother did not introduce into his remarks, but which I know he thoroughly believes.

It is the great Bible teaching that the Kingdom of the Lord Jesus Christ is an earthly kingdom. It is the kingdom of the heavens. It is so in all its principles and it is so for other reasons. At the same time it is a kingdom essentially of mankind so far as certain principles are concerned, and to show that, God made a special covenant with David, a royal covenant, and it is by virtue of that covenant that the Lord Jesus Christ inherits his kingdom from David himself.

You may ask, why was it necessary that the Lord Jesus Christ should come to us with the distinct aspect that he is an heir of David. Now because the Scriptures make much of that I think that therefore we ought to make much of it too and feel the importance of it. The Lord Jesus represented himself in the parable when he said that a nobleman went into a far country to get his kingdom and when he should get his kingdom he would return bringing his kingdom with him, which shows us that the kingdom and the church are two distinct things. I want to fix your attention specially on the fact that God has presented to us the idea of the royalty of Jesus Christ as our king, in His receiving that kingdom from the Father through His lineal descent from David.

In the 7th chapter of the second book of Samuel we have an account of the covenant God made with David. That covenant states expressly in the language of the Father that David should have a son; that that son should build a house for God's name and that God would establish his throne, the throne of His kingdom forever. But, wasn't that Solomon? So I suppose nine out of ten of all those who read this account would say. Then they come upon this verse and they say: that is proof that Solomon was the one referred to. "If he commit iniquity (that is, this son that is to be the heir of David and whose throne shall be established forever) I will chasten him with the rod of men and with the stripes of the children of men." The question is asked : How can that refer to the Lord Jesus Christ?

Well, I was puzzled by that when my mind was all aglow with the great Bible evidences, as far as I had attained to them at that time with reference to this glorious truth of the Lord's second coming. I came upon the verse and I was very much puzzled, but I happened one day to take down from a shelf in my library one of the volumes of Bishop Horseley's Commentaries on the Scriptures.

Turning to that passage I was perfectly aroused, for he said : "This verse is mistranslated. Our revisers under King James did not get at the proper meaning of the Hebrew, which reads thus : If he bear iniquity and is chastened with the rod of men and with the stripes of the children of men." Why, there is a recognition at once of the vicarious sufferings of the Lord Jesus Christ; the very sufferings, the passion, in which was grounded the very kingdom that he shall possess. Then, feeling a little anxious about it still, I came across a Jew, a learned man in the Hebrew, and I asked him one day if he would kindly translate that verse for me. He said he would, but he would go home and after looking at it carefully write out the translation and send it to me by mail. After perhaps two or three days I got the communication through the mail and to my great delight I found that he, though giving it in some different terms, gave it precisely as to its meaning according to the translation of Bishop Horseley. When he received this promise from God what effect did it have on David? In the 17th chapter of 1 Chronicles we have a second account of the very same royal covenant. We are told that David, the king, came and sat before the Lord and said "Who am I, oh Lord God, and what is mine house that Thou hast brought me hitherto, and yet this was a small thing in Thine eyes, oh Lord, for Thou hast also spoken of Thy servant's house for a great while to come." Now follow the words which I want you to notice "and hast regarded me in the arrangement about the man from above, oh God Jehovah." That you will not find in the rendering here but that is the true sense of the Hebrew. He thanked God that God had regarded him, that is his house, in the arrangement about the man from above.

The Lord Jesus comes to us as a king, under the sanction and by virtue of this very covenant that God made with David, and when we turn to Isaiah and read the expression "the mercies of David" what do they mean? You cannot explain that expression properly without reference to this covenant. The question comes again, as I have said, why should the Lord Jesus be presented to us as a king under the idea of his descending and lineally inheriting from a mere man? The Lord Jesus Christ was God, the incarnate, eternal Son of God. Why was it necessary that he should thus be presented to us? Because, my friends, just as under the Levitical arrangement the great truths that we now glory in as constituting the gospel of our salvation, were symbolized and represented in the sacrifices and the various ceremonies that were ordained, so God meant to present to our attention this great truth of the kingdom of Jesus Christ in an exceedingly emphatic manner. He put emphasis on it by presenting him as the heir of king David.

So we learn that the kingdom of the Lord Jesus Christ when established in this world, will be a visible kingdom here, a real kingdom, and the king upon his throne will be the Lord Jesus Christ in his glory and his grandeur. It does not derogate at all from the glory of deity, for, as has been already said, the antitype very far excels in many instances the type. So it is here, the Lord Jesus, the king, while reigning on David's throne, will yet be a very different king from what king David was. This is the truth. May God bless it.

PROF. W. G. MOOREHEAD.

I have only a word or two to say to you, and let me read a little Scripture as the basis of what I am going to say. In Paul's Epistle to Titus 2: 11 we find this language : "For the grace of God that bringeth salvation hath appeared to all men, teaching us that denying ungodliness and worldly lusts we should live spiritually, righteously and godly, in this present world, looking for that blessed hope and the glorious appearing of the great God and our Saviour, Jesus Christ."

That is the attitude of a child of God. We believers look back to the grace of Christ that brought us salvation; we look around on present duty; we look forward to the coming glory. The blessedness, the preciousness and the glad joy of this blessed hope for me, lies particularly in these things : First, that when He shall come again all them that sleep in Him shall be raised up and made like unto His glorious body, and we who are alive and remain shall be changed into the likeness of the body of His glory, and together with the raised ones be caught up in clouds to meet Him in the air. I am fast growing to be an old man. I have buried some that were very dear and precious to me, and the gladness and the blessedness of this hope lies in this : that they who fell asleep in Him, and one of them sleeps in Florence, Italy, shall be raised up, and if I have fallen asleep be raised up also together with them and enter into the infinite glory. Therefore it is a blessed hope for me.

Then there is one other reason why it is blessed that I want to mention now. Never will we get the deliverance of groaning creation until the Lord comes again. In the 8th chapter of Romans, to which reference has been made during the sessions of this conference again and again, we are assured by the inspired apostle that the whole creation groans and travails in pain until now, as if it were a living and sentient thing, in their suffering, doom and corruption and expressing its sad state by groans. My brethren, you know perfectly well that that is true. I had a friend who died at Wooster, Ohio, some few years ago, who was one of the finest musicians we had in that part of the State, in fact, I think the finest in the western part of the United States, Prof. Karl Merz, a German. He said to me one day: "If your ear was attuned and musical as I think I may say without boasting mine is, you would discover that all the sounds in nature nearly are in the minor key. Nearly all the animals express themselves in their voice in the minor, and we almost unconsciously, you know, talk about the sighing of the wind, and if you have lived on the sea shore you will have observed again and again, that the waves that break on the shingle, break with the solemn moan of the sea. Nearly all the music of the uncultivated peoples is music in the minor key."

As a missionary I used to listen to the poor peasant women in the Apennine mountains of central Italy, as they came home from their day's toil when the sun was going down and all the western slopes of the mountains were clothed in gorgeous purple that we never see in our country. They came singing, with their burdens on their head; and invariably they sang in the minor. Creation groans, animals groan, we groan likewise together with them, but the assurance of the inspired apostle is, that nature herself shall be delivered from the bondage of corruption into the glorious liberty of the children of God, and that comes when He comes.

Therefore it is a blessed hope. My brethren, let us wait for it, look for it, watch for it. It is a familiar saying in Southern India, that the cocoanut tree yields only as it seems to listen for the footsteps of its owner, and we grow and we bear fruit and we are faithful, as we listen and watch for the footfall of Him who has promised to come and not to tarry.

REV. DR. JOHN H. PRUGH.

We have listened to these words of testimony from the teachers, and I would like to ask that we, the students, may have the privilege of giving a word of testimony. I wish to make a motion, and I do it because I had no part at all in the arranging of this conference, knew nothing about it save as I saw the notices in the daily press, but as one of the students at this conference I am sure I voice the feeling of all here, to-night, in what I say.

You began the meeting this evening, Sir, by saying that these men who have been our teachers, came with this thought in their hearts: That God might be glorified. You need not have said that. After sitting four days at their feet, after listening to these splendid Scriptural addresses, we know that they came with that grand purpose, and, also, that the children of God might see the truth more clearly. Some of these Doctors were our teachers in other days, and we loved them then. And, during these past four days having sat at their feet again, and at the feet of those who companied with them, we delight, to-night, to pay honor to them all.

I voice the sentiment of every one here when I say, that these addresses have startled some of us like bugle blasts from heaven. They have been to others like revelations. Whether we shall all come to see alike, I know not, but this conference, I am sure, will serve as a mighty stimulant to renewed Bible study on our part, and on the part of the people of this community, and that will be a magnificent blessing.

I now move that, by a rising vote, we be allowed to express our high appreciation of the efforts of your committee in arranging this conference and of the efforts of our teachers; that by this vote we may be allowed to express our deep gratitude to you. As the Chairman of the evening is included in the motion you may consider it put by me.

Unanimously carried.

APPENDIX.

BRIEF REVIEW OF "MILLENNIAL DAWN."

REV. W. G. MOOREHEAD, D. D.

Three volumes of a book with the above title have been published at Pittsburgh, Pa. The author of this large work is Mr. C. T. Russell, editor of *Zion's Watch Tower*, a monthly devoted to the dissemination of the same religious notions as those contained in the book.

On the title page of each of these volumes are the words, "For Bible Students." The student of the Bible will not need to read far till he discovers that the title, "Millennial Dawn," is a misnomer; that a more fitting one would be, "Dark Dreams," or "Nocturnal Hallucinations."

One would be indisposed to say anything about the book if it were not for the fact that it is being pushed into the hands of the public with remarkable persistency. Agents carry it from house to house, and sell it for the ridiculously small sum of twenty-five cents a volume. The effort seems to be to put it into the hands of every person in our country and Canada. That it has done harm is certain; that it is calculated to undermine the faith of readers cannot be denied, for the book is essentially anti-Scriptural, and a wretched perversion of the Gospel of Christ.

The character of the book will appear from the following summary of the more prominent errors and heresies which it inculcates:

1. Jesus in his pre-existent state was a mere creature (Vol. I, pp. 174, 176, 184). The book expressly teaches that our Lord, prior to his incarnation and during his earthly life, was only a creature, higher indeed in the rank of being than the angels, yet,

like the angels, a created being. This is the doctrine of Arius, which the Council of Nicea solemnly condemned; the doctrine of Socinians, which the reformers rejected with abhorrence; of modern Unitarians, which all evangelical Christians repudiate. Over against this fatal error we set the majestic words of the inspired John, 1:1: "In the beginning was the word, and the word was with God, and the word was God." By the *Word* in this great text, of course, is meant the Lord Jesus Christ. Three things are asserted of Him: 1. His eternity: "In beginning the word was existent." There is no article before the term *beginning;* it is altogether indefinite and unmarked duration that is meant, and the verb is the substantive verb *to be.* 2. His eternal separate existence: "The word was with God." 3. His Deity: "And the word was God." Most emphatic is the order of the words in the original: "And *God* was the word." Besides, the prophets uniformly testify that the Messiah who was to come should be Jehovah, the great God himself, and no other. (Isa. 9:6; 40:3; Jere. 23:6; Mal. 3:1, etc.)

2. In the incarnation our Lord had but one nature, not two natures, as Christians have always held (Vol. I., p. 175.) We quote: "Neither was Jesus a combination of two natures—human and spiritual. The blending of two natures produces neither the one nor the other, but an imperfect, hybrid thing, which is obnoxious to the divine arrangement. When Jesus was in the flesh he was a perfect human being; previous to that, he was a perfect spiritual being, and since his resurrection, he is a perfect spiritual being of the highest or divine order" (Vol. I., p. 175.) We ask, was there, then, any incarnation at all? The book asserts with a positiveness that error always uses, that in Jesus "there was no mixture of natures." (Vol. I., p. 176.) Plainly, this means that Jesus dropped his "spirit nature" when He became man, and was only man and nothing more during the whole time of His sojourn on earth. This is to deny the vital doctrine of the incarnation of the Son of God, and to degrade the eternal word to the level of Adam before his fall. In short, according to "Millennial Dawn," there was no incarnation whatever!

3. The atonement of Jesus was that of a mere man, was purely human, without in any sense being divine (Vol. I., chap. 9.) His death, therefore, was a creature's death; His sacrifice only a human

sacrifice; His atonement a mere man's. What a wretched caricature of Christ's person and work! What an inadequate and puerile view of divine justice and law, and of man's guilt and ruin by sin! Everywhere in Scripture the ground of the sinner's justification before God is what Paul calls "the righteousness of God." (See Rom. 3 ; II. Cor. 5 : 21; Phil. 3, etc.) That is, it is *divine righteousness*, God's own righteousness, provided by Him in His Son Jesus Christ, and received by faith. I want something infinitely more and better than creature righteousness if I am to be saved; and this I have in Christ, God's eternal and co-equal Son. Paul writes to the Galatians: "If any man preach any other Gospel unto you than that ye have received, let him be accursed." 1 : 8, 9. If "Millennial Dawn" teaches the Gospel of the Son of God, then all Christians are wrong, and all the Apostles were wrong; but if they are right, this book is wrong, fundamentally, and totally, and fatally wrong, and Paul's tremendous *anathema* falls upon it.

4. The body of Jesus was not raised from the grave (Vol. II., pp. 126–129.) To explain the disappearance of the crucified body the book says: "Our Lord's human body was, however, supernaturally removed from the tomb * * *. Whether it was dissolved into gases, or whether it is still preserved somewhere as the grand memorial of God's love, of Christ's obedience, and of our redemption, no one knows." (Vol. II., pp. 129, 130). This squarely contradicts the teaching of Paul in I. Cor. chap. 15. In that chapter everything is made to turn on the grand fact of Christ's literal, bodily resurrection. If Christ be not raised, then Christianity is wiped out as a supernatural system, and Christians are of all men the most pitiable, the most fearfully deceived! It contradicts also the four Gospels.

5. After His resurrection Jesus became divine. (Vol. I.,pp. 173–176 ; Vol. II., p. 132). The book teaches that, as the reward of his perfect obedience, Jesus was exalted after His death to be divine. That is, he received a sort of *apotheosis*, as the pagan Romans deified their heroes. For this there is not one particle of Scripture. Even God cannot exalt another to be God, for the Divine Essence is incommunicable. Nor is this satement contradicted by II. Peter, 1 : 4—"partakers of the divine nature," as believers are said to be—for it is *holiness*, perfect deliverance

from every taint and stain of sin, that is meant, as the context in Peter clearly shows. No inspired writer teaches *Pantheism*, nor that believers become sharers of the Divine Essence. A creature can never become God, though Budhism and Millennial Dawn both teach it. God will never give His glory to another. (Isa. 42 : 8).

6. The Lord's coming took place in 1874 (Vol. II., pp. 158–172, 240). Scripture teaches that the Millennium begins with the return of the Lord Jesus to the earth. According to this book, that blessed age has been going on for twenty years. Lawlessness, apostasy, organized evil, Satan unbound, and the Millennium all co-existent and running side by side! A blind man can see the absurdity of this statement.

7. The end of the present order of things takes place in 1914 (Vol. II., chap. 4). One grows weary of the everlasting effort to fix dates and name the very day when the end shall come. Poor William Miller tried it, to his deep discomfiture. Prof. Totten also announced that the day of grace terminated last year, and that the end will come in 1899½. So, too, this book. All of them are no doubt mistaken, for the exact time of the end is concealed (Mark 13 : 32).

8. At the resurrection, which is simultaneous for all the dead, the Gospel will be preached to the unsaved among them, and the great mass will accept it and be saved (Vol. I., chaps. 6, 9). On this great error three remarks are submitted: 1. The Bible distinguishes between the resurrection of the righteous and the wicked (Rev. 20 : 1–6). Mr. Russell labors to show that the words, "But the rest of the dead lived not again until the thousand years were finished" (Rev. 20 : 5), are spurious. He is altogether mistaken. Every unicial Greek copy has these words, except the Sinai MS., which omits them by oversight of the copyist, as Alford has shown, and every editor of the Greek text, and every version retains them. 2. Acts 3 : 19 is the basis for this false view of the resurrection. Nothing can be more crude and shallow than the exegesis of this passage in Millennial Dawn. Peter says "the restitution" was foretold by all the prophets; but what prophet predicts the offer of life to the impenitent dead? Not one. Ezekiel 16 does not mean what is read into it by the author of this book. What the prophet teaches is the utter and total repudiation of Sodom,

Gomorrah and all apostate Hebrews alike. There is no redemption for them, but judgment! 3. Paul emphatically declares the irreparable loss of heathen sinners, Rom. 2 : 12 : "For as many as have sinned without law (*i. e.*, without a written revelation,) shall also perish without law." Does *perish* mean salvation? Which will you believe, Paul or Millennial Dawn?

Such is the "Millennial Dawn," a mixture of Unitarianism, Universalism, Second Probation and the Swedenborgian method of exegesis.

What infinite dishonor it does the Son of God, whom it first represents as a spiritual creature, then makes a mere man, and finally tries to compensate for so great a loss by exalting Him after His death to be divine! Shocking! most shocking! He who died on Calvary was a man—only a man! Our redemption rests on the work of a human being like one of ourselves, except that He was without sin! The Bible assures me that my salvation has been wrought out by one who is both God and man, the Divine Mediator, Jesus Christ (Acts 20 : 28). He who is now at the right hand of God has nothing human about Him, for His body, we are told, was never raised. How much better is this than the words of the infidel Renan: "The stone from His sepulchre was never rolled away!" And yet there is inscribed on the covers of these pretentious volumes, "For Bible Students." The author is fond of charging those whose shoe-latchet he is not worthy to unloose with misunderstanding and misinterpreting the Scripture. Perhaps among all the books of the English-speaking world there is not another which contains as many errors as the "Millennial Dawn." May God, in infinite mercy, preserve His people from being poisoned by it!